Simon
Wiesenthal

Also by Tom Segev

Soldiers of Evil: The Commandants of the Nazi Concentration Camps

1949: The First Israelis

The Seventh Million: The Israelis and the Holocaust

One Palestine, Complete: Jews and Arabs Under the British Mandate

Elvis in Jerusalem: Post-Zionism and the Americanization of Israel

1967: Israel, the War, and the Year That Transformed the Middle East

Simon Wiesenthal

The Life and Legends

Tom Segev

Doubleday
New York London Toronto
Sydney Auckland

DD

DOUBLEDAY

Translation copyright © 2010 by Ronnie Hope

All rights reserved. Published in the United States by Doubleday,
a division of Random House, Inc., New York, and in Canada
by Random House of Canada Limited, Toronto.

www.doubleday.com

DOUBLEDAY and the DD colophon are registered trademarks
of Random House, Inc.

This translation is based on an unpublished Hebrew-language work
by Tom Segev. Copyright © by Tom Segev.

Book design by Michael Collica

Frontispiece by Alain Nogues

Library of Congress Cataloging-in-Publication Data

Segev, Tom, 1945–
Simon Wiesenthal : the life and legends / Tom Segev.—1st ed.
    p.   cm.
Includes bibliographical references and index.
I. Wiesenthal, Simon.   2. Holocaust survivors—Austria—Vienna—
Biography.   3. Nazi hunters—Biography.   4. Jews—Austria—
Vienna—Biography.   5. War criminals.   6. Austria—
Politics and government—1945–   I. Title.
DS135.A93W537 2010
940.53'18092—dc22
[B]
2009053480

ISBN 978-0-385-51946-5

PRINTED IN THE UNITED STATES OF AMERICA

1 3 5 7 9 10 8 6 4 2

First Edition

Contents

Simon Wiesenthal

Introduction

The Glass Box

Never before had there been such a funeral. Never before had the remains of so many people been buried in one grave. The procession began in Tel Aviv, on June 26, 1949. The horror enveloping the city's Great Synagogue was almost unbearable, and hysterical shrieks rose from people crowding around the building. The newspapers reported that there were tens of thousands present and described heartbreaking scenes. There were cries of "Mama! Papa!" and many fainted. Small children were also to be seen.

In the main hall of the synagogue stood a glass box, five feet long. In it were thirty porcelain urns, painted with blue and white stripes. According to the newspapers, they contained the ashes of 200,000 Jews who had been murdered in the Holocaust. The mayor was there, as well as other dignitaries and rabbis. Speeches were made and prayers intoned, and then the glass box was loaded onto a police vehicle, to be carried through some of the city's streets; the vehicle had trouble making its way through the crowds. Along the route that the box traveled, people closed their shops and workshops and lined the sidewalks, watching the procession in silent awe.

The first stop on the route was Rehovot, where President Chaim Weizmann had his home. Classes were canceled in the town's schools, and the students were sent to see the box. Weizmann, aged and frail and almost blind, said a few words. Then the box was taken to Jerusalem, and at the entrance to the city there were once again thousands, waiting and weeping. Some of them brought bars of soap. They mistakenly believed that the soap had been made out of the bodies of Jews and wanted to bury it with the glass box, in the soil of the ancient cemetery of Sanhedria, among graves that had been hewn out of rock two thousand years before.

The man who organized this historic spectacle was Simon Wiesenthal, then forty-one years old. From the day he was released from the Mauthausen concentration camp in Austria he had lived in the nearby city of Linz and occupied himself with searching out Nazi war criminals. The ashes of the dead had been collected at his initiative at concentration camps and other detention sites across Austria.

"The glass box," he wrote later, "had suddenly become a kind of looking-glass, in which the faces of many, many were reflected—friends from the ghetto, companions from the concentration camps, people who had been beaten to death, died of starvation, been hounded into the electrified fence. I could see the panicked faces of Jews who were whipped and clubbed into the gas chambers, chased from behind by human animals devoid of conscience or feelings, who would not hear their lone plea: to let them live."[1]

By then Wiesenthal already knew several Israelis, but not many Israelis knew him. The mayor of Tel Aviv, Yisrael Rokach, for one, didn't know who he was when Wiesenthal first contacted him, in Yiddish, a few months before. But Rokach seems to have been impressed by Wiesenthal's assertive style. It was more like an order than a query, request, or suggestion: the Association of Former Concentration Camp Inmates in Austria had decided to transfer the ashes of the martyrs to Israel and to honor the city of Tel Aviv by making it the recipient, Wiesenthal wrote. There was no way to refuse, and Rokach replied that Tel Aviv would accept the urns with a "tremor of sanctity," although he had no idea what to do with them.

The annihilation of the Jews haunted many of the inhabitants of Israel. They were tormented by the pain. Already in 1946, ashes brought from a camp in Poland had been interred in Israel. But even in 1949, nobody really knew the right way to go about mourning six million dead or how to perpetuate their memory. The law on prosecuting Nazis and their collaborators would only be enacted a year later; the official Holocaust Memorial Day would be designated two years later, and the law establishing the State Memorial Authority, Yad Vashem, would be passed only in 1953.

When Wiesenthal came to Israel, the Holocaust was still wrapped in silence. Parents never told their children what they had experienced; the children never dared to ask. Holocaust survivors made people flinch with anxiety, embarrassment, and feelings of guilt. They were not easy to live with: How can you share an apartment building with them, work with them, go to the movies or the beach with them? How can you fall in love with them and marry them? How can their children go to school with yours? It's doubtful that any other society ever faced so difficult or painful an encounter with "the Other," to use a phrase that came into currency later.

Many of the Israelis who had settled in the country before World War II, or were born there, tended to relate condescendingly to Holocaust victims and survivors, identifying them with the Jews of the Diaspora, whom they despised as the polar opposite of the "new Hebrews" they were trying to create in the Land of Israel, in the spirit of the Zionist vision. It was customary to blame the victims for not coming to the country beforehand, remaining in Europe instead and waiting to be slaughtered without doing anything to prevent it.

They were despised for their weakness, because most of them had not fought against the Nazis but had gone to their deaths "like lambs to the slaughter." Many Holocaust survivors found neither a sympathetic ear nor any compassion; often they were not even believed when they related what had happened to them.

For their part, the survivors had plenty to say to the Israelis. Why, they would ask, had the Zionist movement not made greater efforts to rescue them from the Nazis? Implicit in this question was a terrible accusation, and the leaders of the movement found it difficult to explain their powerlessness. Besides the question of what they could have done, there was the far more embarrassing one of whether they had taken any interest at all in the plight of European Jews. Many survivors of the Holocaust were shocked to discover after the war that Jews in the United States and in Palestine had lived through the war in relative complacency; reports about the destruction of their brethren concerned them only to the extent that their day-to-day lives were affected.

Wiesenthal once described how, soon after the war, he had seen Jewish newspapers from America and Palestine printed in the summer of 1943, when he was a concentration camp inmate. "And what I read was terribly depressing to me," he wrote. For the papers described the routines of community life, politics, economic prosperity, culture, entertainment, and family celebrations. Only here and there did Wiesenthal find items about the murder of the Jews in Poland, based usually on BBC reports. In the papers from Palestine, he found big headlines about Arabs who attacked a kibbutz and killed two cows. A report about what was happening in Poland, by a refugee who had made it to Palestine, was relegated to page seven. "I started asking myself, are we still one people, the same people?" he wrote.

In 1946, Wiesenthal attended the first Zionist Congress since the Holocaust, held in Basel, Switzerland, and the thought ran through his mind that the leaders of the Zionist movement deserved to be put on trial, like the heads of the Nazi regime who were tried in Nuremberg. "I took a good look at those who were our 'leadership' and had done very little to save Jews," he related.[2] He was referring to Israel's first prime minister, David Ben-Gurion, among others. By bringing the ashes of the victims to Jerusalem for burial, Wiesenthal was demanding of the Israelis that they at long last confront the Holocaust, in the same way that in days to come he was to demand it of the other nations of the world.

The institutions and the officials involved in organizing the funeral tended to look upon the matter as a nuisance, but Wiesenthal would not let them alone. At first he had written to Yad Vashem, but at that time it was only a private society operating out of a three-room office and having a hard time paying the rent. "We regret that our project is as yet unable to receive this sacred consignment," the organization wrote to Wiesenthal, and so he turned to the Tel Aviv municipality. The heads of Yad Vashem had no choice but to acquiesce, but they soon changed their minds and demanded that the glass box be buried in Jerusalem. Wiesenthal went along with that as well: "We believe that for diplomatic and national reasons at this time we must do everything to concentrate in Jerusalem all things and all projects that symbolize the link between the Diaspora of our people and the State of Israel," he wrote, using the first-person plural, as was his custom.

But now the need arose to decide who would finance the project. Wiesenthal assured Mayor Rokach that the organization he was acting for would cover all the shipping costs, but he requested funding for airplane tickets and a ten-day stay for himself and one companion. Yad Vashem replied immediately that it had no money. The request led to a lengthy correspondence, and eighteen months went by. It was a dramatic and bloody period. Between his first letter to Yad Vashem in January 1948 and the funeral, a war had been waged and the State of Israel had been declared. Wiesenthal, who was a keen stamp collector, had an idea: the Israeli Postal Service should issue stamps in memory of the Holocaust, and the revenue would be used to cover the expenses of the memorial project.

But it was not only the issue of funding that held up his initiative. The fledgling state needed an aura of heroic glory, and some of the officials handling the matter thought the remains of Theodor Herzl, the founder of the Zionist movement, should be brought from Vienna for reinterment in Jerusalem before the ashes of the Holocaust victims from Austria; Herzl was a symbol of triumph, the Holocaust represented defeat. So this is what was done. An argument also arose as to the respective roles of the state and the Chief Rabbinate in burying the ashes of those who perished in the Holocaust, an echo of the ever-present confrontation between the secular and the religious. And out of this arose the question of whether the urns that Wiesenthal wanted to bury in a Jewish cemetery in Israel really contained only the ashes of Jews, or whether there were also ashes of gentiles mixed in with them.

In the end, Wiesenthal lost his patience. He cabled Yad Vashem that he was on his way to Rome, where he would board an Italian airliner with the ashes and fly to Israel. Please make all the preparations, he demanded. Only now did Yad Vashem convene a committee, which hastily organized the ceremony as mutual recriminations flew through the air between the various parties involved. These found their way into the newspapers. There was a scandal, but at the last minute the speaker of the Knesset managed to read into the parliamentary record a state declaration of mourning, and the papers gave the event extensive coverage.[3]

This was Wiesenthal's first visit to Israel. He entered the country on a Polish passport. He was welcomed respectfully and no one troubled him with the obvious questions: Where exactly were the ashes collected? How can we know if they are really the ashes of the victims? And how did you determine that the number of Jews who were killed in Austrian concentration camps was 200,000? One newspaper apparently thought this wasn't enough, and wrote 250,000. The papers tended to conceal the fact that these were in fact symbolic samples of ash and described the urns as containing all the ashes of the hundreds of thousands of victims.[4]

Wiesenthal was very emotional. "As I followed the box of ashes," he wrote, "I remembered my family members, my friends and companions, and all those who paid with their lives for one single sin—being born Jewish. I looked at the box, and I saw my mother's face the way it looked the last time I saw her on that fateful day when I left home in the morning for forced labor outside the ghetto and I did not know that I would not see her when I returned in the evening, nor ever again."[5]

The burial of the ashes was meant to be only the first stage in a much more ambitious program: Wiesenthal hoped to have a huge structure erected in memory of the Jews who perished in the Holocaust, what he called a mausoleum. Before the Nazi occupation of Poland, he had studied architecture, and he designed a memorial site that he proposed should be built in a forest outside Jerusalem, to which the ashes should eventually be moved from Sanhedria. He sketched a kind of platform paved with marble, topped with two menacing towers, an exact replica of the gate of the Mauthausen camp, and a stone dome over a round memorial hall with a black floor.

This was the first time he tackled what was to become a vast enterprise. He radiated resourcefulness, self-confidence, and conviction. He was already revealing his innate skill at public relations. Before leaving for Israel he had sent the design for the mausoleum to a large number of Jewish organizations and individuals in various countries. The project was also meant to mark the closing of the Jewish displaced persons' camps in Austria, and the migration of their inmates to Israel. He received many pledges of help. When he sent a copy of the plan to Ben-Gurion in April 1952, he asserted: "We can raise the sum of money needed for this within two years." The prime minister's office informed him politely that it had conveyed his proposal to Yad Vashem.[6]

Wiesenthal did not demand to be appointed the architect of the project, but probably assumed that he would be. If his proposal had been accepted, he might have settled in Israel and practiced architecture, instead of remaining in Austria. Ohel Yizkor—the Tabernacle of Remembrance, which would eventually be built at the Yad Vashem complex in Jerusalem—resembles the memorial hall that Wiesenthal had sketched. Some of the ash that he had brought was later transferred from

Sanhedria to Ohel Yizkor, but he was not given a role in its design, and he never returned to architecture.

The drama of Simon Wiesenthal's life is stored in hundreds of files containing some 300,000 pieces of paper: letters he received and, mainly, copies of letters he wrote in his sixty years of work as a "Nazi hunter." The first file begins in 1945, when he was a walking skeleton, weighing ninety-seven pounds, who had just left Mauthausen with no hope and no future. About sixty feet down on the same shelf, there's a file from the 1980s, containing the following handwritten note: "Darling Simon, Take good care of yourself and stay happy. I love you and we all need you, Elizabeth Taylor."[7]

A tireless warrior against evil and a central figure in the struggle for human rights, Wiesenthal enjoyed worldwide admiration. Hollywood adopted him as a cultural hero, as did the scores of universities that awarded him honorary degrees. American presidents hosted him in the White House. Wiesenthal relished every moment of acclaim, but when he said that President Jimmy Carter needed him more than he needed Carter, he was right. One of the officials of the Wiesenthal Center in Los Angeles observed that if he had not existed, Wiesenthal would have had to be invented, because people all over the world, both Jews and gentiles, needed him as an emblem and a source of hope.

He sparked their imaginations, he enchanted them, thrilled them, and frightened them, weighed on their consciences, and granted them a consoling faith in good. A lone Jew, he had taken it upon himself to make sure that even the last of the Nazis would not die free, or at least free of anxiety, because he, the Jew Wiesenthal, would hunt him down and do his very best to have him brought to trial and punished. And justice would prevail.

A quixotic romantic with a James Bond image and a soaring ego, a tendency to fantasize, and a penchant for crude jokes in Yiddish, he was a brave man who launched some breathtaking ventures. But contrary to the myth he spun around himself, he never operated a worldwide dragnet, but worked almost on his own from a small apartment, surrounded by high piles of old newspapers and yellowing index cards. This was the Documentation Center that he established in Vienna, not far from where the Nazis had set up the headquarters of the Gestapo secret police in the luxurious Hotel Metropol.

On one of the walls of his office hung a large map of Europe, with the names of all the hundreds of Nazi death and concentration camps on it; Wiesenthal himself had been held in some of them. He used historical documents, municipal population registries, and even telephone books in order to gather personal details about Nazi criminals and information about their possible whereabouts. This was his life's goal. Sometimes he would go out on small detective missions, extracting leads from talkative neighbors or barmen, mailmen, waiters, and barbers. An acquaintance compared him to Inspector Clouseau, the bumbling detective in *The Pink Panther*.

His faith in the liberal system of justice and in America, combined with his communication skills, made him very much a man of the twentieth century. The concept of Holocaust commemoration that he developed was a broad, humanistic one. In contrast to the memorializing of only the Nazis' Jewish victims fostered in Israel and by the Jewish establishment in the United States, Wiesenthal tended to view the murder of the Jews as a crime against the whole of humanity, and he tied it in with the atrocities committed by the Nazis against other groups, such as incurable invalids, Gypsies, homosexuals, and Jehovah's Witnesses. In his eyes, the Holocaust was not only a Jewish tragedy, but a human one.

Wiesenthal's broad humanity was anchored in the story of his life. He always lived within more than one sphere of identity. He was born in a Jewish shtetl and until his dying day he defined himself first and foremost as a Jew. But he grew up in the Austro-Hungarian Empire and chose to live in Austria, which he saw as his cultural and political homeland. He kept one foot within the Israeli sphere, too; he looked upon Israel as a second homeland. And with the passage of time he developed a deep sense of identity with America. Living within different circles of identity gave him a certain cosmopolitan openness.

On more than one occasion he had to show great courage. One of the rooms in his office housed hundreds of files containing threatening letters and anti-Semitic abuse that he received. Wiesenthal marked these files with the letter *m* for *meshuganers*—lunatics, in Yiddish. Once a letter addressed to "The Jew Pig, Austria" was delivered to his office. Wiesenthal phoned the posts minister to ask how they knew that it was meant for him. But they knew, always. Nonetheless, Wiesenthal chose to live in Austria and to tie his life and fate to that country. It is not easy to explain why he did so.

In 1953 Wiesenthal discovered and reported to the Israeli authorities that Adolf Eichmann, one of the main Nazi criminals, was hiding in Argentina.

Seven years later, Israel sent its agents to Buenos Aires to seize Eichmann and bring him to Jerusalem. He was put on trial, convicted, and executed. Wiesenthal's role in the affair gave him a heroic aura, as if he had captured Eichmann single-handedly. Some Israelis never forgave him for this, and one of them compared him to a hitchhiker who took over the driver's seat. Others likened him to the legendary liar Baron Munchhausen.[8] Actually, Wiesenthal worked for years in the service of Israel's secret intelligence agency, the Mossad.

He was involved in efforts to locate and prosecute hundreds of Nazi criminals, and assisted in the conviction of dozens. His endeavors were remarkable, especially in view of the fact that after the defeat of the Third Reich, most of those involved in Nazi atrocities had gone unpunished. They had integrated themselves into the lives of their communities in Germany and Austria and other countries and were not called upon to answer for their crimes. Some of them had done well in politics, in the civil service, in the judiciary, and in the educational and economic systems.

This happened not only because the Germans and the Austrians took an indulgent attitude toward the criminals, but also because of the Cold War. More than once Wiesenthal saw that offenders he had located and wanted to prosecute were employed as secret agents in the service of the United States or other countries and, in at least one case, of Israel. "The Nazis lost the war, but we lost the postwar period," Wiesenthal used to say.[9]

Wiesenthal died in September 2005, at the age of ninety-six. His daughter, Paulinka Kreisberg, was flooded with consolation messages. Beatrix, queen of the Netherlands, and Abdullah, king of Jordan, were among those who wrote, as were Laura and George Bush, as well as presidents and prime ministers, legislators and mayors from all over the world. The U.S. Senate unanimously passed a resolution commemorating his life and accomplishments.

Someone sent condolences on behalf of Muhammad Ali, the legendary boxer. That may have happened because of the constant and repeated pressure that Wiesenthal had exerted on the city of Berlin until it gave in to him and named a street after Jesse Owens, the black sprinter who defeated Hitler's athletes in the "Nazi Olympics" in Berlin in 1936.

From Jerusalem, Prime Minister Ariel Sharon wrote: "The State of Israel, the Jewish people and all of humankind owe a great debt to Simon

Wiesenthal who devoted his life to ensuring that the Nazi atrocities will not be repeated and that the murderers will not go unpunished."[10]

But his daughter's heart was touched most by the private letters she received from innumerable individuals, among them hundreds of members of the "second generation"—the children of survivors, for whom the heritage of the Holocaust was a key part of their identity. Many of those children felt a deep identification with Wiesenthal. Esti Cohen, a native of Israel, wrote to Paulinka Kreisberg, "At the age of six, I used to have shoes ready next to my bed so that if the Nazis came in the night, at least I would have shoes, and not be like my mother in the 'death march' from the concentration camps at the end of World War II." She attached to her letter a photocopy of her Israeli ID card, with a yellow star stuck onto it.

Wiesenthal related that once when he was a prisoner at the Janowska concentration camp in Lvov, in Ukraine, he was in a group of inmates ordered to dig a deep ditch. "We knew that soon the ditch would be full of bodies," he said. "The victims were already being marched up. Women and girls. Then I caught the desperate eye of one of the girls. 'Don't forget us,' is what that look said to me." On another occasion, he said, he imagined meeting with the victims in heaven, and he was determined to say only four words, "I didn't forget you," the phrase that became his personal motto.[11]

More than anything else, Wiesenthal deserves to be remembered for his contribution to the culture of memory and the belief that remembering the dead is sanctifying life. Ironically, the more years went by and the more unlikely it became that the surviving Nazi criminals would be brought to justice, the more the Holocaust became a universal synonym for evil, a warning sign for every nation and every person. This happened, to a large extent, thanks to the efforts of Simon Wiesenthal. Nobody did more than he did in this respect. But even at the height of his fame as a "Nazi hunter" and as a humanist authority, he remained a lonely man, haunted throughout his adult life by memories of the horror. He was a tragic hero, always cloaked in the mysteries of his life; it is no easy task to decipher his secrets.

As he walked behind the glass box in Jerusalem, Wiesenthal thought not only about the murdered millions, but also about the murderers: "I was reminded of Eichmann," he wrote later. "That it was possible that the following day he would read in the newspaper about the ceremony and that a smile of satisfaction would come to his lips . . . In my mind's eye, I foresaw the day when my silent prayer would be heard, the day on which the murderer of my people would be taken to the land of the Hebrews. I swore that I would not remain silent and I would not rest until that longed-for day came."[12] This was a statement that was both true and untrue, like much of what Wiesenthal wrote.

I.

"Eichmann Is My Passion"

1. Between Vengeance and Justice

A dolf Eichmann was the most senior Nazi official to speak to Jewish leaders before the war, first in Berlin and afterward in Vienna and Prague. At first he worked in the Nazi party's security service and later in the Reich Central Security Office. He also talked to several representatives of the Zionist movement. The object of these contacts was to arrange for the transfer of Jews from Germany and some of the territories conquered by the Nazis. As of 1941, Eichmann directed the deportation of the Jews of Europe, first to ghettos and then to systematic annihilation in the death camps.

In January 1942, Eichmann attended an interdepartmental conference held in the Berlin suburb of Wannsee to discuss the organization of the extermination. He was never a maker of policy; he implemented it. He was one of those Nazi killers who as a rule did their work sitting behind a desk, but he also took many trips into the field. In his memoirs he mentioned an incident that occurred near the city of Minsk in the German-occupied Soviet republic of Byelorussia. As a group of Jews was being readied for execution, Eichmann wrote, he saw a woman with a baby in her arms. He tried to pull the infant away to save it, he wrote, but someone opened fire and it was killed. Fragments of its brain splashed onto his leather coat, and his driver helped him clean them off.[1] The Jews, who never encountered a more senior Nazi than him, looked upon him and Hitler as the two Adolfs who perpetrated the Holocaust.

———

The leaders of the Jewish people kept a watch on Eichmann's activities. Three months after the war broke out, Ben-Gurion recorded in his diary a report he had received from a Czechoslovakian Zionist official, to the effect that the condition of the Jews in Prague had deteriorated greatly since Eichmann arrived there. Ben-Gurion noted that Eichmann was directly subordinate to the head of the Gestapo, Heinrich Himmler.[2] This was not accurate, but it reflected the prevalent notion that Eichmann was a very senior Nazi official.

Indeed, as late as April 1944, Eichmann appeared to be omnipotent, as he initiated negotiations that were to decide not only the fate of Hungary's Jews, but perhaps also the outcome of the whole war. Some of the leaders of Budapest's Jews, among them Rezso Kastner, heard him offer them a deal: the lives of a million Jews in exchange for an assortment of goods, including several thousand trucks. Kastner said that Eichmann had told him the Jews were being sent to be exterminated at Auschwitz, but that he, Eichmann, was prepared to stop this. The proposal was conveyed to the Western Allies by an emissary.

The story of the "blood for trucks" affair was retold many times, and although fewer than two thousand Jews were saved as a result of a deal between Kastner and Eichmann, the proposition contributed to the inflation of Eichmann's image and his identification with the Holocaust. "He is the guiltiest of all in the extermination of millions of Jews in Europe," wrote a Jewish journalist in Palestine soon after the war ended.[3]

The Jewish Agency, which functioned as the government of the Jewish state in the making, began to collect material on the Nazi criminals toward the end of the war from refugees who had managed to reach Palestine, and from other sources.[4] Based on this information, in June 1945 a standard form for war criminals was filled out at the Agency under Eichmann's name; out of several hundred such forms filled out, Eichmann was listed as the most senior of the wanted Nazis. The information was very incomplete and flawed. Even his first name was missing, and he was erroneously listed as having been born in Sarona, a German colony next to Tel Aviv. In the explanatory remarks, he was accurately described as one of those responsible for the annihilation of the Jews.[5]

A few weeks later, one of the heads of the World Jewish Congress, an international federation of Jewish communities and organizations, petitioned the American prosecutor at the Nuremberg war crimes trials and requested that steps be taken to arrest Eichmann and prosecute him along with the prominent Nazis being tried there.[6] But Eichmann had vanished. Straight after the war, various people had begun searching for him: emissaries from the Jewish community in Palestine, American intelligence agents, and Holocaust survivors, among them Simon Wiesenthal. It was a joint effort and though not always well coordinated, not to mention amateurish, reckless, and replete with mistakes, it was informed entirely by inner passion and devotion to the goal.

Accurate details about Eichmann's life and even a hint as to where he might be hiding were obtained without much difficulty from his deputy, Dieter Wisliceny, who had been arrested in May 1945 by American soldiers. He provided detailed testimony on the destruction of the Jews, placing most of the responsibility on Eichmann's shoulders. Some leaders of the Zionist movement who were in Europe at the time met with Wisliceny; one of them was Gideon Ruffer, who would later change his family name to Rafael and become a top Israeli Foreign Ministry official. What seems to have interested Ruffer most was the cooperation between Eichmann and the Grand Mufti of Palestine, Haj Amin el-Husseini. Wisliceny was extradited to Czechoslovakia, where, in Bratislava Prison, he gave a statement to Arthur Piernikraz, an Austrian-born emissary from Palestine who went by the name of "Pier" and was later to change his name to Asher Ben Natan. In days to come he became one of the heads of the Israeli defense establishment, and the Jewish state's first ambassador to Germany.

Pier was based in Vienna, where he was one of the commanders of the Briha—the operation for getting the Jews who had survived the Holocaust out of Eastern Europe and sending them to Palestine (*briha* is Hebrew for "flight" or "escape"). His mission was not to hunt Nazi criminals, but he nevertheless harbored a hope of trapping Eichmann. Wisliceny told him that Eichmann's chauffer was in detention. The driver was interrogated and gave the names of a number of women whom Eichmann was friendly with. Wisliceny also reported that Eichmann had left his wife and three sons in a village called Altaussee. This was the most significant information that existed then.[7]

In Vienna, Pier had agreed to assist a refugee from the Polish city of

Radom to find the murderers of his family and the other Jews there. The man's name was Tadek (Tuvia) Friedman. Pier gave him a little money and Friedman opened a "center for documentation." His aim was to take revenge on the murderers of Radom's Jews. Pier instructed him to concentrate on one man. "He is the greatest murderer of them all," he told Friedman, and Friedman began the search for Adolf Eichmann.[8]

Wiesenthal heard about Eichmann only after the war, and he later recalled precisely from whom he had heard the name and when: from Aharon Hoter-Yishai, an officer in the Jewish Brigade (which had fought the Axis as part of the British army) and a well-known attorney in Palestine, in July 1945.[9] Wiesenthal, who had begun public activities on behalf of the refugees, was then in touch with the American occupation forces and was helping them locate Nazi war criminals. On one or two occasions, he traveled to Nuremberg to attend the trials.[10]

One of the Briha agents, Avraham Weingarten, put him in touch with Pier, and not long after that Gideon Ruffer also came to see him in Linz. They brought with them the list of Nazi criminals drawn up by the Jewish Agency, and told him that Eichmann was the most important of all.

Eichmann's family had settled in Linz when he was a child. His parents had an electrical goods store on one of the city's main streets. It still bore their family name after the war, and finding them was no problem. But Wiesenthal, who lived nearby in a rented room, was not sure that they were the same Eichmanns. He found out for sure by chance, as he relates in his memoirs. One evening, his landlady was serving him tea, and when she placed the tray on his desk she glanced at the papers lying there.

Her eye caught the name Eichmann. "Eichmann? Isn't that the SS general who persecuted the Jews?" she asked inquisitively, and mentioned that his parents lived nearby. Wiesenthal was excited and he asked her if she was sure. "What do you mean, sure? Don't I know my own neighbors?" the landlady replied. The next day, the police questioned Eichmann's parents, but they said they had no idea where he was.[11]

It may have been this development that led Pier to write to Ruffer, "In the matter of Eichmann, we have begun to address it. So far, only Wiesenthal has done anything, because I was away for a week in Prague and Bratislava. Yesterday he told me that there has been some progress, and that I'd get a letter from him today. In two or three days' time I'll know more."[12] But Pier had also taken action. On the basis of the information divulged by Wisliceny, he sent one of the Jewish refugees in Vienna to get to know one of Eichmann's female friends, in order to get a photograph of him.[13] The man was Manus Diamant, from Katowice in Poland, who was then twenty-four years old.

During the war, Diamant roamed from city to city; the Nazis had killed his mother and his father. After the war he found himself in Vienna, where he met Tuvia Friedman and through him reached Pier. The passion for revenge raged within him. He had known Eichmann's name since 1943. A handsome young man, Diamant posed as an SS officer from Holland and set out to search for Eichmann's girlfriend. It was not an easy task, and when he found her he could not get her to show him her photo album right away. But eventually he managed to get a photograph of Eichmann out of her.

Pier sent Diamant to Linz to work with Wiesenthal, who showed him the Eichmann family's electrical goods store. Diamant began to keep an eye on it. Eichmann's brother also worked there. One day, the brother set out in the direction of the railroad station. Diamant followed him and got onto the same train. They arrived at Altaussee, the village mentioned by Wisliceny. As expected, Eichmann's brother had come to visit his sister-in-law, Veronika; now her address was known to those searching for her husband.

Many years later, Asher Ben Natan wrote to Diamant: "In daring personal actions, you managed to find out where his wife and children were living and to obtain the only photograph of Eichmann, which was the important first step toward trapping the criminal. Eichmann's photograph was used later to identify him in Buenos Aires, before he was abducted."[14]

In the coming weeks, the Jewish refugee impostor managed to make friends with Veronika Eichmann, who was using her maiden name, Liebl, and sometimes he even frolicked with her children on the shore of the lake. Ben Natan would later reveal that at one stage a proposal to kidnap the children had been weighed, "but it was ultimately rejected for fear of possible entanglements."[15]

This was only part of the story. Diamant filled in the gaps. Once, he said, he had gone sailing on the lake, with Eichmann's three children in the boat with him, all happy and full of joy. He remembered a book that he had read, Theodore Dreiser's *An American Tragedy*, the story of a murder on a lake in New York State, and an idea occurred to him: "to drown Eichmann's three children to punish the chief butcher, so that he would feel what millions of Jewish mothers and fathers had felt when their children were torn away from them by force and murdered by his orders." The idea would not leave him alone, he wrote, giving him insomnia and refusing to go away.

All his efforts to locate Eichmann failed, so Diamant decided to return to Vienna and report to Pier. The night before, he slept in Wiesenthal's room in Linz and told him the plan for vengeance that he had thought of. Wiesenthal objected strenuously. "There's no room for revenge," he declared. Diamant tried to convince him. "It's not just revenge, it's punishment. It would be fitting for Eichmann to have to dive into the lake to seek the bodies of his children, the same way we are looking for our million and a half lost children."

Wiesenthal remained adamant. Pier was also opposed to the proposal but nevertheless passed it on to his superiors, who forbade killing Eichmann's children. Diamant was disappointed, but many years later, as a successful Israeli industrialist, he wrote: "When I thought of rocking the boat that I was sitting in with Eichmann's children, I had a vision of my mother shaking her head from side to side, in doubt and in worry; out of respect for her, I threw the oar down and made for the shore."[16]

Many of the survivors of the Holocaust were demanding revenge. Some of them—not many—tried to kill Germans; still fewer succeeded. Jewish Brigade officer Hoter-Yishai described in his memoirs how one survivor had laid before him six golden rings. "These belonged to the six Germans I have killed," the man said. They were prisoners of war. He strangled two of them with his bare hands, stabbed two others to death with their bayonets, and crushed the skulls of the other two with an iron bar.

One of the German soldiers, a young man, pleaded for his life, but the avenger did not heed his supplications and murdered him. "Like this, like this." He demonstrated the stabbing with fury and burning hatred, wrote Hoter-Yishai. The avenger showed him the mementos he had taken, the rings and also a gold tooth he had pulled out of the mouth of one of the Germans whose skulls he had smashed. "In those days," wrote Hoter-Yishai, "I shared with him, the avenger, the feeling of the need for vengeance and the satisfaction that it supplied."[17]

Some of the Brigade's soldiers saw their principal goal as wreaking vengeance. They managed to put together a list of former Gestapo policemen and went to their homes dressed in the uniforms of the British military police, arrested them, and disposed of them on the road. Shimon Avidan, who was to become a senior officer in the Israeli military, went to Europe specifically to liquidate Eichmann, but killed someone else instead by mistake. Another of the avengers was Haim Laskov, later to become chief of the general staff of the Israel Defense Forces.

The best-known and most ambitious plan for revenge was conceived by some survivors who found themselves in the Polish city of Lublin after the war. They developed their lust for vengeance into a moral national-historic doctrine, and decided to poison no fewer than six million Germans. Their leader was Pasha Reichman, who would later change his name to Yitzhak Avidov and serve in Israel's embassy in Poland. The spiritual leader of the group was the much-admired Abba Kovner, a former ghetto fighter and a visionary poet with a charismatic personality.

Their plan to poison the water reservoirs in several German cities failed, but the group did manage to spread poison on loaves of bread distributed in a POW camp; several hundred German prisoners contracted food poisoning. Many years later, Kovner wrote in a letter to Avidov: "It seems as if we risked our lives for things that were devoid of any significance. It was only our readiness to take that risk that gave those things any meaning."

This was the approach that crystallized in Israel as well. Vengeance is a basic feature of our emotional makeup, like fear and joy, and perhaps even hunger and thirst, wrote one columnist, but "supreme European and Jewish morality defines it as a base instinct that should be rooted out of our hearts." The appropriate response to the Nazi crimes, the newspaper *Ha'aretz* asserted, cannot be revenge, but only "full and just punishment, after a trial."

And this was Wiesenthal's position too. *Justice, Not Vengeance* is the name he would eventually give to his autobiography, and speaking shortly after the war at a survivors' conference in Paris, he described the arrest and prosecution of war criminals as the main part of the moral restitution that the Jews deserved. "We must not give the Nazis the chance to say that the Jews are no better than they are," he used to say.[18]

Years later, Wiesenthal was furious about a book on the avengers written by the Israeli historian Michael Bar Zohar. Everything in the book was wrong, Wiesenthal said, including the claim that Kovner's people had managed to poison the bread that was given to former SS personnel in a POW camp. In fact, Wiesenthal said, this had been an attempt made by two non-Jewish kitchen workers who tried to poison the soup but had not harmed anyone. Wiesenthal feared that spreading the story about Jewish vengeance would damage Jewish interests, and the Israeli ambassador in

Vienna tended to agree with him; an extreme right-wing newspaper in Germany had already jumped at the opportunity, the ambassador reported.

Manus Diamant meanwhile kept up his efforts to locate Eichmann's girl-friends but never managed to trace the Nazi officer's tracks. Wiesenthal recorded every scrap of information about Eichmann that he could get his hands on. During the Zionist Congress that was convened in Basel in 1946, he met Rezso Kastner and heard an account of his meetings with Eichmann, and how thanks to this encounter he had managed to save the lives of thousands of Jews. Wiesenthal believed him.[19]

Tadek Friedman was still in Vienna, and the Eichmann file that he had opened at his documentation center was expanding, thanks in part to material that Wiesenthal had obtained in Nuremberg. While there, he said, he had the chance to ask the Nazi criminal Hermann Krumey where Eich-mann was, and Krumey had told him that he was in Egypt or Palestine.[20] In May 1948, Wiesenthal reported that Eichmann had been held for a while in an American POW camp, but had gone under the alias of Eck-man and had managed to escape.[21]

Before the establishment of the State of Israel in May 1948, most of the agents from Palestine had gone home. Arthur Pier departed in July 1947. "Those who replaced him were occupied with other mat-ters and their zeal for catching war criminals was, in my humble opinion, questionable," Wiesenthal wrote later.[22] It seemed as though only he and Tadek Friedman were still taking an interest in Eichmann. "Eichmann is my passion," Wiesenthal wrote in *Aufbau*, the New York weekly for Jews from Germany.[23] In the meantime, he kept up the surveillance of Veronika Liebl-Eichmann in Altaussee; sometimes he even went there himself.

2. A Night in the Snow (Version I)

The village of Altaussee lies three miles north of the town of Bad Aussee. The residents of the two places are proud of their location in the heart of Austria. They are surrounded by awe-inspiring mountain peaks and lakes with mirrorlike surfaces. Scattered among them are yellowish houses that radiate bourgeois respectability and wooden cabins with tiled roofs. The high point of local history is a love story that happened in 1829: the Archduke Johann fell in love with the daughter of the postmaster and she with him, and they got married. Guest books at the local hotels show that Hugo von Hofmannsthal liked spending his time here; a well-known author, he wrote the librettos for Richard Strauss operas and was one of the founders of the music festival at nearby Salzburg.

Others who came from Vienna were the Jewish writers Arthur Schnitzler, Jakob Wassermann, and Hermann Broch, and Theodor Herzl, with his family. He liked to ride a bicycle here. The clear air of Aussee certainly could not have left the thoughts of the founder of political Zionism unaffected, according to the local historian.[24] One forest path is named after another frequent guest, Sigmund Freud. Some of the leaders of the Nazi regime chose Aussee as their last bastion; in better times they had spent their vacations here.

In 1947, Wiesenthal initiated a police search of Eichmann's wife's home in Altaussee but instead of going to the right house, at Fischerndorf 8, they mistakenly went to number 38, where another Nazi criminal, Anton Burger, was found. In one of his annual reports, Wiesenthal wrote that he took part in the raid and that he had escorted Burger to an American prison camp himself.

Burger had belonged to Eichmann's team, and served as his representative in Greece. For several months he had also been commander of the Theresienstadt concentration camp in Czechoslovakia. When the police realized they had gone to the wrong address, they went back to Fischerndorf 8. Veronika Liebl-Eichmann claimed that she and her husband had parted in March 1945 and she had not seen him since.[25]

Toward the end of 1947, Wiesenthal learned that she had petitioned the district court at Bad Ischl for her husband to be declared dead, "for the good of the children." Many wives were doing the same thing at the time, ostensibly in order to be able to collect their husbands' pensions, or to remarry. Naturally, the courts tended to grant their requests. "To me it was clear what this meant," wrote Wiesenthal. "If Eichmann was declared deceased in this way, his name would be erased from the wanted lists, and all official searches for him would be halted."

An American intelligence agent approached the judge and heard from him that a man by the name of Karl Lukas who lived in Prague had testified under oath that he had seen Eichmann shot dead. At the request of the agent, the judge agreed to postpone his decision, and in the meantime Wiesenthal contacted the Jewish community in Prague. It turned out that Lukas was married to Veronika Liebl-Eichmann's sister. The petition for a declaration that Adolf Eichmann was deceased was turned down.

Wiesenthal would later deem this his most important contribution to the efforts to capture Eichmann. "We would never have managed to find him if he had been declared dead, because each of the failures we were to have would have confirmed to us that he was indeed no longer alive."[26] One such failure made Wiesenthal's blood boil, right until the day he died, so great was his fury and so stinging the shame.

It happened toward the end of 1949, he related. A senior Austrian police officer called on him on December 20, and then again the next day, to tell him that Eichmann planned to spend New Year's Eve with his family in Altaussee. "This time we will capture him," said the officer, and he invited Wiesenthal to take part in the operation. Wiesenthal celebrated his birthday on January 1; "I could not imagine a more suitable gift," he wrote. They arranged to meet on December 28. "That week seemed so long to me that I will never forget it. I remembered my visit to Israel half a year before, the weeping crowds in the streets of Tel Aviv and Jerusalem, the ashes of the martyrs . . . and my vision of bringing Eichmann to Israel in handcuffs. At last, my wish was coming true . . ."

Wiesenthal worked in coordination with an Israeli diplomat based in Salzburg, Kurt Lewin. At Lewin's request Wiesenthal sent him certain photographs, and shared with him his hope that Eichmann would soon be caught. "You are always so optimistic," the Israeli diplomat remarked, half in jest, half seriously. Wiesenthal replied that without his optimism he would not have been able to survive in the concentration camps.

A few days before the planned operation, a visitor from Israel came to see Wiesenthal. This happened every now and again, he later recounted. The Israelis asked him about his working methods, leafed through his files on war criminals, studied the documents. Wiesenthal did not say who these Israelis were.

The Israeli who turned up before the Aussee operation was of medium height, with black hair and sparkling eyes, all youthful enthusiasm. According to Wiesenthal he constantly emphasized his pride in being an Israeli. He had fought in the War of Independence and talked a lot about how he had stood out as a courageous soldier on the battlefield. "He really had an admirable talent for storytelling and he thrilled everybody with his realistic descriptions," Wiesenthal wrote.

Like most of his Israeli visitors, this young man asked about Eichmann. Wiesenthal told him that he would soon be captured, and the visitor immediately understood that Wiesenthal was talking about an imminent operation and begged to be taken along.

Wiesenthal asked the Austrian officer in charge, who did not object. This was a crucial error, Wiesenthal wrote later, but he had sensed that the man would follow him secretly if he did not get permission to join the operation.

They traveled in a jeep, through a mountain pass that not many people dared to drive through at that time of year because of the snow. On arrival at Bad Aussee, they checked in at the Erzherzog Johann Hotel. Wiesenthal said he asked the Israeli not to leave his room, at least until the evening, and not to speak to anyone. But the young man went out to a beer hall and got into a conversation with some girls and thought he would impress them by letting it be known that he had arrived from Israel not long before. Meanwhile, six Austrian secret agents had checked into six inns in the area, and a seventh was about to join them.

On the morning of December 31, Wiesenthal met with the commander of the ambushing party and settled the final details with him. He went back to the hotel and once again warned the young Israeli not to leave his room before midnight, lest he endanger the operation. The man promised that this time he would obey the instructions, and so that he wouldn't get bored, Wiesenthal gave him a detective story to read.

Bad Aussee was already in a New Year's Eve mood. The sounds of revelry and drunken singing could be heard, and Wiesenthal too was in an elated frame of mind. A few more hours, and Eichmann will be in our hands, he thought. He went with one of the secret agents to a phone booth. The agent dialed Veronika Eichmann's number and she picked up the phone. He said nothing. "Tell me," they heard her say, "are you definitely coming tonight?" This was the final confirmation that she was expecting him. The agents took up their positions. One of them was stationed on the road leading from a nearby lake, the Grundlsee. There were a number of isolated houses there. They assumed that Eichmann was using one of them and that he would come from that direction, on foot, before midnight.

Wiesenthal and the officer in charge made their last patrol. It was cold and they had time, so they went into the bar beneath the Erzherzog Johann for a drink. The place was swarming with revelers; Wiesenthal was stunned to see his guest among them. "In the middle of the room, at a large table, the Israeli fellow was sitting surrounded by a whole crowd of people. He was telling them yarns of heroism from the War of Independence." Wiesenthal said his hair stood on end and the Austrian commander said: "I'm afraid your friend has screwed up our operation."

Wiesenthal tried to cheer himself up, but he knew that the game was over. "When we came to the next bar, an agent who had been stationed there whispered to the commander that the guests were saying there was an Israeli in the area. In the third bar, the agent said a rumor had spread that there was a whole group of Israelis in town."

They waited a little longer and then the commander said that there was no point in carrying on. Eichmann had set out, but had been warned and had gone back into hiding. Wiesenthal did not immediately grasp the significance of what he had heard, and the officer repeated: "Someone tipped Eichmann off." Wiesenthal was so shocked that he couldn't utter a sound.

About half a year later, one of the agents told him what had happened. "At 11:30 I saw two men on the road from Grundlsee. It was almost totally dark, but I could see their shadows against the white snow. They were about 150 meters away from me. I was standing hidden in the trees at the side of the road. Suddenly someone appeared and shouted something at them. They stopped and exchanged a few words and immediately the three of them ran off in the direction of Grundlsee." Wiesenthal did not say why they did not try to find Eichmann there.

The next day, Wiesenthal left, very dejected. They were so close to catching Eichmann, so close, he mused. "I never bore a grudge against the young Israeli," he wrote. "I never even complained to him. If someone needed to be scolded and blamed, it was I who deserved it, because I took him with me. For weeks I was depressed and I couldn't forgive myself."[27]

Wiesenthal never gave the young man's name, and never explicitly identified him as an Israeli agent, but the central message of his tale left no room for doubt: Israel was to blame for Eichmann's escape. In his opinion, this was no coincidence, as Israel did almost nothing to capture Nazi criminals. Instead of setting up a powerful organization for this purpose, it published books about the Holocaust, an angry Wiesenthal wrote sarcastically.[28]

3. A Night in the Snow (Version 2)

The story about the abortive attempt to capture Eichmann in snow-covered Altaussee can be found in four versions in Wiesenthal's writings, all different and even contradictory in some key details. First he compiled a report that was never published, possibly written as a kind of book proposal. The summaries in this document mention "an Israeli friend" who accompanied him and do not go into detail about the events, except for one somewhat mysterious sentence: "One of us committed an indiscretion." In his final report, the Israeli isn't mentioned at all. According to the draft of the document, the intention was to hand Eichmann over to the Americans and not to rely on the Austrian authorities, but the final version says that the operation was made possible thanks to the excellent working relations Wiesenthal had with the Austrian security services.[29]

The story of the Israeli visitor was published for the first time in a book that Wiesenthal wrote about his role in the hunt for Eichmann. It came out in Hebrew and in German, between Eichmann's capture early in 1960 and the opening of his trial in 1961. There are significant differences between the German and Hebrew versions, perhaps the result of flawed translation and hasty editing. In another book that he published in 1988, Wiesenthal wrote that the young Israeli was an employee of his office.[30]

Within the close-knit intelligence community of Israel, still a small country where everybody knew everybody else, the story made the rounds in whispers; nearly sixty years on, a veteran of the community could even name the young agent who went to visit Wiesenthal as Michael Bloch. Born in Germany, Bloch had come to Palestine in 1934 at the age of six. After World War II, he studied medicine in Switzerland, but returned to Israel before the War of Independence and became an intelligence officer. He was loaned by the army to the Mossad, as was his twin brother, Gideon, who changed his family name to Yarden and later became deputy to the Israeli ambassador in Vienna.

Bloch's papers include a copy of a report that he wrote after his mission in Austria. Wiesenthal is not mentioned in the document, and neither is the name of Eichmann, who is referred to as "the subject," but Asher Ben Natan ("Pier"), who saw the report only many years afterward, confirmed that it was about the same events. Ben Natan knew what he was talking about: After the establishment of the state he served as head of the Israeli Foreign Ministry's political department, one of the forerunners of the Mossad. It was he who had sent Bloch to Austria on what was code-named Operation Aliyah—the Hebrew word for immigration to Israel.

At the end of November 1948, Bloch wrote in the report, Pier had asked him to take responsibility for the operation. As he was not doing anything else at the time, he agreed, on condition that the operation would not take more than two weeks. The goal was defined as "Receiving the subject from the Austrian secret police and transferring him to Israel." Pier left the modus operandi to his discretion, and was responsible for covering his expenses. In addition, he put two other Israeli agents at Bloch's disposal.

On arrival in Austria, Bloch wrote, he immediately contacted the Israeli diplomat Kurt Lewin, who extended him full assistance. The Austrian secret police were following "the subject" and had managed to obtain information on his whereabouts. Lewin and the head of the secret police in Linz agreed that after he was apprehended, "the subject" would be handed over to the Israelis in exchange for $5,000, and that in addition Israel would cover the costs of the operation.

Bloch explained that "the local secret police agreed to the whole matter for two reasons, although handing someone to a foreign country without the government's approval was a violation of Austrian law. The reasons were: 1. The department handling war criminals did not get sufficient budgets for its employees, and in this case they would turn a decent profit, and 2. They hoped that in this way the 'subject' would get the punishment that he deserved."

Bloch confirmed the main points of Wiesenthal's version. According to information that had been obtained on "the subject," he was supposed to visit his family between Christmas and New Year's Day. Their home had therefore been placed under surveillance. "I lived for a number of days in an isolated and empty cabin four kilometers from the subject's wife's house, so that I would be ready to take delivery of him immediately," Bloch wrote, meaning after Eichmann had been apprehended by the Austrians.

One of the other agents, possibly Wiesenthal, was supposed to be with him, "but because of the discomfort in the hut, 20 degrees below zero, dirty sheets, lack of food, etc. he decided to stay in a hotel in the nearby village." Bloch was furious with Wiesenthal and would later tell his brother: "I lay there in some wooden hut, freezing cold, while Wiesenthal went to fool around with girls." In blunter language, Bloch told the same story to his two sons. The man Wiesenthal said he met in a bar could have been one of the other Israelis whom Pier had put at Bloch's disposal; Bloch wrote that one of them had refused to accept his authority. Either way, "the subject" did not show up. He sent his wife a sum of money as a Christmas present but instead of visiting her he crossed over into the British occupation zone in Germany, Bloch wrote.

The conclusion of this report is quite perplexing. According to Bloch, he knew Eichmann's exact whereabouts, but because he was now living in Germany, the operation had moved into a new stage, which could possibly continue for another few weeks, and Bloch could no longer take part in it. He therefore told Lewin that he was leaving. In his eyes, the whole affair looked like an overly amateurish adventure. In order to catch Eichmann, a professional effort was required instead of relying on amateurs. The latter remark was apparently a reference to Wiesenthal.[31]

Isser Harel, the head of Israel's secret service, also wrote about the affair. He sought to diminish the Israelis' part in the failure. Eichmann would not have been alarmed by the presence of a loudmouthed Israeli in a bar, he contended. Wiesenthal was already quite well-known, he had not kept his passion for capturing Eichmann a secret, and his very presence in the small mountain village was enough to keep Eichmann away. Nevertheless, it was important for Harel to stress that Bloch was not one of his operatives and that everything happened "before my time." The Mossad, which he was to head along with the internal secret service, did not even exist at that time, he pointed out.[32]

This episode would produce yet another version, that of one of the Austrian policemen who took part in the attempt to capture Eichmann. His name was Leo Maier. Just before Christmas 1948, he wrote in his memoirs, he was summoned to his superior officer in the Linz police, who ordered him to travel together with another officer to Altaussee. There's a woman living there by the name of Veronika Liebl and she is the wife of a famous Nazi criminal called Adolf Eichmann, he was told. It's possible that he'll visit his family over Christmas. This was the first time Maier had heard the name. He and his colleague had been picked for the mission because they were young bachelors; it was preferable to let married personnel spend the holiday with their families.

"It was a boring assignment," Maier wrote. There was no sign of Eichmann, and the holiday season was passing them by. They were ordered to stay on for New Year's too, and the two young cops were disgruntled. It was bad enough to have to work on Christmas, but on New Year's Eve they wanted to be with their girlfriends in Linz.

During his stay in Altaussee, Maier spotted Eichmann's six-year-old son and began chatting with him. "Are you going to church?" he asked, and the boy replied politely in the affirmative. "What about Mother?" Maier asked, and the child replied that his mother had no time because she had to cook at home. "And what about your father?" Maier continued the interrogation. "Father is far away over the sea," the boy answered, "but soon we'll go to him, and then I'll be allowed to ride on a pony." When Maier called in to his superior officer, he didn't mention the conversation with the boy, but reported that on the basis of the investigation that he and his colleague had conducted in the village, it was clear to him that Adolf Eichmann was in South America and his family was planning to follow him. When he got back to Linz, he put his report in writing.

Maier became a member of the Austrian secret service and a senior police officer. He wrote his memoirs many years after Wiesenthal published his books, but he never even mentioned the complicated operation described by Wiesenthal and Bloch.[33]

What Wiesenthal wrote should be treated with some caution. He did not always recall things the way they had actually happened and did not always bother to verify his recollections. But the lack of agreement between what he wrote and related at various times does not necessarily reflect only the limitations of human memory and the deceptive tricks it plays. As a man with literary aspirations, Wiesenthal tended to indulge in flights of imagination and more than once preferred to revel in historical drama rather than sticking to pure fact, as if he did not believe in the power of the true story to make enough of an impression on his audience.

Wiesenthal wrote that the attempt to capture Eichmann took place some months after he returned from his visit to Israel, where he had buried those urns full of ashes. That took place in June 1949. But Bloch's report was dated January 3, 1949, six months before the interment ceremonies. It was very likely not by mistake that Wiesenthal switched the dates. The significance of the attempt to capture Eichmann stemmed from the same emotion produced by the burial of the ashes. It was therefore necessary to shift the summer scene in Jerusalem forward, before the winter scene in Altaussee, and not to leave them in the sequence in which they had actually occurred.[34]

A few days after the failure of the Altaussee operation, Wiesenthal wrote, he "received notification" that the search had ceased because Eichmann had disappeared. Tuvia Friedman wrote that in 1950 he had been in touch with another group of agents sent by Arthur Pier, and they had cooperated with American intelligence operatives in Salzburg looking for Nazi criminals. Ben Natan confirmed years later that there had been such an attempt, but it too had failed. It was a bad year for hunting, Wiesenthal wrote.[35]

All of the above does not, in fact, represent a serious operational effort, but it is nevertheless possible to say this about Wiesenthal: he was exceedingly eager to start tracking Eichmann down. He recorded every rumor and tried to verify every scrap of information. This was widely known, including by the U.S. Central Intelligence Agency, which believed Wiesenthal was planning to abduct Eichmann and fly him to Israel. In Linz they called him "Eichmann's Wiesenthal."[36]

Often during this period he asked himself why it was that he had survived, and his answer was: In order to capture Eichmann.

2

"During That Period, We Never Took Hitler Seriously"

I. A Small Town in Galicia

In the Wiesenthals' home, they could hear the stream that ran between the houses of the Jews in the town of Buczacz, a burbling that Shmuel Yosef Czaczkes, later known as S. Y. Agnon, winner of the 1966 Nobel Prize for literature, called the "words of the water." Buczacz was a small town covered in greenery in eastern Galicia, now part of Ukraine. Its church spires and little bridge gave it a picturesque look. "My town is built on mountains and on hills and it goes into forests full of trees and bushes and comes out of them," wrote Agnon, "and the Strypa river runs through the town and around it, and streams take water and irrigate the reeds and the bushes and the trees, and good springs well up with good water, and birds live in the trees, and there they chirp away. Some of these birds are conceived and hatched in our town, and some of them flew into our town and stayed in it, when they saw that our town is finer than all the other towns."[1]

Photographs of Buczacz that Wiesenthal kept convey a sense of tumultuous buying and selling going on around an odd baroque-style structure that stands in the center, a tower on a tower on a gigantic foundation block. Here the city council used to meet. The tower sparked Agnon's imagination, and he embroidered a fairy tale around it. Its hero is the Jewish architect who designed the tower. So perfect was the structure that the governor of the city ordered the architect be locked up at its top, lest he design similar ones for other towns.[2]

A few months after Wiesenthal's birth on the night of December 31, 1908, Agnon, who was already twenty years old, arrived in Palestine and settled in Jaffa. But his descriptions of life as a Jewish kid in Buczacz could also serve as a backdrop for the childhood of Szymek, as the eldest son of Henczel (Asher) and Rosa Wiesenthal was nicknamed.

"I awoke from my sleep, and there was light in the house," Agnon related in a true story about what happened one Sabbath morning when he was a small child.

> I got out of bed and opened a window so that the window boards would not stop the light from entering the house. While I was standing at the window, I wanted to see the light before it came into the house. I washed my hands and my face and put on my Sabbath clothes and went outside. And no one else from the house sees me or hears me going out. Neither my father nor my mother, who never took their eyes off me, saw me going out of the house. I am outside and there is no one else outside. Only the birds, singing their morning song, only they were outside.
>
> I stood there until the birds stopped singing. Then I walked to the well, because I heard the voice of the well water and I said I shall go and see the water talking, because I had never seen the water talking.
>
> I came to the well, and beheld it, and the water was welling up from it. And there was no one there to drink the water. I filled my palms with it and I said the blessing and I drank. Then I walked wherever my legs took me . . . and the town was still peaceful and many Jews and dignitaries were in town, and all the Jews who were slain by the enemy, all of them were still alive.[3]

Wiesenthal described himself as a street child, lonely, friendless.[4]

Galicia had passed from hand to hand many times over the generations. Wiesenthal liked to say that the people went to bed at night without knowing what uniforms the local policemen would be wearing in the morning—Polish, Russian, Ukrainian, or Austro-Hungarian. Indeed, during his lifetime, there were many political upheavals, which produced in him a constant, very Jewish skepticism and uncertainty that justified itself again and again: You never know, anything can happen at any time.

He was born into the final years of an unbroken historical period of relative political stability. For sixty years Galicia had lived under the same ruler, the emperor Franz Josef, who governed his empire from Vienna. The Jews of Galicia had good cause to admire the emperor: he granted them civil liberties, and their position was far better than that of their brethren in Russia or later in Poland. Moreover, the empire had wreathed them in German culture. "We adored the emperor and we were ardent patriots of the Austro-Hungarian Empire," Wiesenthal would assert in days to come; but in fact, what he said applied to his parents' generation. His own life was shaped by revolutions and wars.[5]

Before World War I, there were some 870,000 Jews living in Galicia, making up about 20 percent of the population. Over the generations, they had known discrimination and persecution and many of them were poor. In the three decades that preceded Wiesenthal's birth, approximately a quarter of a million Jews had migrated away from Galicia, mostly to America. But there were also many Jews among the region's wealthy residents. They dealt in banking, import-export, or the petroleum industry, or they leased lands from the aristocracy and collected the peasants' rents and taxes. There were also Jewish doctors and lawyers, and there were Jewish delegates in the parliament and Jewish mayors, one of them in Buczacz.

The Wiesenthals were neither rich nor poor. The father had come to Buczacz from another town, Skala, and worked as the local agent for a sugar-manufacturing company. As a child, Wiesenthal loved spending time in his father's storeroom, building towers out of sugar cubes. His grandmother said that he would surely become an architect, and what she had in mind was probably a Jewish architect in Galicia—not all Jews wanted to immigrate to America.[6]

When they spoke of themselves ironically as Galicianers, the Jews were referring to their ability to survive among the gentiles. In the abundance of different nationalities in the Austro-Hungarian Empire, their first circle of identity was the Jewish circle.

Jewish culture thrived in Galicia, and the constant ferment of new ideas led to ideological and political clashes between the various religious strains, such as Hasidism and its more conservative opponents. Innovative secular trends also appeared: the Enlightenment, socialism, and Zionism. A resident of Buczacz was a delegate to the First Zionist Congress in Basel in 1897. Of the town's population of twenty thousand, seven out of every ten were Jews. They had been there since the year 1500 and spoke many languages—Russian, Ukrainian, Polish, German, and Yiddish, which were the languages that Wiesenthal heard in his childhood.[7]

They spoke German at home and his mother, he related, used to quote from the writings of the classics of that language, works by Goethe, Schiller, and Heine. Agnon, the son of a dealer in furs, said the same thing about his mother. Many years later, Wiesenthal signed a statement under oath declaring that his parents had spoken German to each other and that it was the language that he and his mother spoke to each other.

The statement was made at the request of an acquaintance who was suing for reparations from Germany and had to prove that he belonged to the German cultural sphere; Wiesenthal declared that the situation in his home was the same as in his friend's. "We Jews were the pioneers of German culture in the East," he said in a lecture. Nevertheless, his main day-to-day language was Yiddish. It left its mark on his accent, whatever language he was speaking, and never left him. Until his dying day he was an Eastern European Jew and, by his lights, also a refugee: "A refugee is a person who has lost everything, except his accent," he wrote in one of his books.[8]

His grandparents were very observant. Once his grandmother took him to see a wonder-working rabbi. There, Wiesenthal saw a man whom everyone called "the silent one." His grandmother explained that during a terrible argument with his wife, the man had cursed her and yelled, "I wish you'd burn." The same night, their house caught fire and she perished in the flames. Eaten up by guilt, the man came to the rabbi, whose judgment was that he should never, ever utter another word, and devote his life to silent prayer. Wiesenthal's biographer, Hella Pick, who heard this story from him, linked it to the subject that preoccupied him in his adulthood: guilt and punishment, repentance and forgiveness.[9]

When he was three or four years old, his parents sent him to cheder, religious school for children, where he heard about some of the basics of Jewish law and probably picked up a few words of Hebrew; on Jewish holidays, his parents used to put in an appearance at the synagogue, because that's what the members of the community used to do. He didn't grow up in a religious atmosphere, but at least as long as his grandmother was alive, they would have a seder on Passover. Wiesenthal would later tell how at the seder he always waited for Elijah the prophet to appear, and although he never did, his grandmother would say that Elijah had drunk the wine set aside for him. When her grandchild pointed out that the glass was still full, she said that Elijah never drank more than one teardrop.[10]

Wiesenthal said that among his earliest memories was talk of persecution of the Jews. His grandfather spoke a lot about pogroms. Some five years before he was born, a notorious pogrom occurred in Kishinev, then in Russia.[11] Nonetheless, Wiesenthal grew up in a community that was brimming with vitality.

About a year before he was born, an election meeting had been held in one of the squares in Buczacz, with a well-known politician from Vienna, Nathan Birnbaum. The meeting was recorded for posterity in a photograph in which hundreds of the town's Jews can be seen, mostly bearded men in black hats, some traditional, others in accordance with the dictates of the latest Viennese fashion. Here and there, there's a woman to be seen. Everyone looks serious, in deference to the honored speaker, and probably also because the photographer was there: everyone is staring straight at his camera's lens.

One of the buildings to be seen on the square is a hotel. Sitting on its ornate balcony are several matrons in magnificent hats. A large clock held by a long beam is attached to one of the shops. At the center of the crowd there's a carriage, with two white horses in harness, which apparently brought Birnbaum from the train station.

Jewish politics often boiled over, but the local newspaper, *Der jüdische Wecker* ("The Jewish Awakener"), assailed the townsfolk for their apathy. "Every Buczacz Jew is a world unto himself, and public affairs are of no interest to him," the paper complained and proposed the following thesis to its readers: "Whoever sees how many shops sell soda in this town could think that the people here are enthusiastic and need to cool themselves down by drinking cold liquids, but the truth of the indifference and coolness of our Israelite brothers in this town contradicts this supposition. And who knows if it was not drinking too much soda that caused them to be so frozen?"[12]

Most of Buczacz's former residents have spoken of the poverty of the Jews there, but the community maintained several houses of prayer, including a magnificent synagogue, as well as schools, a hospital, an orphanage, and soup kitchens. The Jewish newspaper carried a literary supplement that published some of the earliest poems of the Czaczkes boy, as he was then known. Shalom Aleichem once visited the town, but never found the time to meet the young Czaczkes. Other writers also came.

A man by the name of Avraham Silberschein used to come from Lvov to give lessons in the Bible, history, and Hebrew. There was a theatrical troupe called *Der Tannenzapf* (The Pinecone). Sometimes a circus came to town, or a menagerie, or a picture show, or a tightrope walker, or a man with a gramophone and records, or a magician. In the summer, people went for strolls in the surrounding forests, or swam in the Strypa, or rowed boats on it. In the winter, they'd skate on the ice.[13]

Describing Jewish life in Buczacz in the early twentieth century, Agnon depicted a day-to-day routine without a sense of impending catastrophe. "The sun shines on the earth and those who live on it, and the earth gives forth its produce with a friendly countenance and an angry countenance and people do their business and run to their affairs, and every single one enjoys himself in his own manner or torments himself in his own manner from the doings of the world and its tricks. And although there is no shortage in the world of world-repairers, we used to believe that nothing would change." But then, in the summer of 1914, all of a sudden, there was a rumor that war had broken out.

At first people in Buczacz found it hard to believe that their emperor would become entangled in such a nonsensical thing. Doesn't he know the price of war? The people therefore tended to agree with those pundits who wrote in the Jewish newspapers that there would be no war. But even as they were writing and reading these thoughts, "the war suddenly enveloped everyone and the roar of the cannon shook the town and its surroundings," wrote Agnon.

The Great War—or World War I as it later came to be called—had broken out. It was not only a matter of battles waged between soldiers on remote front lines; it brought established structures of life and basic values tumbling down almost everywhere. In Buczacz too, as Agnon wrote: "The young men were taken off to the war, and the old men are left without anyone or anything to lean on, the women don't know what to do first, and the children are left to their own devices. The schools were shut down and the cheders too. Young men who have not been called to the war, or have been called and cannot reach their units and attach themselves to the troops, collect money and establish committees and open eating houses to give food to the needy."

Many people left the town.

> Everyone takes his money and hires himself a wagon and loads his goods and chattels onto it and lifts his wife and their tender chicks onto the wagon and he and his sons and older daughters follow behind the wagon and they ride and walk to another place where the evil has not yet reached. And as they reach that place, they see that what has happened to them has also happened to the people of the place to which they have come . . . And Buczacz is already empty of most of its Jewish residents. One-third are entangled in the war and are fighting with the Russians, and another third have scattered everywhere, and the third that have remained in the town are subject to plunder and murder.[14]

World War I took Europe into the twentieth century, and at this point the upheavals of history became the central factor in the life of Wiesenthal, as they did for millions of other children. Within a year and a half, he had lost his father, who belonged to the imperial reserve corps, was called up for active service, and was killed. Wiesenthal would often speak about the death of his mother in World War II; he seldom spoke of the loss of his father in the first, but the irony that accompanied that loss did not escape him: his father fought on the same side as Adolf Hitler.[15] It happened in October 1915. Wiesenthal was seven years old. His brother, Hillel, was five. The war would go on for another three years.

2. The Great Mistake

Henczel Wiesenthal was killed as a soldier in the wrong army. The Russians conquered Galicia and like most residents of Buczacz, Rosa Wiesenthal fled, taking her two small sons and her parents, first to Lvov and then to Vienna. There they lived in a Jewish area known as Mazzesinsel, or "Matza Island," in the Leopoldstadt district, between the Danube Canal and the river, crowded in with tens of thousands of other Jews, Viennese, and outsiders, many of them refugees from the east.

Everything was new and curious in the city, where the streets were paved with stones and, as Agnon wrote, "were uncomfortable for the people from the small towns, especially those who were used to the mud of Buczacz."[16] But in Vienna there were expansive parks, palaces, magnificent boulevards, tall buildings, large stores, coffeehouses, and motor cars. The boy from the small town who had just lost his father was sent to school, which was also a new experience for him. It was a Jewish school, and the language of instruction was German. Wiesenthal in days to come would recall the day in November 1916 when they were let out of school to watch the funeral procession of the emperor Franz Josef.

Among the tens of thousands of children who lined the route of the procession there was another Jewish boy, three years younger than Wiesenthal, who later remembered mainly the freezing cold of that day. His name was Bruno Kreisky, and he was to serve as chancellor of Austria more than half a century later. "When at last the cortege arrived, it seemed to me that the whole world was turning black," Kreisky wrote. "It was a parade that was all black. In people's faces, you could see pain and anxiety: What will happen now?" A few months later, Wiesenthal's grandfather also died.[17]

The death of the emperor and the end of the war heralded a new era. Rosa Wiesenthal took her two sons and went back to Buczacz, as did many other of the town's Jews, "out of their love for the town of their birth and because they had realized that they hadn't found prosperity in the other places where they had lived," as Agnon wrote. The Wiesenthal home was one of the few that had not been damaged, though the storehouse had been looted. The Russians had been defeated and had retreated.

Eastern Galicia became an independent state, but before long it passed into the hands of Poland and its "harsh rulers," in Agnon's words. "As they were not able to act sensibly, they acted with an angry cruelty. They knew no mercy, only harsh decrees . . . Great poverty descended on the town, and livelihoods were getting smaller and smaller. A man did not know what he would eat and what he would give to his tender chicks."[18] A typhus epidemic raged in the town, killing many of the citizens. But despite everything, Rosa Wiesenthal managed to keep her husband's business going. She sent her elder son back to his grandmother's home in Vienna for a few months.

In 1920, the Poles waged war against Bolshevik Russia and they were helped by the cavalry of the Ukrainian leader Symon Petliura, whose soldiers were known for their cruelty to the Jewish population. They ran amok in Buczacz too. Wiesenthal told of one of them who appeared suddenly in their street and stabbed him in the thigh with his sword.

Three years later, at age fifteen, he was sent to high school. This was a decidedly secular move. Classes were in Polish and took place on the Sabbath as well as weekdays. For him personally, apparently, the idea was that he should prepare himself for a professional life in a more promising place than Buczacz. In a photograph from those days, he can be seen in a civilian-looking suit and tie, in the company of other young men wearing uniforms of a Zionist scouting movement for Jewish youths, apparently the socialistic Zionist Hashomer Hatza'ir.

In 1922, his beloved grandmother, who had also returned from Vienna, passed away, and a year later he experienced yet another disaster, when his younger brother, Hillel, fell and sustained a serious spinal injury. Their mother took him to Vienna for treatment, and for almost six months there was almost no contact between Wiesenthal and his mother. When she returned, Hillel was still alive but after a few months he died.

Paulinka Kreisberg, Wiesenthal's daughter, believed that his mother was the dominant factor in his life, and that he harbored a feeling that she loved Hillel more than him. Wiesenthal himself spoke little about these matters, and he never displayed any emotion about his early years—not love, not envy, not frustration, not pain. He never told how he learned of his father's death and how it affected him; he never told of his feelings for his brother and how he felt when he died; he never spoke about the funeral or the seven days of mourning. In interviews with biographers, he would build a protective wall around himself and hide behind it, defending himself with a fixed series of stories, like the one about the Ukrainian cavalryman who wounded him with his sword. The interviewers were satisfied.

In high school, Wiesenthal met the love of his life, Cyla Müller, who was to become his wife. A scion of the Freud family, she too had lost her father. "I was happy," Wiesenthal would later recall. "I had a girlfriend who loved me and whom I loved very much." He said that he used to tell her funny stories, and she would laugh a lot. Once he drew her with a pencil: a plump girl, immersed in a book, her hands covering her ears as if she wanted to cut herself off from her surroundings and protect her private world, a deep sadness on her face.[19] Apparently they spoke Polish and Yiddish to each other. Everyone expected them to get married.

And then something else happened: Rosa Wiesenthal got married again, to Isack Halperin, a Viennese Jew living in the city of Dolina, in the

Carpathian Mountains, and went to live with him there. Wiesenthal was hurt by her remarrying and leaving Buczacz. Before doing so, she saw to it that her son would live in his girlfriend's parents' home. Now and again Wiesenthal would go and visit his mother and stepfather. Halperin had sons from a previous marriage. Wiesenthal's relations with his stepfather were not good. At that time, Wiesenthal was spending a lot of time drawing, and actually wanted to study art. His mother persuaded him to take up architecture, perhaps because his stepfather was a manufacturer of building tiles.

Wiesenthal failed his first attempt at the final high school exams. He said that Jewish students had to try harder to get passing marks. Cyla did better than he did. After he passed the exams, he traveled to Prague to study. He had wanted to study in Lvov, which was nearer to Buczacz, but he said that Jews were intentionally failed in the entrance examinations there.[20] He was now twenty years old and, as a Polish citizen, eligible for conscription into the military; this was perhaps another good reason for going to Prague, unless he could get an exemption from serving, as many young men did. Either way, the golden city of a hundred spires welcomed the young Jew from Buczacz. Cyla remained at home, and he would travel to visit her during vacations.

In Europe, the 1920s were years of hope for a new, democratic world. As a student at the Politechnika, the technical college in Prague, Wiesenthal found himself part of the avant-garde cultural ferment; it was daring, free, spiritually intoxicating. For the first time in his life he saw policemen he did not have to fear. Masses of foreign students gave the city a cosmopolitan atmosphere and, again for the first time, he went drinking and partying with boys and girls of his age who were not Jewish. They painted and sculpted and spent time in a movie studio. These were the best years of his life. Sometimes he would take the stage at a Jewish students' cabaret to tell jokes. The Jewish student organization had a Hebrew name, Hatehiya, the reawakening.

Wiesenthal took an interest in Zionist politics. At first he joined the Revisionists, an opposition group in the Zionist movement led by a well-known journalist, Vladimir Ze'ev Jabotinsky. They demanded a revision of the policies of Chaim Weizmann, the president of the World Zionist Organization, policies that seemed to them too conciliatory. In terms of the politics of those days, the Revisionists were the right wing. Jabotinsky's opponents likened him to Mussolini or even Hitler. Wiesenthal later said that during his student days in Prague he idolized Jabotin-sky and twice met him for conversations. What he meant, apparently, was that he attended a lecture and a press conference given by Jabotinsky.[21]

But he didn't stay with the Revisionists for long. "They were arrogant and behaved as if they had a monopoly on the truth," he explained years later.[22] The Revisionists had split and Wiesenthal shifted his support to a party called the Hebrew State, headed by a journalist-politician by the name of Meir Grossman. Jabotinsky and his followers broke away from the World Zionist Organization in 1935; the Hebrew State stayed within the fold. In political terms, it was closer to the center than to the Revisionists.

Wiesenthal was thus a political person and a Zionist before the Holo-caust; he remained on the right of the political spectrum for the rest of his life. But it was not the internal squabbles in the Zionist movement that preoccupied him during those merry days in Prague. He stayed there until 1932, and then moved to Lvov. His stepfather refused to continue financ-ing his studies in Prague. In Lvov, he had to begin his studies almost from the beginning again.

Lvov, founded in the thirteenth century, was an important city. The influ-ence of Vienna was evident in its center, and it even had an opera house. On the eve of World War II, it had a population of about 300,000 souls; one-third of them Jewish. The only cities in Poland with larger Jewish communities were Warsaw and Lodz. The other inhabitants were Poles and Ukrainians, who were at odds with one another, but both blamed their troubles on the Jews.[23]

When Wiesenthal came to the city he was twenty-four. While studying he worked as a foreman for an architecture and civil engineering firm. For his final project, he designed a sanatorium for lung patients. His biogra-pher wrote that he also designed a number of residential buildings, includ-ing a villa for his mother and stepfather.[24]

At the center of public discourse at the time was the rise of the Nazi party in Germany, where they seized power in January 1933. Wiesenthal recalled that an anti-Semitic mood prevailed among the students and teachers at his college. Once a year, the students declared a "day without Jews" when Jewish students were barred from entering the college, and generally they chose a day that fell during the exam period. Among the students there were bands of fascist thugs who abused the Jews.[25]

In Lvov too, Wiesenthal was active in the student Zionist association, which carried the Hebrew name Bar Giora, and now and again he would publish cartoons in the Polish-language student magazine *Omnibus*. Most were anti-Nazi, but some were also aimed against the British proposal to divide Palestine into two states; he wanted a Jewish state in all of Palestine.[26] "Lvov was really a flourishing city in the cultural sense and there were many talented young people there," Wiesenthal recalled many years later, "with youngsters who, if the days of persecution had not come, and if they had survived, would have become the elite of the country."[27] It was in that optimistic spirit that he married Cyla in September 1936. "We dreamed of a better future," he told interviewers Maria Sporrer and Herbert Steiner, but, as was his wont, he left them outside his inner world.

The interviewers asked him if he had not thought back then of immigrating to Palestine or America, as many of his relatives had done. Wiesenthal included the shared dream that he and his wife had woven together among the reasons for their remaining in Lvov, along with the difficulty of obtaining Palestinian immigration certificates. But apparently he never even tried to get such a certificate, in spite of his Zionist patriotism.[28]

For Wiesenthal's Zionism was an ideological worldview, and a love story. Like most Jews, he did not see it as a moral imperative to get up and leave his country. Jewish Galicia was his home, despite everything. It was here that he hoped to live with his family and to succeed in his profession. But it was an illusion, and he should have known it. The Nazis' persecution of the Jews was common knowledge and there were more and more signs of the impending danger, not least the German occupation of Wiesenthal's beloved Prague and Austria in 1938.

Polish anti-Semitism was also growing from day to day. Jabotinsky called for the evacuation of the Jews from Poland and other Eastern European states.[29] But, like most people at that time, including most Jews, Wiesenthal never grasped the unique nature of the Nazi threat. "During that period, we never took Hitler seriously," he said later. "We only looked upon him as a crisis that would pass." They were in love with progress and believed in the twentieth century, he explained, and their faith in justice was so deep that none of them was terribly concerned about Hitler.[30]

Not everyone shared this faith. Wiesenthal's brother-in-law settled in Palestine. But leaving was no easy matter. Wiesenthal's mother, stepfather, and mother-in-law were still alive, and it's doubtful that Simon and Cyla could have taken them along; and they did not want to leave them behind. Like most of his friends, Wiesenthal preferred to rationalize and delude himself that the circumstances did not require him to uproot himself from the place that gave him his identity, to give up his life's dream, and to become a refugee in a strange land, as he had been in his childhood days. All that remained, therefore, was to believe that better days would come. It was a natural reaction, very human and very Jewish, but by remaining in Poland, Simon and Cyla Wiesenthal made the mistake of their lives.

3. Under the Protection of Nikita Khrushchev

First, the Russians came. The secretary of the Ukrainian Communist Party, Nikita Khrushchev, recalled the first days of the war as a kind of race between the Red Army and the German forces. The Germans had bombed Lvov from the air and were about to take the city. But just before they could, the Russians and the Germans agreed in effect to divide Poland between them, in the pact that bore the names of the respective foreign ministers of the two countries, Vyacheslav Molotov and Joachim von Ribbentrop.[31] For the time being, the Germans made do with the western part of Poland, and Lvov was left to the Russians.

With the Red Army came the Communist ideology, and almost from the day the Russians entered Lvov in late September 1939, things were never the same. The Russians rounded up and exiled thousands of people who in their view represented the evils of the bourgeoisie. Many of them perished in labor camps. The new rulers also nationalized the banks, industrial plants, and even private residences. They imposed a new bureaucracy and a new culture on Lvov, with their flags and songs and thousands of pictures of Stalin hanging everywhere. They also imposed fear. In his memoirs, Khrushchev excitedly describes the readiness of the townsfolk to joyfully adopt the Marxist-Leninist truth. Those who did not do so, he comments dryly, had to be put in prison.[32]

The Communist economy that the Russians imposed harmed the city's Jews, most of whom were merchants. Many of them lost all their assets and became destitute. Khrushchev describes his wonderment at the long line of people that formed outside the office of the Gestapo agent who was permitted to operate in the city under the Soviet-German pact. He said that many of them were Jews wanting to move to the German occupation zone in the west.[33] But naturally most of the traffic was in the opposite direction; more than 100,000 Jews escaped from the German-controlled areas and reached Lvov, and tens of thousands were forced to continue eastward into the territory of the Soviet Union.[34]

Hostility to religion was part of the Communist doctrine, but the Jews were allowed to nurture their culture with a Yiddish newspaper and radio broadcasts. A Yiddish theater staged *Uncle Tom's Cabin*. It was also a good year for the Jewish schools, and the restrictions on Jewish enrollment at the technical college, the one that had refused to accept Wiesenthal, were abolished.[35] The couple lived in an apartment on Janowska Street.

As the stepson of a wealthy manufacturer, Wiesenthal was defined by the authorities as a member of the capitalist class, and they summoned him to the police station for repeated interrogation sessions. He and his wife were given ID papers that categorized them according to the discriminatory Clause 11, compelling them to live at least sixty miles from the city.[36] Wiesenthal managed to bribe a police official to give them a permit to remain in the city, but they had to leave their apartment and move to a neighborhood that later became part of the Jewish ghetto. Wiesenthal was not allowed to continue working for the firm that employed him as an engineer. His stepfather, Isack Halperin, lost his factories, and the villa that Wiesenthal had designed for him was also confiscated. Later on, he was arrested, not because he was a Jew but because he was a capitalist, and he died in a Soviet prison.

Wiesenthal would later depict himself as a victim of the Communist regime. He often equated Stalin and Hitler. The difference between the two, he said, was that Hitler was telling the truth when he said he intended to destroy the Jews, but no one believed him; Stalin lied when he said he had nothing against the Jews, and everyone believed him.[37]

Although the Soviet occupation wreaked economic disaster on many of Lvov's Jews, it also enabled many of them to fill important posts in the administration of the city and its cultural, scientific, and economic life, at least in its early days.[38] Wiesenthal coped somehow. He completed his studies, but in contrast to his professional expectations, he was sent to work as a technician in a bed-spring factory in Odessa and his wife was not allowed to accompany him.

Their separation apparently lasted only for a few months, because a little while later he was appointed chief project engineer for the construction of a food-processing plant, evidently a fairly important position. His work took him to several cities in the Soviet Union. He related that he invented a new insulation material and began the process of patenting it.[39]

The nineteen months of the Soviet occupation were far from pleasant, and there was nowhere to run to. But at least the Germans had not yet arrived.

A few hours before the church bells rang on Sunday, June 22, 1941, the residents of Lvov awoke to the sounds of explosions that shook the city: Adolf Hitler had broken his pact with Stalin and ordered his army to carry out Operation Barbarossa. The objective was Moscow. Thousands of Jews tried to flee Lvov with the retreating Red Army, but Simon and Cyla Wiesenthal were not among them. They thought there was no point in trying, as the Soviet forces refused to allow most of the Jews to accompany them. Meanwhile, whole streets had been reduced to rubble and many buildings were in flames. Wrecked wagons and dead horses lay among the ruins, as well as burned-out tanks, and, here and there, a human corpse.

After the Germans routed the Russians and entered Lemberg, as they called Lvov, there were between 160,000 and 170,000 Jews living there. By the time the Russians returned and drove the Germans out three years later, there were 3,400 Jews left, and one of them was Wiesenthal.[40] During the Nazi occupation he lost track of his mother and his wife, but he was alive. Years later, he recorded his story on tape for the Yad Vashem Archive. The interviewer who made the recording observed in a marginal remark: "This is a chain of riveting events which sounds like an unreal story, with sudden switches that transform the narrator from a condemned victim to a survivor and vice versa."[41] For Wiesenthal lived from one miracle to another.

3.

"See You on the Soap Shelf"

I. Janowska

The first day of the Nazi occupation was the day of the Ukrainians. The Germans brought along with them a Ukrainian battalion that had been set up by an intelligence officer called Theodor Oberländer and was known as the Nightingale unit.[1] On their arrival in Lvov they marched to the city hall, took down from its spire the red flag left by the Russians, and hoisted the swastika and the blue and yellow Ukrainian colors. Crowds welcomed them with a sea of flowers. Then, together with local hooligans, the troops went on a rampage.

Through a window, Wiesenthal saw German soldiers and local civilians, apparently Ukrainians, dragging Jews from their homes, kicking them, and beating them with clubs and iron bars and rifle butts. He remembered in particular a soldier mistreating a boy of about twelve, and two women whom thugs flung onto the sidewalk and dragged along by their hair. A Mercedes convertible appeared with a German officer inside, accompanied by a newsreel photographer. The soldiers saluted the officer. It could have been Oberländer, but Wiesenthal did not mention the name.[2] The attacks he witnessed through his window were relatively minor incidents in a large-scale pogrom. Before leaving Lvov, the Russians had set the prisons afire after killing the inmates, many of whom were Ukrainians. People spoke of piles of burned bodies, and they claimed the Jews had a hand in the act. Now a Ukrainian mob and German soldiers were roaming the streets hunting down anyone who looked like a Jew. They formed gauntlets and forced the Jews to run down the middle as they beat them with sticks. An eyewitness said there were razor blades fixed into the sticks. Old men were murdered with axes, babies' heads were dashed against walls.

The bodies of the prisoners burned by the Russians were put on display in the prison yards; townspeople came to look at them and some tried to identify family members. Jews were brought there and forced to dig pits and bury the bodies; then they were shot. The rampage continued for four days. According to one estimate, some four thousand Jews were murdered during that time.[3]

A German soldier broke into the Wiesenthal family's apartment as well. He was dragging a prostitute behind him, and he threw open the three doors of the closet and told the girl to take whatever clothes she wanted. She began rummaging through the closet, and Wiesenthal and his wife could only stand there watching helplessly. Already, before the gas chambers were working, one of the elements at the core of Nazi evil was the humiliation of their victims. Wiesenthal never forgot this incident, even after everything else that happened to him during the war.[4] Two or three days later he was arrested.

Two German soldiers and a Ukrainian auxiliary policeman dragged Wiesenthal from his home in the early hours of the morning. In the street, he recognized some of his neighbors. Other Jews were taken out of other houses, until there were about 100 to 120 men. They were marched to the rail yard, beaten along the way with batons and fists. On arrival they were made to move heavy sheets of tank armor from place to place. It was hard work. Wiesenthal was a tall, strong man, but he had never before done physical labor. German soldiers supervised them, shoving and yelling. At noon, the soldiers were replaced by others. The Jews were given no time to rest.

In the afternoon, they had to move oxygen tanks weighing 200 to 250 pounds. One man passed out and fell. A soldier kicked him in the face. They worked like this until 9 p.m. and when they returned home, the man who had fainted was not among them. The night curfew was already in force, and they were given special passes. Wiesenthal noticed that the name of the sergeant who signed his document was Schiller, the first name of a Nazi rogue to be etched into his memory. For the next two weeks, he and his neighbors had to report for work every day at the same place. The German soldiers and Ukrainian auxiliary police continued to mistreat them, and when there was no real work to be done, they were made to move locomotive parts from one place to another and then back again.[5]

The Germans, unlike the Communists, never aspired to inculcate the residents of Lvov with their ideology. They meant to exploit them as cheap labor, and to kill the Jews. On July 15, 1941, all Jews were ordered to wear a white armband with a blue Star of David on it. The Jews were barred from traveling on trains and they were allowed to travel in tramcars only if they stood in the rear part of the car. Three weeks after that, all the Jews were ordered to report for forced labor. Meanwhile, occupied Poland had been thrown open to German entrepreneurs who employed the local residents for a pittance, or for no pay at all.

Wiesenthal labored at the repair works of the Ostbahn, the Eastern Railway, a large plant where non-Jews were also employed.[6] At first he was put to work cleaning furnaces, but then he managed to arrange a job more appropriate to his skills: painting various identification signs onto the train cars, as well as the German eagle and swastika insignia. A Polish foreman gave him the job, in exchange for one of his wife's dresses.

One day, the German manager of the plant noticed the quality of his work and asked him where he had studied art. One of the Polish laborers standing nearby heard, and informed on him, saying, "He's not a sign painter, he's an engineer." Wiesenthal was alarmed, not only because he had been caught lying, but because the Nazis' first victims in Lvov had been academics and members of the free professions. This was why he had tried to conceal his real profession. But he was lucky, and the rail yard's director, Heinrich Günthert, let him off the hook. After all, Günthert said, he was also an engineer, and he decided to make use of Wiesenthal's professional skills.[7] Wiesenthal's immediate superior, Adolf Kohlrautz, was another decent German. Cyla Wiesenthal was working at the same plant as a cleaner, and they came to work and returned home together every day.

The situation of the Jews in Lvov deteriorated from month to month. About half a year after they had been distinguished from the general population by the armbands came the second stage in their separation: they were commanded to leave their homes and were concentrated in a poor neighborhood in the north of the city. Simon and Cyla Wiesenthal had to move, as did his mother, who had lived with them since her husband died.

The move to the ghetto was coordinated by a special office but was carried out chaotically, violently, and corruptly. The local citizens transferred their apartments to the Jews in exchange for payment, in many cases receiving the apartment elsewhere in the city that the Jewish family had been forced to vacate. In the process, the Jews' furniture and other belongings were looted. The process lasted a few months, until the winter of 1942. Meanwhile, the area had been surrounded by a wooden fence and had become a kind of large detention camp.

The "Jewish quarter," as the Germans called the new ghetto, was a dismal sight. "Mostly, it was the ruins of ramshackle huts that had been slated for demolition before the war," said one of the survivors. "But even a shanty, with tiny windows, mostly without glass panes but sealed instead with rags and sheets of paper and wooden boards, was considered a luxury. The color of the exterior walls was gray-black, splattered with mire and mud from the passing wagons. The roof was made of wooden slats and the gutters were rotten and falling to pieces. If there were 'conveniences' in the apartment, the faucets were broken. In every room and dark corner there was a stove made of mud, with a smoking, rusty, sooty chimney." Many of the houses weren't connected at all to water, power, or sewage networks.

The crowding was intolerable. Whole families were packed into single rooms or even had to share storerooms, cellars, or attics. Wiesenthal recalled that he and his wife and mother were allocated a room in Block No. 1, together with some other people.[8] Instead of beds, in many places bunks had been built and people had to take turns sleeping in the same beds. Almost all they had to eat was a sticky, doughy bread, and instead of coffee they drank water in which beets had been cooked, and which was sweetened with saccharin. Epidemics of typhus, tuberculosis, and other diseases killed off many of the people living in the ghetto. The winter was especially harsh. Deep snow covered everything, and many houses had no heating.

Now the terrible consequences of the economic disaster that the Russians had inflicted upon the Jews of Lvov became clear. Those who had kept a little money managed to secure better conditions for themselves in the ghetto. A large part of the meager food rations allotted to the residents found its way onto the black market. Profiteers and thugs took over the ghetto, many of them serving on the Judenrat, the Jewish council set up by the Germans.

It is an awkward story: The Germans forced upon the Jews a kind of self-rule for conducting civil affairs and handling problems of housing, food supply, and medical services, among others. The Judenrat had its own police, and hundreds of Jews took part in the massive roundups of those slated for extermination that the Germans organized every several weeks. It is estimated that at a certain stage at least four thousand Jews were employed in the various departments of the Judenrat, some 5 percent of the total population of the ghetto.[9]

That population was constantly diminishing, from one roundup to the next. First to go were the elderly and those without means. They were taken to nearby forests and shot. From March 1942 onward, others were shipped by the thousands some 125 miles northward, to the gas chambers at the Belzec extermination facility. Everything depended on their personal documents and work papers. "Work or death" was what they used to say in the ghetto.

In testimony given at the trial of some of the Lvov war criminals, Wiesenthal recounted how the Germans were at pains to anchor the mass killings within their own bureaucratic logic: They would announce suddenly and without giving a reason that certain documents were no longer valid unless they carried a certain additional stamp that could be obtained at a certain office. Hundreds, and often thousands, of people couldn't obtain the stamp and the next day the police would arrest them as illegal residents and consign them to extermination. Sometimes they were transported from the ghetto crammed into the cars of public tramways, fully visible to passersby in the streets. Wiesenthal testified that he had seen them.

A person's chances of getting the required papers often depended on his or her connections and ability to bribe all kinds of middlemen and profiteers and even the German officials themselves.[10] Chances of getting a work permit improved when the ghetto administration needed workers, for clearing snow from the streets, for example, but a lot depended on luck. Once Jewish policemen came to take Wiesenthal's mother as part of a roundup, but he and his wife managed to persuade them to leave her alone and to take them instead. The police agreed, because they were getting two detainees instead of one. The couple were betting on their work papers saving them and indeed they were allowed to go home.

But then one day in the summer of 1942 they came home from work and found that his mother was not there. Neighbors told them that two Ukrainians had taken her away. They never saw her again and Wiesenthal assumed that she had been murdered in Belzec or had died on the way there. A woman who lived with them in the ghetto, Adela Sygal Milchman, recalled how her family had crowded into one room with the Wiesenthals after his mother had gone. The main topic of conversation was what could be done to get out; they were always trying to think which of their Polish acquaintances could do something to help them. For a little while longer they managed to sell what was left of their jewelry to buy bread, but Wiesenthal, the woman remembered, had lost a lot of weight and already looked like a skeleton.[11]

Many thousands of ghetto residents were worked to death in labor camps. The most infamous of these was set up at the end of Janowska Street, where Simon and Cyla Wiesenthal had once lived. The Germans opened a number of factories there for producing military equipment. Most of the workers would come in the morning and return home at night. At first, the Jewish laborers were allowed to do this also, but as of October 1941 they had to stay at the factories and the site became a closed camp. Watchtowers were erected along the fences, manned by armed SS guards. Nevertheless, Wiesenthal still managed to get out on occasion. "I still had friends in the ghetto," he said, "and I had good relations with the people who ran the labor bureau and I often obtained passes to go from the railway compound into the ghetto."[12]

Living conditions in the camps were particularly harsh; survivors later gave shocking testimony of sadistic mistreatment and mass executions. Until the end of his days, Wiesenthal never forgot the stench of burned flesh that hung over the camp, and he recounted in court the black humor that prevailed among the prisoners: "See you on the soap shelf," they would say to one another, a reference to the rumors that the bodies of dead Jews were being made into soap.[13] The number of workers in the Janowska camp reached a peak of some twenty to thirty thousand, not all of them Jews and not all of them slave laborers. There is no accurate estimate of the number of those who perished there, but it is assumed to have been somewhere in the tens of thousands.[14]

2. Good Germans

Wiesenthal was transferred from the ghetto to Janowska in the spring or summer of 1942, and it seems that even as a prisoner there he continued to go to his previous work at the Eastern Railway works, and at times was still able to return home to the ghetto. Cyla Wiesenthal wrote that she was sent to Janowska in June 1942, but worked there for only a short period as a cleaning woman before she was returned to work at the repair works, with her husband.[15] According to Wiesenthal it was the German inspector Adolf Kohlrautz who had managed to arrange for the couple to come back to the rail yard.

The Jewish forced laborers at Eastern Railway were now also being kept in a closed camp, but the conditions were not as bad as they were at Janowska. Wiesenthal was there for two years; his daily life was still far from being as atrocious as that of most of the other Jews in Lvov. In fact, he used to go around the rail yard almost like a free man. A red armband identified him as a worker in the technical department.[16] He worked in an office with a telephone, he earned a little money, he managed to secure the escape of his wife, and he even got his hands on a firearm. Eventually, he made good his own escape, all with the help of Heinrich Günthert and Adolf Kohlrautz.

In the testimony that Wiesenthal filed with the Yad Vashem Archive, he described an amazing relationship with Kohlrautz. The Jewish slave laborer and the German supervisor created a partnership. They both took bribes. Wiesenthal prepared construction plans for the expansion of factories, and Kohlrautz signed them. Wiesenthal was in direct contact with representatives of the civilian construction companies and contractors competing for the work. They gave the bribes to Kohlrautz and there was something for Wiesenthal too.

As Kohlrautz's assistant, Wiesenthal had free access to various plans, including those for the operation of substitute stations in case of sabotage. He said that he gave these plans to two members of the Polish underground operating in the camp. In his Yad Vashem testimony, he stressed that it was not the pro-Communist underground, Armja Lodowa ("the People's Army"), but the nationalist underground, Armja Krajowa ("the Army of the Motherland"), which was subject to the Polish government in exile.[17]

Sometimes he would leave the railway compound, with an escort, to purchase equipment and supplies. He exploited these excursions to establish contacts with different people, keeping in touch with them by telephone. In this way he managed to obtain weapons for the underground. Firearms could be obtained in the ghetto. The last of the residents even opened fire on the Germans coming to take them away. Wiesenthal kept two pistols for himself, hiding them in a drawer in Kohlrautz's desk. Sometimes he spoke to the inspector about the annihilation of the Jews. The German said that the day would come when the entire German nation would be brought to account and have to pay for the crime.[18]

Given the atrocities taking place in the city at the time, Wiesenthal's account of his relations with his superiors reads as if it could only be a figment of his imagination, but he had no reason to make up a story that would diminish his suffering under the Nazi occupation, and that could even be construed as collaboration with the Germans. The opposite is true: he would have had good reason to hide it. But Wiesenthal repeated the story many times and its essence is that his life was saved by decent Germans. This is possibly a foundation for the principle that guided him later in his efforts to bring Nazi criminals to justice. There's no such thing as "collective guilt," he declared over and over; individuals should be judged by their own deeds. Several people who knew Wiesenthal before and during the war would eventually confirm his story about his job at the rail yard. They praised his personality and his courage.[19]

Aware, however, of the question marks that the story raised, Wiesenthal pointed out that his situation was no different from that of the 250 other Jews employed at the same repair works. They all were treated relatively well, he said. This was due to the fact that Günthert managed the place like a desert island in a sea of evil, and took pains to ensure that his German foremen and supervisors did not harm the Jews. And indeed, most of the Germans in charge there were good people, Wiesenthal stated. But not all of them: one inspector, Peter Arnolds, was a wicked person who perpetrated the murder of a young boy, the child of a Jew by the name of Chasin.

Chasin was responsible for looking after a few horses that were kept in the repair yard and he had permission to sleep in their stable. His wife and son remained in the ghetto. In one of the roundups carried out by the Germans, they killed the woman and the boy was left on his own. Neighbors managed to get a message through to Chasin, and somehow he smuggled his son out of the ghetto and brought him into the railway compound, hidden in a large sack. In the daytime, the boy hid in a box of fodder in the stable. His father drilled holes in the box to give him air. At night, when the German officials had gone home, the boy would come out.

One day someone informed on Chasin, and the inspector Arnolds called in the SS from the Janowska camp. "With my own eyes I saw Arnolds entering the stable with an SS man, and three minutes later I heard a single gunshot," Wiesenthal testified. "When they were gone, I went into the stable and found Chasin crying over the body of his son. He told me that the SS man had pulled the boy out of the box, told Chasin to turn around, and fired. Then he tossed the body onto a pile of manure and ordered Chasin to cover it with a horse blanket."[20]

Among the construction companies operating in the railway compound, there was one from Lublin. Wiesenthal surmised that its manager, a man by the name of Rojanski, was connected with the Polish underground. In any event, the man took Cyla Wiesenthal with him to his home and had her registered as his sister. Rojanski and his wife had a son and Cyla Wiesenthal worked in their home as a nursemaid. She did not look Jewish, and the papers she carried identified her as Irena Kowalska. But at one point she could no longer continue hiding there and somehow managed to get back to Lvov.

She came to the repair works and spoke to Wiesenthal through the fence. With the help of one of the underground members who owed him a favor for weapons he had procured for them, he managed to arrange a hiding place for his wife in Warsaw. For a while he received letters from her, and then their connection was cut off. After the war people who knew the couple at the rail yard confirmed the details of her escape.[21]

3. Three Days in a Closet

By the second half of 1943, there weren't many Jews left in Lvov. The authorities began moving those who had been working in civilian plants in the city to the Janowska camp. Among them were Wiesenthal and the others employed at the railway yard. They continued to work there, returning each night to Janowska, where they were forced to stand for long hours on parade, perform physical exercises like knee bends and pushups, and run and jump, all the while being brutally beaten. They were repeatedly registered, classified, divided into groups, or counted, and then many of them were marched off to an area of the camp covered with sand, where they were shot dead.[22]

At the end of September 1943, Kohlrautz told Wiesenthal that the time had come for him to escape. "Run away from here," he told him. "Run." Wiesenthal decided to do it, together with a fellow forced laborer, Arthur Scheimann, who before the war had been one of the managers of a well-known circus and was married to a non-Jewish Ukrainian woman. The two planned their escape carefully. Kohlrautz gave them permits to leave the camp and go to town to purchase equipment, sending a Ukrainian escort along with them. They entered a building, leaving their escort outside smoking cigarettes that Wiesenthal gave him.

The building had two entrances. They went in the front way and left through the rear, and took a tramcar to the home of a man called Roman Uścienski, an agent for one of the construction companies, who was expecting them. He was risking his life. He did it because he hated the Germans, Wiesenthal wrote forty years later. Thanks to Wiesenthal's recommendation, Uścienski was recognized as a Righteous Gentile, an award granted by the State of Israel through Yad Vashem to people who rescued Jews during the Holocaust.[23]

Wiesenthal and Scheimann hid in Uścienski's home for only a few hours. In the evening, a woman who worked as a cleaner at the repair works came and took them to her parents' home in the country. They stayed there together for a while, hiding in the attic, until Scheimann's wife came and took him away. Wiesenthal was on his own. After a few weeks, the village was surrounded by Ukrainian soldiers, there to conduct a search. Wiesenthal managed to escape and made his way to Scheimann's home.[24] A few days later, he was to become part of the life story of a Jewish woman whose destiny took her from one drama to another until she finally found a new life in Israel.

Paulina Busch was the wife of a bookkeeper named Max. Their daughter, Basia, was three. Paulina's sister Lola had a good reputation as a dressmaker. When the war broke out, the family settled in the city of Khodorov, where they were given shelter in a sugar factory whose owner wanted to help them, and whose wife bought her dresses from Lola.

A Jewish family, the Sternbergs, had lived not far from the sugar factory, where their son, Yitzhak, then age twenty, had worked. When the Germans killed his brother and took his mother away, he was left alone and ran away to Lvov. He called himself Olek and, using forged papers, passed as a non-Jew. The owner of the apartment Sternberg rented in Lvov was one of the Polish gentiles who worked at the Eastern Railway works. He knew Wiesenthal, who arranged a job for Sternberg at the rail yard, thereby saving his life.[25]

Walking in the street one day, Sternberg bumped into Paulina Busch, his former neighbor in Khodorov. She had returned to Lvov with her daughter and, like Olek, was concealing the fact that she was a Jew. She had a birth certificate under the name of the sugar factory owner in Khodorov, Maria Krodkiewska, who was living at the time in Warsaw.

Paulina had found work at a kindergarten run by nuns, who had also found her an apartment on Balanowa Street. Once, she was arrested on suspicion of being a Jew posing as a gentile. In prison she was beaten but eventually released. The birth certificate she had was not sufficient any longer and she needed an identity card. Olek had heard that Wiesenthal could forge documents. This was true, and Olek brought him Paulina's old ID card; she got a new one, also under the name of Maria Krodkiewska.

In the meantime, her sister Lola had also come back from Khodorov, and one day Paulina's husband Max also turned up. At first he was given shelter by Olek and then he moved into his wife's apartment, so that now there were three adults and a little girl living there. It was imperative that the neighbors not know, lest they suspect she was sheltering Jews. It was all very difficult.

Olek had meanwhile established a unique relationship with an eleven-year-old girl named Krysia. One day he had seen her through the rail yard fence. She had waved to one of the Jewish workers, who waved back with a limp hand. She came to the fence every day to wave at the worker and would then leave. She was the worker's daughter, and had been left to her own devices. Every night she would find somewhere to sleep, in a stairwell. In the mornings she came to visit her father and in the afternoons she would go into a movie theater. Olek helped her. He bought her food and they roamed the streets together.

They shared their plight, their worries and their fears, and embroidered dreams together. Krysia would tell him what had happened to her the night before: Quite often she was discovered sleeping in her stairwell, woken up, and thrown out into the cold night, and also questioned about whether she was Jewish. She always insisted she wasn't. One day her father disappeared from the railway works; Olek assumed he was dead.

A little while later, Krysia herself also vanished. Olek wondered what had happened to her. A rumor had spread through Lvov about a gang of child kidnappers. They murdered them and sold their flesh in the markets, people said. Olek feared that this is what had happened to his Krysia. The fact that Sternberg could believe such a thing until the day he died shows something about the situation that prevailed in Lvov at that time, whether the story was true or not.[26]

Around the same time, a woman came to Paulina's door and gave her a letter from Wiesenthal. She was Scheimann's Ukrainian wife. Wiesenthal knew Paulina's address, since he had forged her identity document. Now he was asking her to help him find a place to hide, because he could not stay where he was any longer.

Scheimann's wife was on the verge of hysteria. She was working as a seamstress, she told Paulina, and her customers came to her apartment to be measured and to try on their garments. Whenever they came, she would hide her husband in a closet. He sat there on a little stool, sometimes for hours. The slightest cough could have given him away. Now Wiesenthal had joined them. "They put another stool there for me," he recounted later. "And that's how I sat in that closet for three days. We couldn't even breathe out loud because the distance between the closet and the table where the strangers were sitting was less than a meter and a half. In the end I said, I can't take this any longer."[27]

Paulina didn't know how she could take a fifth person into her apartment, but she promised Scheimann's wife that she would try to find some way to help. Two days later, the woman came back. Paulina said she couldn't do anything, but Mrs. Scheimann said that in that case, she would have no choice but to inform on all of them to the Germans. She had demanded that Wiesenthal leave, but he had refused, she said. "He's got two guns, he'll kill us," she shouted, tearing at her hair.

Paulina Bush, alias Maria Krodkiewska, gave in. "You know what? Let him come," she said. Her husband was far from pleased. "What are you doing?" he asked. "I'm getting out. Let Lola stay!" Paulina retorted: "Where will you go? Listen, there are two of you—so there'll be three. It's not for long." In fact, a quite intolerable situation arose in the apartment. "Wiesenthal didn't want to leave," she told a Yad Vashem interviewer.

Most difficult of all was to hide the situation from the little girl; Basia would not be able to keep the secret, they feared. As much as possible, she was kept at the nuns' kindergarten. In the evening they all hid in the bedroom and Paulina kept Basia in the kitchen—the bedroom was out of bounds. Sometimes she heard noises and asked her mother what they were. Paulina would make something up. There are mice in there, she told her once.

The lavatory was on a shared balcony, outside the apartment. Wiesenthal, Max, and Lola could not use it. Paulina gave them a bucket, and emptied it secretly. "I had an awful time," she said later. In the room itself, there was a basin with a faucet and running water that sometimes also served as a toilet bowl. Laundry, cooking, everything had to be done in a way that would give nothing away to the neighbors.

Throughout this time Paulina went on working at the nuns' kindergarten, careful to keep up her pose as a Catholic named Maria. Once, the Germans came to check on the residents of the house and were satisfied by the papers that Wiesenthal had forged. On another evening, three men in German uniforms came to the door and said they had come for the Jews she was hiding. Wiesenthal, Lola, and Max were hiding in the attic and the men found no one. They turned out to be Ukrainian extortionists. They came back once more, but were not heard from again.

Olek, who was still working at the repair works, came to visit them every day, bringing food, newspapers, and paper and colored pencils for Wiesenthal, who would draw people and situations at Janowska from memory, as well as scenes from the daily life in Paulina's apartment. Everyone hoped the arrangement would last.

Wiesenthal took up some of the wooden floorboards in the apartment and dug out a hiding place big enough to take three people lying down. "I took the dirt out in buckets and pots and dumped it in other houses' yards," Paulina recounted. "I also put some inside the stove. I had a large tiled stove that didn't work. And some in the cellar and some in the attic." When he was done digging, Wiesenthal put the boards back and placed the bed over them. When a neighbor came to visit, Wiesenthal and Lola hid in the closet and Max in the laundry basket—the "submarine" as he called it. They followed the developments on the front lines in the newspapers, and called themselves "the general staff" when they discussed them. Sometimes Wiesenthal sent Olek to his friend Scheimann and to his prewar acquaintances, hoping they would be able to help.

Seven months passed. Many years later Yitzhak Sternberg, Olek, wrote: "Human beings are not capable of maintaining a steady level of alertness all day long in conditions of danger that persist for months and years, without moments of relief from the boredom and tension: The adolescent daughter of neighbors used to come to talk to Paulina and share with her the secrets of her great love. It never occurred to her that there were three other people listening in."

Wiesenthal himself never spoke in later years about the dynamics of the relationships that must have grown up between himself and Lola, Paulina, and Max. Paulina bore him a grudge, but the Yad Vashem interviewer who took down her story many years later never managed to get any details out of her. "I don't want to talk about that" was all she would say.[28]

4. Under SS Protection

Throughout all those months, they had no idea that their neighbor, a Ukrainian woman, was hiding seven other Jews in her cellar. One day, they were discovered. Large numbers of policemen arrived and arrested them and made a careful search of the entire building. Wiesenthal, Lola, and Max hurriedly hid in their hiding place under the floorboards.

Wiesenthal recounted: "We lay there under the floor, and they began feeling the walls and tearing up floorboards. When they came to the part where I was lying, I gripped the pistol that I was keeping under my head, but I felt a boot on my head and I couldn't move. They pulled me out, two Polish agents and an SS man. In the meantime, they found the others too. Now, here's what happened next. The Polish agents were involved in a very lively traffic in weapons. They stole the two pistols that I had, because if they had written in their report that they found guns on me, they would have had to hand them over."[29] Wiesenthal was arrested, along with Lola, Max, and Paulina. The agents also took some of Simon's drawings. It happened on June 13, 1944. Many years later, Wiesenthal obtained a copy of the police report on his arrest.[30]

He was taken to Janowska first, and from there to prison. He was scared of being tortured and tried to commit suicide with a razor blade. They took him to the infirmary for treatment so he would be able to face interrogation. One of the last prisoners in Janowska would in days to come tell of an engineer who was arrested with some pictures that he had drawn. She did not remember his name, but remembered that he had cut his veins because he was frightened of being tortured under questioning.[31]

Wiesenthal spoke of two additional unsuccessful suicide attempts that he made, both in order to gain time and put off being interrogated. Once he stole a bottle of pills from a doctor and swallowed them all, but they turned out to be the artificial sweetener saccharin. The second time he tried to hang himself with a noose made of his trousers, but they tore under his weight.

The Red Army was meanwhile advancing toward Lvov, and the Germans began to retreat. One day, the Russians bombed the prison's surroundings. A riot broke out and some prisoners managed to escape, including Paulina, Max, and Lola. The others, including Wiesenthal, were taken quickly to Janowska. That was apparently in July 1944. There were only about a hundred prisoners still in the camp then.

From this point on, it seems as though Wiesenthal owes his life no longer to his resourcefulness or to good fortune, but mainly to the absurd. Some of the last prisoners in Janowska, Wiesenthal among them, tried to escape. But just then a Russian bombardment began. Two of the fleeing prisoners were killed, and the others, including Wiesenthal, returned to the camp to take cover. In normal circumstances, they would certainly have been shot, but this time one of the last officers in charge there, Friedrich Warzok, went up to them and explained that things were different now. According to Wiesenthal, he also explained why: "You are coming with us, and together we'll get through the war." Warzok took them to a storeroom and told them to stock up with food. One man tried to run away and he was shot, as was a woman who complained that her leg was hurting.

They were taken to the railway station and placed on a train. They thought they were being taken to a death camp, but before the train started moving, all of a sudden one of the officers came and put a puppy and his beloved canary in its cage into their freight car. If anything happened to his pets, he warned, he would kill all the prisoners in the car with his own hands. Wiesenthal described this episode many years later at the trial of some of the Janowska criminals.[32]

They were on one of the last German trains to leave Lvov. A few days later the town was taken over by the Russians. Wiesenthal and his fellow prisoners were transported to the west, to a town called Przemyśl. Here it became clear why they had not been killed in Janowska: Warzok and his comrades needed live prisoners to guard, so they could show they had a duty to fulfill and not be sent to the front.

Wiesenthal recounted that there were some fifty prisoners and thirty SS personnel. First, the prisoners' uniforms were exchanged for blue work overalls, and Warzok warned them that he would kill them if they disclosed to anyone that they were Jews. For a few days they were made to work on fortifications. When the Russians drew near to Przemyśl, Warzok took the Jews and set off for the next camp. On the way they encountered a convoy of German civilians, also fleeing the Russians. Warzok ordered them to get off their horse-drawn wagons and commandeered them for his own party, two prisoners and one SS man to a wagon.

They slept in abandoned work camps and, in Wiesenthal's words, they became one big party of war tramps. They ate together and slept together and stole potatoes from farmers' fields, Jews and SS men on the run. They had enough to eat and the SS men shared their cigarettes and hard drink with the Jews. Once or twice they ran into retreating Wehrmacht soldiers, who cursed the SS men and told them to go to the front instead of messing with Jews.

Sometimes they slept a few nights in camps that they set up for themselves, for which Wiesenthal made signs bearing names like "Camp Venus" or "Camp Mercury" as if they were secret installations. Once they abducted a few dozen farmers from their homes and forced them to build dirt embankments to serve as fortifications. Wiesenthal understood right away that this was a phony project aimed at creating the impression that their SS guards were taking part in the war effort, in the hope of buying time, avoiding contact with the German army, and not being sent to the front. Defeat was close. Wiesenthal weighed running away but calculated that as long as he was under SS protection his prospects of surviving were better. "Our situation at that time was excellent," he observed. "They didn't curse us, they didn't hit us. We never heard an unkind word." And they didn't even guard them.

Wiesenthal biographer Hella Pick quotes his account of a conversation he had with one of the SS men in Warzok's gang. The man asked what Wiesenthal would say about the concentration camps if somehow he managed to reach the United States. Wiesenthal replied that he would tell the truth. "They'd think you were crazy," said the German. "No one would believe you." At that moment, Wiesenthal decided that if he stayed alive, he would make sure that the world knew.[33]

Wiesenthal knew that this story of his survival sounded altogether delusional. "I am aware that the tales of my escape sound too adventurous, but at that time everything depended on chance," he explained later.[34] And on another occasion he remarked, "I had so many miracles happen to me that I already don't believe them myself. How can others believe them?"[35]

At least two of the SS men whom Wiesenthal mentioned by name survived to deny certain details of his story, but three Janowska prisoners testified after the war that they were in the group of inmates who were taken out at the last moment by SS officer Warzok and forced to accompany him in his flight from the Russians. Their stories are less colorful than Wiesenthal's but the details, including the itinerary, correspond.

When they arrived at a bridge over the San River, they found their path blocked by a unit of Wehrmacht troops. They also wanted to cross the bridge, but in the distance the voices of Russian soldiers could already be heard. Warzok's men shoved the soldiers aside, crossed the bridge, and when they got to the other side blew it up. The Wehrmacht men were taken prisoner by the Russians.[36]

One of the Janowska prisoners who roamed the countryside with Wiesenthal under SS protection was Leon Sohn. He was one of the seven Jews who had been hiding in the apartment under Paulina Busch's and whose discovery had led to Wiesenthal's arrest. At one stage, Sohn ran away from Warzok's group and made his way back to Lvov, which was by then in Russian hands. There he found Paulina, who had managed to survive detention by the Germans, and married her. Her husband Max had disappeared and was never seen again. Sohn adopted Paulina's daughter, Basia, and later they had another daughter. They lived in Poland as Christians for more than fifteen years. In 1962 they immigrated to Israel and began a new life, as Jews once more.

Yitzhak "Olek" Sternberg kept in touch with them. He left Poland right after the war, but before that he learned what had happened to Arthur Scheimann, Wiesenthal's friend. Scheimann went back to the circus that he had managed before the war. He was a sad clown, Sternberg wrote. Scheimann offered him a job with the circus, but Sternberg preferred to build a new life as a member of Kibbutz Lohamei Hagetaot in Israel.[37]

Warzok's great attempt at deception failed. His band fell into the hands of a special unit whose task it was to hunt down shirkers like them, and they were dispatched to the front. That was in September 1944. "Actually, I was sorry about it," Wiesenthal wrote. "We had the feeling that we were close to seeing the end of the war."[38] But now he was about to experience the ten most terrible months of his life.

5. Płaszów, Gross-Rosen, Mauthausen

After they were separated from Warzok's band, Wiesenthal and his companions were sent to Płaszów, a concentration camp that had been set up in the Jewish cemetery in the city of Kraków in southern Poland. Płaszów has entered contemporary Holocaust consciousness thanks to Steven Spielberg's film *Schindler's List*. At its peak, Płaszów had some twenty-four thousand inmates; an estimated eight thousand were murdered there.[39]

Wiesenthal apparently did not get to know the camp's fearsome commandant, Amon Göth, but he remembered another Nazi officer, Tony Fehringer, very well, for his cruel mistreatment of prisoners. Fehringer was the commander of a special prisoner group (*Sonderkommando* in German), composed entirely of former Janowska inmates who had left there with Warzok. There were thirty-four of them left. "The regime was atrocious," said Wiesenthal, and the task they were assigned was atrocious as well: to take corpses out of a mass grave and to burn them, so as to conceal from the approaching Russians the fact that they had been murdered.

They worked in a pit where 1,200 bodies had been dumped. In certain places, the bodies were covered in sand, and were preserved as if they had been mummified. Some of the corpses were floating in sewage. Wiesenthal and his companions had to remove the bodies from the pit, cover them with a layer of timber, then place another layer of bodies on the logs, and then more bodies and so on, and then pour gasoline over the pile and set it alight. "The smell of the bodies clung to us and permeated us until we couldn't eat anything," Wiesenthal recounted. The members of the group were housed in a special hut.

The stench was so strong that even the SS guards never came close. But "Tony the blond," as they called him, used to come. "He kept in his boot a pair of pliers, like a dentist's forceps," Wiesenthal wrote, "and he used them to break the teeth of the dead bodies to find gold fillings that the SS personnel had missed. When he discovered one, he would slip the tooth into his pocket. Afterward he would swap the gold for glasses of schnapps. He always had a lot of schnapps."[40] This went on for about a month, until October 15, 1944, or thereabouts.

The Russians drew nearer and the Germans evacuated Płaszów as well. Wiesenthal and his party now shared the secret of the crime, and they therefore assumed that they would be put to death. They knew about Auschwitz and expected to be sent there, but instead they were taken to the Gross-Rosen concentration camp, also in southern Poland. There were as many as 100,000 inmates there at one time, and an estimated forty thousand perished there.[41] From Wiesenthal's point of view, the third camp in which he was held was the worst of all. He was imprisoned there for three months in unbearably overcrowded conditions and on a starvation diet. Some of the prisoners were forced to march around the parade ground for hours in order to break in boots manufactured for soldiers at the front. Many died from exhaustion.

Wiesenthal was put to work in the nearby granite quarry. A large rock fell on his right foot and he was taken to the infirmary where a doctor, whose devotion Wiesenthal praised, told him his big toe would have to be amputated. He had no anesthetics. Wiesenthal related: "They lay me on a table. Someone sat on my head. They tied me to the table with two belts, and with a regular pair of scissors he cut my big toe off. They dressed it with paper bandages, and put me in bed in the next room. The pain was atrocious."[42] The further treatment was also carried out without painkillers and his suffering was great.

Wiesenthal stayed in the infirmary until Gross-Rosen was evacuated in early January 1945. Someone helped him get up. Instead of a shoe, he wrapped his injured foot in the sleeve of an old coat. He used a broomstick to help him walk. Together with several thousands of other prisoners, he set off on one of the infamous death marches of the last surviving camp inmates to camps inside German territory.

For four days they slogged through snow, about twelve miles a day, until they arrived at the city of Chemnitz in eastern Germany. From there they were taken by train to the Buchenwald concentration camp near Weimar, loaded onto open freight cars. Many prisoners died on the way, and their bodies were tossed off the train. Citizens living near the railway line complained, so the Jews were ordered to leave the corpses in the cars. Wiesenthal recalled that some of them were put to use as something to sit on.[43]

Buchenwald was only a way station; after a stopover of a few days, the journey continued, southward, in the direction of the Mauthausen concentration camp in Austria. At that time it was at its peak, in terms of the number of prisoners—some eighty-five thousand. An estimated 200,000 people perished in the camp.[44] Wiesenthal had great difficulty making it to the gate; his foot was frozen, he was on the verge of death. When he arrived, his name was listed in the prisoners register. He was given the number 127371 and sent to the "Russian Camp," as the sick quarters were called.[45] That was in mid-February 1945. There were close to three months to go before the camp was liberated.

The last weeks in Mauthausen were preserved in his memory as a kind of race between death and liberation, Wiesenthal said. Every morning, one of the supervisors came to the door of the hut and asked in a shout how many prisoners had "croaked" during the night. The supervisors rarely came into the room itself for fear they would pick up a disease, and because of the disgusting stench inside. Once a day, the inmates of the Russian Camp received a bowl of turbid liquid that was passed off on them as "soup."

The Americans arrived on May 5, 1945. Wiesenthal saw the first tanks at about 10 a.m. "There was great excitement," he related. "The people ran up to the tanks. I also ran. But I was so weak that I couldn't walk back. I crawled back, on all fours."

As was his custom, Wiesenthal never revealed his inner feelings, never bared in public what he went through at that moment, after four years of suffering, sometimes on the brink of death, not knowing what had happened to his wife. Instead of describing his personal emotions, he described the collective elation. Some prisoners waved flags that the Poles and Czechs had prepared in advance. He also saw some who had joined the sleeve of a white shirt and the sleeve of a blue shirt and hoisted them on a stick. "I don't know if there has ever in the history of the Jewish people been a more beautiful flag than that one," he said.[46]

4.

"Who Knows Her? Who Has Seen Her?"

I. The American Connection

The city of Linz has lain on the banks of the Danube in Upper Austria since the days of the Romans, flourishing in the Middle Ages. Mozart, Beethoven, and Bruckner wrote symphonies here. The city is also famous for its jam torte, and it was Adolf Hitler's favorite place; he wasn't born there, but he had some happy years in Linz as a schoolboy. When he grew up, he dreamed of spending his last years and being buried there.[1] His parents are buried in Leonding, their home village on the outskirts of the city. Leonding was also Simon Wiesenthal's first stop on his way to a new life as a free man.

He arrived there a few days after being liberated from Mauthausen, and could not bear the sight of the home of Hitler's family. He had terrible nightmares every night: thousands of prisoners naked, lined up in rows, waiting to die. He heard the shouts of the SS guards, the sound of gunfire, the groans of the victims. So he left Leonding and moved into the city. A tall man, but very emaciated, he suffered from pains all over his body, especially in his wounded foot, and, like all the freed camp inmates, he was in shock. His life seemed pointless, and he was alone in a strange land. He no longer had his wife, his parents, his friends. He did not mean to stay long in Linz, but by the time he left fifteen years had passed.[2]

Compared to other prisoners, he rehabilitated himself very quickly. Ten days after the camp was liberated, he had a slip of paper signed by the mayor of the town of Mauthausen confirming that he had registered there as being "on his way home."[3] And after another ten days, he signed an eight-page document listing the names of close to 150 Nazi war criminals. This list was based on his personal knowledge: many of the persons whom he listed had committed their crimes in Galicia. The document was addressed to "the U.S. Camp Commander, Camp Mauthausen."

Wiesenthal must have needed a few days to get his information together and ready it for submission, so he clearly began working on the list within a day or two after the liberation. It seems that he already had most of the names arrayed in his mind even before he saw the American tanks at the camp's gates. The document did not contain detailed information, and not all the names and the particulars were accurate, but it reflected a faith in the basic value of a just society: criminals must be brought to justice and receive their due punishment. It was therefore not because he planned a career as a "Nazi hunter" that he listed the names, but because he felt that this was the right thing to do. In an accompanying letter, he offered his services to the U.S. authorities, despite the fact that he was a Polish citizen who wanted to return home, as he wrote.[4]

In retrospect, it seems as though at this point he was tying his fate to the United States; until his dying day he remained within the circle of American influence. His relationship to America was very personal and very emotional. The Americans defeated Nazi Germany and liberated him from a concentration camp; it was also natural that he should admire them as the defenders of the free world against the Communist menace. He would one day travel to Luxembourg to place flowers on the grave of General George Patton, the liberator of Europe.[5]

This was the prevalent attitude among many survivors of Mauthausen. In a letter to the U.S. authorities, a group of them wrote: "America! To this magic word we were clutching with all our fears, with all our hopes."[6] In turn, the Americans needed people like Wiesenthal, an intelligent thirty-seven-year-old German speaker who quickly picked up rudimentary English.

Wiesenthal embellished on this relationship with a tale. Two or three days after the liberation, he applied to a Polish prisoner who had been put in charge of issuing exit permits to camp inmates. The man, Rusinek, cursed him in anti-Semitic language and even struck him. Wiesenthal went to the Americans to complain and met an officer by the name of Abby Mann, who was later to become a well-known Hollywood screenwriter. Mann wanted to punish Rusinek, but Wiesenthal agreed to make do with an apology, at the suggestion of another Polish prisoner, Józef Cyrankie-wicz, who was later to serve as prime minister of Poland.

Just as they did in Germany, the Allied Powers divided Austria into zones of occupation. The American zone was under the control of the U.S. Army's Counter Intelligence Corps (CIC). The corps' officers in Mauthausen tack-led the task of locating the Nazi camp staff, in order to have them prosecuted in one of the trials the U.S. Army planned to hold in the town of Dachau in Germany. In the corridors of the unit's offices, Wiesenthal saw captured SS personnel being brought for interrogation. He asked to be allowed to help with the arrests. At first he was turned down because of his poor physical condition, but he kept coming back. The sight of the prisoners filled him with an elation akin to that evoked by divine worship, he related.

An active and ambitious man by nature, Wiesenthal wanted nothing more than to get involved in some kind of activity as quickly as possible. Gradually he also began displaying an interest in other people. This was a characteristic quality of his before the war. When he was practicing archi-tecture, he was never satisfied with merely designing a building, he said. He was always curious about the people who would inhabit it. This inter-est was snuffed out during his imprisonment in the Nazi camps, but now it was reignited. The Americans were impressed by the list of names of Nazi criminals that he brought them, and also by his stubborn insistence on working with them. After a few days of his importuning, they attached him to one of the officers in charge of carrying out arrests. The officer did not know German, and Wiesenthal served as his interpreter.

Physically, he was still weak. Once he went out with two American military policemen to arrest a suspect who lived on the third floor of a building. They told him to go up and bring the man down. He found this very difficult to do. On the second floor, he had to rest. Gasping and panting, clutching the banister, he managed to make it to the third floor. He knocked on the door and it was opened. He confirmed the identity of the suspect, frisked him to see if he was armed, and ordered him to accompany him. But Wiesenthal could hardly get down the stairs. His prisoner took him by the arm and supported him carefully down to the street, where the man was placed under arrest.[7]

Not long after the end of the war, Mauthausen was made part of the Soviet occupation zone and the Americans' operations there were stopped.[8] Wiesenthal was transferred to another American intelligence service, the

Office of Strategic Services (OSS). Until now, he had been involved in arresting suspects whose whereabouts were known; now he was to focus on wanted individuals who had gone into hiding. This assignment too did not last very long. The OSS was dismantled at the end of 1945, but Wiesenthal kept up his link with the Americans. His position was defined as "adviser."[9]

2. The Displaced

His work with the Americans rapidly restored Wiesenthal's mental strength, and gave him a unique status among the refugees. Three weeks after the end of the war, he was already able to travel to Munich to attend the first conference of representatives of camp survivors. There he met a man by the name of Shimshon Junicman, who was close to the Zionist Revisionist "State Party," the same party Wiesenthal had supported before the war. Junicman was later to be a member of the Israeli parliament, the Knesset, for Menachem Begin's Herut party.[10]

The document that Wiesenthal took with him to Munich identified him as a member of the "authorized Jewish committee for Upper Austria." The document bore the signature of a representative of the JDC (the Joint Distribution Committee, popularly known as "the Joint," one of the Jewish welfare organizations operating among the refugees), as well as the imposing seal of the U.S. military government.[11]

This was a chaotic twilight period. Vast regions of the European continent were under the control of foreign military occupation powers, and there were no arrangements in place for orderly governance. Europe was like one big traffic jam, with fourteen million displaced persons (DPs) trying to make their way home or find a new one. They trekked by train, by wagon, in motor vehicles, on motorcycles, and on animals; millions wandered by foot from country to country, crossing one border and then another—endless convoys and straggling processions of refugees. Among them were many Jewish survivors.

Altogether about one million Jews were still alive in the areas that had been under Nazi occupation or influence, besides those living in the territory of the Soviet Union. Most were in Romania, Hungary, Czechoslovakia, Bulgaria, and Poland. Many of them were now on the roads. Many thousands of the Jews who had been liberated from the camps went back to their homes, but most of them found that their houses and businesses had been plundered and destroyed.

The chances that the Communist authorities in Eastern Europe would arrange for the restoration of their property were close to zero. Almost everywhere, the Jews encountered manifestations of anti-Semitism, and here and there they were greeted with outbursts of violence. Many of them failed to find their missing relatives. In these circumstances, they saw no reason to remain in what had been their homelands. So they trekked westward to seek new lives, far from the realms of the catastrophe. Many mixed with the waves of German refugees who had been driven out of the Communist countries in the East. This is how they turned up at transit camps in Germany and Austria.

By the spring of 1947, the number of displaced Jews was close to a quarter of a million. Almost 160,000 were living in the American occupation zone in Germany, another 40,000 in Austria, and some 20,000 in Italy. "The situation in the camps is awful," wrote Yehezke'el Sahar, who started out as an emissary from Palestine and later became Israeli ambassador to Austria. He pointed out that many thousands of people who had survived the Holocaust were dying now. "There isn't a single blanket or item of warm clothing for the people, most of whom are living in wooden huts without heating stoves," he wrote. "The weather here is wintry, with frost at night . . . and there are a great many pregnant women here and children, and no one is doing anything for them." He was convinced that the occupation authorities were ignoring the refugees' distress out of anti-Semitic motives. "My impression is that they are trying to make the refugees' lives so miserable that they will agree to go back to Poland," he wrote.

The food they were given was bad and not always sufficient. Many people slept on the same bunks that had been used in the Nazi camps; many others slept on the floor. There were not enough lavatories or showers. Other sources also reported on the harsh conditions in the DP camps. Earl Harrison, the American representative on the Intergovernmental Commission on Refugees, informed President Harry S. Truman that the only difference between the U.S. military's and the Nazi's treatment of the Jewish refugees was that the Americans were not exterminating them.[12]

In the wake of protests over the plight of displaced persons, several thousand residents of the Bindermichl neighborhood in southern Linz were forced to leave their homes, which were then handed over to the refugees. The district, named for an ancient farm, was built during World War II to house workers at the Hermann Göring industrial center. It resembled a large barracks, with houses in straight rows in a kind of beehive of rectangular compounds.[13] One of the residents of Bindermichl was Wiesenthal. He drew a series of cartoons that seem to express the sad irony of idleness.[14]

The Jewish refugees at Bindermichl were looked after by various international organizations, with most of the care dispensed by Jewish welfare associations. Families lived together, under often very overcrowded conditions, with two families to a room and several families sharing bathrooms and kitchens. They received food and medical care and there was a postal service. Mostly they did not work, and only some of the children attended classes occasionally. The refugees were free to come and go as they wished.

The Zionist movement and other groups sent emissaries, some of them from Palestine. They tried to get the refugees interested in social and cultural activities. They set up synagogues and clubhouses where Jewish holidays were celebrated and lectures and concerts were given; once Yehudi Menuhin performed. Libraries were opened and newsletters printed.[15] Wiesenthal ran the Jewish Committee, in effect a one-man body.

The Americans put two rooms at his disposal to serve as an office; it was kind of an information center, and long lines formed outside during most hours of the day. Someone needed dental care, someone else a winter coat, or a document to support a U.S. visa application. The papers that accumulated during Wiesenthal's work included thousands of letters reflecting a broad spectrum of activities, some public or political, concerning the needs of the refugees in general, and others treating particular individuals' problems. One frequent request was for documents required to submit a claim for restitution from Germany.[16]

All this activity gave Wiesenthal increasing influence over the fate of other people. In dealing with the case of a man involved in a dispute with his wife, Wiesenthal wrote to the representative of the JDC that it was not advisable for him to live in Bindermichl as the woman tended to have temper tantrums, and in any case the man had an Australian immigrant's visa.[17] Moreover, apparently a nod from Wiesenthal could be useful in securing immigration visas for non-Jews. The International Refugee Organization sent him long lists with names of people applying to immigrate to Canada and Australia, asking him to give his opinion as to whether they had been Nazi collaborators.

One man who identified himself as a distant relative of Wiesenthal's applied to move to Bindermichl from another DP camp where the conditions were worse. Wiesenthal gave him the ID card of another resident who had left the camp. The man moved in, using the fake identity, but when the time came for him to immigrate to the United States he did not dare to admit that he had done so. And so he continued using it in New York, for the rest of his life, a full half century, well into his eighties, not daring to divulge his secret lest he be deprived of his American citizenship.[18]

Wiesenthal saw every one of the refugees as a potential agent in the search for Nazi criminals. He approached them through advertisements and he distributed questionnaires among them: Where were you? When? Which Nazis do you remember? What was each one's family name, first name, nickname, rank, hometown, distinguishing features, hair, eyes, face, approximate age? Where was he active, what ghetto, what camp? With the help of the Americans he organized an exhibition of photographs and documents to encourage people to come forward with information.[19] The names that the survivors of the camps provided formed the foundation of the card index that in days to come would contain details about thousands of suspected Nazis.

Wiesenthal was not the first to tackle the issue. A man by the name of Majlech Bakalchuck set up the first "documentation center" in Linz, but he was apparently more interested in the historical record than in the search for criminals, and he did not stay in Linz for long.[20] The attempt to trace war criminals was at first part of the endeavor to establish what had happened to their victims; it was in fact one single enterprise. But most of the refugees were more interested in looking for their relatives.

Their time spent in Bindermichl helped many refugees recover their physical health, but they remained emotional wrecks. Memories of the horror haunted them without letup, and the loss of their loved ones tormented them. If they had known with certainty that their relatives were dead, they could at least have mourned them, but many were ignorant of their fate. Nothing bothered them more than the lack of certainty.[21]

For hours they would cluster around the notice boards, scrutinizing lists of names supplied by the Red Cross. Some tried private initiatives. "Who knows her? Who has seen her?" one man asked on copies he distributed of a black-and-white photograph of a woman who was pretty and evidently knew it, striking an alluring pose for the camera. Her name was Edit Katharina and she was from Budapest.[22]

This quest occupied the refugees more than anything else. One of them, Leon Zelman, described it as an experience everyone shared. When a camp survivor found the name of, say, her sister, or received a postcard from her uncle, everyone was happy for her. But disappointments had to be borne by each one separately.[23] Wiesenthal told of a man and a woman fighting over a piece of paper with new names of survivors. He grabbed it from her and she grabbed it back and it tore, and suddenly they looked at each other and realized that they were man and wife who hadn't seen each other since the war.[24]

Wiesenthal's daily routine was heartrending. "Moses Kurtzweil, violin teacher, and his sister Hermina, Jews from Prossnitz in Moravia, Czechoslovakia, were brought in July 1942 to Theresienstadt and from that point no sign of life has been received from them," said one of the letters that he received.

> Two letters and food parcels that I sent to their address at the camp went without an answer. All of their belongings, clothing, bedding, furniture, jewelry, tableware, his valuable musical instruments, including two violins, one in a leather case, a violoncello, valuable sheet music, violin strings and other accessories, expensive down bed covers, and many more items, were first listed and then declared confiscated property. They were permitted to take with them only one package weighing 10 kilograms, including a blanket. I request that you try to find out what happened to these two wretched people, and I thank you in advance for your efforts.[25]

Wiesenthal sent the letter to the Jewish community in Vienna, as he did hundreds of similar communications.*

Frequently, he would turn to the Red Cross or to various governmental authorities to try to find out what had happened to people. Again and

---

*In Europe the phrase translated here as "Jewish community" or "community" often refers to both the community's residents and to an elected leadership that administers its affairs. In Austrian cities, the term for this—encompassing both the community as a whole and its leaders—is *israelitische Kultusgemeinde*, and has no exact equivalent in English.

again, he had to file away their negative replies, couched in dry bureau-cratic language, with entire tragedies sometimes compressed into a single sentence: "The missing person does not appear in our lists of survivors." Wiesenthal received a letter like this when he wrote to the Red Cross about his wife. No one knew where she was. One day, he found her.

Cyla Wiesenthal, posing as a non-Jewish Pole, had reached Warsaw, using the forged papers her husband had obtained for her with the help of his supervisors in Lvov. She worked in a German radio factory there. In August 1944, she was deported to a Polish labor camp, where she spent about four weeks, and in September she was transferred to an ammunition manufacturing plant near the city of Solingen in Ger-many.

Conditions were very hard. Her physical health was left permanently damaged.[26] She was freed about three weeks before her husband and she went back to Poland to look for him. She heard that he was dead, but never gave up hope. Wiesenthal used to tell the tale of their reunion with a great deal of romantic charm. It was one of his best stories.

He thought that she had been killed in Warsaw. After the war he found the name of an acquaintance on one of the lists of survivors, a dentist he had known back in Buczacz who had settled in Kraków after the war. Wiesenthal asked him to travel to Warsaw to find out what had happened to Cyla. He found out that she was alive. Wiesenthal was beside himself with joy. With the help of his American connections, he arranged an Aus-trian entry permit for her and sent someone to bring her.

The emissary did not know Cyla. Wiesenthal wrote her address on a piece of paper. At the border crossing into Poland, the man was seized by anxiety at the presence of a Soviet KGB agent and he destroyed the paper with the address on it. When he came to Warsaw, he had no way of finding Cyla, so he hung a notice in the offices of the Jewish community, saying that Simon Wiesenthal wanted his wife to identify herself to him so that he could take her to her husband in Austria. No fewer than three women introduced themselves as Cyla Wiesenthal in the hope that they would be able to leave for the West.

The emissary didn't know which woman was the real Mrs. Wiesenthal, the story goes, so he picked the prettiest of the three and took her back to Linz. Before allowing the couple to meet, he went up to Wiesenthal's apartment and warned him that perhaps he had not brought the right woman, and if this was the case, he would take her for himself. Wiesenthal went down to the street. It really was his Cyla.[27]

They had a great deal to tell each other. When they drew up a list of the relatives they had lost, the number of names reached eighty-nine, Wiesenthal recounted. Cyla's mother had been arrested in Buczacz by a Ukrainian policeman and when she failed to walk fast enough he shot her dead.[28] The Holocaust had left its mark on each of them, and on the relationship between the two of them. They were both now thirty-seven years old. A year later, on September 5, 1946, a daughter, Paulinka, was born to them. The refugees in the camps attained the highest birthrate in the world. Wiesenthal had really wanted a son.[29]

3. The President of the Jews

The survivors of the Holocaust split into innumerable organizations and sometimes competed or even fought with one another on political or personal grounds. Wiesenthal tended to get involved in petty squabbles and to fight them ardently, as if the fate of the world depended on their outcome.[30]

He printed calling cards, first identifying himself as "President of the Organization of Jewish Concentration Camp Prisoners in Austria" and later, in a fancier typeface, "Chairman of the International Union of Former Political Prisoners of Concentration Camps in Austria (American Zone)." The first card carried the address of his apartment in Bindermichl, the second of the office on Goethe Street. On both cards, his name was preceded by his professional title, "Dipl. Ing." They both carried phone numbers. At that time, he carried what appeared in all respects to be an official identity booklet. On the cover were the words "The Jewish Central Committee for the American Zone of Austria," in German and English. Inside, there was a photograph and an impressive seal, and personal details. Under "Function" appeared the word *President*.

Wiesenthal used the first-person plural, as if there were an actual organization behind him, and he very quickly picked up the jargon of the former Austro-Hungarian bureaucracy. Although he did not always know the difference between the German language's syntactical rules and those of Yiddish, he took pains to get the official honorifics of the functionaries correct and closely observed the rules of etiquette. He always ended his letters with the phrase "with the highest esteem" and when he wrote to Jewish organizations he would use "with Zion's greeting" (*Zionsgruss* in German).

As is customary in Germany and Austria, he sometimes refrained from signing his name, using instead a bureaucratic title like "department head," often abbreviated, as is also customary in those countries.[31] He never forgot to make copies of his correspondence and diligently filed it all away in exemplary order. He mostly did everything himself but sometimes used a typist. He seems to have enjoyed his work. The fragments of hope that he found among the refugees, and his ability to help relieve their despair, bolstered his spirits; there could have been no better way to rehabilitate himself.[32] Many residents of the camp were grateful to him, but naturally there were also many who bore him grudges. One of these was Leon Zelman.

Zelman began his life in Austria like Wiesenthal himself, a concentration camp survivor living in a refugee camp near Linz. Not far from that camp, a prisoner-of-war camp was set up. The doctor who cared for the refugees also looked after the POWs, who included SS personnel. The refugees protested about this and held a hunger strike, Zelman wrote in his memoirs. He was chosen to represent the refugees of his camp and went to the American military headquarters in Linz to present their objections. While he was talking, a man in civilian clothes came out of a back room and silenced him, ordering in a stern stone: "You people must eat!" "Who are you to tell us what to do?" Zelman asked. "I was also in the camps," the man replied.[33] That should have been enough of a reason for him to support the hunger strikers, Zelman thought, but Wiesenthal thought otherwise, he wrote.

Many years after that incident Zelman had not yet forgiven Wiesenthal, and in an interview he assailed him as if the two were still refugees in Linz. The refugees were afraid of him, Zelman charged, because they were selling things they got from the Americans, like coffee, nylon stockings, and cigarettes, on the black market, and, according to Zelman, Wiesenthal demanded they pay him a commission and threatened to give them up to the authorities if they did not pay.[34]

A similar accusation was leveled in a weekly newspaper in 1948; Wiesenthal sued for libel and the paper apologized.[35] Among his important papers, Wiesenthal kept a report by a three-member panel exonerating him of a charge that he had informed on employees of the JDC who were suspected of profiteering.[36] The black market was booming at that time and many of the refugees were involved, some of them in organized gangs.[37]

The Israeli intelligence agent Michael Bloch sent a long report to his superiors on the black market in Austria, writing, among other things, that emissaries of Israel's political parties working with the refugees were also involved in it: "I saw the flourishing black market in and around the camps with my own eyes, and it is not limited to dealings in cigarettes by a few individuals, but all of the Israeli parties almost without exception are involved.

"There is an attitude prevalent here in certain circles that it's a mitz-vah to get money out of the gentiles and bring it to our country, which needs foreign currency, and that the legality of the money's source does not have to be checked. The parties support themselves by black market deals, so they encourage individuals to trade on it."[38] Once Wiesenthal was detained for twenty-four hours on suspicion of dealing on the black market, but he was released without being penalized. At least once he had to respond to a private suit.

The plaintiff, a man by the name of Gottfried, was living in Tel Aviv. He claimed through an attorney that Wiesenthal owed him $200. Wiesenthal denied this and told a story that reflected the daily routine of his work: Gottfried arrived from Poland immediately after the war and "fell upon" Wiesenthal with a demand that he help him leave Austria. Wiesenthal never understood why it was so urgent, but he called the Italian immigration officer and arranged for him to issue forged papers to Gottfried that would enable him to enter Italy.

Gottfried's case required a great deal of running around, and the man nagged Wiesenthal day and night. Before leaving, he paid Wiesenthal $125. Wiesenthal said Gottfried did this at his own initiative and that he, Wiesenthal, did not ask for any fee.

A little while later, Gottfried sent a nephew to demand $500 from Wiesenthal, claiming that he had given that amount to the Italian immigration officer, in addition to what he had paid Wiesenthal. In the meantime Wiesenthal heard that Gottfried had served in the ghetto police of his hometown, and some people accused Wiesenthal of helping him escape. In the end, Wiesenthal agreed to return $100 to Gottfried, in exchange for a declaration that he had no further claims.[39] Gottfried was not alone. A man by the name of Schulim Mandel left a six-page document with his sons that contained shocking allegations against Wiesenthal, including extortion, arbitrary victimization of refugees, and also a claim that Wiesenthal had had a sexual affair with a married woman. Mandel's complaints first reached the Jewish community office in Vienna, which sent it on to Wiesenthal, who described Mandel as a crook, blackmailer, and informer.[40]

A few months after he began to work with the refugees, Wiesenthal's connections in Linz became a two-way street: various authorities, including the Interior Ministry and the police, international organizations, and foreign consulates began turning to him for information and various documents. He was careful to adorn his correspondence with a multitude of seals and stamps, giving them a somewhat consular appearance.[41]

His activities also caught the attention of the agents of the Briha. And so, almost by accident, Wiesenthal found himself a partner in a daring enterprise, different from anything he had ever expected to find himself doing. He joined in eagerly.

4. Foundation Stones

The Hebrew word *briha* ("escape") was first used to describe the mass migration of Jewish survivors from Eastern Europe westward on their own initiative, led by Jews who had fought the Nazis as partisans. It was later adopted as the name of the organization set up to help the refugees reach Palestine, which helped lay the foundation for the State of Israel.

Palestine was still under British rule, and the mandate authorities were doing their best to prevent the entry of the refugees. Most of the would-be immigrants were therefore sent on ships that sailed from Europe and landed them secretly on the shores of the country. At first the operation was organized by soldiers of the Jewish Brigade who had served in the war as part of the British army. Later they were joined by agents and emissaries from the Jewish community in Palestine, a total of four hundred persons sent to Europe for this purpose by the Zionist movement.

It was a complex operation. Transport timetables had to be planned, accommodations arranged, food and blankets supplied. The refugees were organized into groups, and before setting out they had to be briefed about what to take with them and what to leave behind and how to behave on the road. Reliable guides had to be located and recruited, and the operation spawned an entire document-forging industry for people and vehicles.

For the most part the refugees were transported toward their departure points in the West in trains and vehicles, but before reaching the camps in Germany and Austria they often had to hike through forests and over remote mountain paths, sometimes at night. Among them were old people, pregnant women, and newborn infants. Many were in need of medical care.

On their way to the West the groups had to steal across frontiers and avoid the efforts of the various governments and occupation authorities to prevent them either from leaving or from entering. But everywhere there were also local officials, police officers, and border patrolmen who were ready to help them on their way because they thought everything was legal and in order, because they had been bribed, because they sympathized with the refugees, because they wanted to get rid of them, or because they simply didn't care. The success of the Briha depended upon its ability to make the most of each and all of these motives. It usually took several days for the refugees to arrive at the displaced persons' camps in Germany and Austria. From there they were transferred to Italy, where they were put on boats bound for Palestine. Most of the funding for the operation came from donations raised in the United States.[42] The commander of the Briha in Austria, Arthur Piernikraz, later Asher Ben Natan, was among the founders of Israel's intelligence services, as were many of the other emissaries.[43]

The success of the huge project depended to a large extent on the ability of its operatives to mobilize as much wisdom, resourcefulness, and courage as they could. Wiesenthal's status in the refugee camps and his connections with the American military administration and the various Austrian authorities, as well as his Zionist background and his will to help, made him an ideal partner.

He knew who to talk to in order to obtain ID papers, entry visas, and transit documents and he knew which official wanted dollars and which border policeman would be happy with a carton of American cigarettes. He knew how to smuggle the emissaries of the Briha into the camps with fake identities as refugees so they could organize the next stage in the journey to the Land of Israel.

The transfer of these masses of people also required screening would-be immigrants before they could be consigned to Palestine. To ensure that they were all Jews, doctors checked the males to see if they had been circumcised. Other probes revealed that, as noted in one report, many of the Jews wanting to emigrate were involved in criminal activity and at least some of these were not accepted.[44]

In addition, the emissaries had to make sure that the states of the Communist bloc weren't taking advantage of the operation to plant spies inside the future State of Israel. Romania, for example, agreed to allow the emigration of several thousand Jews of military conscription age only on condition that it could decide whom to send.

On the diplomatic level, the Zionist movement tried to persuade the world that the only way to solve the problem of the Jewish refugees was to settle them in Palestine. It was a combined endeavor: the first part was conducted in New York and Washington, D.C., through the pressure of public opinion and lobbying by Jewish organizations; the second part went on inside the camps, where the emissaries tried to convince the refugees that their place was in the Land of Israel. Wiesenthal helped in this effort. There are photographs of him addressing a Zionist meeting in a refugee camp with a large picture of Herzl behind him and above it a slogan in Yiddish—"The Land Is Calling You." One of the goals was to enlist soldiers to fight in the coming war for the establishment of the Jewish state.

In the first half of 1946, an Anglo-American committee of enquiry was tasked with studying the political situation in Palestine as well as the conditions in the displaced persons' camps in Europe. Before they arrived, the camp inmates were surveyed and the results were clear-cut—almost everyone said they wanted to live in the Land of Israel. Richard Crossman, a British parliamentarian who was a member of the commission, asked himself if they would still want to go there if they were offered the choice between Palestine and the United States, but he knew the question was irrelevant: the United States did not want to take most of the refugees in.[45]

Wiesenthal submitted a memo to the commission declaring that 99 percent of those surveyed had expressed a desire to live in the Land of Israel; this was his first political action on behalf of the Zionist movement.[46] In the corridors of the Zionist Congress held in Basel in 1946, Wiesenthal met a number of interesting personalities. Ironically, it was there that he came across the foundation stone for building his future in Austria.

Wiesenthal was not a delegate to the congress. "I was a poor refugee, and I did not have the money for a hotel," he wrote later. "I slept on a bench in a school, and I ate in a workers' kitchen."[47] But he was already quite well-known, thanks in part to the first book that he published. It was a sixty-page, large-format collection of black-and-white drawings inspired by his imprisonment in Mauthausen.[48]

One of the people he met in Basel was Avraham Silberschein, the man from Lvov who had taught history, Torah, and Hebrew in Buczacz before the war. Silberschein agreed to help Wiesenthal set up his projected documentation center. A lawyer and an economist, Silberschein was one of those Jewish leaders whose names have sunk into oblivion. He initiated a series of projects to help improve the condition of the Jews in Galicia and in Poland after the First World War, including securing credit for cooperative factories. In the early 1920s he was elected a member of the Sejm, the Polish parliament.

In the second half of August 1939, Silberschein had traveled to Geneva to take part in the Zionist Congress that was being held there. Within two weeks, World War II broke out and instead of going home, Silberschein remained in Switzerland. During the war he launched a number of projects aimed at rescuing and assisting Jewish refugees. He set up an organization called Relico, or Relief Committee, whose main functions were funded by the World Jewish Congress.[49]

Wiesenthal gave Silberschein a copy of his Mauthausen drawings and told him about his experiences during the war, his work with the refugees, and his efforts to find Nazi criminals. Unlike the pesky spongers and supplicants who used to importune Silberschein, he seemed to be a serious person, one who worked with the American intelligence services and with the Briha. Silberschein was impressed by his personality. He asked Wiesenthal for an organized plan of operations.

Wiesenthal thought big. He had in mind an organization based in Linz, with branches in three other cities. The documentation center was supposed to employ some fifty staffers, including a spokesperson. He described to Silberschein the enthusiasm of the refugees when they saw the names of wanted Nazis that he hung on the notice boards, especially the names of the first to be arrested. These announcements did more for the refugees than a calorie supplement, he said.

Silberschein, generous but also tempered by experience, disappointed him. He agreed to fund only a much more limited operation. According to Wiesenthal, he was allocated only forty dollars a month to cover office expenses like the phone bill and stamps. Sometimes Silberschein remarked that the budget he had received from Wiesenthal was too large, or not organized well enough, but more than once he promised to continue his support. The connection between the two lasted for years.[50]

5

"The Duty of an Austrian Patriot"

I. A New Homeland

A few months after they were reunited, Simon and Cyla Wiesenthal were planning to immigrate to the United States. Wiesenthal's uncle, David, had sent the required affidavits and also paid the boat fare, via the Hebrew Immigrant Aid Society (HIAS), an American Jewish charity. "We are eagerly awaiting your arrival to this country," wrote Uncle David. But Wiesenthal did not go, and apparently his relatives never forgave him for it. "Everybody but you is boycotting me," Wiesenthal complained in a letter to his cousin Rosa Pick in New York, in January 1948. "I gave up the idea of going to America a long time ago," he added, and said that he and his wife wanted to settle in Palestine.[1]

A little over a year later, Wiesenthal signed a business agreement with two partners, who were also survivors of the camps. They purchased heavy machinery, including trucks, tractors, and a concrete mixer, intending to take them to what was now Israel. It was a good deal from Wiesenthal's point of view. The estimated cost of the project came to $6,500; he invested $1,000 but received a third of the ownership rights. Not many of the one million Jews who settled in Israel in the early years of its existence brought heavy mechanical equipment with them, and there is reason to believe that Wiesenthal would have prospered and made his mark as one of those Holocaust survivors whose personal resurrection served as an emblem for the revival of the Jewish people in their own state.

In May 1951, he wrote to a friend in Israel that he would be there by the end of the year. He hoped to acquire a three-room apartment with a garden in a housing project in Haifa or Ramat Gan. He did not as yet have enough money, but he hoped it would work out. A few months later, he had a visit from his brother-in-law, who had settled in Palestine before the war. "I've heard that recently the situation in the country has deteriorated sharply," he wrote to his friend, and remained in Austria.[2]

There were many Jews who chose not to settle in Israel; most of those who did go went because they had no other alternative, and most of the camp survivors were in this category. They did not want to go back to their own countries, and other countries did not want them. The Jews in the Arab lands could not stay there because of the war between Israel and her neighbors. Only a handful of Jews from America and other Western countries chose to immigrate to the new state that in the late 1940s and early 1950s was struggling with economic austerity and whose future seemed far from secure.

Wiesenthal built his new life in the motherland of Hitler and Eichmann, something that relatively few Jews decided to do. Most of the surviving Jews who had lived in Austria before the war made no attempt to go back there. Considering his work among the refugees, it was natural that Wiesenthal would be one of the last Jews in the camps, but they were disbanded fairly quickly and almost all the inmates left Austria, so his task was in fact over. Nevertheless, he stayed on.

In the days to come, he was asked over and over again why he had done so. All his answers explained only why it was necessary for him to be in Austria after the hunt for Nazi criminals became his major occupation, beginning in the 1960s. There was nothing in his replies to explain why he had not left soon after the end of the war. The status that he had fashioned for himself in the refugee camps pleased him. As early as 1948 his request for a permit to carry a pistol had been granted.[3] But of course he could have carried a gun in Israel too, had he so wished.

Sometimes he tried to evade the issue with sarcastic wisecracks. "The reason I don't live in Israel," he answered an Israeli who asked him about it, "is that there are no Nazis or anti-Semites there."[4] And he told one of his acquaintances at Yad Vashem that he'd move to Israel when Ben-Gurion was no longer prime minister.[5]

Some of Wiesenthal's Jewish friends in Vienna, both natives of the city and immigrants from the East, tended toward the end of their lives to say that they had never intended to go back and live there but they had simply "gotten stuck." One had a home there, another a fur business; one wanted to stay only until he arranged his restitution payments, another "sat on his suitcases" all his life, waiting for economic conditions in Israel to get better, or for the wars with the Arabs to come to an end. One was too old and felt that it was too late to move, while others simply wanted to rebuild their lives in the land of their birth, where they felt at home despite everything.[6] This was also the main reason that Wiesenthal stayed in Austria: he felt at home there.

From very early on, when he was growing up in a small town in the easternmost province of the Austro-Hungarian Empire, Wiesenthal sensed that Vienna was the center of his cultural and political world. It was indeed ironic that he reached the city via the Nazi concentration camps, but the hardships he had undergone didn't erase what had been engraved on his consciousness as a child in Buczacz and as a student in Prague and Lvov.

Many years later, he published a novel in German, the heroes of which are Jews whose stories are very similar to his own, including that of his period of imprisonment in Janowska. Some of the SS personnel appearing in the book do so under their actual names. But the plot centers on Vienna and the book reflects a deep identification with the fate of the city's Jews, as if Wiesenthal were one of them.[7] "As someone who was born in the old Austria, not only did I go to elementary school in Vienna and did my father fall as an Austrian soldier . . . I really do not feel like a stranger in this country," he wrote.[8] And as a native son, he also tried to clear his country of anti-Semitism.

In early January 1946, Wiesenthal wanted to travel from Linz to Vienna. He bought a ticket and tried to get onto a bus. The driver did not want to take him. "No foreigners," he said. Wiesenthal complained to the bus company, but the clerk told him: "We'd be happy if all the foreigners would leave Austria." He wrote a letter to the minister of transport, signing it as usual with the name of his organization, protesting against "this insult to our chairman," as if it had happened to someone else.[9]

This was not an uncommon incident. The Austrians found it difficult to rid themselves of their hatred of Jews. In the first months after the war they were still in the grip of the shock of defeat. Tens of thousands of families were bereft of fathers and sons, and the country was under foreign occupation and divided up into zones, as was Germany. Unlike the Germans, however, most Austrians did not acknowledge any national guilt but instead fostered the notion that they too had been the victims of Nazi occupation.

Many of them felt no need to conceal the hatred they felt for Jews in general and the inhabitants of the camps in particular. Linz had been bombed during the war, and in various places in the city the ruins were still to be seen. The refugees were foreign Jews walking around under the protection of the American occupying forces, and many of them were black-market profiteers. The evacuation of the local residents from their homes in Bindermichl to make room for the refugees had also contributed to the hostility.

In the Austrian press, items sometimes appeared that stereotyped the refugees as black-market profiteers or even drug dealers. Wiesenthal objected bitterly, writing: "People who are still walking about in stolen Jewish clothes and living in apartments furnished with Jewish furniture from all parts of Europe begrudge the Jews their woolen blankets in the camp barracks."[10]

As their representative, Wiesenthal frequently protested attitudes toward the refugees. On one occasion, dozens of Austrian policemen raided one of the camps to search for smuggled goods. Wiesenthal complained that they had concentrated on the living quarters of Jews although there were also people of other ethnicities in the camp. He claimed that the police had behaved rudely and threatened refugees with their weapons. This was collective punishment that had reminded many camp residents of the Nazi days, Wiesenthal wrote to the district governor.[11]

In another incident, the Jews at a certain camp were ordered to pay rent for a room that was being used as a synagogue. Wiesenthal objected to the request itself, but his protest was directed mainly at the words of the Austrian official handling the matter: "If the Jews want to dance like lunatics, let them do it on the lawn, and if they want to do it in a closed room that does not belong to them, then they must pay for it."[12]

In another incident, a Jew went with his wife to a beer hall in Graz. No sooner had they sat down than somebody at a nearby table began making crude anti-Semitic remarks. The Jew first complained to the proprietor, who refused to intervene, and then called the police. A policeman was dispatched to the bar, but when he arrived the owner and his customers grabbed hold of the Jewish couple and threw them into the street, together with the officer, and warned them not to come back.[13]

There were anti-Semitic curses to be heard from the stands at soccer matches, and at least one man was forced to declare that he was not a Jew in order to obtain a license to own a radio, because the old forms from the Nazi administration were still in use.[14]

The Linz municipality erected a monument to a humorist who had organized an anti-Semitic show during the Nazi period.[15] Austrian movie theaters decided not to screen Charlie Chaplin's *The Great Dictator* but did show the films of Veit Harlan, the director of the anti-Semitic Nazi propaganda film *Jew Süss*.[16] The Braunau municipality listed the birthplace of Adolf Hitler among the city's tourist attractions.[17]

As a Zionist, Wiesenthal could have espoused the position that Jews should not be living in Austria at all, and those who nevertheless chose to do so knew that they were living in an anti-Semitic country. But Wiesenthal wanted to purge Austria of its racism. Once his endeavors brought him to the hamlet of Rinn in the Tyrol, which, thanks to an anti-Semitic blood libel connected to the local church, was a big attraction for pilgrims.

By the 1940s, Wiesenthal already tended to try to solve problems by going straight to the top people. He took pains to word his letters with all due deference but never refrained from stressing that it was his right to address the recipient as an equal and that he was not asking for favors. His demand to ban the rites at Rinn was directed to Cardinal Theodor Innizer. He signed as chairman of the camp survivors, but the reason he gave for his request didn't have to do with being Jewish: he wrote that the Rinn pilgrimages should be stopped for the sake of the children of Austria.[18]

As a Jew, he could have told himself that the Austrians did not deserve his efforts to save them from themselves, but he saw himself as one of them. "It is the duty of an Austrian patriot," he wrote in a letter to the editor of the *Salzburger Nachrichten*, "to uproot all of the wild growths of Nazism."[19]

Wiesenthal's efforts to cleanse the society he had chosen to join did not bear immediate results. The Nazis crawled out of their holes and took up positions of influence throughout the governmental apparatus, including the schools and the courts, and all the parties integrated them in key positions. Wiesenthal spoke at length about this at the general meeting of the committee of Jewish communities in Austria, but stressed that the danger springing from the rise of Nazism and neo-Nazism was a menace not only to the small number of Jews in the country but to all Austrians. Only someone who believes in his country can criticize it as Wiesenthal did in his speech, out of disappointment and concern, but also hope.[20]

As an Austrian patriot, Wiesenthal wrote to the minister for education, Ernst Kolb, and demanded that his daughter and the other Jewish children in Linz be provided with a teacher for religious instruction despite the fact that there were only a few of them.[21] Once, when his wife went to enroll Paulinka at a new school, the principal looked at them and said, "And I thought that they had already killed all the Jews."[22]

It was not easy growing up as a Jewish girl in Linz, Paulinka Kreisberg recalled many years later. The other children teased her about being Jewish, drew Stars of David on her desk, and asked her if it was true that she had a tail. Her mother told her to keep to herself, and not to respond. At a certain stage, she internalized the anti-Semitic animosity and began to believe that she was different and inferior to the others. It took years for her to free herself of these feelings. Cyla Wiesenthal also tended to keep to herself; she saw the outside world as hostile and anti-Semitic. Paulinka was allowed to play with the neighbors' children, but only under the supervision of her mother or the housemaid. She had no real connection with her surroundings. "There were only the three of us. Father, Mother, and I," she said.

Her parents never spoke to her about the Holocaust. When Paulinka was seven, she asked why she had no grandparents like the other kids. Her parents said they would tell her sometime, perhaps in a year or two, but she wanted to know right away. "So I told her, and then I went into another room and wept," Wiesenthal recalled. He told a friend that he used to ask strangers to call and say they were relatives to make Paulinka happy. Nothing better illustrates his feeling of belonging to Austrian society than his decision to raise his daughter there. Until age six, she recalled later, her father spoke Yiddish with her. Then they spoke German.[23]

The decision to force life in Linz on his wife and daughter was cruel. In the wake of the Holocaust, there was something perverse about it. It is possible that Wiesenthal was aware of this. Despite his sense of belonging in Austria, he also clung to the foreign elements in his identity and even nurtured them, taking pains to belong and not belong at one and the same time.

2. Help from a Friend

During the struggle for the establishment of the State of Israel and in the early years of its existence, there was a tendency among Jews to identify the Arabs and especially the Palestinian leader Haj Amin el-Husseini with the Nazis. Husseini, whom the British had appointed Grand Mufti of Jerusalem, had offered his assistance to Hitler and had even met with him and some of the heads of his regime, including Heinrich Himmler, the head of the SS, and apparently also Eichmann.

In a profile of Eichmann published in a Hebrew paper in Palestine in 1946, the writer stated that the Nazi official had come to the country in the mid-1930s to organize the Arab rebellion. "It was in the Land of Israel that the first signs of his cruelty were revealed," the article said. This was not an accurate report, but it reflected the tendency to identify the Arabs with the Nazis.[24] Rezso Kastner, the man who negotiated with Eichmann over saving the Jews of Hungary, told Wiesenthal about the connection between the Nazi and the mufti. According to Wiesenthal, he began to take an interest in Husseini in the hope that through him he would be able to trace Eichmann's tracks.[25]

Wiesenthal apparently obtained material on the mufti's links with the Nazis from members of the prosecution in the Nuremberg war crimes trials, and in 1947 he published a book about Husseini. He said that the mufti accompanied Eichmann on his visits to Auschwitz and Majdanek "to study the efficiency of the functioning of the crematoria." Several extermination camp staff members were introduced to Husseini, and he praised them, Wiesenthal wrote. He was evidently the first to disseminate this story, which was to be repeated innumerable times by others. Some attributed it to Eichmann's aide Wisliceny, but there is no reliable evidence for its veracity.[26]

This was Wiesenthal's second book. To publish it he required and obtained the permission of the American occupation authorities. He took the manuscript with him to Basel in the hope that among the delegates to the Zionist Congress he would find a publisher prepared to put the book out in English. He claimed to have found such a person, but that a writer by the name of Maurice (Moshe) Pearlman, who was later to serve as spokesman for the Israel Defense Forces, stole his information about the mufti and published his own book, with the assistance of Asher Ben Natan and others. "The Briha people can't stand me because I know much too much and I cannot be bought," he wrote to the director of Yad Vashem.[27] Wiesenthal's own book about the mufti never came out in English.

Nonetheless, despite his resentment and hurt feelings, Wiesenthal continued gathering material on the mufti's activities, and every now and again he would share it with Avraham Silberschein. An American acquaintance put him in touch with a former Nazi Foreign Ministry official by the name of Gerhard Roth, who, according to Wiesenthal, provided him with, among other things, a list of Nazi agents in Arab countries. The trouble was he didn't do it for free. "I need money urgently," he wrote to Silberschein. "You have no idea how much this Dr. Gerhard Roth is costing."

Wiesenthal conveyed the information he obtained about the mufti to Silberschein, as if he were a spy and Silberschein his handler.[28] Sometimes he also sent him scraps of information about goings-on in the Arab world—something about Saudi Arabia, something about Iraq. On some of these communications he stamped the word CONFIDENTIAL.[29] He assumed, or perhaps knew, that Silberschein passed the information on to Israel.

Toward the end of 1950, Wiesenthal wrote to the editors of a Buenos Aires Jewish weekly and proposed a kind of information exchange agreement. He was interested in the activities of Nazis in Argentina and the nature of their relations with Arab circles in South America, he wrote. He added, as usual in the first-person plural, "We are aware that SS personnel are traveling from Argentina to Syria, bringing with them references from Muslim committees in South America."[30] He received this information from Ahmed Bigi, one of the many mysterious characters who figure in his life story.

In his book about the hunt for Eichmann, Wiesenthal disguised Bigi's identity, calling him Mussa Ali Bey. He wrote that the man was a Turk born in the Crimean peninsula who fought as a captain in the Red Army, was taken prisoner by the Germans, and somehow reached Mauthausen, where Wiesenthal met and befriended him. The connection between them was renewed after his book about the mufti was published, Wiesenthal said.

"Mussa surprised me when he informed me that he corresponded regularly with the mufti. The mufti asked Mussa if he was interested in coming to the Middle East and promised him a high rank in his new army," Wiesenthal wrote.[31] Among Wiesenthal's papers is a copy of a letter written to him by Bigi in 1949, from which it emerges that he had met with the mufti; however, it was not the mufti who had written to him from Damascus but another man, a Muslim who had worked in the German Foreign Ministry during the war and settled in Syria. Bigi said that this man had indeed proposed to him that he come to Damascus and had once asked him if he knew what had happened to several Nazi functionaries, including Eichmann.[32]

Bigi was a devout Muslim, the son of a well-known religious scholar of Tartar origins, Mussa Jurallah, who was living at that time in Cairo. Bigi had apparently served as a fighter pilot in the Soviet air force. Like Wiesenthal, he presented himself to the Americans after the war, and gave them information about the Red forces. He tried to build a reputation as an expert on the Soviet Union, publishing articles under different names as well as two books.

Bigi's widow remembered Wiesenthal as a friend of the family, a pleasant person to talk to, full of entertaining stories. He often visited their apartment in Munich, enjoying good meals and meeting exiles from the Soviet Union, including soldiers in the pro-German army of Andrei Andreiewitsch Wlassow. Perhaps he hoped that among them he would light upon the tracks of Nazi criminals. The widow recalled that Wiesenthal and her husband often talked about the mufti. In one of his letters, Bigi mentioned a meeting in Munich with the Israeli consul Dr. Chaim Hoffman, later Yahil. Once Bigi told Wiesenthal about a group of German officers who were planning to join the Syrian army.[33]

However, the friendship between the Jewish refugee and the Muslim pilot does not look like the cooperative effort of disciplined espionage agents, but rather like the result of displaced persons wandering among the same ruins of Munich in a twilight era. It was as if they were searching for themselves and for a place in the new world, trying to rebuild their lives, while still captives of their problems and their dreams, somewhere between imagination and reality, truth and fiction.

Bigi was infected by Wiesenthal's obsession with catching Eichmann, and apparently he also believed that the mufti could lead them to him. Thus the two became friends, tied together by the romance of a mystery, not quite secret agents, nor real writers, but mostly dreamer-adventurers. Once a German journalist told Wiesenthal that he had spoken with the mufti in Cairo, and Husseini had complained that there was some guy named Wiesenthal over there in Europe spreading lies about him.[34]

The Israeli consul in Vienna, Arye Eshel, took Wiesenthal's information seriously. In 1952, Wiesenthal told him about a conversation between the mufti and a diplomat serving in the Soviet embassy in Cairo. It was the sort of thing that Wiesenthal could have picked up from Bigi's guests in Munich. The mufti had objected to the fact that the Soviets had supported the establishment of the State of Israel, and the diplomat assured him that at the first opportunity the Soviet Union would assist in the liquidation of Israel.

Eshel, Israel's senior diplomat in Austria, saw this as "a plan to uproot the Israelis" and transmitted the information urgently to his superiors, but they did not believe that the report had any basis in fact. Eshel requested permission to ask for clarification from Wiesenthal and to explore the possibility of obtaining more information.[35] It is not easy to determine how reliable Wiesenthal's reports to Silberschein and the Israeli consulate were, but it is possible to learn this from them: he very badly wanted Israel to need him, and he felt a need to help Israel. In fact, Israel did not yet have many agents abroad, and it made use of him.

Wiesenthal would later say that when he traveled to Israel for the first time in 1949 it was with the intention of settling there, but a member of the Foreign Ministry political staff, Boris Guriel, persuaded him that Israel needed him in Europe. The political department was then a branch of Israeli intelligence, and one of its heads, Asher Ben Natan, was known to Wiesenthal from the period of the Briha. Guriel's appeal aroused the patriotism Wiesenthal felt for "our state," in his words, and he complied. Shortly after that, Israel reorganized its intelligence services, and the Mossad was established.[36]

Wiesenthal wrote that Guriel recruited him out of appreciation for his previous activities on behalf of the Jewish people and the Zionist movement, including his work with the Briha. In the course of his work with the American secret services, he explained, he had brought about the arrest of hundreds of Nazi criminals. Moreover, as president of the International Organization of Concentration Camp Survivors, he had traveled to Paris to attend a conference on the fate of the gold that the Nazis had plundered from the Jews and told the delegates that the only body worthy of receiving it was the Jewish Agency. He had also persuaded the refugees to demand that they be sent to Palestine, spoken on their behalf to the Anglo-American commission, and convinced many of them to enlist in the Israel Defense Forces.

When he came to Israel, be brought with him not only urns full of ashes, but also documents attesting to cooperation between Arabs and the

Nazis, as well as evidence that the heads of the German Christian community in Palestine, the Templars, had collaborated with the Arabs. This information would help the state when the Templars demanded the return of the houses that were now serving as offices for the general staff and government ministries. Guriel told one of his staffers to take Wiesenthal on a tour of the country and invited him to a reception attended by some of the heads of Israel's defense establishment, including Professor Ernst David Bergmann, who was later to become the father of Israel's nuclear project.

Among his successes in his early years as a secret agent for Israel, Wiesenthal mentioned a plot conceived by one of the French intelligence agencies to help ex-Nazi officers reach Syria, which was then ruled by a pro-French government. According to Wiesenthal, he foiled the plot and all the German officers were taken into American custody.

Wiesenthal wrote to the Israeli consul about this, so there are grounds to assume that he did not simply make it all up. Among his papers, there are many more details than those he gave the consul, including the names of the German officers slated to serve in Syria, including some members of the Nazi air force. One of these, Johann Schlemmer, was supposed to become head of Syria's military forces, according to Wiesenthal.[37]

The operation was managed, Wiesenthal's notes say, by a bogus businessman, a Syrian who served in the SS during the war, by the name of Acram Tabbara.[38] He acted in concert with the French espionage service. Wiesenthal told the consul that the French were aware of his involvement in thwarting the operation and they had therefore banned him from entering France.

Other documents found among Wiesenthal's papers confirm that he had indeed encountered difficulties in obtaining a French entry visa and he had written an emotional protest to the president of France, Vincent Auriol. The French said they were not letting him in because he was a Communist.[39]

3. A Second Homeland

As a recruit in Israel's secret services, Wiesenthal was given an Israeli travel document that had the same validity as a regular passport and it enabled him to obtain an Austrian residency permit, which was periodically extended; hitherto he had had the status of a refugee. Like other refugees, he first carried a provisional identification card that identified him as a former inmate of Mauthausen, and all kinds of additional documents bearing his fingerprints. His permission to reside in Linz was based on the assumption that his stay there would be temporary. He had declared that he intended to return to Poland. The Israeli travel document made it easier for him to remain in the city.

It seems that Wiesenthal received payment for the services he rendered to Israel. His superiors in Tel Aviv informed him that they were insuring his life with the Migdal company, and it's likely that they also arranged for him to get a press card that he kept among his personal papers. Bound in red cardboard, it identifies him as a correspondent for *Davar*, which was a semi-official daily newspaper. The office of the chancellor in Vienna notified him that he had been accredited as a foreign correspondent, as requested by the Israeli consulate. Another document identified him as a correspondent for *Yediot Hayom*, a daily paper published in Tel Aviv in German.[40]

In the first half of 1952, the Israeli government intended to cease its connection with Wiesenthal and not to renew his travel documents. Wiesenthal objected strenuously and very emotionally. He refused to acknowledge that the document had been given to him by special arrangement and did not afford him Israeli citizenship. Everyone recognized that he was an Israeli, he said. Even at his daughter's ballet classes she was known to be an Israeli child. "Must I now register as a political refugee from Israel?" he asked bitterly. "After all, without a valid passport, I cannot get a permit to remain in Austria."

In his efforts to get his travel document renewed, Wiesenthal retained an attorney and he also recruited Simon Junicman, Menachem Begin's associate, whom he had met at the refugees' conference in Munich. He felt offended, betrayed, partly because the people in "the department," as he called it, using the Hebrew word, had not heeded his demand for remuneration.

At the same time he was endeavoring to get Israeli citizenship, Wiesenthal was exploring the possibility of migrating to Latin America; Argentina, Uruguay, and Panama were the options.[41] But the Israeli consul eventually came around, and it can therefore be assumed his superiors in Jerusalem affirmed that Wiesenthal had indeed helped Israel, as attested to by the innumerable letters that he sent to the consulate.

He sent in many reports about anti-Semitic acts he had learned of, including violent attacks on Jews and victimization of all kinds, as well as press clippings and accounts of his own experiences. When he went to see a film about events in Israel, there was applause from the audience when Arabs were shown slaughtering Jews. He quickly filed a report.[42] Once Wiesenthal warned the consulate that a representative of a large Israeli building concern, Sollel Boneh, which was owned by the Histadrut trade union federation, was getting involved in a deal with a bank whose owner did not hide his anti-Jewish views.[43]

Sometimes he conveyed political information to the Israelis. Once he learned that the People's Party of the district governor, Heinrich Gleisner, was negotiating with an individual identified with veteran Nazis who was also in touch with the Egyptian embassy. Perhaps it would be worth it for him to meet Gleisner and warn him. In any event, he would send the consul a summary of their conversation.[44]

Sometimes he consulted the consulate to avoid getting into trouble. On one occasion he asked if it would be risky for him to meet a delegation of veterans of the anti-Nazi underground due to arrive from Israel, because of "a slight odor of Communism" emanating from the conference they were to attend.[45] From time to time, he asked for advance approval of articles he wanted to publish, and sometimes he arranged for newspapers to publish material that he sent them, usually hostile to the Arab countries.

When the papers reported that the interior minister, Oskar Helmer, was besmirching Israel's efforts to acquire arms, Wiesenthal immediately offered to organize a press conference for the consulate. "I have excellent relations with the press and I have already organized several press conferences," he assured them.[46]

He also warned the consulate that there was a stream of migrants coming to Austria from Israel and seeking to get assistance as refugees. He proposed demanding that the Austrian consulate in Israel cease giving such persons visas and suggested taking steps against the travel agencies that sold them tickets and publishing advertisements in the Israeli press warning those intending to leave that they should expect no assistance from the Jewish community institutions.[47]

One time he demanded that the consulate act against an Israeli, a native of Iraq who tried to get assistance in Austria. Another time he informed them about someone who had returned from Israel and gone to the Joint's offices asking for aid but aroused suspicion and was soon unmasked as an SS man who had managed to pose as a Jew and even been granted Israeli citizenship.[48]

Israel's diplomatic representatives saw in Wiesenthal a partner, and they welcomed his assistance. Among other things, they asked him to gather information on anti-Semitic incidents and on the presumptive strength of the Nazis.[49] The consul shared the concern that the immigration of Israelis to Austria could harm the good name of his country and requested additional information from Wiesenthal.[50]

At a certain stage, Wiesenthal hoped to institutionalize his relationship with the consulate and offered to provide it with information on a permanent basis, and to be paid for it. His offer was turned down, as was his request to be employed in the press department. The consul answered him that regrettably there was no such department, and he had to do everything on his own.[51] Sometimes, the consulate sent him stamps for his private collection, something that made him happy. His passport was extended until the end of 1953, and in the interim Wiesenthal managed to get Austrian citizenship, no easy accomplishment.[52]

In his application for citizenship, Wiesenthal wrote that he intended to remain in Austria and work in his original profession. An Austrian entrepreneur had acquired two of his patents in the field of construction, he said. In this context, Wiesenthal faced another obstacle: his Polish engineering diploma was not recognized in Austria and by law he was forbidden to put the abbreviation "Dipl. Ing." in front of his name; for the rest of his life he would put the letters behind it.[53]

Apparently his difficulty in getting Austrian citizenship arose from a 1950 report found in the Interior Ministry files stating that Wiesenthal had set up an intelligence organization and placed it at the disposal of the Israeli consulate, and that it was possible he was working for the French as well. In addition, the report said that he was suspected of smuggling foreign currency and that he had been involved in a fistfight with some other Jews.[54]

But Wiesenthal, who was already well connected in the local establishment, managed to get District Governor Gleisner, a seasoned politician from the conservative People's Party, which Wiesenthal supported, to intervene on his behalf. Before Austria's annexation to Germany, Gleisner had opposed the Nazis, and when they took over he was incarcerated in concentration camps; freed eventually, he apparently joined the Nazi Party, and even ran a factory owned by the SS. He therefore had good reasons to demonstrate sympathy for Wiesenthal and give him support.[55] His connections with the powerful governor show how far Wiesenthal had come since his liberation from Mauthausen.

Even after the Holocaust and after the establishment of the State of Israel, Wiesenthal's Zionism remained what it had been before the war, in Lvov: a sense of shared fate and worldwide Jewish solidarity, and now there was also identification with the Jewish state, but no obligation to go and live there. Until his dying day, he saw himself as a Zionist, but as the days went by he tended to also espouse the view that the Jews had a historic mission to be everywhere, in order to impart to all humanity their moral values and to act to make the world a better place to live. That included Austria too.

As a Jew, Wiesenthal was entitled to receive Israeli citizenship at any time he wished, by the country's Law of Return. But he wanted to live in Austria, not in Israel. "What would I do there," he wrote in 1979, "I whose self-imposed task in life has been to hunt down Nazi murderers?" In Vienna his very presence was "a constant irritant" for the Nazis, he asserted, and that was a good thing.[56]

6.

"That's How I Became a Stamp Collector"

I. The Big Scoop

One night in September 1947, Wiesenthal was woken by fists pounding on the door of his home. Two former partisan fighters had come to tell him that they had discovered Eichmann's hiding place. The men were living in the large displaced persons' camp at Admont, and while waiting for the chance to immigrate to Palestine they were making a living by dealing on the black market. It was the week before Yom Kippur—the Day of Atonement—and the observant among the refugees needed chickens for the *kapparot* ritual, in which sins are symbolically transferred to a live fowl. At the time there was still a general shortage of food in Austria and chickens were hard to get. The egg market was still subject to controls and farmers feared they would be fined if they were caught selling chickens.

The farmers directed the refugees to a large farm on a mountain slope near the town of Gaishorn am See, but warned them that the owner had been a top Nazi official and he hated Jews. The refugees immediately thought it might be Eichmann. The man had two thousand birds, he hated Jews, why shouldn't it be him? "We were all obsessed with Eichmann," Wiesenthal wrote.

In the morning, the three men traveled to Gaishorn am See and went to the local police station. Wiesenthal left a colorful description of the scene: an ancient rural cottage, two farmers in lederhosen sitting in the hallway and chatting with a cheerful duty officer sporting a big white mustache.

He looked like a relic from the Hapsburg days, Wiesenthal wrote. The policeman got up, went to a wall map, and looked for the farm that the Jewish visitors had described. "Murer," he said, finally. "It's Murer's farm." Wiesenthal was stunned. Franz Murer was a vicious Nazi criminal, known as "the butcher of Vilna."

Wiesenthal already had a file of evidence against him. In Vilna (Vilnius), the capital of Lithuania, there had been an ancient, flourishing Jewish community before the war. Some eighty thousand of its members were murdered by the Nazis and their local collaborators. Wiesenthal submitted an official complaint to the police and the farmer Murer was arrested.[1] Gaishorn was in the British occupation zone and the British handed Murer over to the Russians because Vilna was in the Soviet Union. He was sentenced to twenty-five years in prison. Not Eichmann, but a cause for satisfaction.[2]

When he recounted his efforts to find Eichmann, Wiesenthal would create the impression that he was receiving a continuous flow of information from a number of sources, whose identity he concealed or whom he identified only by their first names: "Hans," "Stefan," "Alex," and so on. They seem to have been figments of his imagination, or perhaps composites of real people's identities. Either way, for several years he did have at least one agent, who lived in Altaussee.

In the tortuous web of Wiesenthal's relations with Austrian society, Valentin Tarra stood out as "the good Austrian." The picturesque summer resort village where so many writers and musicians had found inspiration also provided a suitable backdrop for the captivating tale of the relationship between the Holocaust refugee and the rural gendarme—as inveterate a romantic as Wiesenthal himself, and as devoted as him to the goal.

Born into a conservative Catholic family, the son of a carpenter, Tarra had intended to become a merchant. In days to come he would recall exactly how, during World War I, he had first internalized the principles of socialist humanism that guided him from then on. Tarra fought on the eastern front. One day he was in an occupied Russian village and he saw a man crossing the street. He lifted his rifle and was about to shoot the man when a fellow soldier told him, "Hold on. That Russian's also got a mother, just like we've got mothers. Imagine how your mother would feel if they told her you'd been killed." Tarra did not shoot. His friend, who was a socialist, told him that they were at the front only to serve the interests of the arms manufacturers and that they shouldn't really be there at all. Tarra was persuaded, and that is how he too became a socialist.

He was wounded, taken to the rear, returned to the front, and wounded again. The army surgeons wanted to amputate his leg, but a physician in Vienna managed to save the limb. Tarra remembered that the doctor was a Jew. No longer fit for combat, he joined the local gendarmerie. His commander was a well-known anti-Nazi, as was Tarra.

From 1934 on, political tension was building in Austria, and Tarra had to arrest both right- and left-wing activists; more than once, he sent his wife to warn the left-wingers. He was twice decorated with gold medals, principally for his activities against the Nazis. He was promoted and became a commander. The gendarmerie often used volunteers; once one of them went out with Tarra to break up a particularly violent Nazi demonstration and was killed. He was a Jewish student from Vienna, Hermann Eisler, and Tarra used to say that it was not true that the Jews were cowards, as the anti-Semites often claimed.

Austria would be annexed to the Third Reich in March 1938, but the local Nazis in Bad Aussee didn't wait for the Germans to arrive. They seized control of the government apparatus and arrested their enemy, the commander of the gendarmerie. Tarra was taken from jail to jail and for a while was imprisoned in the concentration camp at Dachau, near Munich. He managed to get out and toward the end of the war he returned to his village and joined the anti-Nazi underground.

After the war, former members of the underground told about a large salt mine that had been used for storing crates holding works of art as well as gold, jewels, and other treasures that the Nazis had pillaged all over Europe. They said they had saved the works of art from destruction at the hands of the Nazis. One piece they mentioned in particular was a jewel-studded imperial crown, and they also mistakenly believed that one of the crates contained Leonardo da Vinci's *Mona Lisa*.

The treasure of Altaussee was to ignite the imagination of many people, including Simon Wiesenthal. But the political nub of the story was this: Just as the residents of Bad Aussee and others in the vicinity had not waited for the Nazis to come and impose their regime but had established it themselves, so they prepared everything for the arrival of the Americans. Both armies were welcomed with open arms, like liberators.

Among the papers Tarra left behind were various documents indicating that he had collaborated with the U.S. Counter Intelligence Corps, an organization that Wiesenthal was also linked to for a while. Under the American occupation, Tarra's powers were broadened and he became a member of a quasi-judicial committee for "de-Nazification," whose task was to probe the conduct of certain people during the Nazi period and to determine whether they should be integrated back into society. Tarra's days as a man of authority did not last long. He had to retire in 1949, leaving him with plenty of time to keep an eye on what was happening in the village and report on it to Wiesenthal.[3]

In his bid to find Eichmann, it was only natural for Wiesenthal to connect with the anti-Nazi retiree in Altaussee, and Tarra put himself at his disposal. The house that Veronika Liebl-Eichmann rented on a mountain slope could be seen from a nearby shoemaker's workshop, where Tarra spent quite a few hours. A car arrived, Tarra wrote down the number, and it turned out that it belonged to her brother-in-law, Eichmann's brother, from the electrical goods store in Linz. The mailman delivered a letter from abroad. Unfortunately, he forgot to check the stamp; perhaps it was from some Latin American country. Tarra briefed him to be more careful next time: it would be best if he told the woman that he collected stamps and asked for the envelope. Once Tarra hid behind a tree and watched a strange man loitering suspiciously. Tarra was sure it was Eichmann, but as he was no longer authorized to make arrests, there was nothing he could do. He looked for the police, but they were on their lunch break and by the time they got back, the man had gone. Tarra wrote everything down diligently. Almost certain it was Eichmann, he reported to Wiesenthal.

Tarra's son Walter, who later became a journalist, remembered accompanying his father on visits to Wiesenthal in Linz and recalled that Wiesenthal sometimes visited them. He brought small gifts: a few yards of cloth to please Mrs. Tarra, a bottle of Israeli wine. Over time, the two men grew to like each other. Both were intrigued by their detective work and both enjoyed barroom humor. Both hated Nazis. Wiesenthal also gave Tarra money, but judging from the tone of his letters to Wiesenthal, Tarra didn't become absorbed in the hunt because of the money or simply because he had nothing else to do with himself, but mainly because he wanted to see the war criminals punished. One of them, for whom he bore a particular hatred, was a resident of the village by the name of Wilhelm Höttl.

Höttl was one of the first members of the SS and later became an intelligence officer in the Nazi army. He was involved in the extermination of Hungarian Jewry and had a hand in the plunder of their property. Toward the end of the war, he sought and found a link to the OSS, the U.S. espionage service, and gave them information about Eichmann and the killing of Jews, among other things. But the Americans reached the conclusion that Höttl could not be relied on and they broke off the connection. After the war, Höttl went into education, establishing the secondary school in Bad Aussee, for which the municipality honored him with a memorial plaque. Tarra was furious every time he saw the ex-Nazi walking his dog, and wasted no time sharing his feelings with Wiesenthal.

The information the former gendarme supplied was not intelligence data, but more in the nature of local gossip. From the many letters Wiesenthal received from Tarra and from his own investigations, he managed to ascertain that Eichmann's wife was in touch with someone overseas, perhaps in South America.

Like the police officer Leo Maier, who had to spend New Year's Eve in Aussee in 1949, Tarra also reported that one of Eichmann's children told him that his mother had promised they would see their father soon, apparently abroad. One day Tarra reported that the woman had taken the children out of school without asking for certificates attesting to the grades they had completed. This was an important piece of information: without such certificates it would be difficult to enroll them in any other school in Europe—hence the conclusion that Liebl-Eichmann was planning to emigrate overseas.

And then she vanished. Tarra saw that the furniture and other belongings were still in the house. Her brother-in-law continued to pay the rent. They wanted people to think she was coming back. But an investigator like him would not be led astray by such patent deceptions, and on January 1, 1953, Tarra wrote to Wiesenthal: "An hour ago, I learned that in July 1952 Vera Liebl-Eichmann [Veronika's nickname] did in fact immigrate with her children to South America, where her husband is employed in a water plant."

This information appeared to be genuine, and eventually proved to be more or less accurate. Eichmann's wife had relocated to Argentina, and he was working at a hydroelectric plant near Buenos Aires. Wiesenthal did what was right: he transferred a copy of Tarra's letter to the Israeli consul in Vienna, Arye Eshel, who had been aware of Tarra's activities for a number of months.

The consul also did the right thing. He gave the information he had received from Wiesenthal to two Israeli secret service agents in Europe, Shaikeh Dan and Yonah Rosen. During the war, both of them had been among the Palestinian Jews whom the British Royal Air Force had parachuted into Eastern Europe on secret missions behind Nazi lines. Now they were busy setting up clandestine networks between Israel and Jews in Eastern Europe.

Dan and Rosen gave Eshel $200 out of the budget at their disposal to help cover the expenses of running Tarra's operations; the consul added an amount from his own funds. It was possible that Tarra was on the right track, Eshel wrote to his superiors, and requested approval to continue the investigation in a way that would be "quiet and systematic, with minimal expenses, in the next stage." Less than two months later, Wiesenthal informed the consul that Eichmann was indeed in Argentina.[4]

It was the biggest scoop of his life, the first authentic piece of information on Eichmann's hiding place. In his memoirs, Wiesenthal transferred this revelation into the realm of legend. He shrouded the story in a cloud of mystery and fantasy, incorporating details from other attempts he had made to verify various rumors and scraps of information. He would one day be required to prove that the scoop wasn't a bluff. The documentation available to researchers indicates that it was not.

2. Spy Talk

According to Wiesenthal he began suffering from insomnia in 1948, his nerves ragged from the pursuit of Nazi criminals. His doctor suggested that he take up a hobby to help him relax. "That's how I became a stamp collector," he wrote, and his nervous tension actually did ease up. In 1953, when he was on vacation in the region of Innsbruck, he heard by chance of another philatelist who wanted to sell part of his collection. Wiesenthal called him and they set up a meeting.

His host turned out to be an elderly baron who in the course of the conversation depicted himself as having been opposed to the Nazi regime, although he had served as an intelligence officer in the Wehrmacht during the war. He realized that Wiesenthal was a Jew and Wiesenthal told him about his camp experiences. The baron went to a bookshelf, got a bundle of letters tied up with string, and showed one of them to Wiesenthal.

It was from an acquaintance of his in Buenos Aires and contained three sentences that Wiesenthal wrote down as soon as he left the baron's house: "Who do you think I have already seen twice, and I also know someone who has spoken to him? That filthy swine Eichmann, who dealt with the Jews. He is living near Buenos Aires and working for a water supply company." Wiesenthal could hardly control his excitement and quickly took his leave of the baron. The same day, he reported the matter to his official Israeli contact, consul Arye Eshel.[5]

This story appeared for the first time in the book Wiesenthal published after Eichmann was captured, and it made the man in charge of Israel's security services, Isser Harel, very angry—and quite naturally so, for if in fact Wiesenthal had reported as early as 1953 that Eichmann was in Argentina, Harel would have to explain how it came to pass that it took another seven years before his agents set out for Buenos Aires to apprehend him.

Harel analyzed the story about the baron, sentence by sentence, word by word. He did his best to prove Wiesenthal was lying. Had he met the baron in "late autumn" of 1953, as he wrote in the book, or as early as May, as he wrote in a letter to the president of the World Jewish Congress, Nahum Goldmann? Wiesenthal had written to Eshel in March, ostensibly the day of his meeting with the baron. In the letter to Eshel he wrote that the letter the baron showed him from Buenos Aires was written on February 24, but to Goldmann he wrote that it was written in May.

Harel was jubilant. How was it that Wiesenthal never asked the baron who had written the letter from Argentina that mentioned Eichmann? How was it that Wiesenthal's curiosity never led him to pay another visit to the baron? "If true, this whole affair would have been Wiesenthal's worst blunder in the entire history of his hunt for Eichmann, a blunder for which there could be no atoning," Harel argued.[6] Seemingly a curious failure indeed, but the true story is more complicated.

In his books, Wiesenthal never gave the baron's name and in his letter to Eshel he identified him only as "M," but in the letter to Goldmann he did give the name, and added some details about the man. He was Baron Heinrich Mast, who had been a German intelligence officer and also worked for the Americans after the war. In his letter to Eshel, Wiesenthal said that he knew him well, and in fact he had described a meeting with him a year before, in a letter to one of his Israeli friends.

Someone, Wiesenthal was never certain who, had spread a rumor that he and Mast were working as spies for Poland and Czechoslovakia.

According to Wiesenthal, Mast came to his office and said that he was giving information to the organization run by Reinhard Gehlen, a former Wehrmacht general who was working for American intelligence.[7] Contrary to what Wiesenthal said in his memoirs, therefore, his contacts with Mast did not result from a chance encounter between stamp collectors.

This episode illustrates the kind of people Wiesenthal mixed with in Linz: shadowy figures, adventurers, all of whom had something to hide. Scheming intriguers, secret agents—at least in their own soaring imaginations—they met in the same cafés, drank in the same bars, everyone gossiping about everyone else and spying on everyone else. They acted more like dreamers and amateurs than professional espionage agents.

Leo Maier, Wiesenthal's friend in the Linz police, once told him about a network of suppliers of counterfeit documents that was helping Nazi criminals create new identities and escape overseas. Maier said they operated from a certain café in Linz. Wiesenthal went there but never observed anything untoward. Soon afterward, the police raided the establishment and detained a man who was carrying a quantity of forged documents. His name was Josef Urban, and he had been one of Eichmann's top aides in Budapest. Wiesenthal said that he had been allowed to attend Urban's interrogation, and he had asserted that one of his agents in the Hungarian capital had been Rezso Kastner, the Jewish community leader now living in Israel. Wiesenthal wrote to Kastner and asked for more information, but did not receive a reply.[8]

Two days after Urban's arrest, American agents came to the Linz police station, took him away with them, and then released him. One of the Americans told the Austrians that Urban ran a network of agents supplying information about what was happening in the Soviet Union. Maier saw him almost every day around the city, despite his past as a Nazi criminal and his role in the distribution of forged documents to help other Nazis escape justice. This disturbed the policeman and he began checking into the sources of Urban's information.

What emerged was that Urban had set up a garbage-collection operation in Austria's Soviet zone. His workers concentrated on gathering discarded paper, and it was brought to an apartment in Linz, where it was examined. If, for example, a letter was found from a woman telling her husband about her job at a new tractor plant, Urban would tell his American handlers that his "local agents" had reported on the opening of a new factory for the production of tanks. The Americans paid him in dollars. Maier never revealed precisely how he had gotten onto this story, but remarked only that he had reported his findings to his superior, who had smiled under his mustache and decided not to tell the Americans about it.[9]

Wiesenthal fit into this atmosphere of intrigue as if it were designed especially to satisfy his excessive appetite for secretive machinations. Once he even found himself caught up in an affair involving two Jewish soldiers in the U.S. Army who were accused of spying for the Soviet Union. The suspects, Curt Ponger and his brother-in-law, Otto Verber, were well-known to Wiesenthal. Ponger, who had served as an investigator for the prosecution in the Nuremberg trials, helped Wiesenthal gather information about Eichmann, and in 1948 he took down a sworn statement from Wiesenthal outlining his life story, apparently a prerequisite to Wiesenthal's being recruited to work with the CIA. The two men were friends and planned joint business ventures, including the publication of a book and the export of wooden prefabs to Israel to house the new immigrants.[10]

Among those questioned in the case was Wilhelm Höttl, the man with the dog who had infuriated Valentin Tarra in Altaussee. He told the CIA that Ponger had contacted him some time before and told him that the Joint "or some other international Jewish organization" had put a prize of $100,000 on Eichmann's head. Höttl got the impression that Ponger was acting on behalf of Israel and refused to cooperate.[11]

According to one CIA report, Wiesenthal offered a prize of 100,000 Austrian schillings for information leading to the capture of Eichmann. He apparently knew Höttl, although he denied it. In the early 1960s an article about Höttl implying that he had worked for Wiesenthal appeared in the German weekly magazine *Stern*. Wiesenthal sued for libel, claiming he did not even know Höttl, and won. However, in a taped conversation Wiesenthal told his biographer, Hella Pick, that he did in fact know him.[12]

Höttl himself also knew Baron Heinrich Mast, and Mast knew Ponger. When Mast learned about the arrest of Ponger and his brother-in-law he wrote to Höttl: "I certainly got the impression that they might be doing a little work for the Israeli intelligence service."

In 1955, the CIA filed away a progress report from an unnamed source who had been invited to take part in an attempt to capture "one Adolf

Eichmann," a notorious war criminal, and to hand him over to Israel. According to the report, Eichmann had been located, apprehended, and handed to Wiesenthal, who chartered a plane to take him to Israel. It was a sophisticated operation. The plane was given a destination somewhere in the Middle East but dropped Eichmann in Israel before going on to its declared destination without revealing that it had landed in Israel first. The source is quoted in the report as saying that "the crew received a considerable sum of money to maintain silence."

Up to this point, the CIA report was written in the past tense and from then on in the conditional. Israel would announce that Eichmann had been discovered as an officer in one of the Arab armies and six months later it would announce that he had been taken prisoner. This would disguise the fact that he had been kidnapped in Europe. The unidentified informant said he had been paid for his part in the operation and that Wiesenthal had promised him a generous bonus as well.

It took almost two months before someone in the CIA noticed the flaws in the report, and then the anonymous source is quoted as asking to straighten out the incorrect impression arising from his earlier statements by clarifying that this was not an operation that had been carried out, but a plan for a future operation.[13] Against the background of this fantastic and complex network of relationships, Mast may have had some reason to disclose to Wiesenthal that Eichmann was in Argentina.

The fact is that on March 24, 1953, Wiesenthal wrote to the Israeli consul Eshel that Eichmann was living near Buenos Aires and maintaining contacts with some members of the German community in the city. This also confirmed what Valentin Tarra had reported, Wiesenthal remarked. Four weeks later, Wiesenthal again wrote to Eshel: he had learned that in a raid on a neo-Nazi group in Germany correspondence with Eichmann had been seized that also indicated that Eichmann was in Argentina.[14]

From this point on, the Israeli authorities should have known that Eichmann was living in Argentina. But as Wiesenthal would later be astonished to learn, his letter had been filed away in an archive; no one had grasped its significance and taken it seriously. As a young state battling for its own survival, Israel was looking ahead to the future and paid almost no attention to the matter of Nazi criminals. The security services gave top priority to other tasks. Moreover, the Israelis found it difficult to confront the Holocaust. In sum, as Moshe Pearlman declared later, the search for Eichmann was only "half serious" and never went beyond the realm of amateurism: "A sniff here and a sniff there: and no more than that." Pearlman knew whereof he spoke: he had served as Israeli military spokesman, director of the government press office, and media adviser to the prime minister. Ben-Gurion himself gave Pearlman permission to publish his book on the Eichmann affair.[15] Therefore one cannot say that in 1953 Israel knew Eichmann was in Argentina: only the file knew.

3. ODESSA

Eichmann was in Altaussee in May 1945, a day or two before Wiesenthal was liberated from Mauthausen, and a few days later he was apprehended by a U.S. patrol. He was taken to a detention camp but managed to conceal his identity and escape, just after his erstwhile aide Dieter Wisliceny had given his name in testimony at Nuremberg. With the help of former SS comrades, Eichmann succeeded in hiding at first in southern and then in northern Germany. He worked as a woodchopper and he raised chickens. In the early 1950s he sneaked across the border into Italy. A Franciscan monk in Genoa gave him a passport under the name of Ricardo Klement and an Argentinean entry visa.[16]

Many other Nazi criminals did the same, reaching lands of refuge thanks to links with Nazi friends and help from various sources, including senior Roman Catholic clergy, the governments of Argentina and other countries, various intelligence agencies, including American ones, and different individuals and groups. Some helped them in exchange for money; others because they hoped to derive some other benefit, such as enlisting them as agents; others as part of their humanitarian efforts for refugees, without knowing precisely whom they were assisting. There were also those who helped the criminals knowingly, out of their identification with Nazi ideology.

It is a very complicated tale, and one shrouded in mystery. Over the years, there have been attempts to unravel and shed light on it, but the whole truth has never been bared.[17] Soon after the war ended, a rumor spread that there was a clandestine organization called ODESSA helping Nazi criminals reach countries of asylum. Wiesenthal did not invent the name, but he did a great deal to disseminate it. Almost certainly, he believed in its existence. He never revealed who told him about it, and even many years later he would refer to his source only as "Hans," describing him as a successful German industrialist who wanted to remain anonymous. He said they had met in Nuremberg, in 1948.

The details of the story differ from version to version, but the essence is the same: ODESSA was believed to be an acronym for the Organisation der ehemaligen SS-Angehörigen ("Organization of Former SS Members"), which was seeking ways for Nazi criminals to escape and helping to smuggle them to places of refuge, mainly in South America. It was said to be an underground network with worldwide connections that worked like a well-oiled machine.

Later on, "Hans" sent a messenger to Wiesenthal with more details: ODESSA had broken off from another, similar association called Die Spinne, German for "the spider," based in the Syrian embassy in Rome, where a pro-Nazi Austrian bishop called Alois Hudal was also lending a helping hand to Nazis on the run.[18] Among the leaders of ODESSA, Wiesenthal mentioned the names of certain Nazis who were to keep him occupied for many years to come, including Walter Rauff, the man who invented and supervised the operation of the gas vans, the mobile gas chambers in which Jews were poisoned by exhaust fumes.

Wiesenthal's involvement in the Briha made it easier for him to visualize how the Nazis were being smuggled across borders in the backs of trucks, hidden under piles of newspapers or other goods, like hundreds of thousands of other refugees on the move, some of them Jews on the way to Palestine.

Reconstructing the escape routes of the Nazis from Germany to Italy, he found that they used the same mountain paths that the Briha used, and the same roadside inns. On occasion the two groups found themselves in the same lodgings at the same time, the Nazis in the cellar, the Jews on the floor above them, both groups keeping utterly silent, lest they be discovered.[19]

Wiesenthal could cleave to the ODESSA story because, for one thing, the U.S. intelligence services did not rule out the possibility that there was such an organization. At the end of 1946, the Americans had heard not only that it existed but that it was named the Skorzeni Organization, after the infamous SS officer Otto Skorzeni. The U.S. agents warned themselves that the organization was perhaps using his name to bolster its prestige, and he himself was not its leader. The rumors came from various sources, but in retrospect it seems as if nobody really knew what it was all about.

In one of the American files, there is an assessment that the Nazi smugglers were Communists, as well as a list of macho code names the organization's members used, such as "Bloody Johnny" and others. One report said that the Soviet Union gave the escapees not only money but also drugs, and it contained a warning: a prostitute with syphilis working for the Communists was trying to infect American soldiers with the disease.

An American agent based in Bamberg in southern Germany wrote to his superiors that he had found no evidence of ODESSA's existence, that it could have been a product of the imagination of the person who first reported it, and that the source may even have been joking. He proposed that the case be closed.[20]

The existence of ODESSA has in fact never been proven. Nevertheless, some top Nazis did in fact disappear, and it was by no means unreasonable to assume that they were helping one another and were also receiving assistance from other sources. A few years after the death of Bishop Hudal his memoirs were published and it turned out that he had indeed established a "ratline" to help Nazis escape justice.[21] Therefore, as long as they had not been proven dead, the Nazis had to be believed alive, as was the case with Eichmann.

4. The First Hunting Season

By chance, Wiesenthal met a genealogist in 1947 and commissioned him to do a study of the Fehringer family. The aim was to find "Tony the blond," who had been the commander of his work gang in the Płaszów camp. Wiesenthal devoted a considerable amount of time to looking for Nazis who had mistreated him personally, including those who had been active in Buczacz and Lvov.

It turned out that there were several Fehringers in the area of Linz, and one of them was twenty-four and fit Tony's description. Wiesenthal wrote that he arranged for him to be photographed secretly, and that he made a positive identification from the picture. Fehringer was arrested, tried, and sentenced to seven years' imprisonment; he died in prison three years later.[22]

Tuvia Friedman, who had established the first documentation center in Vienna, wrote to the directorate of Yad Vashem that by the end of 1952 Wiesenthal had found hundreds of war criminals and caused them to be prosecuted. In a letter to Friedman many years later, Wiesenthal said that the number was about two hundred.[23] The two men were in touch on an almost daily basis. Among other things, they sought out Jewish collaborators with the Nazis: Judenrat members.[24] In 1947, Friedman wrote more than eighty letters to Wiesenthal, and Wiesenthal wrote some one hundred to Friedman. They adhered to a formal, matter-of-fact style, mostly in German, sometimes in Polish, always on official letterhead, always ending with *"Mit Zionsgruss,"* with Zion's greetings. The content hardly ever deviated from a single subject: they exchanged testimony by survivors and information about suspected Nazi criminals and asked each other to investigate or gather evidence on cases they were working on.

Friedman worked with four or five assistants and Wiesenthal was helped by two or three volunteers, but both did most of the work themselves. Apparently it wasn't very difficult to get evidence—quite often people came to them of their own accord. One particularly brutal guard in the Gusen II concentration camp, known as "Hansl," used to enjoy waking the prisoners, exhausted from their day's labors, in the middle of the night and tormenting, beating, and killing them. Two survivors of the camp discovered in May 1946 that he was working in the kitchen of the Post Hotel in Bad Hall in Upper Austria and immediately informed Wiesenthal. He conveyed their evidence to the police and notified Friedman.[25] That year, the two exchanged the names of some 250 suspects. Friedman would later report that his center had located about sixty Nazi criminals and some of them had been prosecuted in Austria or handed over to the Soviets, like Murer.[26]

At that time, Wiesenthal already knew the names of some of the most vicious Nazi criminals, including Franz Stangl, commander of the Treblinka death camp, and Dr. Josef Mengele, the physician known for the horrifying experiments he carried out on inmates in Auschwitz. Mengele's name was well-known. About a year after the war, the Austrian Jewish community newspaper reported that he had been arrested and called for witnesses against him to come forward. This report was not correct; the American army had indeed arrested Mengele but failed to identify him and let him go after a few weeks in custody, in the summer of 1945.[27]

Stangl was not so famous. The first time Wiesenthal came across his name was in 1948, when he was going over a list of SS officers who had been decorated. A German journalist back from a trip to the Arab countries informed him that Stangl was living in Damascus.[28] Wiesenthal was also very eager to catch Martin Bormann, Hitler's closest associate.

Meanwhile, Wiesenthal was developing working relationships with the prosecution authorities in Austria and West Germany, and he also took the initiative in turning to the "people's courts" that were functioning in Austria.[29] They were established when Austria's provisional government decided to outlaw Nazism three days after the liberation of Mauthausen, on May 8, 1945. Several weeks later, a special law for this purpose was enacted.

The trials of war criminals engendered sharp discussions about the limits of justice. "I realize that the crimes of the Nazis cannot be punished, that every sentence can only be symbolic because these crimes were so monstrous that they cannot be addressed by any penal code," said Wiesenthal. Unlike Israel's Nazis and Nazi Collaborators (Punishment) Law of 1950, the legislation in Austria and Germany did not recognize the unique nature of Nazi crimes and handled them as regular criminal offenses, trying the perpetrators under the standard laws of evidence. Wiesenthal therefore considered the testimony against war criminals to be more important than the punishment meted out to them. "We need trials as historical lessons and warnings for the future murderers," he asserted later.[30]

But two and a half years after the war, Wiesenthal was in the throes of deep frustration. He went from prosecutor to prosecutor, from one investigating magistrate to another, but no one wanted to handle the subject and in the meantime the refugees had left and scattered to the four corners of the earth, and from year to year it became harder to take their testimony.[31]

The figures justify his frustration. Austria and Germany opened about a quarter of a million files against suspects but only some 10 percent developed into indictments and less than half of those ended in convictions. The great majority of those convicted were sentenced to short jail terms; several dozen death sentences—most of which were never carried out—and some life terms were lost in the sea of closed cases, acquittals, commutations of sentences, and pardons.[32]

Wiesenthal was also bitterly disappointed by the Allied occupation forces; their courts sentenced several hundred Nazi war criminals to death, but their activities were halted shortly after the war. While he was working with the Americans, Wiesenthal took part in preparations for trials held at the former concentration camp at Dachau, including those of the criminals from the Mauthausen camp. By his reckoning, two thousand of them were investigated, but only two hundred were prosecuted. Over half of these were acquitted for lack of evidence and witnesses. Over the years most of those who were convicted were released before their terms were up, because the Cold War caused Americans to lose interest in dispensing justice to Nazi war criminals. Already in 1951 a number of sentences, including death sentences, were commuted, pardons awarded, and criminals freed.[33] The Americans wanted to bolster their standing in West Germany, and they also employed not a few Nazis within their own ranks.

A man by the name of Dr. Karl Joseph Fischer, whom Wiesenthal identified as having been a doctor at Auschwitz and two other camps, was located and arrested, but he was let go for some reason. Wiesenthal wrote to his longtime supporter Silberschein that apparently someone had paid for Fischer's release, but he also discerned that the U.S. authorities did not seem interested in prosecuting him. When he tried to organize a demonstration on this matter, the Americans told him to let it drop. Wiesenthal sent a letter of protest to the Austrian minister of justice. The Americans also handed out many immigration visas to war criminals from Russia, Ukraine, and the Baltic states; Wiesenthal protested both to the authorities and in the press.[34]

The British did even less. "The dumbest Nazis were those who committed suicide after the fall of the Third Reich," said Wiesenthal. Even he, an opponent of acts of vengeance, identified at that time with the widespread feeling that it would have been better simply to liquidate the Nazis straight after the liberation. "Unfortunately, there is a great deal of truth to that notion," he wrote.[35]

The formal connection between Wiesenthal and the American occupation authorities lasted less than two years, and the spirit in which it ended was apparently not good. The front-line troops and officers who had defeated the Nazis and liberated the camps had gone home, and those who replaced them did not show the same degree of understanding for the refugees. Wiesenthal had the impression that instead of looking for Nazi criminals they were taking in the scenery and spending time with the local girls.

A U.S. intelligence report on Wiesenthal's view of the Americans, dated July 1955, said he looked upon them as "children playing at world politics" and he believed that "fate has given them immense power, but the Americans are hardly in a position to use it logically . . . one cannot take the Americans any too seriously for they are as changeable as weathercocks." The report also said that Wiesenthal "charged the Americans in their policies in Germany and Austria . . . with being guided to a great extent by biased reports fed to them by German informants."

According to Wiesenthal, one of the Americans once asked him why he didn't immigrate to the United States. "You can make a career with us," the man said. "Red and green lights rule our streets, but the Jews run everything else." Wiesenthal was offended, and he said that this is what made him sever his ties to the Americans.[36] Nonetheless, deep in his heart, he continued to admire them.

The truth is that Wiesenthal's frustration was so profound because it was not only the Americans, British, Germans, and Austrians who were neglecting the pursuit of the Nazi criminals, but even the institutions of the Jewish people: "It seems that we were asleep during the first years after the war," he asserted. "We were busy with all kinds of things, except finding the war criminals; for that, the Jews didn't have enough money." Nine out of ten of them got away, he estimated, and added: "One day, we'll have to provide an alibi for this."[37]

The World Jewish Congress (WJC) was among the organizations that failed to do anything, and one of its officials in Austria, Oskar Karbach, explained to Wiesenthal that there were political reasons for this. The world needed Austria as a neutral meeting place between the East and West, he said, and it was not possible to operate international organizations, including those of the United Nations, against a background of lurid trials of monstrous Nazi war criminals.

Karbach did not say it in so many words, but as a neutral capital, Vienna was an ideal city for spies from every country. They all needed such a place. "I shouldn't wonder," he wrote, "if one day some historian discovers that the Austrians received an explicit order not to take the prosecution of war criminals too seriously." Wiesenthal surely knew more about this than he did, he added.[38]

5. The Blunder

After he informed Eshel that Eichmann was in Argentina, Wiesenthal was frantic with excitement and sure that Israel would act immediately. He imagined someone coming to ask him for the address of his informant. He would go back to the baron, who would not refuse to help, and would perhaps even give him a letter of recommendation. Someone would start keeping an eye on Eichmann without delay, either an agent from Israel or a local Jew, perhaps in coordination with the WJC. Now Wiesenthal felt that he had done his bit; he knew he could not continue hunting Eichmann down on his own. The task at hand required governmental action. But a whole year went by, and Wiesenthal heard nothing.

In March 1954, Eshel came to Linz and told Wiesenthal that the president of the WJC, Nahum Goldmann, wanted a report on the status of the search for Eichmann. Goldmann had asked for the consul's assistance a few months earlier, saying that he was acting in response to a request from American intelligence. Eshel said he would speak to Wiesenthal but neglected to do so and received a written scolding from Goldmann, who reminded him about the matter, saying that "the American Intelligence Service is very much interested in any information you could give them."

Wiesenthal hurriedly summed up everything he knew about Eichmann. Goldmann was a highly influential individual; until then, Wiesenthal had not had direct contact with anyone this important. Feeling the burden of the responsibility placed on him, Wiesenthal chose cautious language: "I cannot, of course, guarantee one hundred percent that Eichmann is indeed in Argentina, or that he was there in 1953, but all of the indications convinced me that this is the case."[39]

The interest in Eichmann's whereabouts revealed by the CIA did not exactly reflect a sudden urge to see justice done; rather, it arose from the realms of politics and the media. Wiesenthal also had an indirect role in engendering it by espousing the idea that Eichmann had been in close touch with the Palestinian mufti, Haj Amin al-Husseini. The WJC gave the link between the two as one of the reasons for its proposal that Eichmann be tried at Nuremberg.

Meanwhile, a theory had crystallized that Nazi war criminals were finding refuge in Arab countries so they could carry on from there what they had begun at Auschwitz. Not everything that was published on this matter was accurate. At least one report was fabricated, as Wiesenthal disclosed, with a wink, to one of his acquaintances: "The report that Eichmann is in Cairo was snatched out of thin air," he wrote, and recounted how he begat this canard: He was sitting with an old friend, a correspondent for United Press International, and the two decided that the time had come "to lump the Arabs together with a suitable ally." The two came up with a story saying that Eichmann had called his family from Cairo. Wiesenthal recounted with glee how the report had snowballed from Radio Austria to the Israeli media and from there, via another news agency, spread everywhere from Berlin to Moscow. "I believe that I have served the Jewish cause with this, propaganda-wise," he boasted.[40]

In the summer of 1953, another item of this type was published, saying that Eichmann had been seen in the Damascus region, in the company of the ex-mufti. It caught the attention of Rabbi Abraham Kalmanowitz, the

president and dean of the Hasidic Mir yeshiva in Brooklyn, who immediately wrote an emotional letter to then president Dwight Eisenhower
requesting that steps be taken to arrest Eichmann. The yeshiva of Mir,
a small town in eastern Poland, had been considered one of the most
important centers of Jewish learning in Eastern Europe for over a century,
and Kalmanowitz had the status of an exalted Torah scholar and leader. In
1940 he had reached New York, and from there he participated in a successful effort to get the six hundred students of the yeshiva out of harm's
way into safe havens in Japan and China. After the war he oversaw their
immigration to the United States, and the yeshiva began functioning again
in Brooklyn.[41]

Kalmanowitz also wrote to the State Department, and he received one
answer to both appeals: "The United States has of course no power to
arrest an individual in another country. In any event it is by no means clear
what country Eichmann is now in or what he may be doing. Under these
circumstances it is not possible for this Government to make any represen-
tations to any other government concerning his activities, or to take any
other action in the matter."[42]

Rabbi Kalmanowitz had no intention of making do with this reply, and
the result was a thick file of letters to the State Department. "This man is
a terrible threat to all nations who fight to achieve a true democracy," he
wrote to the official who had signed the first reply.[43] But the main argument was that by teaming up with the Arabs Eichmann was threatening
the well-being of Israel.

Kalmanowitz did what he knew how to do: he mobilized a number
of senators and congressmen and got them to lobby the director of the
CIA, Allen Dulles. After a stream of requests in writing and over the
telephone, Kalmanowitz was invited to a meeting with a CIA official.
The rabbi spoke from the bottom of his heart, warning of another Holocaust; the officials responded with cold formality. Apparently it was all
one big nuisance for them, but they were careful not to insult the rabbi.

Nahum Goldmann could have become involved in this episode through
Kalmanowitz or one of the politicians the rabbi had mobilized. But apparently he too saw it as a bother. In any event, Goldmann would have been
dubious about Kalmanowitz's claim that Eichmann was the driving force
behind Arab aggression against Israel. Nonetheless, he does seem to have
been impressed by the connection Kalmanowitz had established with the
CIA, and this was why he asked Eshel to update him.

When Goldmann received Wiesenthal's report he passed it on to Kalmanowitz, and the next day he also shared with him information that he had received from Berlin to the effect that Eichmann was in Syria. Goldmann never believed that this information was particularly accurate, but he asked Kalmanowitz to convey it to the proper authorities in Washington. Kalmanowitz sent it all to Dulles, and in his accompanying letter he mentioned only Syria, and not Argentina. In a letter to the State Department, he mentioned both countries.[44]

From this point on, then, the United States also "knew" that Eichmann was in Argentina, as Wiesenthal's letter was now in its possession. But in Washington, just as in Tel Aviv, the knowledge was filed away, and no action was taken. There is no basis for accusations that the Americans intentionally refrained from doing anything to capture Eichmann; like the Israelis, they had other priorities.

Wiesenthal knew nothing about all this. The request for information from one of the most prominent leaders of world Jewry via the Israeli consul aroused a great hope in his heart: soon things would at last begin to move, and it would be only a matter of days before Eichmann was captured. But two weeks went by and there was no answer from New York. Wiesenthal wondered to himself if his letter, or the reply to it, had not gone astray. Four weeks went by and New York was still silent. Wiesenthal still entertained the hope that Goldmann would send some agent who would go with him to see the baron and get the address of the informant in Buenos Aires.

Again and again Wiesenthal contacted Eshel, who repeatedly advised him to be patient. "For nine years, I had toiled at locating Eichmann," he would write later. "I acted of my own accord, without much help from the outside. Now that Dr. Goldmann began showing an interest in my activities and in capturing Eichmann, I put at his disposal all of the material that I had obtained through painstaking and nerve-wracking labor throughout all of those years."

His anger grew, and knew no bounds. "I made mistakes, even stupid blunders, I failed more than once," he wrote. "But eventually I succeeded! I knew where Eichmann was and where he was working. I reached a man who knew someone who had seen him in the flesh and who knew a man who had even spoken to him. This is the time for immediate action that has a real chance—and, lo and behold, there's no one listening."[45]

One can only guess what Wiesenthal would have said if he knew how the CIA treated his letter to Goldmann. It was a six-page document in German, in which Wiesenthal summed up Eichmann's life story, recounted the various attempts he had made to catch him, and, on the next-to-last page, explained the likelihood that he was in Argentina. He attached a copy of the file he had assembled, which contained many documents on Eichmann, also in German. There is no evidence today in the CIA archives of this material ever being translated into English, so there are good reasons to accept the hypothesis suggested later by the head of the U.S. Office of Special Investigations, Eli Rosenbaum, that no one in the CIA ever read Wiesenthal's letter to Goldmann. Isser Harel would also claim later that he never saw a copy of the letter.[46]

In September 1954, a rumor spread that an Israeli "revenge squad" had assassinated Eichmann, originating probably in an incorrect item that appeared in the Israeli daily *Ha'aretz*. Wiesenthal hurriedly informed Goldmann that it wasn't true.[47] He was very tense. In the meantime he had begun to learn Spanish and acquired a map of Argentina, and he was gathering all the news he could about the country: he called it his "Argentinean mania."

Some months before, he had received a letter from a rabbi in New York whom he did not know, and whose name meant nothing to him. Kalmanowitz wrote that he had received Wiesenthal's report from Goldmann and wanted to know Eichmann's exact address in Argentina, as if this were some minor detail that Wiesenthal had somehow forgotten to mention. Wiesenthal replied that it was possible to send someone to Buenos Aires to find out, and that it would not cost more than $500, perhaps less. Kalmanowitz responded that he would first have to get some concrete information from Wiesenthal. And so they corresponded, back and forth, until the autumn of 1954. Aside from the rabbi, nobody contacted Wiesenthal, and he said he understood from this that once again no one was looking for Eichmann. "I was shocked to the depths of my soul," he wrote, and he never forgave Nahum Goldmann.[48]

If nothing else, curiosity could (and perhaps should) have motivated Wiesenthal to have another talk with Baron Mast. As long as he was waiting for the State of Israel or the WJC to take action of their own accord, or to at least give him instructions on how to proceed, he refrained from doing anything. Once he saw the baron in a café, but he didn't go up to him. Years later he called at his home, only to be told that, regrettably, the baron had passed away.

In a draft recounting his role in the capture of Eichmann, Wiesenthal wrote that Goldmann's silence had made him decide to close down his documentation center and call a halt to his efforts to find Nazi criminals. "From my point of view, the matter was closed," he declared.[49]

About two years after closing the center, Wiesenthal packed his archive into two crates and dispatched them to the Yad Vashem Archive in Jerusalem. They contained hundreds of files, tens of thousands of documents, including a card index with the names of three thousand survivors, and a number of books. He knew the people at Yad Vashem and had good relations with them. He hoped to get money for the archive, and to this end he enlisted Tuvia Friedman, who had already settled in Israel and was on the staff of Yad Vashem.

Friedman faithfully carried out his mission. He estimated that Wiesenthal's archive was worth $5,000, but Wiesenthal thought it was worth less. If he had been able to afford it, he would have parted with his papers for nothing, he wrote, and asked for $2,400, including packing and shipping expenses. Yad Vashem offered $2,000. Friedman wanted to sell his own documents to the Jewish community in Vienna and asked Wiesenthal to help him make the deal. He was not satisfied with the result and the two men quarreled.

A few days after he sent his archive to Jerusalem, Wiesenthal received a letter from Nehemia Robinson, a WJC official, asking for his opinion of Friedman's reliability; Friedman had apparently applied for a job. Wiesenthal replied that Friedman had dedicated himself to the search for Nazi criminals and that "in spite of his limited intelligence" he had worked with enthusiasm and diligence "in order to make up for the lack." But one day Wiesenthal was warned not to nurture his relationship with Friedman anymore. An Israeli diplomat in Vienna and a security officer at the consulate told him that Friedman was maintaining close contact with the Soviets in the Austrian capital. Wiesenthal investigated and discovered that toward the end of the war Friedman had served in the Polish department of the Soviet secret police, the NKVD.

Wiesenthal suggested the possibility that "while he was in Vienna, Friedman was subjected to Russian blackmail and pressured to perform all kinds of services for them." It was a fact, Wiesenthal wrote, that although Friedman was a refugee, he was a frequent caller at the Polish legation in Vienna and had, apparently without any apprehension, also entered the Soviet occupation zone several times.

According to Wiesenthal, he did not tell Friedman about the Israeli warning to keep his distance. Friedman would occasionally turn to him for information on war criminals, and Wiesenthal tried to help him as much as he could. At the end of his letter to Robinson, Wiesenthal mentioned that he had asked the Claims Conference (the body set up by Jewish organizations to handle restitution from Germany) for assistance with his research on the postal links in the ghettos. "Perhaps you don't know, but I am an expert in philately," he wrote.[50]

When he closed his documentation center in Linz, Wiesenthal said, he prepared precise statistics, according to which the information he had collected in his nearly eight years of work had led to the investigation and arrest of almost eight hundred war criminals.[51]

7.

"I Hope You're Not Coming to See Me"

I. The Secrets of the Lake

When other children asked Paulinka Wiesenthal what her father did, she felt embarrassed because she herself didn't really know, so she used to say he was a journalist.[1] This was not true, but his work with American intelligence, his involvement in the arrests of Nazi war criminals, his activities among the refugees, and his links with the authorities did in fact give him a quite natural connection with the world of journalism.

He was a curious man, an inquirer, and a hard worker blessed with an excellent memory, and he loved knowing more than others. He liked telling stories, and surprising his listeners. He liked easygoing, noncommittal relationships with new acquaintances and more than once he persuaded journalists to carry out all kinds of investigative detective work for him. Occasionally he published articles himself. He had a special liking for mysteries and, like many others, he was captivated by rumors about treasure that the Nazis had sunk in Lake Toplitz, not far from Altaussee.

This small, enchanting body of water lies almost hidden among towering snowy cliffs, its silvery, opaque surface radiating tranquillity and reflecting the sky and the mountain slopes and the foliage along its shores in myriad shades of blue and gray and green. Anyone looking at the lake can only surmise what secrets lie hidden in its depths. Wiesenthal was one of the first people to tackle the subject of the treasure, while he was still working for American intelligence.

Various documents, fragments of evidence, and, mainly, waves of rumors gave birth to the notion that shortly before their defeat, the Nazis

had taken steps to ensure their survival after the war, their flight to countries of asylum, and perhaps even a return to power one day. According to
Wiesenthal, he saw and copied, but unfortunately did not keep, a document that summed up a discussion of the matter.[2] He was referring to the
minutes of a meeting of Nazi leaders held in the Maison Rouge Hotel in
Strasbourg, France, in August 1944.

The working assumption of the participants was that Germany was
facing defeat, and it was therefore necessary to ensure that funds would
be available to allow the heads of the Nazi regime to flee to safe havens
through the ODESSA organization as well as other channels. In days
to come, doubts arose as to whether such a meeting actually took place,
just as there is no certainty that the Nazis actually used any organization
like ODESSA to help them escape. But the minutes that Wiesenthal said
he saw do exist: even General Dwight D. Eisenhower, the supreme commander of the Allied forces in Europe and later president of the United
States, thought they were interesting.[3]

It is possible that the document was a forgery, but Wiesenthal could not
have known that. Just as he believed in the existence of a central organization that smuggled Nazis out of Europe, he believed in the Strasbourg
plan to finance their escape. In August 1946, he published an article in a
local newspaper in which he reported on the Nazi escape fund. He did
so, he asserted, at the initiative of his superiors in the OSS, who hoped
that publication of the article would provoke comments by readers that
would help in the investigation. This did indeed happen, he related, but
the Americans took the responses from the newspaper offices and he himself never saw them.[4]

It is not clear to what extent the article stimulated the rumors about the
treasure, but at some stage everybody "knew" that as their defeat approached,
the Nazis had sunk twenty crates of gold, jewelry, and banknotes worth
many millions in Lake Toplitz. Perhaps Wiesenthal hoped the crates also
contained secret documents that were of special interest to him. Among
the sources from whom he heard about the treasure was his acquaintance
Valentin Tarra, the retired policeman from Altaussee. The two fantasized
about finding the crates. Meanwhile, Wiesenthal sold a series of articles on
the subject to *Aufbau*, the German-language Jewish newspaper in New York.[5]

The Nazi treasure of Lake Toplitz attracted adventurers from all over
the world and was the subject of innumerable articles in the world press,
including reports that printing blocks for forging counterfeit dollars were
also to be found on the lake bed. Mysterious divers and parachutists

who landed and then vanished starred in these stories, as did all kinds of inquisitive types who fell off the cliffs to their deaths before they could solve the mystery of the lake.[6]

Wiesenthal linked the lake treasure to several cases of robbery, including one in which a French occupation court in the city of Innsbruck meted out prison sentences to some farmers who had stumbled across nine crates containing gold and precious stones that had been hidden in a forest, and had not reported the find to the authorities. The trove was confiscated. Wiesenthal reported on this to Silberschein and suggested that he demand the treasure be handed over to a Jewish organization, as it was reasonable to assume that it was looted Jewish property.[7]

Early in 1954, he reported that he had learned about a quantity of gold the Nazis had pillaged from non-Jews, and he hoped to obtain some of it as a reward for his discovery. Wiesenthal requested advice from Fanny Silberschein, who was supporting his efforts after the death of her husband in 1951. He wrote to her that seven crates of gold had been located in Switzerland, and the part belonging to Jews was negligible. He wanted to reach an agreement with the government of Switzerland assuring him a certain percentage of the treasure. He asked Mrs. Silberschein to put him in touch with a suitable attorney.[8]

A few years later, he told the Israeli ambassador in Austria, Yehezke'el Sahar, about the treasure in the lake, and Sahar replied: "I am surprised that the Austrian authorities don't take any initiative to get the crates out of the lake."[9] Wiesenthal also wrote to Yad Vashem about the matter and received a rather excited letter of thanks. The matter had been handed over to "a competent government authority," it said, probably meaning the Shin Bet security service. Wiesenthal noted that he had foolishly acted without getting anything in return.[10]

The magic lake kept its secret. In his book about the hunt for Eichmann, Wiesenthal wrote that the gold had never really sparked his imagination and that he had merely used it as a pretext for his presence in Altaussee: "Why should I not pretend that I am looking for treasure in the Altaussee district and use this as a pretext for continuing the search for Eichmann?"[11] And years later he wrote: "It may well be supposed that the real gold treasure was not sunk in Lake Toplitz at all . . . The lake may have become the focus of public interest because of the romantic nature of that theory."[12]

But Wiesenthal himself apparently did fall captive to a romance: Apart from the secrets of the lake, he tried to solve the secret of Nazi evil. This was an obsessive need that never left him alone and was never satisfied. Wiesenthal was not the only one: the desire to explain the mystery of Nazism was at the center of intellectual discourse all over the world. The journalistic impulses that motivated Wiesenthal were similar to those that led William Shirer to write *The Rise and Fall of the Third Reich*—to try to be the fly on the wall of Hitler's office, to see it all, to know it all, to relive his fall and tell the tale.

Addicted to uncovering the tiniest of details, Wiesenthal never wearied of checking their veracity, but nevertheless his own reports were often inaccurate. Sometimes he clouded them intentionally and sometimes he came out with things that quite simply had never happened, as in his articles repeating the claim that Nazis had used the bodies of Jews to manufacture soap. Later he corrected himself, but in the 1950s he really believed it was so; as was usual at that time, he tended to emphasize the monstrous aspects of Nazism.[13] His articles were printed in a local daily newspaper, in *Aufbau*, and in the newspaper of the Vienna Jewish community; some also appeared in Israel. He used a pen name, Dr. Simoni, and he also published, among others, articles analyzing events in the Arab world.[14] But his usual subject was the lessons of the Holocaust and the needs of the refugees.[15]

2. Belonging and Not Belonging

Early in the 1950s, Wiesenthal began working full-time for two international Jewish welfare organizations, ORT and the Joint Distribution Committee, and he also did jobs for HIAS, which handled the emigration of Jews.[16] By now he was a citizen of Austria, but his life remained centered on Jews and he made his living from Jewish organizations headquartered outside Austria—belonging and not belonging.

The number of displaced persons decreased in the early 1950s and most of the refugee camps closed down, but Jewish refugees were still arriving in Austria, mainly in the wake of the 1956 revolts against Communist regimes in Hungary and Poland. Most of the new refugees were housed in the Asten camp, in a suburb of Linz. Most of them did not remain in Austria, but while they were there they received assistance from ORT and the JDC.

ORT was founded in Russia in 1880 to train Jews to work in agriculture and the trades. In the refugee camps, its representatives worked on vocational training projects in cooperation with the United States government.[17]

Wiesenthal was in charge of the training projects in the Asten camp and the vicinity. His main task was to organize courses, handling enrollment and administrative control of the instructors. Several hundred refugees underwent training as radio technicians and hairdressers, cooks and mechanics, seamstresses, bookkeepers, and photographers, and in many other trades that would enable them to begin new lives and earn a livelihood for themselves.

The documents on Wiesenthal's work for ORT indicate dissatisfaction on his part; the job seems not to have really interested him. There was constant tension between him and the management of the organization. He was impatient with and contemptuous of what appeared to him to be overly strict supervision of his work. His superiors complained repeatedly that the reports he sent them, including the financial ones, were not accurate. They repeatedly returned them to him and requested additional explanations.

ORT was operating as a kind of subcontractor for the U.S. government and therefore had to be sure its reports were accurate, and its correspondence with Wiesenthal does reveal a certain pettiness and even a suspicion of wrongdoing. For his part, Wiesenthal claimed that he was not being permitted to do his job, and his superiors objected to his tone. "I have the feeling that whatever reaches you from Vienna you take as a personal attack on yourself," wrote the manager of the office in the Austrian capital, a Mrs. Goldmann.[18]

Wiesenthal hated being rebuked, especially by female secretaries. He replied with sarcastic sharpness, provoking another rebuke, this time from the director of ORT, Mr. Goldmann: "Your manner of writing was really very shocking, for after all it is the tone that makes the music." He demanded that Wiesenthal stick to the accepted etiquette in correspondence between an employee and his superior.[19] Wiesenthal was no organization man but a lone wolf, an egocentric person who did not like getting instructions from anyone.

As of 1948, Wiesenthal also worked for the JDC. This American-based organization was set up in 1914 to save the Jews of Palestine from starvation and had expanded its activities to rescue Jews in distress in many countries. The new stream of Jews from Eastern Europe required a redoubling of assistance: they had to be taken in, sometimes in the middle of the night, housed in hotels, and provided with all their needs, including medical care. They received subsistence allowances, coupons for the purchase of clothing, and assistance in solving personal problems: one person needed glasses, another one needed a prosthetic leg, another wanted to settle only in Sweden, and another needed treatment for alcoholism.[20]

The paperwork that survives from Wiesenthal's time with the JDC reflects a human drama of the kind that engaged him. In contrast to the drab administrative work that he had to endure in his position with ORT, his duties with the JDC required initiative, improvisation, human understanding, and both a degree of skepticism and compassion. Once again, as in his days of working with displaced persons, he built up a measure of influence, even of power, in deciding the fate of human beings.

He treated the refugees with both official bossiness and paternal warmth: "This letter will cause you no pleasure," he wrote to a refugee named Sonnenschein. "Since the day I met you, you have not managed with the stipend that you get from the Joint. And you know that the Joint gives you special treatment, better than the others." Sonnenschein had to acknowledge once and for all that the Joint was not to blame for his dismal situation, Wiesenthal wrote, and he continued: "I have to use harsh words so that you will get hold of yourself and accept at least some of the responsibility for your fate. I know that you have made many attempts, but they were not good. I did not want to tell you, so as not to discourage you." He recommended that the man find a partner and open a business, aided by one of the loans available to the refugees, and, "as a friend," suggested that he "at long last put a stop to your monthly wailing."[21]

Many of the problems Wiesenthal was called upon to solve sprang from the fact that some of the refugees were ultra-Orthodox Jews. Officials of the Jewish community of Innsbruck wrote to him about the distress suffered by one Bernard Frucht, a refugee from Romania who was being held in prison on suspicion of smuggling. He was an ultra-Orthodox Jew who could eat only kosher food. The Innsbruck community lacked the funds to supply his needs and asked for the Joint's help.[22] One community wanted to restore its ritual bath, another its Torah scroll: the holy lettering had faded and was no longer legible.[23]

And then there were the fifteen ultra-Orthodox men in the camp without families who couldn't manage on the allocation they were getting. Wiesenthal tried to get them to share with existing households, but this endeavor failed and he requested a special allotment for them.[24] Representatives of ultra-Orthodox welfare associations and individual philanthropists would come to the camp and distribute money to their own people; Wiesenthal regarded them as competition. When he saw them, it was difficult for him not to lose his temper, Wiesenthal wrote.[25]

Many of the refugees treated the Joint ungratefully and tried to deceive it. Meilach Cohn, who received funds from the organization, moved to Germany, where he got married. The Joint in Germany invested several thousand dollars in acquiring an apartment for him. A little while later, Cohn returned to Linz and told Wiesenthal he wanted to divorce his wife, who was not Jewish, and leave her the apartment. Wiesenthal objected. There was no reason to allow him to do what he wished with an apartment purchased by the Joint, as if it were his own property. As far as Wiesenthal knew, the marriage to the woman could have been part of a business scheme that had not worked out, and now Cohn wanted to exploit the apartment in order to compensate the woman.[26]

As part of his job, Wiesenthal also had to cope with anti-Semitic incidents and hostile articles in the press, including one piece which disclosed that the government of Israel was paying the government of Hungary several hundred dollars for each Jew who was allowed to leave. This was an arrangement that Israel had tried to keep a state secret.[27]

His work with the two Jewish welfare organizations improved the conditions of the Wiesenthals' life in Linz. Moreover, the American Jewish Committee, an organization that defended the rights of Jews all over the world, began to commission reports from him on the state of the Jews in Austria, paying him the modest sum of thirty-five dollars a month as a retainer.[28] At first, Wiesenthal and his wife and daughter had a small apartment in a working-class neighborhood in the south of the city, but even then they had a housemaid, a Catholic woman from Yugoslavia, whose son had the impression that she was working for wealthy people. During the war, mother and son had lost touch with each other and she had somehow ended up in Linz. Soon after she began working in his home, Wiesenthal managed to locate the boy and, using his connections in the Red Cross, reunite him with his mother in Linz. The boy, Helmar Sartor, later recalled that his mother did all the housework, cleaning, ironing, and cooking. He warmly remembered Wiesenthal, who, he said, had functioned as his father. Paulinka had been like a sister to him.

Wiesenthal also earned money by mediating various deals, including the return of property looted from Jews. Once a Jewish Holocaust survivor recognized a man in the street as an SS member who had robbed him in Kraków. Instead of filing a lawsuit, which would have cost both of them time and money, the Jew got the Austrian to agree to submit to Wiesenthal's arbitration. The man was involved in illegal trading with the American occupation authorities and apparently wanted the allegations not to appear on his record. Wiesenthal ruled that he must give the Jew a radio, a watch, and a golden tobacco box.[29]

Toward the end of 1950, Wiesenthal represented relatives of his wife in negotiations over the sale of a house that belonged to them in the resort town of Bad Goisern in Upper Austria. It had been confiscated by the Nazis and the owners had fled to England. After the war, the building served for a time as a hospital for concentration camp survivors. Wiesenthal negotiated its sale to the district health fund and it became a convalescent home.[30] Legal documents among his papers indicate that he also represented heirs to property who were living in Israel.[31]

All of this never made him wealthy. His books were not yet bestsellers and the occasional lecture he gave or article he wrote during that period could not have added much to his income. But the Wiesenthals led a relatively comfortable life. Toward the end of the 1950s, they began receiving monthly restitution payments from Germany, as compensation for their suffering in the camps. Wiesenthal claimed that he did not want to take this money, but his wife said they owed it to their daughter and, after all, everyone was taking it. His personal papers reveal that it took a prolonged legal battle before the Germans agreed to pay him.[32] By this time, Wiesenthal had his own car, a Citroën, according to a license in his personal papers. From time to time the family went on holidays in the resort town of Bad Ischl, taking their housemaid and her son along.[33]

3. Intrigue on Bethlehem Street

Along with his work with the refugees, his efforts to locate war criminals, and the plethora of other matters that kept him occupied in Linz, Wiesenthal also immersed himself in the affairs of the tiny Jewish community in the city. In the early 1950s it numbered some five hundred members;

by 1960 there were only 156 left. Jewish refugees staying in Linz on their way to other countries were not included in these figures.

His involvement deepened from year to year, and his influence increased. He conducted a protracted political and legal struggle aimed at giving the Holocaust refugees full membership and voting rights in community institutions, and in 1957 he was elected vice president.[34] By virtue of his position, Wiesenthal ran the day-to-day affairs of the community, whose headquarters, used for both religious and cultural activities, were in a small house in Bethlehem Street.[35] He represented the community as a spokesman, vis-à-vis both the press and the authorities. Once he advised the director of the community in Vienna to keep his press releases short. Journalists, he said, are used to copying from each other, and the less they had to work the more likely it was that the community's announcements would be published in full, as they had been worded originally.[36]

The atmosphere in the Bethlehem Street office was awful; most of Wiesenthal's time was spent on intrigues and plots. The community functionaries did everything they could to undermine and obstruct one another, hurling accusations of fraud and corruption, extortion, bribe taking, and sexual harassment.[37] They cursed and threatened and dragged one another into all kinds of inquiries and even libel suits. Rival factions tried now and again to win the Israeli diplomatic representatives in Austria over to their side.

Wiesenthal was involved in all this virtually from the day he arrived in Linz. In 1949 he fired off an angry letter to consul Kurt Lewin, accusing Lewin of discrediting him. As far as it is possible to reconstruct this little scandal, it seems that the consul had in fact attacked someone else, but this someone was a supporter of Wiesenthal and the latter therefore felt that he had been the target. "This is the first time that I am being attacked in public," Wiesenthal wrote, "and how unfortunate it is that you are doing it as the Israeli consul."[38]

The next consul dispatched a report to the Foreign Ministry in Jerusalem, describing in detail what Wiesenthal had claimed was a campaign of vilification against him organized by his rivals in the community.[39] They also badmouthed him to the heads of the JDC in the hope that he would be fired; for his part, he spoke ill of them to the district governor, Gleisner. Complaining about his rivals in the community, Wiesenthal once wrote: "You can ask yourself whether these people are criminals or idiots." But he never wanted to give up his activities there. On the contrary, he meant to get rid of his rivals—"the crooks"—he wrote.[40]

As the spokesman for the community, Wiesenthal tended to express his positions more emphatically than the other leaders. He demanded an open campaign against manifestations of anti-Semitism, while his colleagues tended to keep quiet about the subject. They claimed that he was harming the Jews, even endangering them, while he accused them of groveling.

Wiesenthal alleged that the heads of the community had sold the authorities some of its properties, including parts of the Jewish cemetery, at prices that were too low and had even agreed to give up the demand for compensation for the victims of the Nazis, all because they supported the Social Democratic Party. He also charged that they were employing a Communist as a cantor.[41] His rivals accused him of being corrupt, among other things, for his attempt to build a luxurious home for the use of the vice president and his family. He submitted a detailed plan for the construction of the residence, but it was rejected.[42]

The atmosphere of intrigue in Bethlehem Street combined with other elements that could have made Wiesenthal sick of his life in Austria, but as vice president of the community he had access to government leaders. From time to time, he had meetings with ministers. He was flattered by these connections, which deepened his feeling and that of his acquaintances that he had a special status in Austria.

As early as 1946, he received a letter from the office of the chancellor containing a sharp protest against a proposal that the concentration camp survivors turn to the United Nations and demand that Austrian independence should not be restored, because the country was still full of Nazis. This had not been Wiesenthal's idea, and he was actually being asked what could be done to oppose it. Even at that point officials in the office of the Austrian prime minister appear to have seen Wiesenthal as someone worth consulting.[43]

Wiesenthal hoped to persuade the government to pay restitution to victims of the Nazis, as the Germans were doing. It was a complicated question, from both the legal and the political points of view. In a letter to Chancellor Leopold Figl, he wrote: "It is self-evident to us that Austria is not responsible for the actions of the Third Reich."[44] He thereby in fact recognized Austria's denial of its role in the crimes of the Nazis. However, he did believe that Austria must compensate those former concentration camp inmates who had worked as slave labor in Austrian factories. He also urged Israel to demand compensation but was disappointed: Israel's foreign minister, Moshe Sharett, explained to him that from the legal point of view, Israel had no standing in this matter. Given the negotiations between Israel and Germany over reparations to German-Jewish victims of the Nazis, Wiesenthal felt that the Jewish state was abandoning the Jews of Austria.[45]

The Israeli consul was also critical of his government's position, stating in a memorandum that read as if it were written by Wiesenthal that the Austrians were laying the blame on Germany, but some 600,000 of them had been registered members of the Nazi Party. The proportion of Austrians among the Nazi war criminals was much higher than their percentage in the population of the Reich, and many of them had been employed in the machinery of the extermination of the Jews.

Approximately one-third of Austria's Jews, some 100,000 in number, were killed, Eshel wrote. The Austrians claimed that those who survived and returned had been fully recompensed. Austria had in fact not encouraged the Jews to come back and had not arranged for the restitution of their property. The Social Democratic Party was trying to get a majority in Parliament and was therefore currying favor with the Nazis. "The socialists are betraying the principles of their movement," Eshel summed up.[46]

In November 1958 Wiesenthal took part in a meeting between the heads of the Jewish community and the chancellor, Julius Raab. On their way up the staircase to the chancellor's office, the Jewish delegation met the secretary of state and introduced themselves. "I hope you're not coming to see me," he said. It was Bruno Kreisky, a Jewish politician who was to become chancellor of Austria, and a bitter enemy of Wiesenthal.[47]

The meeting with Raab was dismal. The chancellor addressed the Jews condescendingly, and once he even raised his voice. "Nobody will tell me what to do," he thundered. The minister of finance was also at the meeting. The government had set aside a certain amount to compensate Jews living abroad; the representatives of the Jewish community wanted compensation for the Jews who were living in Austria, too. They did not demand that the sum prescribed by the government be increased, however. They only requested, almost pleaded, that part of the amount already budgeted for Jews abroad be allotted to them. Wiesenthal was disgusted. When they left the chancellor's office, he told his colleagues that they should not have tried to get for themselves money that had been allocated for other Jews. "Let them kiss my ass," replied one of the delegates.[48]

4. Jewish Criminals

Although he no longer had his archives, in the late 1950s Wiesenthal still occupied himself with war criminals. But instead of hunting for Nazis, he was now targeting Jewish collaborators. Ironically, the chances of getting them punished were now greater than the chances of securing the conviction of Nazi war criminals.

A few weeks before the first judgments were handed down by the war crimes tribunal at Nuremberg, the Austrian Jewish Central Committee turned to the American occupation authorities and asked for permission to try Jews who had cooperated with the Nazis, including members of the "Jewish councils" that the Nazis set up in each area under their control, members of the Jewish police units, Jews who had served as kapos in the concentration camps, and others. The committee members, including Wiesenthal, promised that the Jewish courts they wanted to set up would function in accordance with the liberal principles of justice as practiced in America. Along with permission to investigate and to try suspects, the committee also requested permission to impose penalties on the collaborators, including prison terms.[49]

The Americans permitted the refugees to set up honorary courts to conduct trials of collaborators whom the refugees identified, but the most severe sentence allowed was a communal boycott of those found guilty. The hearings were held before a bench of three volunteer judges, and the transcripts and judgments were typed in Yiddish. Several such judgments are to be found among Wiesenthal's papers.[50]

On November 7, 1947, in the Bindermichl camp, a man named Schlomo Zimmerman was found guilty and sentenced to an indefinite "lengthy term" of ostracism from the community. According to the judgment, he had been a kapo in a number of camps and had mistreated Jews and other inmates. The sentence included cancellation of his rights as a refugee and, if this was not legally possible, his transfer to another camp. In the meantime, he lost his right to vote or run in elections for the camp institutions, as well as his right to immigrate to Israel.

The latter penalty was mainly symbolic, as the refugees did not have the legal authority to bar Zimmerman from going to Israel. But it was able to publish its ruling and to preserve the testimonies of the witnesses, and that is what it decided to do.[51]

In the years that followed, Wiesenthal spent a lot of time dealing with Zimmerman, who was perhaps a symbol, perhaps a personal enemy, or perhaps both. In 1951, he heard that Zimmerman had received a U.S. immigration visa, and he protested against this to the International Refugee Organization.[52] Wiesenthal's protest apparently succeeded and Zimmerman remained in Linz. The affair grew into a drawn-out quarrel within the Jewish community because its leaders, for some reason, refrained from ostracizing Zimmerman and even allowed him to live in the community's house in Bethlehem Street.

At a public meeting held by the community, which Zimmerman attended, Wiesenthal and some other members got up and demanded that he be removed from the hall. The community leaders said that they had a letter from the Israeli consulate stating that it did not recognize the decisions of the refugee courts. Wiesenthal wrote to the consul, who denied this.[53] In 1957, Wiesenthal wrote to the West German government and requested that no restitution be paid to Zimmerman and his family.[54] Zimmerman sued him for libel. Wiesenthal represented himself with great ardor and won.[55]

The hunt for Jewish collaborators was no less important to him than the search for Nazi war criminals. One of the files that he transferred to Yad Vashem in Jerusalem contained thirty-three names and was titled "Jewish Criminals."[56] Wiesenthal tended to believe that if no Jews had cooperated with the Nazis, more Jews would have stayed alive, and he rejected the distinction between "good" and "bad" Jewish councils.[57]

This was an exceedingly sensitive subject, but it could not be avoided; for one thing, concentration camp survivors kept on bumping into Jews who had abused them in the ghettos or in the camps. After the war, they mingled with the other refugees and tried to hide among them. When David Ben-Gurion visited the displaced persons' camps, he witnessed an incident in which some of the refugees suddenly discovered a kapo in their midst and attacked him. In Ben-Gurion's words, their "eyes were blood red" and they appeared capable of killing the man. The incident shocked the leader of the Jews in Palestine; it was the first time he had come across this embarrassing aspect of the Holocaust.

Jews who collaborated with the Nazis were also discovered in Israel itself. The police were flooded with complaints, but at first there was no law under which they could be prosecuted. Filling this gap was the goal of the Nazis and Nazi Collaborators (Punishment) Law enacted by the Knesset in 1950. Several dozen people were prosecuted and convicted under its provisions, but only a few Israelis were capable of grasping the historical, judicial, and ethical complexity of the phenomenon.

Beginning in 1952, a horrendous case took center stage in Israeli politics, entailing an agonizing process of picking at the scabs of the sores left by the cooperation between some Hungarian Jewish leaders and the Nazis. One of them, Rezso Kastner, was publicly accused of working with Eichmann and abandoning hundreds of thousands of Jews to be destroyed at Auschwitz in exchange for being allowed to save a few hundred of his associates and relatives in the wake of the "blood for trucks" deal proposed by Eichmann.

Kastner, now a member of David Ben-Gurion's ruling Labor party, the Mapai, was the most well-known Israeli to be accused of collaborating with the Nazis. The state decided to defend his reputation and prosecuted the man who leveled the accusations, Malkiel Grünwald, for libel. The case rapidly snowballed into an assault on the government, with Ben-Gurion himself called upon to defend himself against charges that he had neglected to take action to rescue Jews from the Holocaust. At the same time, he was under fire for deciding to establish diplomatic relations between Israel and West Germany. This was one of the most painful episodes of soul-searching that the Israelis had ever undergone.

Wiesenthal, who considered himself a political opponent of Ben-Gurion, agreed to help Grünwald's defense attorney, Shmuel Tamir, find grounds for the accusations against Kastner, although he had accepted Kastner's version. Tamir sent him some Israeli stamps for his collection.[58] In June 1955, the Jerusalem District Court ruled that Kastner had "sold his soul to the devil" in the person of Eichmann. An appeal was filed and the Supreme Court cleared Kastner, but before it did so, he was assassinated outside his home in Tel Aviv.

In the wake of the first judgment Wiesenthal published a major scoop that he had picked up in May 1948. While in Nuremberg to attend the trials of several commanders of Nazi Germany's armed forces, he discovered an astonishing document, and on his return to Linz he sent it to Silberschein. "Thank God no one has yet taken notice of the contents of this document," he wrote, asking Silberschein to "pass it on" and to keep it a secret, for "it certainly does not give us any honor."

Wiesenthal was right. The document he had happened upon had been written by Nazi intelligence officials, and it recorded in detail discussions with one Feivel Polkes, who was described as a senior member of the Haganah, the military organization of the Jewish community in Palestine. The German secret services had brought him to Berlin before the war, although there is no certainty that he knew who his hosts really were. They asked him for information about Jewish and Zionist organizations in the hope that he would help them foil plans to assassinate Hitler and other top Nazis.

A few months earlier, the leader of the Nazis in Switzerland, Willhelm Gustloff, had been killed by a Jewish assailant, David Frankfurter, and Polkes's interlocutors in Berlin sensed that he knew something about the affair. Polkes agreed to give them the information, on condition that the Nazis make it easier for Jews to emigrate. The man who conducted the talks with Polkes was Adolf Eichmann. His superiors were considering the possibility of sending him to Palestine to continue the contacts. It is possible that Polkes spoke to the Nazis with the knowledge of the Haganah's chiefs, but he also may have been a double agent.[59]

Either way, Wiesenthal was shocked: lo and behold, a Haganah man had held talks with Eichmann and no one in Israel had acted to have him prosecuted. He guessed that Polkes had been operating with the authority and permission of the Israeli establishment, which was now protecting him in order to avoid a scandal. Years later, Wiesenthal tried to sell the story to the mass-circulation Israeli dailies *Yedioth Aharonoth* and *Maariv*; the editors of both papers said the material was indeed riveting but they did not believe it was true. The documents Wiesenthal sent them failed to persuade them to the contrary.

In the winter of 1954 Wiesenthal told the story to a writer for the antiestablishment weekly *Ha'olam Hazeh*, Amos Keinan, who later became a well-known Israeli author. Keinan had come to visit him in Linz, and Wiesenthal told him that he knew of an agent of Eichmann's who was also in the service of the Haganah. But he would not divulge the details unless someone would invite him to Israel and pay his airfare.

Naturally enough, Keinan was angry, and he described Wiesenthal as a Jew with cunning eyes who was trying to get rich by selling Holocaust secrets. "I couldn't get anything out of him," he wrote, and explained why Wiesenthal had refused to give him this scoop: "Who knows, maybe he can make a little money out of it? . . . Perhaps the Jews are ready to pay to find out who helped to murder them? . . . Perhaps it's better to sit in Austria, in a handsome cottage, to dabble occasionally in some little Jewish affair, to live in comfort on top of some documents waiting for them to hatch into money? And perhaps history would be so kind as to wait until Mr. Wiesenthal decides the best way to fix a deal, and anyway, who says you can't be a Zionist in the Diaspora?"

Keinan was also offended because Wiesenthal didn't offer him a bed for the night, but booked him a room in a hotel. "Don't worry, he said, it's not expensive. He showed me to the door. I walked six kilometers in the pouring rain, in a deserted city, and I gave the matter no more thought."[60] In September 1955, Wiesenthal mentioned the Polkes affair in a letter to the Swiss Jewish newspaper *Jüdische Rundschau*. *Yedioth Aharonoth* reprinted the letter under a banner headline, but the affair died away.[61]

Wiesenthal placed the Jewish collaborators in the same category as the people in various countries who cooperated with the Nazis: the Norwegians had Quisling, the French had Pétain, the Belgians had Léon Degrelle, and the Russians had Andrey Vlasov. Psychologically and sociologically, he asserted, there is no difference between the Jews and other peoples, and therefore however sad and disgraceful it was, it was not surprising that there were collaborators among them too. In his historical survey, Wiesenthal also mentioned Josephus Flavius, the Jewish historian who collaborated with the Romans after they destroyed Jerusalem in the first century CE.[62]

From time to time, he mentioned Jewish collaborators in testimony before courts in Germany and Austria. During the 1966 trial of some Lvov war criminals, Wiesenthal touched on the fate of some of the city's Judenrat members: in September 1942, they were executed by hanging. The Gestapo then appointed a new "Jewish council" and the first demand that was made of them was to pay for the rope that had been used to hang their predecessors.[63] Despite this incident and other similar ones, Wiesenthal flatly refused to accept suggestions that at least some of the Jewish collaborators were also victims of Nazi evil. In his eyes they were all scoundrels.

Because of this he demanded that a "Wiesenthal Law"—as he called it—be applied: whoever cooperated with the Nazis in any way should not be allowed to have any role at all in the Jewish community. There were those, he observed, who raised mitigating circumstances, pointing out that the Nazis forced Jews to cooperate, and after all, one could not expect everyone to be a hero. That might be true for just anybody, he responded, but the leader of a community is expected to lead. As for those who said that collaborators should be treated leniently because they were young and inexperienced, that too might have been true, but community leaders are expected to be responsible.[64]

Although he had decided to stop searching for war criminals, he spent a lot of time in the Linz public library, poring over old Nazi newspapers, studying family announcements along with everything else. Mostly, it was routine work, gathering names, dates, ranks, units, addresses. This habit of collection had become a part of him. His daughter would later recall that when they went on outings, he never knew how to just enjoy the scenery; he would always try to gather wild berries.[65] In that period, Wiesenthal used to describe his Nazi-hunting work as a hobby, but he wrote that no work could have given him greater satisfaction.[66]

In fact, he could not do without it. "My work kept me occupied all day until late at night," he wrote. "When I went to bed and tried to sleep, things I'd read and heard during the day would fuse with memories of the past. Often, after a bad dream, I woke unable to separate the dream from reality."[67] And now and again, he would locate one criminal or another.

Once Wiesenthal was traveling by train to Geneva, and in the buffet car he met a man from Denmark, an officer who had, like him, been a prisoner at Gross-Rosen. They began to talk, Wiesenthal wrote, and the man mentioned the names of certain wanted criminals who were of interest to Wiesenthal at that time, among them Richard Rokita, one of the senior staff at Janowska. The man from Denmark said Rokita was living in Hamburg at that time. At Janowska, Rokita had identified himself as a violinist. The Hamburg police sent an investigator to the musicians' union, but they had never had a member with that name. Nevertheless, Rokita was found to be working under an alias as a night watchman and was arrested.[68]

In 1958, Wiesenthal succeeded in getting onto the track of Peter Arnolds, the inspector at the Lvov rail yard who had informed the SS about the Jewish boy hiding in the stable there. Wiesenthal heard by chance that Arnolds was working at an office of the railway in the town of Paderborn in central Germany. He submitted a complaint to the police and was summoned for a confrontation with Arnolds, who denied everything. Wiesenthal tried to find additional witnesses from the staff of the rail yard.

Everyone knew about the incident, he wrote, but almost everyone denied it and claimed they knew nothing, except for one man, Eugen Jetter of Stuttgart. "If there were more people like you, things may have worked out completely differently," Wiesenthal wrote to him. But despite

Jetter's testimony, Arnolds managed to evade punishment. On the other hand, Wiesenthal managed to locate the SS man who actually shot the boy, and he was arrested.[69] He also made an effort to find Oskar Waltke, "the swine who tortured me in interrogation and made me want to commit suicide," as he wrote.[70]

Although he was not officially involved in finding criminals, various authorities turned to him more than once for help in such matters. A court in Cologne asked for his help in several investigations of personnel from the Mauthausen camp. The Frankfurt District Court asked him if he knew two of Eichmann's aides, Herman Krumey and Otto Hunsche.[71] He was in fact interested in both of them, and he wrote that "the old impulse" that had pushed him to search for Eichmann had not been extinguished.[72]

8

"I Always Said He's in Buenos Aires"

I. Letter from an Anxious Father

Early in 1956, Tuvia Friedman urged Nahum Goldmann to post a $10,000 reward for information leading to the apprehension of Adolf Eichmann. Four years earlier, Friedman had closed his documentation institute in Vienna and settled in Haifa. He worked for a while at Yad Vashem, gathered various documents, and, whenever he could, initiated news items and articles in the press, the gist of which was: Eichmann is alive and he must be caught.

The president of the World Jewish Congress was not enthusiastic, but he promised to persuade the JDC to put up the required amount. Friedman found a few Knesset members ready to raise the matter and eventually he wrote to Ben-Gurion. He proposed that a special body be set up to handle the search for Nazi criminals. He received many polite responses and headlines in the press. Other than that, nothing happened.[1]

Isser Harel, the head of Israel's security services, has written that he began to think about Eichmann in late 1957, or four years after Wiesenthal reported that Eichmann was in Argentina. Harel had visited Argentina in late 1955, but he never claimed that he was involved with the search for Nazi criminals during that visit. When he did begin to take an interest in Eichmann, he first spent a great deal of time reading about the case to get an accurate picture of who this Eichmann actually was. Harel's interest was aroused not by his own curiosity but by the initiative of the prosecutor-general of the West German state of Hesse, Fritz Bauer, a Jew who had returned to Germany after the war and was now living in

Frankfurt. If Bauer had not found out independently where Eichmann was living and pressured Israel into catching him, Eichmann may well have died a free man.

The first person to tell Bauer that Eichmann was in Argentina was an almost completely blind German Jew who had been an inmate of the Dachau camp and had found refuge in Buenos Aires, Lothar Herman. One day, Herman noticed that a boy his daughter was friendly with was named Nicholas Eichmann. That was in 1957. At the same time, Eichmann's name came up in one of the trials of Nazi criminals under way in Frankfurt. Herman read about it in a newspaper, put two and two together, realized that Nicholas was going under his father's original name, and wrote to Bauer that he knew where Eichmann could be found.

Bauer went on the alert, but was very careful. For some time, there had been a warrant out in Frankfurt for the arrest of Eichmann, but Bauer feared that if he began formal extradition proceedings Eichmann would hear about it and escape. So he conveyed the information to Israel. At first, he refused to divulge its source.

Harel sent an agent to Buenos Aires to check the address that Bauer had given him. The agent reached the conclusion that it was not Eichmann's residence. Bauer agreed to reveal Herman's identity to the Israelis, and Harel sent his agent to see him. Herman had in the meantime discovered that one of the electricity meters in the house he had mentioned was registered in the name Klement or Klemens, but the Israeli agent never managed to establish that Klement was Eichmann.

The very powerful director of the State of Israel's secret services would not admit that his men had failed. Just as he had once accused Wiesenthal of messing up the Baron Mast affair, Harel now accused the elderly, almost sightless Jewish man: Lothar Herman never explicitly stated that Klement was Eichmann, Harel wrote.[2]

The Mossad agent who failed to discover the truth returned home in March 1958. The same week, the name "Clemens" turned up in a memorandum revealing that the CIA was also displaying only a marginal interest in Eichmann. This is what it said: "Adolf Eichmann was born in Israel and became an SS-Obersturmbannführer. He is reported to have lived in Argentina under the alias Clemens since 1952. One rumor has it that despite the fact that he was responsible for mass deportations of Jews he now lives in Jerusalem." The information reached the CIA via the German secret service.[3]

Astonishing as the sheer stupidity of this document might be, the person who wrote it was looking for Germans working for Arab countries, not hunting down Nazi criminals. It is not clear whether the "rumor" about Eichmann living in Jerusalem originated in Germany. The Germans themselves were also negligent. A German document summing up Eichmann's career identified him incorrectly as the commander of Auschwitz.[4]

Whatever the case, in April 1958, the Federal Office for the Protection of the Constitution, as the German secret service was called, was not sure that Eichmann was in Buenos Aires; it may be that the failure of the Mossad to verify the information Bauer gave them led the Germans to check it again. The German embassy in the Argentinean capital was asked to look into it and replied that it too could not locate Eichmann. It was more reasonable to assume that he was somewhere in the Near East, the embassy suggested, and with that, the investigation was discontinued.[5]

At this stage, the professional forces of neither Israel, the United States, nor Germany seem to have invested their best efforts in the pursuit of Eichmann. Given this situation, the roles played by Friedman and Wiesenthal are significant: the former ensured that Eichmann's name stayed in the headlines, the latter did everything within his limited capabilities to track him down.

In late April 1959, Wiesenthal saw a newspaper announcement of the death of Eichmann's stepmother. One of the signatories was his wife, Veronika Eichmann. This was evidence that she was still married to him, but apparently Wiesenthal never notified anyone about this. In his book, he wrote: "What use was this discovery to me, when I never even had anyone to report it to? I kept the news to myself, and I never imagined what a significant part it was destined to play in the preparations for the capture of Eichmann a few months later."[6] In fact, Wiesenthal was in constant contact with Israel's representatives in Austria, and it is not clear why he did not give them this particular news item.

In the spring of 1959, the German secret service picked up information to the effect that Eichmann's wife and children were in South America while he himself was somewhere in Europe.[7] In the meantime, Friedman wrote to the West German authorities demanding that they search for Eichmann. His contact was Erwin Schüle, who headed a special central federal agency for dealing with Nazi criminals based in Ludwigsburg.[8] Apparently the Germans did not know exactly who Friedman was and, assuming that he was the head of an actual research institute, treated him with respect.

At the end of July 1959, Schüle wrote him that according to one version Eichmann was hiding in Argentina and according to another version he was in an Arab country. Four weeks later, Schüle wrote again, this time sharing with Friedman secret information that had come to his attention: Eichmann was apparently living in Kuwait. It appears that Schüle saw in Friedman a partner in the endeavor and relied on him to keep this information a secret, but Friedman conveyed the letter to *Maariv*, which published it as its lead news story on the eve of Yom Kippur. From there, it was relayed to the entire world.[9]

It is not easy to explain how it happened that one German prosecutor reported that Eichmann was in Kuwait while another was urging Israel to capture him in Argentina. This does not appear to have been intentional deception, but a case of faulty internal communications. Wiesenthal assumed that Schüle was misled by an incorrect newspaper report, of the kind he himself had sometimes helped to plant.

In a letter to the Israeli ambassador, Yehezke'el Sahar, Wiesenthal explained the source of the report: A German journalist by the name of Heinz Weibel-Altmeyer had been digging around for the whereabouts of one of Eichmann's aides, Alois Brunner, for an article in the Cologne magazine *Neue Illustrierte*. He went to Cairo, Beirut, and Damascus, and there, in the Syrian capital, someone told him that Eichmann was in Kuwait. According to Wiesenthal, Weibel-Altmeyer gave this information to Schüle, who passed it on to Friedman.[10]

The archives of the Ludwigsburg agency attribute the Kuwait report to a member of the German security services by the name of Kaesberger.[11] In September 1959, the security services registered a report that Eichmann was in Damascus or in the emirate of Qatar, and that a plan to employ him in a project of one of the oil companies in Kuwait had fallen through because of Friedman's publication of the information from Schüle. The source for this report said that he met both Alois

Brunner and Eichmann himself, but in the German secret service report it does not say where.[12]

The source may have been Weibel-Altmeyer. The journalist had a close relationship with Wiesenthal, so the possibility that Wiesenthal put him on the Arab track should not be ruled out. In any case, the files of the central agency in Ludwigsburg reflect a lack of coordination. Schüle believed that Eichmann was indeed in Kuwait and knew nothing of Bauer's efforts to get the Israelis to capture him in Argentina.

Prosecutor-general Bauer was very upset when the item about Eichmann being in Kuwait was published. Any mention of Eichmann's name could have thwarted his capture, he feared. Israel's diplomatic representative in Germany was also shocked. In both Germany and Israel efforts were made to hush the affair up, but it refused to disappear from the headlines. Bauer tried to minimize the damage through an act of deception: he called an urgent press conference on the day before Christmas and announced that Germany had decided to demand the extradition of Eichmann from Kuwait.

Valentin Tarra, the upright policeman from Altaussee, wrote to Bauer saying it was inconceivable that Eichmann was in Kuwait, because toward the end of the war he had stolen no fewer than twenty-two crates full of gold, so why should he now go to work in Kuwait? Bauer replied politely that he had found much of interest in the letter.[13]

Lothar Herman, the blind German Jew who had written to Bauer, now wrote to Friedman that the report was not true and Eichmann was not in Kuwait but in Argentina. Friedman believed that no one else knew this, and this time he did not leak the information. At the end of October 1959, Ben-Gurion appeared at an election rally in Tel Aviv. Friedman took to the platform and once again demanded that a prize be placed on Eichmann's head. The audience knew him as the man who had for years been speaking about the need to find Eichmann and had recently disclosed that he was in Kuwait. Ben-Gurion did not respond, but six weeks later he wrote in his diary: "Bauer, the prosecutor-general of Hesse, came and said that Eichmann had been found and he is in Argentina . . . I suggested that he be asked not to tell anyone and not to request his extradition but to give us his address and if we find that he is there we shall catch him and bring him here."[14]

It is not clear how the Germans learned that Eichmann was calling himself Klement. It appears that Wiesenthal could not resist the temptation to claim the discovery for himself. He claimed to have sent someone to Eichmann's mother-in-law, who let slip that her daughter had left Germany and was married to a man with an English-sounding name, something like Klems or Klemt. He said he had passed this on to Israel close to a year before Bauer turned up with his information.

There are grounds for casting doubt on this tale. The Hebrew edition of his book on the hunt for Eichmann says that the visit to the mother-in-law took place early in 1959; the German version says it happened in October. The German secret services were aware of the name "Clemens" as early as 1958, but of course Wiesenthal could not have known this when he claimed to have made the discovery.

From the book, it is not clear who spoke to the woman. The Hebrew version says: "I decided to send someone." In German, it says: "a good acquaintance from Germany." In his other books, he wrote that he sent "one of my people" or "one of my men." The first version of the internal report Wiesenthal wrote after Eichmann was apprehended says that Eichmann went by an English-sounding name, but his mother-in-law did not recall it; the third version of the same report says that she mentioned the names "Klems" or "Klemt."[15]

In view of these multiple and conflicting sources, the most trustworthy account is probably a letter Wiesenthal wrote to Ambassador Sahar before Eichmann was abducted, that is to say, before everyone knew that he was calling himself Ricardo Klement. In his letter, Wiesenthal didn't say that the man who got Eichmann's mother-in-law talking was "one of his men" but simply said who it was: the journalist Heinz Weibel-Altmeyer. And he wrote that the woman had said her daughter was married to someone with an English-sounding name, but one can safely assume that if she had indeed said "Klemens" or "Klement" and that if Wiesenthal knew this, he would have reported it to the ambassador. He did not do so, and therefore it appears that he was wrong to claim credit for it later.[16]

2. The Way to Garibaldi Street

Wiesenthal maintained his constant surveillance of the Eichmann family. A few weeks after the appearance of the report that Eichmann was in Kuwait, Wiesenthal informed Ambassador Sahar of the status of his investigation and stated that he had paid his travel expenses himself. He did not ask to be reimbursed but wrote, "From my experience, I know that inquiries like these stop when they entail a lot of traveling."

In November 1959, Sahar returned from a visit to Israel and wrote to Wiesenthal: "I had some talks on the Eichmann matter, and our people told me how much they appreciate your assistance." As a partner who could be relied upon, the ambassador divulged to him what should have been one of the State of Israel's most closely guarded secrets at that time: according to the information in Israel's hands, the Eichmann family was in Argentina. His wife was pretending that her husband was no longer among the living and that she had married another German, but all indications were that this was a fictitious marriage contracted only to confuse the enemy. This information was incorrect: Veronika Eichmann did not remarry.[17] All Wiesenthal could do was wonder what was going on—after all, he had said all this years ago. Still, the ambassador had flattered him by sharing such important state secrets.

Wiesenthal composed a highly detailed report on the Eichmann family, including dates of birth, marriage, and death and similar facts, information that was required for an absolutely positive identification of the quarry. In December, the ambassador told him that the report had made a very positive impression in Israel, and he passed on to Wiesenthal a lengthy questionnaire he had received from Israel, asking him for additional clarification. With the possible apprehension of Eichmann in the air, Wiesenthal went to Frankfurt to ensure that the prosecution authorities in Germany and Austria would coordinate their activities in the matter.[18]

Two months later, in February 1960, Wiesenthal heard that Eichmann's father had died. This time, too, he learned it from a mourning notice published by the family, and Vera Eichmann was again one of the signatories. Wiesenthal had sent two press photographers to the funeral, and he was now in possession of up-to-date photographs of Eichmann's family, including his brother Otto, who closely resembled him. Wiesenthal reported to Sahar: "There's almost no chance that it will help, but it is a matter of routine that has to be done, so that there won't be some reason later on to blame ourselves."

The pictures were passed on to the Mossad, and one of the agents who actually took part in the abduction of Eichmann, Zvi Aharoni, said later on that he had them with him in Buenos Aires and they helped him to ascertain that Klement was actually Eichmann. Harel, on the other hand, tried to belittle the importance of the photos, writing, "No one was excited by them."[19]

Wiesenthal himself was very excited. By all indications things were moving forward, and he was a part of it. Two Mossad operatives called on him more than once. Harel confirmed that these visits were necessary in order to verify that Ricardo Klement was actually Adolf Eichmann.[20] These visits from Mossad agents, the list of questions that were passed on to him, and the things that he heard from the ambassador all indicated that his dream was about to come true, fifteen years after he began his hunt for Eichmann. Now Wiesenthal was facing the hardest test of all: he had to keep the secret to himself.

He found it very difficult to restrain himself, especially because Tuvia Friedman was getting so much publicity. In late January 1960 he almost broke. In a letter to his friends at Yad Vashem, he dismissed the headlines that Friedman was making and he added: "Some of the inquiries are now going through me and there are two governments involved in them, but I cannot refer to this in writing."[21] And to Friedman himself, Wiesenthal wrote with a certain exuberance: "Certain possibilities are coming closer that I do not wish to refer to in writing," adding, "I can assure you that I have not neglected the mission and in some matters I have made far greater progress than the people who are searching for him officially."[22]

In the evening hours of May 11, 1960, the man whom his neighbors knew as Ricardo Klement returned from work to his home on Garibaldi Street, in a suburb of Buenos Aires. Two cars were waiting at the corner. When the man drew close, the bright lights of one of the cars were turned on in order to blind him. Two men jumped out at him, knocking him to the ground, and within seconds he had been bundled into the second car.

The man was gagged and his hands and feet were bound. Dark glasses were placed over his eyes, and he was laid on the floor of the car and covered with a blanket. He was not sedated: a physician accompanying the abductors had warned that unsupervised sedation could kill him. They took him to one of the safe houses that they had rented for the purpose, some forty-five minutes' drive away. On arrival, they asked him who he was. He tried to conceal his real name at first, but soon realized there was no point. "My name is Adolf Eichmann," he said.

He immediately identified his abductors as Israeli agents. "I know

Hebrew," he told them, and to their astonishment began reciting the first verse of the Bible: *Bereshit bara Elohim et hashamayim v'et ha'aretz . . .* ("In the beginning God created the heavens and the earth . . ."). He also knew the most important Jewish prayer, the Shema. After a few days, he signed a declaration that he was ready to stand trial in Israel. He was then dressed in a steward's uniform, given the necessary documents, drugged, and taken aboard a passenger plane of the Israeli airline, El Al, which was waiting at the international airport of Buenos Aires. It had come on a special flight, carrying the Israeli delegation to festivities marking the 150th anniversary of Argentinean independence.[23]

In retrospect, there were quite a few people who knew Eichmann in Argentina and were aware that he was using a false name to hide from his pursuers. Eichmann mixed with other former Nazis, and he even dictated his memoirs to one of them. Any of these people could have informed on him. The name "Ricardo Clement" even appeared in the 1952 Buenos Aires phone directory.[24]

It is reasonable to assume that if they had given the case a higher priority, the CIA or the German secret services or the Mossad could have found Eichmann. The fact that they did not do so reflects the marginality of the Holocaust in the consciousness of the world in the 1950s. Mossad operatives grabbed him and brought him to Israel, but the information on his whereabouts was not the result of a professional intelligence effort, but rather of the dedication of four Jewish Holocaust survivors.

Fritz Bauer emerges as a man of conscience, wise and courageous. In view of the contradictory fragments of information in the files of the various agencies, one may assume that Bauer too was not sure Eichmann was in Argentina, but he gambled on one of the possibilities. After the Israelis began planning the abduction operation on the basis of the information they had obtained from him, they acted too slowly, in his opinion. There is a letter in his archives from a deputy head of the Mossad, Shlomo Cohen-Abarbanel, asking him to be patient.[25]

A few years later, Isser Harel asked for permission to mention Bauer's name in his book about the Eichmann case. The cabinet secretary wrote to Cohen-Abarbanel and asked him to find out if it was correct that Bauer was interested, for history's sake, in having his name published. The deputy head of the Mossad made a special trip to Frankfurt and apparently heard that Bauer had no objections, and that he left the matter to the discretion of the Israeli cabinet, to decide in accordance with its interests.

But the cabinet barred the publication of Harel's book, and he appealed its decision to the Supreme Court, sitting as the High Court of Justice. Cohen-Abarbanel told the court that there were grounds for keeping Bauer's name a secret: "Is there no danger implicit," he asked rhetorically in an affidavit, "when it emerges that the prosecutor-general of a state in Federal Germany, who had already been a target for the arrows of the neo-Nazis, and who stood alone and isolated in the campaign to discover and prosecute Nazi criminals, does not believe in the efficacy of justice in Germany and serves in effect as an agent of Israel and hands Eichmann over to it?" He went on: "This is a man who continued to provide the State of Israel with many and varied services on vital matters." By the time these hearings were being conducted, however, Bauer was no longer alive, and the discussion was now purely theoretical.[26]

Bauer was acting on the basis of material he obtained from Lothar Herman. Herman was moved to act by a desire to put an end to the connection between his daughter and Eichmann's son, and he wanted the reward offered by the World Jewish Congress. The prize had been posted thanks to the efforts of Tuvia Friedman. Only one of the four men saw the pursuit of Nazi criminals as the main purpose of his life, and that was Simon Wiesenthal.

In the spring of 1960, Wiesenthal's life seemed to have hit a dead end. On top of the loathsome squabbles in the Jewish community came the news that both ORT and the Joint Distribution Committee were about to terminate his employment in Linz. There were only a few Jewish refugees left in the city and serving their needs did not justify keeping a full-time salaried worker there. Documents filed in the JDC's archives reveal admiration of and appreciation for Wiesenthal and explain his dismissal by the decrease in the amount of work to be done in Linz. His personnel file reveals that, officially, he wasn't even employed by the Joint but by ORT, but he would nevertheless receive severance compensation, and there was a chance that he would get work in the Jewish community of Vienna.[27]

According to one biographer, Alan Levy, Wiesenthal discovered that the Joint was employing in its Paris branch a Jew who had been in charge of part of the extermination process at one of the camps. The director of the organization at first refused to fire the man and ultimately agreed to do so only because Wiesenthal threatened to stir up a scandal.[28] It is not clear whether there was a connection between this affair and the termination of his employment with the Joint.

Either way, Wiesenthal took the dismissal very bitterly and tried to fight for his job in the ways he knew best; among other moves, he had a meeting with the director-general of the organization, Charles Jordan. "In the years that have gone by since the war," Wiesenthal wrote to Jordan, "I have been far too occupied by efforts to defend myself against Nazi plots, and in this sphere I have attained perfection. In contrast, I have not yet learned how to defend myself against Jewish plots, but believe me I am a good student and I will still learn. I will have no choice, for my own benefit and moreover, I also have a family that I am responsible for."[29]

At a certain stage, he activated all his contacts in the hope that at least he could get a transfer to the Joint office in Vienna, but to no avail. Wiesenthal felt that he was the victim of an injustice. "I will still come up against the Joint, perhaps on another level," he wrote in a threatening tone to an American acquaintance who had also failed to get his dismissal canceled.[30]

At around the same time, his relations with ORT, which had always been tense, snapped, and he was fired in September 1960. Albert Goldman, director of the organization's operations in Austria, wrote a letter to his superiors marked "personal and confidential" explaining his relationship with Wiesenthal, in which he said Wiesenthal had an "envious and jealous character."

According to Goldman, he had continued to employ Wiesenthal not only because it was hard to find a replacement but also because he feared that if Wiesenthal was fired he would publicize the fact that ORT had in effect cheated the U.S. government by taking more funds than it actually spent on vocational training of the refugees. Wiesenthal himself had inflated the number of students in Linz so that he could employ instructors who were in fact superfluous, Goldman said. "His work was very superficial," he concluded, "and dishonest against our organization." He also accused Wiesenthal of responsibility for "irregularities."[31]

Officially, ORT explained his dismissal by citing a demand by the American authorities. In the files there is a long report on an inspection the Americans conducted of the organization's operations in Linz, an inspection that Wiesenthal charged was conducted using "methods of the Gestapo," including intimidation, threats, and secret wiretaps.[32] But this too did not help him. He received warm letters of recommendation, but it seemed as though his life in Linz was falling to pieces.[33]

He was now fifty-two years old, too late to begin a new life. But as a man who never knew the meaning of the word despair, he invented a job to suit his skills and experience: coordinator of Yad Vashem's activities in Germany. His friends in Jerusalem agreed to study the proposal but did no more than that.[34] These were difficult times; there were no real prospects on the horizon.

And then, on May 23, 1960, Prime Minister David Ben-Gurion announced that Adolf Eichmann was in Israel. Wiesenthal may not have grasped it immediately, but Eichmann's capture was going to change his life. The next day he received a cable from Jerusalem: HEARTY CONGRATULATIONS ON YOUR BRILLIANT ACHIEVEMENT. It came from Yad Vashem. Until the day he died he never received a message that made him happier. He kept the cable among his most treasured personal papers: yellowing snapshots of the town of his birth, Buczacz, a list of the concentration camps where he had been an inmate during the war, an old Israeli passport, and one of the affectionate notes that Elizabeth Taylor sent him.

3. The Seeds of Glory

Some four months after the capture of Eichmann and half a year before the start of his trial, Wiesenthal was invited to come to Jerusalem in order to tell his story at a press conference organized by Yad Vashem. His involvement in the affair was already known all over the world. All at once, he had become famous.

Although Ben-Gurion announced that Eichmann had been found by Israel's security services, at first Israel refrained from admitting that its agents had abducted him. Officially, it claimed that he had been captured by Jewish volunteers, Holocaust survivors. This version was concocted in order to placate Argentina, which was demanding that Eichmann be returned to his home in Buenos Aires and had even complained to the United Nations Security Council.[35] As long as Israel hid the true story, the media focused on Wiesenthal and Friedman.

The frenzy began with the Reuters news agency reporting that Eichmann had been trapped thanks to someone who lived in Austria and dealt with war criminals. Journalists made inquiries at the Austrian Interior Ministry and were given his phone number, Wiesenthal related. The Israeli embassy in Vienna also referred reporters to him.

And that's how it gathered momentum: New York, Berlin, Buenos Aires—they all wanted news, he said. The cable from Yad Vashem also arrived precisely when some reporters were sitting with him, and when he opened it he broke into tears of excitement. The reporters insisted on seeing the cable and he managed to conceal it only with difficulty. After the news came out, he received further messages of congratulations.

But the media assault also made Wiesenthal feel, he later wrote, as if he had been hit by a snowball. He was very angry, he wrote to Yad Vashem. At first he didn't want to speak at all, then he realized that his silence merely intensified the curiosity of the reporters and that it was therefore better to tell them about his work. He did so, but they distorted everything he told them, he lamented, and every day he had to deny something or correct something else.

The truth was that he relished finding himself at the center of this tale. But already, less than four weeks after the announcement that Eichmann had been taken, Wiesenthal sensed the stirrings of a future war for the glory, and he was very careful not to ascribe the actual abduction operation to himself. "My part in the final phase of the operation was more than modest," he wrote to Yad Vashem. "Perhaps the best way to describe my achievement is that last autumn I revived the matter with new evidence." In another letter, Wiesenthal said that the press had exaggerated in describing his role and that he was uncomfortable stealing the glory of those involved in the last stage of the operation, that is to say the Mossad agents.[36]

Isser Harel was furious but had to remain silent. For his part, Wiesenthal tried to silence Tuvia Friedman and warned the Israeli embassy in Vienna against television appearances and press conferences by Friedman. "He does not have enough intelligence to refrain from saying things that will harm Israel," he wrote.[37] Friedman had recently quarreled with Yad Vashem, and its staff therefore preferred working with Wiesenthal.

In the months leading up to the Eichmann trial, Wiesenthal helped the Israeli police and the prosecution prepare their case. He was asked if he could add to the information about Eichmann's relations with the mufti, Haj Amin el-Husseini. The police asked him to check various documents in the Justice Ministry in Vienna and offered payment, and he also gave them information he had obtained from journalists, including reports about the tactics Eichmann's defense team was planning to employ, and pieces of information he had received from people who contacted him on their own initiative in the wake of all the publicity.[38]

At this time, Wiesenthal said, he sent the prosecution a uniquely riveting document: the transcripts of a biographical interview with Eichmann conducted by Willem Sassen, an SS man from Holland who had also settled in Argentina, where he worked at publishing and disseminating neo-Nazi propaganda. Sassen had persuaded Eichmann to record his memoirs, and Eichmann had complied out of vanity, greed, and fool-hardiness.[39] It is not exactly clear how the original transcripts reached the hands of the prosecution. Wiesenthal may well have been involved in it, as he claimed; at one point, he mentioned this as a fact in a letter to the chief prosecutor, Gideon Hausner.[40]

It is difficult to determine how useful the material that Wiesenthal supplied the prosecution was, but there is no doubt that the Israeli authorities preparing for the trial took it seriously. Ben-Gurion was worried by reports from Wiesenthal, among others, that neo-Nazis were planning to try to disrupt the trial of Eichmann in Jerusalem.[41] Someone whom Wiesenthal identified, as was his custom, only by the first letter of his name, had disclosed to him that there was a plan to secure Eichmann's freedom in exchange for a well-known person the neo-Nazis intended to kidnap for this purpose in Bonn, the capital of West Germany. Wiesenthal's source attributed the plan to Alois Brunner, Eichmann's former aide, who was living in Damascus. The hostage was meant to be none other than Nahum Goldmann.

The information Wiesenthal cited was very detailed and included the times for the projected snatch, the way the operation was to be financed, and the identities of some of those involved, among them one of the liaison personnel of the Algerian FLN underground movement. Wiesenthal said that he had managed to verify some of the details passed on to him by his informant but he was not absolutely certain the plan was operational. Nevertheless, he brought it to the attention of the people who to the best of his knowledge were in charge of Goldmann's security, obviously referring to the Mossad.[42]

As the trial drew nearer, Wiesenthal worked on the book that was meant to recount his role in the hunt; among other revelations, he intended to divulge the exchange of letters between himself and Goldmann. Wiesenthal wanted to settle accounts with the Zionist leader and he sent a copy of the correspondence to Yad Vashem. "As you shall see," he wrote, "we wasted six years for nothing." He pointed out that he no longer had any reason to remain silent. The affair had never stopped upsetting him—he wrote about it twice to his friends at Yad Vashem, on two successive days.[43]

He worked diligently on his book and managed to finish it for publication with perfect timing, about six weeks before the opening of the trial. The book received a great deal of publicity, including a banner headline across six columns in the Israeli daily *Yedioth Aharonoth*: I ALWAYS SAID HE'S IN BUENOS AIRES. The journalist Haim Mass, who helped Wiesenthal prepare the Hebrew edition of the book, emphasized Goldmann's mistake.

The World Jewish Congress tried at first to deny the story, but Goldmann later confirmed it. Ben-Gurion was also interested in the affair and noted it down in his diary. Goldmann said that he had passed the information he received from Wiesenthal to the CIA. This was the first that Wiesenthal had heard of this, and he was furious that no one had ever told him.[44]

Otherwise, he was elated. "I felt endless happiness in being with you," he wrote to the people at Yad Vashem and pointed out that it had been many years since he had enjoyed an outpouring of friendship such as those that had been heaped upon him in Jerusalem.[45] Not since the birth of his daughter had he been so happy: Eichmann had been caught, he had played a part in it, his part had been acknowledged, everything was marvelous.

4. Justice in Jerusalem

The trial of Adolf Eichmann began in Jerusalem on April 11, 1961, in an auditorium specially equipped to enable coverage by the world media, and several weeks later Wiesenthal saw him face-to-face for the first time. He was stunned. The man sitting opposite him in the dock behind armored glass did not in any way resemble the monster everyone was expecting to see. He did not have "terrifying eyes" as the prosecutor Gideon Hausner wrote later, nor "predatory hands." He was simply a man in a suit, fifty-five years old, balding, bespectacled, with a nervous twitch on one side of his mouth, paging ceaselessly through documents in front of him, all drab and colorless.

"The prince of darkness posing as a gentleman," said Hausner, alluding to Shakespeare's *King Lear*. But Wiesenthal grasped right away that the trial would make a greater impression if Eichmann looked more like a Nazi criminal. He therefore suggested to Hausner that Eichmann be made to wear an SS uniform. If it were only possible, he said, the accused should be made to answer six million times to the question of whether he pled guilty or not guilty to the charges.[46]

Wiesenthal was also unhappy with the slow pace at which the trial began. The German counsel for the defense, Robert Servatius, had many preliminary motions, and some of the stars of the international media who had come to cover the trial were threatening to go home. Hausner was aware of this, and he began his opening speech with words that generated headlines and entered history: "In the place where I stand before you, judges of Israel, to plead for the prosecution against Adolf Eichmann, I do not stand alone. With me, standing here, at this hour, are six million prosecutors."

This opening clearly indicated the nature of the trial: it was designed as an emotional spectacle more than a way of teaching history. Thus, it was to touch only incidentally on the reasons for the rise to power of the Nazi regime, on the components of its power, and on what led millions of people to believe in it and support it. It did not analyze the nature of racism in general nor that of German anti-Semitism in particular; it did not go into what it was that enabled the Nazis to utilize the machinery of governmental bureaucracy to murder the Jews. In Hausner's words, it was Eichmann who "planned, initiated, organized, and ordered others to spill the ocean of blood," but the first sentences of his opening speech showed that Eichmann would not be at the center of the trial, but rather the suffering of the Jewish people.

In letters he wrote and interviews he gave before the trial, Ben-Gurion emphasized that Eichmann the individual was of no interest to him at all. Ben-Gurion saw significance only in the historical value of the trial itself. He hoped the trial would overshadow claims that the leaders of the Jewish community in Palestine had neglected to try to rescue the Jews from the Nazis, and that it would also neutralize the arguments against his government's establishment of ties with West Germany.

More than anything else, Ben-Gurion felt that the young State of Israel had not yet shaped its identity, and he therefore wanted to provide it with an overwhelming collective experience, patriotic and purifying, a national catharsis. Beyond this, he hoped that the trial in Jerusalem would drive home to the consciousness of the rest of the world the idea that Israel was the sole heir to the legacy of the six million and that the Arab states plotting its destruction were trying to complete the crime that Nazi Germany had begun.[47]

Wiesenthal stayed in Jerusalem for a few weeks as a guest of the Israeli government. The testimony he heard from the witnesses for the prosecution were horrendous but did not add much to what he already knew from his own experiences, as well as what he had learned from others. It was a good thing Eichmann had not been caught earlier, he said. If he had been tried by the Nuremberg tribunals, together with the other war criminals, and executed by the Americans, the destruction of the Jews would not have received the prominence that it deserved in the annals of history; in Wiesenthal's words, "not a cock would have crowed."[48]

The Nuremberg trials were held against the backdrop of the deaths of close to seventy-five million people, among them fifty million civilians, more than in any previous war. The killing of millions of Jews was not suppressed at Nuremberg, but the Holocaust was mentioned mainly as one aspect of crimes against peace and against humanity. The arguments were generally based on documents and focused on the accused. The Eichmann trial dealt mainly with crimes against the Jewish people, was generally based on the testimony of survivors, and focused on the suffering of the victims.[49]

Wiesenthal did not object to the tendency to present the extermination of the Jews as a vindication of Zionist ideology and as justification for the existence of the State of Israel. But Israel's goal of gaining a monopoly over the legacy of the Holocaust aroused a sense of discomfort in him. The longer he followed the hearings the deeper he delved into the essence of Nazi evil, and sitting opposite the glass dock, he was overtaken by a great curiosity and a powerful inner need to understand Eichmann's motives and the components of his personality.

Eichmann emerged as a witness who did not do himself much good. He spoke in long rambling sentences full of the bureaucratic jargon of the Nazi regime's inner circles and he tried to please the judges, as if he had somehow fallen victim to a misunderstanding and he had to explain his way out of it: No, it was not in his department that they had decided to murder the Jews but in some other department, and what they did decide in his department was not decided by him but by his superiors. He only carried out the orders that he was given, an instrument of forces stronger than himself. There was therefore no room for the question of whether he was sorry.

He acknowledged, of course, that the extermination of the Jews was one of the most terrible crimes in human history, but he himself was only a small cog in a large machine. Therefore, like Pontius Pilate, the governor of Judea when Jesus was crucified, he could wash his hands of the matter. If he had been ordered to carry out the mass killings at Auschwitz, for example, he would have put a bullet through his own head to resolve the contradiction between his conscience and his duty as a soldier, he said.[50]

The more he listened to Eichmann, Wiesenthal's impression grew that here was a hollow man, totally banal. He thus tended to accept the opinion that was later expressed by the philosopher Hannah Arendt in her book on the trial, *Eichmann in Jerusalem*. When she took her seat in the court auditorium, Arendt was already considered one of the most prominent intellectuals in the United States. Her book became famous principally because of the concept expressed in its subtitle, "A Report on the Banality of Evil."

Arendt found in the trial support for her existing line of thought: It was not the sadistic perversions undoubtedly motivating many Nazis that made the evil of their regime unique, but rather its ability to corrupt the morality of the simple man. The evil had seeped so deep that even its victims were not immune to it. The book provoked worldwide debate and shaped the contribution of the Eichmann trial to the political philosophy of the twentieth century.[51]

Wiesenthal was no philosopher, but when he tried to clarify for himself what had motivated Eichmann, he too reached the conclusion that it was not a worldview, not even an ideological anti-Semitism, but merely mechanical obedience. If they told him to kill his father he would have done it, Wiesenthal opined. "He is not a moral man and neither is he anti-moral, he is amoral, a highly sophisticated type of robot," states the introduction to the Hebrew version of his book about the hunt for Eichmann.[52]

Wiesenthal also read and agreed with what Arendt had to say about the Jewish councils set up by the Nazis. "Over and over, one thought keeps returning: that without the help of the 'Jewish councils' and the Jewish police, the Nazis would not have been able to carry out their plans, certainly not on this scale," he wrote.[53]

When Arendt spoke of "the banality of evil" she was expressing a very pessimistic view of human nature; in its popular sense, the term sustained the notion that everyone is capable of being as evil as a Nazi, and this opinion also found its way into scholarly literature. But in March 2000, when Israel permitted the publication of an autobiographical manuscript written by Eichmann in prison, a different picture emerged: he was a more ideological person than the "banality" theory had been capable of discerning. And he did not carry out orders like a robot. The Nazis were his idols, and he wanted to call his book *The Idols*.[54]

The manuscript was a personal account as well as eyewitness testimony. Eichmann described in great detail the liquidation of the Jews and stated that the program was executed according to explicit orders from Hitler himself. There is no reason to assume that he did not believe this, although historical research has never confirmed the existence of such an order. Eichmann depicted the extermination of the Jews as hell, and he related that it was only through the strength he derived from alcohol and nicotine that he was able to face up to the horror. It was important for him to persuade the reader that he was not an anti-Semite. He had a Jewish friend and once he had even kissed a cousin who was half-Jewish, he wrote.

His memoirs reflect a deep, conscious, and reasoned identification with Nazi ideology. He knew how to explain to himself why he espoused the principles of Nazism. He was interested in politics and read newspapers. The humiliating defeat suffered by the Germans in World War I had made his blood boil, and he embraced the idea of racial purity and thought that the Jews must be removed. He did not obey automatically; he did what he thought was the right thing to do. As a man who identified with the principles of humanistic ethics, Wiesenthal found it difficult to accept this, so he preferred Arendt's thesis. She too refused to see in Eichmann a thinking person; she therefore erred in her assessment of him, as did Wiesenthal.

Eichmann was sentenced to death and executed by hanging in May 1962. Beforehand, a group of intellectuals wrote to Ben-Gurion and proposed that Eichmann should not be hanged. Two cabinet ministers also opposed it. But these were isolated voices.[55] Not many knew it, but Wiesenthal also thought that Eichmann should be left alive. "In my opinion, the question is not all that important, because there is no value to his continued life and there is no value to his death," he wrote a few months before Eichmann was executed.

What he feared was that if Eichmann was killed, his crimes would be forgotten, and as long as he was still in prison they would come up for debate every now and again. Eichmann had not yet told everything that he knew, and his future testimony could be useful. For one thing, it could lead to the conviction of other criminals, and, moreover, he had not yet expressed regret. Wiesenthal appears to have ascribed importance to

Eichmann's expressing regret in public. Either way, life in prison is a more severe sentence than the death penalty, he thought.[56]

Wiesenthal wrote all this in his reply to a letter he had received from New York; people were now writing to him from all over the world. His book on the hunt for Eichmann had been translated into several languages, sold very well, and was beginning to earn him some money.[57] Others also wrote books on the subject, and one of them in particular infuriated Wiesenthal. This was the book by Moshe Pearlman.

Wiesenthal charged that Pearlman had used material that had come from him and he fired off an angry protest to the Israeli minister of justice, Pinhas Rosen. Pearlman was the man who years before had written a book about the mufti, and Wiesenthal had accused him then, too, of using his material.[58] Pearlman also aroused the ire of Tuvia Friedman, who had written his own book about the search for Eichmann and alleged that the Israeli consulate in New York had sabotaged the chances of his book being published so as not to harm Pearlman's book.[59]

And all the while, somewhere in a small town south of Buenos Aires, sat a half-blind, elderly Jew feeling, justifiably, that the representatives of the Jewish people had deceived him. Lothar Herman, the man whose letter to the German prosecutor Fritz Bauer had ignited the process that led to the capture of Eichmann, waited in vain for the World Jewish Congress to award him the promised reward, $10,000. He also wrote to Wiesenthal.

It appears that Herman was not given his money so that Isser Harel's ego would not be hurt. Harel gave himself credit for the operation and felt deep frustration over the need to keep its details a secret. Some people, including Friedman, tried to arrange for Herman to get the reward, but ten years went by before Prime Minister Golda Meir, a sworn enemy of Harel, ordered that Herman be paid.[60]

The trial and execution of Eichmann ignited a process that turned the Holocaust into a central component of Israeli identity. The wide coverage of the trial also introduced the destruction of the Jews into the culture of memory in West Germany and to a certain extent in Austria as well, in the form of books, films, plays, and other works.[61] A special department in the Mossad that followed these developments listed a series of events that the Eichmann trial had begotten, including the resignation of a German government minister, Theodor Oberländer, who had been involved in the conquest of Lvov; a purge in the police department of Rhineland-Palatinate, and the termination of the employment of twenty-three judges in Baden-Württemberg.

For a while the Eichmann trial boosted the readiness of the German and Austrian authorities to arrest, investigate, and prosecute Nazi criminals. The Mossad determined that in the year after the end of the trial the number of arrests doubled from forty to eighty, as did the number of judgments. In the two years prior to the trial, five people were given life sentences, and in the first year after the trial, an additional seven.

A similar process took place in other countries. In the two years before the trial, one Nazi criminal was sentenced to death in Poland; in the first year following the trial, twelve were sentenced to death, seven in the USSR, two in Poland, two in East Germany, and one in France. Wiesenthal compiled a report on the reactions in Austria and concluded that the trial had aroused positive responses there too.[62] Buoyed by this climate, Wiesenthal left Linz and set up a new documentation center in Vienna. At the same time, he secretly worked for the Mossad. The ten years that followed were the most important and the most exciting of his life.

9.

"Sleuth with 6 Million Clients"

1. Figaro Here, Figaro There

Half a year after he began working in Vienna, Wiesenthal had already compiled a quite impressive report, sixteen pages long, in which he included, among other accomplishments, an announcement that he had managed to locate the residence of one of Eichmann's staff officers, Erich Rajakowitsch. The effort to bring him to trial made headlines the likes of which had been seen only before the trial of Eichmann himself.[1]

This was a success that Wiesenthal needed. His move to Vienna had not been a smooth one. The Eichmann trial had made the heads of the city's Jewish community more prepared to demand the prosecution of Nazi criminals, and they respected Wiesenthal's prestige. After consulting with the Israeli embassy, they agreed to set up a documentation center with a threefold purpose: to combat anti-Semitism, gather evidence on the extermination of the Jews, and track down Nazi criminals and bring them to justice.[2] This was Wiesenthal's first chance to concentrate all his time on his life's goal. His friends at Yad Vashem sent him a cable of congratulations.

But Wiesenthal was still officially vice president of the Linz Jewish community with at least one foot still stuck in that dung heap of intrigue. Naturally, he was treated with suspicion.[3] The communities that were supposed to jointly fund the activities of the new center, including his salary, allocated for this purpose less than half the sum he had demanded.

House number 4 on Zelinkagasse in central Vienna radiated bourgeois solidity with its neoclassical marble pillars and heavy wooden front door, and a lobby with a mosaic floor and a ceiling decorated with floral frescoes. But Wiesenthal received only two small rooms there and a half-time secretary, as if he were a minor community official. He saw this as an insult. Wiesenthal thought big and did not intend to limit himself to the narrow confines of Vienna's Jewish community.[4]

He began work in October 1961 and in the first weeks he established connections with the law-enforcement authorities in the capital. It was important for him to stress that he did not see himself as operating in lieu of the governmental agencies, and he always was at pains to remind the Austrians of their obligation to cleanse themselves of the stains of their past. But reality soon taught him that the chances of a Nazi criminal being put on trial depended on someone conducting a preliminary investigation and submitting authenticated, concrete findings that would not leave the authorities any choice but to continue with the inquiry.[5]

He also strengthened his ties with West Germany's central agency for Nazi crimes, with the Israeli police, and also with a number of research institutes. Among other activities, he systematically went over the names that had been mentioned in the Eichmann trial, aiming at capturing his aides.

Erich Rajakowitsch was an attorney and businessman. The first services he provided to the Nazis after they annexed Austria in 1938 were aimed at curbing the economic activities of Vienna's Jews, including the confiscation of their property. Eichmann encouraged him to join the Nazi security services and dispatched him to occupied Holland. According to documents submitted by the prosecution at the Eichmann trial, Rajakowitsch was involved in the transport of Dutch Jews to extermination camps.[6]

Wiesenthal was not the first to look for Rajakowitsch. The CIA had taken an interest in him before, in connection with the confiscation of Jewish property, but did not persist in its search. Rajakowitsch managed to evade punishment. He settled down in Italy, changed his name to Raja, and set up business links with the countries of the Communist bloc, including East Germany and China. Because of this he once again attracted the attention of the CIA, but it seems that at this stage the Americans were not aware that Raja was Rajakowitsch, or were not interested in knowing. Indeed, they tried to exploit his ties across the Iron Curtain. Raja rebuffed them, but in the meantime Wiesenthal got on his trail.

During his interrogation Eichmann had mentioned a conversation with Rajakowitsch in Argentina, and Wiesenthal therefore assumed at first that Rajakowitsch was hiding there too. Nevertheless, he submitted the evidence he had gathered against the former Eichmann aide to the Austrian authorities and managed to obtain an arrest warrant. From time to time, he spoke to veteran lawyers in Vienna who had handled cases involving Jewish property, and one day, he later related, someone told him that Rajakowitsch was now a businessman and living in Milan. Wiesenthal did not divulge exactly how he found this out, but he made no secret of his efforts to catch the man. It would require a great deal of patience.

In his first annual bulletin, issued in April 1962, Wiesenthal noted that although he had located Raja's address, the center lacked the funds to pay for the measures needed to have him arrested. In a report he issued two years later, he related that he had managed to get financing for the trip and had gone to Italy himself. Before leaving, he said, he had received important information from one of the banks that did business with Raja. Wiesenthal had pretended he also wanted to do business with him, and the bank had given him not only Raja's address in Milan but also, for some reason, his car registration number.

In Milan, Wiesenthal went to see the chief of police after the head of the Jewish community there had made introductions. His fame was proving useful. The Italian officer asked him if he was the same person involved in the abduction of Eichmann, and when Wiesenthal replied in the affirmative, the officer asked him if he intended to abduct Raja in a plane or on a boat.

The Italians displayed sympathy toward him, Wiesenthal wrote, but they explained that they could not arrest Raja as he was not an Italian citizen and he was not suspected of an offense against Italian law. A delegation representing the Jewish community appealed to the Italian minister of justice, who agreed to consider issuing a sixty-day arrest warrant against Raja on condition that he receive an official request from Austria. Now it was up to Wiesenthal to navigate his way through Vienna's bureaucratic and political maze.

Getting the Austrian government to request Raja's arrest was no easy matter. Wiesenthal sensed that officials were trying to avoid him. He would get vague replies to direct questions. The investigation was going on, they assured him, but there was as yet no final evidence, they would say, or offer other similar excuses.

"Whoever sets up a concentration camp is doing a swinish thing, there's no doubt about that, but today it is not a punishable offense anymore," a public prosecutor by the name of Pallin told Wiesenthal. Pallin was in no hurry. His office informed Wiesenthal that a final decision could not be expected before he returned from his Easter vacation. "Only afterward did I learn that Pallin and Rajakowitsch had studied at the same school in Graz," Wiesenthal wrote later.[7]

He could think of only one way to move ahead, and in his experience it was an effective one. He called up a correspondent for the Italian daily *Corriere della Sera* and told him the whole tale. Within hours, a reporter for the paper showed up at Raja's front door in Milan and asked for a reaction. Wiesenthal knew that Raja was liable to flee, and indeed the next day he went to his bank, withdrew a large sum of money, and made off in his red Fiat coupe. Now Wiesenthal was happy he had the car's registration number.

More newspapers began taking an interest in the story, but Wiesenthal kept the faith with *Corriere della Sera*. One of its reporters phoned to tell him that Raja had crossed the border into Switzerland, where he had a villa. Wiesenthal passed the information on to the police. Raja never arrived at his home, but a chambermaid at a hotel in Lugano identified him after seeing a photograph in a newspaper. The Swiss police asked him to leave. He tried to get back into Italy but was denied entry. France and Germany did the same.

Wiesenthal rejoiced, but the chase wasn't over yet. From time to time he received news of Raja being seen in various places, but before he could check it out, Raja had vanished. Wiesenthal was reminded of Rossini's opera, he wrote, and the line "Figaro here, Figaro there." Finally he heard that Raja was due to arrive in Vienna on a flight from Zurich. He joined a number of reporters who drove to the airport to cover his arrival. Raja did not show up. He had taken a flight with a stopover in Munich, where he disembarked and vanished once more.

Prosecutor Pallin had meanwhile returned from his vacation. Wiesenthal went to see him and demanded that Raja be arrested the moment he set foot on Austrian soil. Pallin hesitated. There was not enough evidence in the material he had received from Wiesenthal, he claimed once again. Wiesenthal said that the Jews were celebrating Passover that week. Would the prosecutor permit him to use his office to say Kaddish, the mourner's prayer, for the 100,000 Jews of Holland who had been shipped to death camps?

Pallin lost his temper and raised his voice: "What do you want from me?" he asked. Wiesenthal replied that he wanted justice. "And if it turns out that Raja is innocent?" the prosecutor continued. Wiesenthal replied that it would be better to arrest him and then try and acquit him than to do nothing. At the end of the same month, Raja returned from Germany by car, arriving in Vienna without being apprehended, and turned himself in to the police.[8] It was a big news story. *Time* magazine reported that Raja was arrested thanks to Wiesenthal and reminded its millions of readers who he was: "The man who helped track down Eichmann."[9]

There's no way of knowing if the tale actually happened as recounted by Wiesenthal, but this was his mode of operating: poking around the files, rummaging through the documents, calling people up and sometimes writing to them, putting scraps of information together like a great big jigsaw puzzle, and always depending on coincidence and luck as well. He almost always had to struggle with the authorities. He often made use of the media. He was always aware of the ironic aspects of his work. His emotional involvement was deeper than even he understood, but he believed that it was only the quest for justice that motivated him. When he succeeded in locating a criminal and seeing him brought to justice, he was satisfied; if he failed, he moved on to the next case.

Raja's arrest did not develop into a success story. Wiesenthal did his best, helped by the Israeli law-enforcement authorities, among others, but the material that he managed to supply to the Austrian prosecution was insufficient. Raja was acquitted of murder charges and convicted only for his role in the deportation of Holland's Jews to the death camps.

His trial illustrated the limitations of Wiesenthal's methods: the rules of the game as applied by the courts were meant to work in favor of the accused, just as they are in any criminal trial. Raja's case was decided by a jury. He was sentenced to thirty months in prison and released. He later sued Wiesenthal and won: a German publisher was forced to remove from one of Wiesenthal's books several lines implying that Raja was a Communist agent. Raja celebrated his victory by publishing a book of his own.[10]

2. Code Name "Theocrat"

Within months of opening, Wiesenthal's Jewish Documentation Center in Vienna was flooded with letters. He painstakingly listed every item of incoming and outgoing mail. Within months he had received 1,374 letters and his office had sent out 1,507. The flow only increased with time. The center had acquired a reputation.

People from all over the world wrote to him about what had happened to them during the Holocaust, not because they expected him to do anything with the information, but because many of them felt closed in by walls of indifference and lacked what they needed most: a sympathetic ear. Some of the letters contained unbearable descriptions.

A man from Jerusalem by the name of Samy Rachmut explained to Wiesenthal why he had stopped believing in God. God had allowed SS troops to snatch a baby from his mother and then use it as a football. When it was a torn lump of flesh they tossed it to their dogs. The mother was forced to watch. Then they ripped off her blouse and made her use it to clean the blood off their boots. Wiesenthal needed tremendous mental strength to withstand an inflow of letters like this.[11]

He was not able to handle all the matters brought to his attention. He opened hundreds of files and managed to locate several dozen Nazi criminals. About half a dozen of them were arrested on his initiative. In this context, Wiesenthal took pride in a minor success when he managed to have an arrest warrant issued against Otto Skorzeny, the Austrian SS officer who became famous for his exploits in daring commando operations during the war. In one such raid, he freed Italian dictator Benito Mussolini from the underground fighters who had captured him.

After the war, Skorzeny became something of a celebrity. The media did a great deal of fantasizing about his deeds, dreaming up abortive plans to abduct Winston Churchill and Joseph Stalin. Wiesenthal thought he was the leader of the organization known as the Spider, which was believed to have been the forerunner of the ODESSA network in helping Nazi war criminals evade punishment and build new lives in countries of asylum. In the 1960s, Skorzeny lived in Madrid, enjoying the protection and friendship of the Spanish dictator Francisco Franco and hatching international arms deals. One of his customers was Egypt.

In his first bulletin, Wiesenthal linked Skorzeny with the events of Kristallnacht, the night in November 1938 when synagogues and Jewish businesses in the cities of Germany and Austria were vandalized and torched.[12] Soon after that, Wiesenthal found himself in the service of an organization that was also employing Skorzeny: the Israeli Mossad.

On the last page of Wiesenthal's Israeli travel document appeared the signature of an Israeli official, Rafael Meidan, who was described as the acting immigration officer in Vienna. Meidan was a Mossad operative, and it may be that Wiesenthal was aware of it. The two knew each other well. In

September 1955 Meidan wrote a farewell letter to Wiesenthal and promised that his successor, Giora Ra'anan, would visit him soon.[13]

At the end of his stint in Vienna, Meidan was sent to New York, returning to Israel in 1960. Inside the Mossad at the time there was a small department that handled Jewish matters. It was mostly involved with protecting Jewish institutions abroad; in late 1959 there had been a wave of anti-Semitic incidents in Europe, including the painting of swastikas on tombstones in Jewish cemeteries. Consequently, the Mossad was keeping an eye on neo-Nazi organizations.

Meidan thought it wasn't the Mossad's job to hunt down Nazi criminals and this view was shared by Meir Amit, the head of Israeli military intelligence who replaced Isser Harel as director of the Mossad.

Rafi Meidan was sent to Europe, tasked with preparing a reliable report for Amit about possible links between German rocket scientists working in Egypt, veterans of the Nazi regime, and neo-Nazi organizations. Naturally one of the people he questioned was Wiesenthal, and he shared a closely guarded secret with him: the Mossad wanted to recruit Otto Skorzeny with the aim of using him to reach one of the security officers on the Egyptian missile project.

The connection with Skorzeny was set up by Meidan himself. The path that led to him was tortuous, as befits the world of the secret services—it passed through Skorzeny's second wife, who knew a Jewish businessman living in Finland who did a great deal to help Israel. It was not difficult to obtain Skorzeny's agreement to cooperate with Israel; he had already been working for the Americans.

Skorzeny was willing to cooperate with the CIA on the condition that the Americans provide him with written confirmation that he had not been involved in smuggling Eichmann out of Europe.

The former SS officer now presented Meidan with a condition: he would work with Israel if Wiesenthal would erase him from his list of wanted Nazis. He denied that he had been involved in the Kristallnacht pogroms, and he wanted Wiesenthal to act to have the arrest warrant against him canceled, as it was preventing him from entering Austria. He had business dealings in Austria and a daughter there whom he wanted to visit, he explained.

And so, Meidan came to Wiesenthal and solemnly told him: "The State of Israel needs your help." Wiesenthal was shocked to the core of his soul. By that time, he was already well aware that there were Nazis working for the Americans and he himself had obtained information from ex-Nazis, but even in his worst nightmares he probably never pictured Israel making a request like this. He was confronted by a terrible dilemma, forced to choose between his commitment to justice as a Jew and as a human being, and the deep identification he had felt with the security needs of the State of Israel since the days of the Briha.

It was one of the most difficult choices of his life. He weighed it in his mind and struggled with it over and over again before finally deciding to reject the Mossad's proposal. Many years later, Wiesenthal was still certain that on Kristallnacht Skorzeny had set two synagogues on fire in Vienna, but no longer believed that Skorzeny was involved in the ratline operations of the Spider or ODESSA networks. Meidan respected Wiesenthal's refusal to comply with his request, and in the end Skorzeny agreed to work for the Mossad anyway, as did Wiesenthal himself.[14]

By the end of the 1950s, not many vestiges remained of the destruction wrought in Vienna by the bombers of the Allied air forces. The people of the city had begun rebuilding their lives right after the war. In the opera house, voices soared again; in St. Stephen's Cathedral, sacred worship resumed; in the Prater park, the famous giant Ferris wheel turned as if it had never stopped; and in the cafés, *Apfelstrudel* was being dished up as if there had never been a war.

It was back to normal for Viennese philatelists also, and they would meet once a week, every Sunday morning, in the café of the Josephinum Medical School; after a few years they moved to the Café Museum, a venerable Viennese coffee shop. Wiesenthal was a regular guest. Everyone there knew everyone else. They all had regular tables where they would spread out their albums and trade their stamps.

Wiesenthal's main interest was the postal service between the provinces of the Austro-Hungarian Empire, and he waited with the patience of a hunter stalking his prey until someone offered to sell or exchange stamps from nineteenth-century Galicia. It was a kind of market, and one day Wiesenthal would be asked to explain his stamp dealing to the income tax authorities.[15] But Wiesenthal did not go to the gatherings only in order to buy, sell, or exchange stamps. He went mainly to be in the company of the other philatelists, fellow slaves to the collectors' urge. They drank beer or coffee as they traded and then went home for lunch.

It may also be that Wiesenthal used these meetings to get information from his colleagues that could be helpful in his work, but it is likely that the philatelists never spoke about much apart from stamp collecting. They therefore probably displayed little interest in a young man who sometimes came with Wiesenthal. If they had asked Wiesenthal who his young visitor was, he wouldn't have been lying if he introduced him as a student from Israel studying veterinary medicine in Vienna. He also could have told them that in addition to his studies he worked as a gardener, something that was also true.

Many years later, Dr. Dov Uchovsky could appreciate how ironic this was. The Cold War had made Vienna into a paradise for clandestine international intrigue, as immortalized by Graham Greene's 1949 screenplay for *The Third Man*. This atmosphere gave rise to the popular jest that the top KGB agent in any given capital city was the gardener in the Soviet embassy. Uchovsky was not the Mossad's senior agent in Vienna, but a short while after he had started work as a gardener he was recruited to carry out various tasks, among them acting as a liaison between the Mossad and Wiesenthal.

Wiesenthal was not considered a Mossad agent, but he was a regular operative. He received a monthly retainer and he had a code name: "Theocrat." His brain functioned as a reservoir of names. His memory—and the hundreds of personal files that he kept in his office—enabled him to identify points where the paths of people who interested the Mossad crossed. Among other information, he was able to give his handlers the name of a female scientist working for one of the Max Planck Institutes who, he knew, had a connection with one of the German scientists working in Egypt. This item made it possible to exert pressure on the scientist with the aim of getting him to go home.

Once Wiesenthal asked a German reporter by the name of Othmar Katz to find out the current address of a German businessman who had been involved in the construction of the Aswan Dam in Egypt. "It is very important to me," he stressed.[16]

Wiesenthal's connections in the Austrian police and Interior Ministry were useful, among other reasons, because in those days in Austria, hotels carefully registered the personal details of all foreigners checking in. To comply, guests had to hand over their passports, and more than once Wiesenthal was able to provide his handlers with details of the arrivals and departures of targeted people, including some traveling to and from Arab lands.

———

Wiesenthal was thirty years older than Uchovsky, and the youthful student admired him and related to him like a son to his father. He visited the Wiesenthal home and treated Paulinka's Spitz puppy. He recalled Wiesenthal as a man who radiated restlessness, who was always looking over his shoulder, perhaps in apprehension, perhaps out of caution.

Spending time with him could be pleasant—Wiesenthal used to crack jokes and reminisce and he knew a lot about many subjects—but it could also be oppressive. "He wasn't always nice," Uchovsky would recall in days to come. Wiesenthal could be rude, self-absorbed, offensive. The two met once or even twice a week. If he didn't go with him to the Sunday stamp collectors' meeting, Uchovsky would meet Wiesenthal at Café Korb, another traditional coffeehouse that evoked the ease and pleasantness of the days of Emperor Franz Josef.

3. Where's Mengele?

The assistance Wiesenthal gave the Mossad on the case of the German scientists was not part of his major tasks. Although the Mossad was admittedly more interested in neo-Nazis than in Nazis of the past, it did not totally neglect the latter, and it paid Wiesenthal mainly to search for war criminals, among them Martin Bormann. He was asked to find out whether Bormann's son, who had become a Catholic priest, was in touch with Josef Mengele, the doctor from Auschwitz.[17]

Mossad director Harel had hoped to catch Mengele together with Eichmann, but failed. Apparently, in the course of this effort an Israeli woman agent was killed.[18] In an attempt to explain away his failure, Harel claimed that Mengele had escaped from Buenos Aires because of Wiesenthal. He said that it was Wiesenthal who initiated proceedings for the extradition of Mengele from Argentina to West Germany. An official of the Nazi-infested West German embassy in Buenos Aires tipped Mengele off in time.[19] Harel placed this occurrence in 1959. It is difficult to be certain whether his version is true, but one thing is certain: Wiesenthal wanted very much to track Mengele down.

In the summer of 1960, Wiesenthal phoned the West German central war crimes agency in Ludwigsburg to reveal that according to information he had recently received, Mengele was hiding on the Greek island of Kythnos. On the same day, he imparted the same information to Yad Vashem by letter. This was a peculiar affair: "A few minutes ago I received a piece of news," he began dramatically. Two days later he added further information: Mengele, who had escaped from Argentina to Chile, had tried to obtain political asylum in Egypt but was turned down and had gone to Kythnos, where he was hiding in a monastery.

It is not clear why Wiesenthal chose to notify Yad Vashem, or why he did it by mail in so urgent a matter. He wrote that Mengele did not intend to remain on the island for long and that a neo-Nazi organization operating in Germany intended to smuggle him into another country. He proposed that the Greek diplomatic legation in Israel be contacted immediately—rather a surprising proposal because it was precisely such a diplomatic move that had permitted Mengele's flight from Buenos Aires. A few days later, Wiesenthal sent this information to the Israeli embassy in Vienna.[20]

Yad Vashem acknowledged receipt of his letters by cable. They were very excited: "It is unnecessary to note that we immediately took the required action. If it succeeds, then you will have bestowed a great service upon our nation and we the archives staff can only take this opportunity to once again express our great appreciation for you."[21]

In a later account, Wiesenthal left out his efforts to notify Germany and Yad Vashem, including his proposal to turn to the Greek legation in Israel, writing: "If I notified the Greek authorities through normal diplomatic channels, several weeks would be lost. This time, as often in the past, I chose to take an unconventional approach."

What he did was to call the German magazine *Quick*, which agreed to send the journalist Othmar Katz to Kythnos. This too was a peculiar step because, as Wiesenthal himself had written to the Israeli embassy, everything depended on the matter being kept secret, and if it were leaked to the press Mengele would simply vanish again.[22] Wiesenthal obviously trusted his friends at *Quick*. In any case, he later explained, the magazine was interested in the story and he was interested in the man.

It is not clear what Katz was supposed to have done if he had located Mengele on Kythnos, but he did not find him. Mengele had departed the island twelve hours before Katz arrived, according to Wiesenthal. The reporter showed the owner of a local inn a photograph, and he gave a positive identification of Mengele. Katz later confirmed that he had gone to Kythnos at the initiative of Wiesenthal but claimed that Mengele had not been there at all. He had told Wiesenthal of this on his return, he said, and read Wiesenthal's version in his book only years later.

Wiesenthal never revealed who had told him that Mengele was hiding on Kythnos, identifying his source only as "Johann T.," an elderly German who had been a member of the Nazi Party. Perhaps he invented the story in order to make up for his part in Mengele's escape from Buenos Aires, but it is also very possible that he actually had information and believed that it was genuine. The Israeli embassy in Vienna took his letter seriously and passed the information on to Jerusalem.[23] The entire affair is therefore somewhat odd and amateurish, but Wiesenthal never gave up hope.

The Mossad continued with its efforts to find Mengele. One of the agents who took part in the Eichmann abduction, Zvi Aharoni, claimed that in 1962 he had located Mengele in Paraguay. He said he had immediately notified Harel, but the latter preferred to use Aharoni in the search for an Israeli child who had been kidnapped by his grandfather and taken to New York. The documentation that could confirm this is not open to researchers, but Aharoni's claim has been repeated by other Israeli agents.

Mossad operative Rafi Meidan found a way of entering the home of Rolf Mengele, a son of the fugitive criminal who was a lawyer in Freiburg, West Germany, and dealt in real estate. Meidan posed as a rich German living in Canada who wanted to buy a home for his mistress. Mengele showed him a few places and then invited him home for fresh asparagus. On one of the walls, Meidan saw a photograph of a man in uniform. His host refused to speak of him, and would say only, "That's my late father." The Mossad agent believed him, but the search for Mengele continued and Wiesenthal also kept up his efforts to find him for many years.[24]

In late 1963, some of the criminals of Auschwitz went on trial in Frankfurt. The prosecutor was Fritz Bauer. Josef Mengele's name came up several times during the hearings and was also mentioned in the newspapers. Wiesenthal's papers are replete with letters from people claiming to know where he was; most of these claims were groundless. There are also documents attesting to the efforts made by Wiesenthal and Bauer to find Mengele.

The Mengele family owned a factory that made agricultural machinery. In July 1964, Wiesenthal wrote to Bauer that the plant's bookkeeper, Hans Sedelmeier, was in regular contact with Mengele. Bauer replied that he was aware there had been such contacts in the past, but he did not know that they were ongoing. Sedelmeier had already been questioned in the past, Bauer wrote, saying, "It is possible that we could try something."

During those months, Wiesenthal was linked to a plan, a fantastic one, to discover Mengele's address in Asunción, the capital of Paraguay, and to have a woman agent infiltrate his home. He devoted an entire fairly detailed chapter to this in his book. The woman, he said, was middle-aged and had turned up at his office in April 1964. He called her "Frau Maria" but said that wasn't her real name. She had come to find out details about certain people who had disappeared during the war. He knew that Mengele's relatives were looking for a woman to run his household, he wrote, and it occurred to him that Frau Maria could fill the role.

He suggested it to her, and after giving it some thought she accepted. "Two weeks later, we met in Salzburg and planned our strategy," Wiesenthal wrote. In May 1964, "Frau Maria" sat down in a bar in Günzburg, Bavaria, Mengele's birthplace, where his family still lived. She made some loud anti-Jewish remarks and attracted the attention of a man whom Wiesenthal also gave a fictitious name, "Herr Ludwig."

The man told her that he worked in the Mengele family's factory and she said, "I hope they never catch him." Incidentally, she let drop that she loved traveling abroad. Ludwig kept in touch and a few weeks later he suggested that she take the post of housekeeper for Mengele in Asunción. She agreed. The connection between her and Ludwig continued. Once he even tried to send her to Vienna to try to make friends with Wiesenthal and find out what he knew about Mengele. She refused, and a short while later the connection between the two ended.

This is another story that sounds as if it was dreamed up. But as with the tale about the abortive attempt to trap Eichmann in Altaussee, documents in Wiesenthal's archive show that this story about Mengele is not completely imaginary. Ludwig was apparently Sedelmeier, and the real name of "Frau Maria" was Else Marcus.

In the summer of 1964, Wiesenthal traveled to Frankfurt, where he visited Bauer's office and told him about the connection between Marcus and Sedelmeier. Bauer promised to look at the documents, and the same evening the two met at Café Kranzler. Bauer brought a number of questions along with him; for one thing, he wanted to know what the relationship was between Wiesenthal and Marcus. Wiesenthal told him that her late husband had been a distant cousin of his own mother-in-law.

Bauer took the matter seriously. He assumed that Mengele's friends and family knew of her background and may have wanted Marcus pre-

cisely because she was a convert to Judaism and had been married to a
Jew, just as Mengele himself had, according to Bauer, equipped himself
with testimonials from Jews who said he had treated them well. The two
discussed the possibility of taping the conversations between Marcus and
Sedelmeier and also the dangers to her personal safety in Paraguay if her
identity as an agent were to be discovered. Bauer said that he could personally contact the West German ambassador in Asunción to ensure that in
case of trouble she would receive asylum at the embassy. They decided to
put this off for a further meeting.[25]

4. Who's Afraid of Anne Frank?

In the first two years of his operation in Vienna, Wiesenthal handled some
one hundred cases. Most of his activities involved assistance to various
prosecution agencies, particularly in West Germany and Austria. Wiesenthal knew how to locate witnesses and to supply incriminating documents.
About a dozen suspects were arrested thanks to his initiatives. He reconstructed the escape routes taken by war criminals and located some of
them in distant lands, from Ecuador to Ethiopia, and from Ireland to
Syria. He found one in Nepal and another in the Canary Islands.

Now and then he organized searches, such as dispatching Katz to look
for Mengele. "We sent a contact to the Schwammberger family in Innsbruck and we discovered that Schwammberger was living under an alias
near Heidelberg," Wiesenthal reported. Josef Schwammberger had been
the commander of the ghetto at Przemyśl in southern Poland. But by this
time, he was already living in Argentina. A few months later Wiesenthal
reported that he had sent two people to Eberbach, near Heidelberg, where
Schwammberger's wife was living. The local postmaster told them that the
woman regularly received mail from Argentina.[26]

As a rule, he would not go out on sleuthing missions himself, but it did
happen occasionally. The World Jewish Congress in New York sent him
testimony about a Gestapo officer by the name of Julius Gabler. Only
one detail about him was known: in civilian life he sold shoes. Wiesenthal
reported: "We called up a few shoe stores and we also activated some
private individuals to look for the man in the shoe trade. As this report
was being finalized, we were informed that he has been found and this
information has been passed on to the prosecution."[27]

Later on, the witness in New York remembered another detail: during
the war, Gabler had a friend whose name the witness recalled and he was a

building contractor. "In the phone book we found three companies with this name," Wiesenthal reported to the security authorities.[28]

Wiesenthal reported on several other cases as well, increasingly using the first-person plural "we" as if he headed a vast organization; only rarely did he write "I." Thus, in the plural, he reported on his discovery of the reappearance of Franz Murer, the "Butcher of Vilna," whom Wiesenthal had located on a chicken farm back in 1947 when he had gone hunting for Eichmann with some veterans of the partisans.

As far as Wiesenthal knew, Murer was still sitting in a Soviet prison serving out a twenty-five-year jail term. But in 1955, Murer had been released and had returned to his farm. His neighbors welcomed him with open arms and had even elected him chairman of the district's farmers' association. Wiesenthal heard about it by chance. He called a press conference and demanded that Murer be prosecuted. Nothing happened then, but after Murer's name came up during the Eichmann trial the authorities were compelled to arrest him. Wiesenthal handed the prosecution evidence that he obtained from Yad Vashem.[29]

The trial opened in June 1961 before a jury in the city of Graz. Murer was charged with the murder of sixteen Jews. The Austrian prosecution flew in witnesses from Israel and America. They gave hair-raising testimony. One of them described the murder of his little son, who was shot dead before his eyes. He had never forgotten the killer, and he pointed him out in court.

Murer, then age fifty-two, denied everything. His two sons sat in the courtroom and now and again laughed and made mocking faces at the jury. Wiesenthal complained to the judge about their behavior, but the atmosphere in the courtroom remained sympathetic toward the accused. Some of the witnesses got tangled up in contradictions. Murer was acquitted. Wiesenthal received abusive anti-Semitic letters and threats to his life. He passed them on to Yad Vashem, together with an anonymous letter informing him that the judge in the Murer trial had been a member of the Nazi Party.

Here and there, objections to the acquittal were voiced in Austria, and some Christian youths staged a demonstration. The prosecution appealed to the Supreme Court. The Israeli press responded in fury: "I believe that even Eichmann would have been acquitted if he had been tried in Graz," wrote the correspondent for *Ha'aretz* in Vienna, and in an editorial the paper declared, "This acquittal arouses with absolute justification feelings of disgust and anger among the Jewish people."

The paper attributed the acquittal of Murer to the anti-Semitic atmosphere prevailing in Graz and demanded that Murer be tried again in another city. Wiesenthal suggested to Yad Vashem that a symbolic trial be staged in New York. Holding such an event entailed spending money, but the Eichmann trial also cost money and from the historical point of view it had proved worthwhile, he wrote, adding that a symbolic trial in New York could lead the Austrians to hold a second trial for Murer.

And indeed, the Austrian Supreme Court ruled that Murer must be tried again on the basis of a technical flaw in the lower court proceedings. But the case was not retried. Wiesenthal was frustrated. "In the matter of Murer, we are not making progress," he wrote. "We must get hold of something that will make an impression on people. Regrettably the material that we have managed to find so far is not very impressive." But he refused to give up. An invitation to a reception at the Soviet embassy filled him with hope. He would try to persuade the ambassador to arrange a trip to Vilna for him so he himself could find evidence against Murer.

Nothing came of it. Wiesenthal tried again and again to have the case retried, but he did not succeed and could console himself only with the thought that the efforts to bring Murer to justice were causing him and all other Nazi criminals sleepless nights. In April 1975, Wiesenthal notified the Israeli ambassador that the authorities had closed the case against Murer together with hundreds of other files. But in Wiesenthal's office the case remained open.[30]

Then, between one disappointment and the next, Wiesenthal came upon one of his most important scoops: he found the policeman who arrested Anne Frank, an old dream from his days in Linz.

One evening in late October 1957, a friend phoned Wiesenthal and told him about an uproar that had occurred in a Linz theater during a performance of the play based on the diary of Anne Frank. Wiesenthal hurried to the theater. While he was parking his car he saw a police patrol car and a crowd of onlookers. When he reached the theater he saw that a group of some twenty young people around the age of fifteen, apparently high school students, were being taken out. Meanwhile, the performance had resumed and Wiesenthal waited in the lobby until it was over, when some members of the audience told him what had happened: An organized group of youngsters had started shouting and scattering leaflets that said Anne Frank had never existed and it was all an invention meant to enable the Jews to get more compensation. While some in the audience were shocked, most responded with indifference, Wiesenthal wrote. As for himself, the incident stunned him. He could not grasp what had motivated the youths, who had not yet been born when the Nazis took Anne Frank into captivity in Amsterdam in 1944.

A few days later he was sitting with a friend in a café, and a group of youths were at a nearby table. Wiesenthal's friend knew one of them, a boy named Fritz, and he asked if he had been part of the group that had disrupted the play. Fritz said that he hadn't been there but some of his classmates had. "What have you got to say about it?" asked Wiesenthal's companion, and Fritz replied: "What is there to say? There's no proof that Anne Frank lived. They say she's buried in some mass grave in Germany, but they can't prove it." Wiesenthal entered the conversation and asked the boy, "Young man, how in your opinion would it be possible to prove that Anne Frank ever lived?" Fritz did not reply but just shrugged and said, "Do you still need me?" before going back to his friends.

Wiesenthal looked at them. They were drinking Cokes and apparently talking about something else. Then he had an idea. "What would you say if the man who arrested Anne Frank was found?" he asked his companion. "Would these young people believe him if he admitted that he had arrested her?" The man was enthusiastic and said it would be a body blow against neo-Nazi propaganda. This was an expression of faith in human reason and in the readiness of people to change their beliefs on the basis of factual information—a faith that Wiesenthal held all his life.[31]

If Anne Frank had lived, gone home, and published the diary that she had kept in her youth, she might not have become an icon. But toward the end of the war, she perished in the Bergen-Belsen concentration camp. She was sixteen years old.

A short time after the Nazis took over the government in Germany, Anne Frank's parents left Frankfurt and migrated to Holland. In July 1942, after the Germans took Amsterdam, the family went into hiding in a secret apartment behind a bookcase and stayed there, with some other Jews, in rather difficult conditions. Anne, who was then thirteen, kept a diary. In it she described the day-to-day routine of their lives as well as her fears, dreams, fantasies, and desires. As an adolescent, she dreamed of becoming a journalist and wrote her diary with the intention of publishing it one day. In August 1944, the hiding place was discovered, apparently as the result of a betrayal. The identity of the man or woman who informed on the Frank family has never been revealed, but the name of the German security police officer who came to arrest them was known to be something like Silber, Silbernagel, or Silberthaler. The family members were sent to Auschwitz, Mauthausen, and Bergen-Belsen. Only the father survived.

On his return to Holland, he discovered that the family's housemaid had found Anne's diary and kept it. He published it, first in an abridged form. The tale of one young girl illustrated the horror of the Holocaust more than any other work of literature or film had done. It touched people's hearts in almost every country and sold many millions of copies in almost every language. Accordingly, it also became a target of neo-Nazis and Holocaust deniers, who endeavored to undermine the reliability of the diary.

His pursuit of Erich Rajakowitsch, Eichmann's man in Holland, had made Wiesenthal very popular in that country and connected him with people engaged in research into Nazism and war crimes. On a visit to Amsterdam one day, Wiesenthal was given a copy of the internal phone directory of the onetime Nazi security service in the city. In the plane on his way back to Vienna, he went over the names and noticed one in particular: Karl Silberbauer. This could have been the man who arrested Anne Frank, he realized.

In Vienna, he began to look for Silberbauer in his many telephone books, and he asked the Interior Ministry to check if there was such a person in the population registry. As usual, the ministry held things up, and on November 10, 1963, Wiesenthal was amazed to read in the Communist newspaper *Volksstimme* that Silberbauer had been located and was still serving in the Vienna police force. As had happened more than once in the past, Wiesenthal felt cheated: someone had stolen his scoop.

In the days that followed, Wiesenthal spoke a great deal to the media and on November 21, the story appeared in the *New York Times*. The timing could not have been worse for Wiesenthal in terms of publicity, because the next day President John F. Kennedy was assassinated. Nevertheless, CBS television found room on the evening news for a report from its correspondent Daniel Schorr, starring Wiesenthal. This was an important step up in the formation of his public standing. About two months later, the *New York Times* ran a long profile of him under the title "Sleuth with 6 Million Clients." Not since Eichmann was caught had Wiesenthal received such prominent recognition for his endeavors.[32]

The policeman Karl Silberbauer was at first suspended from the force, but he was not prosecuted and after the affair quieted down he was reinstated. The struggle over the veracity of Anne Frank's diary had therefore not ended. Holocaust deniers continued to argue that it had been fabricated after the war and Wiesenthal continued to fight them, with only partial success. One day he discovered that the Ullstein publishing house, owned by the German media mogul Axel Springer, which had published the diary, had also published a book by David Irving, who was then still considered a serious historian but later turned out to be an inveterate Holocaust denier, in which he listed the Anne Frank diary as a forgery. Wiesenthal wrote to Springer, and the Ullstein publishing house apologized.

Once an Austrian newspaper also alleged that the diary was phony. Wiesenthal urged Otto Frank to sue the paper, the *Österreichische Nachrichten*, but Anne's father preferred to make do with an apology from the paper. Neo-Nazi demonstrators continued to disrupt performances of the dramatized version of the diary, as they had done in Linz, and almost two decades after that incident Wiesenthal found it necessary to write to the Austrian interior minister, Karl Blecha, to demand that steps be taken against the deniers of the diary's authenticity; Blecha's office replied politely, as usual.[33]

10.

"You May Have Thought He Was Happy, but He Also Cried Sometimes"

I. The Mare of Majdanek

Soon after Wiesenthal's successes began giving him a reputation in the international media, the tension between him and the heads of the Vienna Jewish community increased. The strongman in the community organization was its director, Wilhelm Krell. The two men knew each other from the time when they were both inmates of the Płaszów and Gross-Rosen camps.

When Wiesenthal lost his jobs in Linz, Krell helped him move to Vienna. But Wiesenthal found it very difficult to work for anyone, and Krell was a domineering person. Their friendship gave way to terrible quarrels. It was only to be expected. "Things will develop into a public scandal, something that will certainly not gain respect for the Jewish community in general," foresaw an official of the Israeli embassy, and that is what happened.[1]

Wiesenthal alleged that the community officials were picking on him out of sheer meanness. "Each of my successes made them envious and miserable," he wrote. "Each mention of my name in the press bothered them." He accused Krell of carrying on "a reign of terror" in the community. He obtained a sworn statement from a man whom Krell tried to plant in his Documentation Center to spy on him in exchange for payment. Krell was a Communist and he traded illegally in gold, Wiesenthal charged. He left a memorandum in his papers according to which Krell told the West German ambassador that the community had reservations about Wiesenthal;

knowledge of this reached the central war crimes agency in Ludwigsburg and interfered with his work, Wiesenthal claimed.[2]

This was an embarrassing time in the life of a small community that was struggling for its place in a society that had not yet shaken off the profound influences of Nazism. It was also an embarrassing time for Wiesenthal; he wallowed in the intrigues of the Vienna Jewish community with a fervor that was not cooled even by his initial successes and the publicity he had received in America.

In the middle of 1963, the community was preparing to elect representatives to its institutions. Wiesenthal set up a new organization, the Association of Jewish Victims of the Nazi Regime, with a membership, he claimed, of 1,200. One of the community's wealthy members helped fund its activities, which included Yiddish song recitals and lectures; one guest was the West German prosecutor Fritz Bauer.

The Israeli embassy reckoned that Wiesenthal aimed to be elected president of the community. "The war over control of the community is being waged sharply and with excessive crudeness on both sides, with personal smears mostly against the community president, who is being accused of highly doubtful conduct during the Nazi period, and there may be a grain of truth in this," the Israeli ambassador, Michael Simon, reported to the Foreign Ministry in Jerusalem.[3]

The president of the community was Dr. Ernst Feldsberg. Wiesenthal circulated a document signed by an Eichmann aide from which it emerged that in 1939 Feldsberg took part in the selection of the Jews whom the Nazis transferred from Vienna to the vicinity of the town of Nisco in southeast Poland, a stopover on their way to extermination. This was the most terrible of the accusations leveled during the election campaign.[4] "The Vienna community seems to be the only Jewish community in the world headed by a person who also held a position during the period of the Nazi regime," Wiesenthal wrote.

He never claimed that the president of the community had knowingly lent a hand in the extermination of Jews, but by the provisions of the "Wiesenthal Law" that he had tried to introduce while still in Linz, he believed every manifestation of cooperation with the Nazis should be condemned. When he was in Israel, Wiesenthal related, he had realized what a wide abyss had opened up between Israeli youth and the Jews of the Diaspora; it was a gap that originated, he said, in the fact that Jews had collaborated with the Nazis, and the fact that one of these collaborators was at the head of the Vienna community deepened the chasm still further.

These were arguably substantive points of contention, but in fact almost everything about the conflict was personal, with ego battling ego. As he had done in Linz, Wiesenthal claimed that the heads of the Vienna community were prisoners in the hands of the Social Democratic Party. "The Jewish community in Vienna lies like a cancer in the lives of the Jews," he wrote. The Israeli ambassador agreed with him: "Of all the communities that I have known in my service abroad," he wrote to Jerusalem, "the Vienna community is certainly the worst, and the same goes for its leaders."[5]

Wiesenthal tried to mobilize the support of journalists and members of the Knesset as well as that of the World Jewish Congress. Nahum Goldmann refused to get involved. "In matters like this, there are two approaches," Wiesenthal wrote in open hostility. "An approach with feeling and respect for the dead, and one of realpolitik. When it comes to politics, I cannot compete with Dr. Goldmann."[6]

The final blow came a few months later, when the community organization took over Wiesenthal's Documentation Center, and even though it offered to double his salary, it also demanded that he obey its leaders. He preferred to resign. "They wanted me to be Krell's servant," he wrote.[7] Ambassador Simon backed him. "It must be emphasized that this move by the president and the director-general of the Vienna community was carried out with great cunning and in the guise of pure democracy, but not very wisely," he wrote. He presumed that the heads of the community were not aware of Wiesenthal's considerable power. "As a professional Nazi hunter, he has managed to instill fear in very large circles in Austria, including members of the government, and he has free access to all the ministers," wrote Simon.

The ambassador also explained the political background of the affair to his superiors: The minister of the interior, Franz Olah, a Social Democratic Party leader, was in charge of the police and, in the eyes of the public, responsible for the fact that Karl Silberbauer, the police officer who arrested Anne Frank, had been permitted to return to the police force shortly after Wiesenthal had exposed his identity. According to the ambassador, the Silberbauer affair had caused the interior minister a great deal of discomfort and he had therefore instructed his people in the Jewish community to put a curb on Wiesenthal "and this request or order was immediately fulfilled by his Jewish lackeys," in Simon's words.

Wiesenthal's response was fraught with pathos. In an article titled

"*J'accuse*" he declared: "Since 1945 I have been working only in the service of my Jewish conscience, my loyalty to the Jewish people, and the memory of the dead—and I shall continue to do so."[8]

The community leaders didn't wait a moment. Wiesenthal was asked to vacate his office, his request to rent it was turned down, and the locks were changed. At first he was not even allowed to make use of the material that he had gathered through such great efforts. In an official letter, the community notified the Israeli embassy that the management of the center was now in its own hands. It sent a similar notice to the media and in April 1964 it published an activity report implying that Wiesenthal had done nothing and had left a big mess behind him.[9] In fact, he had been working on a lead that was going to develop into one of his most dramatic successes.

The facts of this story are not totally clear, but Wiesenthal's version is reasonable. Early in 1964, he was sitting in the upscale Café Rowal in Tel Aviv, basking in the Mediterranean sunshine and musing about the snow covering Vienna. He was waiting for a friend who had studied architecture with him, Ze'ev Porat. Porat couldn't make it, and he called the café. As was the custom in Israeli cafés and hotels at the time, Wiesenthal was paged by loudspeaker. When he got up to go to the phone, a number of people who knew his name from the media turned to look at him. By the time he got back to his table, there were three women sitting there. One of them apologized in Polish and asked for his help: Did he by any chance know "the Mare of Majdanek"?

Her excitement grew as she spoke. She would never forget the child, she said. He was in a backpack carried by one of the new arrivals at the camp. The SS inspector, a woman nicknamed "the Mare," ordered the man to empty the pack and noticed the child. The man picked him up and tried to run away. The Mare ran after him, caught up with him, and killed the child with a shot from her pistol. She also carried a whip that she would use to lash the inmates viciously, left and right. The woman at Café Rowal knew that the Mare's name was Hermine Braunsteiner.

On his return to Vienna, Wiesenthal found Braunsteiner's name in one of his files. She had been tried for her actions in the women's camp at Ravensbruck and given a three-year sentence. A newspaper published in Vienna reported on the 1949 trial. Her crimes at Majdanek were barely mentioned at this trial. Wiesenthal assumed that if he could find her, it would be possible to have her tried again. He found her address in the trial records, went to the house in Vienna, and found an old woman who remembered her as a child and was able to direct him to relatives of hers.

According to Wiesenthal, he sent someone to the family's home, a young man whose name he did not give. He rang the doorbell and said he was traveling in the area and wondered if he had found the home of some distant relatives. He was asked to come in, and he chatted about the scenery and the weather and let drop incidentally that he had an uncle who had been sentenced to five years for so-called crimes that he had committed during the war, although he was absolutely innocent. That's exactly what they did to a relative of ours, the members of the family said, adding that luckily she was now living in Halifax, Canada, with her American husband. They also disclosed that her new name was Ryan.

An acquaintance of Wiesenthal's, a Holocaust survivor living in Toronto, managed to find out that Hermine Braunsteiner-Ryan had moved with her husband to Queens, New York. On July 9, 1964, Wiesenthal passed her address on to the Israeli police. Meanwhile, he also did what he had done before in such cases: he phoned the *New York Times* reporter who had written the profile of him and on July 14 the *Times* carried a story headlined FORMER NAZI CAMP GUARD IS NOW A HOUSEWIFE IN QUEENS.[10] The paper attributed the discovery to Wiesenthal. This was the start of a saga that unfolded very slowly over several years. The timing of the publication left no room for doubt: Wiesenthal was carrying on with his activities, regardless of the Vienna Jewish community's effort to block him.

2. 7 Rudolf Square

A few weeks after he was evicted from his office, Wiesenthal issued a new bulletin, as if everything had remained the way it was, apart from a change of address to 7 Rudolfsplatz, third floor.[11] Readers of the report learned that the Documentation Center was now operating under the aegis of the Association of Jewish Victims of the Nazi Regime, which Wiesenthal had set up in the hope of using it to gain control of the Vienna Jewish community in its forthcoming elections. The "association," which existed on paper alone, was also the publisher of a journal that Wiesenthal put out occasionally, by the name of *Unser Weg*, German for "Our Way."

Meanwhile, Wiesenthal announced that he had picked up the trail of Kurt Wiese, an SS officer who was posted during the war at Grodno and Bialystok in Poland and had murdered hundreds of people there, including scores of children. After the war he had lived for a number of years without being bothered, but was then located and brought to trial in Cologne. The court released him on bail and he escaped to Austria. Wiesenthal heard about it on the radio and began looking for him. With the help of a reporter for the Soviet news agency Tass in Vienna, he first gathered evidence against Wiese and later related in detail his efforts to find him.

Wiese was a frequent caller at the Egyptian embassy in Vienna, he wrote, and apparently hoped to reach Cairo. "But he didn't get far," Wiesenthal observed. After a long surveillance operation—"some of it hazardous"—Wiese was located living with Nazi friends. "From his necktie to his phony name, we managed to give the police all the details," Wiesenthal wrote, and some time later Wiese was sentenced to life imprisonment.[12] During the same year, Wiesenthal was invited to visit Prague to give his opinion of certain Nazi documents that had been salvaged from the bottom of a lake. He was also shown part of the operational log of the SS brigade named Das Reich. Events such as these pleased him.[13]

Wiesenthal didn't maintain his center at his own expense. Ambassador Simon reported in late February 1964 that "the superiors of Mordechai Elazar have decided in the meanwhile to take Mr. Wiesenthal into their ranks, to pay him a salary, and to put an office at his disposal."[14] "Elazar" was not his real name. He was the Mossad's man in Vienna.

As far as Elazar remembered, Wiesenthal learned his real name only many years later, but documents in his private archive in Vienna show that Wiesenthal was aware of Elazar's true role. The two began to work together in 1962. Like his superiors, Elazar did not place the search for Nazis at the head of his order of priorities; Arab agents were more interesting to him. But he did see Wiesenthal often. Once a month he handed him a cash amount equivalent to three or four hundred dollars and Wiesenthal signed receipts.

They used to meet in the Café Mozart, and the relationship was something like love at first sight. Like the young Uchovsky, Elazar, too, tended to see a father figure in Wiesenthal. They became friends. The letters they wrote each other attest to their friendship being dear to both of them. "Wiesenthal was a man with many identities—like a diamond with many facets," Elazar recalled after he retired. They spoke Yiddish. In the eyes of his Israeli friend, "Wiesenthal was the ultimate Jew and there was nothing that was more Jewish than he was." He was referring to, among other qualities, Wiesenthal's willingness and ability to live out of choice in a country where Jews were not wanted and to his inclination to feel at home there.

Elazar had good reasons to admire Wiesenthal: a short time before he began to work with him, Wiesenthal was instrumental in exposing the identity of Robert Jan Verbelen, a Belgian who had collaborated during the Nazi occupation of his country. Elazar was impressed by his capture not so much because during the war Verbelen had betrayed members of the Belgian underground, but because according to Wiesenthal's information he was involved in neo-Nazi activities.

One day Wiesenthal took Elazar to see Mauthausen. They walked around the detention cells and the gas chamber that had been constructed under one of the infirmary huts. Wiesenthal talked a lot, and was silent a lot, and wept. It was an experience the Israeli agent never forgot.[15]

Meanwhile, campaign season in the Jewish community continued. Just before the elections, Ambassador Simon reported a "horror story" he had heard from a man by the name of Karl Kahane, whom he described as a wealthy industrialist, the biggest single contributor to the Israeli fundraising organization Keren Hayesod, and the partner of Edmond de Rothschild in a number of enterprises in Israel—in brief, "a highly trustworthy man and devoted to Israel," in Simon's words.

A week before Yom Kippur, the Day of Atonement, Kahane had met the Austrian chancellor, Josef Klaus, and invited him to be present at the Kol Nidrei prayer service at the start of the holy day. The head of the Austrian government accepted on condition that he receive an official invitation from the Jewish community. But the leaders of the community refused to invite him. The ambassador informed Jerusalem of the excuse, as reported by Wiesenthal: the chancellor belonged to the People's Party, and the community leaders were anxious that their "masters" in the Social Democratic Party would not be happy about it.

Wiesenthal told the ambassador that the chancellor had been disappointed and insulted. The heads of the Foreign Ministry in Jerusalem could hardly believe their ears. "This story is so fantastic that if you told me someone had made it up I would find it more reasonable than the dry facts," one of them wrote, and he tried to console the ambassador by adding: "After what you have related, you and your predecessors, about the quality of the leaders of this community—why should I be surprised? I feel sorry for you."[16]

The ambassador tried to keep out of the Jewish community election campaign, and his superiors urged him to do so, but the correspondence between Jerusalem and Vienna leaves no room for doubt that Israel supported Wiesenthal. The extensive correspondence on this issue shows that it was not only the well-being of the community that mattered to the Israelis. "Our interests are identical to the activities of Wiesenthal," the officials explained, and instructed the ambassador to intimate to Krell— "and this totally incidentally"—that from a "general Jewish" point of view it was very important that those activities continue. In order to remove any possible doubts from the ambassador's mind, the ministry stressed that "this is also the opinion of the interested parties in the Mossad."[17]

And thus the election campaign for the committee of the Jewish community of Vienna took the form of a behind-the-scenes struggle between Wiesenthal and the Mossad on the one hand, and the community and the Social Democratic Party on the other. The election was held in late 1964, and the Mossad was defeated. The Socialists won a clear majority, with almost double the 863 votes won by Wiesenthal.[18]

Wiesenthal was now fifty-six, balding, mustached, always attired in a suit and necktie. He lived with his wife and daughter in a working-class neighborhood in Vienna's tenth district, on Van-der-Nüll-Gasse at the corner of Davidgasse. They rented a three-room apartment. A visitor from Poland who lunched with them in May 1965 thought it was nicely furnished. The man knew Wiesenthal from Mauthausen and said he had come to attend a memorial service at the camp. On his return home, he gave a detailed report to the Polish secret service. The report identified him as "Agent No. 156."

He arrived at Wiesenthal's home in a taxicab, and Wiesenthal came out to the street and paid the driver. They embraced warmly; the reunion was an emotional one for both of them. First each told the other what had happened to him since they had last been together. Meanwhile Cyla Wiesenthal prepared the meal. Wiesenthal told his guest how he had found her after the war. The story was similar, although not identical in all its details, to the version that he gave in his memoirs. Paulinka, then nineteen and a student, dreamed of becoming a journalist, the agent reported.

He got the impression that the Wiesenthal family was well-off. They had a government allowance, and their apartment had a kitchen and a bathroom, he reported. In Warsaw at the time these things were not taken for granted. Wiesenthal drove his friend in his own car, a Ford Consul, which he was careful to park in a guarded parking lot, not in the street outside his home. He was scared of terrorists, the agent reported.

Wiesenthal did his best to impress his friend, taking him to see his

new four-room house, which was still under construction, and telling him
about his trips abroad. Then they went to a clothing store whose owner
spoke Polish and sold wholesale. The agent chose a nylon jacket for his
son and four shirts. Wiesenthal took one of them from him, as if it were
for himself, and paid the whole bill. In the evening he took his guest to
the opera, where they saw *Madam Butterfly*. The next day, Wiesenthal's guest
came to his new office on Rudolfsplatz, west of the Danube canal.

Crown Prince Rudolf was the only son of Emperor Franz Joseph and the
empress Elizabeth ("Sissi"), and in the square bearing his name the Vienna
municipality tried to create an atmosphere that would recall the days of
the empire. Between the trees it placed ornate green wrought-iron benches
and lampposts, a poster column, and a water fountain. Elderly people
strolling and children frolicking and pigeons fluttering on the cobblestone
pavement give the square a pastoral tranquillity and a carefree, bourgeois
restfulness, the way things were in the days before World War I.

The building at No. 7 stood next to the house where the prominent
author Hermann Broch was born. Four houses away was the birthplace of
the philosopher Martin Buber. But in Wiesenthal's time, the house stood
out because of its bland white facade and lack of distinguishing features.
It was built after World War II, apparently to replace an older structure
wrecked in the bombing of the city.

Wiesenthal began his day at the office reading the newspapers. Then he
would go over his mail. Many of the letters he received contained checks
or small amounts of cash. The contributions came from organizations of
supporters or from individuals, mostly in Holland and the United States.
Wiesenthal painstakingly wrote to thank each and every one of them, even
if they had sent only twenty-five dollars, or even ten, as many did. He
frequently reported that his center was short of funds. After going over
the mail, he would sort out the invitations to travel and speak, and then
attend to his visitors.

Agent No. 156 noted that the center was identified by a plaque at the
entrance to the building and lacked security measures, apart from a mirror.
There was no doorman. He committed to memory the internal division of
the office and on his return to Warsaw he sketched the three rooms. They
contained many books and piles of newspapers and a card file cabinet. He
also took note of a large map on which the sites of concentration and
extermination camps were marked.

In the front room sat a secretary, who the agent said was in her thirties and did not look Jewish. Another room was occupied by a short man of about thirty-five to forty, whom the agent identified as a Jew, apparently one of the volunteers who worked in the office. Wiesenthal sat in the smallest room at the end of the hallway, with windows overlooking a backyard.

Other visitors gave similar descriptions. Wiesenthal's desk was cluttered with papers, photographs, and newspaper clippings as well as a telephone, a typewriter, and a very large ashtray. Sitting there was "a burly man, over six feet tall, wearing a thick tweed jacket, stooping as if permanently looking for a mislaid piece of paper," in the words of the British writer Frederick Forsyth.[19] But in a period before the computer age, Wiesenthal was blessed with an excellent memory and he knew exactly where to find the material that he needed. He smoked a lot and loved candy. In one of the desk drawers he kept a Smith & Wesson Bodyguard Airweight .38 revolver that he was licensed to carry.

The Polish agent's report reflected a typical morning. All kinds of visitors came and telephone calls were received. The agent noted a conversation with Bonn and one with the secretary of the Soviet embassy in Stockholm. The man Wiesenthal wanted to talk to wasn't in and he left a message for him.

Wiesenthal's daily routine led him from the drabness of his file cards to the atrocious documents on his desk. "He is immersed in his work all the time and thinking about it all the time, always as if he is somewhere else," wrote Agent 156. Usually he drove home for lunch. His wife was a sickly, depressive woman. Wiesenthal did not share his work with her and she never asked about it. His world was not her world. "I am not married to a man. I am married to thousands, maybe millions, of dead," Wiesenthal quoted her as saying.[20] After lunch he would go back to the office. The agent got the impression that Wiesenthal did everything himself; the secretary and the other man were there only to help him with technical matters.[21]

3. The Mouse That Roared

The better known Wiesenthal became, the more young people came to ask to be taken on as volunteers; he employed them as researchers and as clerks to correct the style and spelling of his letters. More and more letters were coming from America and Wiesenthal did not yet have a command of English. He also put his aides to work as messengers, to do chores, to go to the post office or the bank. He paid them pocket money, always punctually.

One of these volunteers was Peter Michael Lingens, who was to become a well-known journalist. He was in his early twenties then and wondering what to do with his life, when his mother asked him if he wouldn't like to work in Wiesenthal's office for a while. She was a physician and a jurist who had opposed the Nazis, helped some Viennese Jews to escape abroad, and been in touch with the underground. In 1943 she was arrested and sent to Auschwitz, and then to Dachau. After the war she was active in camp survivor circles and befriended Wiesenthal.[22] Lingens, who supported the Social Democratic Party, was slighted when Wiesenthal's secretary rejected his romantic advances, and he couldn't really make heads or tails out of the quarrel between Wiesenthal and the Jewish community, but he found in Wiesenthal what others had before him: a father figure.

"I grew up without my father," Lingens would later say. "First he was in the war and when he came back he divorced my mother and left for America. I needed a father. Wiesenthal was overflowing with fatherliness and warmth. A great deal of warmth. He radiated the sense that you could come to him with any problem. I called him Simon and I used the familiar *du* with him." But he also related to him with a certain awe: "When he called me into his room, I was always tense." The rest of the office staff called him respectfully by his academic title, "Herr Ingenieur." Among themselves the young volunteers called him "Wizi." Everybody agreed that he was very egocentric, overly concerned for his dignity.

Once Wiesenthal took Lingens to Bad Aussee. "How nice it is that you and I are sitting here now, and not Göring and Eichmann," he said to the young man, and shared his reflections on the nature of human evil, on crime and punishment, justice and vengeance, good and bad. He seemed to have a need for Lingens's awe, for his attention and his company, and it may be that just as Lingens saw a substitute father in him, Wiesenthal saw in Lingens the son he had hoped to father.

In the office, Wiesenthal sometimes raised his voice in impatience because his helpers didn't promptly bring him the file he needed and he found it before they did. They were not upset. "He loved good food and laughed a lot, knew how to marvel at a sunset. You may have thought he was happy," Lingens recalled, "but he also cried sometimes."

Another volunteer, Alexander Friedman, mainly remembered a characteristic hand movement of Wiesenthal's. Every few minutes he would put his hands to his temples and move them backwards, perhaps smoothing his hair into shape, perhaps erasing images of horror that had entered his mind at that moment.

One day Wiesenthal phoned Friedman with an urgent request to go to the Israeli embassy. Two young French speakers had turned up there and asked that a meeting be arranged with Wiesenthal. The embassy staff would not allow them in and would not give them Wiesenthal's unlisted phone number, but one official called him and asked him what to do. Wiesenthal told him to have the people wait outside and he asked Friedman to meet them.

Friedman made his way to the embassy and found two people between the ages of twenty-five and thirty. He told them he worked for Wiesenthal and invited them to a café. He had arranged to have a friend wait in the same café, and Friedman sat down with the two strangers at an adjacent table. The two said that they belonged to an organization called Les Enfants de Résistance, and that they had come to tell Wiesenthal they had captured Martin Bormann.

Friedman asked why they didn't go to the police and the two said they wanted to hand Bormann to the Israelis through Wiesenthal. Friedman got up and went to phone Wiesenthal, who immediately decided that the two had to be crooks. He told Friedman to ask them for Bormann's fingerprints. The two were a little disappointed but promised to come back in two days' time. They didn't.

During this period Wiesenthal occasionally made use of a Dutch journalist, Jules Huf, who had come to him on his own initiative. His father, a doctor, had saved some Jews in Amsterdam during the war. Huf admired Wiesenthal, among other reasons because he was prepared to live in a country swarming with Nazis. Huf himself detested Austria. Once Wiesenthal told him that there were a million people waiting for him in heaven who would ask him what he had done for them while he was able to. "That's a line that could appear in a play by Shakespeare," Huf gushed.

Wiesenthal shared some of his trade secrets with Huf, such as the various ways that public sources like telephone books could be useful. Sometimes he sent him out to check names on mailboxes, question neighbors, or do similar bits of detective work.[23]

———

Sometimes Wiesenthal spoke as if he had gigantic forces backing him, making himself akin to the mouse that roared. The more people believed in the myth he had built up around his work, the greater his ability to function effectively and, at least partially, the closer the reality came to resemble the myth.

One of the most important aspects of his life's work was the worldwide struggle he waged against the application of statutes of limitations to Nazi crimes. In both Germany and Austria, the law was such that twenty years after the end of the war it was nearly impossible to prosecute these crimes unless the legal process had begun before the cutoff date, in May 1965. And for less serious offenses, the statutes went into effect only ten years after the end of the war.[24]

Governments, organizations, and individuals all over the world applied pressure from the outside on the authorities in Vienna and Bonn to change the laws, but because this seemed like a dry legal issue it was not easy to transform it into a headline-maker. Wiesenthal worked from the inside, expressing in yet another way his sense of belonging to Austrian society. This was not a Jewish matter, he believed, but rather a moral test of the readiness of Germans and Austrians to rid themselves of Nazi criminals, and it was therefore up to him to get them interested in the subject. He invested a great deal of energy and a not insignificant sum of money to this end.

The effort to have statutes of limitations on crimes of murder lifted began in the early 1960s, right after the capture of Eichmann. There were contacts between the World Jewish Congress and the German authorities, there were debates in the Israeli press and the Knesset. One of the Israelis who raised the subject was Tuvia Friedman. Later, the topic became one of the first diplomatic issues between the two governments.[25]

The Germans were well prepared for the struggle. In late 1963, the Bonn Press and Information Office put out a booklet containing details on the trials of war criminals in West Germany. More than 480 of them had been executed by the Allies, it said. Moreover, thirty thousand indictments had been filed and five thousand persons indicted. Soon after that, the German authorities published even more impressive figures: investigations had been opened against more than sixty thousand suspects, twelve had been sentenced to death in German courts before 1948, and more than six thousand had been sentenced to jail terms, including seventy-seven years to life.

When these facts were published, one of the most important war crimes trials was under way in Frankfurt, the crowning achievement of the prosecutor Bauer. This was known as the first Auschwitz trial, and it was to be followed by a second. In anticipation of the struggle over extending the statute of limitations, it was important for the Germans to stress that the preparations for these trials had begun before the Eichmann trial and that the debate process had not affected the Auschwitz trial in any way.[26]

It later emerged that nine out of every ten persons suspected of Nazi crimes were never even put on trial, and more than half of those actually charged were acquitted, generally because of "lack of evidence." Only 6,656 Germans were found guilty and only two hundred of them were convicted of murder. Most of the guilty were given fairly light sentences.[27] The tiny number of accused reflected not only the limitations of the legal system but also the public atmosphere in which the trials were held. There was a tendency to be lenient toward the Nazis, especially those who murdered Jews.

Defense counsel in these trials used to break everything down into the smallest of details: Did the witness see the accused from the left side or the right side? Did he see if the uniform he wore was green, black, or brown? If it was brown, then it could not have been this man, because in his unit they wore green uniforms, or vice versa. If the crime took place early in the morning, perhaps there hadn't been enough light to identify the accused and if the accused was holding the whip in his right hand, as the witness alleged, then it could not have been him because he was left-handed, or the other way around, and if the witness was wrong about this detail then perhaps he or she was wrong about all the other details too.

Once, a German court traveled to Israel to hear witnesses who could not or would not go to Germany. One of the defense attorneys, Ludwig Bock, demanded that the Tel Aviv district court judge who presided over the hearings recuse himself because he was a Jew. The judge, Bruno Nachman Ya'acobi, visibly shocked, termed the demand impertinent and warned that it could be seen as contempt of court. If the lawyer meant that an Arab judge would relate with greater sympathy to Nazi criminals, then he was insulting Arab judges, Ya'acobi stated. Such were the rules of the judicial game that Wiesenthal himself espoused and considered almost sacred. As a law-abiding citizen, he fired off a protest over Bock's conduct to the head of the German bar association.[28]

Most Germans opposed extension of the statute of limitations, including the minister of justice, Ewald Bucher, himself a former member of the

Nazi Party. In July 1964, Bucher wrote a long letter to Nahum Gold-mann at the World Jewish Congress explaining that the principles govern-ing statutes of limitations are among the fundamental values of justice. Most of his reasons were legalistic. Goldmann replied in a political vein, dwelling on the damage that application of the statute would do to West Germany's efforts to return to the family of nations, and warned that East Germany would exploit the statute for its own ends.[29]

Wiesenthal maintained that this confrontation was not between Jews and Germans, but between the Germans and themselves. He turned to a number of writers, educators, jurists, scientists, artists, and other well-known Germans and asked for their help in the struggle. This was no easy task. First, he had to draw up a list of suitable people, then he had to locate all their addresses and send each one a personal appeal.

He also wrote to people in Israel, from Golda Meir to S. Y. Agnon, and in the United States, receiving letters of support from Arthur Miller and Robert Kennedy.[30] In all, he received 360 replies, of which he decided to publish 200, all by influential Germans and Austrians, adhering to the line that Wiesenthal had formulated for the struggle: this was a moral issue that the Germans themselves had to address.

Among the people who wrote to him were two Nobel laureates, Werner Heisenberg and Max Born; children's author Erich Kästner supported his struggle, as did Professor Joseph Alois Ratzinger, the future Pope Bene-dict XVI. Wiesenthal submitted the letters to the justice ministers of West Germany and Austria, and also published them in a book.[31] This was the biggest project he had initiated to date.

The postponement of the application of the statute of limitations required legislation, and before the vote in the Bundestag a public debate raged in Germany in which soul-searching, collective conscience, and party politics all played a role. Justice Minister Bucher resigned over the issue. In March 1965, a parliamentary compromise was reached that enabled the Germans to avoid the moral question confronting them. Instead, a legalistic formulation was found that led to a postponement of the issue for five years.[32] "We shall unfortunately have to face the issue again only too soon," Robert Kennedy wrote to Wiesenthal, and he was right.

Now Wiesenthal turned to the fight to get the statute of limitations postponed in Austria as well. He wrote to the justice minister and a num-ber of other politicians and received evasive and also hostile replies. Even-tually, a similar resolution was attained in Austria too.[33]

4. Admiration and Disappointment

The success of Wiesenthal's public struggle against the statutes of limitations gave both his work and his status a new dimension. From now on he was no longer seen as an amateur sleuth or as a pest running from one official to another, or from one courtroom to another or one journalist to another, but as a personage to whom many doors were open and who had something to say on fundamental questions of society and politics in West Germany.

When he had no real news, Wiesenthal would resort to names that always made headlines, like that of Hitler's top aide, Martin Bormann. "We have received authoritative evidence that Bormann is alive," he once announced. When Charles de Gaulle visited Paraguay, Wiesenthal wired him Mengele's name and address and a request: perhaps the French president would be so kind as to discuss the matter with his counterpart in Asunción.[34] Writing directly to heads of state was something that Wiesenthal had been doing since he was liberated from Mauthausen.

In October 1966, Wiesenthal sent a long memorandum to the Austrian chancellor, Josef Klaus, in which he asserted that the role of the Austrians in the crimes of the Nazis was immeasurably out of proportion to their numbers in the population of the Third Reich. He said that although they accounted for only 8.5 percent of the population of the Reich, the Austrians were guilty of the murder of three million Jews, although he did admit that his arithmetic may well have been faulty. He demanded that more officials, more lawyers, and more funds be allocated to step up the pace of prosecution of Nazi criminals. The memorandum was framed as an internal communication from one Austrian to another; he was worried about "our country's" international image, Wiesenthal wrote, not as a Jew coming to settle accounts with the murderers of his people, but as a concerned citizen who wanted to repair his own society.[35]

More and more people wanted to meet him, among them ambassadors, and he was being written up in more and more newspaper articles. He was frequently invited to lecture, in the United States and other countries as well, and this became an extra source of income in addition to the retainer from the Mossad, the monthly pensions he and his wife received from Germany, and the royalties from the sales of his book about his part in the capture of Eichmann. Various organizations began asking him to contribute money. One letter of this nature was filed away, probably with a special satisfaction: it came from the Joint Distribution Committee, which only a few years before had fired him.[36]

All this happened mainly because he radiated an idealistic commitment to the principles of law and justice, uncompromising devotion to duty, courage, and faith in himself.

The interest and admiration he aroused also reflected the social, cultural, and political trends of the late 1960s. In Europe, a generation born toward the end of World War II and immediately afterward was coming of age; many of them felt that their parents had denied their guilt, had lied to them, and had not eradicated the roots of Nazi evil from their inner selves.

In spite of the growing admiration, Wiesenthal experienced a great deal of disappointment and frustration; this was particularly true of his searches for the Nazis who had mistreated him personally. Some twenty years after SS officer Friedrich Warzok led the last inmates of the Janowska labor camp westward, Wiesenthal believed that he was hot on his trail. In June 1966, Warzok was sighted in Hamburg, Wiesenthal reported, and he had managed to locate a former lover of Warzok's in Austria. She was questioned by the police and she confirmed that she had been with Warzok in 1945. "We are continuing to act in this matter," Wiesenthal wrote. "We are talking about an important criminal."[37] He looked for him in Egypt and Sudan and various agencies tried to help him, but Warzok was never captured.[38]

Prosecution agencies made use of Wiesenthal's ability to find witnesses and also of his historical knowledge. "You can be sure that I shall try to the best of my ability to help, precisely because I myself am from Buczacz and my family and my wife's family were murdered there," Wiesenthal promised one of the prosecutors.[39]

One day Wiesenthal was interviewed for television. As usual, he tried to use the occasion to advance his searches. He held up to the camera a letter he said he had received that same day from an old woman living in northern Germany. She wanted to draw his attention to a policeman who seemed suspicious to her. His name was Pahl. This was one advantage he derived from all the publicity. The more well-known he became, the more threatening and obscene letters he received, but he also received more letters from people wanting to inform on others—their neighbors, debtors, sometimes even relatives against whom they sought revenge, often anonymously. This letter from the old lady sent a chill up his spine.

He had been hunting for Pahl since 1946. In those early days in Linz he had sometimes come across refugees from his hometown, Buczacz, who gave him details of the murder of its Jews. That is how he heard about the slaying of his wife Cyla's mother, shot dead by a Ukrainian policeman, and about how his uncle, Israel Wiesenthal, a bakery owner, and his wife, Chaya, had been shot inside the oven in which they were hiding. In these stories told by the refugees, the name of the policeman, Pahl, kept cropping up.

As the years went by, Wiesenthal noted down scraps of information of all kinds that he heard about the man. People wrote to him in Yiddish, English, Russian, and German, from Chicago and Hadera, London and Montevideo, many informing him of atrocities committed by Pahl. He had also shot children dead. From Canada, Wiesenthal received the testimony of a former resident of Buczacz who described the killing of the Jews on the Fedor, a hill on the outskirts of the village, and asserted that the perpetrator was the same Pahl. But Wiesenthal never managed to track him down, and even the Pahl that the old lady wrote about turned out, on investigation, not to be the right Pahl.

In the meantime, the possibility arose that the real name of the man Wiesenthal had been seeking for so many years was in fact not Pahl but Pal.[40] In the file documenting the case, the names Pahl and Pal both appear repeatedly. The file contains a letter from the prosecution authorities suggesting the possibility that the correct name was neither of these, but actually Paul.[41]

A survivor living in Montreal wrote: "I have spoken to people who knew Pal. The one in Buczacz seems to be spelled Pahl or vice versa, I don't know which is and which is not under arrest (I hope all)."[42] Wiesenthal tried to convince himself: "In the last twenty years, we have followed many false trails and found many Pahls," he wrote in December 1965, "but now the right man has been arrested."[43]

Eventually, Peter Johann Pahl and Richard Pal were found to be two different individuals who had both been active in the Buczacz region. Their lawyers were jubilant: How does the witness know the name of the man who crushed the skull of the baby with his boot, as he claims? How does he know whether it was Pahl or Pal? Perhaps it was someone else entirely and perhaps that baby is even still alive to this very day?

As in many other trials, the accused in this case too contended that they had not been at the site of the crimes at the time when they were committed because they had been on leave, and that the events as described by the witnesses had not fallen within their sphere of responsibility or that the witnesses could not say with certainty that it was them and not someone else who had done the deed, or whether it was Pahl or Pal.

This thick file was no different from hundreds of other files stacked up in Wiesenthal's little office, and like them its final entry is a newspaper clipping. The date was 1979, more than thirty years after Wiesenthal first came across the name. The pensioner Richard Pal, sixty-six, was acquitted of any wrongdoing. The court in Stuttgart ordered that he be compensated for the years he had spent in prison.

It is not hard to guess how Wiesenthal felt when he read that item, but in the meantime, he had racked up his greatest success since the capture of Eichmann: he had located Franz Stangl, the commander of the Treblinka death camp, where an estimated 850,000 Jews were murdered.[44]

II.

"A Huge Mass of Rotten Flesh"

I. School for Murderers

Near the village of Alkoven, north of Linz and south of one of the bends in the Danube, stands a massive white castle, four stories high, with many windows and a red tiled roof. There is a tower at each of its four corners with a pointed lead roof, and a fifth tower, higher than the others, has an onion-shaped dome. The inner courtyard is surrounded by row upon row of arches, adorned with all kinds of ornate decorations.

The castle, Schloss Hartheim, is named for the family that laid its foundations in the twelfth century. The building was enlarged during the Renaissance, but toward the end of the nineteenth century it fell into disrepair and the prince who owned it gave it to a local charity, which used it for an "asylum for idiots and cretins," as sanatoriums for the mentally ill were called then.[1] During World War II, it became known as the "Castle of Death," and American forces approached the building cautiously, as they assumed there were SS troops occupying it. It turned out that there were only a few nuns looking after several dozen orphans.

While he was still in Mauthausen, Wiesenthal heard of sick inmates who had been sent to Hartheim and never returned. But it was only after the war that he learned about the Nazis' plan for systematic euthanasia, or "mercy killing."

The commander of Mauthausen, Franz Ziereis, who was taken prisoner by the Americans, provided information about Schloss Hartheim under questioning.

The Americans estimated that about thirty thousand people were killed at the castle, most of them chronically ill. The victims included mentally retarded persons, among them children. They were either poisoned with pills or injections, or they were gassed in a chamber installed for that purpose on the ground floor.

The euthanasia program was rooted in the Nazi concept of life and death. It was an ideology that sanctified not life, but racial purity. At first, this approach led to laws that mandated the surgical sterilization of anyone found to be suffering from hereditary illness, and abortions when a pregnant woman or her husband was found to be tainted with such a disease. A little while later, the Nuremberg laws were enacted, forbidding sexual relations between gentile "Aryan" Germans and Jews. Meanwhile, at various concentration camps in Germany medical experiments were being carried out on inmates.

The mercy killings were perpetrated mainly between the beginning of the war and the autumn of 1941. Often, they were not preceded by medical examinations. It was sufficient for physician-officials to issue administrative orders without even seeing the people they were condemning to death. Sometimes they were influenced by economic or even political considerations. Close to four hundred people, including doctors, psychiatrists, nurses, administrators, maintenance personnel, and security staff, were involved in the program.

In 1946, an American military tribunal convened at the former concentration camp of Dachau convicted sixty-one members of the Mauthausen staff of war crimes and crimes against humanity. Some of them had been involved in the atrocities of Hartheim. Fifty-eight were sentenced to death and executed by hanging at the Landsberg prison, where Adolf Hitler wrote *Mein Kampf* while he was imprisoned in the 1920s.

This was the first war crimes trial. It was followed by the Nuremberg Trials and the Nazi Doctors' Trial, at which the euthanasia program was described in some detail. The two men in charge of the project were found guilty and hanged. But in Austria, when a number of people who worked at Schloss Hartheim were put on trial before "people's courts" in 1947, they were acquitted or given light sentences.[2] The Austrians tried to obliterate what happened at the "Castle of Death" from the collective memory. Many people never knew that their relatives had been murdered there, and those who knew tended to be ashamed and anxious that rumors would circulate about a hereditary mental disorder running in their family.

In the summer of 1962, Wiesenthal received the first of a series of heart-rending letters from an elderly woman living in London, Stephanie Alberti. She had previously written to Judge Moshe Landau, who had presided over the Eichmann trial. Her letter was forwarded to the Israeli police in Tel Aviv, and they responded by advising her to contact Simon Wiesenthal, at No. 4 Zelinka Lane, Vienna I, which she did.

Her brother Leo Alberti, a native of Budapest, had been arrested by the Germans for political reasons, apparently after being informed on, and taken to Mauthausen. She never heard from him again. After the war, former inmates told her that he had been murdered at Hartheim. This knowledge gave her no rest. "I am seventy-five and I will not and cannot die as long as I have not brought the murderers of my brother to the earthly punishment they deserve," she wrote to Wiesenthal.

He replied politely, asking for more information. She wrote back that one of the people who had notified her that her brother had been killed at Hartheim was a doctor by the name of Zoltan Klar. He had been liberated from Mauthausen and on his return to Budapest he told her that her brother had contracted pneumonia and had made a terrible mistake: he reported his illness and asked for medical treatment. He had instantly been removed to Hartheim. Wiesenthal replied that he knew Klar; they had been in the same barracks in Mauthausen. He promised to try to find out more details. Apparently he failed, but Stephanie Alberti kept on writing.

She also published advertisements in the Austrian press offering a reward to anyone who helped her, and she turned to others, including Yad Vashem and the German federal government's central agency for Nazi crimes in Ludwigsburg. But again and again she was referred back to the same address: Simon Wiesenthal, 4 Zelinka Lane, Vienna I. "In my opinion, it would be better to give Frau Alberti a concrete answer as to whether and how we can help her and not, out of politeness, to give her evasive promises that cannot be kept," a World Jewish Congress official to whom she had also appealed for assistance wrote to Wiesenthal.

This was the one and only thing that occupied her. When Wiesenthal was late replying to one of her letters, she would write in a near panic, begging him not to neglect her request. She also got another brother, Erwin, who lived in Vienna, to become involved, and he wrote to Wiesenthal on paper bearing the letterhead of Centropa, a movie production company. "Please, do me a great favor, answer her, and calm her down with a few lines. You, who bravely and with such great genius hunted down Eichmann, can understand the mental condition of this old and stubborn woman, even if she is making your important work more difficult—and needlessly, apparently."

Wiesenthal did reply to her, again and again. She also came to see him in Vienna. He received her and her brother courteously. He referred her to the prosecution authorities in Vienna, where they took a statement from her. The officials asked her if she had been present herself when her brother was executed at Hartheim or was relying on hearsay, which to their great regret had no real legal value. Wiesenthal's address had become a beacon for Holocaust survivors in distress. He could identify with the woman whose search for the men who sent her brother to his death was the purpose of her life, just as the search for the murderers of all the Jews was the purpose of his.[3]

He had dealt with Hartheim before. In November 1961 he tried to interest Othmar Katz, the reporter for *Quick*, in the diary of a nurse, the mother of an incurably ill child, who described how she had traveled to Berlin and pleaded that the child not be gassed, but put to death with a lethal injection. Wiesenthal gave her name and he promised he would provide illustrations. He asked for a prompt reply, pointing out in his characteristic way of handling the media that there was another weekly interested in stories of this nature, but assuring Katz that he preferred him. In March 1962, he sent his findings about the site to the prosecutors in Ludwigsburg.[4]

Now Stephanie Alberti's plight bolstered his interest in Hartheim. It was not difficult to conjure up the horrors of the site. Many people, residents of the village, knew of the mercy killings and many of them had been employed on the project. Wiesenthal went there, got the neighbors talking, read whatever he could find on the subject, and did some thinking. Most of the murder victims of Hartheim were not Jewish, but Wiesenthal figured that the number of personnel staffing the location was far higher than what was needed, and he concluded that they were there in order to undergo training for a far greater project: the Final Solution, or the extermination of the Jews. In his second bulletin, in 1962, he had already used the phrase "school for murderers."[5] Preparing for the trial of a suspected war criminal, he had studied the service files of personnel at extermination camps and noticed that many of them were Austrians and many of them had previously been stationed at one of the euthanasia centers, Hadamar in Germany or Hartheim.

In the meantime, Wiesenthal was shaping a worldview that would guide him until the end of his life and anger many other people: The Jews were not the only victims, and not the first ones. The extermination of the Jews could not be understood without understanding the Nazi race doctrine as a whole, and it was doubtful that it could have been possible to destroy the Jews so efficiently had the Nazis not first murdered other groups in the guise of euthanasia, virtually all of them non-Jewish Germans.

In February 1964 Wiesenthal held a news conference in the Vienna press club. Over one hundred reporters turned up, some of them from abroad. He distributed a letter he had sent a few days before to the Austrian justice minister, Christian Broda. In it he stated that the Nazi mercy killings constituted a kind of dress rehearsal for the annihilation of the Jews.

A few weeks later, he went a step further and declared that genocide had threatened not only the Jews: the Nazis had wiped out Gypsies and members of other groups who they believed were endangering the purity of the Aryan race. From now on, this was his basic premise. The Holocaust was not a crime against the Jewish people alone, but a crime against humanity in its entirety, including the Germans themselves.[6]

Among the "graduates" of Hartheim who had later been employed killing Jews, Wiesenthal mentioned a man by the name of Christian Wirth, who was to become the commander of the camps at Belzec, Sobibor, and Treblinka, and another man, whose first name he apparently didn't know: Stangl.[7] The Austrian media gave his statements extensive coverage.

2. Stangl

Franz Stangl was a Nazi, and his political convictions explain his readiness to take an active part in the extermination of hundreds of thousands of Jews. He developed the callousness required to do this gradually, stage by stage, beginning in his childhood. His story was similar to those of many other commanders of death camps.

If in 1938 he had been told that three years later he would be the commander of two death camps, Stangl would probably have dismissed such a possibility—he did not have much of an imagination. But if he had been told that the only way to get rid of the Jews was to destroy them, he almost certainly would not have ruled out the idea. For Stangl did not act like a robot without opinions of his own; neither was he a sadist in the narrow sense of the word. He knew what he was doing and he believed that it was the right thing to do.

His father was a night watchman in Altmünster, a resort town on a lake in Upper Austria. Stangl described his father as a man who often talked proudly about having been a soldier in the Austro-Hungarian imperial army.

He ruled over his family with an iron fist and in a military fashion. He often beat his son, sometimes until blood flowed, for some act of mischief. "I was frightened to death of him," Stangl recalled many years later. "I felt as if he never wanted me at all. Once I heard him talking to my mother. He distrusted her, suspecting I was not really his son."

When he was about eight, his father died after a severe illness. That was in 1916, two years into the Great War. Two years later, his mother remarried. Her second husband, a widower, was a metalworker who had two sons from his previous marriage, one of them Stangl's age. When he was fifteen, Stangl was apprenticed at a textile plant and did well. Within three years he had passed all the tests and became a master weaver, the youngest in all of Austria.

By the age of twenty, he was a foreman in charge of fifteen workers. In the evenings, he gave lessons on the zither and on weekends he built sailboats. "Those were the happiest days of my life," he would say later, and his wife added that they were in fact the first years of happiness that he knew, after the misery of his childhood.

In 1931, after five years as a master weaver, Stangl found himself at a crossroads. "I saw the thirty-five-year-old workers around me. They had begun work in the factory at my age and already they looked old. The work conditions had harmed their health. I asked myself, do I really want to work at weaving for the rest of my life?"

By this time he apparently already knew the girl who would, in a few years' time, become his wife. Her family owned a cosmetics shop. The young textile worker therefore had good reason to try to improve his social and economic standing, to match those of the woman he loved. He tried to enlist in the police force.

As a policeman, he would share in the power of government. He would wear a uniform and carry a weapon. His economic future as a state employee would be assured, with prospects for getting ahead that a factory worker could never have. It was a challenge. The entrance exams were difficult and it took months before he received the reply, but finally he was accepted. Then came a yearlong course at the police academy, also not an easy hurdle to clear.

"They drilled into us the belief that all people are evil by nature," he recounted. He met all the requirements and was posted to various assignments, from directing traffic to breaking up demonstrations. He was very good at the latter. "In February 1934," he recalled, "terrible street battles broke out in Linz. A group of socialists who organized the demonstrations occupied the cinema and we had to fight them for hours to get them out. The battle went on for more than twelve hours. I was one of those who took part from the beginning to the end. I won a citation, a silver medal."

In July 1934, Stangl found a cache of weapons the Nazis had hidden in a forest. His superiors saw that he was a diligent policeman and he won a second decoration, an Austrian Eagle with a green and white ribbon. He was sent to take a course for undercover police officers, and a year later he was posted to the political department of the secret police in the city of Wels, not far from Linz, and a center of illegal Nazi ferment. Stangl was now a plainclothesman and his job was to conduct surveillance of the underground activities of the Social Democrats, the Communists, and the Nazis. It was a large step forward in the career of the former textile worker, who was now twenty-seven years old. At the end of the year he got married.

When asked forty years later how he related to the activities of the Nazi Party in those days, he evaded the question: "I was a policeman and I did my job" was all he said. This was three years before the Anschluss, when Austria was annexed to Nazi Germany. When that event occurred, Stangl was seized by anxiety. The Austrian Eagle decoration that had been awarded to him for his discovery of the Nazi arms cache could now cost him his life. Three of the five policemen who received the award together with him were executed the day after the Anschluss, he told his biographer, British writer and historian Gitta Sereny.

Stangl hurried to consult a lawyer, a member of the Nazi Party who owed him a favor; the man obliged by adding his name to the list of party members who had joined when it was still illegal, before the Anschluss. Thus, Stangl said, he saved his life and at the same time became a Nazi. It is possible that this is what happened, and it is possible that Stangl lied. Either way, party member Stangl went on serving in the political department of the secret police, which after the annexation became part of the Gestapo headquarters in Linz.

A short time later, Stangl signed a declaration identifying him as "a believer in God" in the Nazi style, and no longer a member of the Catholic faith. This was an important stage in his gradual integration into the Nazi system of values. When World War II broke out, Stangl was categorized as an essential worker and therefore not conscripted into the army.

If he had stopped to work out an interim balance sheet for his life so far, Stangl would have had good reason to be satisfied. He was living with his wife in a nice house with a garden. A year after they married, their eldest daughter, Brigitte, was born. He had the happy family life he had lacked in his parents' home. He also enjoyed his work and he was promoted rapidly, reaching a far higher status than could have been predicted when he was young. What he had achieved he achieved on his own, and not easily. Moreover, as a party member he had reason to believe that he would continue to advance.

In November 1940, Stangl was summoned to Berlin to receive new orders. The summons was signed by Heinrich Himmler, the head of the SS, whose powers were second only to those of Hitler himself. Stangl presented himself at the national police headquarters. One of the officers, by the name of Werner, Stangl recounted, told him it had been decided that he would be given a most difficult assignment. "Werner said that both Russia and America had had for some considerable time a law that permitted them to carry out 'mercy killings' on people who were hopelessly insane or monstrously deformed. He said this law was going to be passed in Germany, as everywhere else in the civilized world—in the near future."

Out of consideration for the sensibilities of the population, Werner told Stangl, euthanasia would be introduced only gradually and only after the public was psychologically prepared. But he added that the harsh task had already begun, under a heavy cloak of secrecy. "Mercy killings," he promised, were being carried out only after strict examination of the subjects by at least two doctors, so that there would be no shadow of a doubt that they were indeed incurable. They were being killed painlessly and thereby liberated from the terrible suffering they would undergo if they stayed alive.

According to Stangl, he tried to turn down the post he was being offered: "The officer was very friendly and sympathetic. He said he understood well that that would be my first reaction, but that I had to remember that my being asked to take this job showed proof of their exceptional trust in me. It was a most difficult task. They fully recognized this, but I myself would have nothing whatever to do with the actual operation. This was carried out entirely by doctors and nurses. I was merely to be responsible for law and order."

This was a turning point in his life. He agreed to take up the position for several reasons, he said. "It was already being done by law in America and Russia; the fact that doctors and nurses were involved; the careful examination of the patients; the concern for the feelings of the population." And he was also scared: He had had some trouble with his superior officer and was facing a disciplinary trial. He very much wanted to leave Linz.

The position entailed promotion. As the security officer at Schloss Hartheim, and now once again in a green police uniform, Stangl was given a higher rank than that of the police chief of the nearby city.

At Hartheim he did not face agonizing struggles with his conscience, because what he had to do did not contradict the moral values that guided him. As far as he knew and wanted to know, the patients who were brought to Hartheim were not worthy of living. Everything was legal, in accord with Nazi ethics and government policy, and his involvement with what was going on was indirect. He did not kill anyone with his own hands. He was responsible for security, and all he had to do was to make sure that each patient had the right papers and that death certificates were issued in conformance with regulations.

In days to come, Stangl told of a visit he paid, as part of his job, to a home for retarded children run by nuns. One of them showed him a little child who looked as if he was about five years old. "Do you know how old he is?" she asked him, and then she told him: "That boy is sixteen, and he will never change." The nun complained that for some reason the doctors at Hartheim had refused to take him and free him from his suffering. Stangl said he was amazed. Here was a Catholic nun demanding that an incurable imbecile be put to death. "A Catholic nun! Who was I to doubt what was being done?"

In August 1941, it was decided that the euthanasia program would be ended, partly because of pressure by the Church and public opinion. It is estimated that by then some 80,000 to 100,000 people had been killed. Even after that date, several thousand retarded children, political prisoners, criminals, homosexuals, and Jews were put to death at the euthanasia facilities.

With the end of the Hartheim operation, Stangl was dispatched to help with the dismantling of a similar facility, at Bernburg in northern Germany. He spent a short time there taking care of administrative matters. The director of the institution was Dr. Imfried Eberl, who later became the first commander of the Treblinka death camp. Stangl's superiors then gave him the choice of returning to Linz or serving in Lublin, Poland, under police chief Odilo Globocnik. Stangl, mindful of the tension between himself and his commander in Linz, preferred the transfer to Lublin. It was the spring of 1942. His work at Hartheim had prepared him mentally for his new post: to set up the Sobibor death camp. Globocnik had told him it would be a military supply camp.

Soon after his arrival, Stangl noticed a gas installation similar to the one that he had seen at Hartheim. This was at Belzec. Christian Wirth, an officer he had met previously at Hartheim, told him what the building was for. "I went there by car," Stangl recalled. "As one arrived, one first reached the Belzec railway station on the left side of the road. The camp itself was on the same side, but up a hill. The headquarters was 200 meters away, on the other side of the road. It was a one-story building. The smell . . . Oh God, the smell. It was everywhere."

Wirth wasn't in his office. Stangl was brought to the officer, who was standing on a hill with pits at its foot. They were full of corpses. Stangl estimated there were thousands of them. Wirth told him what was happening at Sobibor and put him in charge of the camp.

According to Stangl, he told Wirth on the spot that he was not suitable for the job, just as he had said when he was told that he was going to Hartheim. Wirth promised to pass on his reply to those in the upper echelons. They did not accept his refusal, and he did not insist.

The next morning Wirth went to Sobibor to try out one of the new gas chambers. For this purpose, twenty-five Jewish laborers were put into it and killed. Stangl was there as well. He was in charge of Sobibor from March to September 1942, and from then until August of the following year he served as commander of Treblinka.

Thirty years after that, Stangl remembered his first day at Treblinka. It was a lot worse than Sobibor, he said. "In Sobibor unless one was actually working in the forest, one could live without actually seeing; most of us never saw anybody dying or dead. Treblinka that day was the most awful thing I saw during all of the Third Reich . . . the hundreds, no, thousands of bodies everywhere, decomposing, putrefying . . ." Stangl was sent to Treblinka, among other things, to impose order. For one thing, he had to put a stop to corruption in the camp headquarters. His predecessors had been helping themselves to at least part of the money and valuables found on the people sent there to be murdered. He saw himself as a policeman the whole time, he said.

If he had wanted to he could have gotten up and left. But leaving would have entailed some inconvenience and perhaps even some risks. They may have sent him to the front. The career he had built with such great effort could have come to an end. It is doubtful that he thought much about all this. There was no reason to. Everything he was doing was intended to advance the ideology he believed in and the regime he was serving with full awareness of its aims.

Among the personnel of the camps, there were opportunists and sadists and there were those devoid of feeling who acted out of blind obedience. Many of them were indeed mediocrities, men with shallow personalities, lacking in imagination, daring, or initiative, the way Hannah Arendt described Eichmann. But most of the SS officers who ran the death camps were not Germans like all the other Germans. They were political soldiers.

Their military service provided them with employment, careers, a way of life, and self-expression. The power and the sense of togetherness attracted them, the loyalty, the mission, and the challenge—all within the framework of an all-conquering male companionship. Almost each one of them had personal emotional reasons for joining the movement that fed their identification with it. But most of those involved in the killing of the Jews had also been among the first members of the Nazi movement and had stood out early on in their ideological fanaticism.

The majority of Germans and Austrians never joined the Nazi Party, and the majority of party members did not join the SS. Most of those involved in the extermination belonged to SS units that were considered the elite of the elite: the Death's Head regiments. It was not a "banality of evil" that was at the core of their actions, as Arendt wrote, but rather a conscious and particularly intense identification with the evil itself. It was a gradual process.

The "mercy killings" prepared Stangl for his task at the death camps, psychologically and otherwise. From one posting to the next, he rose in rank, and the more responsible the post the greater his identification with what was being done. As the war went on, the level of brutality in the camps rose, until at a certain point Stangl ceased to see the inmates as human beings like himself, and that made it easier for him to manage their destruction.

When he saw Wirth standing over a pit full of corpses, Stangl told his biographer, there was nothing human about it. "It was always a huge mass of rotten flesh," he said. "I rarely saw them as individuals. I sometimes stood on the wall and saw them below in the ditch. But—how can I explain it—they were naked, packed together, running, being driven with whips . . ." To him they were cargo, he said. Many years on, in Brazil, he was riding in a train, and Treblinka came into his mind: "My train stopped next to a slaughterhouse. The cattle in the pens, hearing the noise of the train, trotted up to the fence and stared at the train. They were very close to my window, one crowding the other, looking at me through that fence. I thought then, 'Look at this, this reminds me of Poland; that's just how the people looked, trustingly, just before they went into the gas chambers.'"

That was the key point: as the brutality grew and the camp inmates lost the semblance of humanity, it was as if the racist doctrine was fulfilling itself. "At a certain stage, they were killing human beings in the camps the way we swat a pesky fly or a bedbug," said the defense counsel for one of the camp commanders. And that is also what Stangl said. It took him a few months, but ultimately he got used to Treblinka, just as he had gotten used to Hartheim and Sobibor.[8]

3. A Race Against Time

When Wiesenthal told of his efforts to capture Stangl, he recalled that he had first seen his name in 1948 on a list of senior SS officers who had been decorated. And in fact, he could easily have encountered the man himself: Stangl had been arrested after the war and held in an American prisoner-of-war camp at Glasenbach that Wiesenthal occasionally visited. After a while he was transferred to prison in Linz, from which he succeeded in escaping. Apparently he had not yet been identified as a death camp commander. It is not clear when Wiesenthal began to take an interest in Stangl, but he said that he used the same method that had helped him find Eichmann: he kept Stangl's wife, who lived in Wels, under surveillance.

One day in 1949, three men from a well-known Austrian haulage firm came to her home and left with two large crates. On the sides of the crates they had written the word *Damascus*. Frau Stangl's neighbors apparently knew what was going on.

In 1959, Wiesenthal heard that Stangl was still in Damascus, ostensibly from Heinz Weibel-Altmayer, the German journalist who had spread the rumor that Eichmann was in Kuwait. It may well be that it was not the reporter who told Wiesenthal the news, but the other way around. Perhaps Wiesenthal gave the story to Weibel-Altmayer so that he could help verify it. Either way, the information was in fact already inaccurate. Since 1951 Stangl had been living in Brazil with his family. According to Wiesenthal, as of 1960 he knew that Stangl was in South America, but he did not know precisely where.

A few days after the press conference Wiesenthal held in February 1964, a woman who appeared to be very agitated came to his office. She had just read what Wiesenthal had said about the link between the "school for murderers" in Hartheim and the extermination of the Jews, and his mention of Franz Stangl. "I never knew at all that my cousin Teresa was married to such a terrible man, a mass murderer," she said, and burst into tears. Wiesenthal asked her where her cousin was, and she exclaimed: "Where? In Brazil, of course." Once again Wiesenthal could tell himself that one of the best ways to attract information was through newspaper publicity.

The day after the woman's visit, a guest arrived whom Wiesenthal described as a man with shifty eyes. He said he had served in the Gestapo, and complained that his colleagues had abandoned him. "The big shots, the Stangls, the Eichmanns, they got all the help when they needed it," he said. "They were smuggled overseas, they got money and jobs and forged papers. And who helps people like me?" He pointed to his shabby attire and continued: "I have no work, I have no money, I can't even afford a glass of wine." Wiesenthal could smell the strong whiff of alcohol on his breath, but did not argue.

Then the man came to the point: for $25,000 he would give Wiesenthal Stangl's address. Wiesenthal said that he didn't have that kind of money at his disposal, and they settled on $7,000. According to Wiesenthal, they reached that sum on the basis of the number of Jews that Stangl was esti-mated to have murdered, 700,000—one cent for each Jew. "I had to make an effort to keep my hands on the table," Wiesenthal wrote, "otherwise I would have lost my temper and slapped him." But he understood that this was the only chance he had of trapping Stangl, and he agreed to pay. The visitor told him that Stangl was working as a mechanic at the Volkswagen works in São Paulo, Brazil.[9]

There is nothing in Wiesenthal's papers to bear this version of the story out. On the basis of other sources, there are grounds to assume that he made it up to conceal the true identity of the informant. It is highly prob-able that the person who told Wiesenthal where to find Stangl had been sent by Stangl's former son-in-law, Herbert Habel.

When Stangl's daughter left him, Habel sought revenge. Stangl's wife told his biographer that Habel had explicitly threatened to inform on Stangl to Wiesenthal. That was in 1964, not long after Wiesenthal had mentioned Stangl at his press conference on Hartheim. Stangl himself had also read Wiesenthal's statements; according to his wife, since Eich-mann's capture he had lived in the certainty that his day would come.

Stangl himself would later claim at his trial that his former son-in-law had betrayed him to Wiesenthal. Wiesenthal was present in court and dur-ing a recess reporters asked him if it was true. At least one newspaper quoted him as saying that Habel was indeed his source and that he had paid him $7,000 for the information. Habel apparently threatened to sue him and demanded a retraction. Wiesenthal said he had been misun-derstood and that he had no connection with Habel, but he was unable to rule out the possibility that Habel had sent the man who told him of Stangl's whereabouts.[10]

But this was apparently not enough for Habel, and Wiesenthal had to send him a clarification that looks as if it was formulated in consultation with a lawyer. It read: "I hereby wish to state publicly that you have no connection whatsoever to this affair and that I have never been in contact with you, not in person, not by telephone and not in writing."[11] Stangl's family was not convinced. They believed that the man who came to Wie-senthal was Habel's uncle. Sereny points out that the uncle lived in Vienna and that he was of Jewish descent.[12]

The Mossad agent who used the alias "Mordechai Elazar" would state years later that Stangl was located by Wiesenthal alone, and that is also what Alfred Spiess, the prosecutor in the Stangl case, wrote.[13] This could explain why it took so long from the time he received the information in 1964 until Stangl was arrested in 1967.

Among other reasons, the question arose because in the bulletin dealing with the case Wiesenthal wrote that Stangl's "exact address" had been known to him for three years. In one of his books he wrote that he got hold of the address "several weeks after" he learned that Stangl was in São Paulo.[14] He appears to have gotten carried away, as he occasionally did. He learned of Stangl's exact address only a few weeks before the arrest, but he did know that his quarry was working at the Volkswagen plant in 1964.

Documents he left behind testify to a sleuthing effort conducted and financed by Wiesenthal from his Vienna base via letters, cables, and phone conversations through August 1964, and ultimately also through a special emissary he dispatched to Brazil. He sent a check for $100 and promised $400 more to someone who managed to get his hands on a list of the workers at the Volkswagen plant, and to draw up a list of those whose first name was Franz. But none of these was Stangl. Wiesenthal hired other investigators, and he paid them too. It turned out that Stangl was using "Paul" as his first name.

By this time, Wiesenthal already had established ties with officials of survivors' and Jewish organizations in various countries, including the representative of the World Jewish Congress in Brazil, Dr. Vojtech Winterstein, a former leader of Slovakian Jewry and a Holocaust survivor. Winterstein set up a connection between Wiesenthal and a member of the Brazilian Senate, a Jew by the name of Arao Steinbruch; the two had met at a conference in Brussels and after that kept in touch by corresponding. At a certain stage, Wiesenthal sent the senator $3,000 "to cover expenses." Winterstein rebuked him; $1,000 would have been enough, he wrote. Either way, Steinbruch put his contacts into action.

Wiesenthal himself had begun a race against time to persuade the Austrian government to request the extradition of Stangl. There was already a warrant out for his arrest, but as was only to be expected, the officials had to be pressured into doing what had to be done. A number of telegrams among Wiesenthal's papers are fraught with urgency: Steinbruch needed documents. Meanwhile Wiesenthal also turned to the Israeli police and asked them to immediately begin taking evidence from Treblinka survivors.

The great fear was that there would be a leak and that Stangl would go into hiding. "I did not want to operate through official channels after the unfortunate experiences in the Mengele case and others," he wrote to the Israeli police. The more people who shared the knowledge of the upcoming arrest, the more Wiesenthal worried. The letters and cables he exchanged with his contacts in Brazil were written in code. At one stage he was weighing flying to Brazil himself.

The Austrian warrant for the arrest of Stangl had meanwhile been translated into Portuguese and passed on to the Austrian embassy in Brazil, opening the way to have Stangl detained. The Brazilian government waited for Carnival to end, but in mid-February 1967, Stangl's home was already under surveillance.

And two weeks later he was arrested, in an operation full of high drama. Three police agents and a press photographer went to a São Paulo hospital, identified themselves, and instructed one of the nurses to put a telephone call through to the Volkswagen plant and tell Stangl that his daughter had been injured in a car crash and was in the hospital, and that he should come immediately. Within half an hour he was there, and was placed under arrest. It was a worldwide sensation and in Israel it was the lead story in the news.

Wiesenthal heard of the arrest at the airport in Amsterdam. He was on his way to the United States. He worried that Brazil would avoid extraditing Stangl and he went to the telephone. First he called a number of friends in various countries and asked them to organize demonstrations outside the Brazilian embassies there. Then he got hold of the justice minister of the West German state of North Rhine–Westphalia and urged him to demand Stangl's extradition. He also called contacts in Poland, with a view to getting Warsaw to demand Stangl's extradition as well. In South America, he explained later, there have to be as many extradition demands as possible. When he got to New York, his renown enabled him to get a meeting with Senator Robert Kennedy, who, according to Wiesenthal, immediately called up the Brazilian ambassador to the United States and demanded that Stangl be handed over.

Brazil complied, and Stangl was extradited to Germany. Soon it became clear that throughout the years he had used his real name. He and his family were registered at the Austrian consulate in São Paulo, although his name was also on the list of wanted criminals. If the consul's officials had done their job properly, they would have come across his name on both lists and requested his arrest and extradition themselves. One of them disingenuously told Stangl's biographer later: "If Herr Wiesenthal thought that Stangl was living in São Paulo, why didn't he in fact address himself to us?"[15] On the other hand, the Volkswagen Corporation went to great lengths to convince Wiesenthal that it had not known Stangl was on its payroll, and it recruited a prominent member of the Bundestag, Walther Leisler Kiep, to express its regrets to him.[16]

Stangl's trial opened in Düsseldorf in May 1970, and a few months later he was sentenced to life imprisonment. A year later he died in prison, so it might be said that he got off easily. But Wiesenthal was not disappointed. Stangl was one of the major war criminals and no one did more than Wiesenthal to track him down. He had only his inner faith, his devotion to the mission, his connections, and his fame to rely on. If Stangl had been the only Nazi war criminal that he managed to bring to justice, he could have told himself that his life had not been lived in vain.

12.

"Auschwitz Lines"

1. Common Fate

In May 1966, Wiesenthal was on a flight from Vienna to Amsterdam. The attendants knew him and greeted him by name. The man sitting next to him asked him in English if he was the person whose name he heard sometimes in the news. Wiesenthal replied in the affirmative and his neighbor introduced himself: Tamari, of Ramallah, Jordan, a Palestinian Christian businessman on his way to New York. For some reason, Wiesenthal compiled a detailed report of their conversation. Apparently, Tamari spoke most of the time and Wiesenthal listened.

Quite naturally, the conversation turned to the Israeli-Arab conflict. The son of a family that had fled from Jaffa, Tamari said that Israel had made a serious mistake by not compensating the Palestinian refugees for the property they abandoned. King Hussein of Jordan also did not treat them properly; he feared them, particularly the intelligentsia. Wiesenthal asked about the mufti, and Tamari replied that he had no influence. As for Al Fatah, there was nothing that could be done against them, although Jordan suffered from the militant organization's operation a great deal more than Israel.

Tamari told Wiesenthal about himself and his family. He mentioned a Jewish friend, a doctor living in the Israeli part of divided Jerusalem. He sent him regards via people who crossed between the Jordanian and Israeli parts of the city. He spoke of a book he had read recently, the diary of Norman Bentwich, the attorney general of the British Mandatory government in Palestine, a Jew known for his moderate political views. Tamari had been very impressed. And Wiesenthal was impressed by Tamari: "It seems to me that I have spoken to an Arab whose level of intelligence and candor is above average, and he is no extreme nationalist," he wrote, evidently with some surprise.

Tamari asked Wiesenthal if he had ever spoken to an Arab before. Wiesenthal was cautious: "I did not give him a direct reply," he wrote. It is very possible that Tamari was the first Arab he had ever spoken with, and that he thought there was some intelligence value to the conversation and therefore wrote down all the details. Tamari said that he believed in peace, but there was only one man who was being listened to and that was Nasser, president of Egypt. There was no chance that Nasser would make peace.[1]

During that period, Wiesenthal did not expect that Israel's borders would change. Like most Israelis, he had learned to live with the armistice lines of 1949, and like them he believed that the Arabs had not given up on the dream of wiping Israel off the map and that therefore another war was in the cards. And in June 1967, the Six-Day War broke out.

The crisis that led up to the war began with Al Fatah terrorist incursions across Israel's northern border. The resulting tension between Israel and Syria soon spread to the southern border, between Israel and Egypt. The Egyptians threatened to destroy Israel, and most Israelis believed them. A dreadful anxiety gripped them; many thought of the Holocaust. In the cities, rabbis consecrated parks and sports fields to be used as cemeteries; hundreds of thousands of casualties were expected.[2] Wiesenthal tried to find out what was happening. He telephoned the embassy and some of his friends in Israel. No one could calm him down. There was a sense of doom. The harrowing memories he carried within him came to the surface and overwhelmed him, too.

During those weeks, the flow of incoming mail increased greatly. Many Holocaust survivors wrote to share their anxiety with him; evidently it did not occur to them that he too was in a panic, and they expected him to encourage them. Despite the profound dread, he tried to maintain his usual work routine. On June 5, the day the war broke out, he wrote to the Hamburg public prosecutors to notify them that he had located a witness in Riverdale, New York, who was willing to testify in a case they were preparing against a Nazi criminal from the ghetto in Przmyśl, Poland.[3]

But on the same day, perhaps for the first time in his life, Wiesenthal turned down a request for an interview. "You will surely understand that in Israel's present circumstances I do not have the head for interviews," he wrote to the journalist who had contacted him.[4] He wanted to help Israel in its most difficult hour and he knew only one way to do so: he pulled out his "Egypt" file and booked the Concordia press club in Vienna.

It was on June 5 that Israeli air force jets destroyed almost all Egypt's military aircraft on the ground. Like most Israelis, and millions of Jews and non-Jews across the world, Wiesenthal was engulfed by an almost boundless euphoria. This time, they all felt, the Jews had defended themselves and a second Holocaust had been averted, at the eleventh hour. On June 7, Israeli forces operating on the Jordanian front captured the Old City of Jerusalem and the Wailing Wall. At almost the same time, Wiesenthal arrived at the press club, where records indicate that more than 130 journalists had assembled for his press conference.

Wiesenthal presented them with a list of twenty-nine names of Nazi criminals who he said had taken refuge in Arab countries. It was evidently prepared hastily, like the list he had given the Americans in 1945. This was a subject that had always concerned him; Nazis living among the Arabs, he declared, saw the war as an opportunity to complete the murder of the Jews that had been halted twenty years before.

At the head of the list was Alois Brunner, one of Eichmann's assistants, who had at first lived in Damascus and was now in Cairo, Wiesenthal stated. He had played host to the mufti at Auschwitz during the war, Wiesenthal claimed, and now the Palestinians were putting out propaganda that called explicitly for the extermination of the Jews. He told the reporters that Franz Stangl, the commander of Treblinka who had been arrested in Brazil, had gone to Damascus after the war. Among the other names he mentioned was Friedrich Warzok, the SS officer from the Janowska camp, who, according to Wiesenthal, was living peacefully in Cairo.

Between six and seven thousand Nazi criminals were living in Arab lands, Wiesenthal asserted. Some had arrived there before the war, others managed to escape from British prisoner-of-war camps in Egypt, and still others reached the Middle East with the help of various escape ratlines—Wiesenthal mentioned ODESSA. The Arabs needed the Nazis' professional skills. At first they used them to organize their police forces and propaganda apparatus, which was responsible for, among other things, the translation of *Mein Kampf* into Arabic, and now they were integrating them into the production of missiles and chemical weapons, Wiesenthal said.

Over the years, the Nazis who were living in the Arab world expanded their activities into Europe. Wiesenthal said they were helping neo-Nazi organizations, providing them with weapons and sabotage materials and helping them spread propaganda against the restitution agreements between West Germany and Israel, the establishment of diplomatic relations between the two countries, and the postponement of the application of the statute of limitations to Nazi war crimes. He was able to provide the Arabic names taken by some of the men on his list, and he also named the government departments in which some of them were employed.[5]

The material preserved in his archives does not make it possible to know for sure how Wiesenthal managed to obtain the names on his list. It is reasonable to assume that he did it the same way he found those of other Nazi criminals, by relying on open sources, such as items in the press, and information he got from diplomats, businessmen, and journalists who traveled to and from Arab countries and met the Germans there.

The Egypt file in the Wiesenthal archive contains a very detailed report compiled by a British journalist, Norman Barrymaine. He went to Egypt in 1953 to look for a man he identified in his account using a false name and the initial of his real name, B. It is possible that he meant Martin Bormann, Hitler's close associate. It is not clear who sent Barrymaine to Cairo and financed his mission, but his report is replete with information about Germans living in the Egyptian capital. Apparently Wiesenthal passed the names on to Israel, and he may also have obtained some names from Israel that he did not have before. At least some of the names on his list came from a similar list drawn up by an organization for veterans of the anti-Nazi underground.[6]

About two months after he published his list, Wiesenthal received a rather embarrassing letter from West Germany's central war crimes agency in Ludwigsburg. The chief of the agency, Adalbert Rückerl, could identify only ten out of the twenty-nine names on the list Wiesenthal had presented at the press conference. The details Wiesenthal provided for those ten were more or less the same as those known to the agency, but apart from Alois Brunner, Rückerl could not confirm that any of the men on his list had actually been living in an Arab country. Moreover, nineteen of the names provided by Wiesenthal were entirely unknown to Rückerl, and he stated emphatically that one of the persons named had never existed. There are also no records of these people in the Wiesenthal archive or at Yad Vashem. This naturally brings to mind the "news item" Wiesenthal had invented and planted in the press years before to the effect that Eichmann was in Egypt.

Israel's victory produced a stream of congratulatory messages to Wiesenthal, as if it had been his personal triumph. Many came from Germans he didn't know who did not distinguish between Israelis and Jews. Wiesenthal did not disabuse them of their error, and thanked them as if they had indeed sent their congratulations to the correct address.

The feared "second Holocaust" that had menaced Israel before the war and the unexpected victory—which included the conquest of the Western Wall and holy places on the West Bank—actually did, at least for a while, smooth over the estrangement between Israelis and Jews of the Diaspora. Instead of the alienation Wiesenthal had felt once he realized how little the Zionist movement had done to rescue the Jews during the Holocaust, there now was a deep sense of shared destiny. Wiesenthal particularly identified with Menachem Begin, who until the Six-Day War was the leader of Israel's parliamentary opposition.

As an admirer of Begin's mentor, Ze'ev Jabotinsky, Wiesenthal supported Begin's politics, although he did not share his opposition to the restitution agreements with Germany. Once or twice he had visited Begin and his wife, Aliza, in their Tel Aviv apartment. They seemed somewhat more Jewish to him than many Israelis, whose language, Hebrew, he could not speak. With the Begins, he spoke Yiddish.[7] On the eve of the outbreak of the war, a national unity government had been set up and Begin served in it as a minister without portfolio, making him one of the fathers of the victory.

After the war, Wiesenthal could identify not only with the State of Israel but also with the policies of its government. He adopted its declared position: there would be no withdrawal from occupied territories without peace and no peace without direct negotiations; there would be no return to the prewar borders; East Jerusalem would remain under Israeli control and the entire, united city would be Israel's capital forever. This was what most Israelis wanted. That same summer, Wiesenthal toured the cities of the West Bank accompanied by Elazar, the Mossad agent, who had by now told him his real name.

———

The Six-Day War placed the dispute between the Arabs and Israel, particularly the Israeli-Palestinian conflict, squarely at the center of international public discourse, and it became intertwined with the political, social, cultural, and ethical upheaval that typified the 1960s. The New Left created a storm of rebellion that swept over the United States and Europe, bringing down the entire system of existing conventions, so that at a certain stage it seemed as though there was a need to define good and evil anew, to affirm what was permitted and what was forbidden.

More and more people also felt a need to take a position "for Israel" or "against Israel" and even tended to define their moral identity on the basis of their attitude toward the conflict with the Palestinians. The topic found its way into party politics in many countries. Wiesenthal's efforts to defend Israel's positions were, in his eyes, part of his moral and political struggle to defend the basic concepts of Judaism and Zionism that had shaped his life.

Sometimes he felt confused. The birth of the New Left in Germany came about partly as a protest against the role of former Nazis in German society; Wiesenthal therefore had every reason to support this political orientation. But many of the movement's leaders backed the Palestinians, and Wiesenthal imagined that he detected an anti-Semitic tone in their writings. The European social democratic movement, on the other hand, tended to support Israel, while the socialists in Austria were lenient toward former Nazis. Things became even more complicated when, after the Six-Day War, more and more Israelis began demanding withdrawal from the territories conquered in the war. They too spoke in the name of Israeli interests and defined themselves as patriots.

One of these was Uri Avneri. Born in Germany, he settled in Palestine as a child and was now editor of the antiestablishment weekly *Ha'olam Hazeh*. Wiesenthal actually had good reason to respect him. The magazine had opposed Prime Minister Ben-Gurion's regime, which Wiesenthal also despised, and it had led the campaign against Rezso Kastner, together with Shmuel Tamir, whom Wiesenthal had helped. Avneri advocated the establishment of an independent Palestinian state alongside Israel. And even at that early date he was not alone: the then chief of the general staff, Yitzhak Rabin, also supported the idea.[8]

In 1969, Avneri gave an interview to a leftist journal published in Berlin, and he was asked for his opinion on a number of people who supported right-wing circles in Germany, among them Wiesenthal. "I hardly know him," Avneri replied, "but I don't like him. I simply have the impression that he makes a business out of it. That he lives off the Nazi crimes. If a state agency carried out these investigations—fine. But if what we have is a private enterprise that makes money—then the whole thing, from a purely emotional point of view, is not so nice, in my opinion."

Wiesenthal dashed off a long letter to Avneri, in which he described his own position among the various ideological camps. He did not expect Avneri to like him, he wrote. The old right hated him because he prevented the obliteration of Nazi war crimes, and the New Left hated him because he supported Israel.

As a member of the Jewish people who was well aware of its history of suffering, he continued, he knew that at each historical juncture there were Jews who paraded the streets with a sign around their necks saying "Down with Us." In the final analysis, they were consigned to the garbage bin of history. "Longing for the garbage bin may also be what motivates you," Wiesenthal wrote to Avneri, and he signed off, "With contempt."[9]

The occupation of the Palestinian areas returned the arguments back to square one of the conflict: 1948. "Isn't it tragic," a young German asked Wiesenthal, "that the creation of Israel, that attempt to redress the injustice done to the Jews, has only given rise to fresh injustice: Israel has a national home, but aren't the expelled Palestinians the new Jews?"

This young German no doubt regarded himself as a great moralist, Wiesenthal wrote sarcastically, and continued, "No, it is not tragic. The creation of Israel was the only possible and the only correct reaction to Auschwitz. There had to be a country in the world were the Jews were the landlords instead of tolerated guests."[10] Wiesenthal may have been sorry that it was not he but rather Israel's foreign minister, Abba Eban, who defined the old borders as "Auschwitz lines," but he certainly identified with this definition and mobilized to broadcast it. He put his voice, which by now had moral weight, at Israel's disposal, as well as his connections with the media and an increasingly large portion of his time. Wiesenthal was now the focus of worldwide interest. His autobiography had appeared in some twenty languages.

2. Life Stories

Wiesenthal was good at telling stories, but he never wrote well. His literary agent, Charles Ronsac of the Opera Mundi agency in Paris, correctly believed that it would be wrong to leave such a dramatic tale up to him alone and looked for a ghostwriter to write his autobiography. The choice

fell upon an acquaintance of Wiesenthal's, Josef Wechsberg. A native of
Czechoslovakia, he had written for *The New Yorker* and as of the 1950s was
living in Vienna. "Wechsberg was a wonderful man," Wiesenthal would
recall in years to come. "I wrote a report, and he transformed it into
a work of literature." A Jew who, like Wiesenthal, had made Vienna his
home, and only one year younger than his subject, Wechsberg expertly discerned what Wiesenthal wanted to say and what the world wanted to hear.

The Murderers Among Us was framed as a series of exciting suspense tales,
such as the discovery of a cache of Jewish prayer books after the war.
They were piled up in the dark cellar of an ancient castle in a dense forest,
thousands of books. "For a long while we stood there, without being able
to utter a sound," Wechsberg related, writing for Wiesenthal. Someone
took some of the books, brought them to his lips, and put them back on
the pile. "Suddenly I heard a groan. I turned around. The young rabbi
was holding a prayer book. He was looking at its first page and his face
was white as a sheet. Suddenly he collapsed onto the ground . . .

"I picked up the prayer book and opened it. On the first page there was
something written in a woman's handwriting. There was no doubt that she
had written it in a very emotional state: 'They have just come to our town.
In a few minutes they will be in our house. If anyone finds this prayer
book, please notify my dear brother . . . don't forget us and don't forget
our murderers. They . . .' The rest was illegible. I closed the prayer book
and looked at the young man. He was still pale, but now he was tranquil.
'If you don't mind,' he said, 'I would like to keep this prayer book myself.
It belonged to my sister. She died in the camp at Treblinka.'"

Wechsberg apparently thought this was one of those stories it was
not wise to endanger by checking its authenticity. The Austrian historian
Evelyn Adunka asked Wiesenthal where exactly this castle was, who the
man was who found the prayer book, and what happened to the books.
Wiesenthal could not answer.[11] Old books and works of art pillaged by
the Nazis sparked his imagination and preoccupied him. His book is full
of such tales; many of them cannot be verified.

Newsmagazines like *Time* and *Der Spiegel* covered the book and published
extracts from it, and it became a worldwide bestseller. In the Unites States
about a quarter of a million copies were sold and in France and Holland
about forty-five thousand each. In Sweden, Norway, Finland, Italy, and
Germany a total of sixty thousand were sold. Carmen Hofbauer, who has
researched Wiesenthal's literary output, never managed to find the sales
figures for the rest of Europe, or for Brazil, Japan, or Israel, but altogether

close to half a million copies were sold.[12] The book came out with perfect timing, a few months before the arrest of Franz Stangl. Wiesenthal's agent quickly made sure to include this story in a new edition.[13]

Wiesenthal's successes, like his role in the capture of Eichmann, and his tracking down the police officer who arrested Anne Frank, reflected devotion to his mission, resourcefulness, and courage, and Wechsberg depicted it all excellently. Part of the book's success came from the fact that Wiesenthal included as yet unsolved cases. This added a dimension of suspense to his story and left open the promise of more to come, as in the Stangl case. Among the Nazi criminals not yet caught was Gestapo head Heinrich Müller, as well as Mengele and Bormann.

Müller was, in Wiesenthal's eyes, the most wanted Nazi war criminal. "He may have found refuge in Russia, but I doubt that he remained alive," he noted.[14] As a rule, Wiesenthal did not tend to presume that his quarries were dead, but given his connection with the Mossad, it may not have been a coincidence that he voiced the hypothesis that Müller was no longer alive, because the Mossad was still trying to catch him. In August 1966, Mossad chief Meir Amit reported to Prime Minister Levi Eshkol on the attempts to track down Müller and Bormann and presented various possibilities for further action. Eshkol said he would think about it.[15]

On the night of November 5, 1967, the neighbors of Frau Sophie Müller heard suspicious sounds coming from her apartment in a residential block at Manzigerweg 4 in the Pasing neighborhood of Munich. The wife of the former Gestapo chief was not at home, and the neighbors called the police. Two men were arrested in the building's stairwell and they identified themselves as Israelis. The case was widely covered in the media, and it gave Wiesenthal's book a timely dimension.

Isser Harel took advantage of the failure of the Müller operation to run down his successor and rival, Amit. Harel claimed that Amit was motivated not by the moral importance of capturing Nazi war criminals, but the desire to win glory by taking credit for an operation like the capture of Eichmann. The Müller file in Wiesenthal's archive provides no evidence of any involvement on his part in this abortive attempt to get on the Gestapo chief's trail.[16]

The Mossad also kept up its interest in Mengele. Wiesenthal now had a new liaison officer, who identified himself as A. Livnat and corresponded with him in English from POB 7027 Tel Aviv. "Concerning the woman who had come back from Paraguay and has lived for years with Mengele I undertook all the necessary steps. But it will take a little longer before one will be able to speak openly with her," Wiesenthal wrote to him.[17] He maintained contacts with people who gave him information about Mengele's wife; they may have been either paid detectives or volunteers. Wiesenthal briefed them not to sign their letters with their own names but to use the code names he gave them, like "Xavier" and "Felix."[18] It was efforts of this kind that were still the center of his life.

The book's success created a dramatic improvement in the economic situation of Simon and Cyla Wiesenthal. They were now living in their own house in Mestrozigasse in the upscale nineteenth district in northern Vienna. The house exuded middle-class comfort, but not wealth. Their daughter, Paulinka, was no longer living with them. She had married in December 1965, and moved to Holland. Her mother was now lonelier than ever. Wiesenthal had always wanted another child, but his wife had refused. Now it was too late.[19]

About two and a half months after the Six-Day War, Wiesenthal received a personal letter from a relative that confronted him in one fell swoop with the upheavals of Jewish destiny. A woman by the name of Theolinde Rapp wrote to him from Cairo. She was the wife of his uncle on his mother's side, James, a dentist who had left Galicia in the 1920s and, in a characteristically Jewish odyssey, ended up in Egypt. For the past forty-five years the couple had been living in Port Said, at the northern end of the Suez Canal.

Wiesenthal did not know much about Rapp. There had been a picture of him on the wall of his parents' home in Buczacz, and he remembered him as a handsome man. He was eighteen years older than Wiesenthal, who had still been a child when Rapp completed his dentistry studies. When Wiesenthal was liberated from Mauthausen he had tried to contact him, but could not find him.

Now he learned that they had gone to Egypt while the British were still ruling there and remained there after their departure, after King Farouk was deposed and the Free Officers' revolt placed Nasser in power. James and Theolinde Rapp had remained behind even when most of the Jews left Egypt in the exodus that followed the 1956 Suez War. Now he was seventy-seven, half blind, and ill. His wife, now eighty-one, wrote to his famous relative from the Austrian embassy in Cairo and the letter was passed on to Wiesenthal via the Foreign Ministry in Vienna. In the wake of the Six-Day War, she related, she and her husband had been forced to give up their apartment in Port Said and they had lost all their possessions. They were now living as penniless refugees in the embassy.[20]

The Foreign Ministry added some details: the embassy had rented a room for the couple with an Egyptian family in Cairo but they had not gotten along well there, and now the embassy was thinking of arranging a place for them at an old-age home run by Italian nuns in Alexandria. Returning to Port Said was out of the question, as a war of attrition was raging along the Suez Canal and the Egyptians were evacuating the residents of all the cities along the canal.[21] Thus had the Six-Day War, along with everything else that it wrought, destroyed what remained of the lives of an elderly Jew from Galicia who had lived with his wife among the Egyptians and fixed their teeth for almost half a century, two decades of which had seen war against the Jewish state that had risen on the other side of the desert.

Wiesenthal could appreciate the tragic irony of this story. He promised to help the Rapps and sent them a few hundred dollars. Then he rummaged through his lists of addresses for the names of family members in America—in New York, Chicago, and Oakland, California. Most of them hardly ever saw him and some were hurt by this fact. They would have been happy to host their relative, the famous Nazi hunter. One of them was well-known in his own right—the screenwriter Philip Rapp, who wrote film scripts for Danny Kaye and popular TV comedies. For Rapp, who lived in Beverly Hills, Wiesenthal found time, while the rest of his relatives mostly had to make do with letters of apology. But now, Wiesenthal shared with them the sad story of how their relatives were stranded in Cairo, and they all pitched in to help.[22]

In the meantime, Wiesenthal had achieved a degree of prominence in the Cold War.

3. Operation Danube

Wiesenthal's enlistment in Israel's struggle to improve its standing in world public opinion placed him in opposition to the mighty propaganda machinery of the Communist states. Following the Six-Day War, these states, apart from Romania, cut their diplomatic ties with Israel and a period of open hostility ensued. Wiesenthal thought in historical terms and he tended to relate to history according to the way it affected his life. On the face of things, he had good reason to be grateful to the Red Army and its commanders and to Stalin, who had sent them to crush Nazi

Germany. But Wiesenthal remembered the oppressive regime of the Soviets in Lvov. As early as 1953, he turned to the Human Rights League in Austria to protest against the anti-Semitism that characterized the last days of Stalin's reign.[23]

He fought Stalinism in his accustomed way: just as in his youth he had drawn cartoons against Hitler, in 1962 he published a book full of trenchant anti-Communist jokes. He saw humor as the weapon of the weak and the oppressed, almost the only means that they had to fight back against Communism and its ideological hypocrisy, its stagnant economics, its corrupt bureaucracy, its stale culture, its imbecilic propaganda, and its abasement of humanity.

Some of the jokes were ones that he made up himself, others he had heard or read somewhere: "How do we know Adam and Eve were in the Soviet Union? Because they were naked and barefoot and they thought they were in Paradise."

"Three inmates in a Soviet concentration camp are chatting. 'Why are you here?' asks one. 'Because in 1939 I insulted Comrade Popov,' says the other, 'And you?' 'I am here because in 1943 I praised Popov.' 'What about you?' they ask the third inmate. 'I'm Popov,' he says."

"Nikita Khrushchev and John F. Kennedy have a car race. Kennedy comes in first in his Cadillac and Khrushchev follows a long time later in his Popjeda. The next day's *Pravda*, the party newspaper, reports that Khrushchev came in second and Kennedy second last."

"Leonid Brezhnev is walking along the Chinese border with a goat. Mao appears on the other side and asks: 'Why are you walking with a pig?'

" 'It isn't a pig, it's a goat,' says Brezhnev.

" 'You shut up,' says Mao. 'I wasn't talking to you.' "

"One day, Brezhnev got sick of hearing criticism about the persecution of Jews in the USSR. To get the world to drop the subject he calls in his minister of culture, Yekaterina Furtseva, and gives her three months to build thirty synagogues and appoint thirty rabbis. When the three months are up he demands a report. 'The synagogues have been built,' says Furtseva, 'But we haven't got any rabbis, because all the applicants were Jews.' "

According to Wiesenthal, sixty-five thousand copies of the book were sold and many were smuggled into the countries behind the Iron Curtain. This was his contribution to the breakdown of Communism. Wiesenthal was proud of this, but he preferred not to be identified with the book and he used a pen name, Mischa Kukin. In light of his work for the CIA, it is possible that the Americans financed the publication of the book and its circulation in Eastern Europe. Wiesenthal also cultivated relations with American radio stations, such as Radio Free Europe, that broadcast to the Communist countries.[24] Until the Six-Day War, nonetheless, he had managed to maintain useful relations with the Eastern European states through their embassies in Vienna, as well as the Soviet ambassador. Following the war, however, he had no doubt as to where he stood. Now he began to focus on Nazi criminals who had found refuge in Communist countries.

In September 1968 Wiesenthal issued a list of thirty-nine former Nazis working as journalists in East Germany. He said he did it because the East German press was publishing anti-Semitic attacks on Israel. A British correspondent, Jonathan Steele, checked the names and found that they included several people who even before the end of the Nazi era had crossed over to the Communist opposition, and that two of them had even been tried by the Nazis and sentenced to death in absentia.[25]

The Yugoslav minister of justice received a letter from Wiesenthal protesting against the granting of asylum to a Nazi criminal.[26] The Soviet authorities received a list of names of war criminals with a request for information on their activities. After a year passed by without a response, Wiesenthal condemned them. To Israeli foreign minister Abba Eban he sent documents purporting to prove that the Soviet Union had malevolently neglected the rescue of Jews during the Holocaust.[27]

In January 1970, he published a booklet containing the names of senior figures in the Polish government who, he claimed, were anti-Semites. He sent it to all the members of the U.S. Senate, among others. One of the people mentioned was the Polish deputy minister of culture, Kazimierz Rusinek, with whom Wiesenthal had a long-standing personal score to settle. He alleged that it was Rusinek who had cursed him and struck him on the day after his release from Mauthausen.[28] Two years later he published another list of former Nazis active in East Germany, this time university faculty members.[29]

And so the Holocaust became part of the Cold War. The hostility of the Soviet Union and its satellites toward Israel and the rise of anti-Semitism in these countries intensified this process. "Because Hitler and Stalin gave anti-Semitism a bad name, a substitute has been found," Wiesenthal said in a speech. "Today they no longer say, 'It's the Jew's fault'; they say 'It's the Zionist's fault.' "[30] Along with many other individuals, he too enlisted in the struggle against the oppression of the Jews in the Soviet Union and for their right to leave. He lobbied foreign ambassadors and he gave speeches.[31]

The Cold War, which had already hampered the search for Nazi war criminals in the 1950s, also forced Wiesenthal to compromise. He knew that the United States employed war criminals. More than once he restrained himself from exposing former Nazis in senior positions in West Germany. In at least one case he held back to advance Israel's interests. This was the case of Hans Globke.

In the Nazi era, Globke had been involved in enforcing the notorious Nuremberg laws. Together with Eichmann's staff he had a hand in the expulsion of Germany's Jews and the pillaging of their property. In the 1950s, he served as one of Chancellor Konrad Adenauer's top aides, and he was involved in the establishment of relations with Israel and the restitution agreements. Wiesenthal attacked Nahum Goldmann for having anything to do with Globke, but he did so only in a private letter.[32]

Before the Eichmann trial, Ben-Gurion instructed the prosecutor, Gideon Hausner, to steer clear of mentioning Globke's role. He did not want to offend Adenauer, Hausner explained later. East Germany had offered to supply the court with much material on Globke, through an attorney by the name of Friedrich Kaul. Wiesenthal, who was in Jerusalem for the trial, confronted him at a press conference and said it was all Communist propaganda.

A few months after the Six-Day War, he also responded with cool hostility to information coming from East Germany, according to which the president of West Germany, Heinrich Leubke, was involved in the construction of Nazi concentration camps. "East Germany specializes in withholding documentation and putting it on the market only when the persons concerned attain senior posts in West Germany," Wiesenthal wrote. This was during Leubke's second term, and in 1969 the allegations compelled him to resign.[33]

The Communists saw Wiesenthal as an imperialist agent, and they did not underestimate his influence. In Poland articles appeared describing him variously as an agent of Israel, West Germany, and the United States. One of them included an implicit threat: there were people who knew Wiesenthal and his wife during the war, and they were liable to tell what they knew. The Polish embassy in Vienna distributed these articles in German translation. Wiesenthal protested to Austrian foreign minister Kurt Waldheim, but this incident was only the tip of the iceberg.[34]

Beginning in 1963, and for more than ten years after that, the Polish secret service conducted close surveillance of Wiesenthal and his activities. They called it Operation Danube. Wiesenthal's code name was Izmir. The main object of the exercise was to recruit Wiesenthal as an agent. This was also the aim of the man identified as Agent No. 156 who visited Wiesenthal at home and in his office. He was not the only one.

The Poles maintained a network of spies in Vienna whose duties included keeping Wiesenthal under surveillance. They drew up lists of people who were in touch with him and gathered reams of material on these people, mostly Holocaust survivors. They looked into Wiesenthal's sources of funding in the United States and surmised that the Mossad was also financing him. They read all the correspondence addressed to him from Poland, including mail from the Auschwitz museum. They regarded his Documentation Center as nothing more than a front. One of their sources is described in their documents as being an employee of the Mossad by the name of Greta. According to Greta, Wiesenthal never kept important documents in the office, but in a safe in the Israeli embassy.

In tandem with the work done by their agents in Vienna, the Poles also invested considerable effort in attempts to find evidence that Wiesenthal had collaborated with the Nazis. This failed, and in 1974 the Polish secret service reached the conclusion that there was no point in continuing the operation, as Wiesenthal hated the Communists and would never serve them. The Danube file was sent to the archive.[35]

The East German regime also tried to tackle Wiesenthal. For one thing, they checked the names of the journalists and faculty members that Wiesenthal alleged had been Nazi sympathizers. Here and there, a note of admiration for his struggle against the Nazis crept into their reports. The need to check his accusations arose after their fellow Communist parties in other countries asked if there was anything to them. To their great embarrassment it turned out the answer was positive. Officials of the East German security service, the Stasi, explained that in some cases the subjects had been very young during the Nazi period, but in others, their examinations revealed that Wiesenthal was right. So the question arose, what was to be done about it?

The Stasi officials realized that Wiesenthal would not have any great difficulty in proving many of his claims, so they recommended to the minister in charge of their organization not to deny them. They proposed instead that East Germany publish two lists of its own: one of senior members of the Communist regime whose past was clean and another that would expose former Nazis serving in senior posts in West Germany. Moreover, they would look into Wiesenthal's past, to see if they could discover that he had collaborated with the Nazis.

They probed as far back as his childhood and up to his incarceration in the Nazi camps; their reports said, among other things, that Wiesenthal served as an agent of the Israeli secret service, but there was nothing to show he served the Nazis. The Stasi therefore decided to seek the help of their counterparts in Poland, and two officers were specially dispatched to Warsaw.

Major Kramer and NCO Muregger, both of Department IX/10, were made very welcome in the Polish capital. The atmosphere was cordial and the Poles got down to work right away, again sifting through old files. After three days, they met up for a concluding session. The Poles knew that Wiesenthal was an Israeli spy, they reported, but to their great regret this time too they failed to come up with anything to show he had worked with the Germans. The two Stasi men went back to East Germany and asked for the help of the Soviet Union.

The comrades in Moscow also hurried to report that Wiesenthal was known to be an imperialist agent. They knew that he was in touch with the press attaché at the Israeli consulate in Vienna and that he also worked for the Austrian secret service, where he was known as Ovid. They mentioned a certain lack of clarity as to the date when he was first arrested in Lvov. But they too could not uncover any devastating secrets.[36]

In the meantime, Wiesenthal was devoting a great deal of thought to his wartime memories and immersing himself in one of his most ambitious projects.

13.

"What Would You Have Done?"

I. The Sunflower

One day during the war, Wiesenthal's forced-labor unit stopped near a German military cemetery in Lvov. On each of the graves blossomed a sunflower, as erect as a soldier at attention, face to the sun. Brightly colored butterflies flitted from flower to flower, from grave to grave. Wiesenthal imagined he was watching a kind of secret communications network between the world of the dead and the world of the living, and suddenly he was filled with envy, he wrote, because his body would be dumped onto the corpses of others, and the corpses of others would be dumped onto his; the grave would perhaps be covered, but no sunflower would blossom on it.

Wiesenthal was a frustrated writer. The chase after Nazi criminals and the legal and political struggles did not satisfy him. He wanted also to take part in the ethical, philosophical, theological, and literary discourse that the Holocaust had inspired. But his literary talent was meager, and deep inside he must have known it. So he wrote a kind of autobiographical tale, with a moral dilemma at its core.

When it was done, in 1968, he sent this work to a large number of writers and intellectuals and asked for their comments. Several dozen agreed to allow him to publish their remarks together with his tale. Thus, he placed himself alongside them, and them alongside himself; one of them, or perhaps not.

The Sunflower, as he called the book that came out of this project, described a part of what happened to Wiesenthal during the war. At its climax, there is a dramatic encounter between him and an SS man. It happened at a time when Wiesenthal's routine took him from Janowska to the rail yard and back. The forced laborers were marched to and from work along the streets that he knew well. Passersby would look at them and occasionally some would wave at them, as if in greeting, but would stop immediately because they were scared of the SS guards. Once Wiesenthal saw a man he knew from his days as a student at the technical college. The man recognized him too but was afraid of greeting him with even a nod of his head. Wiesenthal noticed how surprised the man was to see that he was still alive. "We could read on the faces of the people in the streets that we were doomed," he wrote.

They reached the Polytechnic, an impressive neoclassical edifice with six marble pillars gracing its facade. Wiesenthal was reminded of his years as a student and how his gentile fellow students would declare "Jew-free days." Now the building was a military hospital. The Jewish slave laborers passed by the well-kept lawns and into the rear courtyard. Ambulances were coming in and out and the Jews had to stand up against the walls to make room for them. They were put in the charge of a German orderly.

"I had a curious feeling of strangeness in these surroundings, although I had spent several years here," Wiesenthal wrote. "I tried to remember if I had even been in this back courtyard. What would have brought me here?" There were large concrete containers full of blood-soaked bandages in the yard, and boxes, sacks, and packing material strewn all around. The prisoners loaded them onto trucks. The stench of medicines, disinfectants, and putrefaction hung in the air.

Red Cross sisters and orderlies were hurrying to and fro. Some lightly wounded soldiers were sitting on a bench. One of them got up and approached Wiesenthal and the other prisoners. "He looked at us as though we were animals in a zoo. Probably he was wondering how long we had to live," Wiesenthal wrote. The soldier's arm was in a sling. With his other hand he picked up a stone and threw it at Wiesenthal, shouting, "You Jewish swine." Wiesenthal stepped aside and the stone missed. A nurse who saw what was happening went up to him and asked if he was a Jew, and told him to follow her.

They went into the building and up the stairs, and again Wiesenthal couldn't remember if he'd been there or not. He thought that when he was a student he had used another staircase. The nurses and doctors were sur-

The famous "Nazi hunter" at work on a typical day. Wiesenthal conducted his search for Nazi criminals from a small apartment, surrounded by high piles of old newspapers and yellowing index cards. But his efforts brought dozens of Nazi criminals to justice. *(Luigi Caputo)*

Simon and Cyla Wiesenthal, soon after their marriage in 1936. They met in high school and remained together until her death in 2003. *(Simon Wiesenthal Archive, Vienna)*

In the 1920s, Wiesenthal was the leader of a Zionist youth movement in his hometown, Buczacz. Referring to this photograph, Wiesenthal later remarked that, even as a young boy, he detested uniforms and never wore one. *(Simon Wiesenthal Archive, Vienna)*

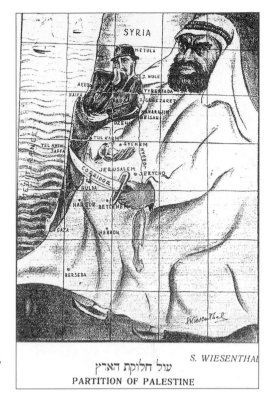

Later, as a student in Prague and Lvov in the 1930s, Wiesenthal supported the so-called revisionist Zionists, and occasionally drew cartoons protesting the partition of Palestine between Jews and Arabs. (*Simon Wiesenthal Archive, Vienna*)

S. WIESENTHAL

עול חלוקת הארץ
PARTITION OF PALESTINE

A German soldier in the Lvov ghetto during the war. Between 160,000 and 170,000 Jews were living in Lvov when the Germans took the city in 1941. By the end of the war, there were fewer than 4,000. (*Yad Vashem Archive*)

Jewish forced laborers at Plaszow concentration camp, where Wiesenthal was held in 1944. The camp gained international infamy as a result of Steven Spielberg's film *Schindler's List*, based on the novel by Thomas Keneally. *(Yad Vashem Archive)*

Hartheim Castle near Linz, Austria, where many staff members of the extermination camps received their training.

Shortly after his liberation from Mauthausen, Wiesenthal published a collection of graphic works depicting the Nazis and their crimes. This image shows Hitler setting off to turn the whole world into a single concentration camp. *(Paulinka Kreisberg)*

Mauthausen concentration camp, May 6, 1945, the day after its liberation by the U.S. Army. On May 3, approximately 80,000 people were officially registered as inmates, including Simon Wiesenthal. For the rest of his life, Wiesenthal remained grateful to America. *(United States Holocaust Memorial Museum)*

Surviving inmates of Mauthausen. An estimated 200,000 perished in the camp before liberation. Many others died immediately afterward. *(United States Holocaust Memorial Museum)*

Wiesenthal addressing a Zionist rally in a displaced persons' camp in 1948. The banner, in Yiddish, says: "The Country is calling you," meaning Israel. Wiesenthal always regarded himself as a Zionist, but never lived in Israel. *(Simon Wiesenthal Archive, Vienna)*

Simon and Cyla Wiesenthal, in 1946. Each had thought the other was dead, but after the war they miraculously found each other again. *(Simon Wiesenthal Archive, Vienna)*

Wiesenthal on his way to Israel in 1949, in a memorial procession he organized, with a glass box containing the remains of Holocaust victims. "The glass box," he wrote after the funeral in Jerusalem, "had suddenly become a kind of looking-glass . . . I could see the panicked faces of Jews who were whipped and clubbed into the gas chambers." *(Simon Wiesenthal Archive, Vienna)*

Adolf Eichmann, the architect of the Final Solution. After the war, Wiesenthal devoted his life to hunting down Eichmann and other Nazi criminals, and was the first to report Eichmann's whereabouts. *(Yad Vashem Archive)*

Wiesenthal in his office, with pictures of two suspected war criminals. He frequently shared details of his work with reporters, hoping the publicity would get him more information about the people he was seeking. It often did. *(Gérard Rancian)*

Over the years, Wiesenthal received thousands of anti-Semitic letters, most of which he kept in files marked *M* for "meshuganers," or crazy people.

Many Hollywood celebrities admired Wiesenthal. Here he is in 1982 with Elizabeth Taylor, who wrote to him: "I love you and we all need you." Frank Sinatra once sang "My Way" for him. *(Arthur Waldinger)*

During his pursuit of Nazi criminals, Wiesenthal made contact with numerous heads of state. Here he is with U.S. President Ronald Reagan in 1984. He also met and received support from Presidents Jimmy Carter and Bill Clinton. *(The White House)*

Wiesenthal with Israeli Prime Minister Menachem Begin (center) and Rabbi Marvin Hier, founder of the Simon Wiesenthal Center in Los Angeles. Wiesenthal admired Begin and had stormy differences of opinion with Hier. *(Simon Wiesenthal Center, Los Angeles)*

So was darf nie verjähren!
¡Esto no debe prescribir jamás! This must never prescribe!

In 1970, Wiesenthal led a worldwide postcard campaign protesting the statute of limitation that would have discontinued trials against Nazi criminals in Germany and Austria. The text under the photograph reads: "Such things must never happen again." The campaign was successful: the statute of limitation was abolished. *(Simon Wiesenthal Archive, Vienna)*

Among Wiesenthal's papers is an official portrait of Austrian Chancellor Bruno Kreisky defaced by a swastika scribbled on Kreisky's lapel. In 1975, Kreisky had falsely accused Wiesenthal of collaboration with the Nazis. *(Simon Wiesenthal Archive, Vienna)*

AMERICA SAYS NO TO WALDHEIM!

Waldheim—May 22, 1943, Yugoslavia.

SIMON WIESENTHAL CENTER
9760 WEST PICO BLVD., LOS ANGELES, CA 90035 / (213) 553-9036

In 1986, the Wiesenthal Center in Los Angeles joined the World Jewish Congress in a postcard campaign against former UN Secretary-General Kurt Waldheim, who was running for the Austrian presidency, and accused him of war crimes. Wiesenthal himself refused to accuse Waldheim of murder and suggested the matter be put before an international commission, which was done. *(Simon Wiesenthal Archive, Vienna)*

Wiesenthal had enemies and admirers, but few friends. In the 1970s, he found love with Eva Dukes. Living in New York, she was almost fifty when they met, and in her second marriage. *(Courtesy of Eva Dukes)*

Wiesenthal at his seventieth birthday party in Los Angeles in 1978. *(Arthur Waldinger)*

Wiesenthal's sixty years as a "Nazi hunter" gained him particular respect in Holland, where his daughter and her family lived for several years and where he felt at home. Here he is at age eighty-seven, on a bench in the town of Utrecht in 1995. *(Sjaak Ramakers/Sjaak Ramakers Photography)*

prised to see him there. They soon reached a hall Wiesenthal remembered well—it was here that he had received his diploma. The nurse stopped to talk to another nurse. Wiesenthal weighed trying to escape. He was familiar with all the corridors. Suddenly he forgot about himself and the nurse and he was back with his anti-Semitic teachers, who tried over and over again to make life difficult for him. He saw the hand of one of them holding a pencil and making thick lines across his drawings.

The nurse signaled Wiesenthal to wait and he returned to reality. He leaned on the railing and looked at the hall below, at the wounded soldiers being carried in on stretchers, lying on their backs, looking up, their eyes meeting his. Again his mind wandered back to his student days, but the nurse returned and was evidently happy to see he was still there. She pulled him into the dean's office, but instead of the desk and cupboards that he remembered there was a single white bed, with a night table beside it. "Something white was looking at me out of the blankets. At first I could not grasp the situation," Wiesenthal wrote.

The nurse bent over the bed and whispered something and Wiesenthal heard a deeper voice whispering back. In the darkness of the room, he could now see a motionless figure wrapped in white. He tried to make out its head. The nurse told him to remain where he was and left the room. Then he heard a voice from the bed saying, "Please come nearer. I can't speak loudly."

Now Wiesenthal could see him more clearly. White, bloodless hands, head completely bandaged with openings only for mouth, nose, and ears. Wiesenthal was not sure that this "uncanny situation" was actually occurring, there in the dean's room, him wearing a prison uniform, alone with the "corpselike figure." He had no idea who the man was.

He sat hesitantly on the edge of the bed and the patient asked him to come closer. "I have not much longer to live, I know the end is near," he whispered and then fell silent. Wiesenthal too said nothing. The wounded man said he knew people were dying everywhere, but before he died he wanted to talk about an experience that was tormenting him. Otherwise he would not be able to die in peace.

Wiesenthal felt that the man was staring at him through the bandage covering his eyes. He said that one of the nurses, who had brought him a letter from his mother and read it to him, had told him there were Jewish prisoners in the courtyard. He had asked her to bring one of them to his bedside. Wiesenthal assumed the man was a Jew and that before he died he wanted to see a Jew for the last time.

The man introduced himself. Wiesenthal would identify him only by his first name, Karl. He was a member of the SS. He gripped Wiesenthal's hand and held it tightly and said that he had to tell him about a dreadful crime he had committed a year before. His mother must not hear of it, he said, but he had to tell a Jew about it. Wiesenthal was not alarmed—there wasn't an atrocity he was not familiar with—but he did feel uneasy. He understood that the German soldier wanted to confess and it occurred to him that one day a sunflower would grow on his grave.

"I was not born a murderer," the soldier began. He was from Stuttgart and he was twenty-one. "That is too soon to die. I have had very little out of life," he said. Wiesenthal thought about the Jewish children the Nazis had murdered, and the dying SS man seemed to guess what was on his mind: "I know what you are thinking and I understand. But may I not still say that I am too young . . . ?" His father, a factory manager, was a Social Democrat and with the rise of the Nazis he got into difficulties, like many others. His mother brought him up as a Catholic, but he nevertheless joined the Hitler Youth and when war broke out he volunteered for the SS. Outside, Wiesenthal heard the voice of the nurse who had brought him there.

The wounded man told his story in great detail. Wiesenthal wondered why he didn't tell him what he wanted. Finally he reached a summer's day in August 1941. He had taken part in the conquest of Dnepropetrovsk, a large city in eastern Ukraine. He described the fierce house-to-house fighting. In one street stood a group of 150 or 200 Jews, some of them women holding babies.

A truck carrying gasoline cans drove up, and the SS men ordered some Jewish youths to take them into one of the houses and they obeyed. Then the SS troops began pushing the Jews into the house, cursing and kicking them; one of them used a whip. It was not a very large house, but soon all the Jews had been crammed into it.

"He was silent and my heart started to beat violently," wrote Wiesenthal, adding that he thought he knew how the story would end. "I might have been among those who were forced into that house." The wounded man went on. Another truck drove up loaded with Jews and they too were forced into the house. Then the doors were locked. Wiesenthal wanted to go and stood up, but the man asked him to stay and went on with his story. The troops were ordered to back away a few yards and then take the pins out of hand grenades and throw them through the windows into the house. It began burning.

At a window on the second floor, there was a man with a child in his arms, and a woman. The man covered the child's eyes with his free hand and jumped out the window. The woman followed. The SS men shot them. Others jumped, some of them in flames, and they too were shot.

Wiesenthal was reminded of Eli, a six-year-old boy he had sometimes seen in the Lvov ghetto. One day he had seen him next to a house, standing on the tips of his toes to scrape up some crumbs from a windowsill that someone had left there for the birds to eat. Wiesenthal never forgot what he looked like. "He had large questioning eyes that could not understand—accusing eyes," he wrote.

The wounded SS man went on talking. He acknowledged his guilt. He would die soon. To die in peace he needed a Jew to forgive him. He asked Wiesenthal to forgive him.

Wiesenthal looked through the window. Outside there was glorious sunshine. Inside, he wrote, "two men who had never known each other had been brought together for a few hours by Fate. One asked the other for help. But the other was himself helpless and able to do nothing for him." He got up and looked at the wounded man. His hands were folded and Wiesenthal imagined that he saw a sunflower between them. "At last I made up my mind and without a word I left the room," he wrote. The nurse who brought him wasn't there. He walked down the stairs, and the doctors and nurses once again looked at him in surprise. He returned to his comrades in the courtyard.

While he was a prisoner, Artur and Josek, a religious Jew, were Wiesenthal's two good friends. Wiesenthal jokingly called Josek "Rabbi" and wrote that "his faith gave him answers to all questions, and I could only envy him." Once they were talking about the creation of man, and one of them wondered if the inmates and the camp commander "were truly made of the same stuff." They asked themselves how God allowed a place like the camp to exist. Artur, the skeptic, said God had apparently taken a vacation; Wiesenthal went to sleep and asked them to wake him up when God came back. Everyone laughed but Wiesenthal internalized the idea: God was on vacation and had not left anyone to replace him.

When he told his friends the story about what had happened at the hospital, they were pleased the German was dying. "One less," they said. One said he envied Wiesenthal. He would like to watch ten murderers dying every day. Josek, the "Rabbi," was pleased that Wiesenthal had not forgiven the SS man. "You would have had no right to do this," he said.

"What people have done to you yourself you can, if you like, forgive and forget. But it would have been a terrible sin to burden your conscience with other people's sufferings." Wiesenthal wasn't sure: "But aren't we a single community with the same destiny and one must answer for the other?" he asked.

Josek tried to cheer him up. He would have done the same, because he believed in life after death, and what would Wiesenthal tell the dead people of Dnepropetrovsk if they demanded to know who gave him the right to forgive their murderer? Wiesenthal found it difficult to be persuaded. He felt that the murderer showed a deep and genuine repentance. Did this not carry any weight? Now Artur joined in: "If you had forgiven him, you would never have forgiven yourself all your life," he said. He thought Wiesenthal was making too much fuss over his SS man.

His doubts and misgivings gave him no rest, and he asked himself if all this had really happened at all. The work in the hospital courtyard continued and a few days later, the same nurse came back and ordered Wiesenthal to come with her. She led him to a storeroom and gave him a parcel wrapped in green paper. A piece of cloth was attached to it with an address on it. The wounded SS man had died and asked the nurse to give his possessions to Wiesenthal. He refused to accept them. He told the nurse to send them to the dead man's mother at the attached address. She did not insist and he went back to work.

Two years later, Artur and Josek were dead. Wiesenthal had been transferred from one camp to another and at Mauthausen he met a Pole by the name of Bolek. He told him the story of the dying SS man. Bolek asked if he had shown signs of regret and said that if he had, then he deserved the mercy of forgiveness. Bolek was a Catholic, a student of theology. Wiesenthal continued to agonize over his decision.

Some time after the war, he decided to look for the SS man's mother. He said that he remembered the address attached to the package. He went to Stuttgart and after wandering around the ruins of the city for a while, he found her. She said that her son had been a good boy. Wiesenthal did not tell her about his crime. At this point, he identified him by the first letter of his family name. He thought often about Karl S., he wrote: every time he went into a hospital and saw a doctor or a nurse, or saw a sunflower. And then the question of forgiveness returned. He decided he could not handle it on his own, and he turned to the greatest writers and intellectuals of his generation. "What would you have done?" he asked.[1]

2. An F from Heinrich Böll

The hunt for Nazi war criminals and their prosecution entailed many basic legal and ethical questions and demanded new definitions of crime, guilt, responsibility, punishment, and justice. Most of the accused claimed that they were only obeying orders, making it necessary to distinguish between legal and illegal orders, which in turn raised the question of whether the Nazi regime itself was legal, as well as a debate over the degree of personal responsibility borne by each individual soldier. In addition it was necessary to clarify whether there was such a thing as collective guilt, and to restore the value of human life to its rightful place among other basic values. The nature of Nazi evil was scrutinized by many thinkers and Wiesenthal too was preoccupied by the question.

The concepts of confession and absolution added a theological dimension to the discussion. They have foundations in both Judaism and Christianity, but in the absence of a belief in God, they lack meaning. The Holocaust led many people to reexamine their faith. Wiesenthal was a secular person before it happened and he had no personal need to wrestle with the question "Where was God?" Instead he turned to the professionals: academics, philosophers, authors, religious leaders, and some statesmen.

Many of them encouraged him. "I think I would have acted the way you did," the philosopher Herbert Marcuse wrote from America. "One cannot and should not go around happily killing and torturing and then, when the moment has come, simply ask, and receive, forgiveness. In my view, this perpetuates the crime." The American author Cynthia Ozick went further, questioning the idea that "vengeance brutalizes, forgiveness refines." She ended the long and reasoned essay she sent Wiesenthal with the words: "Let the SS man die unshriven. Let him go to hell."

The Italian writer Primo Levi, himself a survivor of the camps, assured Wiesenthal that he well understood the doubts that were tormenting him, but in the circumstances that he described, his decision represented the lesser evil. If he had forgiven the dying man, feeling as he did that he represented the entire Jewish people, he could have done so only by lying or by inflicting upon himself a terrible moral violence. Levi doubted that the SS man was truly repentant. The very fact that he had demanded a

Jewish prisoner be brought to him showed that he remained a Nazi and an anti-Semite, seeing the Jew as "an abnormal being, half-devil, half miracle worker." Some of the Christians who contributed to the debate wrote in the same vein as Levi, including the German Lutheran theologian Martin Niemöller.

But their belief in repentance and absolution made it difficult for some other religious leaders to support Wiesenthal's conduct. The Austrian prelate Franz Cardinal König required supreme verbal skill to meet Wiesenthal halfway without getting himself into theological hot water. Jesus preached that there was no limit to forgiveness, he wrote, but in view of the horrors Wiesenthal experienced, he understood that "an explicit pardon would have surpassed our concept of the human." The dying man still believed in God, the cardinal asserted, and Wiesenthal had listened to him and showed him sympathy, so that he "somehow felt accepted" by Wiesenthal, otherwise he would not have bequeathed him his personal belongings. Some wrote that Wiesenthal's question had no answer: both the American author Herman Wouk and the Israeli historian Saul Friedländer wrote that they could not answer the question.

The Sunflower was a very ambitious project. Wiesenthal wanted big names, but some never replied, among them Hannah Arendt, David Ben-Gurion, Habib Bourguiba, Jomo Kenyatta, Günter Grass, Arthur Miller, Julian Huxley, Erich Kästner, and Charlie Chaplin.

The responses of those who bothered to explain their refusal to take part are no less interesting, from Graham Greene to Barbara Tuchman. Elias Canetti wrote that only someone who had experienced the horrors as Wiesenthal had could relate to the question that he raised, and he himself had been living securely in England. "Perhaps I should be ashamed of that," he wrote.[2]

The British historian A. J. P. Taylor wrote that he could not provide any sort of moral judgment about the behavior of others: "I have difficulty enough in laying down moral judgments about my own behavior." Bertrand Russell's secretary sent a postcard: he received so many such requests that it was impossible to agree to them all. Elie Wiesel said that he didn't like debates.[3]

Wiesenthal later recalled that he had thought of the book as the twenty-fifth anniversary of the end of the war approached. At the time, everyone was speaking of the need to forgive. In Germany a new generation had grown up that demanded to be freed from its parents' guilt. "I wanted to show that it was a totally personal matter," Wiesenthal wrote. "I can forgive only what has been done to me, but I do not have the right to forgive in the name of others." He said the reason he turned to so many thinkers was not because he was unsure of his own position, but rather because he had found in his story a matter of principle that touched everyone in the world.[4] He was right: the book was translated into twenty languages. In each country, the list of contributors was changed, according to local interest.

In the American edition, Archbishop Desmond Tutu told about Nelson Mandela, who sat in prison for twenty-seven years and, when he was elected president of South Africa, invited his white prison warden to be his guest at the inauguration ceremony. Tutu was aware of the political significance of forgiveness. He was the driving spirit behind the Truth and Reconciliation Commission, which heard testimony on the atrocities of apartheid. Many of the victims expressed willingness to forgive their tormentors. "Forgiveness is not some nebulous thing. Forgiveness is practical politics. Without forgiveness there is no future," Tutu wrote.

The Sunflower became a textbook in many schools. Pupils were asked to write what they would have done in Wiesenthal's place. Hundreds of them sent him their essays. They made him very happy, and he replied to them almost until his dying day. "My response to the dying soldier would be no different today—and I am now ninety-three years old—than it was then," he wrote to the schoolchildren of Congregation Shaarei Zedek in Tampa, Florida.[5]

One of the figures whom Wiesenthal asked, "What would you have done?" was the German author Heinrich Böll. After sending a handwritten note to Wiesenthal asking him for more time to think, he wrote him a long letter that never related at all to the moral question. Böll thought that Wiesenthal had missed an opportunity to introduce the crimes committed by the German army, the Wehrmacht, into the discourse on Nazi war crimes. There's no argument about the crimes of the SS, he wrote, but the Wehrmacht's misdeeds were not exposed in the Eichmann trial or at other trials. This was not by chance, Böll wrote. The Wehrmacht's crimes had been covered up in order to protect West Germany and the reputation of its armed forces. It would have been better to make the SS man in Wiesenthal's story a high officer in the Wehrmacht who before dying would have given the narrator a historic mission: to lay bare the truth about the crimes committed by the German army.

Böll also thought the narrator should not have spared the SS man's mother from hearing the truth. The Germans who claimed they knew nothing about the Nazis' crimes would adopt this mother as a symbol and say that like her, they did not know. Germans would also be happy to adopt the SS man as a symbol. Böll thought that he was too "unambiguous" a good boy from a good home who didn't really mean to harm anyone.

It may well be, Böll added, that he was investing too much intellectual speculation in Wiesenthal's story, but it was important for Wiesenthal to take into account the effect of the book on a public that had not yet confronted its past. On this point, Böll suggested a literary alteration. He would stress the sunflower motif still more, he wrote. He shuddered every time he saw how carefully the Germans tended their military cemeteries.

Wiesenthal could have taken Böll's response as a compliment. One of the great writers of the century had written to him, author to author. But he preferred just to file the letter away. For Böll's working hypothesis was that *The Sunflower* was a work of fiction; he graded it the way a teacher of literature would grade a student's short story, and he gave him an F for "failed." If it had been a true account, he would have respected its content and its form, and he would never have dared to examine its literary value, Böll wrote.[6]

Böll was the first person to doubt the authenticity of Wiesenthal's story, but he was not the only one. Another German, Franz Smerdka, of Weidenstetten in southern Germany, wrote to say that he had served in a military unit stationed in Dnepropetrovsk. He never heard of the fire that Wiesenthal described. He spoke to some of the town's residents, one of whom had a Jewish wife. They certainly would have told him. He wanted to know when it happened. He also wanted to point out that a Jewish prisoner could never have reached the bedside of a wounded SS man to hear a confession of his crimes.

Wiesenthal replied within days. The incident occurred a year before Smerdka's unit reached the city, and it is doubtful that any of the inhabitants would have dared to speak about it to a German soldier, particularly one married to a Jew. And yes, under normal circumstances a concentration camp inmate would not have reached the bedside of a wounded SS soldier, but in this case the inmate had been sent to work at the hospital where the soldier was a patient. He was alone in a separate room and it was therefore possible for the nurse to fulfill his wish without anyone knowing.[7]

A reader named Mark Alper, of Brighton, Massachusetts, also wondered if the story was true. "Yes, of course it really happened," Wiesenthal replied. "It happened to me." All the stories he published were based on facts; he changed only the names sometimes, so as not to harm those involved, he wrote.[8] Children from various countries who read the story also wanted to know if it was true, and Wiesenthal assured them too that he had not made it up.

This is also what he told volunteers who worked with him. "Wiesenthal told us the story was true and we believe him," said two of them, Paul Sills and Michael Stergar, and others agreed. Some of the last friends who outlived him tended to respond to the question with an indulgent smile. Sometimes he wove tales out of things that happened to him or others, or that he saw in his imagination, they said.[9]

Wiesenthal was the only source for the story. There is nothing among his papers that can independently confirm or refute it. He apparently never gave the SS man's full name. In the film based on his autobiography, *The Murderers Among Us*, the patient mutters a name that sounds like Seidel or Seidler. In the copy of the film script in Wiesenthal's files, there is an ellipsis where the name would normally appear.[10]

It is not clear why Wiesenthal, who had devoted his life to exposing war criminals like this one, chose to protect the anonymity of this particular SS man. It is astounding that he managed to remember the address after everything he went through in the five years that followed, for if everything happened as he described it, he caught only a glimpse of the address when the nurse tried to hand him the package.

Neither is it clear why Wiesenthal went to the trouble of looking for the man's mother. Alexander Friedman, who in his youth worked as a volunteer at the Documentation Center and later became a psychiatrist whose patients included Holocaust survivors, suggested the following explanation: "Wiesenthal knew, of course, that the whole part about the visit to Stuttgart was not credible. The fact that he did not drop it therefore strengthens the possibility that it really happened."[11]

One more question remains: Would a Nazi war criminal ask a Jewish prisoner to forgive him? Peter Michael Lingens mentioned a scene his mother, Ella Lingens, described in her memoir: Maria Mandel was a forewoman in one of the Auschwitz subcamps. After the war, she was tried in Poland and sentenced to death. Before her execution, she met one of the former camp inmates. "Tomorrow I will die," Mandel said, "and I am happy about it. In recent weeks I have understood the enormity of the crime that I was involved in. I cannot live with this burden. Will you pardon me?" And the former prisoner said yes, she forgave her.[12]

In Wiesenthal's own eyes, *The Sunflower* was his best book. It was his third bestseller. Along with the money it earned him, it also brought a flood of invitations for speaking engagements in the United States and elsewhere. More and more people across the globe were attributing a moral authority to Wiesenthal, accepting the lessons that he proposed should be drawn from the Holocaust. These included the need to support the State of Israel, which was tantamount to supporting the policies of its government. But then Wiesenthal became entangled in a very embarrassing affair, and once again his relations with Israel were involved.

14.

"Kreisky Is Going Mad"

1. Enemy of the People

Vienna, so relaxed a city and neutral in the Cold War rivalry, offered ideal conditions for spies from anywhere—but sometimes they were caught and put on trial. One of these was Johann Ableitinger, a former investigator for the internal security service, the Staatspolizei, who had become a private detective in 1962. His experience and his connections in the police and the Interior Ministry stood him in good stead. He knew whom to bribe and could therefore illegally offer his clients classified information on the people who interested them. In 1968 he was arrested and sentenced to two and a half years in jail.

Ableitinger was more private eye than spy, but he also provided services to a number of Western espionage agencies and legations. One of these was the Israeli embassy, which was identified in his files as "Niko" and "Brass," while his contacts there were "Winter" and "Paul." The link with the embassy, he said under interrogation, was set up by another client, Simon Wiesenthal. The two were old acquaintances; Ableitinger used to supply Wiesenthal with information about Nazi criminals.

For a while the affair was at the center of Austrian politics. Christian Broda, a leader of the Social Democratic opposition who had served as justice minister in the past and was to do so again in the future, attacked Wiesenthal sharply, accusing him of having a "private police force." This attack was primarily aimed at the Conservative government, which Wiesenthal supported.

Wiesenthal responded by exposing some embarrassing aspects of Broda's past. While still in high school he had been a Communist, during the war he had written a doctoral thesis espousing Nazi ideas, and when he took part in the hunt for ex-Nazis after the war, he had been suspected of being involved in the murder of two of them while they were under investigation. The file on Broda in Wiesenthal's office reflected tireless diligence, even containing a copy of his doctorate.[1]

Wiesenthal was questioned about the charges against Ableitinger. The detective cooperated with his interrogators and was not charged himself, but the affair led to the establishment of a parliamentary inquiry committee. In its minority report it alleged that Ableitinger had supplied Wiesenthal with services that did not belong within the purview of the Documentation Center. This formulation left no room for doubt: they were speaking about espionage. The minority report reflected the position of the Social Democratic Party and was signed, among others, by Christian Broda and Leopold Gratz, who was later to serve as education minister and then mayor of Vienna.

Throughout the case, Wiesenthal was in close contact with the Israeli embassy. The letters he wrote to the ambassador, Ze'ev Shek, had one goal: to establish that not only was he implicated up to his neck in this affair, but the embassy was as well.[2] Internal documents of the Foreign Ministry in Jerusalem also confirm that Ableitinger did indeed do work for Israel.

The embassy reported on its efforts to have the committee's report toned down.

> In the minority report it is stated that in addition to Ableitinger being a spy for the East, he was also Wiesenthal's "personal spy" and that he "supplied materials in improper ways to Israeli espionage agents." We immediately protested against these assertions, arguing that asking a private detective for details on the character of a citizen and his past is an absolutely legal act, for that is what it says on a private detective's license. How the detective obtains such material and whether he transgressed the law in his contacts with the Interior Ministry—this is not the concern of the Israeli embassy. We succeeded in getting the sentence concerning Israel removed from the parliamentary report, but everything else concerning Wiesenthal remained in.[3]

Wiesenthal did not conceal the fact that he employed Ableitinger, but he denied using him for espionage missions. He wrote to one of the heads of the Jewish community and to the head of the Social Democratic Party, Bruno Kreisky, but gave the most detailed explanation to the foreign minister, Kurt Waldheim. He said he had hired Ableitinger to carry out forty-six investigations over a period of six years. All except four were aimed at exposing the past of Nazi criminals. He chose Ableitinger because he did not have a Nazi past and because he had a reputation for being a good detective.

He needed a private detective because at that time his relations with the Interior Ministry were poor. Among other things, the department that was supposed to reply to his inquiries was understaffed and did not supply him with the information he needed to advance the legal process against Nazi criminals in Germany. Ableitinger knew how to get hold of material that a private citizen would never be able to obtain.

The four cases that did not concern Nazi criminals, Wiesenthal explained, were "Jewish matters" that interested him personally and had no political significance. One of them had to do with a vice scandal at a youth club and the other three were attempts to find out the backgrounds of Jews living in Vienna.

In his letter to Waldheim, Wiesenthal also explained the nature of the connection between Ableitinger and the Israeli embassy. Austrian citizens wanting to visit Israel at that time still required entry visas, and in order to ensure that they were not liable to be arrested there under the law for the punishment of Nazis, the Israeli consulate often had recourse to Wiesenthal's services. When the workload became too heavy, he suggested that the consulate hire a private detective to do the job, and he recommended Ableitinger. Wiesenthal tried to present the publicity the affair received as an attempt to smear Israel, and in a letter to Kreisky he warned that it could lead to attempts to have the Documentation Center closed down.[4]

The Eastern bloc countries exploited the affair and sought to present it as evidence that Wiesenthal was a spy and an extortionist. They claimed that the material he got from Ableitinger included embarrassing facts about politicians and senior officials. There is no way of verifying this allegation. The case became an issue in the parliamentary elections of March 1970, as the right-wing Austrian People's Party, which Wiesenthal supported, conducted a campaign against Kreisky that was not free of anti-Semitism, including hints that it was better to vote for a "true" Austrian.

The Social Democrats emerged as the largest party in Parliament, but Kreisky was unable to win the support of a parliamentary majority. Instead, he reached an arrangement with the Liberal Party that enabled him to form a minority coalition. He thus ensured himself the chancellorship, but in doing so placed himself in a disgraceful situation: some of the ministers in his government turned out to be former supporters of the Nazis, including the minister of agriculture, Hans Öllinger.

One of Kreisky's aides, Heinz Fischer, recalled later how everything had been done in a makeshift manner. Somehow, Kreisky had been stuck without an agriculture minister and one of his colleagues suggested over the phone that he take Öllinger. Kreisky asked what his first name was and what qualified him for the position. It took a few calls to clarify things. Öllinger himself was speechless with surprise when he was offered the job.[5] Nobody remembered to check into what he had done under the Nazi regime.

The news about his past was first published in an Austrian weekly and reached the international media. It is not clear whether Wiesenthal was the source for the item. Either way, he was quick to announce that there were other former Nazis serving in Kreisky's cabinet: housing minister Joseph Moser, transportation minister Erwin Frühbauer, and interior minister Otto Rösch. The latter case was particularly shameful, as Rösch had also indulged in neo-Nazi activity after the war.

The first Jewish chancellor in Austria's history was furious, and he ardently defended the right of former Nazis to serve in public positions, as long as they had not been convicted of any crime. When Öllinger resigned for what were termed "health reasons" Kreisky appointed another former member of the Nazi Party in his stead, Oskar Weihs. Most of the Austrian press supported Kreisky. The time had come to draw the line regarding the past, the papers stated. And that meant Wiesenthal should too.

"I have now learned of a new kind of anti-Semitism," Wiesenthal wrote to one of his supporters, Victor Matejka, an artist and writer and a well-known figure on the Austrian cultural and political scene. Wiesenthal compared Kreisky and his supporters to his rivals in the Jewish community who opposed him because he wanted to purge the community of Jews who had collaborated with the Nazis. The attacks on him were aimed at all Jews, friends or rivals, he contended, and not only at Jews. Some young people had urged him to leave Austria and move to Israel, and Wiesenthal replied: "What will you suggest to the Austrian citizen who is not a Jew and who objects to the Nazi policies of the government?"[6]

2. Bruno's Friends

On June 11, 1970, in a speech at the Social Democratic Party convention, education minister Leopold Gratz bitterly attacked Wiesenthal. "The so-called Documentation Center," the minister railed, "serves as a private police force for informers and slanderers, and before long it will be clarified whether Austria still needs a Wiesenthal organization."

Wiesenthal was already used to the abuse of ex-Nazis and neo-Nazis in all countries, including his own, but this was the first time a cabinet minister had badmouthed him in public. Kreisky, who was behind Gratz's verbal assault, told reporters: "I'm just waiting for Herr Wiesenthal to prove that I was also a member of the SS." Kreisky allowed a Dutch newspaper to quote him as saying, "Wiesenthal is a Jewish fascist." A top official of the Israeli Foreign Ministry said in an internal communication, "I see that Kreisky is going mad."[7]

Kreisky denied calling Wiesenthal a Jewish fascist. The paper said the chancellor had seen the text of the interview before it was published and approved it. But before it could produce the document as proof, it was destroyed in a mysterious fire. The Israeli embassy in Vienna was able, however, to pass on to the Foreign Ministry in Jerusalem a photocopy in Kreisky's handwriting that apparently confirmed the words ascribed to him in the interview. The chancellor's office got the Vienna police to investigate the possibility of a forgery. A long memorandum in the Bruno Kreisky Archive documents the handling of the affair as if it were of great national importance.

Among other things, the memo mentions that in 1930 a fascistic Zionist movement under the leadership of Ze'ev Jabotinsky was active in Austria. In an interview with another paper, Kreisky tried to place things within a broader context: he had meant to say that the Jewish nation was not different from any other nation and that among the Jews there were also murderers and prostitutes and fascists. After all, the socialist Zionist movement leader had been murdered by a Jewish fascist in Tel Aviv, Kreisky said, referring to the assassination of Haim Arlosorov in 1933.

Kreisky's remarks about Jewish fascism were apparently the product of a traumatic experience he underwent in his youth when he attended a rally in Vienna addressed by Jabotinsky, the Zionist leader who had so greatly influenced Wiesenthal's world outlook. Kreisky remembered that Jabotinsky's supporters appeared in black shirts, black trousers, and black boots. Actually, the shirts worn by members of Betar, the Revisionist youth movement, were brown, not black. Evidently it was not Kreisky's memory that guided him here, but his enmity.

The rally opened with words of praise for Mussolini, and Kreisky then realized that Jews too could be fascists, and even Nazis, if only they were allowed to. He said he remembered Jabotinsky well as a "tough one-armed man." Kreisky was mistaken, of course. Jabotinsky had both of his arms. Kreisky was apparently mixing him up with Joseph Trumpeldor, who had been killed in 1920 defending the settlement of Tel Hai in Upper Galilee against Arab marauders, and after whom the Jabotinsky youth movement was named, Betar being an acronym for Brit Trumpeldor, the Hebrew name of the Trumpeldor League.[8]

Wiesenthal located the origin of his rivalry with Kreisky in a televised debate a few years before. Kreisky was then serving as foreign minister and Wiesenthal accused him of being overly sympathetic toward the Arabs. At that time, some German-speaking residents of the Italian province of South Tyrol were demanding greater autonomy, and the Austrian government had rejected their request for assistance. Wiesenthal had said that Kreisky was willing to do more for the Arabs than he was for the Germans of the Tyrol. Kreisky never forgave him, Wiesenthal said.[9]

He depicted the attack on him as an attempt to have his center closed down, and he defended himself in his customary manner: He called the *New York Times*, and within a short time a wave of hundreds of cables of protest flooded the chancellor's office. Jewish organizations and a number of U.S. senators issued statements of support for Wiesenthal, who collected all the responses and published them in a booklet. Kreisky instructed his attorney to examine the possibility of suing Wiesenthal for libel.[10] The chancellor's office denied there was any intention to close the Documentation Center, but the protests continued and Kreisky was forced to cancel a planned visit to the United States.

Kreisky and his people saw Wiesenthal as a dangerous enemy. Wiesenthal was kept under surveillance and his phones were tapped, as if he were an enemy of the state. Justice minister Broda sent Kreisky a detailed report about what Wiesenthal had said to a passenger who sat next to him on a plane: he was going to step up the fight against Kreisky not only because he put Nazis into his government but also because of his hostile attitude toward Israel.[11]

In Israeli background papers of the time, Kreisky was said to have always been cool toward the Jewish state, although he claimed that he was neutral in the Israeli-Arab dispute. His attitude was expressed during a visit he paid to Egypt in 1964. At that time, he refused to go on an official visit to Israel. Wiesenthal reported to the embassy that Kreisky had praised Egypt as a country with a four-thousand-year history, in contrast to its neighbor, a country that had arisen only yesterday and that, as far as anyone knew, might be gone the day after tomorrow. Kreisky denied having said this, and Wiesenthal declared, "I am ready to go to court on this matter."

In the Six-Day War, the Social Democratic Party had taken Israel's side, and although the party was in opposition at the time, Kreisky saw fit to back the government, which also supported Israel. According to some of his friends, he followed the war closely and showed great sympathy for the Israeli side. The Israeli ambassador in Vienna reported that Kreisky admired Israel's achievements and that before 1970 he had never taken a "concrete anti-Israel step."

Israeli diplomats believed that the attack on Wiesenthal entailed the need for a psychological explanation, and that Kreisky had "a deep Jewish complex." More than anything, he feared that his compatriots did not accept him as a true Austrian. To the Israelis it was clear that this "complex" was at work during Kreisky's dispute with Wiesenthal as well.[12]

The Israeli embassy in Vienna followed the situation closely. Everyone assumed that Kreisky's minority government would not last long and interpreted the attack on Wiesenthal as an attempt to pander to the Nazi sympathizers and the right in the run-up to the next elections.

However, the Israeli diplomats also mentioned that Wiesenthal had been running down the Social Democrats on behalf of the right-wing People's Party, which had lost the elections, and whose ex-Nazi ministers he had overlooked. This was a popular criticism Wiesenthal denied by pointing out that he had also protested the shortcomings of the Austrian legal system during the previous administration in a memorandum to Chancellor Josef Klaus.

In Jerusalem officials began doubting whether Wiesenthal was worth supporting. "On the personal level, Wiesenthal is known to be dedicated body and soul to his goal, but also as an ambitious, loudmouthed publicity hound who often makes claims he is unable to back up," said a briefing paper sent out from the Foreign Ministry to Israeli ambassadors all over the world. Wiesenthal also "arrogates to himself" credit for capturing Eichmann, the paper continued, but the following also needed to be remembered: "Those who know the truth about operations aimed at discovering Nazi criminals tell of Wiesenthal's irresponsibility, which springs from his publicity seeking and egocentricity, which knows no bounds."

Wiesenthal alleged that education minister Leopold Gratz had been a Nazi, but Foreign Ministry officials did some elementary arithmetic and realized that at the end of the war Gratz was only fifteen years old. "Altogether, he had only been a member of the Hitler Youth, in conformity with the obligation that was imposed on all Austrian high school students," the Israeli background paper said.[13]

Three months after the quarrel between Kreisky and Wiesenthal broke out, Israel deployed its best diplomatic brains in an attempt to square the circle and advance its political interests without neglecting its obligations as a Jewish state. "It's an unpleasant business," asserted one of the heads of the Foreign Ministry. The aim was to separate the quarrel from Austria's positions on the Middle East, and the chief cause for concern was Wiesenthal's attacks on Interior Minister Rösch. "This man is one of our most ardent supporters in the Austrian government," the Israeli officer stated. "He helps us with immigration [from Eastern Europe] and with everything to do with the security of the embassy, El Al, Jewish institutions, etcetera."

Until then, Israeli representatives had always said that although they did not interfere in Austria's internal affairs, as Jews and as Israelis they supported Wiesenthal's enterprise. Now a senior Foreign Ministry official, Gershon Avner, was not at all sure it was possible to moderate "such profound psychological complications," but he advised the ambassador in Vienna to desist from openly supporting Wiesenthal and to say no more than that Israel was "aware of the dispute."

In contrast to the days of the conflict between Wiesenthal and the Vienna Jewish community, this time the Mossad refrained from dictating Israeli policy to the Foreign Ministry. "Israel's interest is to be preferred over intellectual precision here," Avner wrote. "We must take care of ourselves and he—Wiesenthal—is so nasty, unpopular, and tactless in some of his activities that we have the right to do what is good for us." Ambassador Shek had his doubts: "I still want to think about it," he wrote to his superiors. Meanwhile, Shek heard that Kreisky's associates were trying to calm him down.

A few days later, Shek had good news: toward the end of a reception that he gave for the visiting Romanian ruler Nicolae Ceauşescu, Kreisky spotted the Israeli ambassador and came over to greet him. "Since he was elected chancellor, nothing like this has happened in public," Shek reported. During the friendly conversation that developed, Kreisky repeated his wish to visit Israel. Shek refrained from mentioning Wiesenthal.

Kreisky also tried to get the heads of the Jewish community on his side. On the eve of Rosh Hashanah, the Jewish New Year, he met with two of them, Wilhelm Krell and Anton Pick, and according to a report the Israeli ambassador sent to Jerusalem, the chancellor began by saying: "I see myself as a Jewish chancellor." Although he was a member of the Austrian nation and had no loyalty other than to Austria, he had never denied his Jewish origins, he said. He was proud of having been elected to his position despite the fact that some of his opponents had used anti-Semitic arguments against him. He had heard, the chancellor added, that the community was experiencing financial difficulties. The government would help. Education Minister Gratz would increase the allocation that it received.

The Jews thanked Kreisky, and then he began to talk about Wiesenthal. In the ambassador's words, the chancellor "poured out the bitterness he harbored toward the man in quite an extreme manner." He had never intended to shut Wiesenthal's center down, even though it was becoming a headquarters of the People's Party and acting against government ministers and against him personally, but he had to defend himself.

The community heads mentioned the former Nazis whom Kreisky had appointed as ministers, and he focused on Interior Minister Rösch. In his youth Rösch had joined the Nazi Party but he had never held any position in it, and there was no one in Vienna who was doing more for the Jews and for Israel than he. The community heads confirmed this and thanked the chancellor for the increased security at synagogues for the coming holiday season. They had meant to raise the plight of Soviet and Iraqi Jewry, but the chancellor was pressed for time. Before dismissing them, he reiterated: "I see myself as a Jewish chancellor and if you need anything, speak to me."

Ambassador Shek summed up by saying that the impression received by Krell, a sworn enemy of Wiesenthal, was similar to what he had heard from Karl Kahane, the influential Jewish millionaire who lived in Vienna and was close to Kreisky: it appeared that the chancellor was learning to separate his dispute with Wiesenthal from everything to do with the

Jewish community and Israel. "Whether he has acquired wisdom or he is behaving according to coldly calculated self-interest, this is a positive development, but I am not sure it will last," the ambassador concluded, and someone in Jerusalem wrote on his report: "The days of the Messiah are here, but it's very hard to know how long they will last."[14]

3. The Mills of Justice

The dispute with Kreisky caused Wiesenthal great pain. He reckoned that most, if not all, Austrians were happy that someone had taken upon himself to free them at long last from their Nazi past—and was more able to do so than a Jewish chancellor. "I am their bad conscience," he wrote some time later, "because each one of them should have taken upon himself what I have done for Austrian society."[15] Never had he felt so alone.

He tried to console himself with the thought that eventually the Nazis would also lose faith in Kreisky. Meanwhile, he tried to recover from the affair in his usual manner: he wrote a detailed memorandum in which he once again described how Austria had evaded its duty to punish Nazi criminals. He charged that the Kreisky government had closed hundreds of cases under investigation for political reasons. He described this as a kind of "cold amnesty" and stated that Austria was not ascribing any more value to human life than Nazi Germany had.

It was a rather dry document, eighteen pages long. The facts spoke for themselves, placing Austrian society in a shameful light. Judicial statistics showed that in the 1960s Austria had convicted thirteen thousand persons for crimes committed during the Nazi period, but Wiesenthal's research revealed that almost all of them had been tried for belonging to forbidden organizations and not for acts of murder. Meanwhile, prosecution witnesses were growing old, Wiesenthal pointed out, their ability to testify was diminishing, and public prosecutors familiar with the cases were retiring. There were insufficient personnel and funds. Investigations of those identified as Nazi criminals sometimes took ten years or more.

This was the case with Ernst Lerch, the owner of a café in Klagenfurt, Austria, who had been an officer in Operation Reinhard, which focused on extermination of the Jews in Poland. This was not a case that required Wiesenthal's sleuthing abilities. Lerch lived openly under his true identity and his café bore his name. Starting in 1962, Wiesenthal demanded that he be tried for the murder of two million people and declared that this was the worst case in the history of Austria's criminal justice. Nothing happened, and the years passed by.

The witnesses who could have had Lerch convicted died, one after the other, and his café flourished. In 1971, he was finally arrested, but a bid to have his trial moved from his hometown to Vienna failed, and there was no real chance of his being found guilty in Klagenfurt. When the trial began he was immediately released until the end of the proceedings. He denied everything, and the trial was deferred and eventually discontinued under orders from Justice Minister Broda.[16]

Wiesenthal's memorandum didn't change anything, but he might have been surprised to learn that Broda did not dismiss it. In a letter to Kreisky, Broda said he had read it very attentively and that the facts Wiesenthal cited deserved to be considered.[17] Yet the Justice Ministry must have also "considered" the letters it received every year from Wiesenthal about Franz Murer, "the butcher of Vilna," who was supposed to have faced a retrial, and here, too, nothing happened. Still, the work Wiesenthal put into the memorandum had the effect of returning him to his main purpose in life. He also used it to express his anger about the conduct of other governments.[18]

On December 7, 1970, the West German chancellor, Willy Brandt, came to Warsaw and placed a wreath at the monument to the Warsaw Ghetto uprising. He stood at attention for a moment, and then dropped to his knees and remained motionless in this position for several long minutes. "I did what people do when words fail them," Brandt wrote later.[19] He had come to Poland within the framework of his attempts to thaw the Cold War between the East and the West. In Germany, his genuflection sparked a stormy argument. Almost everywhere else in the world it elicited wonderment and admiration. A year later, Brandt was awarded the Nobel Peace Prize.

Wiesenthal waited a few weeks and then wrote to Brandt saying that he too had been very impressed by the chancellor's gesture in Warsaw. The criticism it aroused in Germany was shameful. But his praise for the German leader took up only two paragraphs of the five densely typed pages in which he expressed his bitterness over ten years of foot-dragging by the German judicial system in the case of the Nazi criminal Ludwig Hahn, as well as delays in other cases.

Hahn was under investigation for his role in the deportation of hundreds of thousands of Jews from the Warsaw Ghetto to the Treblinka extermination camp. Since the file was opened in 1966, it had swelled to 130 volumes containing two thousand pieces of evidence, and still no decision had been taken to indict him. Hahn and other suspects were not being kept in detention. Wiesenthal gave the names of six of them. Some had been investigated not only for their role in suppressing the uprising in the Warsaw Ghetto, but also for acts of murder they personally had carried out. This was not the only investigation being dragged out in Hamburg. Twelve years had passed since the authorities had begun looking into the murder of the twenty-two thousand Jews of the town of Slonim, today in western Belarus. The chief suspect in this case, Gerhard Erren, had been allowed to become a teacher after the war. Six years had passed since the beginning of the investigation into the murder of the twenty-eight thousand Jews of Przemyśl, in southeastern Poland, and the suspects were not in detention; neither were those implicated in the crimes committed in Lublin, another case where the investigation had been strung out.

Bruno Streckenbach, the deputy to the head of the Nazi security services, Reinhard Heydrich, was functioning as a successful businessman in Hamburg, with the investigation against him dawdling along. "It is difficult to find the words to adequately describe the conduct of the Hamburg prosecution," Wiesenthal wrote to Brandt, who knew something about how words could fail a man, asking him to intervene so the world would see that the man who knelt to honor the victims also cared about the punishment of their murderers.[20]

The frustration so evident in his letter to Brandt was also reflected in the more than two hundred cases he listed in his bulletins for the early 1970s. These were difficult years. The reports document the reams of excuses and constraints that enabled hundreds if not thousands of Nazi criminals to go unpunished. All that Wiesenthal could do was issue reports.

There was the case of an SS man by the name of Max Täubner who together with some comrades killed more than nine hundred Jewish civilians. He recorded some of these killings with his camera, sending the photos home to his wife, who showed them to their friends. For this, an SS tribunal sentenced him to ten years' imprisonment.

Täubner was arrested after the war, but a court in Memmingen ruled that he need not stand trial for murdering the Jews because the SS court had already tried and convicted him. A court in Munich confirmed this ruling. Here were courts in the new Germany recognizing the legality of a judgment handed down by an SS tribunal. Wiesenthal found this "grotesque." He managed to get hold of a copy of the SS court's judgment, which explicitly stated that Täubner was being tried not for killing Jews, but for disobeying orders by taking photographs of the action.

Wiesenthal's demands that he be tried for murder were turned down again and again. While this was going on, one of Täubner's subordinates who also took part in the killing was discovered and put on trial. Täubner was called as a witness, but naturally didn't remember a thing, Wiesenthal observed. The man was sentenced to two and a half years in prison.[21] From time to time Wiesenthal found Nazis in prominent positions—one a lecturer in political science in Hamburg, another a professor in Stuttgart—and generally nothing happened.[22] Other countries were no less apathetic.

The countries of Eastern Europe no longer cooperated with Wiesenthal, but even countries that usually displayed sympathy for his activities stuck closely to the letter of the law, at the expense of justice. In 1973, Wiesenthal announced that after searching for years he had located a Nazi criminal by the name of Karlis Lobe, who had been responsible for the murder of tens of thousands of Latvian Jews. He was living in Stockholm. The Swedes, like other nations, did not distinguish between the crime of murder and war crimes and applied the statute of limitations to the latter as well. There was no possibility of prosecuting Lobe, though he was compelled to sue a newspaper for calling him a murderer. He did so and lost, but was not penalized.[23]

One of the perpetrators of the massacre at Babi Yar was a Norwegian, Harald Frederik Skasppel. After the war, proceedings against him were started in Norway, but he escaped to Brazil and the file was closed. Wiesenthal tried to get him arrested on the grounds that he had used a false Swedish passport, but the Swedish embassy in Vienna informed him that the statute of limitations also applied to this offense.[24]

Nor did the Netherlands, where so many of his admirers lived, do everything Wiesenthal thought should be done. In the Dutch town of Herten, on February 9, 1945, German paratroops had found two brothers by the name of Moors, aged eighteen and twenty-three, hiding in the cellar of a priest's house together with two girls. British troops were already surrounding the village and its liberation was imminent. The four young people were taken to the German commander, Helmut Behagel von Flammerdinghe, who ordered that the girls be transferred to Germany. The soldier ordered to do so took them in the direction of the border but let them go after a few miles. The brothers were shot dead. A few hours later, the British took the village and found their bodies.

Wiesenthal located von Flammerdinghe in the city of Graz. An identification lineup was held and one of the girls identified him positively. The fear of death he had instilled in her did not allow her to forget him, Wiesenthal wrote. He initiated an investigation against the man, but the case ended without an indictment. Wiesenthal found that the Dutch were not too interested in the case. And in the United States, law enforcement authorities allowed Hermine Braunsteiner, the Mare of Majdanek, almost ten years of legal wrangling before she was extradited to Germany in 1972.

Wiesenthal enjoyed a few successes. Ludwig Hahn was sentenced to life imprisonment, as were Gerhard Erren and some of the other criminals whose cases Wiesenthal handled.[25]

He also exposed criminals who were unknown to the authorities. From time to time, if not very frequently, he could report on their home addresses, and some of them were arrested. He produced more and more testimony by survivors, which led to several indictments and strengthened the prosecution in cases that were already under way. But more than anything else, in the early 1970s, Wiesenthal experienced disappointment. He badly needed a success.

15.

"Better Than Any Monster"

1. The Forsyth File

In the spring of 1971, Wiesenthal had a visit from a man who was already a well-known journalist and was soon to become famous as the author of the political suspense novel *The Day of the Jackal*. Frederick Forsyth worked for the Reuters news agency and the BBC. He had previously served as a pilot in the Royal Air Force. His first political thriller dealt with a plot to assassinate the French president, Charles de Gaulle, and before it was published Forsyth was already working on his next book. He had come to get information from Wiesenthal about the ODESSA organization.

Forsyth was familiar with Wiesenthal's memoirs, but Wiesenthal had not heard of Forsyth. In the wake of the success of the memoirs and *The Sunflower*, he frequently found himself in the company of well-known authors. Leon Uris had also asked to meet him. Wiesenthal prepared a file for Uris on the case of the Swedish diplomat Raoul Wallenberg, who had saved thousands of Hungarian Jews from the Nazis and then vanished in a Soviet prison. Wiesenthal tried to persuade Uris to incorporate the story into one of his novels.[1] In contrast, he was hesitant about meeting Forsyth.

Almost thirty years after he had first heard the rumors about ODESSA and transformed them into one of the pillars of his own renown, he had good reason for fearing that Forsyth would steal the story from him and turn it into a fictional thriller; then no one would believe that the clandestine organization had actually existed. But Wiesenthal hardly ever turned away a journalist empty-handed, and Forsyth had a riveting story that

Wiesenthal found difficult to ignore. He asked for a night to sleep on it, as he wanted to preserve his own credibility as well as that of the ODESSA story. The next day, he suggested to Forsyth that he incorporate into his book the tale of a real-life Nazi. He rummaged around in his metal cabinets and pulled out a file bearing the name of Eduard Roschmann, otherwise known as the Butcher of Riga.

Forsyth was wary. A living person could sue for libel, he warned, but Wiesenthal assuaged his fear. In order to sue, he would have to appear in court and the moment he showed his face he would be arrested. Forsyth also worried that Roschmann wasn't famous enough. "But nobody's ever heard of Riga," he said. Nevertheless, Wiesenthal managed to persuade him that this was a true horror story. Tens of thousands of Jews were slaughtered there, many of them by Roschmann himself, with his own hands. He was hiding in Argentina under an assumed name, Wiesenthal said.

"I've got it all here," he cried, and added a reason that Forsyth found hard to withstand: "Not only that. We know that he came back to Europe in the mid-1950s and was exposed by his first wife. He'd let her think he was still being loyal to her while he had bigamously married his secretary."

Now it was Forsyth's turn to sleep on it. The next day he said, "This is tremendous. Far better than any monster we could invent."[2] He would also make Wiesenthal himself one of the heroes of his book, he decided. Thus, Wiesenthal's life story was to become a postmodern blend of reality and imagination, history and entertainment, fundamental beliefs and celebrity. Wiesenthal was agog. He thought the book could well bring about the discovery of Roschmann, whose name he had first heard in 1946. That was also the year when Orson Welles made and starred in the movie *The Stranger*, which had created the mold for thrillers of this genre, about a Nazi criminal in hiding from the law being hunted and exposed.[3] In fact, together with other books and films, Forsyth's *The Odessa File* and the 1974 film based on it would consolidate the place of the Holocaust in popular culture.

Born in Graz, Roschmann was the second commander of the ghetto in Riga, the capital of Latvia. By Wiesenthal's count, he was responsible for the deaths of thirty-five thousand people. After the war he returned home and was arrested on suspicion of belonging to a neo-Nazi organization. Graz was then under British occupation. Wiesenthal hastily notified the Americans of the arrest and they requested Roschmann's extradition. The British put Roschmann on a train to Dachau, where the Americans were holding war crimes tribunals, but on the way he escaped his guards by jumping out of a lavatory window.

According to Wiesenthal, Roschmann reached Argentina with the help of ODESSA, which smuggled him there from Italy, where he had been sheltered by Bishop Alois Hudal.[4] The Roschmann file in the Wiesenthal archives shows that from time to time he received information about the man, but in the thirty years before he met Forsyth he did not mention him once in his bulletins. Forsyth quotes him as stating that Roschmann was among his "top fifty wanted men."[5]

Forsyth was thirty years younger than Wiesenthal when they met and it was not long before he was a lot more famous. *The Day of the Jackal* became a worldwide bestseller and was made into a movie that was nominated for an Oscar. The two met frequently to work out the plot for *The Odessa File* and they also corresponded, in English and German. Forsyth addressed Wiesenthal as "Simon" and signed his letters "Freddy." Wiesenthal addressed him as "Dear Friend." He went out of his way to help the author, supplying him with much material, setting up a useful connection for him at the archive of the German newspaper *Bild*, and introducing him to a number of survivors of the Riga ghetto.[6] At a certain stage, each one of the two men adopted something of the professional persona of the other: Forsyth tried his hand at some amateur sleuthing, while Wiesenthal attempted to change the plot of the book.

"Not long ago we received some information that seemed quite strange to us," Wiesenthal wrote to Forsyth several months after they met. An American student whom Wiesenthal identified only as "Truitt" had written to say that he had been offered $800 to carry a letter from Spain to London. Wiesenthal assumed this was an attempt by one German in hiding to contact another. He sent Forsyth a copy of Truitt's letter, perhaps to titillate him, or perhaps to exploit his skills and connections in the same way he had exploited other journalists in order to advance his investigations. Truitt's letter carried an address in London. Wiesenthal swore Forsyth to secrecy. Truitt must not by any means be endangered.

Forsyth threw himself into this episode with a great deal of enthusiasm. "Quite fascinating but full of queries and unanswered questions," he wrote back to Wiesenthal only three days later. Why had ten months gone by between the time Truitt was approached to carry the letter and his letter to Wiesenthal? Forsyth wondered.

Truitt's letter implied that someone had also sent him to Italy and Greece. Who could that someone be? Forsyth asked. Perhaps a certain

"Alex" or members of the Shulman family, who were also mentioned in Truitt's letter? Also, who were these people, and what was the relationship between them? Did Alex know about the Shulmans and did they know about Alex? In his mind, he spun the plot of a new thriller, although the letter Wiesenthal sent him had ignited his imagination precisely because it was ostensibly not fictional, but apparently had to do with real people.

It would be worthwhile for Truitt to take more letters, Forsyth wrote to Wiesenthal, so he could open them and photocopy the contents; he would have to be careful not to leave traces on the paper. But first, he would have to be contacted without being put in peril. An "Earl Beauchamp" was also mentioned. Forsyth let Wiesenthal know that not only was there such a man, but he had served as parliamentary secretary to the minister of war in Neville Chamberlain's cabinet.

In the meantime, Truitt had somehow turned up in Bamako, the capital of the West African state of Mali. Forsyth knew the place: "A tiny city and capital of an extremely unpopulated country of devoutly Moslem tribesmen" he called it in a letter to Wiesenthal. It would be impossible to meet Truitt there without attracting attention, although he could of course be flown to Paris.

But then Forsyth had another idea. He composed a vague letter to Truitt replete with American slang, working in regards from "Uncle Simon," who asked that Truitt contact him. Forsyth sent the proposed letter to Wiesenthal and instructed him on what to do: If he decided that he did want to contact Truitt through this letter, he should put it into a white envelope, write Truitt's address on it without putting on postage stamps, and place it into another envelope, which he should then send to an address in London stipulated by Forsyth. There stamps would be placed on the envelope addressed to Truitt, so that it would look as if it were mailed from London. Meanwhile Forsyth went to do some snooping around Truitt's London address.

Wiesenthal carried out Forsyth's instructions but pointed out that in the interim Truitt had returned to the United States; it is not clear how he knew this. Wiesenthal was half apologetic: Truitt's letter had indeed been quite vague, but sometimes it was necessary to examine clues that seemed strange at first glance, or not credible. One could never know, because sometimes totally fantastic situations reveal very interesting facts, he observed.[7] And indeed, in the no-man's-land between real life, drama, and fantasy, the two men learned to like each other.

2. Movie Story

Forsyth began his tale on a date that everyone remembers, November 22, 1963, the day President John F. Kennedy was assassinated. Peter Miller, a German reporter, receives the diary of a Holocaust survivor, Salomon Tauber, from one of his police contacts. Tauber is a resident of Hamburg who sees Eduard Roschmann in the street. He assumes no one will believe him, so he commits suicide. The diary describes what happened to Tauber in Riga and Roschmann's crimes there. Miller sees in the diary that among his other crimes, Roschmann murdered a German army officer.

Although Miller cooperates with a group of Jewish avengers, the hunt for Nazi criminals is not presented in the book as a specifically Jewish mission, but rather as one that the younger generation in Germany has taken upon itself. Miller pursues Roschmann not only because he murdered Jews, but to a large extent also because, as a representative of the New Left, he wants to purge himself of Nazism and because Roschmann killed a German officer. Later it turns out that this officer was Miller's father.

Before he sets out to find Roschmann, Miller goes to Vienna to consult Wiesenthal. He has sex with a girl there, asks her to marry him, and goes off to confront Roschmann, who manages to escape and reach Argentina. The plot thickens when members of ODESSA conspiring to supply Egypt with biological weapons so that it will be able to destroy Israel also, for some reason, blow up the journalist in his yellow Jaguar. In the end, a Mossad agent, Uri Ben Shaul, takes Tauber's diary to Yad Vashem, where he says Kaddish, the mourner's prayer, for him, then goes off to fight in the Six-Day War and is killed on his way to conquer the Wailing Wall with his fellow paratroopers.

Wiesenthal tried to have a share in shaping the plot. "I have thought about it again, and I have reached the conclusion that Miller can't take the diary to the meeting with Roschmann, because then the diary will be destroyed, along with Miller," he wrote to Forsyth. "Therefore, to get around this problem, we can play a trick. Miller will tear out of the diary a page that particularly impresses him, make a copy of it, and carry it with him all the time. The reader doesn't know why Miller does this but imagines that this page has some part to play. When Miller reaches Roschmann, he forces Roschmann to read the page aloud, and so the reader will know what it's all about."[8]

Wiesenthal was happy with the book's ending. The fact that Roschmann escapes, as he did in reality, would encourage readers to go out and try to find his trail and—who knows?—perhaps discover where he was hiding.

The Odessa File, which became an instant bestseller, was made into a film released in 1974, two years after the book appeared, but to Wiesenthal's disgruntlement the director, Ronald Neame, decided to change the ending. "He explained to me that it was impossible to present moviegoers with a despicable Nazi criminal for two hours and then let him get away," Wiesenthal wrote. "At a film's end, people want satisfaction and to see justice triumph." So in the movie, Roschmann is shot dead. The cast included Jon Voight (*Midnight Cowboy*) as Miller and Maximilian Schell (*Judgment at Nuremberg*) as Roschmann, as well as Maria Schell and Derek Jacobi.

Wiesenthal said that he declined an offer to play himself in the movie "for a lot of money" because he did not want to be identified to such an extent with the entertainment industry. Instead, a well-known Israeli stage actor, Shmuel Rodensky, portrayed him.

Wiesenthal's predictions about the reaction to the movie weren't too far off the mark: readers and moviegoers all over the world sent him bits of information on Roschmann's whereabouts, some even claiming they had seen him. Wiesenthal tried to check these reports, and it turned out that often it was not Roschmann who had been spotted but someone who looked like Schell. A tourist couple who believed they had discovered Roschmann in a restaurant in Santa Cruz, Bolivia, played at being secret agents. They struck up a conversation with their suspect, invited him to have some of their champagne, and sent his glass to Wiesenthal so he could check the fingerprints.[9]

Wiesenthal related this episode with a smile, but there are letters from Forsyth in his archives showing that the author did not settle for just writing thrillers, but seriously wanted to trap Roschmann—and found someone to finance the search. He also sent Wiesenthal fingerprints, using "Our Spaniard" as a code name for their quarry. He sent pictures and requested that measurements be made to determine if they were of "Edward." He was impatient: "Please let me know the instant they have a reply for you," he urged. But the results of the examinations were disappointing.

The "Spaniard" was a man called Hernández living in La Paz, the capital of Bolivia. Someone Forsyth identified as "Karl" managed to obtain from the Bolivian Interior Ministry a document bearing Hernández's fingerprints. But unfortunately they were not the same as Roschmann's. There was of course a possibility that nonetheless, the man was in fact Roschmann, Forsyth fantasized—perhaps he had used someone else's document.

But in order to find out the truth someone would have to go to La Paz again. To his great regret, his friends were no longer willing to provide the funds for this escapade.

In the course of the Forsyth-Wiesenthal correspondence, Hernández was also spotted in a restaurant. Forsyth wrote that Karl should steal a cup, plate, or ashtray that Hernández had touched, but he did not succeed in this mission. As in the plot of one of his thrillers, everything now depended on a mystery man called Brown, but Brown had vanished. "If we could have found him I would even have taken him back to La Paz and asked him to point out both the informant and the man identified as Roschmann, then hired a local private detective to fingerprint the man in secret. But this is not possible," Forsyth wrote. "Anyway, it was a good try."[10]

The *New York Times* review of *The Odessa File* was devastating: "Were Forsyth a better novelist he would not have had to use the real Roschmann," the critic wrote. "He would have reinvented him and we would not as likely still be trying to digest his vulgar stew of hideous documented fact and flimsy melodrama." The paper's film critic also derided the movie, but remarked that at least it doesn't include cabaret scenes, and the Nazis enjoy themselves less than they do in *The Night Porter*, the film by Liliana Cavani that depicts a sadomasochistic relationship between a former SS man and a female Holocaust survivor.[11]

The sarcastic observations reflected a new cultural phenomenon: more and more movies were exploiting the Holocaust for entertainment purposes, and serious criticism failed to block their commercial success.[12]

Before the film was made, Maximilian Schell received an embarrassing letter that he quickly passed on to Wiesenthal. A Gertrude Schneider wrote from New York to say that as a survivor of the Riga ghetto who had written her doctorate on the subject, she wanted to advise the actor that there was no truth in the statement that Roschmann was the Butcher of Riga. He had been commander of the ghetto for less than a year, from January to November 1943, and had shot only one boy.

She was not condoning this act, she wrote—one murder was as bad as thousands—but it was preposterous to call Roschmann the Butcher of Riga. According to her, he was considered a joke. Moreover, whereas Tauber's diary mentions Jews who served as kapos, Schneider wrote that only a few had done so and Forsyth's book tarnished all the victims of the Holocaust. "Very soon we will have to bear the guilt of having killed each other with the kind Germans providing the ammunition," she observed. "The survivors will most strenuously object to a film containing such nonsense and would consider it libel and slander."

Wiesenthal tried to calm her down: one should not relate to a thriller as exact historical documentation and it was important only that the historical background be accurate, he wrote. Moreover, the Roschmann story was based not on the murder of one boy but on a warrant by the Austrian court that cited him for the murder of three thousand Jews and the murder of eight hundred children under ten years of age. Not everyone who was in the Riga ghetto could know about everything that happened there, he remarked, and pointed out that the diary of Salomon Tauber as depicted in *The Odessa File* was based on testimony by a number of people.

However, Wiesenthal did admit that the crimes of Roschmann as described in this thriller were "somewhat exaggerated." He accepted responsibility for this, explaining: "We had hoped that Roschmann would show up somewhere in the world and protest or at least that millions of readers would start to search for him. This might be a chance to find him."[13] He hoped to cause friction between Roschmann and the people who were helping him to hide. This was the reason for exposing Roschmann's bigamy and for inserting the scene where Roschmann kills a German officer.

It happens close to the end of the German occupation. One last German ship is docked in Riga's port, loaded with wounded troops. Roschmann orders a Wehrmacht officer to take them off the ship to make room for SS personnel and enable them to save their skins. The officer refuses and Roschmann shoots him. "The scene started out as pure invention. It was intended to strip away any sympathy his friends may have left toward him," Wiesenthal said. The hope was that they would inform on him, or at least stop helping him.

In time, Wiesenthal would reveal that the inspiration for the scene was the incident that occurred during his forced flight from Gross-Rosen, when SS officer Warzok blew up a bridge over the San River to save his own SS men, leaving Wehrmacht troops stranded at the mercy of the Russians.[14]

Wiesenthal wanted to believe that Roschmann had become a hunted animal. He imagined him walking down a street, sitting in a café, doing his shopping—and stricken by a terrible fear every time someone glanced at him, unable to trust even his closest friends not to betray him. In fact, the huge amount of publicity generated by the film did produce results. For one thing, it led an international crime syndicate to look for the fugitive Nazi with the aim of handing him over for a ransom. And one day, in July 1977, someone saw the film in Buenos Aires and went to the police to report that Roschmann was living on his street under an assumed name.

He was arrested and West Germany requested his extradition on the strength of the warrant for his arrest issued in Hamburg. Within twenty-four hours he had disappeared. It turned out that he had escaped to Paraguay, where four weeks later he had a heart attack and died. Wiesenthal's first reaction was skeptical: "I wonder who died there instead of him," he told news agency reporters who contacted him. But a day or two later he issued a statement headlined: "Eduard Roschmann is dead."[15]

3. The Programmed Friend

Among the flood of reactions Wiesenthal received to *The Odessa File* one letter meant more to him than the others. It came from Cyprus and it was signed "Leo Maier." Maier saw himself as a friend of Wiesenthal's, and for a while Wiesenthal seemed to be reciprocating. In the end, though, Wiesenthal had enemies, admirers, and many acquaintances, but no true friends. Leo Maier learned this the hard way.

The two men had met in Linz. Maier was one of the policemen sent to ambush Eichmann in Altaussee. His father had been a Nazi and he himself had volunteered to serve in the Wehrmacht. His work with the police entailed surveillance of Nazi criminals; from time to time he had to go to Wiesenthal's office and his comrades used to tease him: "So you've got to go and run errands for the Jew again?"

Maier had been careful to maintain an official distance. Wiesenthal noticed this and asked him, "You can't stand me, right? Why not, really?" Maier replied honestly that as his father's son it was hard for him to work with a Nazi hunter. "I know they call me a Nazi hunter, but that's not correct," Wiesenthal replied. "I don't hunt Nazis, but rather war criminals. There were also hundreds of thousands of decent Nazis, like your father. Give him my regards." Maier did this, and his father said, "Let him kiss my ass, that Jew swine."

Wiesenthal used to tell jokes about Jews that embarrassed Maier. If he hadn't known that Wiesenthal was a Jew, he would have thought he was an anti-Semite, he wrote, and gave an example: "Two Jews were sitting in a café in Vienna after the war and reminiscing about the Holocaust. 'What happened to Blau?' one asked. 'Did he survive?' The second replied: 'Oh my God! Poor Blau! The Nazis gouged out his eyes! They cut off his nose! They chopped off his hands! Sawed off his legs! But shhh! He's just walked in . . .'"[16]

Gradually they became friendly and sometime after the capture of Eichmann, Maier was summoned to an urgent meeting with the interior minister in Vienna. On his desk was a thick file that included the report Maier had written in 1948 after the abortive ambush. The minister sent him to Jerusalem as an observer at the Eichmann trial.[17] Wiesenthal was also there. In a conversation with mutual friends he said that if he could choose a brother, it would be Leo Maier. "I was so proud when I heard that," Maier would recall in days to come.[18]

In 1967 Maier was involved in one of those shakeups that happen periodically in secret services everywhere. He was suspected of collaborating with the East German intelligence agency and selling secrets about the gigantic Austrian steel concern VOEST. He was not indicted, but there was a scandal and a parliamentary inquiry. Maier was transferred out of his job and forced to join the UN troops in Cyprus as a police officer.

He was forty-three then, embittered, often lonely, and usually bored. He wrote to Wiesenthal again and again, saying that he was in Cyprus against his will and against his conscience, as he was a pacifist and hated uniforms. He felt as if he had become a prostitute, doing everything for money. It was only the salary that kept him there, he wrote. He had debts in Austria, including some money he owed to Wiesenthal, and he had therefore sold his soul. He hoped to save, so that he could build a house. His wife was with him part of the time on the island, where she had given birth to a daughter who gave him great pleasure, a sister to their son who was already a university student, but his wife and daughter often went back to Austria, and then he suffered from loneliness and homesickness.

Now and again he would ask about his former colleagues, although he claimed that no one remembered him and that he had no interest in what was happening in his former department. "The world is becoming more and more insane, the Arabs are developing a new kind of crime," Maier wrote, but he had no desire to go back into the secret service. "What for?" he wrote to Wiesenthal. "For that country? For an Austrian salary?"

Once he came across information about a Nazi criminal living in Damascus, and he passed it on to Wiesenthal. Once or twice he traveled to Israel, where Wiesenthal put him in touch with some of his contacts.

He once addressed Wiesenthal using the Hebrew word *Shalom,* and at one point he offered to work for him. Wiesenthal replied that there would "always be a place" for Maier in his life, but he feared that as a former agent with the Austrian secret service, Maier was not someone he would be able to employ.[19]

Maier described himself as a sporting type who liked women and alcohol, but his letters to Wiesenthal make him sound sensitive and vulnerable. He shared his troubles and his intimate dreams with him, repeatedly described him as a valued and dear friend, and again and again begged his pardon for pouring his heart out to him. His letters indicate a degree of dependence upon Wiesenthal. He usually addressed him as Simon and sometimes used jocular epithets like "old man."

Wiesenthal was more reserved, although Maier was one of the few people with whom he used the familiar second-person *du.* His letters too were replete with friendliness and longing and sometimes more sentimental than he wanted them to be. Let the months of separation pass quickly, he wrote once, and then added in parentheses a kind of self-reproach: "That sounds almost like a love letter." He shared with Maier his joy at the birth of his granddaughter in Holland, adding, "It's a sign that I'm getting old." Maier was seventeen years younger than he, but Wiesenthal affectionately called him "my old man" also. Wiesenthal's work was virtually his entire life, and unlike Maier he had nothing much to speak of apart from it. For his part, Maier wrote a lot about his dream of becoming a writer of thrillers.

During his years of service in Cyprus, Maier followed the tragedy of the island's division with trepidation. All the impotence of humankind was concentrated here, he wrote, and hatred and racism triumphed. Children saw their parents weeping, internalized the injustice, and played soldiers with wooden guns, and it was not hard to see that in a while they would swap the toys for real guns.

He described how Turkish Cypriots were forced to leave the villages in the south where they had lived for three centuries and migrate to the north, and how the Greeks had to leave the north and live in refugee camps in the south or move into the homes evacuated by the Turks. The world had learned nothing since the Eichmann trial, he remarked. Against this background, Maier wrote a suspense novel, followed by another one called *The Programmed Agent,* whose main character was a reporter in Jerusalem covering the Eichmann trial.

As a beginning author, Maier was confident about the stories he had to tell but suffered agonizing doubts about his ability to produce a real book. "I live in great tension that it will come to nothing," he wrote, and tried to console himself: "It probably happens to every author before he actually sees himself in print." He sent his draft manuscripts to Wiesenthal, who promised to read them carefully, line by line, and also sent Maier many instructions about fixing the structure of the plot, its content, and also the personalities of the characters. The character of the journalist must be strengthened, because as he is he looks like just another idiot, and it would be better for Frau Doktor Rabinowitsch not to appear in Beersheba, but instead at the Weizmann Institute in Rehovot.

Maier obeyed. Time and again he erased and rewrote: "I did exactly what you told me to do," he wrote to Wiesenthal. "After all, this book is both of ours, and also I know that your remarks are important and correct." Occasionally he asked for a kind word: "Cheer me up a little, Simon. I need it," he begged. Wiesenthal enjoyed this literary adventure and tried to help. He spoke to agents and publishing houses.

It was not easy to sell the book. Wiesenthal's own agent wondered if these James Bond types fighting the KGB weren't passé in the era of détente, and whether the reconciliation between the blocs did not call for a new kind of plot.[20]

Maier envied Forsyth, and also dreamed of becoming a second Johannes Mario Simmel, a popular Austrian writer who had mentioned Wiesenthal in one of his books.

Maier read *The Odessa File* in Cyprus. The book was rubbish, he thought. It would be a big hit, he figured—it was suitable for American readers. It would do nothing for the anti-Nazi educational and political struggle that he and Wiesenthal were trying so hard to advance. In Germany and Austria, the book would be recognized immediately as garbage. Nazis were to literature like salt to soup, he observed. They have to be used in the correct quantity. And to his taste, Forsyth's soup was just too salty.

It was not easy for him to see the book succeed while he was having trouble finding a publisher for his own work. He was on the verge of giving up. It seemed to him that his books would never appear and that he would never be an author, he wrote to Wiesenthal. He read with satisfaction a stinging review of *The Odessa File* in *Der Spiegel* and wrote, "My *Programmed Agent* is much better, but no one wants to believe me."[21]

In general, Wiesenthal was not open to criticism, but here he agreed with Maier. "I admit that the English version of the book includes a lot of things that someone like you, who knows a lot about such things, cannot accept," he wrote to Maier. Before the German-language version came out, the publisher had asked him to review it and he had already changed a lot and cut a lot. The German version would be far more acceptable, he promised.[22] Meanwhile, he continued his efforts to get Maier's books published, and that began to happen in 1977. Maier chose the pen name Leo Frank. The choice may have been Wiesenthal's idea. Leo Max Frank was an American Jew who was wrongly convicted of the murder of a young woman at the Atlanta factory that he managed, and lynched by an anti-Semitic mob in 1915. Wiesenthal mentioned him in one of his speeches.[23] Some of Maier/Frank's books sold well and were adapted for television.

In time, the link between the two men weakened, and Maier felt that he was losing Wiesenthal. In a 1979 letter Maier had the air of an injured admirer: he had not forgotten what Wiesenthal had said in Jerusalem, that he would choose him to be his brother, and in the years that had passed the "almost infantile adoration" that he felt for Wiesenthal had not lessened. "I permit myself to say that I was always there for you when you needed me, but when I think about it now—apparently I was only one of many and in the last thirty years I have only deluded myself that I have a special role in your life, just as your friendship was (for me) something very special."

He did not know, he wrote, whether Wiesenthal had read *The Programmed Agent*, as if he had forgotten that the book was born as a joint effort. Actually, he had hoped that Wiesenthal would do more to promote its sales by giving it publicity in the media. Now he felt betrayed. "Apparently, I exaggerated in my estimation of your ability and, particularly, your willingness to do something. And why should you? You must certainly have your own problems." He had therefore come to the conclusion that "it was nonsense, an illusion, to hope for anything in this matter, and as they say in English—'No hard feelings.'"

Toward the end of the letter, he compared his relations with Wiesenthal to those with his father. It is a letter that sheds light on both of their characters. Wiesenthal knew how to attract admirers, but was not good at requiting their admiration, at least not to the degree that they expected. And in the meanwhile, he did indeed have other things to worry about.[24]

4. Terror Against Jews

On September 28, 1973, armed Palestinian terrorists got onto a passenger train at Bratislava, then in Czechoslovakia, now the capital of Slovakia. The train was on its way from Moscow to Vienna and among the passengers was a group of thirty-nine Jewish emigrants from the Soviet Union on their way to Israel.

The Arabs took three of the Jews and an Austrian hostage, and demanded that in exchange for their release the Austrian government close down Schönau Castle near Vienna, which was being used as a transit facility for immigrants on their way from the Soviet Union to Israel.

The attack on the train was one of a series of spectacular terror operations carried out by Palestinians against Jews at various places in the world during the 1970s. Some of these attacks were carried out in collaboration with German and other terrorist groups. They hijacked passenger planes and murdered Israeli athletes at the 1972 Munich Olympics. In the train incident, Chancellor Kreisky allowed the terrorists to leave Austria on a plane that eventually flew them to Libya. No blood was spilled, but Wiesenthal was shocked.[25]

A few days later, Israel's prime minister, Golda Meir, came to Vienna to scold Kreisky for giving in to terror. It was a tough encounter. "A glass of water he didn't offer me," said Meir on her return home, and the Israeli press ran the headline: TOTAL BREAK WITH KREISKY.[26] For a moment it wasn't clear what weighed more on relations between Israel and Austria, the surrender to terror or the fact that Meir was left thirsty.

The Austrians were deeply offended. Years later it was still important to Margit Schmidt, Kreisky's loyal aide, to tell for the umpteenth time how she had prepared a room where Meir could have freshened up before the meeting, but she had insisted on seeing Kreisky immediately. It could not be that the chancellor never offered her coffee, said Schmidt, and in Austria they always served water with coffee.[27]

When she said she never got a glass of water, Meir actually meant that Kreisky did not fall into line with any of her demands, but the Israeli minutes of the meeting shows that this was not quite accurate. Kreisky related how the attack on the train and its aftermath unfolded, and he insisted that if he had not surrendered to their conditions, the terrorists would have killed their hostages. Meir spoke mainly of the need to combat terror. She had arrived in Vienna from a conference of the Socialist International in Strasbourg, where she had enjoyed a great deal of support, and she naturally expected warm support from Kreisky as well, as a socialist and a Jew.

But when he insisted that he had been right to give in to the terrorists, Meir felt it necessary to remind him of his duty as a Jew and to instruct him on how to fight terrorism. "Israel has to decide whether it will live or not live," she said. She claimed that Kreisky had bestowed a victory on terrorism by giving in to the demands, and that in the wake of his surrender, the life of not only every Israeli but also the life of every Jew in the world was imperiled. "We Jews and Israelis are a nuisance to the world, we have long experience," she added, and she didn't forget to add: "I witnessed a pogrom as a child."

Kreisky complained that he was receiving abusive letters from Jews and, in particular, Jewish organizations abroad, whereas Austrian industrial workers were sending him messages of congratulations for saving the lives of the Jews. It was a highly personal confrontation. It is hard to imagine two more different people. Meir was a suspicious person with narrow horizons; her working assumption was that the whole world harbored hostility toward Israel and the Jewish people. Kreisky was a statesman who thought in the broadest international terms. There were polar distances between them, he said, and it was clear that they could never agree on many matters. "My conscience could not bear causing the loss of lives," he said, and Meir replied, "Then we will have to fight terror alone."

But in contrast to the impression given by Meir on her return, Kreisky did not say that he would stop the transit of Jews from the Soviet Union through Austria, and he mentioned the waves of refugees who had been given asylum in the past in his country, including Holocaust survivors and those fleeing Romania, Hungary, and Poland. He explained that at Schönau Castle security could no longer be ensured, partly because Israel had given the site too much publicity before the attack. "Without all the publicity about the Jews stopping at Schönau, perhaps nothing would have happened," he said again a few weeks later, to the Israeli ambassador.

Kreisky wanted to share the responsibility for the Jews in transit with other countries, and perhaps involve the UN high commissioner for refugees. Either way, Schönau Castle would not be closed immediately, but it would be "phased out," he said, promising that substitute facilities would be found in Austria. "The whole problem is technical," he tried to reassure Meir, but the technical discussion was not enough for her. She wanted to extract from Kreisky an admission that Arab terrorists must be killed.

Arabs never commit suicide, she explained. That's why they must be killed without getting involved in negotiations with them, otherwise they would come back. Japanese commit suicide, she added, not Arabs. At that stage in the annals of terrorism, this was true, but Kreisky said, "That isn't a scientific contention. It is a matter of psychology and it is arguable." Meir remarked sarcastically that the president of Egypt was already sending a special envoy to Vienna to express his gratitude for the closure of Schönau. Kreisky said this was not correct and added that the envoy was someone who had served in the past as the Egyptian ambassador.[28]

The envoy from Cairo was Ismail Fahmi, soon to be appointed foreign minister. He told Kreisky the Egyptians had reached the conclusion that there was no other option but to go to war with Israel. Kreisky did not want to believe him, and asked if they really had given up on all other possibilities. Fahmi reiterated that Egypt could not continue to live with the defeat they had sustained in the Six-Day War and they had therefore decided that before the end of 1973 they would go to war. Two days later, on October 6, Yom Kippur, the Jewish Day of Atonement, the Egyptians and the Syrians took Israel by surprise, and the Jewish state's toughest conflict since its 1948 War of Independence began.

Kreisky told the Israeli ambassador in Vienna, Yitzhak Patish, about his conversation with Fahmi, about ten days later. He was sorry he had not reported on it right away, he said, but claimed that he had not taken what Fahmi said seriously, and immediately after the meeting he had gone on an election campaign tour of Upper Austria. In Jerusalem a Foreign Ministry official who received Patish's report was shocked: "The man ostensibly knew that the Arab attack was about to take place and didn't bother to warn us," he stated, and observed that because the war was still going on, the prime minister had not yet found time to react to this.[29]

A little while later, Kreisky visited Israel. Toward the end of his visit, he met with the parents of two Israeli prisoners of war held by Syria, both of whom were badly wounded. On his return home, Kreisky notified Meir in total secrecy, and for her ears only, that he had asked the prime minister of Syria to secure their release.[30] One of his supporters related that he had also tried to rescue some Jewish girls who were being forced to work as prostitutes in Syria.[31]

Kreisky also continued to allow the Jews from the Soviet Union to go through Austria in transit to Israel, and there could perhaps have been no greater contribution to the Zionist enterprise. Paradoxically, he did this at least in part because he felt that he shared the Austrians' responsibility for the crimes of the Nazis against the Jews. He was also aware of the surge of neo-Nazi activity in his country. Wiesenthal too sensed it. He employed a special staffer in his center whose task it was to keep track of neo-Nazi publications, a subject that was also of interest to the Mossad.

Wiesenthal tried to battle Holocaust denial in his own particular fashion. Once he entered into a bizarre and quarrelsome correspondence with an American organization that offered him $50,000 if he could prove that one Jew was gassed to death.[32] He also discovered that Hermann Göring was still considered an honorary citizen of the Austrian village of Mauterndorf, near Salzburg, and it took a public struggle to persuade its inhabitants to erase Göring's name from its list of honorees.[33] In a letter to German historian Joachim Fest, Wiesenthal stated that the term "war criminal" had the effect of diminishing Nazi crimes, because most of their crimes had nothing to do with war.[34]

Holocaust deniers of all stripes made him their target, and they profoundly irritated him. When he sued a well-known neo-Nazi activist, Manfred Roeder, a crowd of thugs was waiting for him in the courtroom and he was greeted by anti-Semitic shouts.[35] The more famous he grew, the greater the volume of hate mail he received. Many of the letters were rife with lavatory-wall obscenities. One such item in his papers had a little bar of soap attached. Quite often Wiesenthal could not bear the abuse and broke into tears.[36]

16.

"Mr. Wiesenthal, I Claim, Had Different Relations with the Gestapo from Mine"

I. Toward the Second Round

In mid-1974, Wiesenthal sent one of the volunteers working in his Documentation Center to deposit some checks in the bank. "I went to St. Stephen's Square," recalled Michael Stergar years later, "and the bank's doors were shut. I went back to the office. Wiesenthal panicked. 'What do you mean the bank is closed?' he yelled. 'If the bank is closed we can also shut down.' He hurried off to see for himself and found that the bank, the Allgemeine Wirtschaftsbank, had collapsed. 'That's it,' he said. 'We're finished.'"

It is not clear whether the failure of the bank really endangered the continuation of Wiesenthal's work, but the news that the Documentation Center was to discontinue operations almost overshadowed the news that the bank itself had gone bankrupt. Wiesenthal asked everyone from the queen of the Netherlands and the king of Sweden for help, and a new wave of donations flowed in.[1] The center stayed open and remained so for virtually his entire life.

That same year, Wiesenthal got worried again when he was asked to evacuate the premises on Rudolf Square. The other tenants in the building, many of them private citizens, some of them Jews, had begun to receive threatening letters and they complained to the landlords, who ordered Wiesenthal to leave. "It is not appropriate," they wrote, "that an apartment in a residential block should house activities that could lead to a terrorist attack. Herr Wiesenthal's activities should take place in an office building, where there is less danger that whole families will be harmed."[2]

And so Wiesenthal had to find new premises. It was no easy task. He needed someone who would support his activities, and he found a member of the Negrelli family, building contractors whose forefathers had been involved in the digging of the Suez Canal.[3] Luckily, he did not have far to go. The office building he moved to in Salztorgasse was close to Rudolf Square. Wiesenthal used to say that it had been built on the site of the Gestapo headquarters, and that was almost accurate. He and his staff felt as if they had to begin everything anew; Wiesenthal also took on a new secretary.

Rosa-Maria Austraat had seen a want ad that Wiesenthal placed in a newspaper. He interviewed her about her past. She was married with three children and had to work because her husband was in jail following bankruptcy complications. Wiesenthal asked her if she had also been involved, and she said she hadn't. He asked her if she wasn't afraid to work in a Jewish office. She told him about her father. He had been a member of the Nazi Party during the period when it was still outlawed. He had not joined because he believed in the Nazi ideology but because he thought it would be a good thing for Austria to become part of Germany. In World War II, he fought in Norway, and he had not been implicated in war crimes.

While still at school in Carinthia, Austria's southernmost province, she went with her class on a trip to Vienna, where they saw an exhibit about Auschwitz. It was a defining experience that, she said, confronted her with concrete criteria for differentiating between good and evil. She knew exactly who Wiesenthal was and she was very excited when he gave her the job. She was loyal to him until his dying day, and she loved him dearly.[4]

She used to address him to his face using the formal *Sie* and call him "Boss" or "Herr Ingenieur," though behind his back she called him "Bossie." He used her first name and the familiar *du*, as if she were a child. Sometimes she brought him a *Mehlspeis* pastry from home, sometimes she gave him a haircut, and occasionally she would rub ointment into his aching feet. Wiesenthal needed her. "For a long time I haven't been as busy as I am now," he wrote to an acquaintance in the summer of 1975. "One would have thought that with time there would be less work but on the contrary, there is always more."[5] At around the same time he found himself in the midst of an awkward and disconcerting story that would lead him into one of the worst crises of his life.

Bruno Kreisky had a brother two years older than he, named Paul. According to Kreisky, Paul had contracted polio soon after he was born, and as a result his mental development had been retarded. In another version, he had been hurt in an accident when a metal bar had struck him. In any case, Paul was his mother's favorite, Kreisky wrote, observing that it often happened that afflicted children get more love from their parents.

After the German takeover of Austria in 1938, Paul Kreisky went to live in Palestine. He considered himself a Zionist and a supporter of Ze'ev Jabotinsky's Revisionist movement. He took the name Shaul, Hebrew for Paul, married, and raised a family. In time, his situation deteriorated and a Vienna weekly printed photographs showing the chancellor's brother living alone in Jerusalem in pitiful circumstances, and making a living mending clothes.

In his memoirs, Kreisky saw fit to mention his brother's "oddities" and added that they often caused him a great deal of discomfort, as his political enemies had tried again and again to squeeze embarrassing statements out of Paul. In Israel, there were people helping these rivals and once they had lured his brother into appearing in a movie as a beggar at the Wailing Wall. The pictures were then made public. The truth was, Kreisky wrote, that he sent his brother generous financial assistance. Later on, he hired a Jerusalem lawyer, Yehezke'el Beinish, to act as the legal guardian of the sick man, and he took care of all his needs on a daily basis.[6]

Israel's ambassador in Vienna, Yitzhak Patish, believed that Kreisky's visit to Israel helped him get over his discomfort about his brother. "The fact that his nephew was serving as an officer in the Israel Defense Forces fills his Diaspora Jewish heart with pride, and he boasts about it to his friends," Patish reported. He also mentioned that during his visit to Yad Vashem, Kreisky had asked to see the memorial documents of his relatives who had been killed by the Nazis. Patish therefore imagined that he discerned "a certain favorable development, reconcilement, and even reconciliation."[7] A few months later, Paul Kreisky vanished into thin air.

The details of the case have never been clarified, but the chancellor believed that his brother was abducted with the help of the Israeli secret service. He was convinced that Wiesenthal was behind the kidnapping and that his aim was to extract statements from Kreisky's brother that would embarrass him and that could be used to extort concessions to Wiesenthal. It is difficult to grasp on what basis he reached this conclusion, but he repeated it over and over again. Wiesenthal heard about it from journalists, and the new Israeli ambassador, Avigdor Dagan, heard it from Kreisky himself, apparently more than once.

"Kreisky called me at home, and in a phone conversation of some twenty minutes he ranted in a manner that can only be described as bordering on insanity," the appalled ambassador reported in October 1975. In his cable, which was classified as "urgent and top secret," Dagan said that according to Kreisky, his brother had been missing for over a month. Kreisky suspected that he was being held in Holland, where Wiesenthal had many supporters. He roundly cursed Wiesenthal in terms that the ambassador quoted in their original German: he called him a *Schurke*, or scoundrel, ascribed to him *Lumpereien*, or dirty tricks, and declared that he would not "go onto the cross," meaning that he would fight Wiesenthal to the bitter end. "I sensed that he was at the limit of mental stability and I cut short the conversation," Dagan cabled. But Kreisky would not leave him alone. Several months later Dagan reported on yet another encounter: "At a certain moment, [Kreisky] erupted again and began to speak in the tone that we are familiar with about Wiesenthal and the abduction of his brother." The ambassador asked to be informed "what exactly had happened."[8]

Years later, Wiesenthal wrote to the chancellor's son, Peter Kreisky, to tell him his version of "what exactly had happened": A Jewish businessman from Frankfurt got to know Paul Kreisky in Jerusalem and offered to introduce him to his widowed sister who lived in Frankfurt, perhaps with marriage in mind. The businessman paid Paul Kreisky's traveling expenses. Paul left without telling his son Yossi, who was serving in the army at the time. Paul returned a few days later. The Israeli police had informed the Austrian embassy in Tel Aviv about what had happened, and Wiesenthal also heard about it. "To me, it sounded like an amusing anecdote," Wiesenthal wrote, and he denied that he or any of his acquaintances had anything to do with it.[9]

In his memoirs, Bruno Kreisky wrote that the abduction affair was the basic reason for his falling-out with Wiesenthal. Peter Kreisky also believed that this affair had motivated his father to declare war on Wiesenthal. In any event, the first round five years earlier, when Kreisky had reacted explosively to Wiesenthal outing his agricultural minister, was going to look like nothing compared to the blow that Kreisky was now about to deal Wiesenthal.[10] The scandal reverberated from one end of the globe to the other, born of a conflict between these two Jews that reached to the depths of their souls. Self-regard had made them into larger-than-life figures; in little Vienna, there was no room for both of them.

2. Jules Huf's Scoop

The whole thing may have begun at St. Michael im Lungau, a small town in southern Austria whose two thousand inhabitants made a living from the surrounding skiing sites and were proud of the magnificent sunsets the area enjoyed. After the war ended, one of the residents refused to acknowledge defeat. He set up a commando unit and continued fighting. His name was Richard Hochrainer. Wiesenthal told the story in 1975, in his newspaper: in a meadow close to their village, Hochrainer and the other heroes of St. Michael were alleged to have found nine Jewish concentration camp survivors and murdered them.

In the ten years that ensued, Hochrainer lived under an assumed name until the police discovered his true identity and arrested him. He was convicted by a jury and sentenced to seven years' imprisonment but he appealed and was acquitted. Both decisions were taken by six votes to two. He returned home and was welcomed by the townsfolk with flowers. He joined the Liberal Party and maintained good relations with the Social Democrats. In early 1975, both parties agreed to make Richard Hochrainer mayor.[11] Wiesenthal feared that the whole of Austria would become a St. Michael.

The national elections were approaching. Among Wiesenthal's papers is a leaflet with his signature urging his supporters to vote for the conservative People's Party. It is couched in harsh terms: "Kreisky is a traitor to the Jewish people and to democracy," it says. On the eve of the elections, there was no certainty that Kreisky's Social Democrats would be able to form the next government. Observers reckoned that he would have to form a coalition with the Liberal Party, and in that event the deputy chancellor, Friedrich Peter, would be the head of the Liberals.

Ambassador Dagan urgently requested instructions from Jerusalem. In 1938, Peter had joined the Nazi Party and shortly after that he was inducted into the SS. This was common knowledge, but no one asked what exactly he had done there. The impression he gave was that he had served in the general SS, not all of whose personnel were directly involved in acts of murder.

Somewhere in a file unknown to the public there was more information. In 1969 he was questioned about his past. He confirmed that he had served in the First SS Infantry Brigade but claimed that he knew nothing of that unit's activities against civilians. He said he had left the unit and been sent to an officers' training course, after which he served in another unit, the Fifth Company. He claimed that he had not taken part himself in the murder of Jews and had neither seen nor heard of his company participating in any such operations.[12]

"In the past our attitude to Peter's party has—for obvious reasons—been very cold and I too have not made any effort to change things," wrote the ambassador. For his part, Peter had tried to draw close to the Israeli ambassador whenever they met at social events in Vienna. "He spares no effort to stress his friendly interest," Dagan reported.[13]

Peter also used to take pride in his connections with the heads of the Liberal International, among them one of the leaders of the Israeli Liberal Party, Gideon Hausner, who had served as prosecutor in the Eichmann trial. Before the elections, Peter had accompanied Kreisky on a visit to Auschwitz. Kreisky said later that Peter had "learned an important lesson" there. The Dutch journalist Jules Huf later recalled cynics in Vienna joking that Peter had been in a hurry to leave Auschwitz, before Kreisky could turn on the gas.[14] In mid-September 1975, about two weeks before the elections, Wiesenthal had a file prepared about Peter's service in the SS.

He said this file was the result of a coincidence. He had just returned from a vacation with renewed vigor to tidy up his desk. "Only someone who knows what my desk is like can appreciate the magnitude of this task," he wrote. "As a rule, my desk is loaded with piles of files, and that means that I have to examine every single piece of paper, and then I decide what should be filed away and what needs further action. There are also documents I have already gone over perfunctorily beforehand, and now I must check them thoroughly. Other documents are totally new and I have to classify them."

It was an exhausting task, but also a fruitful one, Wiesenthal continued. "It has something of the treasure hunt about it." His excellent memory, which he compared to that of a computer, almost always helped him come across surprises, and that's what happened this time too: Among the reams of papers he went through, he noticed a list of junior SS commanders who were to be sent to an officers' training course. They belonged to the

First Infantry Brigade, with which Wiesenthal was familiar because of the atrocities they carried out in the Soviet Union. He went down the list and suddenly came across the name Friedrich Peter. "I knew that I had a time bomb in my hands," he wrote. "A short while before I discovered it," he added, "the war diary of the First Infantry Brigade of the SS had been published in Vienna."[15]

That was inaccurate. The diary in question had come out ten years earlier, and it included bloodcurdling details of some of the brigade's atrocities.[16] Jules Huf claimed it was no coincidence that the document implicating Peter had been found by Wiesenthal while he was tidying his desk, as he claimed. According to Huf, it was his own scoop. With Peter's appointment as deputy chancellor in the offing, the Dutch journalist had asked the weekly *Profil* for some background material on him, and what he received included his personal SS file. Because he could not make out the abbreviated names of the units Peter had served in, he gave the material to Wiesenthal, and the fact that Peter had belonged to one of the murder units was revealed.[17]

It may be that Wiesenthal had known about it before. Either way, the question was what to do about the file. Publishing it prior to the elections might increase Peter's popularity and harm both Wiesenthal and the entire Jewish community. Wiesenthal consulted with his friend Paul Grosz, and that wise and experienced Jewish man, who would in the future become president of the community, knew how Jews in the Diaspora could extricate themselves from traps like this. He advised Wiesenthal to pass the time bomb on to the president of Austria, Rudolf Kirchschläger, so that he could ponder what to do about it.[18]

While he was busy with the Peter file, Wiesenthal found himself in a stormy situation that vexed him greatly; the possibility cannot be ruled out that his decision to deal such a disconcerting blow to Austrian politics was motivated by the need for something that would overshadow the troubles that he was facing. For it was just at this time that Isser Harel's book on the Eichmann abduction appeared in Israel, and Wiesenthal's name was not even mentioned in it.[19] Reporters asked the former head of Israel's security services why this was so, and Harel said that Wiesenthal had played no role in the efforts to locate Eichmann. This wasn't the first time that Wiesenthal was called upon to rebut such claims.

Ironically, Wiesenthal had originally tried to help Harel by linking him up with his own literary agent. He sent him the draft contract via his former Mossad handler, "Elazar."[20] But the main reason Harel's claims infuriated him was that they appeared in the *New York Times*. He would now have to start a long campaign to prove his credibility, he wrote.[21] Six days later he went to see President Kirchschläger and presented him with the Peter file.

The Austrian voters gave Kreisky's party a slim majority in Parliament, and he didn't need the support of the Liberals. The Israeli ambassador was jubilant: "I won't have to be in touch with the ministers of that party, whose background is known," he wrote, and he also passed on to Jerusalem a copy of the file Wiesenthal had handed to Kirchschläger before the elections. "It transpires that Peter took part in murder," he reported, and he warned his superiors of the scandal that was about to erupt: that same week, Wiesenthal was going to hold a press conference in Vienna. In Jerusalem they tried to temper the ambassador's excitement, but he replied: "We must not stress our reservations about Wiesenthal. We cannot strengthen him, but in my opinion we must also refrain from weakening him."[22]

Wiesenthal was euphoric. One of his former aides saw him on the way to the press conference. He slammed on the brakes of the battered Peugeot he was using now and shouted excitedly: "Come with me! Quick! Quick! I'm on the way to the Hôtel de France! Press conference! Peter is a murderer!"[23]

Ostensibly, the political need to expose Peter's past was now moot, because Kreisky didn't need his support to form a government. But perhaps Wiesenthal feared that because of his tiny majority Kreisky might nevertheless be tempted to do what the politicians in St. Michael had done. But it is far more likely that Wiesenthal simply couldn't restrain himself from taking this opportunity to avenge himself for what Kreisky had done to him five years before.[24]

3. A Roll of Thunder

Kreisky always denied having a "Jewish complex" and many years after his death his associates were still trying, with touching loyalty, to prove that he was not afflicted with such a thing. But Kreisky was a Jewish chancellor in an Austria in which some of the citizens were still Nazis; everyone was always referring to his being a Jew, and he, too, frequently occupied himself with the significance of the fact. "The Jewish thing positively eats him up," the Israeli ambassador reported.[25] He regarded being a Jew as being a kind of hunchback, something that made life difficult but could not be denied, or as he said once: "One should no more deny being a Jew than deny being a German, or being the offspring of a prostitute."[26]

Bruno Kreisky's family came from Bohemia, but he himself was born in Vienna. In his memoirs he described his parents as not having ascribed much significance to their religious origins. It was important for him to mention that they worked on the Jewish Sabbath, intermarried with gentiles, and ate ham. He remembered only one incident with anti-Semitic undertones: His father took him out of a gymnastics club that boasted that it did not accept Jews. He enrolled in another club where there were a lot of Jews, but he observed: "I have had very few friends of the Jewish persuasion in my life."[27]

Kreisky read many books on the subject and he formed the opinion that the Jews were neither a race nor a nation, but rather had a common religious identity. The Zionist movement, which was also born in Vienna, advocated the opposite view: all Jews belonged to one nation that was exiled from its land, and if they wanted to live on as Jews they had to return to the land of their forefathers and to rebuild their commonwealth. The Holocaust was taken by many as clear proof that Zionism was right.

The Israeli embassy tried on occasion to explore Kreisky's past. One of its reports says that he left the Jewish community in 1935, declaring that he did not believe in the God of the Jews, and he saw himself as a "socialist atheist." The last two words were in quotation marks. The embassy pointed out that Kreisky never converted to Christianity, underlining the last four words.

The next Israeli ambassador corrected this information, probably after asking Kreisky himself about it. He had never left the Jewish community, because he had never belonged to it. He said he stopped seeing himself as a Jew when he was sixteen, when the Social Democratic Party began urging its members to leave the Catholic Church.[28]

He was first arrested for forbidden political activities in 1934. Immediately after Austria's annexation to Germany, he was arrested again and, after a few months in a Gestapo prison, freed on condition that he leave the country. He settled in Sweden, where he married a Jewish woman who had become a Protestant Christian before meeting him. They had a son and a daughter, both of whom were baptized. At home they celebrated Christmas with a tree and gifts. His wife insisted on this, Kreisky himself being more reserved, their son Peter recalled.

After the war, Kreisky was one of a group of Social Democratic exiles whom the party did not encourage to come back, because they were Jews and it feared they would be a liability.[29] Kreisky swallowed this and remained in Sweden in a diplomatic capacity until 1951. His son Peter reckoned that his pleasant years of exile in Sweden prevented his father from comprehending the full significance of the Holocaust. The journalist Peter Michael Lingens believed that his attitude was formed still earlier, when he had Nazi cell mates and he regarded them as victims of persecution for their political views, like himself. This encounter had created "a totally distorted" attitude to the Holocaust, Lingens reasoned.[30]

All the parties, said Peter Kreisky, were trying to win the support of the Nazis; everybody tried to blur the Nazi past, including his father. Sometimes they talked about it. He also heard about relatives who had been killed in the Holocaust. But his father thought in terms of politics. His son organized socialist activities among his schoolmates, and once he scheduled an outing to Mauthausen. His father said: "Don't waste your time. It won't get your group one new member."

Peter Kreisky wasn't a regular churchgoer, but when a Christian leader equated abortions to the extermination of Jews at Auschwitz and refused to condemn apartheid, he decided to leave the Church. His father didn't try to stop him but worried about the political damage that the act could cause him: they'd say the son left the Church under the influence of his Jewish father, he feared. But his son took the step, and nothing happened.

Kreisky and his son spoke about the Nazis who still lived in Austria. Kreisky believed that the problem would have a natural solution, that they would grow old and die out.[31] He also believed that the Jews would disappear one day.

In Kreisky's memoirs, he claimed that months before the elections he had told Friedrich Peter that he would not have ministers who had been Nazis in his government.[32] There is no reason to believe this. There were ministers with a Nazi past in his first government, and he was now defending his links with Peter, although he didn't need his backing, despite the information revealed by Wiesenthal. It was at this point that his political sense fell by the wayside and bare personal emotions came into play.

As long as Peter had not been convicted by a court, he should not be disqualified, Kreisky argued. True, he had erred in his youth but those were days of chaos and confusion, and Peter was only seventeen when he was called upon, like most Austrians, to choose between the Communists and the Nazis. It may be difficult to grasp this in a democratic society forty years onward, Kreisky explained, and declared: "Peter has promised me on his word of honor that he never took part in murder. I have no reason to believe him any less than I believe Wiesenthal."[33]

Wiesenthal never linked Peter himself to any specific crime. Thus far, he had also always held that there was no collective guilt and that each individual should be punished for his own crimes, as determined by the courts. Apparently, his enmity toward Kreisky had blurred the principles of justice that had guided him until this point. There is no need for further proof, he asserted. It was enough that Peter served for twenty months in a murderous SS brigade, and he now publicly confirmed belonging to the First SS Infantry Brigade.[34]

A few days after Wiesenthal's conference, Kreisky also spoke to the press, and he had harsh words for Wiesenthal: "He uses the methods of a quasi-political Mafia." Three days later, Wiesenthal sued Kreisky for libel.[35]

The spectacle of two famous Jews slugging it out in public soon burst out of the narrow confines of Austria and took a prominent place in the world media. Wiesenthal was spending much of his time being interviewed by journalists from almost every country in the world, and he was also flooded by letters and cables of support, especially from the Netherlands and the United States. For his part, Kreisky couldn't stop denouncing Wiesenthal, repeating over and over that he had contributed nothing to the capture of Eichmann. Then one day, the chancellor lost control of himself.

It happened in the Concordia press club, during a briefing for foreign correspondents. The transcript of the conversation is reminiscent of a roll of thunder that begins with a distant rumble and climaxes in an earsplitting crack. Answering a question from an Associated Press correspondent, Kreisky began with a long monologue that was supposed to clarify his attitude to his Jewishness and to Israel. Wiesenthal turns up on page five of the transcript. From that point on, Kreisky's sentences are clumsy, often breaking off without having made a point, and it is clear that his emotional state was disrupting not only his choice of words but also his ability to string the words together into coherent sentences.

"I actually know Wiesenthal only from secret reports and those are bad, very bad, and I as chancellor, and even as chancellor I cannot therefore—and not because we belong to the same religious community that isn't a community at all, because it isn't—we come from an entirely different cultural environment, from different religious communities, and they really were different. There is nothing I have in common with Mr. Wiesenthal and he should not go looking for it, just as I have nothing in common with someone else that I do not tolerate or like. Do you understand me? And Mr. Wiesenthal, I claim, had different relations with the Gestapo from mine, yes, that can be proved."

Everything he had to say about this he would say in the course of the lawsuit that Wiesenthal had initiated, said Kreisky, and here he could have called it a day, but he went on and on: "My relations with the Gestapo are completely clear. I was their prisoner, and I was interrogated. His relations are completely different; I believe that I know this, and it will be possible to clarify this."

He took a brief break, and continued: "After all, it is a grave thing that I am saying here, it cannot suffice for him to just feel offended and sue me. It will not be that simple. It will be a big trial, I hope, because a man like him has no right to appear as a moral authority, I claim, he has no right. He should not live off persecuting people. He has no right."

Here, Kreisky began talking about Peter, reiterating that he trusted him, but almost immediately went back to Wiesenthal: "In my opinion, he is a foreign agent using the methods of the Mafia," he repeated. He mentioned the Ableitinger case, declared that Wiesenthal was not a gentleman, and went back to the allegation that Wiesenthal collaborated with the Nazis.

"All I am saying, and it must be clear, so that he doesn't become a moral authority—and he isn't one—and I understand that he wanted to save his life from the Nazis, everyone tried to do that in his own way, right, but he shouldn't make that into the source of moral authority." Here, the transcript reached page eight and Kreisky apologized for the length of his reply.

The correspondents asked him something else about Peter, and Kreisky again tried to draw them toward the existential dilemmas facing the Austrians prior to the annexation to Nazi Germany. The transcript reached page twelve, and then the United Press International correspondent asked if he had understood correctly, that the chancellor had said that Wiesenthal worked as an agent for the Gestapo during the war.

Kreisky replied: "I contend that during the war Wiesenthal lived in the areas of Nazi influence, without being persecuted. Yes? He lived openly, without being persecuted. Yes? That's clear? And perhaps you know, those who know about these things, that this is a danger that a man could not have taken upon himself, because it wasn't living in the underground, hiding in a hideout, but completely in the open, without being, yes . . . He chose to take a risk. I think I've said enough. There were so many opportunities to work as an agent, it did not have to be precisely a Gestapo agent, there were so many other services."

One of the reporters asked Kreisky if he could share with them the contents of the secret reports he had mentioned, but Kreisky corrected him before he could finish the question: "No, not reports of the secret services, but testimonies of people from that period." The reporter asked who those witnesses were, Austrians or people from other countries, and Kreisky replied: "There are some Austrians, Germans, all kinds of testimony." He took another pause and continued: "Relatively old testimony." The reporters continued to pester him and Kreisky bickered with them and continued vilifying Wiesenthal.[36]

Rumors about Wiesenthal's past had haunted him since he left Mauthausen, and he was constantly called upon to refute them. In 1952 he was asked by the *Forward*, a Jewish newspaper in New York, if it was true that he had served as a kapo during the war. The question apparently arose as the result of a tip received by the paper. "I don't know if that is a tasteless joke or a criminal libel," Wiesenthal replied, and gave a lengthy and detailed account of his activities against Jewish collaborators, including his efforts to prevent them from getting emigration visas. As the years went by, he had to defend himself again and again. Asher Ben Natan, who had worked with the Briha after the war and later served as Israel's first ambassador to West Germany, said many years later, "I have no doubt that Wiesenthal worked in the Judenrat in Lvov," but offered no proof to back this up.[37]

Wiesenthal reacted to Kreisky's tirade with his customary sarcasm. "He's an important politician but doesn't like to be a Jew," he wrote to one of his backers in America. "The only person who doesn't know Kreisky is a Jew is Kreisky himself," he said on another occasion, and also "Kreisky is like a Negro who signs an affidavit that he isn't black." Among his papers there is a photomontage showing an official portrait of Kreisky wearing a swastika in his lapel.[38] He filed another libel suit against the chancellor, and it was incorporated with the first one.

Up to this point, Wiesenthal had seen Kreisky as an opponent, but not as an enemy. Kreisky led the left in Austria; Wiesenthal attacked him from the right. He criticized Kreisky for not doing enough to cleanse the country of its Nazi past, and he rejected the chancellor's censure of Israel's policy in the Palestinian territories. But this political rivalry with Kreisky had never threatened Wiesenthal's identity as an Austrian and a Jew, so he was able to live with him.[39]

Kreisky, for his part, couldn't live with Wiesenthal. He saw him not just as a political opponent but rather as an enemy, because Wiesenthal was a threat to his Austrian identity. Wiesenthal was born in a small village in Galicia and spoke Yiddish with his parents; he was a typical *Ostjude*, a Jew from the East, in his appearance and his accent, and this, plus his refusal to allow Austria to blur its criminal past, made it difficult for the Jew Kreisky to persuade his fellow citizens that he himself was one of them, a true Austrian, who was born in Vienna, spoke like a Viennese, felt like a Viennese. His war against Wiesenthal was therefore a war of survival. And it also affected the way he felt about Israel: "With all the goodwill in the world, I cannot see why the land of my actual forefathers should be less dear to me than a strip of wilderness with which I have no connection," he wrote.[40]

The majority of Austrians lined up on his side. The "Sun King," as they called him, had never been more popular, and Wiesenthal never more detested. Without meaning to do so, Kreisky had made it legitimate for his countrymen to despise Jews who looked and spoke and behaved like Wiesenthal. The fact that Wiesenthal so longed to belong to the Austrian community added a dimension of bitter irony to the story. And that is how the war of verbal abuse between two Viennese Jews erupted out of the local political puddle to become the center of a great historical-philosophical debate about nationality and racism, nationalism and patriotism, Zionism and Judaism.

4. Who's a Jew?

At the height of the worldwide storm aroused by his remarks, Kreisky fantasized aloud about having a meeting with a group of Israeli students ("socialists, of course") and persuading them that Zionism was based on racist principles. In November 1975, the UN General Assembly equated Zionism with racism. Although Austria voted against the resolution, Kreisky agreed with its spirit. He understood that unfortunately he would not be able to meet with those Israeli students, so he made do with granting an interview to Israeli television and the Israeli daily *Maariv*.

He received the two correspondents in one of the halls of the eighteenth-century palace that housed the chancellor's office and residence, under a huge crystal chandelier. His office had allotted a quarter of an hour to the interview. At that stage in his dispute with Wiesenthal, Kreisky had already managed to repeat his position on innumerable occasions, he had his version down pat, and he didn't need more time.

After the interview, the chancellor asked his guests if they would be so kind as to give him a little more of their time, because he wished to explain a serious matter to them. He led them into a back room through tall, narrow wooden doors painted white and adorned with gilt carving and sat on a leather sofa embossed with the imperial eagle, also gilt. He knew how to be charming and create a relaxed atmosphere, and he had a clever wit.

On a coffee table in front of the sofa there was a pile of books lying open with pages marked by slips of paper. The time had come, Kreisky said, for the Israelis and all the other Zionists to understand why they were wrong when they spoke of a Jewish people. There was no such thing. But before he proved this, it was important for him to stress that he did not suffer from the Jewish "self-hatred" of which he had been accused. The only thing he hated was the efforts to make him belong, against his will, to a Jewish people in the spirit of Zionist ideology. It was evident that there was nothing he hated more, and Kreisky knew how to hate.

This was not the first time that he claimed there was no Jewish people. In an interview with another Israeli journalist, he had said the same thing and then let slip a wisecrack that caused him a lot of trouble: "If the Jews are a people, then it's a loathsome people."[41] In his conversation with the two journalists whom he had invited into the back room of his office, Kreisky tried to deliver an orderly lecture grounded in works by some of the Social Democratic movement's ideological fathers, including Victor Adler and Otto Bauer, both of whom were of Jewish origin.

Kreisky said he had not touched these books for at least twenty years. But whenever he picked one of them up to quote from it, a partly eaten Mozart chocolate ball could be seen, evidence that he had prepared himself well for the conversation the night before, while nibbling at one of the famous confections.

A man in a dress suit who was in charge of the chancellor's schedule, official consternation on his face, came in to say that some delegation from the Balkans had arrived for their appointment. Kreisky said they should leave and come back later. Half an hour later, the official came in again and said that a minister had arrived as scheduled, and the chancellor ordered that he too be sent away. An hour went by, Kreisky talked and talked, and his Israeli guests listened. "There is nothing in common between my grandfather, who was a school principal in Bohemia, and a Jewish shoemaker in Yemen," Kreisky said again and again. The U.S. ambassador wanted a word on the phone; the official was ordered to tell him that Kreisky would get back to him later.

Finally, one of the journalists dared to ask if in the chancellor's opinion there was an Austrian people, and if so, since when. Kreisky, a bulky man with a thunderous voice, almost exploded with anger and yelled that his forefathers had felt like members of the Austrian people as early as Napoleon's time. And another hour went by. He wanted to keep going, but the brave man in the dress suit who was in charge of the chancellor's schedule came back, this time with an expression of determination etched on his face, and declared that the next visitor could not be put off by any means or a world war would break out—it was the Soviet ambassador.[42] If he only had time, Kreisky lamented, he would lay out his reasoning in writing; he was to do so later, when he wrote his memoirs.

According to Otto Bauer, Judaism had been a religious communality, and its members experienced a common historical destiny even if they did not practice religion, but he stated that this was not true to the same extent everywhere. Kreisky adopted this position. Certain historical circumstances had enabled the Jews of Austria to give up their religious faith, as his parents had done. By so doing they had given up their Jewishness. They were not connected to other Jews by ties of blood or of race.

Kreisky also espoused the theory that the Jews of Europe were the descendants of the Khazars, who lived near the Caspian Sea and whose leaders were said to have adopted the Jewish religion in the eighth century. The Jews of Yemen, he believed, were also the descendants of the peoples of that area who had converted to Judaism, and the same went for Ethiopian Jewry. The Jews had entered history as a mixed nation, and since then they had not stopped mixing with their neighbors, he asserted, adding: "I have never understood why so many Jews, and particularly scholars who have written about the Jewish question . . . insist on stressing over and over again, with such great stubbornness, the unity and the absolute racial purity of the 'Chosen People.'"

In truth Zionists had never spoken of racial purity of the Jewish people, but nonetheless, Kreisky was sure that if he could only prove there was no "Jewish race" he would also prove there was no Jewish people. Kreisky himself recognized that there were multiracial nations, among them, ironically, the Israeli nation. He equated the Israelis with the Americans.[43]

———

In Jerusalem, officials once again had to rack their brains to decide what to do. Apart from the UN condemnation of Zionism as racism, this was the most powerful attack to date on the ideological foundations of the State of Israel. Kreisky was not the first to accuse the Zionists of inventing a Jewish people; the Israelis themselves had always agonized over the question "Who is a Jew?" and had never reached a consensus. The issue threatened to undermine the theoretical justification of their existence.[44] Kreisky was proposing a pragmatic approach. In his eyes, Israel was an "artificial" state that had been born in the wake of the Holocaust, but once it had arisen there was no alternative but to recognize its right to exist.

As it had done in the previous round of the Kreisky-Wiesenthal fight, official Israel tried to stay outside the ring, but Ambassador Dagan reported time and again that Kreisky was trying to get him involved. "It is difficult to describe the sudden change," he wrote about one of the chancellor's outbursts. "All at once, all reason has vanished, and I have scarcely been given a chance to respond in a sentence or two to the outpouring of anger, complaints and invective."

The Israelis had no idea how much he was suffering because of the Jews, Kreisky carped to the ambassador. He was getting heaps of Nazi-style anti-Semitic letters. And all because of Wiesenthal. "Once again he repeated all of the smears that I have already heard from him before, except this time Wiesenthal was only an agent of the Americans and not the Gestapo. And once again he related details about the affair of his brother, and that no one had persuaded him that it wasn't Wiesenthal who was behind it," Dagan reported.

At a certain stage, Dagan reached the conclusion that he was dealing with a lost cause and he proposed the following policy to his superiors in Jerusalem: "We must get used to the fact—I personally have already done so—that in any matter connected even indirectly to the Jews or to Israel, we are dealing with an instable and unbalanced man, a severe case of love-hate, bordering on a split personality." Some of Kreisky's outbursts are also documented in memorandums written in his office. When he received a protest from the Jewish community, he demanded that it retract the letter within twenty-four hours, or else, he threatened, it would be consigned to the garbage bin.[45]

The two journalists who had interviewed Kreisky also went to see Wiesenthal at his Documentation Center. He stood before his map of the concentration camps, fixed his eyes on the lens of the Israeli television camera, and burst into tears. Kreisky's words had pained him greatly, not only as a Jewish Holocaust survivor but also as someone who had adopted Austria as his motherland, he sobbed. He could live with his memories of the Holocaust, he murmured in a choked voice, he could live with the verbal abuse and the threats he received from neo-Nazis and anti-Semites all over the world, but he could not live with the allegation that he had collaborated with the Nazis; not when it came from a Jewish chancellor.

The tears ran down his cheeks and an oppressive, almost intolerable silence descended on the modest office. For a moment it was as if time had stopped and there was only sadness left in the world. The Israeli television correspondent, Ron Ben Yishai, and his colleague, as well as the photographer and the soundman, both Austrians, were frozen in place. No one dared utter a sound. And then Wiesenthal wiped his eyes and asked in a businesslike manner: "Well? How did I do? Was I okay?" It was as if a bomb had gone off in the room.[46]

Wiesenthal was not a cynic; the tears were genuine. He did not lack reasons for weeping, and he did so frequently, not only before the cameras. But when it came to media manipulation, few could compete with him.

In December 1975, the Organization of Petroleum Exporting Countries, or OPEC, held a conference in Vienna. The Yom Kippur War had brought about a dramatic increase in oil prices and OPEC had become a very powerful body. The oil ministers of most of the member countries were at the conference. Neutral Vienna welcomed them graciously, as it did other international gatherings, but the security arrangements such a meeting required were beyond its abilities and its attention was already focused mainly on the approaching Christmas festivities. Six terrorists took over the building where the conference was being held, taking dozens of people hostage, including the foreign ministers, ambassadors, and officials from various countries. The operation was headed by the legendary terrorist known as Carlos. He was acting on behalf of the extremist Popular Front for the Liberation of Palestine.

Once again, Kreisky was called upon to decide on the best way to respond, and once again he decided to do his level best to avoid bloodshed. After negotiations, the terrorists freed some of the hostages and they were allowed to take the remainder with them on a special plane that took them to Algeria and Libya. And again, Kreisky strongly defended his decision.

At that stage, Kreisky still believed that his country's neutrality and his own personal prestige would enable him to help solve the Palestinian problem. His activities in this matter were in accord with the idealistic concepts of the Social Democratic movement, whose leaders thought that it was their duty to design a better world and divided the job up among themselves. Willy Brandt was in charge of engineering a thaw in the Cold War; Olof Palme, the prime minister of Sweden, coordinated the effort to eliminate apartheid in South Africa; and Kreisky took upon himself the task of bringing peace to the Middle East. In so doing, he established contacts with officials of the Palestine Liberation Organization, a move Israel saw as severely damaging its efforts to wipe out terrorism.

Kreisky had allies inside Israel, peace activists headed by Uri Avneri, editor of the antiestablishment weekly *Ha'olam Hazeh*, who encouraged the chancellor to keep on meeting with Issam Sartawi, a leader of the PLO's armed wing, Fatah, as well as a cardiologist, terrorist, and adviser to Yasser Arafat. These meetings were among the first steps leading up to the eventual mutual recognition of Israel and the PLO. Kreisky arranged meetings between Sartawi and journalists, and one of them, Peter Michael Lingens, tried to introduce Sartawi to Wiesenthal. Wiesenthal refused. "Sartawi has Jewish blood on his hands," he said. He fiercely opposed Kreisky's Palestinian initiatives and frequently reported what he heard about them to Ambassador Dagan.[47]

In May 1977, a dramatic turnabout occurred in Israeli politics: the Labor movement lost its hegemony for the first time, and Menachem Begin became the prime minister. At least two Jews in Vienna received this news very emotionally: Wiesenthal was filled with pride, Kreisky with wrath. He did play a role in bringing about the signing of a peace agreement between Israel and Egypt in 1979, but when the talks ran into difficulties, he told the Dutch newspaper *Trouw* that facing the Egyptians, Begin behaved like "a small-time political shopkeeper." Later he called Begin a "small-time political lawyer" and he tarred him, as he had Wiesenthal, with what was to him the blackest brush of all: *Ostjude*, a Jew from the East. The impression was that in the heat of Kreisky's ire, Wiesenthal and Begin had merged into one. Prime Minister Begin responded immediately: everyone knew, he said, that Kreisky hated his father and his mother.[48]

Apparently by the time he got to the second volume of his memoirs, Kreisky had run out of even the little love for Israel that Ambassador Dagan had attributed to him, and only the hate remained. "What is playing out in Israel at present is so disgusting and ugly that I am truly finding it difficult to keep my blood calm," he wrote, referring to the oppression of the Palestinians. But he never gave up hope: "The Zionists' game is a losing one," he asserted.[49]

Meanwhile, his conflict with Wiesenthal was going ahead full steam, from courtroom to courtroom. Its main question was: Had Wiesenthal been a Nazi agent?

17.

"It's Not Easy to Be My Wife"

I. The Evidence

The first libel suits that Wiesenthal filed against Kreisky ended without any results. Kreisky at first said he would waive his immunity as chancellor, but then he reneged, claiming that his mandate belonged to his party, and it would not release him.

The head of the Social Democratic parliamentary delegation at the time was thirty-seven-year-old Heinz Fischer, who had obtained the position thanks to Kreisky. Quite naturally, the youthful politician was eager to satisfy his new boss, and this extended to the latter's fight against Wiesenthal, which he treated as if it were the business of the party itself. "In this matter, Bruno Kreisky gets very emotional and is not an easy man to tangle with," wrote Fischer.

Consequently, he proposed setting up a parliamentary commission of inquiry into the Documentation Center's "quasi-Mafia methods and its reciprocal relations with the state police."[1] The wording was not coincidental—the center was a private organization and the parliament therefore had no authority to investigate it, but by probing its links with the police it could get access to Wiesenthal's affairs. This was a rather brutal threat; Wiesenthal certainly did not want to see such an inquiry, because he feared it would lead to the closing down of his center.

Prior to this, Wiesenthal had received a warning from his attorney, Hans Perner, very tactfully phrased but quite unequivocal: if a trial were to be held, he could not rule out the possibility that Kreisky would produce evidence that might not reflect the actual facts but would be impossible to refute.[2] Many people tried to dissuade Wiesenthal from proceeding with his suit, and various figures tried to settle the dispute between the two men; one of these was Willy Brandt.[3] There was an almost hour-long phone conversation between Peter Michael Lingens, editor of the weekly *Profil*, and Heinz Fischer, who were childhood friends. The Viennese Jewish tycoon Karl Kahane also intervened, and there was finally a conversation between Ivan Hacker, a future president of the Jewish community, and Kreisky himself.

Together the two formulated a statement that Kreisky would make after Wiesenthal retracted his suit. Kreisky wrote it down in his own handwriting. It said that he had never accused Wiesenthal of collaborating with the Nazis and he therefore saw the whole affair as being closed. In accordance with Wiesenthal's demand, the threat of the inquiry commission was also removed. Ten years later, Fischer expressed regret over the events, and said that in the meanwhile he had learned to act more "maturely."[4]

When Kreisky told journalists he had material indicating that Wiesenthal had collaborated with the Nazis he was not lying, but most of that material was worthless garbage sent to him after he publicized his allegations. He also received letters of support from former Nazis in South America and from neo-Nazis, and all at once he became the hero of Holocaust deniers and anti-Semites all over the world. Kreisky seized upon this material as if it were a treasure trove; the intensity of his hatred for Wiesenthal blinded him, overwhelming his decent instincts and disrupting his judgment. But the allegation that Wiesenthal worked for the Gestapo was not a figment of his imagination. It originated in a report that the Austrian ambassador to Poland had sent to Vienna, and Kreisky found it filed away in an archive.

One day, the ambassador wrote in June 1969, a top official in the Polish Interior Ministry told him about a dispute that had arisen in Warsaw over what action could be taken against Wiesenthal. Ever since Poland cut off diplomatic relations with Israel following the 1967 Six-Day War, Wiesenthal had been exposing former Nazis in leading positions there, which Warsaw regarded as anti-Communist "provocation." The Poles tried to strike back.

According to the Polish official, his ministry was in possession of evidence that Wiesenthal had been an agent for the Gestapo. The security services had suggested publicizing this material, but the Foreign Ministry objected. The official wanted to bypass the foreign ministry of his own country and he asked if the Austrians could not do something to restrain Wiesenthal. The ambassador replied, as was to be expected, that Austria was a free country and it was doubtful that anything could be done.

Half a year later, the Polish foreign minister told Austrian diplomat Franz Karasek that Wiesenthal's activities were harming relations between the two countries. Karasek reiterated that it was difficult to take steps against him, but the Austrian ambassador, who was present at the meeting, suggested that the Poles supply Austria with incriminating evidence against Wiesenthal, and that's what was agreed on.

Karasek thought that this part of his talk with the Polish foreign minister deserved a special report to foreign minister Kurt Waldheim, and copies of his memorandum were sent to Kreisky and other ministers as well. Kreisky's copy is in his archive. It shows that what the Poles once had been unable to provide the East German secret services they were also unable to provide the Austrians, despite the great effort they invested in searching for it. Kreisky, however, appears to have seized upon the Polish charges even though the Poles had failed to back them up with evidence. A few months later, a Polish newspaper reported that Wiesenthal had worked for Nazi Germany's intelligence service. Wiesenthal issued a public denial, but Kreisky's belief that there was something shady about his past was probably strengthened.[5]

Austria's governmental machinery went into action to help the chancellor as soon as he launched his campaign against Wiesenthal, and all kinds of documents that had been pulled out of old files landed on his desk with astonishing efficiency. Among the subjects they dealt with were Wiesenthal's work with Holocaust refugees at Bindermichl and his application for Austrian citizenship, and they also included a bundle of papers he had assembled at the time of his claim for restitution payments from Germany. The material covered all the details of his life story, and one document even pointed out that he was not entitled to put his title as an engineer ("Dipl. Ing.") before his name, but only after it. Evidently, Wiesenthal had been under surveillance by the security services throughout the years that he had been living in Austria. All the results were now laid before the chancellor.

Eavesdropping had also been employed. Kreisky received a report on a conversation between Wiesenthal and two people in an airport restaurant before he left for Frankfurt. He was looking for information about Kreisky's family, he was heard saying. The identity of the two people he was talking to was not noted, but the chancellor's office obtained a full list of passengers on Wiesenthal's flight. Ambassadors and consuls in various countries were also roped in to pass on to Vienna all kinds of rumors they had collected. London, Oslo, Ottawa, Munich—they all did their bit.[6]

The telephones in Kreisky's office didn't stop ringing, as more and more people came forward with material that was supposed to help the chancellor. One of them was a Dr. Willhelm Schaller, and an investigator was dispatched to his home to take down a statement. In 1944, Schaller was serving in the Wehrmacht in the city of Tarnów, in southeastern Poland, where he was in charge of a military prison. While walking around the city, he said, he used to see a man of about thirty, tall and hefty, well dressed, standing at one of the street corners. There was no doubt that he was a Jew, said Schaller. He learned that the man ran a sewing workshop where some twenty to twenty-five women worked. He did not know then what his name was.

After the war, Schaller was living in Linz, and early in 1946 he saw the same man. He could name the exact spot: a corner on Bethlehem Street, where the Jewish community's office building stood. Schaller claimed to be blessed with a photographic memory and he could therefore say without any doubt that it was the same man. He struck up a conversation and indeed, the man confirmed that they had seen each other in Tarnów. When asked what he was doing in Linz, the man replied, "I deal in sewing machines." Years went by and sometime after Eichmann's capture, Schaller saw a photograph of Wiesenthal in a newspaper. And again, he had no doubt—he was the man from Tarnów. In other words, Wiesenthal must have worked with the SS.

The security services investigator who took Schaller's testimony also questioned Karl Heinz Weidnitzer, who had served in the German air force and whose duties had taken him to Tarnów in 1944. He said he was passing a house, looked into a window, and saw a sewing workshop with women working inside. In front of the house there was a man wearing clothes that stood out: striped pants and a dark jacket. The man greeted Weidnitzer and he greeted him back. A German officer who was with him asked him why he was greeting a Jew, and he replied that he didn't know the man was a Jew because he wasn't wearing a yellow patch. The German told him that the man was under the protection of the SS and he was therefore exempt from wearing the star. The officer told him that the Jew ran the workshop and also organized hunting trips for the SS personnel to enjoy, and he tried to persuade them that there was oil to be found in the district. The Jew also knew Eichmann, the German said.

After the war they had met again, in a Vienna street. Weidnitzer was in the company of an American agent, he claimed. The man from Tarnów greeted him with a nod, and the American agent told Weidnitzer that he was the head of the well-known Documentation Center, Simon Wiesenthal. Weidnitzer said he was amazed. Hadn't Wiesenthal been a concentration camp prisoner? he asked, and the American answered, "Yes, but only for a few weeks, to give him an alibi." The investigator who took down the testimony of these men for the chancellor's office also noted his own impressions: Schaller was reliable, but a Jew hater; Weidnitzer was a gasbag, and also an anti-Semite.[7]

The minister of the interior, Otto Rösch, an old enemy of Wiesenthal, suddenly remembered an anonymous letter he had received five years earlier, from Venezuela, and now he passed it on to his chancellor in the hope that it would help him. An attempt was made to find the sender, but without success, he reported. The writer said he had served in the German army. Shortly after Lvov was conquered, he had been summoned to the local headquarters, where he received an order to proceed to the jail and release a collaborator who had been arrested by mistake. He did so, and on the way back the collaborator told him that he had been working with the Germans for a long time, since he was a student.

When they arrived at the headquarters, the letter writer said, he saw that the man was indeed welcomed as an old friend. A few days later, he continued, he was instructed to prepare the papers needed by the collaborator and his wife to enable them to leave the city. In time, he recognized him from photographs in the press: it was Wiesenthal. If he had known then what he knew now he would have killed him, he wrote. The officer who had ordered him to get the collaborator out of jail, he said, was Theodor Oberländer, the commander of the Ukrainian Nachtigall (Nightingale) Battalion, which had taken part in the conquest of Lvov. In other words, Wiesenthal had worked for Oberländer.

2. The Nightingale's Version

Theodor Oberländer was a very well-known man. After the war, he had an impressive political career in Germany; in 1956 he was made minister for refugee affairs in the government of Chancellor Konrad Adenauer. His Nazi past came up sporadically in the press. The possibility that Oberländer and Wiesenthal had known each other in Lvov had accompanied both of them for many years before Kreisky decided to try to take advantage of it.

In October 1959, Wiesenthal wrote to the editor of the German weekly *Die Zeit* in response to an article titled "The Oberländer Affair" that had appeared in the magazine. He described how he had been arrested right after the German conquest of Lvov, how he had escaped execution, and also how Ukrainian thugs had slaughtered thousands of the city's Jews. The men of the Nachtigall Battalion had stood by passively, and there was no basis for Oberländer's claim that not a shot had been fired in the first days of the occupation, Wiesenthal wrote. In an apparent aside, he mentioned that he did not know Oberländer and that he had almost certainly never seen him during the war years.[8]

In 1960, Oberländer was convicted in absentia for the murder of thousands of Jews and sentenced to life imprisonment. The trial was conducted in East Germany and it was dismissed in West Germany as a Communist show trial without any judicial significance, but nevertheless, Oberländer was forced to resign from the government.[9]

In his book about his role in the capture of Eichmann, Wiesenthal wrote that the Nachtigall staff came prepared with lists of people they intended to murder, including several dozen professors and intellectuals. One former member of the unit sued the publishers for libel, and won. Wiesenthal was obliged to drop that sentence from the subsequent edition. Before additional documents were found, it would be impossible to prove it, he wrote. He himself had been beaten in jail by Ukrainians wearing German uniforms and he was sure they were Nachtigall personnel, but unfortunately this too could not be proved.[10]

In the decade that followed, the Oberländer affair cropped up occasionally in the German media and courts. Oberländer consistently claimed that he had never been involved in acts of murder. Wiesenthal took an interest mainly in the killing of the professors, who included some of his own teachers, he said. At a certain stage he reached the conclusion that it was not Oberländer who had been responsible. However, he never cleared Oberländer of his part in other crimes, and when he was asked if he would agree to meet with him, he took it as an insult.[11]

The person who tried to arrange the meeting was Rolf Vogel, a journalist who dealt with relations between Jews and Germans and with promoting links between Germany and Israel, and who also provided various services to the two countries. He also helped Wiesenthal and saw himself as a partner in his struggle against the Communist states, primarily East Germany.

One day Wiesenthal was surprised to receive a letter from Oberländer asking for assistance in clearing his name and proposing a date for a meeting, "although it falls on a Saturday."[12] Wiesenthal replied that he would probably not be in Vienna on that date, but in the meanwhile, if Oberländer wished, he could send him material, although as he was very busy he would not have time in the near future to go over it.[13] Oberländer did not give up; he wanted only to establish the truth, he wrote to Wiesenthal, and meanwhile he complimented him on *The Sunflower* and on his other books. He had been shocked to read about some things that he had not known of, he wrote.[14]

Vogel tried to convince Wiesenthal that Oberländer should be helped, as part of the struggle against East Germany, pleading: "Do me a personal favor, and make an appointment with Dr. Oberländer."[15] That letter is dated February 13, 1973. Wiesenthal replied that letters dated the thirteenth of the month brought him bad luck. He clearly had neither the desire nor the time to meet Oberländer. Nevertheless, he included in his letter a piece of additional information: the real culprit in the murder of the professors was living in Argentina.[16] In June 1975, he said the same thing in an investigative report broadcast on German television.[17]

A few days after the broadcast, a letter arrived at Kreisky's office from a man who identified himself as Max Waller and said that until a few years earlier he had worked as a political adviser to a West German cabinet minister, Josef Ertl. On the basis of his connections with organizations of former Nazi prisoners and underground members, Waller said he was convinced that the key to Wiesenthal's past lay in Oberländer's hands. "Oberländer was Wiesenthal's immediate boss," he asserted, and claimed he knew of a document that contained all the details of the case.[18] Wiesenthal's lawyer managed to obtain an unsigned copy of Waller's letter. The relations between the Jewish survivor from Lvov and the German who had conquered the city were now reversed: Wiesenthal needed Oberländer, and he asked him for an affirmation that they did not know each other.

The former minister replied in a very cautious and impolite letter. He confirmed that he had never employed Wiesenthal as an intelligence agent. He also said that he had never handled intelligence agents in Lvov. The letter did not rule out the possibility that the two had in fact collaborated in another sphere.

Oberländer had no reason to help Wiesenthal. He rebuked him for not coming to his assistance in the past. He could have spared him forty out of the forty-nine trials he had been obliged to undergo in order to clear his name, Oberländer wrote, and he pointed out that he had heard harsh criticism of Wiesenthal in "Jewish circles" for his long silence. Wiesenthal quickly sent a letter of apology: there had indeed been a period during which he had his doubts, as it had taken him years to prove that the man who was responsible for the murder of the professors was Walter Kutschmann.[19]

He had learned Kutschmann's name and his place of residence in Argentina about ten years before that, but he had not then connected him to the murder of the professors in Lvov. The Kutschmann case was one of his failures; all of his efforts to bring him to justice ended fruitlessly, partly because the West German prosecution never did what was necessary to have him extradited. Wiesenthal's explanation for this was that West Germany did not want to try someone for crimes that had already been tried in East Germany.[20]

Wiesenthal asked for Oberländer's help unwillingly, but he felt he had to do so in order to defend himself against Kreisky. The legal battle with the chancellor was now at the center of Wiesenthal's life and took up much of his time, but he tried to keep on working.

One day in May 1978, Wiesenthal picked up a copy of the *New York Daily News* while on a flight from New York to Amsterdam. A small news item from São Paulo, Brazil, caught his eye. It said that on April 20 a group of old-time Nazis had celebrated Hitler's birthday at a hotel in the city. "I tried to picture the festivities in my mind," Wiesenthal wrote some time later. It was in São Paulo that he had found Franz Stangl.

The British journalist Gitta Sereny, who interviewed Stangl, had heard from his widow that after he died in prison, one of his former assistants had come to her home and proposed marriage to her. The man, Gustav Wagner, had been Stangl's deputy at the Sobibor extermination camp. The item about the celebration in São Paulo put Wiesenthal on the alert. "I was convinced that Wagner was one of the participants in that bizarre party. Perhaps some paper had printed a picture of the occasion. That would help me to find him," he wrote in his memoirs.[21]

Documents in Wiesenthal's archive show that he had taken an interest in Wagner several years earlier. Like many other cases he handled, this one attracted his attention by chance. One day he received a letter from a woman by the name of Irene Freudenheim. Born to a Jewish family in

Germany, she spent her childhood in Uruguay and in the 1950s moved to Brazil. Her father was a journalist and broadcaster. She had read Wiesenthal's book *The Murderers Among Us* and she wrote to him to express her appreciation. Like many others who wrote to him, she mentioned that she knew of a man who seemed to her like a fugitive Nazi criminal posing as someone else, and she gave his name.

Wiesenthal never neglected letters like this one. He replied that the name she had given him did not appear in his files, but he asked her to look into some details about Wagner, whose birth date he was able to give her. He said he had heard of her father, the broadcaster Hermann P. Gephardt, but aside from what she had written about herself, and the fact that she imagined a man in São Paulo was a Nazi fugitive, Wiesenthal knew nothing at all about the woman. He had no grounds for assuming that she would want to do any sleuthing, but this was the sort of thing that he often did; he had nothing to lose.

And this time too, he was not wrong. Freudenheim took on the task, and in fact she had connections in the police force and managed to obtain Wagner's immigration papers for Wiesenthal, including a photograph. Wiesenthal asked her to employ a private investigation agency and promised to pay all expenses. She consulted her contact inside the police force, who told her there wasn't a private detective agency in São Paulo that could be trusted.

Wiesenthal asked her to establish contact with Stangl's widow, but this was a task that Freudenheim could not accomplish. She proposed asking for Wagner's address at the German consulate, and Wiesenthal advised caution: She must not by any means tell the consulate officials that Wagner was wanted for war crimes. At most, she should say that she needed him to testify in support of a claim for restitution. Freudenheim adopted the wariness of a secret agent and started writing to Wiesenthal via a third party in Europe, as she feared that someone in the post office might notice she was corresponding with him, and the entire endeavor would collapse.[22]

Irene Freudenheim was one of innumerable "agents" whose imaginations were ignited by Wiesenthal, all of them volunteers like her, curious and, to some extent, adventurers. In this case, as in many others, he also made use of a journalist, Mario Chimanovitch, of the *Jornal do Brasil*.

The two men had met during one of Wiesenthal's visits to Israel. He said that Chimanovitch had agreed to find out if his paper had a picture of the Hitler birthday party. It turned out that while it was in full swing, the police had turned up because they suspected it was a Communist event. When they saw it was only a gathering of Nazis, they calmed down and left. There were also press photographers there, and the merrymakers did not balk at the cameras. But it all happened in the vicinity of Rio de Janeiro, not São Paulo, and Gustav Wagner did not take part in the event at all. Wiesenthal was somewhat disappointed, but he acted in his usual way: he marked one of the people in the picture and claimed that he was Wagner. "Mario swallowed the bait," Wiesenthal wrote.

The journalist's version was different. Indeed, Wiesenthal had offered him a scoop, but Chimanovitch had told him that without a photograph there was no story, because nobody knew who Wagner was. Wiesenthal and he had marked the picture together, and he had agreed to run it together with a story, although he knew it was a fabrication.

Years later, Chimanovitch tried to work out why Wiesenthal had chosen to distort the story in his memoirs. Perhaps he had wanted to get all of whatever credit would be forthcoming, or perhaps he had wanted to protect Chimanovitch's professional reputation, or perhaps both. Either way, the story was published and had a big impact.[23] Wagner heard about the search for him on the radio and turned himself in to the police. He said he did so in order to avert being abducted by Israeli agents.

Now they had to decide what was to be done with him. Several countries, among them Israel, made inquiries about his extradition, but Wagner managed to dodge that fate thanks to some typographical error in West Germany's request that he be handed over for trial. The Brazilian Supreme Court turned down Germany's appeal.

"To the Jews this refusal, coming as it did simultaneously with Brazilian recognition of the PLO, did not create a friendly impression," Wiesenthal wrote. But Wagner, who had used his own name throughout the years in Brazil, could not take the stress. Some time after his identity had been revealed, his body was found on a remote farm. Wiesenthal published two versions of the circumstances surrounding his death. In one, he said Wagner had stabbed himself, and in the other that he had hanged himself. Chimanovitch believed that Wagner was murdered.[24]

3. The Assault

From time to time, Wiesenthal traveled to Düsseldorf in West Germany, where the longest and most expensive war crimes trial ever was being held.

Sixteen persons were charged in connection with their actions at the Majdanek concentration camp. It was a disgraceful spectacle. Some of the accused were released for health reasons, or were acquitted in the early stages of the trial. One passed away, and there were only nine left, including two women. One of them was Hermine Braunsteiner-Ryan, "the Mare," who had been extradited from the United States after Wiesenthal found her living in New York.

Except for her, all the accused were out on bail. Each morning they would show up at the court, greet one another, hang their coats and hats in the cloakroom, have a coffee, look at the papers, and then go into Courtroom III and take their seats until the recess, and then again after it, until the day's hearing was over. It took five years—over five hundred days of hearings.

The prosecution did the best it could. Some 350 witnesses were called, most of them survivors of Majdanek who came from Israel and the United States. Many of them came with tales of vicious atrocities. Braunsteiner had stood out for her cruelty to children. Occasionally she leveled outbursts of anger at the witnesses, but generally the testimony sank into a sleepy routine, before empty public benches. Sometimes groups of soldiers or schoolchildren were brought in to view the proceedings, but apart from its educational and political aspects, it was a wasted effort. The German media also gave the trial little attention.

In contrast, the defense attorneys were given extensive coverage. One of them was the same Ludwig Bock who had caused a stir when he demanded that an Israeli judge withdraw from an evidence-taking process because as a Jew he could not be relied on not to show bias against Nazi defendants. In Düsseldorf, defense attorneys were permitted to demand the arrest of one of the witnesses, a former inmate who testified that the camp guards had forced her to carry gas containers to the killing chambers; she should be prosecuted for abetting murder, the defense argued. In another instance, they insisted that an expert witness be called in order to establish there was a difference between the smell of charred human flesh and that of animals, to prove that at Majdanek it was humans who were being burned and not animal flesh that was being roasted.

The tens of thousands of pages of the trial records and the judgment that was finally handed down in 1981 gave historians one of the most important accounts of the extermination of Jews in the Holocaust, but the sentences showed once again the impotence of liberal justice in the face of crimes of this nature. Braunsteiner-Ryan was sentenced to life, and the others to terms ranging from three and a half to twelve years, except for one man who was acquitted. Wiesenthal called the sentences "the best sign of the devaluation of human life."[25] About half a year later, his own life was saved.

On the evening of Friday, June 11, 1982, Wiesenthal came home from his office and packed a suitcase for a trip to Israel. He went to bed at about 10:30 p.m. and read a few pages of a book about the surrender of the Nazi army, *Operation Sunrise: The Secret Surrender* by Bradley Smith and Elena Agarossi. His wife was already asleep. "Suddenly I heard a huge blast," he told reporters later. All the windows in the house, as well as in the neighboring houses, were shattered, doors were ripped off their hinges, and the house was filled with smoke from the explosion. But he and his wife were not hurt.

He hurried downstairs and saw the heavy damage. He pressed the alarm button and the police and fire brigade were there within five minutes. Someone had placed on the doorstep a primitive but dangerous improvised bomb, built into a cooking pot and detonated by an attached clock. Photographers were quick to arrive on the scene and Wiesenthal and his wife, in their pajamas and dressing gowns, tried to look calm. The attempt on his life made news all over the world, and he was flooded with messages congratulating him on his escape.

The assumption was that the perpetrators belonged to a neo-Nazi group. A few months earlier, a pipe bomb had gone off at the entrance to the home of Vienna's chief rabbi, Akiva Eisenberg. Several years before, a court in Germany had convicted two neo-Nazi activists of conspiring to kidnap Wiesenthal.[26]

The latest attack made it necessary to take security precautions. Policemen were stationed outside his house around the clock, and in time a special hut was built for them, like those outside the homes of ambassadors and other VIPs. A steel door was installed at his office, along with an intercom and a closed-circuit camera, very advanced for the era. A policeman was always on duty in the stairwell. The guard was changed every few hours, but they all must have sat in the same place and leaned the chair and their heads against the wall. The chair chipped a mark in the wall, and their heads left a dark stain. Years later these signs could still be seen, an urban archaeological find.

Nine neo-Nazi activists were arrested and charged with committing a number of attacks against Jewish targets, including Wiesenthal's home.

When Wiesenthal came to court to testify, the primary suspect lunged at him, but the security guards overpowered him before he could cause any harm. The man, Eckerhard Weil, was sentenced to five years in prison and his accomplices received shorter terms. Wiesenthal tended to believe that the attacks were the result of the atmosphere created by Kreisky's attacks against him.[27]

Although he had dropped his first libel suits against Kreisky and the chancellor had retracted his allegation, the dispute between the two men had not been resolved and it continued to occupy Wiesenthal incessantly. Kreisky was offended by something that Peter Michael Lingens wrote about him in *Profil* and sued him. Among the issues in the trial were the motives behind Wiesenthal's work. Kreisky argued that he understood Wiesenthal's "psychological need" for revenge, but ascribed to him a "biblical hatred" for Nazi criminals. This phrase was taken directly from an anti-Semitic publication filed in Kreisky's archive, among other documents set aside for his perusal.[28]

Lingens lost in the initial stages, but did not concede and appealed over and over again until the case reached the European Court of Human Rights, where he was cleared.[29] Friedrich Peter of the Liberal Party also filed a number of lawsuits, including one against a man who spread a joke about him: "If Kreisky had run into Peter in 1942, he wouldn't have been involved in a dispute with Wiesenthal today."[30]

In April 1986, Kreisky told a reporter for *Profil* that if he decided to do so at the time, he could have proved his accusations against Wiesenthal in court. By now he was a private citizen and there was nothing to stop Wiesenthal from suing him for libel, which he did. Kreisky was spending much of his time on the island of Majorca and he saw the whole thing as a nuisance, trying again and again to put off the hearings. "He played the poor persecuted old man who wants nothing more than to be left alone," reported Wiesenthal's lawyer. During one of the hearings he suddenly burst out and claimed it wasn't true that his brother had gone to Frankfurt after a woman.[31] The white beard that Kreisky had grown in the interim made him look more Jewish than ever before in his lifetime.

But this time Wiesenthal was determined. He refused to reach a compromise, and Kreisky's attorneys did their best to prove that Wiesenthal had in fact collaborated with the Nazis. They demanded that Theodor Oberländer be called to testify, but on the strength of the letter he had written to Wiesenthal the court ruled that he had nothing to contribute to the case. The defense attorneys also made use of Wiesenthal's own book to argue that his work in the rail yards at Lvov constituted cooperation with the Nazis, and once again the names of his German benefactors Kohlrautz and Günthert came up.[32]

Many people tried to help Wiesenthal. A woman from Fair Lawn, New Jersey, who remembered him from the Lvov ghetto sent a sworn statement to the effect that she had never seen or heard any hint that Wiesenthal enjoyed a privileged position in the ghetto, and he never had more food than anyone else.[33] From the legal point of view, Wiesenthal did not have to prove anything; the burden of proof was on Kreisky's lawyers.

For over fifteen years, Wiesenthal had been wrangling in this vein with Kreisky, and he was now seventy-eight years old. "Kreisky and I have places in history," he said, "and I do not envy him the place that he has taken."[34] He enjoyed the international limelight, the tumultuous attention of media people who never stopped coming or phoning made him feel good, and he lacked a sufficient degree of perspective to tell himself that the whole business was superfluous and pathetic, sometimes even infantile. In the end, it was just a fight between two Jews divided by a common aspiration: to be part of Austrian society.

Wiesenthal paid a high price. Since his liberation from Mauthausen he had never undergone harder times, he wrote at the height of the dispute.[35] Israel's neutral stance hurt him, and when he read that former and future prime minister Yitzhak Rabin had met with Kreisky, he felt betrayed. Throughout the years, he feared that Kreisky would stop the transit of Jews from the Soviet Union via Austria. The Jewish community expressed anxiety that Kreisky would organize a wave of anti-Semitic measures. All this gave him a feeling of grave responsibility. It harmed his health, and more than anything else it harmed his wife.

For years she had been asking him to desist. Perhaps it was not too late to move to Israel, or to be near their daughter and her family, she begged repeatedly. But she never summoned up the courage to leave him. She was often overcome by fits of depression.[36]

———

In 1982, Wiesenthal published a novel called *Max and Helen: A Tragic and True Love Story*. It was written in the first person, and Wiesenthal included himself in it as a character, under his own name, as well as many plot details taken from his actual experiences, including his imprisonment in Lvov, his connection with the Briha organization and the Joint, and, of course, his pursuit of Nazi criminals. Since it involves so many autobiographical elements, it is possible that the protagonists, Max and Helen, are based on Simon and Cyla.

The plot centers on an investigation Wiesenthal is conducting into something he was told by someone he met on a train. A Polish Jew by the name of Max had been arrested, together with his sweetheart, Helen, and her paralyzed sister. The three were sent to a concentration camp. Max and Helen wanted to run away, but she was not ready to abandon her sister. Max escaped on his own and joined a band of partisans. The commandant of the camp, Schultz, took revenge on Helen by raping her. She became pregnant and Schultz sent her to Kraków, where she gave birth to a son, Mark.

After the war, Max reaches Paris. Only in 1960 does he hear that Helen is alive and married and living in the city of Kassel in Germany. He finds out her address and goes to visit her. The door is opened by a boy whom Max immediately recognizes as strikingly similar to Schultz. Helen is standing behind him. She tells Max what happened, and asks for his mercy. Her son, Mark, doesn't know who his father was. He has grown up as a Jew and he thinks that his father perished in the Holocaust. Max cannot overcome the feeling that Mark is Schultz, and he goes back to Paris.

In the meanwhile, Max finds Schultz. Helen asks Max to leave him alone so as not to wreck Mark's life. Max weighs her request and decides, for the only time in his life, to close his case against a prosecutable war criminal. In 1967, Schultz is killed in a road accident. Mark is studying medicine in Munich and marries a Jewish girl from Canada, and the two go to live there. Helen writes to Max in Paris: now she is alone.[37]

Wiesenthal used to tell his life story down to the last detail, but he never told anyone what happened to his wife after he was separated from her in the war. Indeed, it may be that the drama he added to his actual adventures was meant to camouflage this chapter in their lives. He did not abandon her in the camp, like Max abandoned Helen; on the contrary—with the help of his German foreman he arranged papers for her that enabled her to escape and live as a Christian.

But when they were separated, he must have agonized over what was happening to her among the gentiles as the war raged. The striking similarities between their story and the "true love story" he wrote about Max and Helen may well reflect the anxieties and fantasies that tormented him. Toward the end of the war he had believed that she was dead. His pursuit of Nazis had made her life miserable; for both of them, it was almost like self-punishment.

"Cyla is suffering terribly," he wrote to Viktor Matejka; she had undergone nervous breakdowns, one after the other. Her doctor said she would not be able to cope with another struggle. "It's not easy to be my wife," Wiesenthal remarked. As it grew dark, their home was lit up by spotlights, he carried a gun, and every night he put it under his pillow, he related.[38] It was in times like these that he could find consolation in the love of Eva Dukes, the second woman in his life.

4. The Love of Eva Dukes

This was no romantic springtime love affair, but a mature friendship between a man and a woman who almost from the first moment they met related to each other as if they had been together for years. The letters they wrote to each other convey the sense of a stable routine. When they met for the first time, early in the 1970s, she was almost fifty years old, in her second marriage, and he was sixty-five.

A plump woman with a pug nose, Dukes was born to Jewish parents in Vienna. The family had moved to the United States when she was fourteen. She studied at Hunter College and Columbia University and worked as an editor, translator, and occasional journalist. She read a great many books and gobbled up newspapers. Bouncy and garrulous, she was part of a social circle of Jewish professionals and she took an interest in the sorts of things that also interested the *New York Times* and *The New Yorker*. Her admiration for Wiesenthal knew no bounds, and he needed her.

In October 1973, during the Yom Kippur War, Dukes wrote to Wiesenthal expressing her anxiety over the fate of Israel. She could not free herself from thoughts about the casualties, and she yearned for peace, she wrote in German. Apparently they did not yet know each other. She addressed him respectfully as "Dear Dr. Wiesenthal" and of course she used the nonfamiliar form of the second person, *Sie*, rather than the familiar *du*. She signed her full name.

Less than a year later, "Dr. Wiesenthal" had become "Simon," *Sie* had become *du*, and at the bottom appeared an ornate "Eva." Thus it is possible to calculate when the two became friendly. It probably occurred in New York. From then on they would meet each time he was in town, once every few months. It is difficult to ascertain exactly how this relationship flared up into what it became, but it is preserved in the long, typewritten letters that she sent him. They contain no poetic expressions of love, but there is no mistaking the intimacy that prevailed between them, with Dukes sharing her daily routine with him as if Wiesenthal were her life partner.

She translated *Krystina*, a novel he wrote with the Warsaw Ghetto uprising as the background, and she also went over the English version of *The Sunflower*. She wrote to him about the books she read and films she saw and sent him clippings of articles that interested her. When he told her about a threat to his life, she was frantic: "My whole body is trembling— I wish I could cry to calm myself down—I beg you, be careful—don't walk through the park—how do you get to the office? I am so shocked, at last I have managed to cry out of fear. Even in the car you should not go the same way all the time and when you get out someone should be waiting for you, even if it costs a lot of money. Do you have enough money. Should I begin collecting?"[39]

She wrote at least once a week, and sometimes twice on the same day. Most of the letters were three to five pages long. She discussed current affairs with him—the Vietnam War, gay rights, human rights violations in Africa, nuclear weapons—and she told him she feared the world was becoming like Sodom and Gomorrah and nearing its end. On the news from Israel she wrote: "I believe that we must not give up certain territories," meaning Jerusalem and the Golan Heights.

She told him about her cats and her plants, about a tumor "in a not nice place" on her body, and about her money problems. She wrote about her friends as if they were also his friends: So-and-so did this and so-and-so said that. Someone had called and someone else had dropped in for a visit. "Kay and Bert brought me to the subway in Queens and the connection was fantastic, at 6:50 I was at Lexington and 86th." Sometimes she was girlishly coquettish, sometimes motherly.

Before his trips to New York she warned him to bring warm clothing— a sweater, gloves, and a scarf—and she arranged in advance with his hotel for someone to help him take his bags to his room. In 1975, she told him she was getting divorced from her second husband too. He had already found an apartment; she was having trouble finding one for herself.[40]

Wiesenthal knew about the crisis from earlier letters and he replied cautiously. "You must understand that it is hard for me to give you advice, because I am not objective in this matter."[41] From time to time she traveled to Europe, but not to Vienna. Wiesenthal apparently met her in Amsterdam. In photographs of the two, she looks at him happily and he responds with a relaxed smile. It is clear that they felt good with each other.[42]

His letters were shorter than hers. He showed an interest in the details of her life but never came out of his shell, and it seems that what he needed most was her admiration and her support. Once when he returned from a vacation and there was no letter waiting from her, he wrote: "Please write and tell me how you are. I had to travel again immediately after I returned to Germany to testify in the trial of an anti-Semite and they organized an anti-Semitic demonstration for me there that I can hardly describe for you. Please write to me straight away!!!"[43] That was during the Kreisky affair. She tried unsuccessfully to get the conductor Leonard Bernstein to support him.[44]

Her love never died, but it seems that Wiesenthal did not know how to nurture it, just as he did not preserve other relationships, and the affair somehow faded away.

Meanwhile, the hearings in his case against Kreisky continued. Wiesenthal didn't go to court. One day, while he was sitting in his doctor's waiting room, the door opened and out came the physician, Kurt Polzer, with his previous patient, none other than Bruno Kreisky. The two men faced each other in silence for a moment. Then Wiesenthal turned to Polzer and asked, "How is he?" Kreisky could hardly conceal his smile, and left.[45]

Judge Bruno Weiss tore Kreisky's evidence to shreds. The witness who had claimed that he knew of Wiesenthal's collaboration with Oberländer was no longer among the living, and one of the two men who said they saw Wiesenthal in Tarnów had also died. Karl Heinz Weidnitzer, who the chancellor's office had said in an internal memo was motivated by anti-Semitism, had been called to testify, but the judge ruled that his evidence was worthless; for one thing, he had been stricken by amnesia years before he appeared in court.[46] Kreisky was therefore found guilty of libel and ordered to pay Wiesenthal financial compensation. But nine months later, in July 1990, he died, and his heirs refused to pay.

This trial, although it was initiated by Wiesenthal, represented the most exhaustive effort to prove that he had collaborated with the Nazis. Kreisky had harnessed for this purpose the entire governmental machinery of Austria; his attorney, Günther Blecha, was the brother of the interior minister. He received material gathered by the secret services of several other countries but never managed to prove anything.

The archives of East Germany and Poland were eventually opened for research; they contain no material that proves Wiesenthal collaborated with the Nazis. His photograph was printed frequently in newspapers and he often appeared on television, but despite all this publicity not one concentration camp survivor recognized him as a kapo, and not one veteran of the Nazi machine ever pointed a finger at him as a collaborator.

18

"The Children . . . Were Actually the Same Children"

I. In the Footsteps of Columbus

Between the first and second rounds of his feud with Kreisky, Wiesenthal published a book asserting that Christopher Columbus was a Jew. Just as he was not a novelist, Wiesenthal was also no historian; nonetheless, apart from his stamp collecting there was nothing he loved more than historical riddles. He always tended to seek in history what he imagined was lying at the bottom of those lakes in the Alps—inexhaustible treasures of legendary mystery and heady magic.

The book's theme, which others had examined before him, had occupied his imagination since the days in the 1950s when he had worked with the Americans. He owed his life to the United States and he felt a deep need to repay the debt. How beautiful and symbolic it would be if it transpired that America owed its very discovery by the Old World to a Jew.

In the ensuing two decades Wiesenthal read every book on the discovery of America that he could lay his hands on. He compiled lists of dates and names and all kinds of scraps of information and, when he could afford to do so, he traveled to visit ancient monastery libraries in Spain and Italy. He immersed himself in the mystery of the curlicue that Columbus inscribed in the top left-hand corner of his letters to his son. With a little graphic imagination it is possible to perceive it as the Hebrew letters *bet* and *heh*, which observant Jews are accustomed to putting at the top of everything they write, and that form an acronym for the words *b'ezrat hashem*, or "with God's help."

Columbus's life story is shrouded in mystery. When Wiesenthal began to take an interest in him, scholars were still arguing about basic biographical details such as when and where he was born and what his exact family name was. Perhaps he did come from a Jewish family. There are documents showing that wealthy Jews helped to finance his voyages. Wiesenthal speculated that they were looking for a new land. Columbus set sail on August 3, 1492, one day after the decree ordering the expulsion of the Jews from Spain took effect. Wiesenthal presumed that this was not by coincidence.

One of the men who set out with Columbus was Luis de Torres, who had previously been known as Yosef Ben Halevi Haivri, or "Joseph, the son of Levy the Hebrew." He was Columbus's interpreter. Wiesenthal assumed that a Hebrew speaker was taken along because Columbus thought that he might discover lands populated by Jews, perhaps the descendants of the Ten Lost Tribes. Wiesenthal's research gave him a respite from the storms of his life and calmed him down. He took it seriously and in 1972 he published the results in a book.[1]

Sails of Hope was written in a dry style, and although it came out in several languages, it was a resounding failure. "The Israelis certainly won't publish the book," he wrote to a friend, a former Mossad operative, and indeed it took twenty years before it appeared in a Hebrew version.[2] The important German daily *Die Zeit* ran a devastating review of the book, and a little while later Wiesenthal was subjected to the ultimate humiliation for a writer: one of the publishers demanded that he return the advance he had received because most of the copies were still in the storeroom.[3]

In Austria, there was at least one other Jew who didn't rule out the possibility that Columbus was Jewish—surprisingly, it was Bruno Kreisky. He did not mention Wiesenthal's book but, like him, thought that Jews had supported distant voyages in order to find a country for themselves.[4]

Wiesenthal did not let the subject go and fifteen years later he came up with an idea that combined the expulsion of the Jews of Spain in 1492 and the expulsion of the Jews of Europe in 1942. He wrote a novel, *Flight from Destiny*, in which he gave the inversion of the numbers in the two dates a mystical significance.[5] It is the story of the Torres family: the father, Camillio, his daughter, Ruth, and his son, Felix. Torres is a historian by profession and a resident of Vienna. In 1940, the Nazis expel him and his daughter to Poland.

They manage to escape, but the Soviets return them to the Germans.

They run away again, this time to western Ukraine, but within a short time the Nazis reach there, too. Meanwhile Felix has joined them, and the three escape once more, to Romania, where they are saved by rescuers from Palestine, but on the way there their ship hits a mine. A German boat picks up some of the refugees, among them Ruth and Felix. Camillio dies, but Ruth manages to save a diary in which he has written down the family history. It begins in Spain, and it transpires that Camillio Torres is a descendant of Columbus's interpreter. *Flight from Destiny* didn't sell very well either, but it became linked to a historical and political dispute of which Wiesenthal made himself the center.[6]

Conventional wisdom had it that the Inquisition had left it up to the Jews whether to die or to become Christians and live, whereas the Nazis' race theories obliged them to kill the Jews without leaving them any option. Wiesenthal set out to prove that the Nazi theory had its roots in the hatred of Jews fostered by the Catholics in Spain. Without it, Nazism would not have evolved, he argued.[7] He pointed to a series of anti-Jewish decrees issued in the fifteenth century from which it emerges that Spain's Jews were already considered members of an inferior race at that time. He even found what he believed was the source of the Nuremberg laws—which barred sexual relations between Aryans and Jews—in Spain.[8]

In identifying the origins of the Holocaust in Catholic anti-Semitism, Wiesenthal was supporting the Zionist view that the Nazis' destruction of the Jews was a link in a long chain of persecution. Gideon Hausner, the prosecutor in the Eichmann trial, began his opening speech with the pharaohs of Egypt and the pogroms of Eastern Europe. Anti-Semitism, he explained, was rooted partly in the fact that the Jews had been exiled from their land and had lived as a minority among other peoples.[9] With these remarks, Hausner was expressing the Zionist concept of the Jewish people's common destiny.

In 1986, Wiesenthal published *Every Day Remembrance Day: A Chronicle of Jewish Martyrdom*, a kind of calendar in book form that included some four thousand manifestations of anti-Semitism, including pogroms and other acts of persecution and discrimination perpetrated over two thousand years in almost every place on the face of the globe.[10] But in contrast to the historical approach of the Jewish establishment, Wiesenthal tended to equate the destruction of the Jews with other genocidal episodes.

His interest in Columbus made him curious about the extermination of the Native Americans. "Already a few decades after the discovery of America by Columbus, the population of the entire Caribbean Sea region had been destroyed," he wrote in the introduction to *Sails of Hope*. The discoverers of the New World brought with them the Old World's cruelty and the delight it took in killing.

Native Americans were tortured and slaughtered in every possible manner, and their culture was destroyed. In North America, the survivors were herded onto reservations, where they were condemned to live in ignorance, idleness, and drunkenness. In Brazil, he wrote, they sought refuge in the rain forests, but those forests were being destroyed and whenever geologists discovered natural resources in regions populated by Indians, they were doomed to extinction.[11] Wiesenthal saw this as genocide.

In 1982, he was awarded an honorary doctorate by the City University of New York's John Jay College of Criminal Justice and he suggested they found an institute there for the study of genocide. The first topic he suggested the institute address was the tragedy of the Miskito Indians of Nicaragua. At that time the Sandinistas were in control of the country, and Wiesenthal's initiative on behalf of the Indians dovetailed well with his struggle against world Communism. This obviously anti-Communist intention was apparently why he failed to enlist the support of Willy Brandt, the former West German chancellor, an advocate of détente.[12]

In 1986, however, Wiesenthal heard that Israel was selling arms to Latin American countries, which were using them to exterminate their Indian populations. This was a subject very close to his heart, Wiesenthal wrote to the Israeli ambassador in Vienna, asking for clarification. Similarly, he thought that Israel should acknowledge the Armenian genocide, despite its strategic interest in maintaining good relations with Turkey.[13]

Over the years, Wiesenthal increasingly protested against violations of human rights in places across the globe, from Kurdistan to the Plaza de Mayo in Buenos Aires. He formulated a convention for the protection of political prisoners, joined the campaign against antipersonnel mines, and supported the struggles of a number of prominent figures like the Russian scientist and Soviet dissident Andrei Sakharov and the Dalai Lama, the exiled Tibetan spiritual leader.[14] When Yugoslavia broke up, Wiesenthal stood up for the rights of the Muslims in Bosnia.

The situation in the Balkans was highly complicated. Like many other people, Wiesenthal couldn't immediately decide who was right and who was wrong. As the fiftieth anniversary of the Nuremberg Trials approached, he wrote to U.S. president Bill Clinton demanding that the leader of the Bosnian Serbs, Radovan Karadžić, be put on trial before an international tribunal. "The ethnic cleansing, the murder of civilians regardless of age, the rape of Muslim women, while they do not constitute a Holocaust repeat many of its horrible details," Wiesenthal asserted.[15]

This demand was repeated in a letter to the *New York Times*, which he signed along with others, demanding that Karadžić be prevented from running for public office. "To allow perpetrators of genocide to decide who runs is like having post-1945 German elections with Heinrich Himmler picking the slate," they wrote. Clinton replied to Wiesenthal in a long letter. In the meanwhile, the Serbs had carried out a massacre in Srebrenica, and an indictment was filed against Karadžić. Clinton expressed support for trying him in an international court.[16]

Wiesenthal's involvement in the protests over the Balkan wars stemmed from the terrible sense of helplessness he felt when he learned how the world had remained silent in the face of the extermination of the Jews. It reflected a broad humanistic outlook that also characterized his attitude to the Holocaust, and was in contrast to that of some of the shapers of Jewish memory: unlike them, he would often address the crimes committed by the Nazis against non-Jews.

2. The Others

In the spring of 1964, Wiesenthal was invited to give a lecture in Turin, Italy. When he had finished speaking, an elderly, silver-haired woman wearing mourning clothes came up to him. "I was impressed by her somber, almost stony expression," he recalled later. The woman asked him if he restricted himself to crimes against Jews. Wiesenthal assured her that in his Documentation Center there were many files dealing with crimes committed against others, but in general it was Jews whom the Nazis had murdered.

The woman asked him to give her an hour of his time and the next day she came to his hotel. "Again, I was impressed by her dignified manner and by her profound grief," he wrote. She told him that she had been in mourning since the fall of 1943, when she learned that the Germans had "executed" her son. "Since that day, I have never laughed and until the day

I die I shall not laugh," she said. Of course she knew that the dead could not be brought back to life, and as a pious Christian she had reconciled herself with God's will. But it angered her that no one ever mentioned the thousands of Italian soldiers whom the Nazis had massacred at Kefallinía. Wiesenthal didn't know what she meant, and she was upset. "Even you haven't heard about it?" she exclaimed.

Kefallinía is the largest of the Ionian islands, off the western coast of Greece. A local tradition, which benefits the tourist trade there, has it that it is the birthplace of Homer's hero Odysseus. France and Britain ruled the islands before they became part of Greece. In World War II they were occupied by Italian and German forces. When Italy capitulated to the Allies in 1943, fighting broke out between the two forces on Kefallinía and after the Germans won, they shot some six thousand Italian troops. In Italy, the massacre was well documented. Books were published about it and a Rome court passed judgment, in absentia, on over thirty German officers for their part in it. The story of the silver-haired woman touched Wiesenthal and he began urging the Italians to gather evidence and trying to get the German prosecution authorities interested in the case.[17]

His interest in the link between the Nazi "mercy killings" and the extermination of the Jews also led Wiesenthal to probe the Nazi destruction of Gypsies, Jehovah's Witnesses, and homosexuals.

During his incarceration in the concentration camps, Wiesenthal had frequently come across Gypsies. "I was aware of their plight, but naturally the fate of my own people was closer to my heart," he wrote. But the more he tended to see what happened to the Jews within the context of other genocidal cases, the more closely he felt drawn to the tragedy of the Gypsies.

Nobody knows for sure how many Gypsies the Nazis murdered. Wiesenthal used to speak of half a million; Yad Vashem historian Yehuda Bauer estimated the number at between 90,000 and 150,000. Either way, in comparison with the Jewish Holocaust, the extermination of the Gypsies did not make inroads into the collective memory of the West, and it was almost forgotten. In the first years after the war, almost no concerted effort was made to document the crimes committed against them.

The Gypsies confronted the Nazis with an ideological dilemma because they were of Aryan origin. The Third Reich's policy toward them thus reflected doubts and contradictions.[18] Wiesenthal was most intrigued by the common racist elements in Nazi attitudes toward Jews and Gypsies, including the strictures of the Nuremberg laws that forbade Germans to have sexual relations with both Jews and Gypsies.

In this context he quoted a documented order, issued by Eichmann, to add one car carrying Gypsies to each train taking Jews to Auschwitz. Much of what he knew about the lives of inmates at Auschwitz he had heard from his friend Ella Lingens, and it was she who also told him how the Gypsies were marched, in one large bloc after the other, to the gas chambers, just like the Jews.[19]

At the beginning of 1966, he had handed material on the extermination of the Gypsies to the West German prosecution authorities, but in a judicial survey he initiated in the early 1980s, he found that only twelve people had been found guilty of offenses that included crimes against Gypsies. Two were given life sentences and the remaining ten received terms averaging eight years. Many investigations were discontinued, including a probe into the fate of several dozen Gypsy children who were taken from the St. Joseph Home in Mulfingen, near Stuttgart, and sent to Auschwitz. The central agency for Nazi crimes explained to Wiesenthal why the probe was halted: "It was not possible to clarify under exactly what circumstances the deaths of these children occurred." Wiesenthal could only protest.[20]

After the war, the remnants of the Gypsy people, or the Sinti and Roma as they called themselves, were still subjected to discrimination, oppression, and persecution in Germany and occasionally their central organization asked Wiesenthal for help. Newspapers in Germany and Austria were still publishing anti-Gypsy material, and Wiesenthal wrote to the Austrian cardinal, Franz König, about it.

Time and again, moreover, Wiesenthal found it necessary to protest to German mayors—in Darmstadt, Karlsruhe, Hamburg, and other cities—on the destruction of Gypsy shantytowns. The pretext was that they represented a health hazard, but the real intention was to drive the Gypsies away. When he heard that Gypsies were being persecuted in Holland, Wiesenthal cabled Queen Beatrix.[21]

But his main contribution to the cause of the Gypsies involved remembrance of the victims and recognition of their historical heritage. Apart from efforts by the Gypsies themselves, there was no one who did more than Wiesenthal to preserve their heritage. "The Gypsies are not a properly organized people," he wrote. "Many of them are illiterate. They did not have a Documentation Center." He proposed to a German television network that it produce a film on the extermination of the Gypsies and initiated construction of a monument to the murdered Gypsies at Maut-hausen, and when the erection of the central memorial for the Jewish victims of the Holocaust in Berlin was getting under way, he wrote to the mayor of that city demanding that a central monument to the Gypsies also be built.[22]

In Israel, a woman by the name of Miriam Novitch wrote a book about the extermination of the Gypsies. She was a member of Lohamei Hagetaot, a kibbutz named for the ghetto fighters, some of whom settled there, and the site of a Holocaust museum and research institute. Wiesenthal praised her, but her work made little impact. Israeli Holocaust historian Yehuda Bauer, writing about the Gypsies, observed: "What we have here is a geno-cide, not a Holocaust."[23] Wiesenthal deplored this attitude, and commented: "Regrettably, we the Jews, and even the Holocaust survivors among us, have not displayed the degree of understanding and sensitivity toward the Gyp-sies that they deserve as our brethren in suffering."

Meanwhile, no one found a way to compensate the Gypsies. The usual claim was that they didn't have any property. Wiesenthal rejected this argu-ment: "The Gypsy's wagon that was taken from him was of equal value to him as a Jew's store, and like the store, it was the basis for his livelihood. But the Gypsies remained, now as they were then, second-class human beings." He felt that he shared their destiny: "Auschwitz has been engraved in their history and it has in ours, with a searing flame," he wrote. "From this point of view, I feel tied by emotional bonds to each Gypsy who survived Auschwitz."[24]

In January 1976, Wiesenthal wrote to the president of Malawi, Hastings Kamuzu Banda, that while a prisoner in the concentration camps, he had sometimes encountered members of the Jehovah's Witnesses sect, who were also persecuted and murdered by the Nazis, and he had now heard that they were being maltreated in Malawi. Amnesty International had confirmed the information. He did not know much about Malawi, he wrote to Banda, and it was possible that the material in his possession was not correct, but he nevertheless was requesting that any discrimination be halted. Wiesen-thal estimated that some twelve hundred members of the sect had been murdered in the camps, and though he didn't quite equate their plight with that of the Jews, as the years went by interest in their fate increased and he was frequently questioned about them, and he included their story in the legacy of Nazi persecution.[25]

About a year and a half before his death, Wiesenthal signed a letter supporting a demand that homosexuals persecuted by the Nazis receive some of the money from ownerless deposits in Swiss banks. The distribution of the money among the Nazis' victims was supposed to bring an end to the scandalous concealment and plundering of Holocaust victims' accounts by those banks.

The letter was part of a campaign launched by a group named the Vienna Homosexual Initiative (HOSI), part of the Pink Triangle Coalition. In his letter, Wiesenthal stated that gay men and women who were persecuted by the Nazis because of their sexual orientation were not likely to identify themselves and there was therefore a danger that they would not get what they deserved, perpetuating the discrimination.[26]

Austrian and German government officials learned over the years that it was not worth their while to ignore Wiesenthal's letters, and as his fame spread across the globe, they sometimes tended to relate to him with awe. But when he was handling non-Jewish affairs, they often treated him with condescension, as if to say, "It's none of your business."

Once Wiesenthal wrote to Franz Joseph Strauss, the prime minister of Bavaria, about a matter concerning some Gypsies. Strauss rebuffed him in a scolding tone: "It's about time everyone stopped brandishing the past as a weapon against democratic governments," he wrote back. It later turned out that the state of Bavaria was still registering the Gypsies in the way that had been the custom in Nazi days. Wiesenthal and a group of movie stars and intellectuals published a protest ad in the *New York Times*.[27]

But the strongest resistance that his broad, humanistic approach to the Holocaust elicited came mainly from Jews: the denial of the "uniqueness" of the Holocaust was considered a sin almost as grave as denial of the Holocaust itself. It was a matter of unparalleled sensitivity and it placed Wiesenthal in a severe confrontation with the official shapers of Jewish Holocaust remembrance, headed by Elie Wiesel. Along with the fear that Wiesenthal's approach would lead to a diminishing of Holocaust remembrance, there was also a great deal of ego and no small amount of politics involved.

3. The Rival

In November 1973, a cantata called *Ani Maamin*—"I believe," in Hebrew—with words by Elie Wiesel and music by Darius Milhaud was premiered at Carnegie Hall in New York. After the performance, Wiesel wrote in his memoirs, he was standing surrounded by friends when a "broad shouldered man with a mustache and darting eyes in a massive face" came up to him. "Simon Wiesenthal," he introduced himself. "I shake his hand warmly," Wiesel wrote. "We embrace. I know him by name and admire his work. After all he was in the death camps. He was also the first Nazi hunter of the post war period. I hold him in great esteem."

In subsequent years, Wiesenthal would visit Wiesel in his New York apartment. They spoke about world affairs and Wiesenthal told Wiesel about his continuing efforts to pursue Nazi criminals. One day they began to talk about who should be commemorated. "He preaches the universality of suffering," Wiesel wrote, and observed that Wiesenthal had tried to persuade him that it was not just six million Jews but eleven million human beings who had perished in the death camps, including Poles, Ukrainians, Russians, and Germans, and not one of them must be forgotten. Because Jewish blood had mixed with gentile blood at Auschwitz, all the victims must be united in a single memory, Wiesel quoted Wiesenthal as saying.

Wiesel was incensed. He said that there was no historian who cited the number eleven million and Wiesenthal lost his temper. "You think only of Jews," he exclaimed. "For you, they were all saints. I can prove to you that among them there were the worst kind of scoundrels, worse than the non-Jews."

Wiesel was "stunned and saddened" by the outburst. A red-faced Wiesenthal apologized. He had not expressed himself properly. He did not mean it. He wanted to say something else, Wiesenthal said, according to Wiesel's account. This was not a slip of the tongue, however, but a feeling that over the years had crystallized into a firm opinion: Wiesenthal believed in the brotherhood of all the victims.[28]

In the summer of 1975, Wiesenthal received a letter from the well-known American writer Meyer Levin. As a young reporter, Levin had met Anne Frank's father and had helped him publish her diary in the United States. They had also agreed that Levin would adapt the diary into a play and he did so, but Frank didn't like the result. It was largely an ideological disagreement. Frank had fostered the notion of his daughter's diary as a universal, humanistic, optimistic myth, with an ending that was full of hopefulness and faith in human benevolence. Levin wrote a play that was Jewish, Zionist, very anti-German, and pessimistic. His version was not produced. The eventual Broadway production expressed Otto Frank's approach, and so did the film that followed it.

Levin immersed himself in a legal, public ideological and political campaign, refusing to let go for years. At the center of his struggle, which was documented in several books, was the argument over the nature of the Holocaust, its significance, and the right way to present it. The Broadway version ends with Anne's optimistic words: "I somehow feel that everything will change for the better, that this cruelty too will end, that peace and tranquility will return once more." In the Israeli production, they added the words, "I don't know, my girl, I don't know."[29]

Levin's letters to Wiesenthal reveal that he had reached a rather obsessive stage in his struggle. First he asked for Wiesenthal's opinion on Otto Frank's second wife. Levin had heard that she was not Jewish, but Frank said that she had been a prisoner in a concentration camp. Perhaps she had been arrested for being a Communist? Levin also wondered if the people who had hidden the Frank family were linked to the Communists and if so, was this the reason for the interpretation Otto Frank had chosen to give the diary?

Wiesenthal understood exactly what the issue was. He had never given up his fight against those who denied the authenticity of Anne Frank's diary. This was his own subject, ever since he had discovered the policeman who arrested her. He had seen the film and the theatrical adaptations and he could discern no Communist influence in them, he replied, adding that in his opinion it was "not correct to underline at every occasion" only the number of Jewish victims. He asserted that he "was always against speaking only of the six million" Jews who were killed, and always mentioned that there were eleven million murdered human beings, among them six million Jews. He had met Otto Frank only once, he wrote, and had no information on his personal life, and he preferred to concentrate on the pursuit of Nazi criminals.

Levin agreed that the murder of non-Jews should not be ignored but repeated that the dramatic versions of the diary played down the Jewish part. Anne Frank had written about her Jewishness, and these sentences had been cut or distorted in order to bolster her universal image, Levin wrote, adding that although it was done in the United States, the motive behind this adaptation was Stalinist anti-Semitism. His campaign was for the sake of freedom of expression.

"I do not attack 'communism,'" Levin wrote. "I am concerned with the ideological line against Jews, against Israel." The war against the Jews did not end with the defeat of the Nazis, Levin continued. The Nazis sought the physical destruction of the Jews; the Communists tried to eliminate the Jewish identity, and thereby also put the future of the Jewish people in danger. He also mentioned anti-Israeli statements made by members of the New Left. "The fact that you, like others, didn't recognize 'communist influence' in the film or play is simply an example of successful, smooth propaganda," an evidently disappointed Levin wrote.[30]

He was expressing opinions shared by Wiesenthal; as a Zionist and anti-Communist he too tended to identify at least some of the criticism leveled at Israel with Nazi or neo-Nazi anti-Semitism. Given the profusion of topics that concerned Wiesenthal over the years, his silence in the face of Israeli violations of Palestinian human rights was conspicuous.

But within the discourse on the lessons of the Holocaust, Wiesenthal found himself to the left of center. Once he traveled to Israel to try to persuade the people who shaped the way it was commemorated there. He had a long conversation with Gideon Hausner, among others. He did not confine himself to arguments about historical justice or universal ethics but also contended that Israel and the Jewish people could not stand alone against the dangers they were facing. They needed the world's support and it was therefore necessary to strengthen the world's awareness of the fact that Nazism had imperiled not only the Jews, but the whole of humankind. For this reason too it was important to speak not only about the Jewish victims, but about all of them, six million Jews and five million others. "The Holocaust of the Jews will not become less important nor our tragedy less terrible—on the contrary it makes the tragedy of the Jews an important part of the tragedy of all mankind," he wrote.[31]

It is difficult to ascertain how Wiesenthal reached the conclusion that in addition to the six million Jews, the Nazis also murdered five million non-Jews. The number of non-Jews the Nazis killed in the death camps was much lower, whereas the number of non-Jewish civilians killed in World War II was much higher. "It is definitely possible to state that Nazi anti-Semitism was responsible in no small degree for the deaths of not only close to six million Jews, but also of twenty-nine million non-Jews who died as a result of Nazism," wrote the Israeli historian Yehuda Bauer. "Wiesenthal, as he admitted to me in private, invented the figure in order to create sympathy for the Jews—in order to make the non-Jews feel like they are part of us. A nice sentiment, maybe, but ultimately totally counterproductive, not to mention false."[32]

Wiesenthal may well have taken the number from a famous document drawn up by the Nazis in which they set the number of European Jews who were to be exterminated at eleven million. But it is possible that he did indeed invent the number. Either way, this historical error was adopted by the United States government, as part of the mission statement of the Holocaust Memorial Museum in Washington, D.C.

Once President Jimmy Carter also spoke about the eleven million victims. It occurred at a Holocaust remembrance ceremony in the Capitol.[33] Wiesel, who headed the U.S. Holocaust Memorial Council appointed by the president, was infuriated. After the ceremony, he escorted Carter to the White House and on the way there asked the president where he got the number. Carter replied that he had based his remarks on Wiesenthal's writings and speeches. Wiesel told him that there was no basis for these figures. Carter asked if there had not been any non-Jews in the camps. Wiesel's stock reply to such questions was: Not all the victims were Jews, but all the Jews were victims. He explained to the president that among the non-Jewish camp inmates, there were "heroes of the resistance and brave humanists," but they did not number five million; they were just a fraction of that number. But there were also "fierce anti-Semites and sadistic criminals whom the Nazis released from their prisons in order to supervise the camps" among the other non-Jews. "Would it be just, Mr. President, to honor their memory together with that of my parents?" Wiesel asked, and, he wrote, Carter never used the eleven-million figure again.[34]

Documents in Wiesenthal's archives show that at least when it began, his dispute with Wiesel was very much issue-oriented. Gideon Hausner proposed a meeting between them, but that didn't happen. "It appears that Elie Wiesel, whom I respect, admire, and love, didn't have the time or wasn't interested," Wiesenthal wrote.[35] But within months he was already relating to Wiesel as if he were a rival in a competition: "It seems to me that he is losing ground," he reported.[36]

At that time, the two were corresponding about the possibility that they would iron out their disagreements and publish a book together. Wiesenthal formulated a series of themes for discussion: Is there a punishment to fit the Nazis' crimes? Is there any sense in punishment? What can the young generation expect from trials? What dangers did the Nazis leave behind them? Is there anti-Semitism without Jews? What role do hatred, technology, and bureaucracy play in human relations? Is there a survivor complex? Can one escape the past? The role of the school in Holocaust education. The Cold War and the Nazi past. Collective guilt or collective shame. The failure of religion. Who is authorized to forgive?

Wiesel agreed in principle to carry on the dialogue but suggested adding to the list of themes some of the things that disturbed him about Wiesenthal's speeches in the United States. These included the following passage: "Whoever is seeing pictures of starving Cambodian children in the press or on TV and remembers the pictures of the children in the Warsaw Ghetto, many of whom also died of starvation, will realize that they were actually the same children, the differences in time, place and color of their skin being of no importance."[37]

Wiesenthal was offended by Wiesel's criticism and the disagreement over ideas turned into a personal clash. Because Wiesel had insulted him, he wrote to Hausner, he was no longer interested in meeting with him.[38] A few months later, Henry Kissinger said in an interview on Swedish television that he had heard from Elie Wiesel that the Swedish diplomat Raoul Wallenberg was no longer among the living. Wiesenthal quickly spread this around, implying that Wiesel had deserted from an important campaign.[39]

When Wiesel began working on the Holocaust Museum, Wiesenthal instigated a demand by Gypsy activists that a representative of theirs be added to the Memorial Council headed by Wiesel. The quarrel between the two men left the proposal no chance and indeed Wiesel opposed it. He hid behind a procedural pretext: it was not he but President Reagan who appointed members to the council. When the Gypsies wrote to Reagan, the White House passed their letter on to Wiesel.

In subsequent years, Wiesel was flooded with similar demands but he resisted all of them. One pro-Gypsy activist in the United States, Professor Ian Hancock of the University of Texas at Austin, asked Wiesel to clarify something he had written in his book *Night* where he described a Gypsy kapo beating his father and later said that he would never forgive them. Who did he mean, Hancock asked, the Gypsies or the Germans? He added that many Jews had also served as kapos in the camps, and there had been Gypsies among the prisoners whom they abused.[40]

Wiesenthal also wrote to Wiesel. Despite the differences between them, he reminded him, they had always agreed that the Gypsies deserved to be considered as victims of the Nazis. Adding a representative of theirs to the council would improve the lot of the Gypsies in Germany, and that was his reason for writing, he pointed out.[41]

In December 1984, Wiesenthal observed in one of his letters to Wiesel that he was writing on the issue of the Gypsies despite the hostile remarks that Wiesel and his colleagues on the Memorial Council were making about him. Wiesel responded on the council's letterhead, resplendent with the American eagle: "Unless my memory fails me I have never made such remarks. I neither praise you nor criticize you. In fact I refrain from speaking about you. It is you who have for some time engaged in a campaign of slander about the council, its Jewish members and especially about me. Numerous reporters sought my reactions, but I chose not to respond. I believe in fighting anti-Semites, not Jews." Wiesenthal sent a copy to an acquaintance, saying it was "an example of a chutzpah."[42]

Wiesel made no secret of the abhorrence that he felt for Wiesenthal, including on the personal level. In his memoirs he wrote that Wiesenthal had asked him to review *The Sunflower* for the *New York Times*. "It sounds preposterous to me," he wrote, "but how do I know. I haven't read it yet." In reality Wiesenthal had sent him the story and invited him to take part in the book but Wiesel declined.

During one of Wiesenthal's visits, Wiesel's little son Elisha entered the room and he introduced the boy. "Leave us, we have important matters to discuss!" Wiesenthal told him. "Is it because my son does not show much interest that Wiesenthal becomes angry?" Wiesel wrote. "I did not appreciate this. I don't like to see children humiliated and certainly not my own." After that, there was no further contact between the two.

Wiesel also told of a visit to a Serbian concentration camp at the head of an international mission, where the commander went out of his way to welcome him. He did not understand why he was doing this until it became clear that the commander had confused him with Wiesenthal. The contention was that Wiesenthal was the kind of person whom a concentration camp commander would welcome. "He envied me," said Wiesel, years after Wiesenthal's death. "Simply envied me."[43] But apparently the envy was mutual. They were rivals for the supreme authority to speak for the victims and the survivors of the Holocaust and to formulate its moral and political lessons. The "Holocaust portfolio" gave its possessor influence, prestige, honor, and money. Ego and competition for prestige also fueled the hostility between Wiesenthal and the other Nazi hunters, Tuvia Friedman and Beate Klarsfeld.

4. Hunters' Jealousy

Friedman admired Wiesenthal, longed for his recognition, and envied him. He bombarded him with innumerable letters containing a mixture of adulation, self-abnegation, and, most of all, a searing pain over Wiesenthal's refusal to share his glory with him. "You are the great Nazi hunter, and I am the little puppy," he wrote to him, and in his book he put it like this: "I am the Lilliputian and he is the king, with twenty professorships, and I am nothing compared to him."[44] He never concealed his envy and from time to time hinted that he would bare certain details from Wiesenthal's past that were liable to harm him.

According to Friedman, he once attended a lecture in Toronto where Wiesenthal claimed that he had himself taken part in the capture of Eichmann in Argentina, leaping on him, slapping him a few times, pushing him into a jeep, and participating in his interrogation. Friedman went up to Wiesenthal afterward and asked him why he had told the audience such lies, and Wiesenthal explained himself by pointing out that he had received $500 plus expenses for his lectures. Friedman is the only source for this story. In the version that appears in his book, it happened in Montreal.[45]

Sometimes he called Wiesenthal "Herr Ingenieur," sometimes Szymek, the Polish diminutive of Simon. Again and again, he asked to meet with him. Sometimes Wiesenthal agreed, with a sigh of resignation. He treated Friedman like a poor relation and a nuisance, and sometimes he sent him some money, ostensibly payment for all kinds of publications that Friedman sent him from Haifa. On one occasion it was $300, another time $1,000. Once he told him that if he had settled in Israel he would have become a Tuvia Friedman but because he had stayed in Vienna, he became Simon Wiesenthal.[46]

In November 1968 the student demonstrations in several European capitals reached a climax, and the New Left in Germany was also threatening to overturn the social order. During the conference of the Christian Democratic Party in Berlin, a woman sneaked up behind the chair of the West German chancellor, Kurt Georg Kiesinger, and when he turned his head toward her she slapped his face and shouted, "Nazi! Nazi!" Her name was Beate Klarsfeld. Kiesinger had indeed belonged to the Nazi Party and he had been a senior official of the Third Reich's Foreign Ministry. His past had not harmed his postwar political career and his government enjoyed broad support. His deputy was Willy Brandt.

By the time Kiesinger was elected chancellor in 1966, Klarsfeld had already started her protests, but her activities were not widely reported and she decided that articles, shouting, and pamphlets were not enough. A photographer for the weekly *Stern* supplied her with a pass to the conference. Klarsfeld was tried and sentenced to a year in jail, but the sentence was commuted to four months, suspended.[47]

At the time, Klarsfeld was thirty and the mother of a baby. She was living in Paris with her husband, Serge, a Jewish lawyer whose father had been killed at Auschwitz. The steps she took against Kiesinger before she struck him had led to her dismissal from her job with an organization that fostered relations between the youth of France and Germany. Her husband had tried to establish that the man who instigated her dismissal had been a Nazi supporter himself in the past. He hoped to find incriminating evidence against the man in East Berlin, and on his way there he stopped in Vienna and met with Wiesenthal.

Klarsfeld was one of his admirers. He told Wiesenthal how the year before he had flown to Israel to help the army during the Six-Day War. He had come in time to witness the last battles on the Golan Heights. Wiesenthal was very polite, although he did not share the Klarsfelds' left-wing views. He also thought that slapping Kiesinger was not the right thing to do. But as long as she concentrated on politics in Germany, Beate Klarsfeld was no threat to Wiesenthal. She had, meanwhile, been given an enthusiastic reception in Israel.[48] She lost his support, however, when she invaded his turf and began hunting for Nazi criminals.

The Klarsfelds were interested mainly in Nazis who had been active against the Jews of France. Many of them were living in Germany, and the terms of the extradition treaty between France and West Germany barred their prosecution. One of them was Kurt Lischka, head of the Nazi security police in Paris during the occupation; two others were Herbert Hagen and Ernst Heinrichsohn. The three were living freely in Germany; their names and addresses were in the local phone books.

Beate Klarsfeld was frustrated and she shared her feelings with the Israeli television correspondent in Paris, Yaron London. He suggested making a film about the three, and she thought it a good idea. The Klarsfelds took a photographer to the homes of Lischka and Hagen and tried to question them about their parts in the deportation of some seventy thousand French Jews to the death camps. They both refused to answer.

Four weeks later, the Klarsfelds went back to Cologne, where Lischka lived. They brought along some Jewish youngsters from France and a plan of action reminiscent of a cheap thriller. When Lischka came out, they fell upon him and tried to abduct him. It was an amateurish escapade, and Lischka managed to get away from them. The Klarsfelds succeeded at least in making the headlines, and they were sentenced to two months in prison.

Two years later, in 1973, Serge Klarsfeld again ambushed Lischka outside his home, grabbed him, and put a gun between his eyes before making off without firing.[49] The aim was to gain publicity for a campaign to get the West German parliament to ratify an amendment to the country's extradition treaty with France to enable the prosecution of Nazis who had committed war crimes in France. Ultimately, the amendment was ratified. Hagen was sentenced to twelve years, Lischka to ten, and Heinrichsohn to six.[50]

Some of the material the German prosecution authorities used against the three was provided by Wiesenthal. The Klarsfelds later claimed that he had obtained it from them and concealed this fact.[51] In fact Wiesenthal had spoken about Hagen, Lischka, and Heinrichsohn at a press conference he held on October 3, 1967, when he also demanded that the law be amended so they could be brought to justice. On the same day, an article by Wiesenthal on the same matter was printed in *Le Monde*.[52] By now he had come to regard Beate Klarsfeld as a rival.

"Nobody wanted to speak to her," he wrote following one of her visits to Vienna, referring to the leaders of the Jewish community. "So she got together with a few leftist Jews who also always demonstrated in favor of the PLO, and she also recruited some TV crews for it should be filmed [*sic*] how she is arrested for half an hour. And the Jews say—we needed her like we needed a hole in the head."[53]

They smeared each other in media interviews and Wiesenthal's lawyer, Martin Rosen, asked the United Jewish Appeal not to invite her to address its functions.[54] "At first we had a good relationship, but it did not last," Wiesenthal wrote. "Our methods of operating are very different. We first get the criminal and then we call in the press. Klarsfeld works the other way around," he added. Later on, he wrote to the German authorities and asserted that to the best of his knowledge Beate Klarsfeld was in the employ of the East German secret service, the Stasi.[55] The Klarsfelds said the same thing about Wiesenthal that Elie Wiesel had: "He was jealous of us."[56]

In 1971, Klarsfeld began taking an interest in Klaus Barbie, who had been the head of the Gestapo in the French city of Lyon. As with other hunts for Nazis who had committed war crimes in France, she seems to have given a push forward to a case that Wiesenthal had been aware of for some time but had neglected to handle with the energy that Klarsfeld was prepared to expend. In this case, she emulated him by first turning to the Munich prosecution and demanding that they reopen the case against Barbie, which had been dropped several years before. The prosecutor, Manfred Ludolph, gave her some photos that had been taken in La Paz, Bolivia, and told her that one of the people seen in them was apparently the Butcher of Lyon, as Barbie was known. Ludolph also gave her the names of some of his contacts in Lima, Peru, and in La Paz.

She did what the secret services of Germany, France, or Israel could have done long before: she had the photographs printed in several newspapers, and by late December 1971 the information was in her hands: Barbie was using the alias Klaus Altmann and living in Peru. Her informant also told her he could be reached through a man called Friedrich Schwend, his partner in a variety of shady businesses in Bolivia and Peru, including arms trafficking.[57]

Wiesenthal had known Barbie's name for a long time. In 1968 he wrote that the investigation into the case was progressing and its outcome would be "sensational."[58] About a year later he said he had obtained "important reports" about Barbie's whereabouts. In fact, he apparently had no idea where the man was and as he had done more than once in the past, he reported that he was in Egypt.[59]

Wiesenthal was also well aware of the adventures of Friedrich Schwend. During the war, he had been involved in the Nazis' attempt to wreck the British economy by circulating counterfeit pounds sterling in huge amounts. Wiesenthal linked Schwend with ODESSA, and Schwend once sent him a letter full of anti-Semitic abuse. After the war, Schwend had also worked for the CIA, but it is unlikely that Wiesenthal knew about that.[60]

A short time before Klarsfeld became interested in Barbie, Wiesenthal received a letter from a Swiss businessman by the name of Alfred H. Jenny, who wanted him to help a Jewish friend whose son was in jail in Peru although, he said, he had done nothing wrong. It was a very complicated story. It seems that "Altmann" and Schwend were engaged in extorting money from people, among them Jews, who were smuggling their capital out of Bolivia and Peru.

Jenny's friend had told him that the man who had gotten him and his son into trouble, Altmann, had been a senior officer in the SS. Once again, as often before, this was an investigation of Wiesenthal's that originated in a chance request from a stranger, and was not the result of an intentional premeditated effort to find Barbie.

Wiesenthal did not find the name Altmann on his lists of SS members and he assumed it was an alias. Jenny was one of those people whose imaginations Wiesenthal knew how to ignite. In his contacts with Wiesenthal he used all kinds of tricks that he must have learned from spy movies, like code words and clues. The information he provided indicated that Altmann was indeed a Nazi criminal.

The paper trail in Wiesenthal's archives takes the story into innumerable subplots. There is a road map of Peru, and all of a sudden someone going under the name "Bar Giora" crops up. Ultimately, Wiesenthal did not succeed in identifying Altmann as Barbie. "About Altmann, I know nothing," he wrote to Jenny.[61] This coup was therefore to fall into the hands of the competition.

Beate Klarsfeld dashed off to Peru and Bolivia, and in her inimitable manner she stirred up a scandal in the local media. Responding with more than a hint of sour grapes, Wiesenthal wrote, "I am sure that even without Frau Klarsfeld's trips, the French would have worked this out with Peru." In another letter he remarked, "If we had used Klarsfeld's methods in the case of Franz Stangl, the commandant of Treblinka, he would still be living in São Paulo today."[62]

It took more than ten years before Barbie was extradited to France. His trial there confronted French society with its conduct during the Nazi occupation and led to an episode of historical soul-searching. The United States government admitted in 1981 that it had employed him after the war.[63] In 1987 Barbie was sentenced to life imprisonment, and he died in jail four years later.

Early in 1984, Klarsfeld traveled to Chile and led a small group of local Jews in a demonstration outside the residence of Walter Rauff, the man who, among other war crimes, developed the mobile gas vans used to kill Jews before the gas chambers at the death camps went into use. After the war he stayed in Italy, was held by the Americans, but escaped, finally settling in Chile in the late 1950s.

The Chilean police detained Klarsfeld and then allowed her to leave. Her demonstration inspired a very sympathetic piece in *New York* magazine. When the writer asked her about Wiesenthal she replied, "What does he do about Rauff? He writes letters, that's what he does."[64] Wiesenthal's attorney, Martin Mendelsohn, fired off an angry letter to the magazine. "The Klarsfelds will be measured against Simon Wiesenthal. Does anyone doubt who the most important figure will be?" he asked.[65]

Klarsfeld's remark was indeed unfair. Rauff was one of the criminals on whom Wiesenthal had already set his sights in the early 1960s. In 1962, Wiesenthal reported that Rauff was living in Ecuador, although by then he had actually moved on from there to Chile. He fell off the radar for a while, and in 1972 Wiesenthal discovered his new address. He wrote to Chilean president Salvador Allende and received a courteous reply that did not rule out extraditing Rauff to Germany. Wiesenthal got himself invited to see the German chancellor, Helmut Kohl, and in mid-1984 he spoke about Rauff with U.S. president Ronald Reagan at the White House.[66] He could hardly have been expected to do more. Meanwhile, Rauff was living openly and undisturbed. Journalists saw him and photographed him.

This was not a case that Wiesenthal neglected. He simply found himself facing superior forces. Allende was ousted in September 1973, and the government of Augusto Pinochet gave Rauff immunity. Countries that could have acted to secure his arrest, including Israel, preferred not to endanger their interests in Chile. Israel had another good reason not to want Rauff's past opened to scrutiny: in 1948 it had recruited him as an agent and sent him to Syria. Wiesenthal may have known about this, but there's no evidence of that. In 1984, Rauff died peacefully of cardiac arrest.[67]

19

"Only So That Mengele's Name Would Not Be Forgotten"

I. The Mengele Boys

Laurence Olivier was well established as one of the greatest actors of the twentieth century when he agreed to play the part of Nazi hunter Ezra Lieberman in the 1978 film *The Boys from Brazil*. It was about the pursuit of Josef Mengele, the doctor who selected which of the prisoners arriving at Auschwitz would be kept alive to work and which would go straight to the gas chambers, and who conducted cruel experiments on live prisoners aimed at examining race theories. His specialty was twins.

Lieberman was modeled on Wiesenthal. He receives a phone call in his Vienna office informing him that Mengele has cloned ninety-five children using Adolf Hitler's DNA.

The screenplay was adapted from a bestselling novel of the same name by Ira Levin. Wiesenthal didn't like either. He was embarrassed by the almost pornographic plot, which he termed "an insane fiction." When Levin brought him a copy of the book, Wiesenthal rebuked the author for using him as a model without his permission. Levin said that he was a character who belonged to history, and apparently Wiesenthal was quite happy with that answer.[1]

In Europe, the book was panned by critics; in America the reviews were a little kinder. Wiesenthal was worried that it would damage his credibility, but when Laurence Olivier came to visit him he was flattered and helped him prepare for the role. Two years before, Olivier had played the part of a sadistic Nazi dentist in *Marathon Man*. In *The Boys from Brazil*, Mengele is portrayed by Gregory Peck and James Mason plays a fellow Nazi.

Wiesenthal traveled to attend the premiere in New York, where friends told him that critics had given the film bad reviews and that it would harm him. He was angry, and wrote to a friend: "Laurence Olivier portrays an imaginary Lieberman who is not Wiesenthal. The way Lieberman acts is neither my style nor my way of acting. Lieberman is a scared ghetto Jew. Ira Levin probably did not know any other type."[2]

When he agreed to cooperate with the production, he had perhaps entertained the illusion that it would help him capture Mengele, in the same way that *The Odessa File* had helped find Roschmann. He was about to celebrate his seventieth birthday, and he was consumed by a burning desire to find Mengele. His past failures did not discourage him. He could console himself with the knowledge that the Israeli Mossad and the German prosecutor Fritz Bauer had not succeeded any more than he had. He kept on trying.

When he wrote in 1959 that an agent of his had located Mengele in Buenos Aires, he was stretching the truth a little, as usual, but in fact he was working on the case with someone in the Argentinean capital: José Moskovits, the president of the local organization of concentration camp survivors. They had met shortly after the war at a conference of survivors in Europe. Moskovits, a native of Hungary, had lived in Israel for a while before moving to Argentina, where he dealt with reparations claims, property restitution, and similar matters. He appears to have been involved in some of the technical preparations for the Eichmann operation, such as renting safe houses for the Israeli agents. He always put himself at Wiesenthal's disposal.

Their correspondence touched on a number of Nazi fugitives. Wiesenthal would pass on fragments of information and Moskovits would try to find out if there was any truth to them. He knew some of the heads of the Argentinean security services and sometimes employed professional private investigation agencies. The letters that they exchanged over many years reflect a bond of friendship between the two men. Among the questions Wiesenthal asked over the years were some concerning Mengele.

"I have a report from Israel that a man by the name of Pedro Klein living in Buenos Aires knows something about Mengele and wants to contact me but does not know how to do so," Wiesenthal wrote to Moskovits in the spring of 1972. "I have heard that you know the man or you can easily find out who he is. Can he be relied on? Does he want money?" He asked

Moskovits to contact Klein and give him his address. Three weeks later, Wiesenthal asked Moskovits to find out details about a sixty-five-year-old woman who used to be friendly with former Nazis and had also let Mengele hide in her home.

Moskovits did his best. He did not know Klein, he wrote, but in the Buenos Aires phone directory there were three people who could be the man. Could Wiesenthal get more details from Israel? As for the woman, he knew her and soon he would be able to send more information about her activities. He had ordered up a highly confidential investigation, Moskovits reported in reply to one of Wiesenthal's queries. The investigator was totally reliable and Moskovits had also paid the costs.[3]

In 1972, Wiesenthal wrote that Mengele's son Rolf was due to visit Brazil. He wanted to have him followed by detectives but hadn't managed to raise the money to pay for the operation. He needed $10,000 and had only $2,000. He had tried to get the rest from a Dutch newspaper in exchange for exclusivity on the story, but it didn't want to pay so much.[4]

Every now and again, Wiesenthal would announce that he had obtained new information. "Mengele changes his place of residence frequently; he apparently fears for his life," he declared in 1968. Four years later he reported "on the basis of reliable information" that in 1971 Mengele had been in Spain. "Our agent managed to write down the number of the car Mengele traveled in," he wrote. "It was a German number. But it turned out that the numbers were wrong." He was continuing to check reports on Mengele's whereabouts, "but nothing more than that could be said about it."

Two more years went by and in early 1974 Wiesenthal asserted that Mengele was still living as a free man in Paraguay. "Mengele heads our list of wanted persons," he declared in 1978, and explained that the ruling junta in Paraguay was extending him asylum. The Paraguayan government denied this, but Wiesenthal released for publication documents that attested to Mengele's having received Paraguayan citizenship. "We are trying to keep up the public's interest in Mengele," Wiesenthal noted, and indeed a number of magazines published articles about him, including *Time, Paris Match*, and the Austrian *Profil*. The documents indicating that Mengele had obtained Paraguayan citizenship were also given prominence in the Israeli media.[5]

In the early 1980s, Wiesenthal was once again flooded with scraps of information about Mengele. This happened after he initiated a $50,000 reward for information leading to his capture, plus another $10,000 to be given to the charity of the winner's choice. The result was that Mengele's tracks led to Chile, Bolivia, and Uruguay, with each of the searches receiving media exposure.

Wiesenthal was confident that his quarry would be run to ground. "We now know more about Mengele's circles of friends and hope for success by the end of 1981," he reported. When that didn't happen, the reward money was jacked up to $100,000. "According to the most recent information in our hands, Mengele is in Filadelfia, Paraguay," he stated in 1983, adding that he was publishing this "so that Mengele's friends will know what we know."[6]

Wiesenthal checked all the information generated by the reward offer, and also put various governmental officials into play, including his old acquaintance UN secretary-general Kurt Waldheim. Waldheim asked the Paraguayan government about Mengele and passed the reply he received on to Wiesenthal: the fugitive Nazi had left Paraguay a long time ago, and his citizenship had been annulled.[7] Wiesenthal was doubtful and he wasn't the only one. The Israeli ambassador to Paraguay, Benno Weiser Varon, wrote that he believed Mengele was still there but complained that the massive publicity was making it difficult for him to do his job as ambassador. The West German government also assumed he was there, but when their ambassador asked for his extradition, Paraguayan president Alfredo Stroessner threatened that if it did not drop the subject he would cut diplomatic relations between the two countries.[8]

In March 1985 Wiesenthal received a letter from the West German chancellor, Helmut Kohl. It was on official stationery, but at the top he had written in "Personal!" by hand. As Wiesenthal was no doubt aware, he wrote, the West German government was conducting extensive searches for Mengele all over the world but concentrating on South America. Earlier in the year it had asked a number of countries to step up their search efforts, "especially Paraguay," Kohl noted. He said the Paraguayan government had promised it would extradite Mengele to Germany straight after his capture, but it claimed that he had long ago left the country. However, Kohl undertook to emphasize this matter during Stroessner's upcoming visit to Germany.

Kohl's aim in writing seems to have been to avert statements by Wiesenthal that could spoil the Stroessner visit. He did not say it in so many words, but he mentioned the "interesting statement" Wiesenthal had released to the news agencies in which he said that although he did not know Mengele's exact address, he knew he was in Paraguay, in a restricted military area the name of which he also knew. Kohl requested Wiesenthal's "support": in view of the Paraguayan government's denial, would Herr Wiesenthal kindly place at the disposal of the German government the facts and the surveillance results, and clarify the circumstances that had led to his statement to the press? Naturally, the talks with Stroessner would have a different character if the Germans could present him with solid evidence, the chancellor observed.

But Wiesenthal did not know more than the Germans. He was aware of Germany's efforts to find Mengele ever since the days of Chancellor Adenauer, he wrote to Kohl, and then too the government of Paraguay had claimed he wasn't there. In 1979, he had proved that Mengele had obtained Paraguayan citizenship, and he was therefore not impressed by its denials. Mengele's crimes were well documented, and it was therefore necessary to discuss what should be done to ensure that he nevertheless be brought to trial before a German court, Wiesenthal wrote.[9]

The Mengele files in Wiesenthal's archives contain numerous communications from people who claimed they knew where he was or had seen someone answering to his description. Wiesenthal responded to each one, even when he suspected they were intentionally trying to throw him off the scent. A man by the name of Hermann Hans Wagner of Augsburg, Germany, sent him information purporting to disclose Mengele's movements. Wiesenthal assured Wagner that apart from him and his secretary, no one knew about his letter and he was in no danger. He suggested that he use the alias "Felix" to prevent him from being identified.[10]

In 1981, Wiesenthal instructed his attorney in New York to offer $50,000 to a man in Quito, the capital of Ecuador, who had said he could provide Mengele's address. Wiesenthal had spoken to the man and told him that he did not have to supply the "merchandise," as he wrote—the address would be enough. In the letter to his attorney Wiesenthal added: "Naturally I told him that he must make a considerably lower price. I think we can offer him fifty thousand dollars on condition that we can arrest this man on the basis of the address he gives us, payable after the arrest."[11]

A young German by the name of Ingo Wenzeck suggested that a special unit made up of German and Jewish volunteers be established to search for Mengele. He promised that if this was done he would join it.[12] By this time Wiesenthal was financing the escapades of a woman by the name of Ingrid Rimland of Stockton, California.

2. Roots

After she had heard about Wiesenthal's efforts to find Mengele, Ingrid Rimland read his book *The Murderers Among Us* and wrote him that it affected her deeply. "How little we know of each other," she observed.[13] Wiesenthal knew only what she told him about herself. She represented herself as a "serious writer" with several novels to her credit and she sent him publicity material that included details on her origins.

She was born in Ukraine to farmers who belonged to the Mennonite church, which had formed at the time of the Reformation and was devoted to nonviolence. As a child after World War II, she moved with her family to a remote outpost in the Paraguayan jungle, where she grew up. She got married and had a brain-injured son. In a book called *The Furies and the Flame*, a copy of which she sent to Wiesenthal, she described how she brought the child up until he graduated from high school.

She arrived in the United States in the 1960s. In addition to writing, she worked as a consultant in special education.[14] One of her books, *The Wanderers*, had already been described as "pro-Nazi" but Wiesenthal seems to have chosen to believe her claim that this wasn't so, because until that time no one had told him as much about Mengele as Rimland. She claimed she had reason to believe that he was practicing as a doctor in the Mennonite community she had belonged to in her youth. "I knew him quite well, because my mother used to work for him," she wrote.[15] Wiesenthal wanted to believe that this was a serious breakthrough.

The continuation of the story is typical of almost all his work. Since he usually didn't know where the fugitives he was looking for were hiding, he almost never rejected any offer of help in finding them. Having lived from failure to failure, he tended to turn over every stone, and so he was tempted into sending Ingrid Rimland on a secret mission to Paraguay.

She took along with her a man by the name of Walter Boener, a test pilot from Reno, Nevada, who had been born in Paraguay to a German vice-consul. In the 1940s his father had been summoned to return to Berlin, but he was opposed to the Hitler regime, so he deserted to England and joined the Royal Air Force, only to be shot down and killed. His son

Walter had remained in Germany and was recruited into the Hitler Youth and then the air force. He fought in some aerial battles against Russian planes, but toward the end of the war he was arrested for insulting the military. Rimland planned to write a book about his life.[16] Apparently Wiesenthal neglected to check Boener's story, so excited was he about sending the two on their mission.

At first everything went according to plan. Wiesenthal flew to California and met Rimland. He provided her with background material on Mengele and instructed her to leave it at home, so as not to get into trouble in Paraguay.[17] A cover story was concocted: Rimland and her partner were going on a trip to rediscover their roots in the land where they had grown up. Wiesenthal reported on their journey to the prosecutor general in Frankfurt.[18]

Rimland and Boener were paid. Wiesenthal's American attorney, Martin Rosen, arranged the terms in writing. Each of them received a check for $6,000, half of which was to cover expenses, against receipts. In addition, Rosen paid their air fare. If their work resulted in the capture of Mengele, they would get another $50,000 each. Rosen was named as the person to whom they were to report.[19]

Before setting out, Rimland posed a number of questions to Wiesenthal: Did Mengele have "rather protruding eyes"? Did he have a love affair with a woman by the name of Morgenstern? Was he accustomed to posing as a Jew? Wiesenthal didn't understand the significance of these and other questions.[20]

Three months after they left, the two sleuths returned. They did not find the real Mengele, but Rimland had material for a book. She decided that a doctor named Fertsch was Mengele, describing him as a strange and cruel man, and plied her readers with names of other doctors, one of whom she said had been responsible for her son's brain injury. The first chapter of the book was written almost immediately after her return and she sent it to Wiesenthal, gaily speculating that it would be a hit: "I think the movies and the publishers would pay a fortune if I am right. And I would like to bet you a bottle of Champagne, Mr. Wiesenthal, that I am right and Mengele is Fertsch."

Wiesenthal was furious. Rimland and her partner had not carried the search for Mengele any further. He suspected that the two had not even tried to find him but had instead used the money to come back with a book. He apparently raised his voice when he talked to her. "I am still shaking from our last phone call," she wrote to him.[21]

She tried to explain that she was sure she was right, that soon the truth would come out and then she must be ready with her story: a reporter can't be expected to give up on a scoop like this. She tried to elicit his pity, or perhaps guilt: "I feel wretched over this matter as I have, off and on, ever since I first started working with you," she wrote. "I never felt that you fully trusted me. I know, furthermore, that you could destroy me if you disavow what I say or write or I could destroy myself if I tell a foolish story that turns out to be wrong."[22]

Wiesenthal had good reason to be angry with her, not least because he himself had not held back, and while she was still roaming around the land of her childhood with her companion and dreaming up her bestseller, he had already announced that Mengele had found refuge in a Mennonite community. The members of the church were offended and the branch in Holland, where Wiesenthal enjoyed much support, protested; he was forced to apologize.[23]

Many years later, Wiesenthal once again ran into Ingrid Rimland's name. She had thrown in her lot with one of the most infamous Holocaust deniers, Ernst Zündel, and was working with him on a website that contained many a smear against Wiesenthal.[24]

The statements that Wiesenthal issued about Mengele from time to time were incorrect, and he knew it. In fact, he had no idea where Mengele was. He had indeed spent some time in Paraguay and Argentina, but among the countries Wiesenthal mentioned, the one where Mengele had actually found relatively safe asylum for many years—Brazil—was absent. He had moved there a few months after Eichmann's abduction in 1960. On February 7, 1979, he went for a swim in the sea and drowned.

His relatives knew about his death but kept it a secret for several years. Wiesenthal continued to keep the world busy looking for him. At one stage, hints that he might no longer be alive began appearing in the media. After a thorough investigation, the family finally admitted that he had drowned and revealed where he had been buried in Brazil. The grave was opened and his body was exhumed and identified in June 1985.[25]

Wiesenthal found it difficult to give up. Four years after the body's identification he was still clinging to certain doubts, but no one believed him anymore. Mengele was dead and Wiesenthal's credibility had taken a severe blow. This was the second case of its kind. In 1973, the remains of Martin Bormann, Hitler's closest aide, were found in Berlin. Until then, Wiesenthal had claimed that Bormann was alive and he placed him in various sites across the globe, including Brazil.[26]

The inquiry into Mengele's death revealed that his son Rolf had traveled to Brazil several times, as Wiesenthal had suspected without knowing that he was going to visit his father there. Mengele had corresponded copiously with his relatives in Germany. That was the source of the error, Wiesenthal told himself as a justification. He had assumed that the Germans were keeping an eye on Mengele's family.[27] Other people involved in the case also blamed one another, and almost all of them derided Wiesenthal. One of them was the American attorney Gerald Posner.

Posner and British investigative journalist John Ware received the Mengele family's permission to peruse the diaries and personal letters of Josef Mengele, and they wrote a book about his escape and the failures of the search for him. It was primarily the fault of the Mossad and the secret services and law enforcement authorities of Germany and the United States, they wrote, and Mengele was not found because nobody made a serious effort to find him. Describing Wiesenthal's role in the affair, Posner used rather merciless language, disregarding Wiesenthal's long commitment to the hunt for Mengele. Wiesenthal was deeply offended.

In a letter to Posner he recalled that when he first visited the United States in the 1960s, "there wasn't one person who wanted to hear about Nazi crimes. The Jews were quite content celebrating the remembrance once a year. It was I who managed to keep that little flame of consciousness burning by my lectures, articles and TV interviews." In a poignant sentence that expressed the essence of his entire professional outlook, he added: "When nobody was interested in Mengele anymore I often gave information which I could not check to the press, only so that Mengele's name would not be forgotten." This was more than others had done. Posner wrote to Wiesenthal, saying, "There is no one in the world I respect more than you. You have always been a hero figure to me." [28]

Wiesenthal always figured that as long as the death of one of his quarries had not been established, they must be tracked down as if they were still alive. This was the working assumption of all the organizations that were supposed to be looking for Mengele. Over the years, Mengele had become the symbol of Nazi evil. One of the reasons for this was the impact of the films *Marathon Man* and *The Boys from Brazil*. As the number of fugitive Nazi criminals at large decreased and as long as his fate was unknown, the need grew for the belief that one day he would be caught and punished.

In January 1985, various events were held to mark the fortieth anniversary of the liberation of Auschwitz. In Jerusalem, a mock trial was staged where a number of Mengele's victims testified about the fiendish experiments he had performed on them. The media reported all the details, boosting the identification of the Holocaust with Auschwitz and with Mengele.[29] More financial rewards were pledged for anyone producing information on his whereabouts. Israel, West Germany, and the United States all vowed to renew efforts to hunt him down.

If everyone had tried as hard to find Mengele when he was still alive as they did after he was already dead, perhaps he would have been caught. The sudden interest in the man that materialized in the mid-1980s was a reflection of the importance that the Holocaust was assuming in cultural and ethical public discourse, especially in America. It was a relatively new phenomenon. America had begun to discover the Holocaust only in the second half of the 1960s, and simultaneously it discovered and embraced Simon Wiesenthal as well.

3. Culture Hero

The camp survivors who arrived in America in the late 1940s usually encountered very few people who wanted to hear about their travails during the war. Most of the survivors didn't know English. They wanted to integrate into American life quickly, and they made no attempt to rebel against the silence that was imposed upon them. Wiesenthal was aware of the phenomenon. He had come up against it first in Israel, when he brought those urns of ashes for burial. In America, too, survivors felt called upon to explain again and again how it had happened that they had remained alive, and there was a widespread sense of guilt.

And just as survivors had brought with them to Israel difficult questions about what the Zionist leadership had and had not done to rescue them, the same question weighed heavily on the Jewish establishment in the United States. Many survivors felt that American Jews and their leaders had abandoned them during the war, and had not done everything possible to save at least some of the victims. To a large degree, they were right.[30]

The survivors who reached America, like their counterparts in Israel, and like Wiesenthal himself, were astonished to discover that while they were suffering in the camps the lives of their Jewish brethren had continued in an almost unaffected routine. Having absorbed this traumatic revelation, they seemed to accept that it was best to just keep quiet and carry on. The social anti-Semitism in the United States that was still flourishing in the 1950s was another factor that led many Jews to hide not only their Jewish identities, but also the Holocaust.

The phenomenon was not confined to the Jews. Most non-Jewish Americans could not at first isolate the genocide of the Jews from the other Nazi war crimes. The six million murdered Jews were swallowed up into the total number of civilians killed in Europe, almost twenty-five million.

The myths that grew up around the war in the United States depicted the defeat of the Nazis as the triumph of good over evil. The fate of the Jews was not at its core, just as it had not been the focus of the war crimes trials at Nuremberg. The horrendous photographs taken at the death camps were too hard to bear, and they threatened to overshadow the suffering of the American soldiers, some 400,000 of whom were killed. Very soon, the Cold War broke out and the role of the chief villains was transferred from the Nazis of Hitler's Germany to the Communists in Stalin's Soviet Union.

That was how the Holocaust was at first given a rather marginal place in the American collective memory. A plan to set up a memorial monument in Riverside Park in New York was set aside, partly because of claims that it would likely depress the children playing there.[31] *Anne Frank: The Diary of a Young Girl* became an immediate bestseller when it was published in America in 1952, but the film version was an optimistic though sad tale of one little girl in a war, not the story of the destruction of the Jewish people. The historian Raul Hilberg had trouble finding a publisher for *The Destruction of the European Jews*, one of the most important books ever written about the Holocaust.[32]

In the fifteen years that followed the end of the war, a new generation of Jews reached adulthood in America. They felt more secure as Americans than their parents did, and they also began to seek out their Jewish identity.

Those whose parents were born in America sometimes felt uncomfortable if not guilty over the previous generation's dereliction when it came to trying to save the Jews of Europe. Others wanted to know what their parents had experienced during the war. And then came the abduction of Adolf Eichmann and his trial in Jerusalem.

The Israeli operation in Argentina ignited the imagination of American Jews and filled them with pride. In their eyes, this was an act of Jewish heroism. The decision to put Eichmann on trial jibed with their commitment to the American values of law and justice. Many of them internalized the message that Israel was endeavoring to put across by holding the trial: the extermination of the Jews was the Nazis' worst crime, and the State of Israel was there to ensure that another Holocaust would not happen.

The trial hearings were extensively covered in the American media, and Hannah Arendt's book on the trial placed the Nazis and the Holocaust at the center of public discourse. Like many Israelis, particularly the secular ones, a significant number of American Jews began to see the Holocaust as a central element of their identity.

In June 1967, many American Jews were caught up by the same existential anxiety that gripped Israelis; like them, they feared that a second Holocaust was in the offing. Tens of thousands of them flooded the White House with letters, cables, and phone calls pleading with President Lyndon B. Johnson: "Save Israel." They saw Israel's victory in the Six-Day War as having saved the Jews from another genocidal disaster.[33] Now more and more of them wanted to hear about what had happened to their people in Europe, and to speak about it. They were not alone.

In the six years between the Eichmann trial and the Six-Day War, American society underwent upheavals that necessitated a reassessment of its basic ethical underpinnings. The assassinations of John F. Kennedy and Martin Luther King Jr. in 1963 and 1968, the struggles of the civil rights and student protest movements, and the agony of the war in Vietnam, culminating in the horror of the massacre at My Lai, all cast thinking Americans into a state of shock and then into a period of national soul-searching.

Raul Hilberg later recalled that his students "wanted to know the difference between good and evil." The Holocaust, he said, was "the benchmark, the defining moment in the drama of good and evil," against which "one would assess all other deeds." One after the other, American universities began to open Holocaust studies departments, and the enrollment in them was high.[34]

This Americanization of the heritage of the Holocaust began with Hollywood movies, two of which centered on characters based on Wiesenthal, and reached its height with the television miniseries *Holocaust* in 1978. A year before, the miniseries *Roots*, based on the book by Alex Haley, had topped the ratings when it was screened on ABC. The saga of a black family from the days of slavery up to the present, it is believed to have profoundly affected the way African Americans look at themselves.

Directed by the same man who made *Roots*, Marvin Chomsky, NBC's four-part miniseries *Holocaust* was seen by over 200 million people over a two-year period, thereby placing the destruction of the Jews by the Nazis at the center of the American experience. Wiesenthal praised it, observing that the story of one family made a greater impact on the viewer than descriptions of millions of victims, just as the story of Anne Frank had been more effective than the Nuremberg Trials. Elie Wiesel demolished the series, arguing that it was presented as a documentary rather than what it was, a work of fiction.[35]

In 1978 President Jimmy Carter established the President's Commission on the Holocaust and appointed Wiesel as its first chairperson. It began preparations for the erection of the Holocaust Museum in Washington.[36] Identification with the Holocaust experience fortified the self-image of many Americans as representatives of the good, and of hope. Holocaust survivor and "Nazi hunter" Simon Wiesenthal was perfectly suited to this development.

Wiesenthal traveled to the United States at least once a year to lecture at synagogues, community centers, and universities. Each time he calculated how many people had heard him speak and he sometimes boasted about it. "On my present trip I have lectured before twenty-eight thousand students at twelve universities," he once wrote to Menachem Begin.[37] He was soon to become a cultural hero.

He wore old-fashioned suits and spoke broken English in a heavy Yiddish accent. His sentences were convoluted, like German. This only added to his credibility. People identified with him, just as they had identified with the characters in *Holocaust*. Like the miniseries' protagonists, he spoke mainly about himself. He told his life story, relating his experiences in the camps and, in particular, talking about his efforts to find Nazi fugitives and have them brought to justice. People often thanked him for having caught Eichmann, and he did not correct them. He spoke about the need to remember and to prevent another Holocaust.

He was admired everywhere for his efforts to restore the human dignity of the victims, for being a lone fighter for justice against the evil wrought by the Nazi machine. Like the young girl Anne Frank, Wiesenthal was a symbol of hope. The fact that he could link her story to his enhanced his popularity. "He was a popular hero, everybody's grandfather," said attorney Martin Rosen, who also headed the Jewish Documentation Center in New York.

Wiesenthal used to describe this organization as a branch of his Vienna office. In fact it was a foundation licensed to collect tax-deductible donations. Rosen estimated that between 1965 and 1977 it raised between $1 million and $1.5 million, and another million in the next three years.[38]

The center's address in New York was identical to that of a company that imported a popular sporting-goods brand, Republic Cellini. The owner of the company, Herman "Hy" Katz, was a man with an adventurous spirit who read the profile of Wiesenthal published in the *New York Times* in 1964 and was captivated by his determination and courage, and particularly by the mystery that surrounded his operations. Katz loved hunting trips in Africa, and apparently he mostly admired Wiesenthal the hunter. He funded the search for Stangl, among others. Wiesenthal said that without his help, Stangl would not have been caught. "You can be proud to have helped as much as you did. This case will enter history," he wrote to Katz and urged him to keep the letter, so that his children and grandchildren would also be proud.[39]

Katz was supporting Wiesenthal before most American Jews began taking an interest in the Holocaust, but his commitment, like theirs, deepened after the Six-Day War. He urged Wiesenthal to take more drastic action, and at times he fantasized about spectacular operations against Nazi criminals. The arrest of Hermine Braunsteiner-Ryan in New York thrilled him, and he was infuriated by her legal efforts to delay her extradition to Germany. "I want her sitting in jail," he wrote to Wiesenthal. "It is a personal vendetta . . . Let me have the satisfaction that she dies in jail like Franz Stangl."[40]

Six years after her identity was exposed and legal proceedings against her began, a pipe bomb exploded near Braunsteiner-Ryan's house in Queens, New York. There was some damage, but no one was hurt. Katz wrote to Wiesenthal: "One of our groups here 'The Jewish Resistance Squad' had decided to bomb her house, but they made a mistake and bombed the wrong house six blocks away. As you see they are not too well organized. I hope we get rid of her and throw her out of this country."

When he read about the acquittal of two men whom Wiesenthal had managed to have indicted in Austria, he wrote: "Simon, for these two men I think we should plan a special event." He described them as animals and asked Wiesenthal for operational advice as to how the two could get what was coming to them, "the least of which is to die in jail." And he promised: "If it means money, you can count on me."[41] Although Wiesenthal was against this line of action, he did count on Katz. Moreover, he shared the details of his searches with him and also arranged for the Mossad to host him in Israel.[42]

The American millionaire's adulation developed into a deep relationship between the two men. They went sailing together and they shared news about family celebrations and tragedies. Before Katz died, Wiesenthal tried to boost his spirits. He thanked him for his support and wrote: "For me personally, you are my best friend and like a brother. I just felt like telling you this."[43]

Katz died in 1977. Martin Rosen, who had in the meantime become one of Wiesenthal's lawyers, continued to manage the foundation. Once a month, Wiesenthal received a detailed report listing the donors: Dr. G. S. Levey, Miami, Florida—$200; Dr. and Mrs. Elliot A. Klein, Lawrence, New York—$150; the Freund and Harris families, St. Louis, Missouri—$100. From Skokie, Illinois, a Chicago suburb where the American Nazi Party attempted to stage a demonstration, Mr. and Mrs. Marvin Parsoff sent $1,080. The Adlai E. Stevenson High School, Bronx, New York, sent $10.

In a typical month, about $5,000 was contributed by some twenty-five donors. The number of donors cataloged in the Vienna office was in the thousands. The Jewish Documentation Center in New York also organized Wiesenthal's lectures, which were mostly, but not all, for payment. Sometimes his fee was $2,000, but usually it was around $10,000. At the height of his fame his fee could reach as much as $17,000.[44]

Wiesenthal received many a letter requesting his assistance on a variety of different matters. A lawyer by the name of Kevin Kelly of La Salle, Illinois, asked him to help find his son, Dermond, who had gone missing five years earlier. It was a sad story. One day the boy simply left home and never came back. He was sixteen and a half at the time. According to various reports he was living among the Chicago Jewish community. His father sent Wiesenthal pictures of the boy; he was fair-haired and had a pleasant face. "We all love him dearly and want to hear from him or learn that he is all right," he wrote.

Wiesenthal replied promptly and politely. "Having a daughter of my own I can imagine how you feel," he wrote, but pointed out that he was not a detective. However, he sent the desperate father an address for the director of the Chicago Jewish Federation so he could have the information published in the local Jewish press. "You can say I gave you his address," Wiesenthal noted.[45]

Innumerable Wiesenthals wrote to him hoping to discover that they were relatives of his. He would answer that there were many people with the name who were not related to him. And there were people who came to his office and offered him information on Nazis if he would only give them a discount on a new Mercedes—they thought he was the Wiesenthal who operated the Mercedes franchise in Vienna.[46]

4. Special Investigations

In April 1974, about the time that Braunsteiner-Ryan was extradited to Germany, Congresswoman Elizabeth Holtzman called a press conference where she accused the U.S. government of neglecting the search for Nazi criminals who had managed to enter the United States and obtain U.S. citizenship. Holtzman, a Jewish attorney from Brooklyn, was thirty-three years old at the time. She was one of the most prominent women in American politics, known for her strong liberal views. Apart from Wiesenthal, no one did more than Holtzman to locate Nazi fugitives in America.[47]

The Americans were among the initiators of trials against war criminals in occupied Europe, but they also gave asylum to hundreds if not thousands of immigrants, mainly from Eastern Europe, who had abetted the Nazis; many of them were themselves war criminals. The United States saw these people as anti-Communist refugees and embraced them in the spirit of the Cold War.

Just as it had given asylum to Nazis who provided various services and refrained from pressuring Germany to prosecute more Nazis, the United States never did much to bring the war criminals living there to justice. Its laws did not cover war crimes committed in Europe, and American lawmakers never initiated retroactive legislation along the lines of Israel's Nazi Punishment Law.

Wiesenthal had already begun keeping tabs on Nazis entering the United States in the 1950s and he protested against the phenomenon and exposed some of them.[48]

Until the screening of the *Holocaust* miniseries, the U.S. agency that dealt with Nazi criminals was the Immigration and Naturalization Service (INS). In 1979, the Office of Special Investigations (OSI) was set up for that purpose, amidst much infighting inside the Justice Department.[49] The unit's officials were aware of the political expectations that accompanied their work and they were very eager to succeed. An internal memorandum that analyzed various alternatives for action in one of its cases mentioned "bad publicity" as a possible outcome and it continued: "It could cause hard feelings on the part of the Israeli police and Simon Wiesenthal. The feelings might spread throughout the Jewish community in the United States and lead to political repercussions."[50]

Wiesenthal correctly assumed that one of the reasons for the setting up of the OSI was his public activity in the United States, and he was inclined to see it as the executor of his initiatives. He sometimes briefed officials of the unit as if they were his subordinates. He overwhelmed them with names and addresses of suspects, and the officials thanked him courteously, although they very quickly cottoned on to his problematic modus operandi. He assumed that the authorities would accept his information as verified and accurate, and that all they had to do was to arrest and prosecute. And he tended to convey almost everything to the media, for immediate release.[51]

In 1979, the OSI was dealing with one of Eichmann's assistants, Otto Albrecht von Bolschwing; it was a rather sensitive case. After the war, von Bolschwing had worked with American intelligence and as of 1954 he had been living in California. The investigation was secret, but one day the Israeli English-language daily the *Jerusalem Post* ran an interview with Wiesenthal in which he mentioned that von Bolschwing was in America. Apparently he had been told about it in utter confidence by the OSI.

A few weeks later, he mentioned von Bolschwing in his annual bulletin, although he did not claim credit for finding him. Eventually, von Bolschwing died without being deported, so that the premature publication caused no damage, but OSI staffers learned to take care, not only because Wiesenthal stole their scoops but also because he sometimes gave them incorrect information.[52]

In 1974, Wiesenthal had supplied the INS with details about a man named Frank Walus, who was working at a Chicago car assembly plant. Three years later, the agency tried to strip him of his citizenship, claiming that he had served in the Gestapo and had concealed this from the authorities. A court annulled his citizenship, but he appealed and submitted new material that cleared him. The OSI closed the case.

Wiesenthal kept trying to prove that Walus had lied. After they sued each other for libel an agreed, confidential settlement was reached. Wiesenthal had no reason to feel that he had failed. He thought the OSI had acted too hastily, but they blamed him for misleading them.[53]

The OSI did fail in another similar case, when a man by the name of John Demjanjuk, a Ukrainian living in Cleveland, Ohio, was extradited to Israel amid great fanfare. He had been identified as "Ivan the Terrible," the man who operated the gas chambers at Treblinka. His trial in Jerusalem was intended to be a second Eichmann trial and Demjanjuk was sentenced to death, but before his appeal new material was found that led to his acquittal and return to America. In 2009 he was extradited to Germany, where he was tried again.

This episode illustrated the limits of America's readiness to punish Nazi criminals. They were not deported because they killed Jews, but because they lied to immigration officials. More than meting out justice, it was an act aimed at purging American society. Wiesenthal at first believed that Demjanjuk was guilty but after the acquittal said that he too would have cleared him on the basis of the new evidence.[54]

In his contacts with the OSI, Wiesenthal expected the same degree of cooperation and respect that he was accustomed to receiving from German law enforcement agencies. The ambitious American lawyers in Washington, aware of Wiesenthal's political clout, were at pains to avoid any collisions with him. In 1984, the director of the unit, Neal M. Sher, praised Wiesenthal's "unwavering commitment to the pursuit of justice and tireless efforts to awaken the conscience of the world." Three years later Sher thanked him for his work in a particularly friendly letter.[55]

Wiesenthal's status in America pleased him, especially after so many years of enduring hatred and contempt in Austria. Despite his foreignness in America, he felt at home there, almost as much as in Vienna. One day he had a visitor from Los Angeles who asked his permission to name a new center for Holocaust studies after him. Wiesenthal consulted his attorney, and Rosen told him that the center was a serious enterprise, larger in scope than Yad Vashem and in competition with the Holocaust museum then under construction in Washington. Wiesenthal assented. He did not request and did not receive any payment for agreeing. The project caught his fancy and the proposal that it be named for him was flattering.

20.

"As If I Were Already Dead"

I. Between Hollywood and Disneyland

Marvin Hier may not have been considered a great Torah scholar, but there weren't many other rabbis blessed with his organizational, executive, and communication skills. Born in 1939, the son of immigrants from Poland, he grew up on New York's Lower East Side. In his twenties he got the job of assistant rabbi at the Schara Zedeck Orthodox synagogue in Vancouver, Canada, and he remained there for more than twenty years. The Six-Day War did for him what it did for most North American Jews and shortly afterward he led a group of his congregants on a tour of Eastern Europe. On the way they visited with Simon Wiesenthal in Vienna.

Their Austrian bus driver wasn't happy with the destination. It's time to leave the past alone, he told his Canadian passengers. Hier revered the celebrated "Nazi hunter" and supposed he would give the group only a few minutes of his time. But Wiesenthal was polite and very patient, and Hier sensed that he was a lonely man who needed company. Occasionally he broke into Yiddish; it never occurred to him that Jews from America might not know the language. He made a deep impression on them.

Toward the end of the 1970s, Hier spent some time in Jerusalem, where his belief that God had wanted Israel to be established grew stronger. He was connected to the Ohr Samayach yeshiva, which specializes in making secular Jewish youth religious and fortifying their faith. He returned to America and settled in Los Angeles. A smart, pleasant man, he got to know everyone worth knowing in finance, government, and show business, and the screening of *Holocaust* and the announcement of plans for the Holocaust Memorial Museum in Washington gave him a brilliant idea: a Holocaust center between Hollywood and Disneyland could be a big success, although those may not have been the words he would have chosen to describe it.

Samuel Belzberg, a Canadian billionaire who was grateful to Hier for getting his son Mark involved in the rabbi's synagogue in Vancouver, gave him half a million dollars. Another wealthy man, Holocaust survivor Joseph Tennenbaum, chipped in a similar amount. Hier established a Jewish high school named for Menachem Begin and purchased a building that belonged to Yeshiva University. Wiesenthal's prestige and fame would make his name ideal for the project. Hier took off for Vienna.

Wiesenthal, who was already seventy, did not remember Hier's previous visit a decade earlier. "Apparently I didn't make a deep impression," said Hier years later. But he knew who to take with him in order to impress Wiesenthal: the French-born American Jewish billionaire Roland E. Arnall, who had spent the war years hiding in a monastery and after coming to America founded the Ameriquest Mortgage Company.[1]

Hier's project inspired in Wiesenthal a youthful enthusiasm. He naively believed that the center bearing his name would act according to his instructions, and he immediately began trying to use it in his struggle against the statute of limitations in Germany. This was a subject he knew well since his success in extending for five years its application in murder cases. In 1969, the Germans had decided that such cases would no longer be prosecutable after thirty years, and in 1978 the demand arose to abolish the statute of limitations altogether. This happened partly because of the Majdanek trials and the screening of *Holocaust* in Germany, where an estimated fourteen million people saw the miniseries.[2] But pressure from the outside was also needed and Wiesenthal activated his American connections.

The Jewish Documentation Center in New York ordered up hundreds of thousands of postcards that were meant to be sent to Chancellor Helmut Schmidt in Bonn. On one side there was a picture of a German soldier shooting a woman holding a baby, and on the other side, in German, English, and French, "This must never come under the statute of limitations." Wiesenthal ordered Hier to take part in the campaign. Hier and Rabbi Abraham Cooper, who was working with him on setting up the center, were enthusiastic. A campaign like this was just the sort of public relations the project needed.

Hier was thirty years younger than Wiesenthal, and Cooper was forty years younger. The first letters that they and Wiesenthal exchanged ostensibly reflect a hierarchical relationship, with Wiesenthal giving the orders—or at least that was what he believed. The two rabbis handled him like a rare and delicate porcelain flower, swathing him in respect as only Americans can do.

His letters were very businesslike: Please be in touch with Attorney Rosen—this is his New York address and this is his phone number—to get the printing blocks and have the cards printed. Please make sure that each member of Congress gets a card to send to Chancellor Schmidt, please make sure that each senator signs a card. Wiesenthal was on his way, this was his flight number, he wanted to rest in the afternoon, please don't arrange interviews—that could kill the press conference that he wanted to hold. This was the statement he wanted to issue to the media, it should be printed on the center's letterhead. Don't forget to bring postcards to hand out to the journalists. At each university where he was scheduled to speak, postcards should be available.

He pointed out to Rabbi Cooper that in the letter to President Carter there was an error in the name of the president of the German Supreme Court: please make a correction.[3] He instructed the rabbi to make sure that the chancellor's office was flooded with half a million cards, and he shared a little secret with him, like someone trying to encourage an assistant to work harder: "I have received unofficial information that a certain change of thought is taking place in the Federal Republic of Germany. In any case we have to continue to apply pressure on the German government."

A week later, however, Wiesenthal remarked that the campaign was not working properly. The chancellor's office in Bonn had reported in response to a query from the press that it had received only 5,400 cards. Apparently people were keeping them as souvenirs rather than sending them to Germany. This must be dealt with immediately.[4]

The postcard campaign was one of many activities that Wiesenthal was vigorously pursuing. The link with the center in Los Angeles had given him a sense of being at the head of a worldwide, well-coordinated machine and he frequently sent reports on his actions to his new partners. "I am travelling all over Europe, much more than I would like," he wrote to Ephraim Zuroff, an employee of the center. He notified Hier that the queen of the Netherlands had decorated him as a commander in the Order of Orange-Nassau, adding, "You may wish to use this for PR purposes."[5]

Israeli prime minister Begin also received detailed reports from Wiesenthal on his efforts to have the statute of limitations abolished, covering events in London, Brussels, and Paris. Winston Churchill's son accepted his invitation to head up a demonstration; California governor Jerry Brown, a potential presidential candidate, joined the campaign. In Germany, there were meetings with a number of lawmakers, and a meeting was arranged with the Bavarian leader Franz Josef Strauss. Begin addressed Wiesenthal as "My dear friend," and wrote, in English: "May your efforts in the name of historic justice for our people be forever blessed."[6]

Strauss, the powerful leader of the right-wing Bavarian party CSU and a spokesman for the new German nationalism, was opposed to the abolition of the statute of limitations on Nazi war crimes. Getting a meeting with him was an achievement for Wiesenthal. He took it very seriously and refrained from taking Hier with him, although he had come to Germany at the head of a delegation of Jews from Los Angeles. Hier felt slighted, and Wiesenthal put him in his place, observing: "I assume you will agree with me that such matters can much better be discussed confidentially than in the presence of a large delegation." Each member of the delegation would have felt compelled to say something, he wrote. He did offer Hier a little information from the meeting and hinted—without any basis—that he had succeeded in shifting Strauss from his opposition.

Hier swallowed the insult and Cooper sent Wiesenthal a detailed report on the delegation's meeting with Chancellor Schmidt, who, Cooper wrote with somewhat childish glee, was angry about the postcard campaign. Wiesenthal did not attend that meeting, as if it was beneath his dignity to visit with Schmidt as part of a delegation of that rank. Cooper asked for additional directives: Did Wiesenthal intend to appeal to the pope? Should the center prepare for that?[7]

The public struggle against the application of the statute of limitations to Nazi crimes was also at the top of the agenda for the Israeli embassy in Bonn. Tuvia Friedman did his best to stir up public opinion in Israel, where the Knesset held a special session on the issue. In July 1979, the Bundestag decided to abolish the statute, and Wiesenthal was a happy man.[8]

For a moment, he imagined that it was within his power to solve another critical issue: His political contacts in Germany and Sweden, he reported to Begin, had given him grounds to believe that it would be possible to put together an international spy-exchange deal as part of which the Soviet Union would release the imprisoned Jewish human rights activist Anatoly Sharansky.[9] This was not true, apparently, but Wiesenthal's activity reflected his mood. Never before had he felt so useful and so admired. One of the secretaries at the Los Angeles center wrote him: "Growing up as a child and as an adult I have never looked at anyone as a hero, so to speak. This is no longer so . . . you have captured my heart."[10]

Hier was also satisfied. The postcard campaign had placed his center in a key position on the map of Jewish activism. He arranged for Wiesenthal to fly from one fund-raising function to another, at least once in the supersonic and super-expensive Concorde, and he also arranged for him to receive more and more awards. Some twenty universities and colleges presented him with honorary doctorates, he received the Congressional Gold Medal from President Carter, and the Presidential Medal of Freedom from President Bill Clinton.

During this period Wiesenthal liked Hier and found in him a willing listener to his jokes, although Hier described them as inappropriate for a rabbi's ears, like the one about the three Jews Berl, Cherl, and Shmerl, who arrived in America and applied to change their names. The official who got their application decided Berl would be Buck and Cherl would be Chuck, and Shmerl said that he'd rather go home. Wiesenthal repeated it at least fifty times, and each time he split his sides laughing, said Hier. Wiesenthal trusted Hier and even complied with a request to give him blank pages with his signature so the center could use them for "personal" letters to donors and others.

Before the inauguration of the center, Hier gave Wiesenthal the phone number of Elizabeth Taylor and got him to invite her to the ceremony. She was one of a number of movie stars whom Hier attracted to the center, including Jane Fonda and Dustin Hoffman. In 1982, Hier received an Oscar, together with Arnold Schwartzman, for the documentary they produced titled *Genocide*. He was also involved in the contacts that led to the production of the 1989 Home Box Office film on Wiesenthal's life, *The Murderers Among Us*.

As a result of his disappointment with Laurence Olivier in *The Boys from Brazil*, Wiesenthal decided that this time he had to be involved in the selection of the actor who would portray him. He did not agree to Kirk Douglas, and Paul Newman was not available. The eventual choice was Ben Kingsley, who had won an Oscar for his Gandhi, and Wiesenthal was flattered by his portrayal. He was also satisfied with the movie as a whole and with the $350,000 fee that he received for the rights to his autobiography. One of the producers was Abby Mann, who was among the first American officers Wiesenthal encountered after the liberation of Mauthausen.

The film increased his fame. People recognized him on the streets of New York and emotionally shook his hand and asked for his autograph. The comic Jackie Mason stopped his show when he saw him in the audience and said he felt honored that he was there. Frank Sinatra sang "My Way" for him.

Hier, an expert on the social anthropology of his city, supposed that Wiesenthal had captivated Hollywood not only because the Holocaust had become an "in" thing, but also because he radiated a certain something that was absent from the lives of movie stars. Everything around them was artificial, superficial, phony, commercial, transient; this elderly Holocaust survivor from Vienna, with his Germanic English, radiated something true—true idealism, true courage, true humanity.[11] The standing he achieved in America also influenced European countries and Israel to present him with honors and awards. Austria printed some of the drawings he had made at Mauthausen on the first-day covers for stamps it issued to commemorate the liberation of the camp, and that made him particularly happy.

From time to time he received reports from Los Angeles on the work of the center and its public activities, such as the first efforts to secure the prosecution of Nazi criminals who had taken refuge in America. Cooper assured him that "all of our public statements and actions will only reflect positively on the name of our institution," and thus also Wiesenthal's name. "We anxiously await your insights and suggestions," he wrote him on another occasion.[12] Wiesenthal identified with the center and when its establishment was criticized, he defended it. "Jewish organizations often function like the fire brigade: When a fire breaks out, they come to put it out. But when someone tries to prevent a fire, this arouses opposition," he wrote.[13]

Five years after he launched the project, Hier could boast that his center housed the largest Holocaust museum in America. He was in touch with

150,000 students, ran a radio program with 600,000 listeners a week, and had produced a movie seen by millions.

The Simon Wiesenthal Center in Los Angeles had arisen in competition with the projected Holocaust Memorial Museum in Washington, and it also played a part in the competition between the Jewish establishments of the west and east coasts of the United States. "We have accomplished all this while in Washington they're still talking for five years about building a Holocaust center," Hier wrote.[14] But meanwhile his relationship with Wiesenthal had become strained to the breaking point.

2. The Golden Cage

Wiesenthal's first complaints touched on trivial issues: Why didn't they pass on to him letters that arrived in his name? Why didn't he get all the center's publications?[15] Hier calmed him down. But there was also a financial issue. The U.S. ambassador in Vienna, Milton Wolf, had given him $5,000 for the center in Los Angeles and Wiesenthal demanded that $1,000 be made over to the center in Vienna.[16] This was not a one-time incident.

In March 1981, Wiesenthal wrote to Hier that the number and size of the donations he was receiving had dropped significantly. From the beginning of the year he had received only forty checks, and the total amount was low. People were telling him proudly that they had sent donations to Los Angeles, and he could not of course tell them that it would be better to send the money to Vienna. The condition of the fund in New York was also bad. It had deposited $60,000 in a closed account so that it would be able to give a reward to anyone who provided information leading to Mengele's arrest within twenty-four hours. "Please remember me when I come to Los Angeles that we must discuss this fact," Wiesenthal wrote to Hier in his own brand of English.[17]

Hier, who had meanwhile managed to set up a streamlined fund-raising operation, solved the problem without any difficulty. Starting in 1984, Wiesenthal received $5,000 a month and as of 1994 the sum was raised to $7,500 a month. The money was described as "joint research fees."[18] Wiesenthal had never had such a high regular income, and because he had also never grasped the full financial extent of the multimillion-dollar Los Angeles project, he was satisfied. Hier's earnings and those of some members of his family were ten times higher.[19] Wiesenthal's disaffection, therefore, was not about money. He was angry because he was not being consulted.

Some of the letters he sent to Los Angeles reflected fundamental disagreements, but most of the difficulties arose from his feeling that Hier and his people were showing disrespect by not following his instructions. Hier set the center up and ran it as he saw fit. Wiesenthal had to read about its activities in the newspapers. The center was operating like a one-man enterprise, Wiesenthal complained. "You are making the policy for the educational side, the scientific efforts, for the relationship with other organizations, for the museum, for the library, for the fight against anti-Semitism, for the relationships with political bodies in the United States. This is an impossible situation, because all these problems couldn't be managed by one person," he wrote.

He rebuked Hier for attributing too much importance to the center's public relations, remarking that media projects could be a by-product but should not be allowed to supplant the center's main function as a place of serious, in-depth research. Neither should they skip from project to project, "like partisans taking pot shots at the enemy," but they should operate according to a comprehensive plan, he added.[20] Someone brought him a booklet published by the center in Los Angeles containing his biography. He had not been shown the content before it was published and it angered him that it did not include a full list of his honorary degrees.[21]

When he received a summary of the documentary film Hier was producing, Wiesenthal said that the script had to be rewritten. Hier responded that he was "shocked" by his reaction. The script was written by British historian Martin Gilbert, and Orson Welles had agreed to be the narrator.[22] Wiesenthal thought there were too many naked bodies of women and too few secular Jews, or, as he put it, too little "non-religious Jewish couture (too many beards)."

He told Hier about what he said was a far superior Holocaust documentary, *The Final Solution*, made by the Swiss producer Arthur Cohn. Unlike Hier, he said, Cohn had accepted all the advice that he gave him. Thousands of movie theaters were already screening it, and it cost less to make than Hier's film did. Cohn may not have won the Oscar, but that's not what counts, Wiesenthal wrote. But he was able to forgive Hier his shortcomings as a moviemaker; he couldn't forgive him for trying to build himself up as a moral authority.[23]

Early in 1981 Chancellor Schmidt was due to travel to Saudi Arabia to close a deal for the sale of German tanks to the desert kingdom. Hier issued a press release denouncing the deal in vehement terms.[24] Wiesenthal was insulted. If there was any need for such a protest, he was the man to make it and not the head of the center in Los Angeles. Hier was also publishing articles in which he linked Arab antagonism toward Israel with Nazi anti-Semitism and making passionate speeches against Yasser Arafat. These were also Wiesenthal's opinions, but he feared being pushed out of the limelight by Hier. He felt like the bird in the golden cage, as if the Wiesenthal Center were a monster that had risen up against its master.

In March 1984, Hier notified Wiesenthal that the center was going to award an honorary medallion to President François Mitterrand of France. Everything had been arranged with his office and Wiesenthal would chair the delegation. But Wiesenthal had not been asked in advance; even the date had not been cleared with him and he was fuming. "Politically, I as a European know a little about the relationship of Mitterrand to Israel and his views on the Jewish question," he wrote. Moreover, he did not think it appropriate that he should personally present an award bearing his own name. He would write to Mitterrand, he told Hier.[25]

But what annoyed Wiesenthal more than anything else was when the Los Angeles center's personnel made headlines for its Nazi-hunting ambitions. Apparently, the people in Los Angeles thought that they knew everything and the Vienna office knew nothing, he concluded, and a few weeks later he wrote: "I don't want to hear the words Nazi hunter Rabbi Abraham Cooper from the Simon Wiesenthal Center."[26]

Over the years, his letters became more personal, more bitter, more painful, more hostile. "People from my staff here in Vienna, when they see that I'm very sorry about such situations, say that the relationship between the Center and me is so as if I would be dead and the center is only using my name," he wrote in 1984 and two years later, again, in a letter to Hier: "You have no use for me anymore, the only thing you need is my name."[27]

Gradually Hier began dropping the word *Holocaust* from the name of the organization, until it was only the Simon Wiesenthal Center. The change reflected Hier's intention to convert the center into an active hub of activities to counter anti-Semitism and all forms of racism, and not only a Holocaust research institute. Wiesenthal was angry about it, as people began asking him what the center dealt with and he didn't know what to say. "I must tell you that the development of the last few years makes me unhappy," he wrote to Hier in 1985, adding that he was also upset about the "quarrels of the center with the Jewish organizations in the United States, even when the basis is jealousy."[28]

Hier needed endless patience, psychological improvisation, and diplomatic skills to handle the relationship with Wiesenthal. He realized that he must never lose him. "To begin with, Simon, I think it is important to recognize that both of us want the very same thing," he wrote to him in 1983. "We want the Simon Wiesenthal Center to become a leading institution of its kind which will be a lasting legacy to your life's work."[29] But Hier did not reply in writing to most of Wiesenthal's letters. Instead he phoned him at home, sometimes night after night, and often the calls lasted half an hour or more.

Usually he managed to assuage Wiesenthal's anger. Looking at the experience of the previous nine years as a whole, Wiesenthal wrote in 1987, "my judgment is positive," and despite his reservations about some of their statements, "if today they would ask me again to give my name, I would say yes again."[30]

Basically, Wiesenthal could not find a more dignified way to have his work and his views perpetuated. With his Viennese mind-set, he found it difficult to adapt to the showy multimedia style of the center and of the Hollywood-like Museum of Tolerance that it had opened in 1993. He had envisaged a more academic institution. For example, he had proposed undertaking a comprehensive study of the medical experiments carried out by the Nazis. The ideological tendencies of the center and the museum, though, reflected his own approach: the Holocaust was depicted in the context of a neoconservative, universalist worldview that advocated law and order, the struggle against Islamic fundamentalism, the strengthening of Jewish identity in America, and support for Israel. But all this was not enough, and the wounds to his ego continued to torment him.

Shortly before he turned eighty-five, Wiesenthal learned that the Los Angeles center had supported a rather weird escapade meant to expose the activities of neo-Nazi organizations. It had backed a man representing himself as an Israeli journalist by the name of Yaron Svoray who claimed to have penetrated such an organization in Germany. A report that he compiled enjoyed wide coverage in the international media. Wiesenthal, who had devoted much of his life to combating neo-Nazism, read about it in the newspapers. This was inexcusable. "I can no longer tolerate such disregard for my person," he wrote to Hier. As long as the construction work on the museum was under way, he had tried to restrain himself in order to avoid harming the project, "but now the limit has been reached as far as I am concerned! And only one person is responsible for this, and that is you, Rabbi Hier!" Wiesenthal decided to oust Hier from the center that bore his name.

His ties with the center had made a mockery of him, he wrote. "I have been asked by journalists and other well meaning people if I have sold my name. Others, who are less well disposed towards me have gloatingly told me that the name 'Hilton' can too be obtained for a hotel for the right price." He felt hurt and humiliated, and there was no point in Hier talking to him for hours on the phone.

Some of his friends, he wrote, found it incomprehensible that the museum so closely connected with the center that bore his name presented so little information about him and his work. Although a computer on the third floor could be used to obtain such information, Wiesenthal was never consulted about its contents: "Just as if I were already dead," he wrote. He wanted each visitor to the museum to get the page from his book *Every Day Remembrance Day: A Chronicle of Jewish Martyrdom* that gave details about anti-Semitic persecution that had occurred on the date of the visit. The publisher of the book had also expected this to happen, thereby increasing the book's sales. Hier said the material could be made available by computer. Another attempt to humiliate him, Wiesenthal believed, and he decided to take the most drastic step of all: he would offer the idea to the Holocaust Museum in Washington.

"I also don't like the fact that you are constantly present in the media," Wiesenthal's letter to Hier continued. "Not a week goes by without your commenting on some subject that often has nothing to do with the center, yet always as the 'Dean of the Simon Wiesenthal Center.'" In light of all this, Wiesenthal had concluded that there was no point in maintaining his connection with the center via Hier. He did not believe that Hier would change his attitude, he wrote, and he would therefore ask the center's board of directors to replace the management.[31] But Hier kept his job, and Wiesenthal had to settle for the position of figurehead. Frustration and loneliness were eating away at him. In the 1980s he once again found himself facing a terrible offensive.

21.

"Sleazenthal"

I. Character Reference

Eli Rosenbaum was a lucky Jew: he grew up in a society that regarded the Jewish heritage as part of its national identity. Violent anti-Semitism such as that which shaped Wiesenthal's life was no more than a part of history for Rosenbaum, a native of New York who was twelve years old when America's Jews experienced the anxiety of the days before the Six-Day War and the euphoria that gripped them in its wake. As a high school student, he shared the newfound identification with the Holocaust. Wiesenthal was his hero. He read *The Murderers Among Us* again and again, and he could recite whole passages from it by heart.

As a student at Harvard Law School, Rosenbaum joined Wiesenthal's campaign against the statute of limitations on Nazi crimes in Germany, enlisting the support of well-known law professors all over America. In addition, he tried to combat the failings of Interpol, the international criminal police organization, in the hunt for Nazi fugitives from justice. This was also an issue on Wiesenthal's agenda.

Rosenbaum wrote to him and donated money to help finance his activities in Vienna, and he received a personal note of thanks from Wiesenthal, foreseeing "a fine career as an attorney" for the young American. "I treasured that letter," Rosenbaum wrote years later.[1]

Two years after the screening of the miniseries *Holocaust*, Rosenbaum graduated and got a job as an attorney for the Office of Special Investigations. He was twenty-three. Before he started, he wrote to Wiesenthal about the infighting and intrigue that characterized the work of the unit in the first years of its existence. Its director, Martin Mendelsohn, was forced to resign and he later became one of Wiesenthal's lawyers. He was replaced by Alan E. Ryan. The association of Jewish students at Harvard Law School sent a letter of protest to President Carter about Mendelsohn's ouster.

Rosenbaum told Wiesenthal that he had managed to get the job only with difficulty and that he suspected that he was "a 'marked man' at OSI, much the way Marty [Mendelsohn] was." He said he was "increasingly skeptical of the Justice Department's commitment to pursuing these investigations" and that he was determined to resign should he "become convinced that the Government does not intend to properly prosecute these cases."

He instructed Wiesenthal not to call him directly, but to contact him only through Rabbi Cooper in Los Angeles. Wiesenthal tried to encourage him with a paternal kindliness. "When you'll come to the unit and the people there know that I am a friend of yours—I am sure you will not have any difficulties at the new place," he wrote.[2] Rosenbaum stayed in the OSI for about three years, and in 1985 he became the general counsel for the World Jewish Congress (WJC).

The WJC had built up most of its power and prestige under the presidency of Dr. Nahum Goldmann, who led the organization with great acumen for thirty years. The president during the 1980s, the Canadian whiskey billionaire Edgar Bronfman, also professed to speak for the entire Jewish people and preserved the respect many world leaders had for the WJC.

The congress was an umbrella organization, and its status was founded principally on the myth of worldwide Jewish influence.

And like the myth that Wiesenthal had woven for himself, the WJC myth tended to be self-fulfilling. Bronfman, head of the mighty Seagram empire, projected the authority of the head of a powerful state. He would fly from capital city to capital city in his private jet, and he was used to being received by heads of government everywhere. "It is in our interest that people think we are powerful and strong," he explained in an interview. The more he bolstered his own image, the stronger the WJC became.[3]

Goldmann had also strode among the world's leaders as if he were the king of the Jews, but the people who ran the WJC in the 1980s belonged to a new generation of American Jews. They had internalized the persecution of European Jewry as the experience that had shaped the lives of their parents and they had been nurtured on the two-word imperative "Never again." Awareness of their predecessors' failure to save Europe's Jews during the Holocaust, they often felt ashamed of the feebleness and faintheartedness they attributed to those who led American Jewry during the war. They projected the arrogant belligerency and rebellious aspirations of the young. In January 1986, they went to war against Kurt Waldheim. The former UN secretary-general was running for president of Austria in that year's elections, as the candidate of the Conservative Party.

It all began in the Hilton Hotel in Jerusalem, where the WJC was holding its annual conference, Rosenbaum recalled years later. The organization's secretary-general, Israel Singer, came up to him and without any preliminary remarks said that he was sending him to Vienna. "Vienna? Why?" asked Rosenbaum. Singer lowered his voice and said, "It has to do with Kurt Waldheim." Then, almost in a whisper, he asked Rosenbaum if he knew who Leon Zelman was. Rosenbaum did not know.

A survivor of Auschwitz who settled in Vienna after the war, Zelman wrote articles for Jewish newspapers and headed an organization devoted to improving relations between the Jews and the Austrians and between Austria and Israel, known as the Jewish Welcome Service. Like many of the leaders of the Vienna Jewish community, Zelman was associated with the Social Democratic Party. He was known to be an old rival of Wiesenthal's, dating back to the days in the displaced persons' camps in Linz.

Someone from the Social Democratic Party had sent Zelman to the WJC with information about Waldheim: he had concealed his Nazi past. It would make a bigger splash to publish this in New York than in Austria, his political enemies calculated, correctly. Singer dispatched Rosenbaum to Vienna to look into the allegations. In the next few months Rosenbaum worked behind the scenes of a worldwide scandal that was waged like the war between the Sons of Light and the Sons of Darkness. He set out to establish that Kurt Waldheim was a war criminal. Then he tried to destroy Simon Wiesenthal.

At the time when Austria was annexed to Hitler's Germany, Waldheim was twenty, the son of a Catholic family that did not support the Nazis. To anyone who asked, he used to say that he was conscripted into the army and became an officer, but he was wounded in 1941 and returned to

Vienna and began studying at the university. His relations with Wiesenthal were cordial. In the 1960s, when the Polish embassy in Vienna distributed material accusing Wiesenthal of collaborating with the Nazis, then foreign minister Waldheim promised to help him. Wiesenthal sat with him for an hour and reported on the meeting to the Israeli ambassador in Vienna.

There is of course some irony in the fact that Waldheim, whose own secret Nazi past had not yet been exposed, was ready to act to help Wiesenthal to clear his name. Wiesenthal appreciated it and regarded Waldheim as an honest man.[4] In 1971, Waldheim ran for president for the first time. Wiesenthal, who had always supported the Conservative Party, backed him, but Waldheim failed to win and he was nominated to be the secretary-general of the United Nations. Quite naturally, various people began to look into his past.

In December 1971, Wiesenthal received a letter from the Anti-Defamation League of B'nai B'rith. The organization wanted to know what the new UN secretary-general had done during the war. Wiesenthal replied immediately that everything was fine and there was nothing to worry about. "Nothing prejudicial about him from the war time has been known of," he wrote. "The matter already has been examined in Austria but has been unmask [*sic*] as gossip spread by his political adversaries which could not pass a verification. I myself know Mr. Kurt Waldheim very well. I personally had only the best impression of Mr. Waldheim during my contacts with him."[5]

On the level of the personal relations between the two men this was perfectly correct, but Wiesenthal, who had checked the pasts of so many politicians from other camps, had accepted Waldheim's story at face value. There had been nothing to stop him doing then what he did a few years later: obtaining a copy of Waldheim's personal army service file. But he did not deem it necessary then and chose to believe Waldheim.

Wiesenthal wasn't alone in this. No one seems to have tried digging into Waldheim's past—not the Soviet Union, not the United States, not Israel, and not the World Jewish Congress. Later on, it was rumored that Waldheim may have been blackmailed, but there is no evidence to support it. The incriminating documents that disclosed his lies could have been discovered much earlier on, but apparently, as had happened in the case of Eichmann and some other Nazi criminals, the secrets of Waldheim's past remained untouched in the cardboard files for the simple reason that nobody really cared. Waldheim's official biography sufficed, at least until 1979.[6]

In the 1970s, a strongly hostile attitude toward Israel had crystallized in the United Nations. Waldheim's position as secretary-general made him a partner in this attitude.

In 1974 he allowed Yasser Arafat to address the General Assembly wearing a pistol on his hip. In 1975, the assembly passed a resolution equating Zionism with racism. The following year, Waldheim condemned Israel's action in rescuing the passengers of a hijacked Air France plane who were being held hostage in Entebbe, Uganda. On a visit to Yad Vashem, he had refused to put on a yarmulke in the Hall of Remembrance, although it is considered a consecrated site because the ashes of Jewish Holocaust victims are interred there, including some of those brought by Wiesenthal in 1949.

In 1979, Wiesenthal visited his friends at Yad Vashem. The conversation turned to Waldheim and his negative attitude toward Israel. Someone proposed that his past be subjected to fresh scrutiny. On his return to Vienna, Wiesenthal asked the German publisher Axel Springer to help, assuming that he would be able to get the information more quickly, and indeed within a few days it was there on his desk.

The Berlin Document Center, an American-controlled archive that in those days held the Nazi Party card index and the personal files of SS members, stated that Waldheim had not belonged to the party or to any other Nazi organization. A French archive that held information about the German army reported that he had served in the military and gave details. Wiesenthal phoned his friends at Yad Vashem and told them that Waldheim had not been a Nazi.[7]

The material he obtained from the French archive, however, revealed to Wiesenthal what Eli Rosenbaum learned from it years later: Waldheim had lied. In contrast to what was stated in his official biography, his military service did not end when he was wounded in 1941; instead, he had gone back into active service after a few months. This material also contained the name of the Wehrmacht army group that he served with. Later on, Wiesenthal claimed that he could not check the past of thousands of soldiers and hundreds of officers, but this was not sufficient explanation. The very fact that Waldheim had concealed the continuation of his active service should have aroused Wiesenthal's suspicion. Checking the history of the army group Waldheim served with would have revealed that it had committed war crimes in Greece and elsewhere. Wiesenthal had known about the destruction of Greek Jewry for years and he had even appeared as a witness at one of the trials that dealt with it.[8]

He knew a great deal about Wehrmacht crimes, but as was still the rule in those days, he concentrated mainly on those Germans and Austrians who had volunteered for the SS and he tended to leave regular army personnel alone. As in the case of Friedrich Peter, the very fact that someone had served in the SS tarred him in Wiesenthal's eyes, even if no evidence was found that he had personally taken part in the perpetration of war crimes. Wehrmacht men, on the other hand, were considered innocent until proven guilty. "It would never occur to me to prosecute a soldier who in the face of an enemy defended his life with his weapon," he wrote. He asserted that he was more interested in those who had not dared to reach the front lines, but had instead abused the inmates of concentration camps.[9]

An acquaintance in New York, Hillel Seidman, asked Wiesenthal about Waldheim's past in the wake of rumors that surfaced in 1981. Wiesenthal replied that he "was not very happy about it." He had checked Waldheim's wartime past "and couldn't find anything indicating that he was involved in crimes" against Jews or anyone else, he wrote, and he reiterated his basic view that not every German officer was a Nazi officer.

It was an ideological question, he explained. Waldheim had never been a member of the Nazi Party. After the Germans occupied Austria, they conscripted everyone into the armed forces. There was no alternative: everyone had to join up. "We must concentrate on those who are really guilty. We cannot call anybody a Nazi because he is not a friend of Israel." Some Wehrmacht units "took part in the murdering of Jews, but we must not forget that we search for the individual and not for the collective guilt," he concluded.[10]

As of 1979, then, Wiesenthal knew that Waldheim had lied, but without actually examining what Waldheim had in fact done during his army service, he continued to believe in his innocence. He had known and admired Waldheim for a long time, supported him politically, and, most importantly, had already stated years before that he was clean. His ease of access to the UN secretary-general flattered Wiesenthal, and he recruited Waldheim to help in the effort to catch Mengele. Waldheim promised to help and Wiesenthal heaped praise on him: "You are a true advocate of justice," he wrote to him. For his part, Waldheim lauded Wiesenthal's efforts in "mobilizing world opinion against the crimes of Nazism, insuring that these should not be forgotten and above all should never be repeated," as well as his role in the struggle against genocide and racism, in the spirit of the United Nations.[11] Wiesenthal may have been able to extort something out of Waldheim, but there is no reason to suspect that he actually tried to do so. There is also no reason to assume that Waldheim knew that Wiesenthal had discovered his secret.

2. Deep Throat

Eli Rosenbaum didn't know all this when he arrived in Vienna in January 1986, but the member of the Social Democratic Party whom he met through Zelman laid down one condition: he must not under any circumstances contact Wiesenthal; if he did so, they would break off their connection with him. Rosenbaum was astonished, and the man explained that Wiesenthal supported Waldheim and would therefore cover up for him.

Rosenbaum accepted the condition and in so doing acquired an enemy. There was nothing that would annoy Wiesenthal more than being left out of an investigation like this. When he heard about it, his old animosity toward the WJC over its neglect of the hunt for Eichmann flared up anew. In itself, the probe did not surprise him—he saw it as part of the presidential election battle.

Rosenbaum described his stay in Vienna as being like an episode from a thriller. Although he was now operating behind Wiesenthal's back, he coveted the Nazi hunter's aura of mystery. He camouflaged the name of his contact man, and in his book he described him as a cross between Graham Greene's "Third Man" and "Deep Throat" of Watergate fame. Wiesenthal later believed that he had discovered the identity of this man and gave his name as Peter Schieder, a Social Democratic member of Parliament.[12] Either way, it seems that the informant had no trouble obtaining the material he gave Rosenbaum; Waldheim's file was in a government archive, and the coalition government was then headed by the Social Democratic Party.

The material, including a photograph taken in 1943 of Waldheim in uniform, exposed the former UN secretary-general as a liar. In the ensuing months, Rosenbaum enthusiastically threw himself into the inquiry, as did his colleagues at the WJC. Many years later, Rosenbaum recounted that at no stage did he and his partners ever ask themselves why the WJC should bare Waldheim's past. They saw it as a self-evident moral duty.

As an organization, the WJC had a reason to be annoyed with Austria. In January 1985, it had held a conference in Vienna as a gesture of reconciliation and goodwill. While the conference was under way, a well-known Nazi criminal, Walter Reder, an SS officer who had been in prison in Italy since 1951 for his role in the murder of 1,800 civilians, returned home after his life sentence had been commuted at the request of the Austrian government.

He was accorded something approaching a state welcome. The minister of defense, Friedhelm Frischenschlager, shook his hand. Some WJC delegates demanded that the conference be halted in protest. Leon Zelman hastily arranged for an apology to be conveyed in a phone call from the chancellor, Fred Sinowatz, to WJC president Bronfman. The Jews were persuaded to remain, but they never forgot the insult.[13]

The WJC secretary-general, Israel Singer, also had a personal reason for getting back at Austria. His father had lived in Vienna during the Nazi period, and he had been one of the Jews forced to scrub anti-Nazi slogans off the sidewalks on their knees while crowds looked on and jeered. The humiliating scene was captured in a famous photograph. The congress hated Waldheim. They saw him as a scoundrel who should be punished, and they wanted to take revenge for his unfriendly attitude to Israel.

But Waldheim was no longer UN secretary-general and it was doubtful that torpedoing his election as president of Austria was worth all the effort. It therefore seems as though the WJC officials immersed themselves in this war for another reason: they needed a goal.

In the 1970s, the organization had focused on the struggle for Soviet Jewry. This campaign was accompanied by ferocious competition between Jewish committees and action groups all over America. The more vociferous they were, it seemed, the greater their loyalty to their Jewish identity. In the mid-1980s, the Cold War was nearing its end and the fight for Jewish rights in the Soviet Union was also losing momentum. The campaign against Waldheim enabled the WJC to once again meet the need of American Jews to identify with a lofty and patriotic goal.

The material Rosenbaum brought from Vienna left no room for doubt that Waldheim had lied, but the "young Turks," as Singer characterized the congress's action- and publicity-hungry activists, would not make do with that. They wanted to label Waldheim as a war criminal, so they hired a historian and sent him to rummage through the archives.[14]

Rumors that incriminating evidence against Waldheim would somehow pop up before the elections had been circulating in Vienna for some time, and reached a reporter for the magazine *Profil*, Herbertus Czernin. The editor of the weekly, Peter Michael Lingens, once an aide to Wiesenthal, suggested to Waldheim that he allow Czernin to go over his personal file in the state archives. Waldheim agreed. It turned out that he had been a member of both the Nazi student association and the mounted unit of the SA, or storm troopers, the organization that helped the Nazis seize power.[15] This was a story. It appeared in the media for the first time in March 1986, first in *Profil* and the next day in the *New York Times* in a well-coordinated move.

The story on the front page of the *Times* said that Waldheim had served as a counterintelligence officer in a unit that had been responsible for the deportation of Greek Jews to death camps, and had waged a war of annihilation against the partisans in Yugoslavia. Under the headline FILES SHOW KURT WALDHEIM SERVED UNDER WAR CRIMINAL, the paper, even at that point, said the documents revealed little about Waldheim's actions and it was possible that ultimately the worst allegation against him would be that he had not revealed the truth about his past.[16] That is precisely what happened. In fact, one may assume that if he had not concealed the second part of his military service, no one would have bothered to examine the details. It was all about lying, not about war crimes.

But the headline in that first *Times* story linked Waldheim to war crimes, and a little later his name turned up on a list of war criminals that the Yugoslav government had drawn up as early as 1947. Also, another photograph of Waldheim was found, in uniform at the front, as well as further documents, some of them in his own handwriting. He had been there and he knew everything. Wiesenthal was beside himself with embarrassment.

Within the four walls of his office, Wiesenthal called Waldheim a "dope" and an opportunist. From the day in 1979 when he first discovered that Waldheim had concealed his military past, he knew, or so he claimed, that the affair would blow up in Waldheim's face.[17] But when it did happen, it was as if a gigantic snowball were rolling toward Wiesenthal as well. The phones in his office didn't stop ringing—everyone wanted his comment.

Wiesenthal was very cautious. Even in his very first reaction he did not rule out the possibility that Waldheim had lied. The *Times* quoted him as saying that "he questioned how Mr. Waldheim could have been unaware of the deportations" of the Jews from Salonika, but that "he was convinced Mr. Waldheim had not been a member of the Nazi Party."[18] Wiesenthal believed this, but he realized that the character reference he had given Waldheim years before without checking his past could now cause him a great deal of damage. If it emerged that Waldheim was not only a liar but also a war criminal, Wiesenthal was liable to lose his most important asset—his credibility. In order to minimize the damage, he agreed to help Waldheim. Everything was done clandestinely but wholeheartedly, because Wiesenthal was not only defending Waldheim, he was defending himself.

3. Expert Advice

One of the first people to call Wiesenthal that week was Ferdinand Trautt-mansdorff, an aide in Waldheim's presidential election campaign. A member of one of Austria's old aristocratic families, he was only three years older than Eli Rosenbaum. He was also a lawyer and he too had admired Wiesenthal since he was a teenager. His father, a well-known writer, encouraged him to read Anne Frank's diary, and one day, in June 1966, he took him to hear a lecture by Wiesenthal in the city of Graz. Wiesenthal spoke about the Murer affair, and how the Nazi criminal had time and again managed to evade punishment.

In the hall there were some young men wearing lederhosen; he asked his father who they were, and he told him they were Nazis. They were openly hostile and when question time came they asked Wiesenthal what he thought about the bombing of Dresden. Wiesenthal maintained his poise, Trauttmansdorff recalled, and the main message he derived from the occasion was that the Austrians need not be ashamed to be Austrians, there was no collective guilt, but they were not doing enough to punish Nazi criminals.

After the lecture, his father went up to Wiesenthal and invited him for a drink. All of a sudden, Wiesenthal burst into tears. Why should he have to suffer confrontations with young neo-Nazis twenty years after the Holocaust? he asked, weeping. Trauttmansdorff never forgot that moment. In time he joined the Austrian foreign service and served as his country's ambassador to several countries. Waldheim asked him to join his team of advisers in 1986.

Trauttmansdorff remembered Waldheim as an introverted man, addicted to secrecy. It was said about him that when he read an unfriendly piece about himself in a newspaper, he marked it "classified" and ordered that it be filed away in the archive. When items about his past began to appear, he did not make things easy for his aides. He claimed that he could not remember where he had been and when, what he did and didn't do. He tended to see the first items merely as a nuisance, and an attempt by American Jews to interfere in the elections.

Trauttmansdorff asked Waldheim if he had been a Nazi, and Waldheim assured him he had not. Trauttmansdorff believed him, but in contrast to his boss he grasped that Waldheim was facing a genuine threat. He found it difficult to advise him what to do, partly because he did not know how to interpret the documents the World Jewish Congress had handed to the media. And then he remembered the man who knew how to read such documents, and phoned Wiesenthal.[19]

During the ensuing weeks, Wiesenthal served as a kind of confidential adviser. Trauttmansdorff recalled that he paid at least ten visits to his office, and made innumerable phone calls. Waldheim himself also phoned; usually he called Wiesenthal at home in the late evening hours and in time he also sent him a personal letter of thanks for his "objective attitude."[20]

Wiesenthal's assistance mostly took the form of placing the documents that cast suspicion on Waldheim in their historical context, geographically and chronologically. He knew the abbreviations used to identify military units, he knew who the people mentioned in the documents were, and he could direct Trauttmansdorff to the archives in Germany where he could find evidence to counter the allegations.

Wiesenthal may have known a thing or two about public relations in America, but in the face of the WJC's methods he never had a chance. The Americans produced more and more documents, attaching summaries in English and releasing them for publication in the morning hours, New York time. In Vienna, that was late in the day and by the time Waldheim's staffers had woken up to the need to respond, it was yesterday's news and the congress had already released more documents.

In Vienna, they relied on scholarly study of the texts, as befitted the traditions of Central European historiography. The conclusions were sometimes awkwardly worded and legalistic. For example, when Waldheim's signature was found on certain reports about his unit's activities, Wiesenthal noted that the signature was on the left-hand side of the page, which meant that it was only a signature of confirmation, like that of a notary, and that he had not compiled the report himself.[21] The world's media were not interested in that kind of detail. Similarly, attempts to explain that the Nazi organizations Waldheim belonged to were not criminal organizations like the SS also failed.

Moreover, Wiesenthal's public stance did not meet the requirements of the sensationalist atmosphere surrounding the affair. He kept on asserting that the truth must be established. Accordingly, he asked the Yugoslav government to make public everything it knew, and he also spoke to the man who replaced Waldheim as UN secretary-general, Javier Pérez de Cuéllar. This was an understandable approach for Wiesenthal, who was used to collecting evidence against war criminals. He was also not alone in taking this position. In Jerusalem, the attorney general concluded that the material published by the World Jewish Congress bore investigation but was not in itself sufficient to convict Waldheim under Israel's Nazi Punishment Law.[22]

For its part, the media, as usual, disdained the question marks; it wanted a second Eichmann.[23] Wiesenthal was not satisfying its hunger and it began to turn on him. Meanwhile, in Austria a groundswell of anti-Semitism was gathering momentum; it too was naturally directed against Wiesenthal. He was flooded with hate mail saying things like "Hitler killed far too few Jews." The Jewish community of Vienna also came in for a plethora of abuse and threats.[24]

WJC officials did not consult the heads of the community before they decided to intervene in the Austrian political process. None of them had ever had a taste of life under a dictatorship, nor had they experienced anti-Semitism, hence their lack of understanding for Austrian society and their attitude toward the country's Jews. In an interview with *Profil*, two WJC officials, Singer and Elan Steinberg, warned that if Waldheim were elected president Austria would suffer, as would each one of its citizens. Now the clash was no longer simply between the WJC and Kurt Waldheim, but between "world Jewry" and the Austrian nation. Waldheim's election posters began including the slogan "Now More Than Ever!" Jewish community leaders phoned Singer and objected to his statements. Singer advised them to emigrate.[25]

On the eve of the election, Wiesenthal wrote to Abe Foxman, national director of the Anti-Defamation League, that it seemed as though Waldheim was about to win and that to some extent this would be due to the World Jewish Congress and Mr. Singer. "The only losers in this election no matter who gets elected will be the Jews," Wiesenthal wrote, and added: "Why has Elie Wiesel nothing to say?"[26] And indeed, Waldheim was elected on June 6, 1986. On the same day Wiesenthal proposed that an international panel of historians be set up to examine his past, and his proposal was accepted.

About eighteen months later the panel concluded in its report that Waldheim had been present in regions where war crimes were committed, had
known about them, and had not protested against them. Among these
crimes was the deportation of the Jews of Salonika to death camps. The
panel rejected Waldheim's denials and in so doing declared him to be a
liar. He emerged from the historians' report as an opportunist, exactly
as Wiesenthal had observed earlier. The panel did not find evidence that
Waldheim committed crimes himself, and this too bore out the basic position Wiesenthal had adopted from the beginning: his brief was to hunt
down murderers, not liars, he reiterated time and again. The day after the
publication of the report, he demanded that Waldheim resign.[27]

The World Jewish Congress did not wait for the panel to finish its job.
While it was still studying the evidence, Bronfman declared that Waldheim
was a war criminal and the organization initiated a move to get Waldheim
added to the list of several tens of thousands of people from all over
the world, most of them criminals, who were not permitted to enter the
United States.[28] This was done in April 1987, after a quasi-legal process.[29]
Wiesenthal tried unsuccessfully to get the director of the OSI, the Justice
Department's special unit, to drop the matter.[30] Having his name added
to the watch list was a severe blow to the prestige of the Austrian president and a great victory for the WJC. About a year later, Eli Rosenbaum
rejoined the OSI and after a while he became its director.

The more successful the WJC was in exposing Waldheim's past, the greater
the organization's hostility toward Wiesenthal grew. In internal memos
officials usually called him just "Simon," but in one memo someone came
up with the epithet "Sleazenthal" to express their feelings of disgust at
what they perceived as his crookedness.[31] They saw him as the main obstacle in their struggle against Waldheim and treated him as the enemy.

Rosenbaum cultivated a relationship with a former employee of Wiesenthal's who had deserted, taking with her documents that could have
embarrassed him. Through some mysterious circumstances, the WJC also
got its hands on copies of classified cables from the Israeli ambassador
in Vienna to the Foreign Ministry in Jerusalem. Like Wiesenthal, Ambassador Michel Elitzur thought the crusade against Waldheim was not in
Israel's interests.[32]

Rosenbaum agreed to testify on behalf of a detractor of Wiesenthal who had attacked him in the pages of the *Jerusalem Post*. Wiesenthal had sued the man and the paper for libel and earned an apology. Rosenbaum also filed away attacks on Wiesenthal by Beate Klarsfeld.[33]

With Rosenbaum's return to the Justice Department, the tone that the OSI employed toward Wiesenthal changed. The director of the unit, Neal Sher, sent him a stinging rebuke, as if Wiesenthal were one of his employees who had not done his job properly: "The vast majority of your allegations were of little value . . . you have not provided OSI with any concrete evidence against individuals blamed in your correspondence . . . No allegation which has originated from your office has resulted in a court filing by OSI."[34]

Wiesenthal was trying in the meantime to distance himself from Waldheim. Once the president suddenly appeared at a lecture Wiesenthal was giving at the University of Vienna. Wiesenthal did not know in advance that he was coming. He stopped his address in the middle and walked out.[35] But this did not help him in America. Jews from across the United States kept sending him angry, abusive letters. One of them, who signed himself only as "a Jew," said Wiesenthal was "a Hitler who believes his 'friend' Waldheim is innocent."[36]

Many of the correspondents identified themselves as jurists or judges. A New York State Supreme Court judge, Peter Berkowsky, wrote to say that Wiesenthal's support for Waldheim had deeply hurt not only him but also his in-laws, who were Holocaust survivors. Wiesenthal replied in a five-page letter, saying that he had never defended Waldheim, but he was defending Jewish ethics. "It is against Jewish ethics to voice collective threats and accusations," he wrote. "Not only is it against Jewish ethics, we also may not ignore the fact that for 2,000 years Jews have been victims of collective accusations." He wrote innumerable similar letters. Alfred D. Lerner, another New York State Supreme Court judge, accepted his explanations and apologized, but this was an exception.[37]

4. The Price

When he refused to join in the campaign against Waldheim, Wiesenthal assumed that the Los Angeles center bearing his name would fall into line with him, despite the constant tension between them. But Rabbi Hier was blessed with political instincts of unequaled sensitivity. He discerned the intensity of the hysteria surrounding the issue, and he tried to extract from Wiesenthal statements against Waldheim that were as bellicose as possible.

But the most Wiesenthal would permit Hier to say in his name was that he did not believe Waldheim and he did not support him. Hier feared that Wiesenthal's image would collapse, taking with it the network of sponsors and donors that he had built up. He too had begun to get abusive mail. In April 1986 he wrote to then secretary of state George P. Shultz telling him that he supported an investigation against Waldheim, and he sent a copy to Singer.[38]

About a week before the election, Wiesenthal heard that the Los Angeles center was distributing postcards addressed to President Ronald Reagan demanding that Waldheim's name be placed on the watch list of persons barred from entering the United States. The previous evening he had spoken on the phone with Hier, who had not told him about this campaign. Wiesenthal could barely control his temper: "I am very angry because you seem to think that I am an idiot who can only be told part of the truth," he wrote to Hier, and assured him that this act would not go unanswered.[39]

Two days later he sent another letter to Hier, saying that he had decided to move to Los Angeles for a stay of at least six months so that he could take personal control of the center's activities. "You lack the people who can criticize you," he wrote. "You only have people who say yes to everything." All the arrangements had been made, he said, and he was bringing with him an English-speaking secretary.[40] But Hier seems to have handled this crisis like all those that preceded it, and Wiesenthal remained in Vienna.

Hier believed he had not yet capitalized on Wiesenthal's name to the full extent possible. After securing for him almost every possible honor that it was possible to arrange from Los Angeles, he now set his sights on the highest honor of all, and he began working on getting a Nobel Peace Prize for him. The main rival was Washington's candidate, Elie Wiesel.

In 1985, President Reagan visited the military cemetery at Bitburg in Germany, where a number of Waffen SS personnel were buried. The visit aroused a storm of protests. After the visit, a fierce argument broke out among German historians and the nation began to shape a new attitude toward its past. From the outside, it seemed as though Germany was also beginning to shake off responsibility for the crimes of the Nazis. Against this background, there were rumors that the Nobel Peace Prize for that year, the fortieth anniversary of the war's end, would express the burgeoning awareness of the Holocaust.

Wiesenthal had been nominated for the prize several times before. A group of Dutch parliamentarians and a judge in Chicago had put his name forward in accordance with the regulations.[41] He believed he had a chance, but by March 1985 he had already prepared an explanation in the event that he did not get it: "I know that it will make you happy [if] I receive the Nobel Prize but I won't because the activities of the center and its publicity about it are killing my chances," he complained to Hier. His friends in the Dutch parliament had advised him to keep the matter a secret, because anything that might be perceived as an attempt to influence the judges could be counterproductive.[42]

Hier knew better. "I am not convinced by your analysis that the best thing in terms of the Nobel Prize is simply to remain quiet and let it happen," he wrote to Wiesenthal, and he sent him messages framed as intelligence reports. They knew that Wiesel was engaging in a worldwide effort to promote his candidacy. Not only had a number of professors been asked to back him, but he had "also been advised to step up his high profile in those areas." With this in mind, he had gone to Oslo, where the prize is awarded, for a series of lectures. He would be the featured speaker at a conference on hate and anti-Semitism in France under the auspices of President François Mitterrand. He demanded that Reagan cancel his visit to Bitburg. He was also about to travel to Ethiopia to distribute food to the hungry.

There was no question in Hier's mind that this was a worthwhile effort for Wiesel. The prize would not just happen; it had to be worked for. But Wiesenthal refused to take orders from him. "We too could have written to distinguished parliamentarians and organized speaking engagements for you in Oslo, a mission to Ethiopia; but it is only because we respect your wishes that we have not done so," Hier remarked.[43] Wiesenthal did travel to Oslo, where he spoke about the rights of the Native Americans, and he returned to Vienna full of hope.[44]

While he was in Oslo, a German reporter asked him what he thought about Elie Wiesel. Wiesenthal replied in writing, from Vienna, saying he regarded Wiesel as a great writer, despite the fact that he had attacked him for speaking about the non-Jewish Holocaust victims, like the Gypsies, whom Wiesel had forbidden the Holocaust Museum to mention. "In America, he is a superchauvinist; in Europe, where different winds blow, he plays the humanist," he concluded.[45]

In the months that followed, Wiesenthal ensconced himself in the certainty that he would get the prize. At worst, he would have to share it with

Wiesel, he believed, and it never even occurred to him that Wiesel would win the Nobel on his own. A few hours before the announcement in Oslo, Wiesenthal phoned Martin Rosen, his attorney and friend in New York, and told him to get his tuxedo ready. "You're going to Oslo," he told him solemnly, and added that according to his information, he was going to share the prize with Wiesel.

On Monday, October 15, 1986, Wiesenthal was visibly tense when he arrived at his office. The staff sat around him waiting for the announcement from Oslo. When it came and they heard that Wiesel had won the prize on his own, everyone burst into tears, except Wiesenthal. But he was stunned, and he immediately told himself how it had happened: the World Jewish Congress was to blame.[46]

The deliberations of the Nobel Prize judges remain classified for at least fifty years, so that the records of the committee that selected the 1986 laureate will be opened only in 2036, if at all. But two of the members, including former Norwegian prime minister Odvar Nordli, confirmed that the panel had discussed Wiesenthal's candidacy, but refused to comment on the possibility that anyone had demanded he should not get the prize. The WJC denied having contacted the committee, and that is what its leaders told Wiesenthal as well.

It is reasonable to assume that Wiesenthal didn't get the prize because he was at the center of a raging controversy; the committee wanted a laureate acceptable to everyone, and the lobby that promoted Wiesel's candidacy worked well.[47] This, therefore, was the price Wiesenthal paid for his stance in the Waldheim affair. Missing out on the prize was the biggest disappointment of Wiesenthal's life. He brought it up again and again, as if he had been the victim of a great injustice, until his dying day.[48] Nevertheless, he kept on working.

5. Soul Search

Meanwhile, Eli Rosenbaum was busy on his book about the Waldheim case, whose name said it all: *Betrayal*, with Wiesenthal featured as the betrayer. It was a very personal book. Rosenbaum wrote it in the first person and freely shared his feelings with the reader. The impression was that even in adulthood, Rosenbaum was still the lad who had just discovered the horrors of the Holocaust and managed to find a place for them among the foundations of his Jewish identity, and believed in Wiesenthal. When he needed him, like a Hasid needs his rabbi, or like a son his father, he did not find an outstretched hand. The further he progressed in his work, the greater the obsessive hostility he developed toward Wiesenthal.

When he discovered for the first time that Wiesenthal knew Waldheim had hidden the truth about his military service, he was "flabbergasted."[49] He wrote: "My blood was boiling by now. Despair, exasperation and ire combined to create a fury that frightened even me. I felt a tingling sensation as my face flushed red with anger."[50] He felt a powerful need to explain to himself how his boyhood idol could have let him down so, and he found the reply in a letter to the *New York Times*.

In this letter, Wiesenthal related how in 1979 he had checked into Waldheim's past and learned that he had not been a member of a Nazi organization. He said he had done this at Israel's request. But as he had often done before, he was indulging in dramatic overstatement. Almost certainly it was not "Israel" that had asked him to do it, just as it had not been "Israel" that congratulated him after Eichmann was captured, as he always claimed, but his friends at the Yad Vashem archive. It was these friends who had initiated the probe into Waldheim's record, as Wiesenthal himself recounted later.[51]

Aside from his letter to the *Times*, there is no evidence that he investigated Waldheim's past at the request of Israel. But Rosenbaum thought he had found the answer to the question that had long bothered him, and that he now understood why Israel had not done what he and his colleagues did, and had not exposed the Austrian president's lies. It had refrained from doing so because Wiesenthal had misled the Israelis into thinking there was nothing to expose, Rosenbaum believed. He was now fighting Wiesenthal as if he were a greater enemy than Waldheim. "I was struck by a pathetic irony," he wrote. "Simon Wiesenthal and Kurt Waldheim were two Austrians who shared at least one fault: an inability to tell a consistent story about their wartime experiences."[52]

Indeed, comparisons between Wiesenthal's books and his statements to the media had produced certain inconsistencies, contradictions, and fabrications. Using these, Rosenbaum tried to prove that Wiesenthal had manufactured his identity as a Nazi hunter, and mocked his failure to find Mengele, Bormann, and other Nazis.

Wiesenthal always claimed that he had never accused anyone without having proof of their guilt in his possession.[53] Rosenbaum pointed to a number of cases that apparently proved the opposite. A Canadian governmental commission of inquiry into the search for fugitive Nazi criminals in that country had leveled criticism at material supplied by Wiesenthal. Rosenbaum was indignant over this story not having been widely covered in the American media. "I realized again that the media lacked the stomach (or was it the heart?) to report the truth about Wiesenthal. It was a phenomenon upon which he had successfully relied for decades," he wrote.[54]

It is true that many of the people who were indicted at Wiesenthal's initiative were eventually acquitted, but so were others who were prosecuted at the initiative of law enforcement agencies. Wiesenthal claimed he had handled more than three thousand cases, and that thanks to his actions 1,100 Nazi criminals were brought to trial. He did not disabuse those who wanted to believe that all these were convicted; it is impossible to calculate the exact number who were.[55]

In a special file, Rosenbaum gathered all the publications he could find that attributed the capture of Eichmann to Wiesenthal. These publications also greatly annoyed Wiesenthal's old antagonist, Isser Harel. In 1988, Harel wrote a new account of the Eichmann operation, 278 pages dedicated to proving that Wiesenthal's contribution was zero. He had already stated this more than once, but the manuscript he now produced contained several details about the operation that had not been published before. Some of them proved the opposite of what Harel was contending. The draft was small-minded and quarrelsome, and was never published.

In the twenty-five years that had gone by since he retired as head of Israel's security services, Harel had entered politics and served one term as a member of the Knesset, but he failed as a politician and began to write books. A contentious character, embittered and frustrated, he remained on the sidelines of Israeli history. However, this didn't prevent Rosenbaum from quoting his manuscript as if Harel were an objective authority whose version of events was trustworthy and conclusive proof that Wiesenthal was an impostor, or, as Rosenbaum described him elsewhere, "a faker."[56] Many years later, the Israeli government presented certificates of honor to the people who caught Eichmann, signed by the prime minister. Wiesenthal was one of the recipients, together with Harel and others. By then, both Harel and Wiesenthal were no longer alive.[57]

———

In Austria, the Waldheim affair led to a painful confrontation between parents and children, and liberated the Austrians from some of the myths that had shielded them from the truth about their responsibility for the crimes of the Nazis. Wiesenthal had always longed for such a development. Austria learned to admit that it had not been "the first victim" of Nazi Germany, as they had always claimed, but had willingly been annexed to Hitler's Third Reich, and they also learned that the army, as well as the SS, had played a part in the crimes of the Nazis.

Ferdinand Trauttmansdorff was appointed counsel to the Austrian embassy in Washington; his chief role was to mend fences between his country and the Jewish organizations in America.[58]

But the Waldheim affair also bolstered the extreme right wing in Austria, led by Jörg Haider. Wiesenthal followed these developments apprehensively. The two men provoked each other. Wiesenthal declared that Nazi ideas were still popular in Haider's party, and Haider sued him for libel. Before the hearings began, he sent Wiesenthal a long letter proposing that they meet for a clarifying conversation. Wiesenthal refused, and Haider withdrew his suit.[59]

Wiesenthal filed a complaint with the police against a member of Haider's party, a mayoral candidate who told a local newspaper that crematoria for burning Jews would still be built in Austria, but not for Wiesenthal—for him, "Jörgl's pipe" would have to do. The man, Peter Muller, was sentenced to pay a fine.[60]

Wiesenthal also considered taking legal measures against Rosenbaum's book. *Betrayal,* which carried blurbs from Elie Wiesel and Alan Dershowitz on its cover, enjoyed maximum exposure in the American media, including top television programs, in which Wiesenthal also participated.[61] But reviewers in the leading newspapers expressed reservations about the book, and it did not become a bestseller. Wiesenthal's lawyers therefore advised him to let the matter go. It was not translated into German. Wiesenthal hoped it would be forgotten. Despite his advanced age, he tried to keep on working as usual.[62]

In the late 1980s, as Wiesenthal approached his eightieth birthday, he hoped to receive as a gift something he had wanted for many years: the Argentinean government was about to extradite Josef Schwammberger, the commandant of the Przemyśl ghetto. His name had cropped up in the course of Wiesenthal's work since 1947 and it also had a place in Israel's Holocaust remembrance narrative, thanks to the story of Michael Goldman. As a young boy in Przemyśl, Goldman had been caught stealing some bread and was taken to Schwammberger, who punished him with eighty lashes from his whip. Somehow Goldman survived and reached Israel. When he told his relatives about his punishment, they thought he was lying or exaggerating. If the story was true, they said, he would have been dead. He couldn't persuade them, and this, he said later, was "the eighty-first lash." The tale became a symbol, for fifteen years after his ordeal Israeli police officer Michael Gilead, as he was now named, was one of the interrogators of Adolf Eichmann and, after the trial, one of the witnesses to his execution. Wiesenthal devoted great effort to finding Schwammberger.[63]

At the end of the 1940s, Schwammberger was in detention in Innsbruck, Austria, for a while. When he was arrested, the authorities seized a large quantity of jewelry, including watches and rings, which he had stolen from his victims during the war. It was deposited with the court and was meant to serve as evidence against him in his trial. But Schwammberger managed to escape. Wiesenthal discovered that the jewelry was put up for sale, with the proceeds going to the court.[64]

Schwammberger's name came up several times over the years in a number of trials. In 1972 Wiesenthal discovered that he was living in La Plata, Argentina. At his initiative, West Germany requested Schwammberger's extradition and Argentinean police officers went to arrest him. But someone had tipped him off, and he had disappeared.

Wiesenthal continued to deal with the case, and at a certain stage the German government announced a prize of a quarter of a million deutschmarks for information leading to Schwammberger's indictment. The Wiesenthal Center in Los Angeles published his name in its list of the ten most-wanted war criminals. Wiesenthal's man in Buenos Aires, José Moskovits, placed it in a local newspaper, and one day someone called the German embassy with Schwammberger's address. This time he was arrested.

Wiesenthal didn't get his extradition as a birthday gift because Schwammberger's attorneys succeeded in delaying the process, but he did eventually manage to make it to the opening of the trial in Stuttgart.

The court found Schwammberger guilty and sentenced him to life imprisonment. He died in prison several years later.

Wiesenthal's last annual bulletins mention some of the names that had occupied him from the start of his activities. He never let them go. Here and there, new names cropped up. He still managed to rack up some successes, and as ever, there were many more failures. Again and again, his quarries were acquitted, or simply died, such as Egon Sabukoschek, who had been a vicious war criminal in Yugoslavia. In 1992 Wiesenthal announced that he had been located. Three years later he died. "And so this case was also closed," Wiesenthal wrote.[65] The press conference he convened to announce that he had found Sabukoschek was the last of his life.

In 1994, Wiesenthal helped ABC television find a man named Erich Priebke in Argentina. He had been one of the heads of the Gestapo in Italy. The network's correspondent interviewed Wiesenthal, and Rabbi Abraham Cooper of the Wiesenthal Center traveled to Rome to demand that Prime Minister Silvio Berlusconi initiate extradition proceedings against Priebke, and this was done. Still, it was a shameful affair. Priebke enjoyed the patronage of people in Germany and Italy. He was sentenced to life imprisonment, under house arrest.[66] Wiesenthal was now eighty-seven, and marking the fiftieth anniversary of the start of his endeavors. And then another blow struck.

On February 8, 1996, the German television station ARD devoted an edition of its prestigious *Panorama* investigative program to Rosenbaum's allegations, under the title "The End of a Legend." Wiesenthal was presented as a liar. The impression that was left on viewers was that his entire career, from the day that he was liberated at Mauthausen, was no more than a hoax.

The reporters' attitude was openly hostile and sarcastic. Rosenbaum said in the program, among other things, that he estimated the number of Nazi criminals caught by Wiesenthal was fewer than ten. Asked how he would characterize Wiesenthal, he replied: "Incompetent, egomaniacal, a spreader of false information, a tragic figure."[67]

Minutes after the program ended, Wiesenthal was on the phone to his American attorney, Martin Rosen. Wiesenthal spoke from his sickbed; shortly before the broadcast his physician had ordered that he be hospitalized. "I am in despair," he said. Rosen flew to Washington to demand

Rosenbaum's dismissal from the Justice Department. He also wrote to the Democratic senator from Connecticut, Christopher Dodd, a friend of Wiesenthal's. Dodd's father, who had also been a U.S. senator, served as a prosecutor at the Nuremberg trials. "Words cannot describe our anger," Rosen wrote to Rosenbaum himself.[68]

Rosenbaum argued that he had been speaking as a private person on the broadcast, and pledged not to repeat in public his accusations against Wiesenthal. Wiesenthal's lawyers refused to accept this, and a long correspondence began between them and the heads of the Justice Department. According to Rosen, he was told that if he insisted on Rosenbaum's dismissal, the Senate would take advantage of this as an opportunity to close down the Office of Special Investigations for budgetary reasons, and this would mean the end of the search for Nazis in America. Meanwhile, Elie Wiesel sent a handwritten note to Dodd, marked CONFIDENTIAL in big block letters, saying that Rosenbaum was "a good, honest, decent and reliable man." Dodd replied to Wiesel: "Your word is good enough for me."

So Rosenbaum's job was saved, and a way to placate Wiesenthal was also found: to mark the fiftieth anniversary of the Nuremberg Trials, Attorney General Janet Reno would visit the Wiesenthal Center in Los Angeles and deliver some words of praise for Wiesenthal. Rosen demanded that she use the opportunity to apologize to him. Wiesenthal was kept informed of developments.

Reno did come to the center, but Wiesenthal's lawyers were not happy with her speech, as she refrained from apologizing. Dodd was again called in to help. In January 1997, Wiesenthal received a warm, friendly letter of appreciation from President Bill Clinton.[69] He also received many letters of support from people who had seen the German program, and they were especially important to him. With so many Jewish enemies, he found it easier to get on with Germans.

22.

"We All Made Mistakes in Our Youth"

I. Hitler's Friend

One day in January 1975, Wiesenthal burst out of his office in the Documentation Center in Vienna holding a letter in his hand and yelling to the people sitting in the front room, "You'll never believe who wants to visit us!" He paused, and then said in a near whisper, stressing each syllable: "Albert Speer."[1] His staff detected a mixture of triumph and awe in his voice. Speer had been one of Adolf Hitler's closest friends and a minister in his cabinet.

The possibility that he would climb the stairs to the third floor of the building on Rudolfsplatz and take a seat in the tiny office between the iron stove and the thousands of files bearing the names of his partners in the destruction of the Jews made Wiesenthal tremble with excitement. Years later, Michael Stergar remembered the visit as one of the most dramatic events of his period as a volunteer in the office. He was particularly impressed by Speer's thick eyebrows. "I served the coffee," he said, a slight thrill still noticeable in his voice.[2] The visit was the beginning of the strangest relationship of Wiesenthal's life.

At the time, hearings were under way in a libel suit filed against Wiesenthal by his old enemy, Erich Rajakowitsch, Eichmann's man in Holland. Wiesenthal had quoted a letter from Rajakowitsch in which the term "final solution" was used and stated that Rajakowitsch must have known that it meant the extermination of the Jews. In order to prove his case,

Wiesenthal wrote to Speer and asked him when he had heard the phrase for the first time.[3] Speer replied that Hitler and Himmler did not use the term "final solution," and he himself had heard it for the first time only after the war. He added that he had read *The Sunflower* and it had made a "deeply positive impression" on him.[4]

Wiesenthal was gratified and told Speer that he himself had not managed to overcome the problem he had presented to the participants in the project: to forgive or not to forgive. In passing, he recounted the difficulties he was encountering in having the book adapted for the screen, including money problems. "A good idea in itself does not appeal to film financers today. They want to get sex and crime into everything," he wrote. He also seized the opportunity to lay out a theory about the origins of Hitler's anti-Semitism that had preoccupied him for some time: Did Speer believe it was possible that he hated them because he had been infected with syphilis by a Jewish prostitute? He had heard this from the son of a doctor who had treated Hitler, Wiesenthal wrote, but he assumed he would not get far in probing this matter, he noted.[5] Speer was unable to help.

Wiesenthal may have taken his relationship with Speer as proof of his argument that Nazi criminals should not be executed, because they could supply replies to historical questions, the main reason he had objected to the execution of Eichmann. But his first two letters to Speer also expressed a surprising degree of openness, as if Speer were an old acquaintance. Speer took advantage of the correspondence to invite himself to call on Wiesenthal. He had actually wanted to come two years earlier, he wrote, but hadn't known what the correct approach would be.[6]

At the beginning of Hitler's march to power, Speer was a young architect. Hitler saw in him the artist that he himself had wanted to be, and he gave Speer commissions to design large projects. A deep friendship developed between the two men. In 1942, Hitler appointed Speer minister of armaments and war production. He was involved in, among other things, the deportation of Berlin's Jews, the construction of concentration camps, and the use of forced labor. After the war he was one of the defendants at Nuremberg.

He claimed ignorance of most of the crimes he was charged with, but he accepted political and moral responsibility for all the transgressions of the Third Reich, including the war itself and the extermination of the Jews. This stance made a favorable impression on the judges, and he was sentenced to only twenty years in prison. In 1966 he was discharged from Spandau prison in Berlin. The mayor, Willy Brandt, sent a bouquet to Speer's daughter on the day of his release, and Wiesenthal protested.[7]

After serving his term, Speer published an autobiography that became a bestseller, partly because of his repeated expressions of regret. The media everywhere treated him like a respectable celebrity. Wiesenthal also had a favorable opinion of him: "The man has served his sentence, he has admitted his guilt, he has shown contrition—more than this cannot be demanded of him, and he is therefore acceptable," he wrote.[8]

This was Wiesenthal's attitude toward many Germans, including former Nazis. Its roots were in the special treatment he received from his overseers at the Eastern Railway repair works in Lvov. After the war, he had felt a need to help them. His willingness to do so gave him a feeling of fairness; his ability to do so, a feeling of power. Reconciliation offered hope, a commodity that Wiesenthal needed.

Immediately after the end of the war, he tried to find Adolf Kohlrautz, his direct superior in Lvov. He asked Werner Schmidt, a man who had been on the rail yard staff, about Kohlrautz, and also offered Schmidt his assistance. Schmidt did not know where Kohlrautz was but said he was happy to hear that Wiesenthal was alive. He recalled with fondness and nostalgia their conversations during the war, and he asked for help. His apartment had been ruined, his son was a prisoner of the British, there was a shortage of cigarettes, he was about to lose his job because he had been a member of the Nazi Party. He needed a statement declaring that he had not committed any crimes—in triplicate, please, and make sure to mention that the letter is written by a Jew. Wiesenthal obliged.[9]

Heinrich Günthert, his former superior in Lvov, was located by Wiesenthal without much trouble and, to Wiesenthal's sorrow, he heard from Günthert that Kohlrautz had been killed in the battle for Berlin. Over the years, a warm relationship grew up between Wiesenthal and Günthert. "We all believed then that we were doing our duty," Günthert wrote to him, "but we also knew that without any connection to the requirements of the war, many things were being done that were not right, shameful, and—today it must be said—insane." He took comfort in the fact that he had been able to make life at least somewhat easier for his workers and told Wiesenthal what had happened to him since the war.

His story was the story of the whole of Germany: All his property had been destroyed in air raids, there was anxiety over his livelihood, there was hunger, he had lost weight. But he was also fortunate: he had married a girl he knew from before the war, he was working in the administration of the West German railways, and he was now trying not to put on too much weight.

Wiesenthal asked Günthert for a letter confirming that he had known Wiesenthal as an architect, although he had worked under him as a technician. There were not many people left who could confirm that Wiesenthal held a diploma, he explained, and he needed this confirmation to support his claim for reparations. He noted that all his attempts to go back to working at his beloved profession had failed. Both mentally and physically, he was no longer capable of being an architect. Günthert immediately complied. Later on, he also defended Wiesenthal from Kreisky's allegations that he had collaborated with the Gestapo. In an interview with *Profil*, he said that Wiesenthal had been a prisoner like all the others.[10]

"What a pity that there weren't another hundred thousand Güntherts during the war," Wiesenthal wrote to him. "Everything would have been different." He stuck several stamps onto his letter for Mrs. Günthert, who had started a collection, and advised her how to remove them from the envelope with lukewarm water. In December 1965, he invited Günthert to be a guest at his daughter's wedding, and he once remarked that this showed he was not out to hound all Germans.[11]

Many people found it difficult to come to terms with Wiesenthal's conciliatory attitude. One of them, a resident of San Diego, once tried to convince him that all the Germans should be killed, every last one of them. This happened during the period of anxiety that preceded the Six-Day War. In his response, Wiesenthal patiently repeated the fundamentals of his faith, as if he were using his sanity to protect and fortify himself at that nerve-racking moment in time. "I will going on to hunt down the Nazi criminals," he wrote in his own idiosyncratic English, "but I don't think that one can cover up a crime or injustice in doing other crimes which would be none better than the crimes the Nazis have done to the Jews. Everyday I receive letters from Germans who want to help me in my work. Should I try to kill these people who have done nothing but born as Germans?"[12]

In 1982, the Austrian writer Hans Weigel was reported as saying after the Israeli invasion of Lebanon that "Hebrew is the language of the cluster bomb." Wiesenthal's reaction: "When I first heard about the extermination of the Jews, I never said that German was the language of Zyklon B gas. For me, German was and is the language of Schiller and Goethe."[13]

He was treated with greater esteem in Germany than in Austria. In his own country, he was regarded as merely a local Jew, and his eagerness to become an integral part of Austrian society and, particularly, politics only damaged his standing. In West Germany he was regarded primarily as a Jew who represented the victims of the Holocaust.

The Germans were impressed by the esteem he was accorded in the United States and appreciated the respect he showed for their legal system and for their willingness and ability to cleanse themselves of their criminal past. Unlike the Austrians, they acknowledged their responsibility. Wiesenthal had a better working relationship with the German legal authorities than with those of Austria, and more cooperation from the German media as well.[14]

The enmity between Wiesenthal and the Communist bloc, as well as his conservative views, naturally led him to sympathize with the heads of the right-wing Christian Democratic Party in West Germany, despite the fact that several of those leaders, including some of the ministers in Chancellor Konrad Adenauer's cabinet, had belonged to the Nazi regime. Years after the first postwar chancellor was no longer in office, Wiesenthal wrote in a letter to Adenauer, "For me, you were and you have remained a great moral authority, a man whom I respect and admire."[15]

He was writing to protest the fact that Chancellor Kurt Georg Kiesinger had ignored certain anti-Semitic incidents. This was about a year before the chancellor was slapped by Beate Klarsfeld. But for Wiesenthal, Kiesinger was an exception. Neo-Nazi activities did not undermine his faith in German society as a whole. Later on, friendly relations would prevail between him and Chancellor Helmut Kohl. Kohl, the leader of a Germany that had become a world power, treated Wiesenthal as an embodiment of all of Jewish history and even recommended him for the Nobel Prize.[16] Kohl corresponded with him, telephoned him, and also entertained him at his vacation retreat in the mountains. Once the chancellor asked Wiesenthal about the treasures of the Tyrolean lakes. Each man was apparently flattered by the friendship of the other.

In July 1983, Kohl phoned Wiesenthal from Moscow to report on his efforts to secure the freedom of Soviet dissident Andrei Sakharov, on whose behalf Wiesenthal was active. Kohl expected that in the wake of his intervention, the Soviet authorities would allow Sakharov to return to Moscow from his place of exile, and he attributed his own participation in this matter to Wiesenthal: "You tossed me the ball, and I do not intend to drop it," he said.[17] Two years later, Wiesenthal refrained from joining in the wave of protests that followed Kohl's escorting President Reagan to the Bitburg cemetery.

The chancellor promised Wiesenthal that he would support payment of compensation to the victims of Mengele's "medical experiments." Once he conveyed a message via Wiesenthal to Israeli prime minister Yitzhak Shamir: as far as he knew, Libya did not intend to develop chemical weapons.

Kohl was one of the few world leaders who did not boycott Austrian president Waldheim. He was vehemently attacked by Edgar Bronfman, the president of the World Jewish Congress, and shared his offended feelings with Wiesenthal: "I ask myself if everything I have done for reconciliation between Jews and Germans in the past thirty-five years of political activity has been in vain," he wrote.

In his response, Wiesenthal criticized Bronfman and gave the German leader a lesson in Jewish history: "Before Hitler's rise to power, the Jews had a spiritual aristocracy, one that Hitler largely annihilated. That generation, of which we were so proud, is no more and it has not been replaced. Today we have an 'aristocracy of money' and regretfully we have to admit that actually there is no Jewish leadership." In 1990, Wiesenthal was one of the first to congratulate Kohl on the reunification of Germany. The chancellor's office made an effort to prevent the screening of the devastating *Panorama* documentary about Wiesenthal.[18]

2. The Victim and His Savior

Albert Speer built up his public image in accordance with a detailed plan that included regular contact with Jews, contributions to their charities, and conversations with scholars from the Hebrew University.[19] Naturally he had an interest in cultivating a relationship with Wiesenthal. It began as a kind of common celebrity. "You ought to see the faces of the Viennese when we take walks together," Speer was quoted as saying in the American magazine *People*, though he speedily denied saying it.[20]

"Jewish friends in America," as he wrote, had told him that Wiesenthal mentioned the relationship between them when he lectured at synagogues.

Wiesenthal used to tell his audiences that there were more than a few former Nazis who were angry about Hitler losing the war, but only Speer was angry that he started it. Speer was happy to hear this, but he warned Wiesenthal not to identify too closely with him, in order to avoid unpleasant situations.[21] The Third Reich celebrity and the Holocaust celebrity took advantage of each other. Speer expressed his satisfaction that a certain journal had reviewed their books on the same page.[22]

Wiesenthal could have seen this relationship as a personal triumph for himself as a Holocaust survivor. The friendship with Speer had given his suffering a new meaning because from now on he was dealing not with minor sadists in concentration camps, but with Hitler's own minister for armaments. It was only to be expected that he would try to extract from Speer some intelligence information.

On one occasion he asked Speer to tell him about a well-known German weapons manufacturer, Krieghoff, a supplier of military equipment to the German air force during World War II. He said he "had been asked" about similar companies and about Krieghoff in particular. His archives show that from time to time Wiesenthal was indeed still being asked for information of this nature by various people in Israel.[23] He also entertained the illusion that he was speaking to Speer as one architect to another. Speer sent him copies of the plans for the museum that Hitler had asked him to build in Linz.[24]

Sometimes they spoke to each other as frustrated authors. Wiesenthal told Speer that bookstores in Germany were boycotting his works; Speer complained that his book was not selling as well as he had expected. He promised to ask his publishers if they could do something to promote the sales of one of Wiesenthal's books.[25] Sometimes they spoke to each other as victims of injustice. Wiesenthal told Speer how hard it was to live with Kreisky's smears, and Speer sent Wiesenthal a copy of one of the abusive letters he had received from neo-Nazis.[26]

With time, the relationship between the two men took on an increasingly personal character. Wiesenthal visited Speer and his wife at their home in Heidelberg. Once he told Speer about a family matter that was causing him great anxiety: His six-year-old grandson was suffering from meningitis. Every day he called his daughter in Holland, where she lived with her family before they moved to Israel. He could think about nothing else, he told Speer. When the child recovered, he wrote: "Hopefully there will be no lasting damage; this will be known only after a year's time."[27] It was also important for him to let Speer know that his wife approved of their relationship. "I showed your letter to my wife and I said the content of this letter proves that it was written by an honest man, and she agreed with me," he wrote to Speer.[28]

At that time, Speer was working on his next book, which was to include details about his links to the SS. He was determined to publish an exchange of letters between himself and Himmler that tied him to the concentration camps, he told Wiesenthal, but, he reassured him, he did not expect to be harmed by this. "There is nothing extraordinary or dangerous," he wrote. "On the contrary, it emerges from these documents that I tried successfully to improve the sanitary conditions [in the camps] immediately after I heard of the bad situation."[29]

Two years later, Wiesenthal read in a newspaper article that it was Speer who had instigated the establishment of the Mauthausen concentration camp. He sent the clipping to Speer, who replied that he did not intend to react. "From your own experience you know well that there is no point in challenging smears like this. It happens to you every day, and it is beginning to happen to me also." This was of course, he remarked, a "grotesque allegation" and added that if it had been accurate it would certainly have been published a long time ago.[30] The truth was that Speer had inspected Mauthausen about a year and a half before Wiesenthal arrived there as a prisoner; he came not to improve the sanitary conditions, however, but to make the exploitation of the inmates' work more efficient. He was also quite familiar with Auschwitz.[31]

If Wiesenthal had realized that he was being tricked, he would have found it difficult to get out of the trap, just as he found it difficult to distance himself from Waldheim after the truth about his past came out. Because exactly as he had cleared Waldheim before learning that he had lied, he also cleared Speer: he invited him to participate in a new edition of *The Sunflower*, as if Speer were one of the intellectuals worthy of sharing their ethical musings with the world.

Speer chose his words with great care. He tried to convince Wiesenthal that he, Wiesenthal, had actually forgiven the wounded SS man in the book in the same way that he had forgiven Speer himself; in so doing, he tried to depict himself as a victim. He described their first meeting: "You showed kindness and pity, humanity and benevolence," he wrote. "You did not touch my wounds, you tried to help, you didn't rebuke me, you didn't let loose your anger at me. I looked into your eyes, they reflected each and every one of the murder victims, testimony to all of the suffering, degradation, fatalism, and torments of human beings. But somehow your eyes were not full of hatred. They remained warm, tolerant, full of sympathy for the suffering of the other." He was presumably referring to his own suffering during his incarceration, or perhaps to the defeat of his nation and the death of his friend Hitler.

For a moment, Speer deviated from his self-pity and mentioned in an almost legalistic tone that Wiesenthal had written a dedication in his copy of the book in which he acknowledged that Speer had accepted responsibility. But in the next line he went back to writing as if he had been a victim of Nazi evil, not one of its perpetrators. "It was my trauma that led me to you. You have helped me a lot, as you helped the SS man when you refrained from pulling your hand out of his and from rebuking him. Every man carries his life's burden on his shoulders, no one can take it off for him, but since we met my own burden has been lightened. God's grace has touched me, through you."

This was a very Christian text, and a very calculated one. It was written not by a criminal requesting forgiveness from his victim, but by a victim who had won absolution from his savior. Wiesenthal wrote that he was moved to the depths of his soul. "I believe that thanks to this essay the world will see you as I see you," he told Speer.[32] Speer began sending him handwritten, informal notes, and at one stage he had a personal, almost intimate, request. Would Wiesenthal be so kind as to read the manuscript of his new book before it was published? Wiesenthal obliged.[33] He imagined that he now understood not only Speer but his entire generation, whose "idealism had struck them blind," and when they realized where their chosen path had led them, it was too late. Once Wiesenthal wrote to Speer: "We all made mistakes in our youth."[34] This statement was a key to Wiesenthal's entire story.

3. From Camp to Camp

In October 1994, an official government limousine with a police escort drew up at the site of the Auschwitz death camp. Wiesenthal, now nearly eighty-six years old, had come to Poland on a visit of reconciliation. President Lech Wałesa had presented him with a state decoration, and the Jagiellonian University of Kraków awarded him an honorary doctorate. The visit was heavily loaded with symbolism. Wiesenthal was deeply moved. Again and again tears welled up in his eyes. It was not easy for him to make his peace with the Poles, but the temptation to grant them forgiveness had won his heart over.

When they entered the gate under the notorious motto *"Arbeit Macht Frei,"* Wiesenthal told his biographer, Hella Pick, who was with him on the trip, how he had been brought to Auschwitz on one of the death trains and how he had gotten out alive. They had arrived at Auschwitz from the Płaszów camp, he said, but instead of sending them to the gas chambers to be put to death, the Germans let them wait in the freight cars for three days, and then for some reason sent them to another camp, Gross-Rosen, and that was how he survived. Pick did not doubt his story, but it was apparently not true.[35]

In an autobiographical outline that he drew up in 1947, Wiesenthal described his stay at Auschwitz the same way he told it to Pick. But in the testimony he gave years later at Yad Vashem, he related precisely how it came about that he and his fellow prisoners did not reach Auschwitz. The Russians were nearing Płaszów and chaos reigned at the camp. "The Germans lost their heads," he said. "Apparently they sensed that their end was approaching. By mistake, they failed to couple our car onto the train that was going to Auschwitz and instead coupled it to the train that was taking the regular prisoners, and so we arrived by mistake at the Gross-Rosen camp."[36]

When Wiesenthal testified at the Lvov trial held in Stuttgart in 1966, he once again said explicitly that he was never at Auschwitz.[37] When he submitted his reparations claim to Germany, he attached a sworn statement from the director of the Jewish community organization in Vienna, Willi Krell, who was with him in the camps, in which Krell stated they had left Płaszów together and arrived at Gross-Rosen the next day. Krell was transferred some weeks later to Auschwitz.[38]

Auschwitz, however, had become part of Wiesenthal's public biography. In the United States, where many people tended to identify the Holocaust with Auschwitz, his purported stay at the camp was mentioned in speeches in his honor in the House of Representatives and the Senate, as well as in a background paper prepared for President Carter when Wiesenthal was awarded the Congressional Gold Medal.[39]

Wiesenthal told his life story very frequently, whether in documents he compiled for official purposes, books and letters he wrote, testimony he gave in court, interviews with journalists, or lectures he delivered. In the papers he left behind, there are at least twenty written autobiographical summaries. It is only natural that they differ on certain details, such as dates, places, and people's names.

It is therefore not possible to produce from his accounts a clear chronology of his life in Lvov, between the ghetto, the Janowska camp, and the railway repair works. It is reasonable to assume that he passed from one to the other repeatedly, under varying degrees of coercion, at one point a prisoner, at another a forced laborer, as he testified at the trial of various Janowska war criminals.[40] The story of his escape from the camp and his time in hiding also cannot be reconstructed with any chronological certitude.

This is not surprising. Wiesenthal never kept a diary and it is reasonable to assume he did not remember all the details of each ordeal he underwent, like many other Holocaust survivors who appeared as witnesses at the trials of war criminals. People who were with him in the camps and confirmed his accounts in general terms also contradicted each other on various details—the vagaries of memory are not proof of lying. A comparative study of the plethora of autobiographical material left by Wiesenthal frequently makes it possible to determine what really happened. He was never a prisoner at Auschwitz.

Wiesenthal regarded the testimony he gave at Yad Vashem as sacred, and it is evident to anyone reading this document that he tried to be accurate. He was also careful about what he said when he testified at the trials of war criminals. Again and again he told the judges that certain details were known to him only through hearsay; again and again he warned that his memory might be misleading him on everything to do with dates.

In his evidence at one trial, Wiesenthal said that he had seen a trainload of Jews standing at the platform at Lvov for three days. This may have been the origin of his story of his three days in Auschwitz, which in a later version became four days.[41] Either way, his attempt to place himself at the hub of the catastrophe—Auschwitz—was part of a set pattern, a tendency to magnify his ordeal.

Immediately after being liberated, Wiesenthal gave the names of the camps in which he had been imprisoned as Janowska, Płaszów, Gross-Rosen, and Mauthausen. On the way to the latter, he had also spent some time in a fifth camp, Buchenwald.[42] With the years, the number of camps he claimed to have passed through rose. In résumés he drew up in the 1950s, he once wrote that he had been incarcerated in nine camps, and another time eleven camps.[43] In the 1990s he approved for publication a series of biographical interviews in which it was stated that he had been in twelve camps, and Joseph Wechsberg, who edited his autobiography, wrote in his preface that Wiesenthal had been in "over a dozen" camps.[44]

In the early 1980s, Wiesenthal listed the places of imprisonment he had passed through and arrived at a total of twelve, including Auschwitz. However, six of those places were not concentration camps but small work encampments Wiesenthal passed through on his way from Janowska to Gross-Rosen. They should therefore not be counted as concentration camps in which he was an inmate.[45] He was in fact a prisoner in five camps. In his books on his wartime experiences, he tended not only to aggrandize his ordeal, but also to add a dash of drama to the circumstances of his survival.

4. From Miracle to Miracle

In his Yad Vashem testimony, Wiesenthal said that on the afternoon of July 6, 1941, he was playing chess with a neighbor in Lvov when a man wearing civilian clothes with an armband in the colors of the Ukrainian national flag came in and arrested them. The two were taken to the Brigidki jail, together with several dozen other detainees. They were told to put their hands behind their heads and face a wall. Wiesenthal said he heard shots and the men standing around him were hit and fell, one after the other. He remembered the sound of their bodies hitting the ground. At six o'clock, the shooting stopped.

Those prisoners who were still alive were placed in a cell, among them Wiesenthal and his neighbor. They waited, anticipating their deaths in the morning. During the night, the door opened and a Ukrainian came into the cell, carrying a flashlight. He recognized Wiesenthal among the prisoners and asked, "Mr. Engineer, what are you doing here?" The man was a laborer who had worked on a building site Wiesenthal was overseeing before the war. Wiesenthal said that he had liked the man and had allowed him to sleep in one of the apartments under construction. Now the man returned the favor and got him out of the prison, together with his neighbor.

This story exists in various versions, some very detailed, others more sketchy. Many of the details are not identical, or are even contradictory. In some of them, there is no mention of the shooting and Wiesenthal is simply released after a few hours and returns home. In evidence he gave during one of the trials, the shooting ceased before they reached the prison, or immediately when they arrived there, because it was the end of the working day.

In some earlier versions of the story, Wiesenthal gave different dates in July for his arrest—the fourth, the eighth, the sixteenth. Eventually, he settled on the sixth, a Sunday. This was no coincidence. Joseph Wechsberg wrote that Wiesenthal's life was saved because the bells of a nearby church began ringing and the Ukrainians stopped shooting and went to evening Mass.[46] Thus, his survival was given a dimension of a miraculous divine intervention. In the testimony at Yad Vashem, Wiesenthal made no mention of the bells, but the inclination to give his rescue a celestial meaning was also present in the story of his "rebirth" at Janowska.

On April 20, 1943, Hitler turned fifty-four. Right after the war, Wiesenthal wrote a story that recounted what had happened to him on that day. He was in the Janowska camp. The camp staff were preparing to celebrate the birthday of their leader. At around ten o'clock in the morning an SS officer by the name of Richard Dyga took Wiesenthal and a group of other prisoners, including some women, to a sandy area. They were told to strip bare and to stand alongside a six-foot-deep ditch, inside of which were lying the bodies of prisoners who had already been shot.

It was raining. The SS men started shooting the prisoners in the backs of their necks. Their bodies fell into the ditch, one after the other. Wiesenthal's turn came closer, when suddenly there was a whistle and the shooting stopped. Wiesenthal was wondering if he was alive or already dead, when it turned out that an SS officer, Adolf Kolonko, had come running up to take Wiesenthal back to the camp. "Get out of the line," he ordered, dragging him off, naked and wet.

Wiesenthal looked back. The shooting resumed and stopped again. The entire group had been murdered. On his return to the camp he was given clothing and ordered to make a birthday poster for Hitler. "You are lucky we still need you," said Kolonko. That night, one of his cell mates said to Wiesenthal, "On April 20, two people were born, the Führer and you."[47]

The first version of the story, preserved among Wiesenthal's papers, carried the subtitle "A True Legend from a Thousand and One Hells." In

1955, it was published in the memorial album of the Buczacz community that came out in Tel Aviv, under the title "Birthday in a Concentration Camp," without the subtitle.[48] Over the years, Wiesenthal had internalized the story and fixed it in his biography, as if it were true. When the German media marked Hitler's one hundredth birthday in 1989, he repeated the story and even mentioned it in his annual bulletin.[49]

It may very well be true that Wiesenthal was in Janowska in April 1943, but SS officer Kolonko wasn't there. According to his personal service file he reached Janowska only in July. Richard Dyga arrived in August.[50] When he appeared as a witness for the prosecution in the Stuttgart trial in December 1966, Wiesenthal recounted his experiences in Janowska in great detail, but he never mentioned the tale of his "rebirth" on Hitler's birthday. The story is also absent from the detailed testimony he gave about his Holocaust experiences at Yad Vashem.[51] However, Wiesenthal did not make it all up.

At Janowska camp, prisoners were indeed murdered, including in the way described by Wiesenthal. The historian Philip Friedman has reported that on April 20, 1943, fifty-four Jewish inmates were taken and shot in honor of Hitler's fifty-fourth birthday.[52] A friend of Wiesenthal's, Leon Wells of New Jersey, testified at the Eichmann trial that he had been taken out to the sandy area at the Janowska camp with other prisoners. They were ordered to undress and go down into the prepared grave and then fired at, without any connection to Hitler's birthday.

"When my turn came and I began walking toward the open graves, I was called back and told to return to the camp," Wells told the court. "The reason was that a man had been shot in the camp and they wanted me, with an SS man, to go back to the camp and bring the body so it could be buried with us in the grave." Wells took advantage of the opportunity to evade death.[53] It seems as though Wiesenthal appropriated Wells's story as his own. Of course, it is also possible that Wells heard the story from Wiesenthal.

Wiesenthal was also saved from death at the last minute, but that was a few months after Hitler's birthday. One day before the Janowska camp was due to be closed down, the remaining inmates were going to be shot dead, including Wiesenthal. But instead, the camp staff decided to take the inmates with them on their flight westward, as Wiesenthal often recounted. A German court heard and accepted his evidence on the story of his retreat with the SS personnel, as well as the testimony of two other witnesses who took part in the same forced march.[54]

In his Yad Vashem testimony, Wiesenthal told of an incident at the

Mauthausen camp, two years after he was at Janowska. A kapo entered the barracks and asked if any of the prisoners could draw. Wiesenthal said he could. The kapo said that it was the head kapo's birthday and his colleagues wanted to give him a picture for a present. Wiesenthal did the drawing, and saved his own life.[55] These, therefore, were the components of the "true legend" about how his life was saved, and his "rebirth" on Hitler's birthday.

Many years later, Wiesenthal corrected the story in an authorized biography. He left out the names of the men who had not yet arrived at Janowska when the incident occurred and instead gave the name of another SS officer, Koller. Wiesenthal knew him well. Before Koller's trial, he gave detailed testimony on the officer's sadistic cruelty, but he never mentioned Koller's part in the events of April 20. If he had been involved, Wiesenthal would certainly have said so, but as was his custom when giving evidence in courts, here too he apparently stuck to the facts.

In his amended version of the incident, Wiesenthal said he had survived thanks to his foreman at the Eastern Railway works, Adolf Kohlrautz. It was Kohlrautz who had rescued him from the camp, under the pretext that he needed Wiesenthal to draw congratulatory signs for Hitler's birthday. It is very possible that this is what actually happened, because it is similar to what Wiesenthal wrote years later in a private letter to his attorney.[56]

The 1989 film starring Ben Kingsley depicted the version that Wiesenthal had written right after the war. He was present during the filming in Hungary. Sitting on a folding director's chair bearing his name, watching the line of naked men falling one by one into the death pit, he actually saw for the first time the "true legend" that he had carried within himself for so long, perhaps real, perhaps imaginary. It is within this context that one must also see the booklet of drawings Wiesenthal published immediately after the war, based on what he had undergone in the camp at Mauthausen.

In the front of the booklet there is a picture of Wiesenthal himself, wearing a prisoner's uniform bearing the number 127371, his outstretched right hand pointing an accusing finger and a large sign on his breast bearing the French phrase *J'accuse!* Most of the drawings were designed as posters, some of them incorporating fragments of photographs: Hitler at the camp entrance with a globe of the Earth at his head, wrapped in a ribbon with a swastika at its center; a portrayal of Himmler going up in the smoke coming out of the crematorium chimneys; a watchtower built out of human skulls; and many depictions of atrocities, torture, and murder. The pictures had brief captions, such as "Dante's Hell was an amusement park compared to the camp's stone quarry."

In one drawing, Wiesenthal depicted the execution of three men, apparently by gunfire. "The Marquis de Sade would have felt true satisfaction here," he wrote in the margin. The bodies were hanging from three poles. "Sights like this make good photographs," he wrote, but he must have regretted this remark later, for he was portraying not something that he had seen with his own eyes, but a scene he had copied from photographs that appeared in *Life* magazine in June 1945.

The three men were Nazi spies who had infiltrated the American armed forces. They were discovered, tried, and shot, and it didn't happen in the Mauthausen camp. Talking to his biographer, Wiesenthal denied copying the *Life* photos, and asserted that this accusation was libel. But the similarity between his drawing and the photographs in the popular magazine leaves no room for doubt, and when he published a new edition of the book he left this drawing out.[57]

5. Living with Memory

People may reinvent their biographies when they have something to hide. There is nothing to prove that this is what motivated Wiesenthal. On the other hand, it would be reasonable to assume that he was consumed by a profound sense of guilt. Such feelings tormented many Holocaust survivors. They found it hard to live with the fact that they had remained alive and their loved ones had perished: parents, siblings, spouses, children. Many felt that they had survived at the expense of their relatives and blamed themselves for not having done enough to rescue them.

This feeling deepened in the atmosphere that frequently surrounded them, in Israel and elsewhere. Many people tended to think that those who survived the camps had done so at the expense of their less fortunate fellow prisoners, and labeled them as rogues and scoundrels. "Among the survivors of the German concentration camps," said David Ben-Gurion, "there were those who, had they not been what they were—harsh, evil, and egotistical people—would not have survived, and all they endured rooted out every good part of their souls."[58] It is very possible that Wiesenthal felt guilty about the death of his mother, and he might have also needed a fantasy to cope with such a feeling.

It happened in the Lvov ghetto in August 1942. Each day, Wiesenthal and his wife would go to work, and his mother stayed home. One day he came home and she wasn't there. In his testimony at Yad Vashem he related: "Whenever we went out, the remainder of our jewelry was left with Mother, so if they came to take her she could bribe someone to let her stay." He was talking about a gold watch and some other items, and he was really saying that he had done his best to save her life. He told his biographer that the policeman who came to arrest his mother agreed to take the watch and left. But half an hour later another policeman came. His mother had nothing left to bribe him with, and he took her away.

The version he gave at Yad Vashem was different. His mother was gone when he came home, he said, but the watch and two gold rings were still there. "Apparently my mother didn't want to take away from us our last remaining property, or she was unable to use them to secure her release," he said.[59] This version is the more accurate one, but apparently the intensity of the trauma surrounding his mother's death had led him to conceal the whole truth, even from Yad Vashem. It is to be found in a letter he received in 1946.

The letter was from Werner Schmidt, the man who wanted Wiesenthal to help keep him from being fired from his job because of his Nazi past. Wiesenthal sent him the document he requested, but Schmidt thought it was not enough. He wanted confirmation that during the war, complete trust had prevailed between them, and he gave an example of what he meant: Wiesenthal had trusted Schmidt enough to reveal to him that his gold and other jewels were hidden away in a wall of his ghetto apartment, above the light switch.[60] If the jewels were bricked up in the wall, his mother could not have used them to bribe the police who came to pick her up. Wiesenthal could only torment himself with the thought that he had not done everything he could and should have done to save her.

Guilt feelings could also explain another, still more dramatic, story connected to the death of his mother. When he came to work at the rail yard the day after her disappearance, he saw on the tracks a train full of imprisoned civilians and he was sure his mother was among them. He heard the voices of the people, begging for water. He was not allowed to approach the cars. After half an hour, he had to get back to work. The following day, the train and its passengers were still in the same place, and a few hours later it left for the death camp at Belzec.[61]

In the cinematic version, Ben Kingsley runs alongside the train, banging on the sides of the cars and yelling, "Mrs. Wiesenthal, Mrs. Wiesenthal," over and over again, desperate to save her. It is very possible that Wiesenthal borrowed this story, too, from someone else, like the one about his own escape on Hitler's birthday. This time it was Yitzhak Sternberg of Kibbutz Lohamei Hagetaot.

Sternberg described a very similar scene in an autobiography he published a few years before the film about Wiesenthal's life was produced. He too discovered that his mother was in one of the cars in a freight train standing at a platform—in fact it was the same station and the same platform that Wiesenthal mentioned, because Sternberg also worked there. The next day Sternberg came back to the train and called out his mother's name, but she did not answer.

Until his dying day, he wrote, he would not forget the whistle of the locomotive blending in with the noise of its wheels and the cries of the people in the cars begging for water. The train moved out at midnight, and he learned later that it had arrived at Belzec. Sternberg was none other than the boy Olek whose life Wiesenthal had saved in Lvov and who had helped him while he was in hiding there. After the war he visited Sternberg occasionally at his kibbutz.[62] Of course, it is also possible that Sternberg heard the story from Wiesenthal.

When Tuvia Friedman saw the film, he fired off an angry letter to Wiesenthal. It upset him that Wiesenthal had claimed to have done something no Jew would ever have been allowed to do, because the trains were always surrounded by SS personnel. It upset him to see that Wiesenthal was pretending to have done more for his mother than Friedman had been able to do for his own sister and brother, who had been sent to Treblinka. Only in Hollywood could a Jew run alongside his mother's death train, Friedman wrote. It is very likely that in reality Wiesenthal had been equally helpless, but unlike Friedman, he had managed to give his fantasy a cinematic reality.[63]

Alexander Friedman, who worked with Wiesenthal as a volunteer and later became a psychiatrist whose patients included Holocaust survivors, was very familiar with cases like this. There is no deception involved; it sometimes happens that the memory falsifies itself, Friedman said. He knew survivors who had magnified their suffering, and he had even identified a kind of competition between his patients as to who had suffered most. In this context he used the expression "the aristocracy of suffering." Friedman was also aware of a tendency to exaggerate stories of being rescued, in order to magnify the degree of the danger that had threatened the survivor.

Exaggerating suffering and danger sometimes served the purpose of allowing the survivor to cope with his guilt feelings, as a kind of self-inflicted punishment not only for staying alive but also for having suffered less than others or faced less danger than they had. Friedman had more than once diagnosed survivors who tried to deny their helplessness and the abasement they had undergone by making up deeds of bravery that had never happened.[64] Wiesenthal sometimes said that he had fought in a partisan unit and even had the rank of major, and that he had operated an underground radio station and published a newspaper. But his testimony at Yad Vashem says nothing of such actions.[65]

Exaggerating his suffering and spinning fantasies around his survival may have made it easier for him to push out of his consciousness the real atrocities he had experienced and to preserve his sanity. But it seems as if the main force driving him after the war was the need to prove that he had not been one of the villains. On September 15, 1946, he recorded what had happened to him during the war in a one-page typewritten document. Judging by the creases in the paper, he seems to have carried it around with him, perhaps in his wallet. The tenth line reads: "Throughout my entire period in the ghetto, I never held any position."

This was a surprising statement, because no one had asked him about it. Further on, he related in detail his movements from one camp to another until he was liberated by the Americans. His declaration could have ended here, but he repeated what he had already said: "Throughout my entire period in these numerous concentration camps, I never once held any position, and I preferred to do hard labor rather than receive a preferable position that would have obligated me to act against anyone."[66]

Wiesenthal indeed had no part in the crimes of the Nazis, but he always found it difficult to live with the fact that he had suffered less than others and that he owed his life to the decency of some Germans. His wife had also survived thanks to them. In his Yad Vashem testimony, he even asserted that he had survived Mauthausen thanks to the fact that the kapo who enlisted him to make a drawing had improved his living conditions in the camp and thus saved his life.[67]

One may assume that his conscience troubled him about this. The hunt for Nazis can therefore be seen, perhaps, as a punishment he inflicted upon himself, as well as an attempt to win expiation. He needed to cleanse himself. The consciousness of the Holocaust that he nurtured was meant to cleanse human civilization in its entirety. It was a mission without an end. He used to speak about it to Albert Speer, and once he told Speer that he would like to write a book about the Jewish collaborators.

The Jews, he explained, were still scattered in a hundred different countries and in one way or another, history could repeat itself at any time; a second Holocaust could not be ruled out. It was therefore necessary to condemn the Jewish collaborators just as the Nazi criminals themselves were condemned. The idea of writing a book like this was grounded in the pain that the Jews felt when they saw other Jews working for the Gestapo, Wiesenthal observed, and added: "Precisely as in the case of *The Sunflower* this subject is also rooted in personal experience."[68]

Wiesenthal's bitterness toward Jewish collaborators and the gratitude he displayed toward the Germans who saved him also taught him to judge people by their deeds and merits rather than by their group affiliation. This was the basis for his humanistic views and his faith in justice. It was the basis for his belief in good and his longing for conciliation. It may also explain the strange attraction he felt toward Speer. When Wiesenthal wrote to him, "We all made mistakes in our youth," he was writing as one sinner to another, and he envied Speer because he had found repentance and forgiveness.

Eva Dukes, perhaps the only person who was allowed into Wiesenthal's inner world, believed that deep inside, he had also wanted to forgive the wounded SS man in *The Sunflower*. "You could almost have forgiven him, and as your suffering proves, you were closer to doing so than you realized then," she wrote to him. "It was largely your guilt toward your comrades and toward the dead that held you back, the dread of disloyalty. Apparently you were close to feeling, although incapable of saying, 'Yes I forgive you.'"

If Wiesenthal had been capable of forgiving the man, perhaps he would also have been able to forgive himself, and perhaps he would have shaken off the grip of the Holocaust that pursued him even more relentlessly than he pursued others. This in essence was the tragedy of his life. He, who always tried to prevent the innocent from being punished, punished himself for a crime he didn't commit.

6. Last Supper

In central Vienna, behind the Opera House, there is a metal statue of an old Jew on his knees cleaning the sidewalk with a brush; he looks like a dog. Alfred Hrdlicka, who created the sculpture as part of a monument against fascism and war, drew his inspiration from the famous photograph that recorded the degradation of Viennese Jews forced to brush the sidewalks clean.

Hrdlicka's intention was to show that the road to Auschwitz began with the degradation of human beings, in Vienna. The monument was dedicated in 1988 after a decade of intense argument. Public preoccupation over its location and message became part of the searing national debate over the Waldheim affair and its lessons. Wiesenthal thought that the monument reflected a Stalinist style and that Hrdlicka's use of the word *fascism* instead of *Nazism* was meant to protect the Austrians from the truth about their crimes.

The monument is located near the site of a building that was destroyed in an Allied air raid in which all its inhabitants were killed. Wiesenthal saw this as a bid to blur the difference between victims and murderers. But he realized that in the wake of Waldheim's victory he could not oppose the erection of the monument. "For all that, it's better than nothing," he wrote to *Profil.* He had no choice but to swallow the insult of the Jew on his knees with the brush.[69]

Summer came and went, and then it was autumn. The Viennese and the tourists who filled the city made good use of their Jew: they sat on his back to rest from the heat of the day; children used him as a slide and pet dogs peed on him. It did not look good, so the Jew was sent back to his creator for improvements. To stop people from using him as a bench, Hrdlicka wrapped him in barbed wire, ironically reminiscent of the crown of thorns that the Romans had placed on the head of Jesus.

The most important figures in the original photograph were not the Jews undergoing humiliation, not even the police officers watching them, but of course the Viennese gathered around them, gleefully relishing the scene. A copy of the photograph could have been placed alongside the monument; it could have been positioned so that the images of passersby would be reflected in its glass, and they could see themselves in the photograph. Hrdlicka spared them this unpleasantness. The Jews decided to erect their own monument in the city's Judenplatz (Jewish Square). This too provoked bitter contention, some of it a continuation of the endless disputes between Wiesenthal and community leaders.[70]

The culture of memory had always occupied his thoughts, all the more so as he grew older. When he was almost ninety, he returned to Mauthausen, on the fiftieth anniversary of the liberation of the camp. The Greek composer Mikis Theodorakis requested his permission to use some sentences of Wiesenthal's in his *Mauthausen Cantata*.[71] After many years of contemplation, Wiesenthal had also crystallized his concept of the nature of Nazi evil and the destruction of the Jews. The Holocaust was the combination of hatred and technology, he wrote to the Soviet scientist and human rights activist Andrei Sakharov. He believed that neutralizing hatred would also lead to restraint in the use of lethal technologies.[72]

In 1992, Wiesenthal wrote to the president of Ukraine protesting the naming of a street in Lvov after Symon Petliura, the leader of the armed bands that carried out pogroms against Jews. One of Petliura's soldiers had almost killed Wiesenthal when he was a boy in Buczacz.[73] President Leonid Kravchuk rejected his protest.

In January 1994, Wiesenthal reported the death of Anton Burger, one of Eichmann's lieutenants. He had been arrested in 1947, in Altaussee, in a hiding place not far from the home of Eichmann's wife, when the police had come to his house instead of hers by mistake. Shortly after his arrest he managed to escape, and in the forty-seven years that ensued he hid, apparently in Austria and Germany, under an assumed identity. There was no other wanted man Wiesenthal had hunted for so long.[74]

Even though he was now working fewer hours every day, he was still painstakingly replying to each letter he received, ever aware of the terrible and wonderful dramas that had accompanied the upheavals of his century. The members of his generation were people who could say when and where they had first laid eyes on an automobile; Wiesenthal lived long enough to protest against neo-Nazi games on the Internet.[75]

Some months before his ninetieth birthday, the phone rang in his office. On the line was a survivor of Theresienstadt. He was calling from Canada, and he had information on an SS man by the name of Julius Viel who had shot seven prisoners near the end of the war. Wiesenthal did what he had done often in his fifty-three years of pursuing Nazi criminals—he passed the information on to Germany's central authority for war crimes in Ludwigsburg.

Locating Viel was not a problem. Before retiring, he had been editor of a local newspaper in the town of Schramberg in the Black Forest, in southern Germany. He was also well-known for his guidebooks for hikers and cyclists, for which he had been awarded a state Decoration of Merit. He was the last criminal Wiesenthal brought to justice.[76] Viel died several months after being sentenced to twelve years' imprisonment.

In 1989 Wiesenthal received a letter from a man named Heinz Silberbauer. After seeing an interview with Wiesenthal on television, he wrote to thank him for his courage and, mainly, for adhering to his guiding principle: seeking justice, and not revenge. "My name is surely known to you," he wrote. "When you found the man who arrested Anne Frank, reporters pestered me for many days on the phone. Again and again I had to make it clear to them that it was not my father and not any of my relations. We just happen to have the same name.

"Nevertheless, I somehow felt ashamed. I was ashamed of my father. The incident reminded me that he had been and remained an incorrigible Nazi. Thank God, I never grew up with him. He died four years ago." Wiesenthal replied warmly. Letters like these bolstered his faith in the moral strength of the young and encouraged him to continue in his work, he wrote.[77]

Chaya Friedman, a teacher from Highland Park, New Jersey, sent him letters written by her students. Wiesenthal was delighted. The only way to prevent another genocide lies in young people's willingness to learn about the Holocaust, he wrote back. Of course he understood why so many young people recoiled from dealing with the nightmare he had experienced; he knew that many of them looked away and said, "That's a part of history and has nothing to do with us today."

It was the task of the survivors of the Holocaust to explain to young people over and over again that the destruction of the Jews was far more relevant to their lives than they could ever imagine. They were used to living as free people, but they had to be told how suddenly they could lose their freedom. "Freedom is like health, I always tell young people," Wiesenthal wrote. "You don't recognize its value until you have lost it. Freedom is not a gift from the heavens, you have to fight for it every day of your life."

He was ninety-five, he said, and soon all the Nazi criminals—and the witnesses to their crimes—would be gone. The duty of preventing the next genocide and defending human rights was now passing to the generation of the children in Highland Park, New Jersey.[78]

As his life drew to an end, he sought to make peace with the Wiesenthal Center in Los Angeles. The Museum of Tolerance had evolved into a success story that gave him satisfaction. Tens of thousands of American students, members of the U.S. armed forces, and many others visited it every year. They passed through exhibits that extensively illustrated the horrors of the Holocaust, and others that documented discrimination and persecution involving minority groups in various countries, including the United States. Islamic terror is emphasized, and Wiesenthal appreciated this.

His disagreements with the young and dynamic Americans who ran the center had sprung from the fact that he came from an entirely different world from theirs, he wrote to his attorney. He bequeathed them his desk and the large map of the concentration camps that hung in his office, as well as the carpet, the pictures, and the books whose authors had inscribed them with personal dedications.[79]

Cyla Wiesenthal died at the age of ninety-three in November 2003. A few weeks after that, Wiesenthal came to his office for the last time. His extreme old age had left its mark. He could no longer drive himself, and his faithful secretary, Rosa-Maria Austraat, drove him.

The last year of his life passed in illness and solitude. Two Polish caregivers looked after him. Only his stamp collection still gave him any joy. The stamps were his friends, and he introduced them to his Israeli granddaughter, Rachel Kreisberg, one by one, according to their nominal value in kreutzers, the currency of the Austro-Hungarian empire: This is a 10-kreutzer stamp, this is a 25 kreutzer, this has a perforated edge, this was cut, this carried the image of a ruler, this only a number, this has a round postmark, this a triangular one. All of them were arrayed in albums, in straight lines like soldiers on parade.

There were also envelopes and letters and whole proof sheets of stamps of the Third Reich, bearing Hitler's portrait. From time to time Wiesenthal would say, "Nice, no?" Once his granddaughter took him to the stamp exchange in the Café Museum; he purchased something and returned home with the feeling that he'd gotten a bargain. After he died, the collection was sold at an auction, fetching almost half a million euros. He would certainly have been happy to hear that.[80]

Some of his friends came to pay him farewell visits. Tuvia Friedman came from Haifa, Eva Dukes from New York. Queen Elizabeth of England could still have her ambassador call on him to appoint him a Knight Commander of the Order of the British Empire, and the Austrian president, Heinz Fischer, came to his home to award him the Golden Cross of Honor. He was the same Fischer who had once threatened to set up a commission of inquiry into Wiesenthal's activities. "Nice," said Wiesenthal in Yiddish, and went back into his room. Not long after that, Fischer awarded an Austrian soccer official a higher award, one "with a star"; Rosa-Maria Austraat wrote to the president to protest. It was a good thing that Wiesenthal had died before this, she wrote.[81]

He took with him a happier memory, from his ninetieth birthday. His friends gave him a party in the historic luxury hotel, the Imperial. Although he had always been a secular person, he insisted that the meal be a kosher one; the idea that the hotel that once hosted Adolf Hitler was serving a kosher meal to guests honoring Simon Wiesenthal enchanted him.

Acknowledgments

Simon Wiesenthal dictated the story of his life to a number of writers, but he has never been the subject of a fully documented biography before this one. I was able to write it because of access given me to thousands of files stored in fourteen archives in Austria, Germany, Poland, Britain, the United States, and Israel. The names of the archives appear at the head of the Notes section, and I am grateful to the staff at each of them for their assistance.

Wiesenthal's personal papers are held in his Documentation Center in Vienna, which is kept as he left it when he died. I was given unconditional access to his papers and to the center by the gracious permission of his daughter, Paulinka Kreisberg. His granddaughter Rachel Kreisberg assisted me in finding my way through the family genealogy. I am grateful to both of them. The files Wiesenthal kept on Nazi criminals, and other materials that helped him in his work, are also to be found in the Documentation Center. When I arrived there, most of the material had not yet been catalogued and had not yet been given archival record numbers. I have in my possession copies of all the private papers cited in this book.

Since that time, the Wiesenthal Archive has been established, and much of the material is now catalogued on a computerized database. I am indebted to the staff of the archive, Brigitte Lehner, Gertrude Mergili, and Michaela Vocelka, for their knowledge, patience, and especially the warmth of their welcome. I am particularly thankful to Rosa-Maria

Austraat, who worked with Wiesenthal from 1975. She told me of her admiration and great love for "Bossie," as she sometimes called him. I learned a great deal from her. Some of Wiesenthal's working archives I discovered in the basement of the Jewish community building in Linz. I also received kind assistance at the archive of the Jewish community of Vienna.

At the Bruno Kreisky Archive in Vienna I was given access to material that had not been opened to researchers before me. I appreciate this. Federal prosecutor Kurt Schrimm, the head of Germany's Central Office for the Investigation of Nazi Crimes in Ludwigsburg, also made as yet unopened material available to me, as did the German Federal Office for the Protection of the Constitution.

Hitherto classified material connected to the hunt for Adolf Eichmann reached me thanks to a special ruling by the Israeli High Court of Justice in Jerusalem, and in this matter my gratitude is due to Osnat Mandel, head of the High Court section of the State Attorney's Office. A report by Israeli agent Michael Bloch was placed at my disposal by his sons, Dror and Yuval. I am also grateful to his brother, Ambassador Gideon Yarden. I owe thanks to a number of people who knew Wiesenthal during the period of his work with the Mossad: the late Meir Amit and Dov Ochowski, as well as Rafi Meidan, and a man who asked to be identified only by the name under which he worked in Vienna, "Mordechai Elazar."

I received highly valuable material from Eli M. Rosenbaum, the director of the U.S. Justice Department's Office of Special Investigations. Mr. Rosenbaum was also kind enough to devote long hours of his time to share with me his critical views of Wiesenthal—mainly, but not exclusively, concerning Wiesenthal's conduct in the Waldheim affair. Waldheim himself, who has since died, received me in his home for an interview. I feel deep gratitude to Margit Schmidt, who did her best to explain Bruno Kreisky to me; to Peter Michael Lingens, who explained Wiesenthal; and to Ambassador Ferdinand Trauttmansdorff, who explained Austria.

I am indebted to many others, in ten countries, including people who knew Wiesenthal and to Holocaust survivors: Dan Ashbel, Ines Austern Gander, Avi Avidov, Yehezkel Beinish, Asher Ben-Natan, Ikaros Bigi, Yehuda Blum, John H. Bunzl, Mario Chimanovitch, Dan Diner, Eva Dukes, Alexander Friedman, Tuviah Friedman, Frank Grelka, Jenny and Paul Grosz, Cecilié Grünwald, Christoph Heusgen, Marvin Hier, Avshalom Hodik, Jules Huf, Swanee Hunt, Avner Inbar, Michael John, Omry Kaplan-Feuereisen, Avi Katzman, Beate and Serge Klarsfeld, Erich Klein, Peter Kreisky, Claudia Künher, Avraham Kushnir, Peter Marboe, Martin

Mendelsohn, José Moskovits, Lutz Musner, Håvard M. Nygaard, Hans Popper, Doron Rabinovici, Oliver Rathkolb, Tzali Reshef, Martin Rosen, Helmar Sartor, Heinrich Schmidt, Peter Schwartz, Mark Shraberman, Paul Sills, Michael Stergar, Walter Tarra, Bina Tischler, Richard Trank, Aharon Weiss, Elie Wiesel, Ingo Zechner, Leon Zelman, and Efraim Zuroff. Without their help, information, and advice this book could not have been written.

I very much appreciate the editorial advice of Kristine Puopolo, my editor at Doubleday, as well as the support of Stephanie Bowen, her assistant; Nora Reichard, production editor; Rosalie Wieder, copy editor; and Benjamin Hamilton, foreign language proofreader.

During my stay in Vienna, I was hosted by the International Research Center for Cultural Studies; its staff received me warmly and assisted me in my research with useful advice.

As with all of my books, it is a pleasure once again to thank Deborah Harris, my agent and friend.

Notes

Abbreviations

All cited documents held by the Israeli State Archive (ISA) are contained in files at the Israeli Foreign Office

ASD	Archiv der Sozialen Demokratie, Frankfurt
AIKGW	Archiv der Israelitischen Kultusgemeinde Wien, Vienna
AJA	American Joint Archives, New York/Jerusalem
BGA	Ben-Gurion Archives, Sde Boker
BKA	Stiftung Bruno Kreisky Archiv, Vienna
BSTU	Die Bundesbeauftragte für die Unterlagen des Staatssicherheitsdienstes der ehemaligen Deutschen Demokratischen Republik, Berlin
CAHJP	Central Archive for the History of the Jewish People, Jerusalem
CZA	Central Zionist Archive, Jerusalem
IPN	Institute of National Remembrance, Warsaw
ISA	Israel State Archive, Jerusalem
IWM	Imperial War Museum, London
SWAW	Simon Wiesenthal Archive, Vienna
USNA	Unites States National Archives, Washington, DC
WPP	Wiesenthal Private Papers, Vienna
YVA	Yad Vashem Archive, Jerusalem
ZS	Zentrale Stelle der Landesjustizverwaltungen, Ludwigsburg

Introduction: The Glass Box

1. Simon Wiesenthal, *Ich jagte Eichmann* (Gütersloh, Germany: Siegfried Mohn, 1961), pp. 146–47.

2. Wiesenthal to Leon Wells, June 17, 1987, WPP.

3. Statement by the Speaker, June 22, 1949, Knesset Proceedings, Vol. 6, p. 807; Wiesenthal, correspondence with Yad Vashem and Tel Aviv Municipality and related material: CZA C6/415, S30/4675; YVA M9/68, M9/69, M9/161, M20/182; ISA 2732/24.

4. Description of funeral in press clippings file, CZA S71/642.

5. Wiesenthal, *Ich jagte Eichmann*, pp. 146–47.

6. Wiesenthal to Ben-Gurion, April 24, 1952, ISA 2732/24.

7. Taylor to Wiesenthal, March 28, 1984, WPP.

8. Hella Pick, *Simon Wiesenthal: A Life in Search of Justice* (Boston: Northeastern University Press, 1996), p. 107.

9. Wiesenthal, interview with Hella Pick, IWM, Accession 20823, Reel 23.

10. Condolences file, courtesy of Paulinka Kreisberg.

11. Maria Sporrer and Herbert Steiner (eds.), *Simon Wiesenthal: ein unbequemer Zeitgenosse* (Vienna: Orac, 1992), p. 38.

12. Wiesenthal, *Ich jagte Eichmann*, p. 147.

I: "Eichmann Is My Passion"

1. Adolf Eichmann: "Goetzen," p. 200, ISA (136 AE).

2. Ben-Gurion diary, November 30, 1939, BGA.

3. Kastner to friends, August 31, 1944, CZA S6/555; Yehiam Weitz, *Ha'ish shenirzach pa'amaim* (Jerusalem: Keter, 1995), p. 32ff; "Ma olel Karl Eichmann: Hameratzeah miSharona," *Hamashkif*, May 31, 1946.

4. Memos, CZA S25/10745, S25/10746, S25/22691, S71/2181.

5. Memos, CZA S25/7887.

6. Nehemia Robinson to Jackson, July 27, 1945, AJA, World Jewish Congress Collection (MS-361), Box C106, File 16.

7. Wisliceny's arrest and interrogation, USNA, RG 263, UD-2 Box 1 (Notorious Nazis); Office of United States Chief of Counsel for Prosecution of Axis Criminality, *Nazi Conspiracy and Aggression*, Vol. 8 (Washington, DC: GPO, 1946), p. 606ff. (Dieter Wisliceny, affidavit, November 29, 1946); Wisliceny statement, February 10, 1947, SWAW, Eichmann file; Gideon Ruffer to Steiner, April 10, 1946, CZA S25/3340; Moshe Pearlman, *The Capture of Adolf Eichmann* (London: Weidenfeld & Nicolson, 1961), p. 10ff.

8. Tuvia Friedman, *15 shanim radafti aharei Eichmann* (Netanya: Achiasaf, 1961), p. 23ff.; Tuviah Friedman, *Sixty Years: Nazi Hunter* (Haifa: Institute for the Documentation of Nazi Crimes, 2006), p. 161ff.

9. Simon Wiesenthal, *Ich jagte Eichmann* (Gütersloh, Germany: Siegfried Mohn, 1961), p. 22.

10. Ibid., p. 239.

11. Ibid., p. 27.

12. Pier to Ruffer, March 29, 1946, CZA S25/3343.

13. Asher Ben Natan, *The Audacity to Live* (Jerusalem: Mazo Publishers, 2007), p. 71ff.

14. Ben Natan to Diamant, March 26, 1990, see Manus Diamant, *Hamesima Eichmann*, introduction by Simon Wiesenthal (Tel Aviv: Yaron Golan, 2004), p. 304.

15. Ben Natan, *Audacity to Live*, p. 73.

16. Diamant, *Hamesima Eichmann*, p. 287; see also Manus Diamant, *Ma'avak al hisardut*, ed. Yosef Krost and Yosef Frenkel (Katowice, Poland: Prihata veshkiata shel kehila yehudit [Association for Memorializing Katowice Jewry], 1996), p. 296.

17. Aharon Hoter-Yishai, *Habrigada veshearit haplita* (Tel Aviv: Union of Ex-servicemen, 1999), p. 289ff.

18. Tom Segev, *The Seventh Million: The Israelis and the Holocaust* (New York: Henry Holt, 1993), p. 140ff.; Kovner to Avidov, January 1, 1962, courtesy Avi Avidov; see also Diamant, *Hamesima Eichmann*, p. 260ff.; Simon Wiesenthal, *Justice Not Vengeance* (London: Weidenfeld & Nicolson, 1989); Simon Wiesenthal, "Meine Suche nach Eichmann" (third draft, 1960), p. 7, WPP, Eichmann file; Dina Porat, *Me'ever lagashmi: Parashat hayav shel Abba Kovner* (Tel Aviv: Am Oved, 2000); author interview with Alexander Friedman, January 12, 2006.

19. Wiesenthal to Ze'ev Shek, January 8, 1969, ISA 4167/7; Shek to Foreign Ministry, January 14, 1969, ISA 4167/7; Simon Wiesenthal, *Grossmufti: Grossagent der Achse* (Salzburg, Austria: Ried, 1947), p. 42.

20. Wiesenthal to Silberschein, May 31, 1948, YVA M20/182.

21. Wiesenthal to Silberschein, May 31, 1948, WPP; Wiesenthal, *Justice Not Vengeance*, p. 31; Wiesenthal, *Ich jagte Eichmann*, p. 46; David Cesarani, *Eichmann: His Life and Crimes* (New York: Vintage, 2005), p. 203ff.

22. Wiesenthal, *Ich jagte Eichmann*, p. 150.

23. Wiesenthal to *Aufbau*, June 4, 1947, WPP.

24. Alois Mayrhuber, *Küenstler im Ausseerland* (Graz, Austria: Styria, 1995), p. 117.

25. Wiesenthal, *Justice Not Vengeance*, p. 69; Wiesenthal, bulletin no. 18, January 31, 1988, p. 6, SWAW; SWAW, Burger file; see also Karla Müller-Tupath, *Verschollen in Deutschland: das heimliche Leben des Anton Burger, Lagerkommandant von Theresienstadt* (Berlin: Aufbau-Taschenbuch, 2000).

26. Lukas personal details, handwritten note; Wiesenthal, "Meine Suche nach Eichmann" (third draft), p. 3, SWAW, Eichmann file; Wiesenthal to Goldmann, March 30, 1954, CZA Z6/842; Tara to Bauer, January 6, 1960, WPP; Wiesenthal, *Justice Not Vengeance*, p. 70.

27. Wiesenthal, *Ich jagte Eichmann*, p. 158ff.; Wiesenthal, *Justice Not Vengeance*, p. 70; Wiesenthal to Kurt Lewin, December 10, 1948, WPP.

28. Wiesenthal to Rosenkranz, undated, WPP.

29. Wiesenthal, "Meine Suche nach Eichmann" (third draft), p. 7, and additional notes, SWAW , Eichmann file, p. 2.

30. Wiesenthal, *Justice Not Vengeance*, p. 69.

31. Michael Bloch to head of Intelligence Service, January 3, 1949, courtesy of Yuval Bloch; Asher Ben Natan, author interview, September 5, 2007; Gideon Yarden, author interview, September 17, 2007.

32. "Isser Harel, Simon Wiesenthal and the Capture of Eichmann," unpublished document, p. 130, courtesy of Eli Rosenbaum.

33. Leo Frank, *Geständnis: Das Leben eines Polizisten* (Linz, Austria: Grosser, 1993), p. 25ff.

34. Wiesenthal, *Ich jagte Eichmann*, p. 159; Hevra Kadisha Kehilat Yerushalayim, *Sefer hayovel* (Jerusalem: Hevra Kadisha Kehilat Yerushalayim, 1992), p. 148ff.; see also Maria Sporrer and Herbert Steiner, eds., *Simon Wiesenthal: Ein unbequemer Zeitgenosse* (Vienna: Orac, 1992), p. 123.

35. Wiesenthal, *Justice Not Vengeance*, p. 74; Friedman, *15 shanim*; Asher Ben Natan, author interview, September 5, 2007; Simon Wiesenthal, *The Murderers Among Us*, ed. Joseph Wechsberg (New York: McGraw-Hill, 1967), p. 119.

36. Wiesenthal, *Justice Not Vengeance*, p. 69; CIA progress report, April 24, 1951, USNA, RG 263, UD-2 Box 1 (Notorious Nazis).

2: "During That Period, We Never Took Hitler Seriously"

1. S. Y. Agnon, *Ir u'mlo'a* (Tel Aviv: Schocken, 1973), p. 14.

2. Ibid., p. 233.

3. Ibid., p. 711.

4. Hella Pick, *Simon Wiesenthal: A Life in Search of Justice* (Boston: Northeastern University Press, 1996), p. 40.

5. Maria Sporrer and Herbert Steiner, eds., *Simon Wiesenthal: Ein unbequemer Zeitgenosse* (Vienna: Orac, 1992), p. 16.

6. Alan Levy, *Nazi Hunter: The Wiesenthal File* (New York: Barnes and Noble Books, 2002), p. 17.

7. Yisrael Cohen, ed., *Sefer Buczacz* (Tel Aviv: Am Oved, 1956); Omer Bartov, *Erased: Vanishing Traces of Jewish Galicia in Present-Day Ukraine* (Princeton, NJ: Princeton University Press, 2007), p. 127ff.; Dan Laor, *Agnon* (in Hebrew) (Tel Aviv: Schocken, 1998), p. 13ff.

8. Rolf Vogel, ed., *Das Echo: Widerhall auf Simon Wiesenthal* (Stuttgart, Germany: Seewald, 1979), p. 16; Wiesenthal, statement under oath, May 27, 1981, WPP; Pick, *Simon Wiesenthal*, p. 34; Simon Wiesenthal, *Flucht vor dem Schicksal* (Munich: Nymphenburger Verlagshandlung, 1988), p. 49.

9. Pick, *Simon Wiesenthal*, p. 41.

10. Paulina Kreisberg, author interview, April 23, 2008; Simon Wiesenthal, *The Sunflower: On the Possibilities and Limits of Forgiveness* (New York: Schocken, 1997), p. 43.

11. Sporrer op cit p. 19; see also Wiesenthal, testimony at Yad Vashem, October 27, 1960, YVA 03/1817, p. 1.

12. Cohen, *Sefer Buczacz*, p. 101.

13. Ibid., p. 200.

14. Agnon, *Ir u'mlo'a*, p. 655ff.

15. Levy, *Nazi Hunter*, p. 17.

16. Agnon, *Ir u'mlo'a*, p. 694; Ruth Beckerman, ed., *Die Mazzesinsel: Juden in der Weiner Leopoldstadt 1918–1938* (Vienna: Löcker Verlag, 1992).

17. Levy, *Nazi Hunter*, p. 18; Bruno Kreisky, *Zwischen den Zeiten: Der Memoiren erster Teil* (Vienna: Kremayr und Scheriau, 2000), p. 24.

18. Agnon, *Ir U'mlo'a*, p. 656.

19. Sporrer op cit p. 26; portrait of Cyla Müller, courtesy of Paulinka Kreisberg.

20. Sporrer op cit p. 20; Wiesenthal, interview with Hella Pick, IWM, Accession 20823, Reels 23–24.

21. Wiesenthal, interview with Hella Pick, IWM, Accession 20823, Reels 23–24; Jüedisches Zentralkomite, Activities Report (1946?) with biographical appendix; Wiesenthal to Abe Foxman, November 24, 1988, WPP; Wiesenthal at Jabotinsky Prize award ceremony, November 1988, WPP.

22. Wiesenthal, interview with Hella Pick, IWM, Accession 20823, Reel 4.

23. Bartov, *Erased*, p. 13ff.; Eliyahu Yones, *Smoke in the Sand: The Jews of Lvov in the War Years 1939–1944* (Jerusalem: Gefen, 2004); Shimon Redlich, *Together and Apart in Brzezany: Poles, Jews, and Ukrainians 1919–1945* (Bloomington: Indiana University Press, 2002).

24. Mannes Halpern, statement, April 6, 1946, WPP; Aroni Goldini, statement, April 1946, WPP; Wiesenthal, declaration under oath, May 27, 1981, WPP; Pick, *Simon Wiesenthal*, p. 47; Wiesenthal, certification of studies, Prague, 1929, and diploma, Lvov, 1940, WPP; Paulinka Kreisberg, author interview, April 23, 2008.

25. Sporrer op cit p. 23.

26. Jüedisches Zentralkomite, Activities Report; Wiesenthal to Abe Foxman, November 24, WPP; copies of *Omnibus* (student magazine), WPP; Alexander Gotz to Wiesenthal, February 12, 1964, WPP.

27. Wiesenthal to Anna Cieśla, June 19, 1986, WPP.

28. Sporrer op cit p. 26.

29. Shmuel Katz, *Jabo: Biographia shel Zeev Jabotinsky*, Vol. 2 (in Hebrew) (Tel Aviv: Dvir, 1993), p. 969ff.

30. Sporrer op cit p. 27; Rolf Vogel, ed., *Das Echo: Widerhall auf Simon Wiesenthal* (Stuttgart, Germany: Seewald, 1979), p. 16.

31. Strobe Talbott, *Khrushchev Remembers* (London: Andre Deutsch, 1971), p. 140.

32. Ibid., p. 146.

33. Ibid., p. 141.

34. Yones, *Smoke in the Sand*, p. 130.

35. Ibid., p. 57ff.

36. Ibid., p. 48.

37. Sporrer op cit p. 31.

38. Yones, *Smoke in the Sand*, p. 42.

39. Wiesenthal to commander of U.S. occupation forces, Mauthausen camp, May 25, 1945, courtesy of Eli Rosenbaum; Wiesenthal, curriculum vitae, January 17, 1953, WPP; Wiesenthal, curricula vitae, September 15, 1946, July 16, 1947, and April 10, 1956, WPP; Wiesenthal, testimony at Yad Vashem, October 27, 1960, YVA 03/1817, pp. 1–2.

40. Yones, *Smoke in the Sand*, p. 180.

41. Wiesenthal, testimony at Yad Vashem, October 27, 1960, summary.

3: "See You on the Soap Shelf"

1. Philipp-Christian Wachs, *Der Fall Theodor Oberländer (1905–1998): Ein Lehrstück deutscher Geschichte* (Frankfurt/New York: Campus, 2000), p. 51ff.

2. Wiesenthal's investigation by Ponger, May 27, 1948, USNA, M1019/79/460.

3. Eliyahu Yones, *Smoke in the Sand: The Jews of Lvov in the War Years 1939–1944* (Jerusalem: Gefen, 2004), p. 79.

4. Wiesenthal, declaration under oath, March 17, 1948, YVA M9/818.

5. Wiesenthal's investigation by Ponger, May 27, 1948, USNA, M9/818.

6. Yones, *Smoke in the Sand*, p. 86ff.

7. Wiesenthal at Lvov trial, December 20, 1966, protocol, p. 2291, SWAW, Lvov file.

8. Ibid., p. 2312.

9. Yones, *Smoke in the Sand*, p. 99ff.

10. Wiesenthal at Lvov trial, p. 2363.

11. Adela Cygal-Adelman, statement, January 7, 1976, WPP.

12. Wiesenthal at Lvov trial, p. 2363.

13. Philip Friedman, "Hurban Yehudei Lvov," *Encyclopedia shel galuyot*, Vol. IV, p. 719; Wiesenthal, testimony, June 6, 1961, p. 10, SWAW, Dyga file; Wiesenthal at Lvov trial, p. 2321.

14. Israel Gutman, ed., *Encyclopedia of the Holocaust*, Vol. II (London: Macmillan, 1990), p. 733.

15. Cyla Wiesenthal, Verfolgungsgeschichte, August 12, 1954, WPP.

16. Wiesenthal at Lvov trial, p. 2334.

17. Yones, *Smoke in the Sand*, p. 226ff.

18. Wiesenthal, testimony at Yad Vashem, October 27, 1960, YVA 03/1817, p. 11.

19. Survivors' testimonies: IPN BU, 0665/269 MSW Dep. II, Vol. I; IPN BU, 01419/161 MSW, 1963–1974, Vols. I–III; IPN BU, 01069/247 MSW.

20. SWAW, Peter Arnolds file.

21. Testimony of Polish agent "Stanislaw," December 1964, IPN BU,

01419/161 MSW, 1963–1974, p. 35ff; testimony of Kasimir Sztatkowski, IPN BU, 01419/161 MSW, 1963–1974, pp. 209–10.

22. Maria Sporrer and Herbert Steiner, eds., *Simon Wiesenthal: Ein unbequemer Zeitgenosse* (Vienna: Orac, 1992), p. 41.

23. Wiesenthal to Yad Vashem, December 18, 1986, and accompanying documents, YVA M31/3692.

24. Wiesenthal, testimony at Yad Vashem, October 27, 1960, p. 23ff.

25. Yitzhak Sternberg, *Bezehut aheret* (Beit Lohamei Hagetaot, 1984), p. 39.

26. Ibid., p. 56ff; Paulina Krodkiewska, testimony, September 24, 1992, YVA 033c/2497.

27. Wiesenthal, testimony at Yad Vashem, October 27, 1960, pp. 28–29.

28. Paulina Krodkiewska, testimony, September 24, 1992.

29. Wiesenthal to Yad Vashem, December 18, 1986, p. 32ff.

30. Kommando der Schutzpolizei, Bericht, June 13, 1944, WPP; see also arrest certificate for Paulina Krodkiewska, July 1, 1944, WPP; Sternberg, *Bezehut aheret*, p. 56.

31. Alma Severin, YVA M49.E/605.

32. Wiesenthal to Yad Vashem, December 18, 1986, p. 41ff.; Wiesenthal at Lvov trial, p. 2334; see also p. 2468.

33. Hella Pick, *Simon Wiesenthal: A Life in Search of Justice* (Boston: Northeastern University Press, 1996), p. 68.

34. Sporrer and Steiner, *Simon Wiesenthal: Ein unbequmer Zeitgenosse*, p. 49.

35. Wiesenthal, interview with Hella Pick, IWM, Accession 20823, Reel 32.

36. Edmond Adler, testimony, YVA M49.E/808; Izak and Helena Lehman, testimony, March 22, 1960, SWAW, Dyga file; Engelberger to Joseph Kermish, January 27, 1960, YVA 04/469; see also Simon Wiesenthal, *The Murderers Among Us*, ed. Joseph Wechsberg (New York: McGraw-Hill, 1967), p. 273.

37. Wiesenthal declaration under oath, December 30, 1966, WPP; Yitzhak Sternberg, *Bezehut aheret*, p. 84ff.; Paulina Krodkiewska, testimony, September 24, 1992, YVA 033c/2497.

38. Wiesenthal to Yad Vashem, December 18, 1986, p. 50ff.; Sporrer and Steiner, *Simon Wiesenthal: Ein unbequmer Zeitgenosse*, p. 45f.

39. Gutman, *Encyclopedia of the Holocaust*, Vol. II, p. 623.

40. Simon Wiesenthal, *Doch die Mörder Leben* (Munich: Droemer Knaur, 1967), p. 362; Wiesenthal, testimony at Yad Vashem, October 27, 1960, p. 51.

41. Gutman, *Encyclopedia of the Holocaust*, Vol. III, p. 1139.

42. Wiesenthal, testimony at Yad Vashem, October 27, 1960, p. 56.

43. Wiesenthal, interview with Hella Pick, IWM, Accession 20823, Reel 32.

44. Gutman, *Encyclopedia of the Holocaust*, Vol. II, p. 657.

45. *Mauthausen Nummerbuch*, YVA M8/Mau-3; see also YVA, ITS Central Names Index, W-178; arrest documents at various camps, courtesy of International Tracing Service.

46. Wiesenthal, testimony at Yad Vashem, October 27, 1960, p. 62; Sporrer and Steiner, *Simon Wiesenthal: Ein unbequmer Zeitgenosse*, p. 54.

4: *"Who Knows Her? Who Has Seen Her?"*

1. Ian Kershaw, *Hitler, 1889–1936: Hubris* (London: Allen Lane, 1998), p. 15.

2. Alan Levy, *Nazi Hunter: The Wiesenthal File* (New York: Barnes and Noble Books, 2003), p. 77; Maria Sporrer and Herbert Steiner, eds., *Simon Wiesenthal: Ein unbequemer Zeitgenosse* (Vienna: Orac, 1992), p. 58.

3. Document signed by mayor of Mauthausen, May 15, 1945, WPP.

4. Wiesenthal to American occupation authorities, May 25, 1945, courtesy of Eli Rosenbaum.

5. Wiesenthal, interview with Hella Pick, IWM, Accession 20823, Reel 13.

6. Mauthausen refugees to Clark, March 28, 1946, YVA M9/73.

7. Sporrer and Steiner, *Simon Wiesenthal: Ein unbequmer Zeitgenosse*, p. 59ff.

8. History of US CIC, 430th Division–Austria, USNA, RG 407, E427, Box 18337.

9. Hella Pick, *Simon Wiesenthal: A Life in Search of Justice* (Boston: Northeastern University Press, 1996), p. 103.

10. Junicman to Wiesenthal, May 24, 1952, WPP.

11. Document identifying Wiesenthal ("To Whom it may concern"), June 18, 1945, WPP.

12. Tom Segev, *The Seventh Million: The Israelis and the Holocaust* (New York: Henry Holt, 1993), p. 125; Wiesenthal, recorded testimony, August 1986, YVA 033c/258; Mark Wyman, *DPs: Europe's Displaced Persons 1945–1951* (Ithaca, NY: Cornell University Press), 1998.

13. Michael John, "Gebrochene Kontinuität: Die Kultusgemeinde Linz nach 1945," ed. Eleonore Lappin, in *Jüdische Gemeinden: Kontinuitäten und Brüche* (Berlin: Philo, 2002), p. 144ff.

14. Rolf Vogel, ed., *Das Echo: Wiederhall auf Simon Wiesenthal* (Stuttgart, Germany: Seewald, 1979), p. 17; Simon Wiesenthal, seven caricatures, WPP.

15. Reports on "Jewish Situation" in Upper Austria, February 9 and 14, 1946; memo, May 24, 1946, YVA M9/73; Report on the condition in Bindermichl, February 8 and 14, 1946, CZA S25/6409; Thomas Albrich and Ronald Zweig, eds., *Escape Through Austria: Jewish Refugees and the Austrian Route to Palestine* (London: Frank Cass, 2002); Christine Oertel, *Juden auf der Flucht durch Austria, Jüdische Displaced Persons in der US-Besatzungszone Österreichs* (Vienna: Eichbauer, 1999); Helga Embacher, *Neubeginn ohne Illusionen: Juden in Österreich nach 1945* (Vienna: Picus, 1995), p. 59ff.

16. Jelenke to Wiesenthal, December 31, 1948, YVA M9/52.

17. Wiesenthal to Friedländer, December 31, 1952, YVA M9/28, M9/71, M9/4, M9/31.

18. Anonymous interview with author, October 12, 2007.

19. Pamphlet for former Lvov residents, July 24, 1947, YVA M9/42, see also M9/47; Wiesenthal to Vienna Jewish community, September 15, 1947, CAHJP KAU 958.

20. Bindermichl files, YVA 037/70 (30).

21. Bindermichl files, YVA 037/70 (1–2).

22. Undated notice, YVA M9/10.

23. Leon Zelman, *Ein Leben nach dem Überleben* (Vienna: Kremayr und Scheriau, 2005), p. 119.

24. Simon Wiesenthal: "Vorwort" in Christine Oertel, *Juden auf der Flucht durch Austria, Jüdische Displaced Persons in der US-Besatzungszone Österreichs* (Vienna: Eichbauer, 1999), p. 10.

25. Letter to the Central Committee, January 19, 1946, YVA M9/10.

26. Cyla Wiesenthal, Verfolgungsgeschichte, August 12, 1954; Cyla Wiesenthal, statements under oath, June 20, 1955, April 9, 1956, WPP.

27. Wiesenthal, interview with Hella Pick, IWM, Accession 20823, Reel 30.

28. Levy, *Nazi Hunter*, p. 83.

29. *Hakongres Hazioni Ha Kaf Bet: Din vaheshbon stenografi* (Jerusalem: Zionist Directorate Publishing House, 1946), p. 210; Wiesenthal, interview with Hella Pick, IWM, Accession 20823, Reel 18.

30. Wiesenthal, testimony, November 10, 1960, YVA 03/1817; Wiesenthal, recorded testimony, August 1, 1986, YVA 033c/258; Shlomo Kless, *Bederekh lo slula: Toldot habriha 1944–1948* (Jerusalem: Mossad Bialik, 1995), p. 245; memos, March 27 and 29, 1946, YVA M9/73, see also M/97, M9/15, M9/28, M9/71.

31. Various memos, YVA M9/4, M9/28, M9/71.

32. Pick, *Simon Wiesenthal*, p. 103.

33. Zelman, *Ein Leben nach dem Überleben*, p. 122.

34. Leon Zelman, author interview, May 15, 2006.

35. Zempoli to Wiesenthal, May 22, 1948, WPP.

36. Report summary, February 18, 1949, WPP.

37. Kless, *Bederekh lo slula*, p. 271; Christine Oertel, *Juden auf der Flucht durch Austria, Jüdische Displaced Persons in der US-Besatzungszone Österreichs* (Vienna: Eichbauer, 1999), p. 35ff.; Helga Embacher, *Neubeginn ohne Illusionen: Juden in Österreich nach 1945* (Vienna: Picus, 1995), p. 101ff.

38. Michael Bloch to head of Israeli intelligence service, January 3, 1949, courtesy of Yuval Bloch.

39. Wiesenthal to Weintraub, November 22, 1960.

40. Mandel affidavit, courtesy of Eli Rosenbaum; Wiesenthal to Vienna Jewish community, November 16, 1961, WPP.

41. Memos, YVA M9/51.

42. Segev, *Seventh Million*, p. 123ff.

43. Asher Ben Natan, *The Audacity to Live* (Jerusalem: Mazo, 2007), p. 23ff.

44. Michael Bloch to head of Israeli intelligence service, December 28, 1948, courtesy of Yuval Bloch.

45. Richard Crossman, *Palestine Mission: A Personal Record* (London: Hamish Hamilton, 1946), p. 86.

46. Wiesenthal memorandum, February 14, 1946, CZA S25/6409.

47. Wiesenthal to Kubovy, January 17, 1961, WPP.

48. Simon Wiesenthal, *KZ Mauthausen* (Linz, Austria: IBIS, 1946).

49. Yisrael Cohen and Dov Sadan, eds., *Pirkei Galicia: Sefer zikaron ledoktor Avraham Silberschein* (Tel Aviv: Am Oved, 1957).

50. Wiesenthal to Silberschein, June 30, 1947, YVA M20/183-A; see also YVA M20/182; Wiesenthal, interview with Hella Pick, IWM, Accession 20823, Reel 30.

5: *"The Duty of an Austrian Patriot"*

1. David Wiesenthal to Simon Wiesenthal, May 31, 1946, courtesy of Rachel Kreisberg; Wiesenthal to Rosa Pick, January 10, 1948, courtesy of Rachel Kreisberg.

2. Agreement between Wiesenthal and partners, April 7, 1949, and statement by Majer Spokojny, WPP; Wiesenthal to Schorr, February 14, May 17, June 6, 1951, and January 15, 1952, WPP.

3. Notice on renewal of vehicle license, November 10, 1947, YVA M9/38; reference for pistol license, March 2, 1948, WPP.

4. Wiesenthal to Rafi Cohen, May 30, 1979, WPP.

5. Rosenkranz to Wiesenthal, May 23, 1965, WPP.

6. Heinrich Schmidt, author interview, May 11, 2006; Paul Grosz, author interview, July 3, 2006; see also Ruth Beckermann, *Unzugehörig: Österreicher und Juden nach 1945* (Vienna: Erhard Löcker, 2005).

7. Simon Wiesenthal, *Flucht vor dem Schicksal* (Munich: Nymphenburger Verlagshandlung, 1988).

8. Simon Wiesenthal, "Mahnmal-Denkmal am Judenplatz," *Ausweg*, Vol. 19, no. 2, June 1997, p. 1.

9. Wiesenthal to Ministry of Transport, January 8, 1946, YVA M9/10.

10. Comments on an incident in Salzburg, undated, YVA M9/63; see also Wiesenthal to Eshel, March 13, 1952, and Wiesenthal to Trobe, undated, ISA 2732/24.

11. Wiesenthal to Gleisner, May 23, 1951, YVA M9/28.

12. Wiesenthal to Eshel, September 12, 1952, ISA 2732/24.

13. "Juden Unerwünscht," *Iskult-Presse Nachrichten*, May 25, 1954, courtesy of Linz Jewish community.

14. "Antisemitismus auf dem Fussballfeld," *Der Neue Weg*, No. 9, May 1948; "Dürfen Juden in Österreich Radio hören?" *Der Neue Weg*, No. 4, March 1947.

15. "Ehrengrab für einen Nazi," *Iskult-Presse Nachrichten*, December 30, 1953, courtesy of Linz Jewish community.

16. "Keine Chaplin-Filme in Österreich"; "SPO-Linz lässt Veit Harlan aufführen," *Iskult-Presse Nachrichten*, April 7, 1954, courtesy of Linz Jewish community.

17. "Hitlers Geburtshaus—Attraktion des Fremdenverkehrs," *Iskult-Presse Nachrichten*, May 25, 1954, courtesy of Linz Jewish community; Wiesenthal to Gleisner, September 25, 1951, and Wiesenthal to Eshel, September 26, 1951, YVA M9/28; see also Wiesenthal to Bundesverband der Israelitischen Kultusgemeinden, February 7, 1957, AIKGW, Korrespondenz Bundesverband.

18. Wiesenthal to Cardinal Innizer, undated, YVA M9/64; see also

"Ritualmorddenkmäler in Österreich," *Iskult-Presse Nachrichten*, November 4, 1953, "Ritualmord-Festspiele," *Iskult-Presse Nachrichten*, September 7, 1954, courtesy of Linz Jewish community; Innizer to Wiesenthal, November 1, 1948, YVA M20/182-A.

19. Wiesenthal to Canaval, June 1, 1951, WPP.

20. Wiesenthal at the Generalversammlung des Bundesverbandes der Israelitischen Kultisgemeinden in Österreich, June 22, 1958, WPP.

21. Wiesenthal to Kolb, September 25, 1953, WPP.

22. Paulinka Kreisberg, author interview, September 7, 2006, and autobiographical note, with permission of the writer.

23. Ibid.; Heinrich Schmidt, author interview, May 11, 2006; Wiesenthal, interview with Hella Pick, IWM, Accession 20823, Reel 10.

24. "Ma olel Karl Eichmann: Hameratzeah miSharona," *Hamashkif*, May 31, 1946.

25. Zum Fall Kastner, undated declaration by Wiesenthal, WPP; Simon Wiesenthal, *Ich jagte Eichmann* (Gütersloh, Germany: Siegfried Mohn, 1961), p. 134; CZA S25/3340; Wiesenthal statement, *Yedioth Aharonoth*, September 29, 1955, p. 1; Kastner statement, January 3, 1946, BGA, No. 191565.

26. Simon Wiesenthal, *Gossmufti: Grossagent der Achse* (Salzburg, Austria: Ried, 1947), p. 37.

27. Maurice Pearlman, *The Mufti of Jerusalem* (London: Victor Gollancz, 1947); Wiesenthal to Silberschein, April 11, 1947, YVA M20/182; Wiesenthal to Kubovy, January 9, 1961, WPP; see also manuscript of Wiesenthal's book in English, YVA M20/183.

28. Wiesenthal to Silberschein, December 31, 1947, January 12, 1948, and January 24, 1948, YVA M20/182-A; Wiesenthal to Silberschein, January 12, 1949, WPP; see further correspondence, YVA M9/690, M9/692, M9/693, M9/693a.

29. Wiesenthal to Silberschein, May 31, 1948, June 23, 1948, and June 25, 1948, YVA M20/182-A.

30. Wiesenthal to Swarsensky, December 1, 1950, WPP.

31. Wiesenthal, *Ich jagte Eichmann*, p. 134ff.

32. Bigi to Faln, August 1, 1949, WPP.

33. Ibid.; Wiesenthal to Goldmann, CZA Z6/842; Bigi to Wiesenthal, September 28, 1952, WPP; Ikaros Bigi to author, January 22, 2008.

34. Wiesenthal to Shar, January 19, 1960, WPP.

35. Eshel to Foreign Ministry, February 27, 1952, and January 2, 1953, ISA 2304/17.

36. Hagai Eshed, *Mossad shel ish ehad: Reuven Shiloah, avi hamodi'in haYisraeli* (Tel Aviv: Idanin, 1988), p. 126ff.; Asher Ben Natan, *The Audacity to Live* (Jerusalem: Mazo, 2007), p. 78.

37. Wiesenthal to Eshel, May 10, 1952, WPP.

38. Richard Breitman, with Norman J. W. Goda and Paul Brown, "The Gestapo," in *U.S. Intelligence and the Nazis*, ed. Richard Breitman et al. (Cambridge, UK: Cambridge University Press), pp. 154–55.

39. Wiesenthal to Auriol, May 1, 1952, WPP; Junicman to Wiesenthal, June 3, 1952, WPP; see also Wiesenthal, *Ich jagte Eichmann*, p. 144.

40. Press card and Bundeskanzleramt issued to Wiesenthal, September 30, 1950, WPP.

41. Hardy Swarsensky to Wiesenthal, September 9, 1952, and February 24, 1953, WPP.

42. Wiesenthal to Eshel, March 13, 1952, ISA 2732/24; Wiesenthal to Tabor, March 23, 1952, ISA 2732/24; Wiesenthal to consul, August 25, 1952, ISA 2732/24.

43. Wiesenthal to Eshel, December 2, 1952, WPP.

44. Wiesenthal to Eshel, December 11, 1952, YVA M9/28; Wiesenthal to Eshel, May 15, 1951, ISA 2732/24.

45. Wiesenthal to Tabor, November 29, 1952, WPP.

46. Wiesenthal to Levin, December 20, 1948, WPP.

47. Wiesenthal to Eshel, April 25, 1953, May 11, 1953, and June 6, 1953, ISA 2732/24; Wiesenthal to Eshel, May 22, 1953, WPP.

48. Wiesenthal to Eshel, June 18, 1953, ISA 2732/24; Wiesenthal to Eshel, August 16, 1952, WPP.

49. Tabor to Wiesenthal, March 17, 1952, October 30, 1952, and December 14, 1952, ISA 2732/24.

50. Eshel to Wiesenthal, May 4, 1953, May 14, 1953, and May 25, 1953, ISA 2732/24.

51. Wiesenthal to Eshel, April 30, 1952, and Eshel to Wiesenthal, October 18, 1951, YVA M9/29.

52. Eshel to Wiesenthal, November 12, 1951, YVA M9/29; Wiesenthal to Eshel, April 28, 1952, Eshel to Wiesenthal May 5, 1952, and Wiesenthal to Eshel, May 10, 1952, WPP; Wiesenthal to Eshel, June 14, 1952, Wiesenthal to Tabor, January 14, 1953, Wiesenthal to Eshel, May 7, 1953, and Eshel to Wiesenthal, May 10, 1953, ISA2732/24.

53. Wiesenthal to Oberösterreichische Landesregierung, March 27, 1952, and Rösch to Kreisky, October 28, 1975, BKA, Wiesenthal Box I (Informationen für den Bundeskanzler); biographical summary, May 14, 1969, BKA, Wiesenthal Box II.

54. Interior Ministry report, May 23, 1950, BKA, Wiesenthal Box I (Informationen für den Bundeskanzler).

55. Gleissner to Graf, January 17, 1953, WPP; Walter Schuster, *Politische Restauration und Entnazifizierungspolitik in Oberösterreich*, (Linz, Austria: Historisches Jahrbuch der Stadt Linz, 2002), p. 176ff.

56. Wiesenthal to Rafi Cohen, May 30, 1979, WPP.

6. *"That's How I Became a Stamp Collector"*

1. Simon Wiesenthal, *The Murderers Among Us*, ed. Joseph Wechsberg (New York: McGraw-Hill, 1967), p. 59ff.

2. Maria Sporrer and Herbert Steiner, eds., *Simon Wiesenthal: Ein unbequemer Zeitgenosse* (Vienna: Orac, 1992), p. 100ff.; Thomas Albrich et al., eds., *Holocaust und Kriegsverbrechen vor Gericht: Der Fall Österreich* (Innsbruck, Austria: StudienVerlag, 2006), pp. 134–35.

3. Tarra family papers, courtesy of his son; Walter Tarra, author interview, June 16, 2006; Rot-Weiss-Rot-Buch, Vienna, 1946, Druck und Verlag der

Österreichischen Staatsdruckerei, 1946, Vol. I, p. 146ff.; Um Österreichs Freiheit—
Ein Beitrag zur Geschichte der Abwehrkämpfe des Jahres 1934 in der Steiermark,
Granz (n.d.), Fond zur Unterstützung der Witwen und Waisen der Gefallenen
Bundesheer, Exekutive and Wehrverbandsangehörigen.

4. Tarra to Wiesenthal, September 24, 1952, December 6, 1952, January 1,
1953, and March 22, 1953, WPP; ISA 2732/24; Eshel to director general, February
3, 1953, ISA 2304/17.

5. Simon Wiesenthal, *Ich jagte Eichmann* (Gütersloh, Germany: Siegfried Mohn,
1961), p. 224ff.; Wiesenthal to Eshel, March 24, 1953, WPP.

6. Isser Harel, "Simon Wiesenthal and the Capture of Eichmann," unpublished
document, courtesy of Eli Rosenbaum, p. 130ff.

7. Wiesenthal to Junicman, April 18, 1952, WPP.

8. Wiesenthal to Kastner, December 6, 1948, WPP; see also Simon Wiesenthal,
Justice Not Vengeance (London: Weidenfeld & Nicolson, 1989), p. 45.

9. Leo Frank, *Geständnis: Das Leben eines Polizisten* (Linz, Austria: Grosser, 1993),
p. 22f.

10. Wiesenthal, *Ich jagte Eichmann*, p. 56f.; correspondence between Wiesenthal
and Ponger as well as intelligence records pertaining to Wiesenthal were obtained in
1986 by the World Jewish Congress under the Freedom of Information Act, and are
quoted here with the kind permission of Eli Rosenbaum; "U.S. Sentences 2 as Spies
for Reds," *New York Times*, June 9, 1953, p. 12.

11. CIA report (Dr. Höttl's reaction to the arrest of Verber and Ponger), April 3,
1953, USNA, RG 263, UD-2 Box 1 (Notorious Nazis).

12. Undated memo on the case against Stern, WPP; Wiesenthal, interview with
Hella Pick, IWM, Accession 20823, Reel 47; Norman J. Goda, "The Nazi Peddler:
Wilhelm Höttl and Allied Intelligence," in *U.S. Intelligence and the Nazis*, ed. Richard
Breitman et al. (Cambridge, UK: Cambridge University Press, 2005), p. 265ff.;
The Trial of Adolf Eichmann: Record of Proceedings in the District Court of Jerusalem, Vol. IV
(Jerusalem: State of Israel, Ministry of Justice, 1993), Session 8, July 4, 1961,
p. 1514ff.

13. CIA Progress Report, March 15–April 15, 1955, USNA, RG 263, UD-2
Box 1 (Notorious Nazis).

14. Wiesenthal to Eshel, May 22, 1953, ISA 2732/24.

15. Moshe Sharett, *Yoman ishi*, Vol. 4 (Tel Aviv: Sifriat Maariv, 1978), p. 1,186;
Moshe Pearlman, *Eikh nitpas Eichmann* (Tel Aviv: Am Oved, 1961), p. 87; Ben-Gurion
diary, October 30, 1960, BGA.

16. David Cesarani, *Eichmann: His Life and Crimes* (New York: Vintage, 2005),
p. 200ff.; Neal Bascomb, *Hunting Eichmann* (Boston: Houghton Mifflin Harcourt,
2009).

17. Uki Goni, *The Real Odessa: Smuggling the Nazis to Peron's Argentina* (London: Granta
Books, 2002).

18. Wiesenthal, *Ich jagte Eichmann*, p. 178ff.

19. Wiesenthal, *Justice Not Vengeance* (London: Weidenfeld & Nicolson, 1989), p. 56.

20. Documents relating to Odessa, USNA, RG 319, IRR case files, boxes 39
and 64.

21. Heinz Schneppen, *Odessa und das Vierte Reich: Mythen der Zeitgeschichte* (Berlin: Metropol, 2007), p. 58ff.

22. Simon Wiesenthal, *Doch die Mörder Leben* (Munich: Droemer Knaur, 1967), p. 364.

23. Friedman to Yad Vashem, September 11, 1955, WPP; Wiesenthal to Friedman, May 9, 2003, WPP.

24. A. Frydmann, "Juden welche in der Zeit des Hitler-regimes im Judenrat beschäftigt oder für denselben tätig waren," *Der Neue Weg*, No. 9, May 1948, p. 3.

25. Wiesenthal to Staatspolizei, May 13, 1946, YVA M9/10.

26. Tuwiah Friedman, ed., *Die Korrespondenz der zwei Nazi Forscher Tuwiah Friedman und Simon Wiesenthal in den Jahren 1946–1950* (Haifa: Institute for the Documentation of Nazi Crimes, 2005), Vol. I (no page numbers); see also Friedman report, June 1947, CZA S25/10746.

27. *Der Neue Weg*, No. 43/44, December 1946, p. 3; Wiesenthal to Friedman November 5, 1947; Friedman, *Korrespondenz der zwei Nazi Forscher*, Vol. II (no page numbers); U.S. Department of Justice, Office of Special Investigations, *In the Matter of Josef Mengele: A Report to the Attorney General of the United States* (Washington, DC: Department of Justice, 1992), p. 26ff.

28. Wiesenthal, *Murderers Among Us*, p. 301ff.

29. Wiesenthal to the Linz People's Court (Volksgericht), August 6, 1947, YVA M9/38.

30. Wiesenthal in New York, November 6, 1980, SWAW, speech file.

31. Wiesenthal, interview with Hella Pick, IWM, Accession 20823, Reels 23 and 35.

32. Winfried R. Garscha, "The Trials of Nazi War Criminals in Austria," lecture at U.S. Holocaust Memorial Museum, November 1966, WPP; see also, Thomas Albrich et al., eds., *Holocaust und Kriegsverbrechen vor Gericht: Der Fall Österreich* (Innsbruck: Studien Verlag, 2006); Karl Marschall, *Volksgerichtsbarkeit und Verfolgung von Nationalsozialistischen Gewaltverbrechen in Österreich* (Vienna: Bundesministerium für Justiz, 1987); Andreas Eichmüller, "Die Strafverfolgung von NS-Verbrechen durch westdeutsche Justizbehörden seit 1945," *Vierteljahreshefte für Zeitgeschichte*, 4/2008, p. 621ff.

33. *Landsberg: Ein Dokumentarischer Bericht*, Office of the U.S. High Commissioner for Germany, Munich, 1951; News report, Al Hamishmar, March 5, 1951, CZA 36S 71/4.

34. Wiesenthal to Sobek, December 23, 1947, YVA M20/182; Wiesenthal to Bedo, October 15, 1948, YVA M9/64; Joslow to Shapiro, November 3, 1948, YVA M9/52.

35. Wiesenthal to Swarsensky, December 1, 1950, WPP; Wiesenthal, interview with Hella Pick, IWM, Accession 20823, Reels 27 and 35.

36. Army intelligence report, July 2, 1955, courtesy of Eli Rosenbaum; Simon Wiesenthal, "Meine Suche nach Eichmann" (third draft, 1960), p. 7, WPP, Eichmann file; Wiesenthal, recorded testimony, YVA 033c/258; Wiesenthal, *Justice Not Vengeance*, p. 20; Sporrer and Steiner, eds., *Simon Wiesenthal: Ein unbequemer Zeitgenosse*, p. 78ff.; Schneppen, *Odessa und das Vierte Reich*, p. 87.

37. Wiesenthal to Yad Vashem, May 9, 1960, WPP; Wiesenthal to Yad Vashem, July 1, 1963, YVA 0/4/529.

38. Karbach to Wiesenthal, August 26, 1970, WPP.

39. Goldmann to Eshel, March 12, 1954, ISA Z6/1949; Wiesenthal to Goldmann, March 30, 1954, Z6/842.

40. Wiesenthal to Silberschein, June 22, 1948, YVA M20/182-A.

41. Kalmanowitz obituary, *New York Times*, February 17, 1964, 31:4.

42. Kalmanowitz to Eisenhower, July 20 and 23, 1953, USNA, RG 263, UD-2, Vol. 4; Hart to Kalmanowitz, August 24, 1953, USNA, RG 263, UD-2, Vol. 4.

43. Kalmanowitz to Hart, August 3, 1953, USNA, RG 263, UD-2, Vol. 4.

44. Grossman to Goldmann, April 27, 1954, Goldmann's secretary to Kalmanowitz, April 28, 1954, Goldmann to Kalmanowitz, April 29, 1954, ISA Z6/846; Kalmanowitz to Goldmann, May 9, 1954, Kalmanowitz to Dulles, May 6, 1954, Kalmanowitz to Byroade, May 6, 1954, ISA Z6/843.

45. Wiesenthal, *Ich jagte Eichmann*, p. 231.

46. Rosenbaum, memorandum, March 23, 2007; Isser Harel, "Simon Wiesenthal and the Capture of Eichmann," unpublished document, courtesy of Eli Rosenbaum, p. 81.

47. *Ha'aretz*, September 17, 1954; Wiesenthal to Goldmann, September 21, 1954, CZA Z6/863.

48. Kalmanowitz to Wiesenthal, May 21, June 25, and November 3, 1954, WPP; Wiesenthal to Kalmanowitz, June 12, October 25, and November 10, 1954, WPP.

49. Wiesenthal, "Meine Suche nach Eichmann" (third draft), p. 11, SWAW, Eichmann file.

50. Wiesenthal to Segal, October 3, 1955; Alsberg to Wiesenthal, January 2, 1956; Wiesenthal to Eshel, September 1, 1955; Wiesenthal to Yad Vashem, March 1, 1956; Eshel to Wiesenthal, August 18, 1955; Friedman to Wiesenthal, August 22, 1955; Eshel to Wiesenthal, August 24, 1955, WPP; Tuvia Friedman, author interview, March 30, 2006; Robinson to Wiesenthal, March 22, 1956; Wiesenthal to Robinson, March 27, 1956, WPP.

51. Wiesenthal, "Meine Suche nach Eichmann" (second draft, 1960), p. 4, SWAW, Eichmann file; Wiesenthal, "Meine Suche nach Eichmann" (first draft, 1960), supplement, p. 2, SWAW, Eichmann file.

7: "I Hope You're Not Coming to See Me"

1. Paulinka Kreisberg, author interview, September 7, 2006.

2. Simon Wiesenthal, *Justice Not Vengeance* (London: Weidenfeld & Nicolson, 1989), p. 51.

3. Maria Sporrer and Herbert Steiner, eds., *Simon Wiesenthal: Ein unbequemer Zeitgenosse* (Vienna:: Orac, 1992), p. 78ff.; Heinz Schneppen, *Odessa und das Vierte Reich: Mythen der Zeitgeschichte* (Berlin: Metropol, 2007), p. 71ff.; David Eisenhower, *Eisenhower at War 1943–1945* (New York: Random House, 1986), p. 523.

4. Wiesenthal to Kohl, April 19, 1985, WPP.

5. "Die Schatzgräber von Altaussee," *Aufbau*, July 6, 1951.

6. Wiesenthal to Loehde, September 11, 1959, WPP. See also Flora Lewis, "Nazis Dumped Counterfeit Fortune into Toplitzsee," *Washington Post*, November 24, 1963, E5.

7. Wiesenthal to Silberschein, April 24, 1947, WPP.

8. Wiesenthal to Silberschein, February 8, 1954, WPP.

9. Sahar to Wiesenthal, September 11, 1959, WPP; see also Wiesenthal to Israeli consul, November 11, 1952, YVA M9/31.

10. Wiesenthal to Kermisz, July 30, 1960, WPP; Kermisz to Wiesenthal, August 18, 1960, WPP; see also related material, YVA M9/35.

11. Simon Wiesenthal, *Ich jagte Eichmann* (Gütersloh, Germany: Siegfried Mohn, 1961), p. 37.

12. Wiesenthal, *Justice Not Vengeance*, p. 54.

13. "Nochmals RIF," *Der Neue Weg*, August 15, 1946, SWAW, RIF file.

14. Carmen Hofbauer, "Simon Wiesenthal als Publizist," dissertation, University of Salzburg, 2002.

15. Simon Wiesenthal, "Der Altag," *Der Neue Weg*, August 15, 1946.

16. Wiesenthal to HIAS, December 22, 1956, courtesy of Linz Jewish community.

17. The World ORT Union, USEP activities report on Austria to July 31, 1960, CAHJP, WOU 438.

18. Goldmann to Wiesenthal, October 9, 1956, WPP.

19. Goldmann to Wiesenthal, October 18, 1956, WPP.

20. Wiesenthal to Meir, April 5, 1957, courtesy of Linz Jewish community.

21. Wiesenthal to Sonnenschein, April 3, 1956, courtesy of Linz Jewish community.

22. Innsbruck Jewish community to Wiesenthal, July 4, 1957, courtesy of Linz Jewish community.

23. Wiesenthal to Feder, March 27, 1957, courtesy of Linz Jewish community.

24. Wiesenthal to Feder, November 5, 1957, courtesy of Linz Jewish community.

25. Wiesenthal to JDC, April 4, 1958, courtesy of Linz Jewish community.

26. Wiesenthal to Feder, September 25, 1957, courtesy of Linz Jewish community; see also Wiesenthal to *Yedioth Aharonoth*, October 11, 1954, courtesy of Linz Jewish community.

27. Wiesenthal to Ziegenlaub, February 7, 1957, courtesy of Linz Jewish community.

28. Shuster to Wiesenthal, June 24, 1959, WPP.

29. Wiesenthal memo, June 24, 1953, courtesy of Linz Jewish community.

30. The sale documents are cited courtesy of Dr. Hans Popper, CEO of the Oberösterreichische Gebietskrankenkasse; see also YVA M9/8.

31. Court judgment, November 25, 1960, WPP.

32. Wiesenthal to Kempner, March 30, 1953, courtesy of Linz Jewish community; Evian to Wiesenthal, February 14, 1959, WPP; Wiesenthal, interview with Hella Pick, IWM, Accession 20823, Reel 18.

33. Helmar Sartor, author interview, October 17, 2006.

34. Wiesenthal to Friedler, June 2, 1953; Wiesenthal to Rehm, June 6, 1953, AIKGW, Extern, 53.

35. Michael John, "Gebrochene Kontinuität—Die Kultusgemeinde Linz nach 1945," in *Jüdische Gemeinden: Kontinuitäten und Brüche*, ed. Eleonore Lappin (Berlin: Philo, 2002), p. 172; Helmut Fiereder, "Die Wiedergründung der jüdischen Gemeinde von Linz 1945–1948," ed. Walter Schuster et al., in *Historisches Jahrbuch der Stadt Linz 2003–2004, Archiv der Stadt* (Linz, Austria: Archiv der Stadt Kinz, 2004), p. 583ff.; Kostenvoranschlag für den Bau eines Wohnhauses für Cylia u. Herrn Simon Wiesenthal, courtesy of Linz Jewish community.

36. Wiesenthal to Krell, March 29, 1953, WPP.

37. Wiesenthal to Robetin-Fuchs, March 8, 1957; Schilderung des Tatbestandes, March 12, 1957, WPP.

38. Wiesenthal to Lewin, March 21, 1949, WPP.

39. Wiesenthal to Eshel, May 26, 1953, ISA 2732/24.

40. Wiesenthal to Krell, April 22, 1953, courtesy of Linz Jewish community; Wiesenthal to Krell, June 24, 1953; Wiesenthal to Krell, June 20, 1953, AIKGW, Extern, 53.

41. Wiesenthal to Schwager, April 13, 1953, courtesy of Linz Jewish community; see also Wiesenthal to Schwager, April 10, 1953, AIKGW, Extern, 53.

42. Kostenvoranschlag für den Bau eines Wohnhauses für Cylia u. Herrn Simon Wiesenthal, courtesy of Linz Jewish community.

43. Sobek to Verband der politisch Vefolgten, May 23, 1946, YVA M9/73.

44. Wiesenthal to Figl, July 22, 1952, ISA 2732/24.

45. Wiesenthal to Krell, September 4, 1951, YVA M9/28; Wiesenthal to Eshel, July 16, 1952, ISA 2732/24.

46. Eshel to Foreign Ministry, February 29, 1954, ISA 2304/19.

47. Wiesenthal, interview with Hella Pick, IWM, Accession 20823, Reel 31.

48. Wiesenthal memorandum of meeting with Raab, November 18, 1958, WPP.

49. Jewish Central Committee to military government, November 7, 1947, YVA M9/87.

50. Wiesenthal to Jüdische Historische Dokumentation, April 29, 1947, YVA M9/98; Wiesenthal, testimony, November 6, 1947, YVA M9/121, M9/11, M9/84; Shlomo Kless, *Bederekh lo slula: Toldot habriha 1944–1948* (Tel Aviv: Moreshet, 1995), p. 245.

51. Refugee court judgment, November 18, 1947, WPP; see also Wiesenthal to the committee of the Linz Jewish community, April 21 and 22, 1953, AIKGW, Extern, 53.

52. Wiesenthal to International Relief Organization, June 12, 1951, YVA M9/28.

53. Wiesenthal to Eshel, May 26, 1953, ISA 1732/24; Eshel to Wiesenthal, May 28, 1953, ISA 1732/24.

54. Wiesenthal to West German government, December 14, 1957, WPP.

55. Linz District Court judgment, December 11, 1958, WPP; see also Abraham and Fimek Mandel to Wiesenthal, November 24, 1975, WPP.

56. "Jüdische Verbrecher," YVA M9/88.

57. Wiesenthal at a Yad Vashem conference, 1968, *Jewish Resistance During the Holocaust: Proceedings of the Conference on Manifestations of Jewish Resistance* (Jerusalem: Yad Vashem, 1971), p. 246; Tom Segev, *The Seventh Million: The Israelis and the Holocaust* (New York: Henry Holt, 1993), p. 258.

58. Tamir to Wiesenthal, January 29, 1954, WPP.

59. Yoav Gelber, *Shorshei hahavatzelet: Hamodi'in bayishuv 1947–48* (Tel Aviv: Israel Defense Ministry, 1992), p. 276ff.

60. Amos Keinan, "Sochno shel Eichmann b'Yisrael," *Ha'olam Hazeh*, No. 889, October 27, 1954, p. 8.

61. Wiesenthal to Silberschein, May 31, 1948, YVA M9/583; Bart to Wiesenthal, October 23, 1953, WPP; Wiesenthal to Bart, October 30, 1952, WPP; Simon Wiesenthal, "Zum Fall Kastner," *Jüdische Rundschau*, September 2, 1955, p. 2; Yudkovsky to Wiesenthal, September 25, 1955, WPP.

62. Simon Wiesenthal, "Zum Problem jüdischer Quislinge," YVA M9/87.

63. Wiesenthal at Lvov trial, December 20, 1966, protocol, p. 2291, SWAW, Lvov file; bulletin no. 3, April 1965, p. 2, SWAW.

64. Simon Wiesenthal, "Zum Problem jüdischer Quislinge," YVA M9/87; Wiesenthal to military government, November 7, 1946, YVA M9/87, M9/246.

65. Paulinka Kreisberg, author interview, September 7, 2006; Simon Wiesenthal, *Doch die Mörder Leben* (Munich: Droemer Knaur, 1967), p. 362.

66. Wiesenthal to Eshel, February 15, 1951, YVA M9/28; Wiesenthal to Friedman, March 10, 1960, in *Die Korrespondenz der zwei Nazi Forscher Tuwiah Friedman und Simon Wiesenthal in den Jahren 1946–1950*, ed. Tuwiah Friedman (Haifa: Institute for the Documentation of Nazi Crimes, 2005), Vol. II (no page numbers).

67. Simon Wiesenthal, *The Murderers Among Us*, ed. Joseph Wechsberg (New York: McGraw-Hill, 1967), p. 59.

68. Wiesenthal, *Murderers Among Us*, p. 280; Rokita file, SWAW.

69. Wiesenthal to Padaborn prosecutor's office, January 16, 1958, Wiesenthal to Günthert, January 18, 1958, Wiesenthal to Padaborn prosecutor's office, March 25, 1958, and Wiesenthal to Jetter, July 9, 1958, WPP; Wiesenthal to Friedman, September 8, 1958; Friedman, *Korrespondenz;* Wiesenthal, *Murderers Among Us*, p. 280.

70. Wiesenthal to Silberschein, July 14, 1958, WPP.

71. Frankfurt District Court to Wiesenthal, March 19, 1958, WPP; investigating magistrate of Cologne district court to Wiesenthal, January 26, 1960, WPP.

72. Simon Wiesenthal, "Meine Suche nach Eichmann" (second draft, 1960), p. 4, SWAW, Eichmann file; Wiesenthal, "Meine Suche nach Eichmann" (third draft, 1960), p. 10, SWAW, Eichmann file.

8: *"I Always Said He's in Buenos Aires"*

1. Tuvia Friedman, *15 shanim radafti Aharei Eichmann* (Netanya: Achiasaf, 1961), p. 131; Tuvia Friedman, "Nokem shetafas meot Nazim," *Maariv*, November 7, 1957.

2. Isser Harel, "Simon Wiesenthal and the Capture of Eichmann," unpublished

document, courtesy of Eli Rosenbaum, pp. 19–20; Moshe Sharett, *Yoman ishi*, Vol. 4 (Tel Aviv: Sifriat Maariv, 1978), p. 1,186.

3. "War Eastern Connections," March 19, 1953, USNA, RG 263, UD-2 Box I (Notorious Nazis).

4. Irmtrud Wojak, *Fritz Bauer 1903–1968: Eine Biographie* (Munich: C. H. Beck, 2009), p. 287.

5. Office for the Protection of the Constitution to Foreign Ministry, April 11, 1958; Foreign Ministry to Office for the Protection of the Constitution, July 4, 1958; Office for the Protection of the Constitution to Foreign Ministry, June 9, 1960; all courtesy of the Office for the Protection of the Constitution.

6. Simon Wiesenthal, *Ich jagte Eichmann* (Gütersloh, Germany: Siegfried Mohn, 1961), p. 239.

7. Office for the Protection of the Constitution to Foreign Ministry, June 9 1960, courtesy of the Office for the Protection of the Constitution.

8. Kurt Schrimm/Joachim Riedel: "50 Jahre Zentrale Stelle in Ludwigsburg," *Vierteljahreshefte für Zeitgeschichte*, 4/2008, p. 525ff.

9. Schüle to Friedman, August 20, 1959, in *Die Korrespondenz 1959–1990 zwischen der Zentralstelle in Ludwigsburg und der Dokumentation in Haifa*, ed. Tuwiah Friedman (Haifa: Institute for the Documentation of Nazi Crimes, 1993), no page numbers.

10. Wiesenthal to Sahar, January 19, 1960, WPP; Wiesenthal to Altmayer, January 22 and January 25, 1960, WPP.

11. Kurt Schrimm to Martin Mendelsohn, December 20, courtesy of Martin Mendelsohn, and related materials, ZS, Generalakte III 21 to III 24/93.

12. Office for the Protection of the Constitution to Foreign Ministry, June 9, 1960, courtesy of the Office for the Protection of the Constitution.

13. Memo to Miron, October 18, 1959, ISA 3086/12; Savir to Shinar, October 23, 1959, and Schüle to Israeli mission, November 13, 1959, ISA 293/13; press clippings, ISA 293/13; see also correspondence, CZA C6/549; Tartakower to Nahmias, October 25, 1959, CZA C6/524; Isser Harel, *The House on Garibaldi Street* (New York: Bantam Books, 1976); Irmtrud Wojak, *Eichmanns Memoiren: Ein kritischer Essay* (Frankfurt: Fischer, 2004), p. 16ff.; Tarra to Bauer, January 6, 1960, WPP; Bauer to Tarra, January 11, 1960, WPP.

14. Friedman to Goldmann, February 1, 1956, ISA 6688/8; Friedman to Tartakower, May 13, 1958, ISA C6/549; Friedman to Ben-Gurion, March 4, 1959, ISA 6688/8; Tartakower to Friedman, June 17, 1956, September 19, 1956, September 23, 1956, and September 30, 1956, ISA C6/415; Schüle to Friedman, July 24, 1959, ISA C6/549; Tuvia Friedman, *Helki bemivtza Eichmann* (Haifa: Institute for the Documentation of Nazi Crimes, 2005), no page numbers; *Maariv*, October 11, 1959; Ben-Gurion diary, December 6, 1959, BGA.

15. Wiesenthal, *Ich jagte Eichmann*, p. 245; Simon Wiesenthal, *Justice Not Vengeance* (London: Weidenfeld & Nicolson, 1989), p. 77; Simon Wiesenthal, "Meine Suche nach Eichmann" (first draft, 1960), p. 5, SWAW, Eichmann file; Wiesenthal, "Meine Suche nach Eichmann" (third draft, 1960), p. 5, SWAW, Eichmann file.

16. Wiesenthal to Sahar, January 19, 1960, WPP.

17. Wiesenthal to Sahar, September 23, 1959, and November 2, 1959, WPP; Shar to Wiesenthal, November 10, 1959, WPP.

18. Report on visit to Frankfurt, November 12, 1959, WPP; Shar to Wiesenthal, December 29 1959, with questionnaire, WPP.

19. Wiesenthal to Sahar, February 10, 1960, WPP; Harel, "Simon Wiesenthal," p. 230, courtesy of Eli Rosenbaum; Aharoni in BBC interview.

20. Harel, "Simon Wiesenthal," p. 187, courtesy of Eli Rosenbaum.

21. Wiesenthal to Rosenkranz, January 29, 1960, WPP.

22. Wiesenthal to Friedman, March 10, 1960, WPP.

23. Tom Segev, *The Seventh Million: Israelis and the Holocaust* (New York: Henry Holt, 1993), p. 323.

24. Wojak, *Eichmanns Memoiren,* p. 16ff.

25. Cohen-Abarbanel to Bauer, May 10, 1960, Nachlass Fritz Bauer, ASD.

26. High Court of Justice (the "Bagatz"), judgment in *Isser Harel vs. the Government,* August 27, 1969, no. 130/68, p. 8; affidavit of Shlomo Cohen Abarbanel, July 8, 1968; High Court of Justice, judgments 130/68 and 632/05.

27. Lipian to Haber, January 18, 1961, AJA, AR 45/64 #3229, Admin: Personal W.

28. Alan Levy, *Nazi Hunter: The Wiesenthal File* (New York: Barnes and Noble Books, 2002), p. 93.

29. Wiesenthal to JDC director general, April 6, 1961, WPP.

30. Wiesenthal to Shuster, American Jewish Committee, June 15, 1951, WPP; Shuster to Wiesenthal, June 24, 1959, WPP.

31. Goldman to Halperin, April 6, 1961, and to Max Braude, May 1, 1961, CAHJP, WOU 830.

32. Wiesenthal to Goldman, November 2, 1960, CAHJP, WOU 830.

33. Goldman to Wiesenthal, January 10, 1961, WPP.

34. Rosenkranz to Wiesenthal, February 12, 1960, WPP.

35. Note on the unfolding of the Eichmann affair, August 8, 1960, BGA, no. 166258; see also High Court of Justice, judgment, *Isser Harel vs. the Government of Israel.*

36. Wiesenthal to Rosenkranz, May 30, 1960, WPP; Wiesenthal to Chaimoff, July 2, 1960, WPP.

37. Wiesenthal to Dak, June 17, 1960, WPP.

38. Kiermitsz to Elkana, July 7, 1960, YVA M9/60; Wiesenthal to Sahar, June 8, 1960; Dak to Foreign Ministry, June 15, 1960; Wiesenthal to Dak, June 24, 1960; Hofstetter to Yakhil, July 12, 1960; Yakhil to Israeli embassy in Vienna, July 18, 1960; Wiesenthal to Dak, July 27, 1960; Wiesenthal to Dak, August 30, 1960; Hofstetter to Yakhil, September 19, 1960—all in ISA 2731/2; Dak to director general, Foreign Ministry, July 31, 1960, ISA 2741/2; Wiesenthal to Kiermitsz, July 14, 1960; Hofstetter to Yakhil, August 5, 1960; Dak to director general's bureau, November 7, 1960; Wiesenthal to Hofstetter, December 1 and December 7, 1960—all in ISA 7027/12; affidavit, April 13, 1961, ISA 3071/34; Wiesenthal to Yad Vashem, September 16, 1960, WPP.

39. David Cesarani, *Eichmann: His Life and Crimes* (New York: Vintage, 2005),

p. 217ff.; Uki Goni, *The Real Odessa: Smuggling the Nazis to Peron's Argentina* (London: Granta Books, 2002), p. 306ff.

40. Wiesenthal, interview with Hella Pick, IWM, Accession 20823, Reels 31–32; Wiesenthal to Ben. A. Sijes, December 28, 1970, WPP; Wiesenthal to Hausner, October 5, 1980, WPP.

41. Ben-Gurion diary, July 27, 1960, BGA.

42. Wiesenthal to Roth, June 12, 1962, WPP.

43. Wiesenthal to Yad Vashem, June 8, 1960, and June 9, 1960, WPP.

44. *Yedioth Aharonoth*, February 24, 1961; Ben-Gurion diary, May 12, 1961, BGA; Wiesenthal to *Yedioth Aharonoth*, June 22, 1961.

45. Wiesenthal to Kubovy, November 7, 1960, WPP; Wiesenthal to Rosenkranz, November 7, 1960, WPP.

46. Levy, *Nazi Hunter*, p. 156.

47. Segev, *Seventh Million*, p. 323.

48. Wiesenthal, interview with Hella Pick, IWM, Accession 20823, Reels 34–35.

49. Tim Cole, "The Holocaust and Its (Re)Telling: The Nature of Evidence at the Nuremberg and Eichmann Trials," in *From the Protocols of the Elders of Zion to Holocaust Denial Trials*, ed. Debra Kaufman et al. (London: Vallentine Mitchell, 2007), p. 56ff.

50. Segev, *Seventh Million*, p. 355.

51. Hannah Arendt, *Eichmann in Jerusalem: A Report on the Banality of Evil* (New York: Viking Press, 1968); Steven E. Aschheim, ed., *Hannah Arendt in Jerusalem* (Berkeley: University of California Press, 2001).

52. Simon Wiesenthal, *Haredifa Aharei Eichmann* (Jerusalem: Weiss, 1961), p. x.

53. Wiesenthal, interview with Hella Pick, IWM, Accession 20823, Reel 22.

54. Ben-Gurion diary, December 3, 1961, and February 22 1962, BGA; Wojak, *Eichmanns Memoiren*; see also Tom Segev, "Elilav shel Adolf Eichmann," *Ha'aretz*, March 3, 2000, B4.

55. Ben-Gurion diary, February 26, 1962, BGA.

56. Wiesenthal to Keintzel, October 27, 1961, WPP.

57. Wiesenthal, interview with Hella Pick, IWM, Accession 20823, Reel 21.

58. Ben-Gurion diary, October 30, 1960, BGA; Wiesenthal to Rosen, March 9, 1961, CZA C6/556; Wiesenthal to Tartakower, March 14, 1961, CZA C6/556; Wiesenthal to Kubovy, January 9, 1961, WPP; Wiesenthal to Rosenkranz, January 17, 1961, WPP.

59. Friedman to Ben-Gurion, November 25, 1960, ISA 6688/8; Maroz to Herut, November 13, 1960, ISA 4332/1; Arnon to Manor, January 3, 1962, ISA 6688/8; Ben-Gurion to Friedman, CZA C6/500.

60. Herman to Tartakower, May 30, 1961; Tartakower to Herman, June 10, 1961; Herman to Tartakower, June 19, 1961; Tartakower to Rosen, June 29, 1961; Rosen to Tartakower, August 1, 1961; Tartakower to Herman, August 6, 1961—all in CZA C6/600; see also Mizrahi to Friedman, July 25, 1972, in Friedman, *Healki Bamivtza Eichmann*; Herman to Wiesenthal, April 16, May 8, May 16, and August 8, 1973, SWAW, Eichmann file.

61. Gilad Margalit, *Ashma, sevel vezikaron: Germania zokheret et meteha bemilhemet haolam hashniya* (Haifa: Haifa University Publishing House, 2007).

62. Cohen to Robinson, August 9, 1961, YVA 0–65; Wiesenthal to Shuster, June 15, 1961, and July 27, 1961, WPP; see also Andreas Eichmüller, "Die Strafverfolgung von NS-Verbrechen durch west-deutsche Justizbehörden seit 1945," *Vierteljahreshefte für Zeitgeschichte*, 4/2008, p. 621ff.

9: *"Sleuth with 6 Million Clients"*

1. Bulletin, April 2, 1962, p. 5, SWAW.
2. Dak to Foreign Ministry, March 14, 1961, ISA 3299/47.
3. Minutes of meeting of the Linz Jewish community committee, June 22, 1961, courtesy of Linz Jewish community.
4. Wiesenthal, interview with Hella Pick, IWM, Accession 20823, Reel 20.
5. Bulletin, May 10, 1963, p. 1, WPP.
6. *The Trial of Adolf Eichmann: Record of Proceedings in the District Court of Jerusalem*, Vol. II (Jerusalem: State of Israel, Ministry of Justice, 1993), Session 34, May 10, 1961, p. 624.
7. Bulletin, October 24, 1963, p. 1, WPP.
8. Simon Wiesenthal, *The Murderers Among Us*, ed. Joseph Wechsberg (New York: McGraw-Hill, 1967), p. 201ff.; bulletins, April 2, 1962, p. 5, and April 1, 1963, p. 2, SWAW.
9. "End of Chase," *Time*, April 26, 1963.
10. Thomas Albrich et al., eds., *Holocaust und Kriegsverbrechen vor Gericht: Der Fall Österreich* (Innsbruck: StudienVerlag, 2006), p. 175ff.; Richard Breitman et al., eds., *U.S. Intelligence and the Nazis* (Cambridge, UK: Cambridge University Press, 2005), p. 356ff.; Erich Raja, *Kopfjagd auf Rajakowitsch* (Heusenstamm, Germany: Orion, 1966).
11. Rachmut to Wiesenthal, April 1, 1962, WPP.
12. Bulletins, April 4, 1962, p. 4, and September 30, 1962, p. 3, WPP.
13. Meidan to Wiesenthal, September 22, 1955, WPP.
14. Rafi Meidan, author interview, November 15, 2006; Meir Amit, author interview, January 17, 2006; Nadav Zeevi, "Hakolonel shehatza et hakavim," *Ha'aretz*, December 8, 1995; report from Munich, January 4, 1961, USNA, RG 263 UD-2 Box 2, Vol. 3 (Notorious Nazis).
15. Rosa-Maria Austraat, author interview, May 3, 2006.
16. Wiesenthal to Katz, November 3, 1961, WPP.
17. Dov Ohovsky, author interview, July 26, 2007.
18. Gerald L. Posner and John Ware, *Mengele: The Complete Story* (New York: Cooper Square Press, 2000), pp. 168–69; Wiesenthal, *Murderers Among Us*, p. 201.
19. Jose Moskovits, author interview, October 18, 2007.
20. Wiesenthal to Yad Vashem, July 20, 1960, July 22, 1960, WPP; Wiesenthal to Dak, July 27, 1960, ISA 2731/2.
21. Kermycz to Wiesenthal, August 8, 1960, WPP.
22. Wiesenthal to Dak, July 27, 1060, ISA 2731/2.
23. Wiesenthal, *Murderers Among Us*, p. 159ff.; Posner and Ware, *Mengele*, p. 207; Dak to Foreign Ministry, July 31, 1960, ISA 2731/2.
24. Posner and Ware, *Mengele*, p. 182ff.; Rafi Meidan, author interview, November 15, 2006.

25. Wiesenthal to Bauer, July 20, 1964, and Bauer to Wiesenthal, July 23, 1964; transcript of conversation between Wiesenthal and Bauer, August 25, 1964, SWAW, Mengele file; Wiesenthal, *Murderers Among Us*, p. 168ff.; Irmtrud Wojak, *Fritz Bauer, 1903–1968: Eine Biographie* (Munich: C. H. Beck, 2009), p. 308ff. See also Giordano to Wiesenthal, August 8, 1964, SWAW, Mengele file.

26. Bulletin, September 30, 1962, p. 10, WPP; Aaron Freiwald and Martin Mendelsohn, *The Last Nazi: Josef Schwammberger and the Nazi Past* (New York: Norton, 1994), p. 159ff.

27. Bulletin, September 30, 1962, p. 10, SWAW, Gabler file.

28. Wiesenthal to Sicherheitsdirektion, October 4, 1962, SWAW, Gabler file; bulletin, December 31, 1967, p. 1, WPP.

29. Bulletin, April 2, 1962, WPP; Rosenkranz to Dworzecki, December 16, 1962, YVA 0/4/529; Rosenkranz to Wiesenthal, February 13, 1961, to May 90, 1961, YVA 0/4/529.

30. Interim report on Murer case, June 14, 1963, SWAW; anonymous to Wiesenthal, June 25, 1963, SWAW, anonymous letters, Murer file; "Hamushbai'm heeminu rak larotzhim," June 23, 1963, SWAW; "Franz Murer Must Be Retried," *Ha'aretz*, October 4, 1963; Wiesenthal to Dworzecki, June 20, 1963, YVA 0/4/529; Wiesenthal to Yad Vashem, July 1, 1963, YVA 0/4/529; Wiesenthal to Brand, November 6, 1964, YVA 0/4/529; Wiesenthal to Dagan, April 30, 1975, WPP; see also Wiesenthal, *Murderers Among Us*, p. 68; bulletins, October 24 1963, p. 6, and December 31, 1963, p. 3, WPP.

31. "Die Ziffer vor der Null," WPP; see also Simon Wiesenthal, *Doch Die Mörder Leben* (Munich: Droemer Knaur, 1967), p. 220ff.; Michael John, "Gebrochene Kontinuität: Die Kultusgemeinde Linz nach 1945," in *Jüdische Gemeinden: Kontinuitäten und Brüche*, ed. Eleonore Lappin (Berlin: Philo, 2002), p. 155f; see also Wiesenthal to official in charge of education, October 24, 1957, AIKGW, Korrespondenz, Kultusgemeinden.

32. News clippings and other media summaries, WPP; Hella Pick, *Simon Wiesenthal: A Life in Search of Justice* (Boston: Northeastern University Press, 1996), p. 172; Clyde A. Farnsworth, "Sleuth with 6 Million Clients," *New York Times*, February 2, 1964, Sunday magazine, p. SM11.

33. Wiesenthal to Springer, September 19, 1975; Cramer to Frank, October 27, 1975; Siedler to Wiesenthal, September 30, 1975; Wiesenthal to Frank, February 6, 1976; Frank to Wiesenthal, February 17, 1976; Wiesenthal to Polz, February 6, 1976; Polz to Frank, February 19, 1976; Wiesenthal to Blecha, June 25, 1986; Heindl to Wiesenthal, July 7, 1986—all in WPP.

10: *"You May Have Thought He Was Happy, but He Also Cried Sometimes"*

1. Givton to Foreign Ministry, June 25, 1963, ISA 2731/14.

2. Wiesenthal to Karbach, March 23, 1964, WPP; memorandum, November 8, 1963, WPP; Bemerkungen zur Klage Krell-Wiesenthal-Grabovski, December 11, 1964; Wiesenthal to Roth, May 28, 1963, WPP; Wiesenthal affidavit, August 4, 1964.

3. Simon to Foreign Ministry, November 27, 1963, ISA 2731/14.

4. Wiesenthal to Association of Jewish Victims of the Nazi Regime, January 22, 1963, ISA 2731/14.

5. Wiesenthal memo, March 19, 1963; Wiesenthal to Ehrlich, September 10, 1963; Wiesenthal memo, November 8, 1963; Simon to Shek, November 27, 1963—all in ISA 2731/14.

6. Wiesenthal to Simon, August 10, 1964; Wiesenthal to Bader, June 30, 1966; Wiesenthal to Maas, August 29, 1966; Wiesenthal to *Aufbau*, July 7, 1966; Wiesenthal to Kazman, August 29, 1966—all in WPP.

7. Wiesenthal to Karbach, March 23, 1964, WPP.

8. Simon to Shek, January 7, 1964, ISA 2731/14; see also Wiesenthal to Krell, March 19, 1964, AIKGW, Extern, 85; Simon Wiesenthal, "Ich klage an!" *Der Ausweg*, December 29, 1963, p. 11.

9. Feldsberg to Israeli embassy, March 5, 1964, ISA 2731/16; bulletin, April 13, 1964, SWAW.

10. *New York Times*, July 14, 1964, p. 10; Simon Wiesenthal, *Justice Not Vengeance* (London: Weidenfeld & Nicolson, 1989), p. 139ff.

11. Bulletin, May 1, 1964, p. 1, SWAW; see also meeting protocol, November 15, 1964, AIKGW, XXVII, B,d 1322.

12. Irene Segal-Grande, H. H. Fuchs, and C. F. Rueter, *Justiz und NS Verbrechen* (Amsterdam: Amsterdam University Press, 1978), Vol. XXIX, p. 637ff.

13. Bulletin, October 1964, pp. 1–2, SWAW; Simon Wiesenthal, *The Murderers Among Us*, ed. Joseph Wechsberg (New York: McGraw-Hill, 1967), p. 140ff.

14. Simon to Foreign Ministry, February 13, 1964, ISA 2731/14.

15. "Elazar," author interview, October 8, 2008; bulletins: September 30, 1962, p. 3; May 1, 1964, p. 1; January 31, 1978, p. 4; January 31, 1984, p. 6—all in SWAW; see also Verbelen file, SWAW.

16. Simon to Shek, September 24, 1964, and Shek to Simon, September 29, 1964, ISA 2731/14.

17. Efrati to Simon, January 17, 1964, ISDA 2731/14.

18. Bitan to Foreign Ministry, December 23, 1964, ISA 2731/14; Evelyn Adunka, *Die vierte Gemeinde: Die Geschichte der Wiener Juden von 1945 bis heute* (Berlin: Philo, 2000), p. 269ff.

19. Frederick Forsyth, *The Odessa File* (New York: Bantam Books, 1995), p. 158.

20. Hella Pick, *Simon Wiesenthal: A Life in Search of Justice* (Boston: Northeastern University Press, 1996), p. 93; report by Agent 156, June 14, 1965, IPN BU, 0665/269 MSW Dep. II, Vol. I, p. 150ff.

21. Report by Agent 156, June 14, 1965.

22. Ella Lingens, *Gefangene der Angst: Ein Leben im Zeichen des Widerstandes* (Berlin: BvT, 2005).

23. Peter Michael Lingens, author interview, June 23, 2006; Alexander Friedman, author interview, June 12, 2006; Jules Huf, author interview, March 14, 2006.

24. Adalbert Rückerl, ed., *NS Prozesse* (Karlsruhe, Germany: Müller, 1972), p. 22f.

25. Robinson to Schüle, March 4, 1960, ZS GA III/6 Bd. 1.

26. B'nai B'rith memo, November 19, 1964, YVA 0–65 (Robinson, correspondence related to trials); Rückerl, ed., *NS Prozesse*, p. 22; Schüle to Robinson, April 5, 1963, ZS, GA III-6 Bd. 2; World Jewish Congress, Assessment of a Verdict, September 1965, YVA 0–65 (Robinson, correspondence related to trials).

27. Andreas Eichmüller, "Die Strafverfolgung von NS-Verbrechen durch westdeutsche Justizbehörden seit 1945," *Vierteljahreshefte für Zeitgeschichte*, 4/2008, p. 621ff.

28. Wiesenthal to the president of the Rechtsanwaltkammer, January 3, 1973, WPP.

29. Bucher to Goldmann, July 21, 1964, and Goldmann to Bucher, August 1, 1964, CZA Z6/1233.

30. Miller to Wiesenthal, December 31, 1964, WPP; Kennedy to Wiesenthal, August 11, 1965, WPP.

31. Simon Wiesentha, ed., *Verjährung 200 Persönlichkeiten des Öffentlichen Lebens sagen Nein* (Frankfurt: Europaische Verlagsanstalt, 1965).

32. Protocol of Bundestag debate, February 25, 1965, CZA Z6/1234.

33. Pallin to Wiesenthal, July 1964, WPP; Wiesenthal to Klaus, November 23, 1964, WPP; Thomas Albrich et al., eds., *Holocaust und Kriegsverbrechen vor Gericht der Fall Österreich* (Innsbruck: StudienVerlag, 2006), p. 14f.

34. Bulletin, April 1965, p. 1ff., SWAW.

35. Wiesenthal to Klaus, October 12, 1966, WPP.

36. Warburg to Wiesenthal, July 30, 1968, WPP.

37. Bulletin, April 1967, p. 2, SWAW.

38. Wiesenthal to Osnabrück prosecution, January 2, 1997; Behrendt to Wiesenthal, January 17, 1997, SWAW, Warzok file.

39. Wiesenthal to Hasslocher, June 18, 1960; Schmidt to Wiesenthal, September 22, 1971; Wiesenthal to Schmidt, September 28, 1971; Wiesenthal to Frick, December 15, 1977—all in WPP.

40. Memorandum, August 25, 1965, WPP.

41. Mannheim prosecution, draft appeal for witnesses, undated, WPP.

42. Kace to Wiesenthal, October 20, 1965, WPP.

43. Wiesenthal to Bendler, December 30, 1965, WPP.

44. Yitzhak Arad, *Belsec, Sobibor, Treblinka: The Operation Reinhard Death Camps* (Bloomington: Indiana University Press, 1999).

11: *"A Huge Mass of Rotten Flesh"*

1. Hartmut Reese, ed., *Baugeschichte des Schlosses Hartheim/Alkoven* (Linz, Austria: Trauner, 2003).

2. Tom Matzek, *Das Mordschloss: Auf der Spur von NS Verbrechen in Schloss Hartheim* (Vienna: Kremayr und Scheriau, 2005), p. 261ff.; see also Henry Friedlander, *The Origins of Nazi Genocide from Euthanasia to the Final Solution* (Chapel Hill and London: University of North Carolina Press, 1977).

3. Alberti to Wiesenthal, June 25, 1962 et al., SWAW, Euthanasia box.

4. Wiesenthal to Katz, November 3, 1961, WPP; Wiesenthal to Zweig, March 15, 1962, WPP.

5. Bulletin, September 30, 1962, p. 5, SWAW.

6. Simon Wiesenthal, "Seltsames Interview," *Der Ausweg*, no. 2, March 1964, p. 3.

7. Wiesenthal to Broda, February 14, 1964, WPP; Wiesenthal at press conference and press reports, SWAW, Euthanasia box; bulletins April 2, 1962, p. 11, and September 30, 1962, p. 11, SWAW.

8. Gitta Sereny, *Into That Darkness: From Mercy Killing to Mass Murder* (London: Andre Deutsch, 1974); Tom Segev, *Soldiers of Evil: The Commanders of Nazi Concentration Camps* (New York: McGraw-Hill, 1987), p. 201ff.

9. Simon Wiesenthal, *The Murderers Among Us*, ed. Joseph Wechsberg (New York: McGraw-Hill, 1967), p. 301ff.

10. Wiesenthal to Marbach, June 3, 1970, WPP.

11. Wiesenthal to Habel, July 20, 1970, WPP.

12. Sereny, *Into That Darkness*, p. 351ff.

13. "Elazar," author interview, October 3, 2006; Spiess to the editor of the *Jerusalem Post*, August 20, 1986, WPP.

14. Bulletin, April 1967, p. 1, SWAW; Simon Wiesenthal, *Justice Not Vengeance* (London: Weidenfeld & Nicolson, 1989), p. 86.

15. Sereny, *Into That Darkness*, p. 354.

16. Stangl box, SWAW; Wiesenthal, *Justice Not Vengeance*, p. 80.

12: *"Auschwitz Lines"*

1. F. Tamari (of Ramallah), conversation with author, May 1966, WPP.

2. Tom Segev, *1967: Israel, The War, and the Year That Transformed the Middle East* (New York: Metropolitan, 2007).

3. Wiesenthal to Hamburg prosecution, June 5, 1967, WPP.

4. Wiesenthal to Sitte, June 5, 1967, WPP.

5. Bulletin, June 6, 1967, SWAW; see also Simon Wiesenthal, *Justice Not Vengeance* (London: Weidenfeld & Nicolson, 1989), p. 240.

6. Norman Barrymaine, report on Jose Perez, February 1953, SWAW, Egypt file.

7. Michael Stergar, author interview, June 1, 2006.

8. Tom Segev, *1967*, p. 544.

9. Wiesenthal to Avneri, December 23, 1969, with copy of Avneri interview in *Berliner Extradienst*, December 13, 1969, WPP.

10. Simon Wiesenthal, *Justice Not Vengeance*, p. 224.

11. Wiesenthal, interview with Hella Pick, IWM, Accession 20823, Reel 21; Wiesenthal, *The Murderers Among Us*, ed. Joseph Wechsberg (New York: McGraw-Hill, 1967), p. 288ff.; Evelyn Adunka, *Der Raub der Bücher* (Vienna: Czernin, 2002), p. 9ff.

12. Opera Mundi to the publishers, March 10, 1967, WPP; Carmen Hofbauer, "Simon Wiesenthal als Publizist," dissertation, University of Salzburg, 2002, p. 130ff.

13. Droemische Verlagsanstalt publishers to customers, November 11, 1967, WPP.

14. Wiesenthal, *Murderers Among Us*, p. 78.

15. Yaacov Hertzog diary, August 9, 1966, ISA 4510/16-A.

16. Isser Harel, *Mashber hamadanim baGermania 1962–1963* (Tel Aviv: Sifriat Maariv, 1982), p. 146ff.; SWAW, Muller file; Richard Breitman et al., *U.S. Intelligence and the Nazis* (Cambridge, UK: Cambridge University Press, 2005), p. 148ff.

17. Wiesenthal to Livnat, September 12, 1967, Mengele file, SWAW.

18. Wiesenthal to Weinhold, August 2, 1967, Mengele file, SWAW; see also bulletin no. 12, January 31, 1972, p. 3, and bulletin no. 14, January 31, 1974, p. 4, SWAW.

19. Hella Pick, *Simon Wiesenthal: A Life in Search of Justice* (Boston: Northeastern University Press, 1996), p. 92.

20. Theolinde Rapp to Wiesenthal, August 5, 1967, WPP.

21. Lander to Wiesenthal, October 25, 1967, WPP.

22. Wiesenthal to Philip Rapp, August 28, 1967, WPP; Wiesenthal to John Rapp, August 17, August 28, and November 6, 1967, WPP; John Rapp to Wiesenthal, August 17 and 21, 1967, WPP; Wiesenthal to Martin Rapp, August 28, September 9, and November 6, 1967, WPP; Martin Rapp to Wiesenthal, August 27, 1967, WPP; Wiesenthal to Joe Rapp, September 27, 1967, WPP; Wiesenthal to Pick, August 17, September 28, and November 6, 1967, WPP; Pick to Wiesenthal, August 24 and September 11, 1967, WPP.

23. Wiesenthal to Human Rights League, February 26, 1953, courtesy of Linz Jewish community.

24. Mischka Kukin, *Humor hinter dem Eisernen Vorhang* (Gütersloh, Germany: Signum Verlag, 1962); Carmen Hofbauer, "Simon Wiesenthal als Publizist," dissertation, University of Salzburg, 2002, p. 125ff.; Wiesenthal to Sulzberger, May 2, 1972, WPP.

25. *The Same Language: First for Hitler—Now for Ulbricht* (Bonn: Rolf Vogel, Deutschland Berichte, 1968); Jonathan Steele, *Inside East Germany: The State That Came in from the Cold* (New York: Urizen, 1977), p. 214.

26. Bulletin no. 9, January 31, 1969, p. 1ff., SWAW.

27. Bulletin no. 12, January 31, 1972, p. 8, SWAW; Wiesenthal to Eban, April 26, 1970, WPP.

28. Bulletin no. 10, January 31, 1970, p. 1, SWAW; Kreisky to Wiesenthal, March 26, 1969, WPP; see also bulletin no. 7, December 31, 1967, p. 5, and bulletin no. 8, June 30, 1968, p. 8, SWAW.

29. Simon Wiesenthal, *Anti-Jewish Agitation in Poland: A Documentary Report* (Bonn: Rolf Vogel, no date); Wiesenthal to Javits, February 13, 1970, WPP.

30. "Der Jud' ist Schuld," August 30, 1968, SWAW, speech file.

31. Wiesenthal in Amsterdam, April 19, 1970, SWAW, speech file; Wiesenthal to Italian ambassador, December 23, 1970, WPP.

32. Wiesenthal to Wells, June 17, 1987, WPP; Wiesenthal, interview with Hella Pick, IWM, Accession 20823, Reel 38.

33. Wiesenthal to Durlacher, November 24, 1967, WPP; see also Segev, *The Seventh Million: The Israelis and the Holocaust* (New York: Henry Holt, 1993), pp. 340–41.

34. "Wann wird Wiesenthal Wien verlassen?" *Zyie Literackie*, November 29, 1970, BKA, Wiesenthal Box II; Wiesenthal to Waldheim, November 25, 1969, WPP.

35. Polish documents relating to "Operation Danube," IPN BU, 0665/269 MSW Dep. II, Vol. I; IPN BU, 01419/161 MSW, 1963–1974, Vols. I–III; IPN BU, 01069/247 MSW.

36. Report on Official Journey to the People's Republic of Poland in the Matter of: Wiesenthal, Simon, February 21, 1969, and accompanying documents, Die Bundesbeauftragte für die Unterlagen des Staatssicherheitsdienstes der ehemaligen Deutschen Demokratischen Republik (BSTU), Berlin, Archiv der HA IX/11, AS 236/68, Part I; see also Stasi file, SWAW.

13: *"What Would You Have Done?"*

1. Simon Wiesenthal, *The Sunflower* (New York: Schocken, 1997).

2. Canetti to Wiesenthal, April 28, 1969, WPP.

3. Taylor to Wiesenthal, March 7, 1969, Farley to Wiesenthal, February 11, 1969, and Wiesel to Wiesenthal, December 1, 1968, WPP.

4. Wiesenthal to Hamelman, April 14, 1987, WPP.

5. Wiesenthal to Rubin, June 10, 2002, WPP.

6. Böll to Wiesenthal, August 15, 1969, WPP.

7. Wiesenthal to Smerdka, March 23, 1982, WPP.

8. Alper to Wiesenthal, July 18, 1986, WPP; Wiesenthal to Alper, July 28, 1986, WPP.

9. Paul Sills and Michael Stergar, author interview, June 1, 2006; author interviews with Heinrich Schmidt (May 11, 2006), Paul Grosz (July 3, 2006), and Alexander Friedman (June 12, 2006).

10. Film script, hospital sequence, prepared by E. B. Gerard, WPP.

11. Friedman, author interview, June 12, 2006.

12. Ella Lingens, *Gefangene der Angst: Ein Leben im Zeichen des Widerstandes* (Berlin: BvT, 2005), p. 278.

14: *"Kreisky Is Going Mad"*

1. Broda file, SWAW.

2. Wiesenthal to Shek, August 18, 1970, SWAW; Wiesenthal to Shek, August 25, 1970, WPP.

3. Report of parliamentary inquiry committee, attached to Fischer to Kreisky, October 28, 1975, BKA, Wiesenthal Box II; Kreisky-Wiesenthal dispute, September 17, 1970, ISA 4556/45.

4. Wiesenthal to Kreisky, October 21, 1969; Wiesenthal to Hacker, October 30, 1969; Wiesenthal to Waldheim, November 25, 1969—all in WPP.

5. Heinz Fischer, *Die Kreisky Jahre, 1967–1983* (Vienna: Löcker 1993), p. 67.

6. Wiesenthal to Matejka, August 5, 1970, SWAW, Kreisky box.

7. Avner to Eldar, July 10, 1970, ISA 4556/45.

8. Memorandum, September 9, 1970, BKA, Wiesenthal Box I.

9. Hella Pick, *Simon Wiesenthal: A Life in Search of Justice* (Boston: Northeastern University Press, 1996), p. 248.

10. Eldar to Europe I, July 15 and July 30, 1970; Israeli embassy to Europe I, August 13, 1970; Naim to Europe I, August 21, 1970; Shek to Europe I, October 6, 1970—all in ISA 4556/45; Angriff auf das Dokumentationszentrum und die Reaktion aus aller Welt, SWAW; see also bulletin no. 11, January 31, 1971, SWAW; Kreisky to Prunbauer, November 2, 1970, BKA, Wiesenthal Box II; protest letters to Kreisky, "Jewish fascist" affair, BKA, Wiesenthal Box II.

11. Broda memo, June 6, 1970, BKA, Wiesenthal Box II.

12. Bitan to legations, September 17, 1970, ISA 4556/45.

13. The Kreisky-Wiesenthal dispute, September 17, 1970, ISA 4556/45; Wiesenthal to Broda, November 11, 1970, BKA, Wiesenthal Box II; see also Oliver Rathkolb, *Die paradoxe Republik: Österreich 1945 bis 2005* (Vienna: Paul Zsolnay, 2005), p. 383ff.

14. Avner to Shek, September 4, 1970, and Shek to Avner, September 10, 1970, ISA 4556/45; Kreisky-Wiesenthal dispute, September 17, 1970, ISA 4556/45; Shek to Europe I, September 24, 1970, and October 12, 1970, ISA 4556/45; see also Evelyn Adunka, *Die vierte Gemeinde: Die Wiener Juden in der Zeit von 1945 bis heute* (Vienna: Philo, 2000), p. 390ff.

15. Wiesenthal to Nittel, August 29, 1973, WPP.

16. Bulletin no. 2, September 30, 1962, p. 7; bulletin no. 12, January 31, 1972, p. 2; bulletin no. 13, January 31, 1973, p. 3—all in SWAW; Simon Wiesenthal, *Justice Not Vengeance* (London: Weidenfeld & Nicolson, 1989), p. 96ff.

17. Wiesenthal to Broda, November 11, 1970, and Broda to Kreisky, December 14, 1970, BKA, Wiesenthal Box II.

18. Wiesenthal to Intwald, May 12, 1976, WPP; Wiesenthal to Wistrich, September 1, 1978, WPP.

19. Willy Brandt, *Begegnungen und Einsichten: Die Jahre 1960–1975* (Hamburg: Hoffmann und Campe, 1976), p. 525.

20. Wiesenthal to Brandt, January 22, 1971, WPP; see also bulletin no. 12, January 31, 1972, SWAW.

21. Bulletin no. 12, January 31, 1972, p. 3; bulletin no. 13, January 31, 1973, p. 5; bulletin no. 14, January 31, 1974, p. 5—all in SWAW.

22. Bulletin no. 15, January 31, 1975, p. 4, SWAW; Wiesenthal to van der Steen, December 14, 1974, SWAW, Bahl von Flammerdinghe file; bulletin no. 14, January 31, 1974, p. 1, and bulletin no. 25, January 31, 1985, p. 5, SWAW.

23. Bulletin no. 13, January 31, 1973, p. 10, SWAW.

24. Bulletin no. 15, January 31, 1975, p. 3, SWAW.

25. Ibid., p. 1 (Erren); bulletin no. 12, January 31, 1972, p. 4 (Sobota); bulletin no. 14, January 31, 1974, p. 5 (Nell Bigell)—all in SWAW.

15: *"Better Than Any Monster"*

1. Bulletin no. 14, January 31, 1974, p. 8, and bulletin no. 15, January 31, 1975, p. 2, SWAW; Wiesenthal to Uris, November 25, 1971, WPP.

2. Simon Wiesenthal, "The Hunt for the 'Butcher of Riga,'" as told to Gwynne Roberts, SWAW, Roschmann file.

3. Shlomo Sand, *Hakolnoa kehistoria: Ledamyen u'lvayem et hameah ha'esrim* (Tel Aviv: Am Oved, 2002), p. 242.

4. Simon Wiesenthal, *Justice Not Vengeance* (London: Weidenfeld & Nicolson, 1989), p. 97.

5. Frederick Forsyth, *The Odessa File* (New York: Bantam Books, 1995), p. 159.

6. Wiesenthal to Forsyth, August 27, 1971, November 16, 1971, and November 18, 1971, SWAW, Roschmann file.

7. Wiesenthal to Forsyth, September 2, 1971, SWAW, Roschmann file; Forsyth to Wiesenthal, September 5, 1971, SWAW, Roschmann file; Wiesenthal to Forsyth, September 9, 1971, SWAW, Roschmann file; Forsyth interview in Guy Walters, *Hunting Evil* (London: Bantam Press, 2009), p. 344ff.

8. Wiesenthal to Forsyth, November 8, 1971, SWAW, Roschmann file.

9. Wiesenthal, *Justice Not Vengeance*, pp. 99–100.

10. Forsyth to Wiesenthal, May 3, 1973, and May 23, 1973, SWAW, Roschmann file.

11. Richard P. Brickner, "The Odessa File," *New York Times*, November 5, 1972, p. BR5; Nora Sayre, "Neame's 'Odessa File': Thriller About Secret SS Society Opens," *New York Times*, October 19, 1974, p. 36.

12. Sand, *Hakolnoa kehistoria*, p. 242ff.

13. Schneider to Schell, January 9, 1974, SWAW, Roschmann file; Wiesenthal to Schneider, April 2, 1974, SWAW, Roschmann file; Schneider to Wiesenthal, May 1, 1974, SWAW, Roschmann file; see also Gertrude Schneider, *Journey into Terror: The Story of the Riga Ghetto* (New York: Ark House, 1979).

14. Wiesenthal, "The Hunt for the 'Butcher of Riga.'"

15. Wiesenthal, *Justice Not Vengeance*, p. 101; Uki Goni, *The Real Odessa: Smuggling the Nazis to Peron's Argentina* (London: Granta Books, 2002), p. 243; Wiesenthal statement, September 2, 1977, SWAW, Roschmann file.

16. Leo Frank, *Geständnis: Das Leben eines Polizisten* (Linz, Austria: Grosser, 1993), p. 39ff.

17. Ibid., p. 27.

18. Maier to Wiesenthal, December 9, 1979, August 5, 1972, March 15, 1973, and August 16, 1975, WPP.

19. Wiesenthal to Maier, August 20, 1968, August 5, 1972, August 21, 1972, September 20, 1973, and March 1, 1974, WPP.

20. Ronsac to Maier, March 1, 1974, WPP.

21. Maier to Wiesenthal, December 5, 1972, March 15, 1973, and March 5, 1974, WPP.

22. Wiesenthal to Maier, January 10, 1973, WPP.

23. Wiesenthal at Jabotinsky award ceremony, October 1988, SWAW, speech file.

24. Maier to Wiesenthal, December 9, 1979, WPP; Frank, *Geständnis*, p. 40.

25. Alexander Friedman, author interview, June 12, 2006.

26. Meiron Medzini, *Hayehudiah hageah: Golda Meir vehazon Yisrael* (Tel Aviv: Yedioth Aharonoth, 1990), p. 426; *Ha'aretz*, October 4, 1973, p. 1.

27. Margit Schmidt, author interview, May 27, 2006.

28. Conversation between the prime minister and Chancellor Bruno Kreisky, October 2, 1973, ISA 2726/6; Patish to Foreign Ministry, October 17, 1973, ISA 2726/6.

29. Patish to Meroz, October 17, 1973, ISA 2726/6; Meroz to Patish October 23, 1973, ISA 2726/6.

30. Kreisky to Meir, March 20, 1974, ISA 8525/1.

31. Leon Zelman, author interview, May 15, 2006.

32. Letters between Brandon and Wiesenthal, December 24, 1980, to May 6, 1981, SWAW, Institute for Historical Review file.

33. Wiesenthal to Mayor Mauterndorf, May 6, 1976, WPP; bulletin no. 17, January 31, 1977, p. 7, SWAW.

34. Wiesenthal to Fest, August 24, 1976, WPP.

35. Bulletin no. 14, January 31, 1974, p. 6, SWAW; *Yedioth Aharonoth*, August 31, 1975, p. 3.

36. Loehr to Wiesenthal, undated, WPP; Michael Stergar, author interview, June 1, 2006.

16: "Mr. Wiesenthal, I Claim, Had Different Relations with the Gestapo from Mine"

1. Bulletin no. 15, January 31, 1975, SWAW; Michael Stergar, author interview, June 1, 2006.

2. Pravda to Fried, December 9, 1974, courtesy of Paulinka Kreisberg; see also Wiesenthal to Dukes, December 23, 1974, WPP.

3. Michael Stergar and Paul Sills, author interview, June 1, 2006.

4. Rosa-Maria Austraat, author interview, May 3, 2006.

5. Wiesenthal to Maier, June 4, 1975, WPP; Wiesenthal to Dukes, February 9, 1976, WPP.

6. Bruno Kreisky, *Zwischen den Zeiten: Der Memoiren erster Teil* (Vienna: Kremayr und Scheriau, 2000), p. 64ff.

7. Patish to Foreign Ministry, August 7, 1974, ISA 8525/3.

8. Dagan to Foreign Ministry, October 24, 1975, ISA 4212/9, and June 11, 1976, ISA 6815/10; Shek to head of director general's bureau, October 22, 1967, ISA 8488/1.

9. Wiesenthal to Kreisky, April 14, 1981, SWAW, Kreisky box.

10. Bruno Kreisky, *Der Mensch im Mittelpunkt: Der Memoiren dritter Teil* (Vienna: Kremayr und Scheriau, 2000), p. 233; Peter Kreisky in interview, June 22, 2006.

11. Simon Wiesenthal, "Kreisky's Dilemma: Unser Dilemma," *Der Ausweg*, vol. 13, no. 1, April 1975, p. 1.

12. Interior Ministry report, November 8, 1969, SWAW, Peter file.

13. Dagan to Foreign Ministry, May 2, 1975, ISA 8525/1.

14. Tom Segev, "Miparashat Peter leparashat Wiesenthal," *Maariv*, November 7, 1975, p. 28; Huf, author interview, March 14, 2006.

15. Simon Wiesenthal, *Justice Not Vengeance* (London: Weidenfeld & Nicolson, 1989), p. 294.

16. *Unsere Ehre heisst Treue* (Vienna: Europaverlag, 1965).

17. Huf, author interview, March 14, 2006.

18. Alexander Friedman, author interview, June 12, 2006; Grosz, author interview, July 3, 2006; Wiesenthal to Kirchschläger, September 29, 1975, SWAW, Peter file.

19. Isser Harel, *Habayit berehov Garibaldi* (Tel Aviv: Sifriat Maariv, 1975).

20. Wiesenthal to Ronsac, February 6, 1968; Wiesenthal to "Elazar," July 29, 1966.

21. Wiesenthal to Dukes, September 23, 1975; see also bulletin no. 16, January 31, 1976, p. 10, WPP.

22. Dagan to Foreign Ministry, October 6, 1975, ISA 8525/2.

23. Michael Stergar, author interview, June 1, 2006.

24. Wiesenthal at press conference, October 9, 1975, SWAW, Peter file; bulletin no. 16, January 31, 1976, SWAW.

25. Shek to Foreign Ministry, February 5, 1974, ISA 8525/1.

26. Hella Pick, *Simon Wiesenthal: A Life in Search of Justice* (Boston: Northeastern University Press, 1996), p. 251.

27. Bruno Kreisky, *Im Strom der Politik: Der Memoiren zweiter Teil* (Vienna: Kremayr und Scheriau, 2000), pp. 279–80; Bruno Kreisky, *Zwischen den Zeiten: Der Memoiren erster Teil* (Vienna: Kremayr und Scheriau, 2000), pp. 74, 78.

28. Bitan to Israeli legations, September 17, 1970, ISA 4556/45; Patish to Shek, August 7, 1974, ISA 8525/3.

29. Otto Binder, *Wien-retour: Bericht an die Nachkommen* (Vienna: Bölau, 1997), p. 103.

30. Lingens, author interview, June 23, 2006.

31. Peter Kreisky, author interview, June 22, 2006.

32. Bruno Kreisky, *Der Mensch im Mittelpunkt: Der Memoiren dritter Teil* (Vienna: Kremayr und Scheriau, 2000), p. 233.

33. Segev, "Miparashat Peter leparashat Wiesenthal"; Huf, author interview, March 14, 2006.

34. Wiesenthal to *Aufbau*, December 9, 1975, WPP.

35. Privatanklage, October 7, 1975, SWAW, Kreisky box.

36. Tonbandaufzeichnung, Pressekonferez Bundeskanzler Dr. Kreisky, November 10, 1975, SWAW, Kreisky box; Perner to Wiesenthal, December 5, 1975, SWAW, Kreisky box.

37. Wiesenthal to Marian Zyd, October 16, 1952, WPP; Ben Natan, author interview, February 5, 2006.

38. Wiesenthal to Blech, December 2, 1975, SWAW, Kreisky box; Sills and Stergar, author interview, June 1, 2006; Huf, author interview, March 14, 2006.

39. Wiesenthal to *Profil*, March 8, 1973, WPP.

40. Kreisky, *Im Strom der Politik*, p. 295.

41. Pick, *Simon Wiesenthal*, p. 264.

42. Segev, "Miparashat Peter leparashat Wiesenthal."

43. Kreisky, *Im Strom der Politik*, p. 274ff.

44. Michael Abitboul et al., eds., *Hatzionut umitnagdeha ba'am hayehudi* (Jerusalem:

Hasifriya Hatzionit, 1990); Shlomo Zand, *Matai va'ech humtzah ha'am hayedudi* (Tel Aviv: Resling, 2008).

45. Shek to Dagan, May 11, 1975, ISA 8525/1; Dagan to Foreign Ministry, May 24, 1976, ISA 6815/10; Dagan to Foreign Ministry, October 27 and October 28, 1975, ISA 8525/2; Dagan to Foreign Ministry, December 16, 1975, ISA 2726/4; Dagan to Foreign Ministry, December 17, 1975, ISA 8525/3; Federal Chancellor's Office memorandums, October 27, 1975, BKA, Informationen für den Bundeskanzler, Wiesenthal Box II, File 2.

46. Tom Segev, *Maariv*, November 7, 1975.

47. Uri Avnery: "Der letzte europäische Jude," in *Wer war Bruno Kreisky?*, ed. F. R. Reiter (Vienna: Ephelant, 2000), p. 7ff.; Johnny Bunzel, author interview, May 13, 2006.

48. Bruno Kreisky, *Das Nahostproblem* (Vienna: Europaverlag, 1985), p. 52; BKA, VII.1 (Länderboxen), Israel Box 2.

49. Kreisky, *Im Strom der Politik*, pp. 296 and 300.

17: "It's Not Easy to Be My Wife"

1. Heinz Fischer, *Die Kreisky Jahre, 1967–1983* (Vienna: Löcker, 1993), pp. 146–47.

2. Perner to Wiesenthal, November 18, 1975, SWAW, Kreisky box.

3. Wilke to Kunz, November 28, 1975, BKA, Wiesenthal Box III, File Ia; Wiesenthal to Hacker, March 29, 1984, AIKGW, XXVII, B, d, B21.

4. Fischer, *Die Kreisky Jahre*, p. 147; Peter Michael Lingens, author interview, June 23, 2006; Wiesenthal to Perner, April 30, 1986, SWAW, Kreisky box; Kreisky statement, December 3, 1975, BKA, Wiesenthal Box 2; Fischer statement to press, courtesy of president's office.

5. Schlumberger to Peterlunger, June 24, 1969; Karasek to Soronics, October 13, 1969, and Karasek to Waldheim, October 13, 1969, BKA, Wiesenthal Box I; Wiesenthal statement, March 31, 1970, SWAW, Kreisky box.

6. Information on an overheard conversation, October 17, 1975, BKA, Wiesenthal Box I, File I.

7. Interrogations of Schaller and Weidnitzer, October 23, 1975, BKA, Wiesenthal Box I, Informationen für den Bundeskanzler.

8. Wiesenthal to *Der Zeit*, October 13, 1959, WPP.

9. Philipp-Christian Wachs, *Der Fall Theodor Oberländer 1905–1998: Ein Lehrstück deutscher Geschichte* (Frankfurt: Campus, 2000).

10. Wiesenthal to Ohrenstein, March 13, 1962; Wiesenthal to van Dam, March 1, 1962; Robinson to Wiesenthal, April 5, 1962, WPP.

11. Wiesenthal to Vogel, March 17, 1969, SWAW, Oberländer file.

12. Oberländer to Wiesenthal, October 21, 1972, SWAW, Oberländer file.

13. Wiesenthal to Oberländer, October 30, 1972, SWAW, Oberländer file.

14. Oberländer to Wiesenthal, November 22, 1972, SWAW, Oberländer file.

15. Vogel to Wiesenthal, February 13, 1973, SWAW, Oberländer file.

16. Wiesenthal to Vogel, February 16, 1973, SWAW, Oberländer file.

17. Broadcast transcript, June 1975, SWAW, Oberländer file.

18. Rösch to Kreisky, October 23, 1975; Waller to Kreisky, November 18, 1975, BKA, Wiesenthal Box I, Informationen für den Bundeskanzler.

19. Oberländer to Wiesenthal, August 7, 1976, SWAW, Kutchmann file; Wiesenthal to Oberländer, August 18, 1976, SWAW, Oberländer file.

20. Wiesenthal to Sichting, June 30, 1975, SWAW, Oberländer file; bulletin no. 4, April 1966, p. I; bulletin no. 26, January 31, 1986, p. I; bulletin no. 27, January 31, 1987, p. I—all in SWAW.

21. Gitta Sereny, *Into That Darkness: From Mercy Killing to Mass Murder* (London: Andre Deutsch, 1974), p. 357; Simon Wiesenthal, *Justice Not Vengeance* (London: Weidenfeld & Nicolson, 1989), p. 168ff.

22. Freudenheim to Wiesenthal, April 20, 1973–January 21, 1977, SWAW, Wagner file.

23. Mario Chimanovitch, author interview, October 29, 2008.

24. Wiesenthal, *Justice Not Vengeance*, p. 88ff.

25. SWAW, Braunsteiner-Ryan file.

26. Bulletin 17, January 31, 1977, p. 9; Hella Pick, *Simon Wiesenthal: A Life in Search of Justice* (Boston: Northeastern University Press, 1996), p. 93.

27. Bulletin 23, January 31, 1983, p. 11; bulletin 24, January 31, 1984, p. 8; bulletin 25, January 31, 1985, p. 11—all in SWAW.

28. Landesgericht für Strafsachen Wien, Privatanklage, April 13, 1976, p. 6, SWAW, Kreisky box; Roeder statement to his supporters, September 1975, ABK, Wiesenthal, Box I, Informationen für den Bundeskanzler, File Ia.

29. European Court of Human Rights, Lingens Case (12/1984/84/131), July 8, 1986, SWAW, Kreisky box.

30. Schwager to the president of the Vienna Jewish community, June 24, 1976, AIKGW, 145 (1969–1973).

31. Perner to Wiesenthal, March 27, 1987, Vienna District Court record, March 26, 1979, p. 16, SWAW, Kreisky box.

32. "War Wiesenthal ein Gestapo-Kollaborateur?" *Profil*, November 18, 1975, p. 16ff.

33. Sworn statement by Adela Sygal Milchman, January 7, 1976, WPP.

34. Peter Marboe, author interview, May 23, 2006.

35. Wiesenthal to Sichting, November 20, 1975, WPP.

36. Wiesenthal to Hausner, December 17, 1975; Wiesenthal to Porat, June 24, 1980; Wiesenthal to Dukes, December 15, 1975; Wiesenthal to Dukes, January 20, 1976, WPP; Cyla and Simon Wiesenthal on ZDF TV, March 2, 1978 (transcript), in Rolf Vogel, ed., *Das Echo: Widerhall auf Simon Wiesenthal* (Stuttgart, Germany: Seewald, 1979, 1982), p. 49.

37. Simon Wiesenthal, *Max and Helen, A Tragic and True Love Story* (London: Granada, 1982); Carmen Hofbauer, "Simon Wiesenthal als Publizist," dissertation, University of Salzburg, 2002, p. 152ff.

38. Wiesenthal to Sijes, December 9, 1975, WPP; Wiesenthal to Matejka, April 13, 1976, SWAW, Kreisky box.

39. Dukes to Wiesenthal, August 28, 1974, WPP.

40. Dukes to Wiesenthal, January 30, 1975, May 3, 1975, February 5, 1976, April 2, 1976, and April 13, 1976, WPP.

41. Wiesenthal to Dukes, May 12, 1975.

42. Eva Dukes, author interview, October 25, 2007.

43. Wiesenthal to Dukes, August 29, 1975, WPP.

44. Wiesenthal to Dukes, November 24, 1975, WPP.

45. Alexander Friedman, author interview, June 12, 2006.

46. Vienna District Court judgment, October 19, 1989, SWAW, Kreisky box.

18: *"The Children . . . Were Actually the Same Children"*

1. Simon Wiesenthal, *Sails of Hope* (New York: Macmillan, 1973).

2. Wiesenthal to a friend, September 5, 1972, WPP.

3. Wiesenthal to Prause, October 4, 1972, WPP; Ronsac to Wiesenthal, August 29, 1975, WPP; see also Carmen Hofbauer, "Simon Wiesenthal als Publizist," dissertation, University of Salzburg, 2002, p. 145ff.

4. Bruno Kreisky, *Im Strom der Politik: Der Memoiren zweiter Teil* (Vienna: Kremayr und Scheriau, 2000), p. 289.

5. Simon Wiesenthal, *Flucht vor dem Schiksal* (Munich: Nymphenburger, 1988).

6. Hofbauer, "Simon Wiesenthal als Publizist," p. 175ff.

7. Wiesenthal to Hagelstange, March 18, 1971, WPP.

8. Simon Wiesenthal, *Segel der Hoffnung* (Olten, Switzerland: Walter, 1972), p. 35.

9. *State of Israel vs. Adolf Eichmann*, opening speech, Prime Minister's Office, 1961, pp. 7, 13.

10. Simon Wiesenthal, *Every Day Remembrance Day: A Chronicle of Jewish Martyrdom* (New York: Henry Holt, 1987).

11. Simon Wiesenthal, *Mifrasei Tikva: Ha'im Colombus haya Yehudi?* (Jerusalem: Reuven Mass, 1992), p. 3.

12. Bulletin 25, January 31, 1985, p. 9, SWAW.

13. Wiesenthal to Elitzur, October 2, 1986, WPP.

14. Bulletin 32, January 31, 1992, p. 9 (Kurds); bulletin 38, January 31, 1998, p. 11 (Plaza de Mayo); bulletin 12, January 31, 1972, p. 2 (the rights of political prisoners); bulletin 37, January 31, 1997, p. 5 (mines); bulletin 32, January 31, 1992, p. 10 (Tibet); bulletin 16, January 31, 1976 (Sakharov)—all in SWAW.

15. Wiesenthal to Primorac, September 4, 1992, SWAW, Bosnia box; Wiesenthal to Clinton, July 19, 1995, SWAW, Bosnia box.

16. Wiesenthal, interview, *Profil*, July 26, 1993, SWAW, Bosnia box; Wiesenthal, messages to demonstrations in London, February 12, 1994, and Göttingen, Germany, August 31, 1995, SWAW, Bosnia box; Wiesenthal to Clinton, July 19, 1995, SWAW, Bosnia box; Wiesenthal, Charny, and Fein, *New York Times*, July 7, 1996 (letters to the editor); Clinton to Wiesenthal, August 14, 1995, SWAW, Bosnia box.

17. Bulletin no. 4, April 1966, p. 4, and bulletin 12, January 31, 1972, p. 5, SWAW; see also Simon Wiesenthal, *Doch die Mörder Leben* (Munich: Droemer Knaur, 1967), p. 348.

18. Michael Zimmermann, *Rassenutopie und Genozid: Die nationalsozialistische "Loesung der Zigeunerfrage"* (Göttingen, Germany: Wallstein, 1996).

19. Simon Wiesenthal, *Justice Not Vengeance* (London: Weidenfeld & Nicolson, 1989), p. 220; press release, March 4, 1986, SWAW, Gypsy box; Simon Wiesenthal, *The Murderers Among Us* (New York: McGraw-Hill, 1967), p. 238.

20. Streim to Wiesenthal, February 16, 1981, SWAW, Gypsy box; bulletin 4, April 1966, p. 3, SWAW; Wiesenthal at press conference, October 31, 1984, SWAW, Gypsy box; press release, January 11, 1985, SWAW, Gypsy box; see also Wiesenthal to Kovacs, October 28, 1971, SWAW, Gypsy box.

21. Wiesenthal to Verband Deutscher Sinti, September 3, 1981; Wiesenthal to Gollrad and Kaessar to Wiesenthal, October 12, 1983 (Erhardt case); Wiesenthal to König, and Wiesenthal to Metzger, August 23, 1983; Metzger to Wiesenthal, September 5, 1983; Rose to Wiesenthal August 21, 1983 (Darmstadt); Volz to Wiesenthal, March 25, 1986 (Karlsruhe); Wiesenthal to Voscherau, February 14, 1989 (Hamburg); Wiesenthal to Beatrix, January 19, 1981; director of Queen's Bureau to Wiesenthal, January 19, 1981—all in SWAW, Gypsy box.

22. Wiesenthal to Hübner, November 24, 1982 (TV film); Wiesenthal to Löschnak, October 3, 1994 (Mauthausen monument); Wiesenthal to Diepgen, September 29, 1994 (Berlin monument), SWAW, Gypsy box.

23. Yehuda Bauer, *Rethinking the Holocaust* (New Haven, CT: Yale University Press, 2001), p. 66.

24. Wiesenthal to Novitch, December 24, 1984, SWAW, Gypsy box; Zvika Dror, *Masa Miriam: Sipur hayeha shal Miriam Novitch* (Tel Aviv: Beit Lohamei Hagetaot, 2008); Wiesenthal, *Justice Not Vengeance*, p. 223; see also Romani Rose and Walter Weiss, *Sinti und Roma im "Dritten Reich"* (Göttingen, Germany: Lamuv, 1991).

25. Wiesenthal to Banda, June 1, 1976, Wiesenthal to Hutter, June 1, 1976, and Hutter to Wiesenthal, June 3, 1976, SWAW, Jehovah's Witnesses file; bulletin 17, January 31, 1977, p. 5, and bulletin 40, January 31, 2000, p. 6, SWAW.

26. HOSI to Wiesenthal, February 12, 2004; Wiesenthal to Korman, March 15, 2004; Grande to Mergili, May 11, 2004; Mergili to Grande, May 12, 2004—all in SWAW homosexuals file.

27. Wiesenthal to Strauss, August 29, 1986, and Strauss to Wiesenthal, October 11, 1986, SWAW Gypsy box; *New York Times* ad, April 16, 1999, SWAW, Gypsy box; see also bulletin 22, January 31, 1982, p. 6, SWAW; Gilad Margalit, *Germany and Its Gypsies: A Post-Auschwitz Ordeal* (Madison: University of Wisconsin Press, 2002).

28. Elie Wiesel, *And the Sea Is Never Full* (New York: Schocken, 2000), p. 127ff., pp. 187–88; Wiesenthal to Charny, March 31, 1988, WPP.

29. Dina Porat, "Maarekhet bat 40 shana: Yomana shel Anna Frank umakhshishei hashoah 1958–1998," in *Hashoah hayehudi vehauniversali: Sefer hayovel le'Yehuda Bauer*, ed. Shmuel Almog et al. (Jerusalem: Yad Vashem, 2002), p. 160ff.; Tim Cole, *Selling the Holocaust: From Auschwitz to Schindler* (New York: Routledge, 2000), p. 29ff.

30. Levin to Wiesenthal, May 31, 1975, and Wiesenthal to Levin, June 13, 1975, WPP; Levin to Wiesenthal, July 16, 1975, WPP.

31. Wiesenthal to Grey, July 4, 1980, WPP; Wiesenthal to Hausner, June 24, 1984, WPP; Wiesenthal to Rosensaft, May 5, 1982, WPP.

32. Yehuda Bauer, "Po tamun hahevdel," *Ha'aretz*, November 23, 2005; Yehuda Bauer, "Don't Resist," *Tikkun*, Vol. 4, no. 3, May–June 1989, p. 67ff.

33. Stuart E. Eizenstat, *Imperfect Justice* (New York: Public Affairs, 2003), p. 19.

34. Wiesel, *And the Sea Is Never Full*, p. 127ff., pp. 187–88.

35. Wiesenthal to Hausner, June 24, 1980, WPP; Wiesenthal to Grey, July 4, 1980, WPP.

36. Wiesenthal to Grobman, November 21, 1980, WPP.

37. Wiesel to Wiesenthal, February 5, 1981, and Wiesenthal to Wiesel, August 11, 1981, SWAW, Wiesel file; Wiesenthal in Washington, August 5, 1980, SWAW, speech file.

38. Wiesenthal to Hausner, October 5, 1980, WPP.

39. Wiesenthal to Hier, June 25, 1981, WPP.

40. Hancock to Wiesel, November 25, 1986, SWAW, Wiesel file.

41. Wiesenthal to Wiesel, December 14, 1984, SWAW, Gypsy box.

42. Ibid.; Wiesel to Wiesenthal, January 8, 1985, WPP; Wiesenthal to Hier, January 16, 1985, WPP; Wiesenthal to Charny, March 31, 1988, WPP.

43. Wiesel, *And the Sea Is Never Full*, pp. 128 and 390–91; Wiesel, author interview, June 7, 2007.

44. Friedman to Wiesenthal, August 25, 1988, WPP; Tuviah Friedman, *Sixty Years: Nazi Hunter* (Haifa: Institute for the Documentation of Nazi War Crimes, 2006), p. 37.

45. Friedman to Wiesenthal, February 21, 1999, WPP; Friedman, *Sixty Years*, p. 28.

46. Friedman to Muzykant, July 6, 1999, courtesy of Eli Rosenbaum; Wiesenthal to Friedman, November 28, 1996, and May 9, 1998, WPP; see also Tuwiah Friedman, ed., *Die Korrespondenz der zwei Nazi-Forscher Towiah Friedman und Simon Wiesenthal in den Jahren 1955–2005* (Haifa: Institute for the Documentation of Nazi War Crimes, 2005).

47. Beate Klarsfeld, *Wherever They May Be* (Agincourt, France: Vanguard Press, 1975), p. 50ff.

48. Serge and Beate Klarsfeld, author interview, May 27, 2008.

49. Klarsfeld, *Wherever They May Be*, p. 288.

50. *Frankfurter Allgemeine Zeitung*, February 12, 1980, p. 3.

51. Klarsfeld to Wiesenthal, December 19, 1971, SWAW, Klarsfeld file; Serge and Beate Klarsfeld, author interview, May 27, 2008.

52. Wiesenthal to Kulka, December 1, 1980, SWAW, Klarsfeld file; bulletin 7, December 31, 1967, p. 3, SWAW.

53. Wiesenthal to Foxman, June 6, 1986, SWAW, Waldheim box.

54. Rosen to Kornreich, November 1988, SWAW, Klarsfeld file.

55. Wiesenthal to Leide, June 23, 1994, SWAW, Stasi box.

56. Wiesenthal to Maier, January 9, 1991, SWAW, Klarsfeld file.

57. Klarsfeld, *Wherever They May Be*, p. 58ff.; bulletin 21, January 31, 1981, p. 10, SWAW.

58. Wiesenthal to Faris, May 29, 1968, SWAW, Barbie file.

59. Bulletin 9, January 31, 1969, p. 3, and bulletin 11, January 31, 1971, p. 4, SWAW; see also bulletin 13, 1973, p. 7, SWAW.

60. Richard Breitman, "The Gestapo," in *U.S. Intelligence and the Nazis*, ed. Richard Breitman et al. (Cambridge, UK: Cambridge University Press, 2005), p. 123ff.

61. Wiesenthal to Jenny, November 15, 1971, SWAW, Barbie file.

62. Wiesenthal to Jenny, February 25, 1972, and Wiesenthal to Moskovits, April 19, 1972, SWAW, Barbie file; see also Wiesenthal, interview with Hella Pick, IWM, Accession 20823, Reel 8.

63. "U.S. Says Army Shielded Barbie," *New York Times*, August 17, 1981, p. 1; *Klaus Barbie and the United States Government: A Report to the Attorney General of the United States* (Washington, DC: Criminal Division, U.S. Department of Justice, 1983).

64. Peter Hellman, "Hunting a Nazi," *New York*, March 19, 1984, p. 44ff.

65. Mendelsohn to Koshner, March 16, 1984, SWAW, Klarsfeld file.

66. Bulletin, October 1962–March 1963, p. 7; bulletin 13, January 31, 1973, p. 1; bulletin 14, January 31, 1974, p 4; bulletin 15, January 31, 1975, p. 6—all in SWAW; Wiesenthal to Allende, August 21, 1972, WPP.

67. Wiesenthal, *Justice Not Vengeance*, p. 60; Shraga Elam and Dennis Whitehead, "Ha'ish shelanu be'Damesek," *Ha'aretz Magazine*, March 16, 2007; Breitman, "The Gestapo."

19: *"Only So That Mengele's Name Would Not Be Forgotten"*

1. Wiesenthal to Freudenheim, February 17, 1977, WPP.

2. Wiesenthal to Hier, October 9, 1978, WPP.

3. Wiesenthal to Moskovits, April 5, 1972, and April 25, 1972, WPP; Moskovits to Wiesenthal, May 18, 1972, and March 28, 1973, WPP; Moskovits, author interview, October 18, 2007.

4. Wiesenthal to Posner, August 13, 1986, SWAW, Mengele file.

5. Bulletin 8, June 8, 1968, p. 3; bulletin 12, January 31, 1972, p. 3; bulletin 14, January 31, 1974, p. 4; bulletin 18, January 31, 1978, p. 5—all in SWAW; see also *Maariv*, January 31, 1983, p. 1.

6. Bulletin 21, January 31, 1981, p. 1, and bulletin 23, January 31, 1983, p. 4, SWAW.

7. Waldheim to Wiesenthal, June 13, 1979, and July 23, 1979, WPP; Wiesenthal to Waldheim, July 31, 1979, WPP; Hier to Wiesenthal, July 30, 1979, WPP.

8. Benno Weiser Varon, *Professions of a Lucky Jew* (New York: Cornwall, 1992), p. 380ff.; Simon Wiesenthal, *Justice Not Vengeance* (London: Weidenfeld & Nicolson, 1989), p. 110.

9. Kohl to Wiesenthal, March 8, 1985, and Wiesenthal to Kohl, March 15, 1985, SWAW, Mengele box.

10. Wiesenthal to Wagner, May 22, 1979, SWAW, Mengele box.

11. Wiesenthal to Rosen, February 22, 1981, SWAW, Mengele box.

12. Wenzeck to Wiesenthal, February 27, 1985, SWAW, Mengele box.

13. Rimland to Wiesenthal, November 25, 1984, SWAW, Mengele box.

14. Rimland to Wiesenthal, August 16, 1984, and November 15, 1984, SWAW, Mengele box.

15. Rimland to Wiesenthal, July 21, 1984, SWAW, Mengele box.

16. Rimland to Wiesenthal, November 15, 1984, SWAW, Mengele box; see also Walter Boener, *In Defiance* (New York: Carlton, 1993).

17. Wiesenthal to Rimland and Boener, December 17, 1984, SWAW, Mengele box.

18. Wiesenthal to Klein, August 9, 1984, SWAW, Mengele box.

19. Rosen to Rimland and Boener, January 3, 1985, SWAW, Mengele box.

20. Rimland to Wiesenthal, December 15, 1984, SWAW, Mengele box.

21. Rimland to Wiesenthal, February 24, 1985, and March 4, 1985, and Wiesenthal to Rimland, March 14, 1985, SWAW, Mengele box.

22. Rimland to Wiesenthal, March 4, 1985, SWAW, Mengele box.

23. Speyer to Wiesenthal, January 25, 1984; Wiesenthal to Klein, March 8, 1984; bulletin 23, January 31, 1983, p. 4; bulletin 25, January 31, 1985, p. 2, SWAW.

24. Bulletin 40, January 31, 2000, p. 3.

25. Gerald L. Posner and John Ware, *Mengele: The Complete Story* (New York: Cooper Square Press, 2000), pp. 158, 286ff.

26. Bulletin 3, April 1965, p. 1; bulletin 8, June 30, 1968, p. 3; bulletin 9, January 31, 1969, p. 3; bulletin 14, January 31, 1974, p. 3, SWAW.

27. Bulletin 26, January 31, 1986, p. 2; bulletin 29, January 31, 1989, p. 1, SWAW.

28. Posner to Wiesenthal, June 2, 1986; Wiesenthal to Posner, August 13, 1986, SWAW, Mengele file.

29. Bulletin 25, January 31, 1985, p. 8; bulletin 27, January 31, 1987, p. 7, SWAW.

30. Goli Neeman Arad, *America: Hayehudim, ve'aliyat haNazim* (Tel Aviv: Am Oved, 2006).

31. Tim Cole, *Selling the Holocaust: From Auschwitz to Schindler* (New York: Routledge, 2000), p. 148.

32. Ibid., p. 2.

33. Tom Segev, *1967: Israel, The War, and the Year That Transformed the Middle East* (New York: Metropolitan, 2007), p. 304.

34. Cole, *Selling the Holocaust*, p. 13.

35. Wiesenthal to Springer, February 2, 1979, WPP; Elie Wiesel, *And the Sea Is Never Full* (New York: Schocken, 1999), p. 117ff.

36. Shlomo Zand, *Hakolnoa kahistoria: Ledamyen u'levayem et hameah ha'esrim* (Tel Aviv: Am Oved, 2002), p. 243; Peter Novick, *The Holocaust in American Life* (Boston: Houghton Mifflin, 2000), p. 209ff.; Cole, *Selling the Holocaust*, p. 13; see also Michael Bernbaum, *After Tragedy and Triumph: Modern Jewish Thought and the American Experience* (Cambridge, UK: Cambridge University Press, 1990), p. 17ff.; Edward T. Linenthal, *Preserving Memory: The Struggle to Create America's Holocaust Museum* (New York: Viking, 1995).

37. Wiesenthal to Begin, November 20, 1978, WPP.

38. Martin Rosen, author interview, May 15, 2007.

39. Wiesenthal to Katz, December 28, 1970, WPP.

40. Katz to Wiesenthal, April 15, 1976, WPP.

41. Katz to Wiesenthal, March 17, 1972, WPP.

42. Wiesenthal to "Elazar," May 15, 1967, WPP.

43. Wiesenthal to Katz, April 22, 1976, WPP.

44. Sciulla to Wiesenthal, April 15, 1976, WPP; Martin Rosen, author interview, May 15, 2007.

45. Kelly to Wiesenthal, April 19, 1976; Wiesenthal to Kelly, April 27, 1976, WPP.

46. Wiesenthal to Wiesenthal, July 21, 1978, WPP.

47. Spiegel to Wiesenthal, December 2, 1974, WPP.

48. Lingens to Karbach, April 21, 1964; Karbach to Lingens, April 22, 1964; bulletin 5, December 31, 1963, p. 5; bulletin 13, January 31, 1973, p. 4; bulletin 15, January 31, 1975, p. 4; bulletin 16, January 31, 1976, p. 3; bulletin 20, January 31, 1980, p. 7, SWAW.

49. *U.S. Attorneys' Bulletin*, Office of Special Investigations issue, Vol. 54, no. 1, January 2006.

50. Boylan to Rayan, November 6, 1980, SWAW, Valus file.

51. Wiesenthal to Sher, January 24, 1980; Sher to Wiesenthal, January 20, 1987, et al., SWAW, OSI file.

52. Bulletin 20, January 31, 1980, p. 7, SWAW; Eli M. Rosenbaum with William Hoffer, *Betrayal: The Untold Story of the Kurt Waldheim Investigation and Cover-up* (New York: St. Martin's Press, 1993), pp. 301–2.

53. Martin Mendelsohn, author interview, October 26, 2007; bulletin 24, January 31, 1984, p. 4, SWAW; Eli Rosenbaum, author interview, October 22, 2007.

54. Wiesenthal to Hier, July 29, 1993, SWAW, Demjanjuk file.

55. Sher to Wiesenthal, November 30, 1984, and November 13, 1987, SWAW, OSI file.

20: *"As If I Were Already Dead"*

1. Hier, author interview, March 9, 2007.

2. Tim Cole, *Selling the Holocaust: From Auschwitz to Schindler* (New York: Routledge, 2000), p. 13.

3. Wiesenthal to Hier, July 31, 1978, August 24, 1978, October 9, 1978, and October 15, 1978; Wiesenthal to Cooper, January 16, 1979, WPP.

4. Wiesenthal to Cooper, November 21, 1978, WPP; Wiesenthal to Hier, December 1, 1978, WPP.

5. Wiesenthal to Zuroff, February 27, 1979; Wiesenthal to Hier, March 27, 1979, WPP.

6. Wiesenthal to Begin, February 16, 1979; Begin to Wiesenthal, January 30, 1979, WPP.

7. Wiesenthal to Hier, March 16, 1997; Cooper to Wiesenthal, March 23, 1979, WPP.

8. Yohanan Maroz, *Ha'im haya zeh lashav? Shagrir Yisrael be'Germania mesakem* (Tel Aviv: Sifriat Hapoalim, 1988), p. 133ff.; Tuvia Friedman, *Hamaavak neged hok habityashnut al pishei haNatzim baGermania* (Haifa: Hamachon Ladokumentatzia, 1981); Rolf Vogel, ed., *Das Echo: Widerhall auf Simon Wiesenthal* (Stuttgart, Germany: Seewald, 1979), p. 118ff.

9. Wiesenthal to Begin, April 3, 1979, WPP.

10. Rockman to Wiesenthal, September 5, 1979, WPP.

11. Wiesenthal to Hier, June 7, 1980, WPP; Rosen, author interview, May 15, 2007; Hier, author interview, March 9, 2007; Hier to Wiesenthal, May 26, 1982, WPP.

12. Cooper to Wiesenthal, October 27, 1978, and March 23, 1979, WPP.

13. Wiesenthal to *Aufbau*, December 2, 1985, and to Hier, July 6, 1979, and July 7, 1979, WPP.

14. Hier to Wiesenthal, June 6, 1983, WPP.

15. Wiesenthal to Hier, June 18, 1979, and May 4, 1982, WPP.

16. Wiesenthal to Hier, November 20, 1979, WPP.

17. Wiesenthal to Hier, March 11, 1981, WPP.

18. Zimmerman to Wiesenthal, September 23, 1988, WPP.

19. Form 990, Return of Organization Exempt from Income Tax, 2002 (Simon Wiesenthal Center, Los Angeles), downloaded from http://www.guidestar.org.

20. Wiesenthal to Hier, June 24, 1983, and November 23, 1983, WPP.

21. Wiesenthal to Hier, July 11, 1983, WPP.

22. Wiesenthal to Hier, February 9, 1982, and Hier to Wiesenthal, November 23, 1983, WPP.

23. Wiesenthal to Hier, February 9, 1982, and November 23, 1983, WPP.

24. Hier, press release, April 13, 1981, WPP.

25. Wiesenthal to Hier, March 1, 1984, WPP.

26. Wiesenthal to Hier, July 3, 1985; Wiesenthal to Hier, August 14, 1985, WPP.

27. Wiesenthal to Hier, August 16, 1984, and June 2, 1986, WPP.

28. Wiesenthal to Hier, March 21, 1985, WPP.

29. Hier to Wiesenthal, November 30, 1983, WPP.

30. Wiesenthal to Wells, June 17, 1987, WPP.

31. Wiesenthal to Hier, June 7, 1993, WPP.

21: *"Sleazenthal"*

1. Eli M. Rosenbaum with William Hoffer, *Betrayal: The Untold Story of the Kurt Waldheim Investigation and Cover-up* (New York: St. Martin's Press, 1993), p. 301.

2. Rosenbaum to Wiesenthal, May 28, 1980, and Wiesenthal to Rosenbaum, June 12, 1980, WPP.

3. Bronfman to *Der Spiegel*, 1986/49, p. 150.

4. Wiesenthal to Shek, February 17, 1970, and April 16, 1970, WPP.

5. Rachleff to Wiesenthal, December 23, 1971; Wiesenthal to Rachleff, December 30, 1971, WPP.

6. Robert Edwin Herzstein, *Waldheim: The Missing Years* (New York: Paragon, 1989), p. 265ff.; Oliver Rathkolb, "Waldheims CIA Akte," in *1986: Das Jahr, das Österreich veränderte*, ed. Barbara Toth and Hubertus Czernin (Vienna: Czernin Verlag, 2006), p. 96ff.

7. Berlin Documentation Center, report, March 20, 1979; Simon Wiesenthal, "My Struggle Against Nazis," SWAW, *Panorama* file; Wiesenthal, *Justice Not Vengeance* (London: Weidenfeld & Nicolson, 1989), p. 311.

8. Wiesenthal, interview with Hella Pick, IWM, Accession 20823, Reel 6; Wiesenthal to van Dam, December 22, 1967, WPP.

9. Wiesenthal to Kutschera, July 3, 1967, WPP.

10. Wiesenthal to Seidman, May 6, 1981, WPP.

11. Wiesenthal to Waldheim, July 31, 1979; Waldheim to Wiesenthal, December 5, 1979, WPP.

12. Simon Wiesenthal, "Leon Zelmans Angriffe auf Simon Wiesenthal," *Ausweg*, No. 2, July 1995, p. 3.

13. Wiesenthal to Boutbien, February 15, 1991; Wiesenthal, *Justice Not Vengeance*, p. 311; Leon Zelman, *Ein Leben nach dem Überleben* (Vienna: Kremayr und Scheriau/ Orac, 2005), p. 192.

14. Transcript of conversation between Wiesenthal, Singer, and others, undated; Mendelsohn to Wiesenthal, April 6, 1987, SWAW, Waldheim box.

15. Barbara Toth and Hubertus Czernin, eds., *1986: Das Jahr, das Österreich veränderte* (Vienna: Czernin Verlag 2006), p. 15ff.; Trauttmansdorff, author interview, May 17, 2006.

16. *New York Times*, March 4, 1986, p. 1.

17. Sills and Starger, author interview, June 1, 2006.

18. "Waldheim Says His Past Was Misrepresented," *New York Times*, March 6, 1986, p. A6.

19. Trauttmansdorff, author interview, May 17, 2006.

20. Waldheim to Wiesenthal, October 14, 1997, WPP.

21. Wiesenthal to Elitzur, May 22, 1986, and to Eliot, September 18, 1997, SWAW, Waldheim box.

22. Wiesenthal to Berkowsky, October 8, 1986, SWAW, Waldheim box; Rubinstein to Justice Minister, May 30, 1986, YVA 04/274.

23. Rosenbaum, *Betrayal*, p. 155; see also "Waldheim: War Criminal," *Jewish Press*, June 20, 1986, p. 1.

24. Anonymous letter, undated, SWAW, Waldheim box; Positive und Negative Waldheim Zuschriften, AIKGW, XXX, dfb 85.

25. Wiesenthal, *Justice Not Vengeance* (London: Weidenfeld & Nicolson, 1989), p. 316.

26. Wiesenthal to Foxman, June 6, 1986, SWAW, Waldheim box.

27. Rosenbaum, *Betrayal*, p. 437ff.; Bericht der Internationalen Kommission von Militärhistorikern in Sache des Österreichischen Bundespräsidenten Kurt Waldheim,

February 1988, SWAW, Waldheim box; see also Kurt Waldheim, *Die Antwort* (Vienna: Amalthea, 1996).

28. Bronfman to *Der Spiegel*, 1986/49, p. 47ff.

29. Elisabeth B. White, "Barring Axis Persecutors from the United States: OSI 'Watch List' Program," *U.S. Attorneys' Bulletin*, Office of Special Investigations issue, Vol. 54, no. 1, January 2006, p. 19ff.

30. Sher to Wiesenthal, April 18, 1990, SWAW, OSI file.

31. WJC internal memos, courtesy of Eli Rosenbaum.

32. Konieczny-Oroglia to Singer, May 2, 1986, and accompanying memos, courtesy of Eli Rosenbaum; Elitzur to Jerusalem (copies of cables), courtesy of Eli Rosenbaum.

33. WJC internal memo, December 1, 1986; Rosenbaum to van Leer, October 13, 1987, courtesy of Eli Rosenbaum; Wiesenthal to Tamir, June 4, 1986; Tamir to Wiesenthal, July 10, 1988, WPP.

34. Sher to Wiesenthal, April 18, 1990, SWAW, OSI file.

35. Wiesenthal, interview with Hella Pick, IWM, Accession 20823, Reel 9.

36. "A Jew" to Wiesenthal, May 21, 1986, SWAW, Waldheim box.

37. Berkowsky to Wiesenthal, October 2, 1986; Wiesenthal to Berkowsky, October 8, 1986; Lerner to Wiesenthal, June 17, 1986, SWAW, Waldheim box.

38. Hier to Shultz, April 16, 1986, and to Singer, April 17, 1986, courtesy of Eli Rosenbaum; Shonfeld to Greenberg, May 20, 1986; Wiesenthal statements, April 21, April 22, May 16, and May 19, 1986, courtesy of Eli Rosenbaum.

39. Wiesenthal to Hier, May 28, 1986, WPP.

40. Wiesenthal to Hier, June 2, 1986, WPP.

41. Spijer to Wiesenthal, January 31, 1986; Siegan to Norwegian Nobel Committee, January 15, 1986, WPP.

42. Wiesenthal to Hier, March 21, 1985; Spijer to Wiesenthal, January 31, 1986, WPP.

43. Hier to Wiesenthal, March 27, 1985, WPP.

44. Wiesenthal to Elitzur, October 2, 1986, WPP.

45. Wiesenthal to Schilde, January 17, 1986, WPP.

46. Hier, author interview, March 9, 2007; Rosen, author interview, May 15, 2007; Austraat, author interview, May 3, 2006; Alan Levy, *Nazi Hunter: The Wiesenthal File* (New York: Barnes and Noble, 1993), p. 516.

47. Jacob Weisberg, "How to Get a Nobel Prize," *New Republic*, November 10, 1986, pp. 12–13.

48. Nordeli in conversation with Håvard Nygård, June 2007, and anonymous message to author, August 20, 2007; Wiesenthal in conversation with heads of World Jewish Congress, November 2, 1986, courtesy of Eli Rosenbaum; Eli Wiesel, author interview, June 7, 2007.

49. Rosenbaum, *Betrayal*, p. 456.

50. Ibid., p. 357.

51. Wiesenthal in *New York Times*, May 8, 1988, p. BR44; Rosenbaum, *Betrayal*, p. 456.

52. Rosenbaum, *Betrayal,* p. 303.

53. Wiesenthal to Pelinka, September 22, 1986, WPP.

54. Rosenbaum, *Betrayal,* pp. 372–73; Efraim Zuroff, *Occupation: Nazi Hunter, The Continuing Search for Perpetrators of the Holocaust* (Jersey City, NJ: Ktav, 1994), p. 317ff.

55. Levy, *Nazi Hunter,* p. 233.

56. Rosenbaum, *Betrayal,* p. 450ff. and p. 146.

57. Certificate of honor for apprehending Eichmann, June 25, 2007, courtesy of Paulinka Kreisberg.

58. Barbara Toth and Hubertus Czernin, eds., *1986: Das Jahr, das Österreich veränderte* (Vienna: Czernin Verlag, 2006).

59. Haider to Wiesenthal, December 3, 1991, WPP.

60. Wiesenthal to Hier, and Cooper to Wiesenthal, May 22, 1995; bulletin 30, January 31, 1990, p. 5; bulletin 31, January 31, 1991, p. 8; bulletin 32, January 31, 1992, p. 8, SWAW.

61. Jacob Heilbrun, "Waldheim and His Protectors," *New York Times Book Review,* October 10, 1993, p. 9; see also Rosenbaum to *New York Times,* December 11, 1993 (editorial section); Deborah Lipstadt, "The Evil That Men Do," *Washington Post,* December 9, 1993, "Book World," p. 3).

62. Martin Rosen, author interview, May 15, 2007; see also bulletin 34, January 31, 1994, p. 8ff., SWAW.

63. Tom Segev, *The Seventh Million: The Israelis and the Holocaust* (New York: Henry Holt, 1993), p. 155; bulletin 13, January 31, 1973, p. 6; bulletin 14, January 31, 1974, p. 5; bulletin 28, January 31, 1988, p. 2ff.; bulletin 29, January 31, 1989, p. 2—all in SWAW.

64. Bulletin 13, January 31, 1973, p. 6; bulletin 14, January 31, 1974, p. 5; bulletin 4, October 24, 1963—all in SWAW; Aaron Freiwald with Martin Mendelsohn, *The Last Nazi: Joseph Schwammberger and the Nazi Past* (New York: Norton, 1994), p. 239ff.

65. Bulletin 35, January 31, 1995, p. 3; bulletin 36, January 31, 1996, p. 1, SWAW.

66. Bulletin 35, January 31, 1995, p. 3, SWAW; Uki Goni, *The Real Odessa: Smuggling the Nazis to Peron's Argentina* (London: Granta Books, 2002), p. 264ff.

67. Transcript of *Panorama* program, February 8, 1996, courtesy of Eli Rosenbaum.

68. Rosen to Dodd, February 13, 1996, and Rosen to Rosenbaum, February 13, 1996, courtesy of Martin Rosen.

69. WJC Internal memo ("Wiesenthal chronology"), June 6, 1996, Wiesel to Dodd, February 28, 1996, and WJC internal record, April 12, 1996, courtesy of Eli Rosenbaum; Rosen to Richard, April, 25, 1996, Fois to Dodd, May 22, 1996, Rosen to Dodd, May 24, 1996, Rosen to Wiesenthal, May 31, 1996, and Dodd to Wiesenthal, June 14, 1996, courtesy of Martin Rosen; Clinton to Wiesenthal, September 24, 1996; bulletin 37, January 31, 1997, SWAW; Martin Rosen, author interview, May 15, 2007.

22: *"We All Made Mistakes in Our Youth"*

1. Speer to Wiesenthal, January 12, 1975, WPP.

2. Paul Sills and Michael Stergar, author interview, June 1, 2006.

3. Wiesenthal to Speer, October 25, 1974, WPP.

4. Speer to Wiesenthal, November 1, 1974, WPP.

5. Wiesenthal to Speer, November 7, 1974, WPP.

6. Speer to Wiesenthal, January 12, 1975, WPP.

7. Wiesenthal to Brandt, January 22, 1971, WPP.

8. Wiesenthal to Schwartz, October 8, 1975, SWAW, Eichmann box.

9. Schmidt to Wiesenthal, May 18, 1946, and August 2, 1946, WPP; sworn statement, June 13, 1946, WPP.

10. "War Wiesenthal ein Gestapo-Kollaborateur?" *Profil*, November 18, 1975, p. 16ff.

11. Günthert to Wiesenthal, September 17, 1956; Wiesenthal to Günthert, November 20, 1956; Wiesenthal to Günthert, January 18, 1958, WPP.

12. Wiesenthal to Gans, June 1, 1967, WPP.

13. Copy of letter signed by Wiesenthal (no date or recipient), WPP.

14. Wiesenthal to Cramer, October 23, 1979, WPP.

15. Wiesenthal to Adenauer, February 9, 1967, WPP.

16. Hella Pick, *Simon Wiesenthal: A Life in Search of Justice* (Boston: Northeastern University Press, 1996), p. 244.

17. Wiesenthal to Kirchschläger, July 19, 1983, WPP; see also bulletin 16, January 31, 1976, p. 8, SWAW; Wiesenthal to Sakharov, February 17, 1987, WPP.

18. Wiesenthal to Kohl, June 27 and August 23, 1985 (Mengele); Wiesenthal to Kohl, June 28, 1986 (Berchtesgaden); Kohl to Wiesenthal, December 2, 1986; Wiesenthal to Kohl, December 12, 1986 (World Jewish Congress); Wiesenthal to Shamir, March 29, 1989; Wiesenthal to Kohl, October 5, 1990 (German unification); Joachim Wagner, in press release, February 7, 1996, courtesy of Eli Rosenbaum; Wiesenthal to Kohl, April 19, 1985, WPP; see also Wiesenthal to Ohla, October 23, 1963, WPP.

19. Speer to Wiesenthal, April 25, 1976; Wiesenthal to Speer, February 3, 1977, WPP.

20. Speer to Wiesenthal, April 25, 1976, WPP.

21. Wiesenthal to Speer, April 9, 1976; Speer to Wiesenthal, March 5, 1977, WPP.

22. Speer to Wiesenthal, July 4, 1976, WPP.

23. Wiesenthal to Speer, April 21, 1977; Hausner to Wiesenthal, June 3, 1979; Laden-Waldman to Wiesenthal, January 19, 1987, WPP.

24. Paul Sills and Michael Stergar, author interview, June 1, 2006; Wiesenthal to Speer, July 27, 1977, WPP.

25. Wiesenthal to Speer, January 15, 1975; Speer to Wiesenthal, June 2, 1981, WPP.

26. Speer to Wiesenthal, October 2, 1975; Wiesenthal to Speer, November 4, 1975, WPP.

27. Wiesenthal to Speer, February 3, 1977, WPP.

28. Ibid.

29. Speer to Wiesenthal, March 5, 1977, WPP.

30. Wiesenthal to Speer, March 12, 1979; Speer to Wiesenthal, April 20, 1979, WPP.

31. Mattias Schmidt, *Albert Speer, das Ende eines Mythos* (Berlin: NZ, 2005), p. 206ff.; Gitta Sereny, *Albert Speer: His Battle with Truth* (London: Picador 1995); Albert Speer, *The Slave State: Heinrich Himmler's Masterplan for SS Supremacy* (London: Weidenfeld & Nicolson, 1981), p. 15.

32. Wiesenthal to Speer, April 9, 1976, WPP.

33. Speer to Wiesenthal, July 14, 1976, and March 5, 1977; Wiesenthal to Speer, March 14, 1977, WPP.

34. Wiesenthal to Speer, July 26, 1976, WPP.

35. Hella Pick, *Simon Wiesenthal: A Life in Search of Justice* (Boston: Northeastern University Press, 1996), p. 7ff.; see also Wiesenthal, interview with Hella Pick, IWM, Accession 20823, Reel 13.

36. Wiesenthal, testimony at Yad Vashem, October 27, 1960, p. 56, YVA 03/1817.

37. Wiesenthal at Lvov trial, December 20, 1966, protocol, p. 2,300, SWAW, Lvov file; Wiesenthal to Brandon, January 8, 1981, WPP.

38. Karl in sworn statement, August 13, 1954, BKA, Informationen für den Bundeskanzler, Wiesenthal Box II, file 2.

39. McGovern in the Senate, November 30, 1979, *Congressional Record*, Senate, p. 34,721; Downey in House of Representatives, March 3, 1980, *Congressional Record*, House, p. 4,426; Moses to president, August 4, 1980, courtesy of Eli Rosenbaum.

40. Wiesenthal at Lvov trial, December 20, 1966, pp. 2,292 and 2,321.

41. Ibid., p. 2300; Wiesenthal to Brandon, January 8, 1981, WPP.

42. International Tracing Service Certificate, W-178, SWAW.

43. Wiesenthal, curricula vitae, April 10, 1956, and January 17, 1953, WPP.

44. Simon Wiesenthal, *The Murderers Among Us*, ed. Joseph Wechsberg (New York: McGraw-Hill, 1967), p. 3.

45. Wiesenthal to Brandon, January 8, 1981, WPP.

46. Maria Sporrer and Herbert Steiner, eds., *Simon Wiesenthal: Ein unbequemer Zeitgenosse* (Vienna: Orac, 1992), p. 34 (July 4); Wiesenthal at Lvov trial, December 20, 1966, p. 2290; Wiesenthal testimony at Yad Vashem, October 27, 1960, p. 4; Wiesenthal, interview with American investigator Curt Ponger, May 27, 1948, YVA M9/818; Wiesenthal, *Murderers Among Us*, p. 28.

47. Simon Wiesenthal: "Führergeburtstag," YVA M9/63.

48. Simon Wiesenthal, "Yom Huledet Bemahaneh Ricuz," in *Sefer Buczacz*, ed. Yisrael Cohen (Tel Aviv: Am Oved, 1956), p. 295ff.

49. Pick, *Simon Wiesenthal*, p. 61; Wiesenthal, *Murderers Among Us*, p. 32; bulletin 30, January 31, 1990, p. 8, SWAW.

50. *Indictment vs. Waltke*, Hannover District Court, YVA TR10/48, p. 45.

51. Wiesenthal at Lvov trial, December 20, 1966, p. 2,288ff.; Wiesenthal, testimony at Yad Vashem, October 27, 1960, p. 60.

52. Israel Gutman, ed., *Encyclopedia of the Holocaust*, Vol. II (London: Macmillan, 1990), p. 733.

53. Wells testimony, *The Trial of Adolf Eichmann, Record of Proceedings in the District Court of Jerusalem*, Vol. I (Jerusalem: State of Israel, Ministry of Justice, 1993), Session 22, May 1, 1961, p. 364.

54. Irene Sagal-Grande, H. H. Fuchs, and C. F. Reuter (eds.), *Justiz und NS-Verbrechen* (Amsterdam: Amsterdam University Press, 1978), Vol. XVIII, p. 744ff.

55. Wiesenthal, testimony at Yad Vashem, October 27, 1960, p. 60.

56. Sporrer and Steiner, eds., *Simon Wiesenthal: Ein unbequemer Zeitgenosse*, p. 42; Wiesenthal testimony, June 6, 1961, p. 14, SWAW, Dyga file; Wiesenthal to Perner, May 6, 1967, WPP.

57. Simon Wiesenthal, *KZ Mauthausen* (Linz, Austria: IBIS, 1946); "Firing Squad," *Life*, June 11, 1945, p. 47ff.; Simon Wiesenthal, *Denn sie wussten was sie tun: Zeichnungen und Aufzeichnungen aus dem KZ Mauthausen* (Vienna: Deuticke, 1995); Pick, *Simon Wiesenthal*, p. 76.

58. Tom Segev, *The Seventh Million: The Israelis and the Holocaust* (New York: Henry Holt, 1993), p. 119.

59. Wiesenthal, testimony at Yad Vashem, October 27, 1960, p. 11; Pick, *Simon Wiesenthal*, pp. 31–32.

60. Schmidt to Wiesenthal, August 2, 1946, WPP.

61. Pick, *Simon Wiesenthal*, p. 62.

62. Zvika Dror, ed., *Dapei Edut* (Kibbutz Lohamei Hagetaot, 1984), pp. 732–33.

63. Friedman to Wiesenthal, April 20, 1994, WPP.

64. Friedman, author interview, June 12, 2006.

65. Wiesenthal, interview with American investigator Curt Ponger, May 28, 1948, USNA, M1019/79/460; Wiesenthal, testimony at Yad Vashem, October 27, 1960, p. 60.

66. Wiesenthal, curriculum vitae, September 15, 1946, WPP.

67. Wiesenthal, testimony at Yad Vashem, October 27, 1960, p. 60.

68. Wiesenthal to Speer, July 26, 1976, WPP.

69. Wiesenthal to *Profil*, August 2, 1988, WPP.

70. Simon Wiesenthal, ed., *Projekt Judenplatz Wien: Zur Konstruktion von Erinnerung* (Vienna: Zsolnay, 2000); Matti Bunzel, "On the Politics and Semantics of Austrian Memory: Vienna's Monument against War and Fascism," *History and Memory*, Vol. 7, no. 2 (Fall/Winter 1996), p. 7ff.

71. Bulletin 36, January 31, 1996, p. 7, SWAW.

72. Wiesenthal to Sakharov, February 17, 1987, WPP.

73. Bulletin 33, January 31, 1993, p. 5, SWAW.

74. Bulletin 34, January 31, 1994, p. 1, SWAW.

75. Bulletin 36, January 31, 1996, p. 4, SWAW.

76. Bulletin 39, January 31, 1999, p. 5; bulletin 41, January 31, 2001, p. 1; bulletin 42, January 31, 2002, p. 2, SWAW.

77. Silberbauer to Wiesenthal, November 12, 1989; Wiesenthal to Silberbauer, January 2, 1990, WPP.

78. Wiesenthal to Friedman, September 26, 2002, WPP.

79. Wiesenthal to Rosen, May 22, 2003, courtesy of Rosen.

80. Family video, courtesy of Rachel Kreisberg; catalog and sale results, no. 328 (September 2006), courtesy of Heinrich Köhler Auktionhaus, Wiesbaden; Rosen, author interview, May 15, 2007.

81. Rosa-Maria Austraat, author interview, May 3, 2006; Austraat to Fischer, December 22, 2005, courtesy of Rosa-Maria Austraat.

Index